Recent Advances in Example-Based Machine Translation

Text, Speech and Language Technology

VOLUME 21

The titles published in this series are listed at the end of this volume.

Recent Advances in Example-Based Machine Translation

Edited by

Michael Carl

Institut der Gesellschaft zur Forderung der Angewandten Informationsforschung e.V. an der Universität des Saarlandes, Saarbrücken, Germany

and

Andy Way

School of Computer Applications, Dublin City University, Dublin, Ireland

KLUWER ACADEMIC PUBLISHERS

DORDRECHT / BOSTON / LONDON

A C.I.P. Catalogue record for this book is available from the Library of Congress.

ISBN 1-4020-1400-7

Published by Kluwer Academic Publishers,
P.O. Box 17, 3300 AA Dordrecht, The Netherlands.

Sold and distributed in North, Central and South America
by Kluwer Academic Publishers,
101 Philip Drive, Norwell, MA 02061, U.S.A.

In all other countries, sold and distributed
by Kluwer Academic Publishers,
P.O. Box 322, 3300 AH Dordrecht, The Netherlands.

Printed on acid-free paper

Printed in the Netherlands

Contents

Preface

It gives me great pleasure to be asked to write a preface to this book, *Recent Advances in Example-Based Machine Translation*, which exhibits the current state of the art in research on example-based machine translation.

When I first proposed this idea, I used the term "machine translation by analogy principle". I started my research work in the early 1960s, and was interested in the process of computer learning of the grammatical rules of a language along the lines of the process of learning a second language, particularly English, by Japanese people. I had the idea that grammatical rules will emerge by comparing differences in sentences by first giving the computer very short, simple sentences, and then longer sentences step by step.

The experiment was not successful because computers were too poor in speed and memory capacity at that time. However, I reached the conclusion that the grammatical rules (other than wh-rules to handle embedded sentential structures) could be extracted automatically by simulating the human language learning process. Later on I was asked to take part in an experiment to teach language to chimpanzees, and found out that a chimp can master a language without embedded structure to a certain extent. It was quite an interesting coincidence between the capability of a piece of computer software and that of a chimpanzee!

Another curiosity of mine was to try and simulate the second language learning process by Japanese people. A subject is given lots of short, simple English sentences with Japanese translation. He/she memorizes these sentences and their translations, and then has the ability to translate similar sentences by comparing the differences between a new sentence and sentences in his/her memory. At that time I was engaged in a big machine translation project funded by the Japanese Government, which aimed at translating abstracts of scientific papers from Japanese into English. I adopted the rule-based machine translation schema because the sentences in abstracts were very long and complex. However,

I had a feeling that rule-based MT had a limit that the translated sentences were too rigid, and the readability was not so good. I thought that the utilization of examples with good quality translations was a way to improve the readability of translated sentences.

I presented a paper, 'A Framework of a Mechanical Translation between Japanese and English by Analogy Principle', at the NATO Symposium on Artificial and Human Intelligence in Lyon, France in October 1981 (later published as a book of edited proceedings as Nagao, 1984). There were no significant responses from fellow researchers to this paper at the time, but I believed that MT researchers would become aware of the importance of the idea sometime in the future, and I persuaded colleagues in my laboratory to develop the idea. Dr E. Sumita (cf. Chapter 6, this volume) was one of my research staff, and he brought the idea into being when he moved to *ATR* (the Advanced Telecommunication Research Institute). He applied the idea to the translation of Japanese phrases of the form *A no B*, which are translated sometimes as *B of A*, *B at A*, *B in A*, *B for A*, and so on, according to the combination of A and B. He published the results at TMI, at Austin, 1990, which made the method of MT by analogy principle very famous around the world.

The 'MT by analogy principle' (or EBMT) has several difficult problems to solve. One is the construction of a good thesaurus to be used for the measurement of similarity. Another is how to use grammatical rules to segment a long sentence into phrases to which example phrases are applicable, because the comparison of similarity is easy for short phrases but is almost impossible for long sentences. Other problems include, for example, the accumulation of translation pairs (examples) and the choice of an algorithm capable of selecting the most suitable example depending on different contexts. Translation memory can be regarded as one extreme of EBMT. But the role of the thesaurus is still important, because people always use different terms for the same notion, and it is impossible to store all variations of a long sentence.

Another interesting method of MT by extending the idea of analogy-based MT is the utilization of transcription. By transcription, I mean the rewriting of a sentence by maintaining the core meaning of a sentence by using simpler, more standard expressions rather than complex, redundant ones. When a standard expression is found, it is transcribed into a sentence in another language by EBMT, and then some transcriptions will be performed in order to recover the context of the original sentence. This method may not necessarily produce a good quality translation, but may be used as a human-machine interface in machine translation, for example, where the machine side requires some standard expressions in order to execute certain machine actions.

Language translation is one of the most complicated tasks of the human brain, which utilizes not only linguistic knowledge but also knowledge of the world, and varieties of our sophisticated human senses. EBMT is one of the possible approaches to the mechanism of human translation, and this book represents a considerable contribution to the field. But we have to investigate many other possibilities to approach the level of the complex functions of the human brain.

PROFESSOR MAKOTO NAGAO

References

Nagao, M.A. 1984. A Framework of a Mechanical Translation between Japanese and English by Analogy Principle. In A. Elithorn and R Banerji (eds.) *Artificial and Human Intelligence*, Amsterdam: North-Holland, pp.173–180.

Contributing Authors

Tantely Andriamanankasina
Graduate School of Engineering, Hokkaido University,
Kita 13 Nishi 8, Kita-ku, Sapporo 060-8628, Japan
tantely@mx10.freecom.ne.jp

Kenji Araki
Graduate School of Engineering, Hokkaido University,
Kita 13 Nishi 8, Kita-ku, Sapporo 060-8628, Japan
araki@media.eng.hokudai.ac.jp

Eiji Aramaki
Graduate School of Informatics, Kyoto University,
Yoshida-honmachi, Sakyo, Kyoto 606-8501, Japan
aramaki@pine.kuee.kyoto-u.ac.jp

Francis Bond
NTT Communication Science Laboratories,
Nippon Telegraph and Telephone Corporation,
2-4 Hikari-dai, Seika-cho, Soraku-gun, Kyoto 619-0237, Japan
bond@cslab.kecl.ntt.co.jp

Ralf D. Brown
Language Technologies Institute,
Carnegie Mellon University, Pittsburgh, PA 15213-3890
ralf+@cs.cmu.edu

Michael Carl
IAI–Institut der Gesellschaft zur Förderung der Angewandten Informationsforschung e.V. an der Universität des Saarlandes, Martin-Luther-Straße 14, 66111 Saarbrücken, Germany
carl@iai.uni-sb.de

Ilyas Cicekli
Department of Computer Engineering, Bilkent University, TR-06533 Bilkent, Ankara, Turkey
ilyas@cs.bilkent.edu.tr
Department of Computer Science, University of Central Florida, Orlando, Fl 32816, USA

Bróna Collins
Department of Computer Science, Trinity College, Dublin 2, Ireland
Brona.Collins@ireland.com

Osamu Furuse
NTT Cyber Space Laboratories, Nippon Telegraph and Telephone Corporation, Yokosuka, Japan
furuse.osamu@lab.ntt.co.jp

H. Altay Güvenir
Department of Computer Engineering, Bilkent University, TR-06533 Bilkent, Ankara, Turkey
guvenir@cs.bilkent.edu.tr

Sadao Kurohashi
Graduate School of Information Science and Technology, The University of Tokyo, Hongo 7-3-1, Bunkyo-ku, Tokyo 113-8656, Japan
kuro@kc.t.u-tokyo.ac.jp

Yuji Matsumoto
Graduate School of Information Sciences, Nara Institute of Science and Technology, Japan
matsu@is.aist-nara.ac.jp

Kevin McTait
LIMSI-CNRS, Université de Paris Sud,
91403 Orsay, France
mctait@limsi.fr

Arul Menezes
Microsoft Research, Redmond WA., USA
arulm@microsoft.com

Emmanuel Planas
Groupe d'Etudes pour la Traduction Automatique (GETA),
Laboratoire de Communication Langagière et Interface Personne Système (CLIPS),
Université Joseph Fourier, Grenoble, France
emmanuel.planas@imag.fr

Fred Popowich
gavagai Technology Incorporated and Simon Fraser University,
400-6400 Roberts Street, Burnaby BC, V5G 4C9, Canada
popowich@gavagai.net

Stephen D. Richardson
Microsoft Research, Redmond WA., USA
steveri@microsoft.com

Reinhard Schäler
Localisation Research Centre,
University of Limerick,
Limerick, Ireland
Reinhard.Schaler@ul.ie

Satoshi Shirai
Natural Language Processing Systems Department,
NTT Advanced Technology Corporation,
12-1 Ekimae-honcho, Kawasaki-ku, Kawasaki-shi, Kanagawa 210-0007, Japan
sat@fw.ipsj.or.jp

Harold Somers
Department of Language Engineering,
UMIST,
PO Box 88, Manchester M60 1QD, England
Harold.Somers@umist.ac.uk

Eiichiro Sumita
ATR Spoken Language Translation Research Laboratories,
2-2-2 Hikaridai, Keihanna Science City, Kyoto 619-0288, Japan
eiichiro.sumita@atr.co.jp

Koji Tochinai
Graduate School of Engineering, Hokkaido University,
Kita 13 Nishi 8, Kita-ku, Sapporo 060-8628, Japan
tochinai@media.eng.hokudai.ac.jp

Davide Turcato
gavagai Technology Incorporated and Simon Fraser University,
400-6400 Roberts Street, Burnaby BC, V5G 4C9, Canada
turk@gavagai.net

Hideo Watanabe
IBM Research, Tokyo Research Laboratory,
1623-14 Shimotsuruma, Yamato, Kanagawa 242-8502, Japan
hiwat@jp.ibm.com

Andy Way
School of Computer Applications,
Dublin City University,
Dublin 9, Ireland.
away@computing.dcu.ie

Kaoru Yamamoto
Graduate School of Information Sciences, Nara Institute of Science and Technology,
8916-5, Takayama, Ikoma, Nara 630-0101, Japan
kaoru-ya@is.aist-nara.ac.jp

Foreword

The idea of producing this volume was born following a Workshop on Example-Based Machine Translation (EBMT) held at *MT Summit VIII* on 18th September 2001 in Santiago de Compostela, Spain. Originally, the idea of EBMT dates back to the early 1980s. Despite the 20 intervening years following Nagao's seminal idea of using examples for machine translation (MT), this was the first international workshop on EBMT to ever take place. There was a feeling at the workshop that research in the area of EBMT had achieved a critical mass and that, given the absence of books on the subject, the time was ripe to compile a volume giving a detailed overview of the latest developments in the field.

This volume thus represents the first major attempt at compiling a representative number of EBMT approaches in one volume and gives an up to date overview of the state of the art in the field. It is intended as being of relevance primarily to researchers and program developers in the field of MT and especially EBMT, cross-linguistic information retrieval, and bilingual text processing. We hope that the ideas contained herein will also be of interest to translation technologists, and language and localisation professionals, especially translators, users and developers of Translation Memories and Alignment software.

We could not have compiled this volume without many contributors who helped to make it possible. First of all we would like to thank the authors who contributed to this volume in due time. Without their input there would be no book.

We would also like to thank the anonymous reviewers for the many constructive and helpful comments which served to improve many of the papers as well as the general organisation of the book. We would also like to thank Graham Russell, Nano Gough and Mary Hearne for their careful proofreading of the draft chapters, Lyne Da Sylva for tips on indexing the book, and Aoife Cahill and Mairéad McCarthy for help with the conversion of some of the chapters from Word to LaTeX, all of which led to the improvement of this volume. In addition, we would like to thank our editors in *Kluwer*, Jacqueline Bergsma and Tamara Welschot, for making this an interesting and enjoyable venture. Final thanks are due to Deborah Doherty at *Kluwer* for help with the stylefiles. All remaining errors are those of the authors and editors.

Michael Carl & Andy Way

Introduction

Michael Carl and Andy Way

Rule-based Machine Translation (RBMT), Example-based Machine Translation (EBMT), Statistical Machine Translation (SMT): the number of available paradigms for automatic translation has multiplied in the last decade or so and provoked some confusion and terminological inconsistencies. As Somers states in Chapter 1, we believe that the "dust has settled" since a number of basic technologies within the evolving MT paradigms have been presented and tested and valuable experience has been gained — not only within this book, but also in a number of research papers. In this introduction, we shall distinguish EBMT from RBMT and SMT by discussing and clarifying some of the frequently used terms in this volume. This introduction cannot hope to standardize the terminology, as Machine Translation — and in particular EBMT — subsumes a number of different approaches unifying researchers from heterogeneous domains. We refer readers new to EBMT, as well as more familiar researchers interested in an overview of the field, to Chapter 1, where the different problems presented to the EBMT paradigm can be seen, as well as an introduction to the techniques available for solving them. These are all described in more detail in the remaining chapters in the book.

Finally, we present the structure and contents of this volume. The first part, *Foundations of EBMT*, provides the historical, technological and philosophical background of EBMT. The remaining three parts — *Run-time Approaches to EBMT, Template-Driven EBMT*, and *EBMT and Derivation Trees* — give an in-depth overview of the current state of the art in EBMT.

1. Machine Translation Paradigms

1.1 Rule-based Machine Translation

Rule-Based Machine Translation (RBMT) is characterized by linguistic rules used in translation. RBMT systems typically consist of a series of processes which analyze input text: morphological, syntactic and/or semantic analyses; and a process of generating text as a result of a series of structural conversions based on an internal structure or some interlingua. The steps of each process are controlled by a dictionary and a grammar which are obtained through inspection by one (or a group of) linguist(s). This often entails a slow, time-consuming development process, mainly hindered by what has come to be known as the 'knowledge-acquisition bottleneck', as the team of developers first has to fully understand the problem before it can be described in terms of rules (or their exceptions). However, a number of complex problems in MT are not (yet) sufficiently well understood or rely on a full semantic and pragmatic analysis of the corpus, which is rarely available, including:

- development and maintenance of appropriate large-scale grammatical and lexical resources. In the worst case, the addition of a new rule for some intended improvement may cause the entire edifice to topple and performance to degrade.

- quality and level of linguistic detail required for various cases of disambiguation. This problem shows up in a number of different areas, most notably in discriminating between different senses of a word, but also in modelling context sufficiently accurately to enable the relating of pronouns to their antecedents, for instance.

1.2 Corpus-based Machine Translation

Corpus-based Machine Translation (CBMT, also known as Data-driven Machine Translation) is an alternative direction that has been proposed to overcome the knowledge acquisition problem of RBMT systems. CBMT systems assume the existence of a bilingual parallel corpus (usually a database of translated sentences) which is used and/or consulted to derive the required knowledge for new translations. Within the CBMT paradigm, two main directions can be distinguished: **Statistical Machine Translation** and **Example-Based Machine Translation.**

1.3 Statistical Machine Translation

Statistical Machine Translation (SMT) systems implement a highly developed mathematical theory of probability distribution and probability estimation which is rooted in the work of Frederick Jelinek at IBM T.J. Watson Research Center and — in particular — a seminal paper by Brown *et al.*, 1990 (cf. Chapter 1, p.3 for the reaction that the precursor to this work provoked in MT protagonists at *TMI-88*). SMT systems, in the proper sense, learn a translation model from a bilingual parallel corpus, and a language model from a monolingual corpus. At run-time, the best translation is searched for by maximizing the probability according to the two models. Although there have been a number of modifications and enhancements in the intervening years, the original idea assumes an unsupervised approach merely relying on the surface forms of the text with no further linguistic or human intervention. RBMT and SMT typically generate the target sentence from translations of single words, which, in RBMT, are filtered and constrained via a set of rules, or in SMT, via a probability model.

1.4 Example-Based Machine Translation

Example-Based Machine Translation (EBMT) takes a stance somewhere between RBMT and SMT, as many EBMT approaches integrate both rule-based and data-driven techniques. As it is difficult to find an analytical definition of what EBMT is, this book tries to shed some light on the different facets of EBMT. However, there are some typical features which distinguish EBMT from SMT, and others which distinguish it from RBMT. A more thorough discussion of these points is provided in chapters 1 and 2 of this volume.

1.4.1 Translation Units in EBMT. The ideal *translation unit* in EBMT systems is the sentence. EBMT shares this characteristic with **Translation Memory** technology. Only if the translation of an identical sentence is not available in the bilingual corpus, do EBMT systems make use of some sort of similarity metric to find the best matching translation examples. Suitable sub-sequences are iteratively replaced, substituted, modified or adapted in order to generate the translation. While this replacement, substitution, modification or adaptation may be completely rule-driven or also data-driven, the transfer itself, i.e. the mapping of a source segment into an equivalent target segment, is largely guided by or acquired from translation examples. The fact that its systems use entire sentences as a model for new translations has caused EBMT to also be known by the term 'translation by analogy' (among others).

1.4.2 Representations in EBMT. Some EBMT systems use a bilingual, sentence aligned corpus directly during translation. Such EBMT systems are described in Part II in this volume. EBMT systems may also extract the implicit knowledge from the bilingual corpus in advance so that — in a similar manner to SMT — their translation modules (or 'decoder', to use a term from SMT) can use this extracted knowledge for new translations. Such EBMT systems are described in Parts III and IV in this volume. However, while the extracted translation knowledge in SMT is essentially numeric — it consists of huge probability tables for the translation and the language models — the extracted translation knowledge in EBMT is essentially symbolic. This might make it look like RBMT: however, automatically extracted transfer rules *are* different from those obtained via manual inspection by linguists. As is demonstrated thoughout this book, they are too redundant, too specific, too general or simply too unexpected to be written by linguists.

1.4.3 Theoretical Foundations of EBMT. There is no homogeneous theory or computational technique for the processing steps and representations in EBMT: almost all techniques in Artificial Intelligence (AI) are also found in EBMT and there is no linguistic representation or annotation schema which would be excluded *a priori*. We do not see this a major drawback for the integrity of EBMT. In fact, many concepts and approaches in computer (and other) sciences lack an analytical definition, yet this does not imply the absence of the science itself. For instance, there is no uncontroversal definition of what 'artificial intelligence' is, yet, AI is a subject taught in many schools and universities and it is a scientific reality. To give another example, there is no hard line to be drawn between rule-based and knowledge-based approaches to MT. However, both paradigms feel they are distinct and rely on different insights. An example from mainstream linguistics is the distinction between subcategorizable arguments and non-subcategorizable adjuncts. Linguists (and many MT protagonists) find it useful to distinguish between such material in theory, but coming up with clear, precise definitions of governable grammatical functions and modifiers which are applicable in practice is nigh on impossible when confronted with real corpora.

Similarly, EBMT borrows many ideas from neighbouring disciplines such as SMT and RBMT: a common advantage of SMT and EBMT over RBMT is that being based on probabilities, the statistical methods are robust in the face of new, 'unseen' input, whether this be grammatical strings not seen before, or ill-formed input. An advantage of RBMT over SMT, which many approaches to EBMT also take on board, is the use of 'rules' where it makes sense to do so: the use of generalized templates, where abstractions are made over similar examples in the system's databases, can be seen in many of the contributions in this book. The advantage that EBMT has over RBMT in this regard is that any 'rules' or 'constraints' are generally relaxable in EBMT, whereas they are normally hard-wired in rule-based systems.

Furthermore, EBMT takes advantage of some of the utilities from other computational paradigms (such as Cased-based Reasoning, Machine Learning, Parsing and Tagging, and theories of Syntax and Semantics, to name but a few), as is shown in this book.

The least one can say, therefore, is that EBMT subsumes those approaches and systems which people decide to call 'example-based' (cf. Chapter 2 for more discussion on this topic). In addition, it is clear that the trend towards 'hybrid' systems has been readily taken on board by protagonists in the example-based paradigm. We hope to give a representative overview of the current state of the art of our field in this book.

2. Terminology of EBMT

In the EBMT literature — and also in this volume — different terms are used to mean (pretty much) the same thing. While we cannot hope to give an exhaustive list of the terms with their intended use, we shall attempt to clarify some potentially confusing terms for the uninitiated reader in this section.[1]

2.1 Multi-engine vs. Hybrid Machine Translation

Although different knowledge resources are used within the example-based paradigm (cf. Table I.1), an MT system is said to be **hybrid** if the description focuses on the integration of relatively autonomous subsystems (which often implement various computational techniques)

[1] If further help is required, the reader should consult the index at the back of this book.

to achieve different tasks in the MT process. A **hybrid** MT system stands in contrast with a **multi-engine** MT system, as in the latter different MT systems (often implementing different MT paradigms) run in parallel to accomplish the same task. A supervised process then selects the best translations from among the results produced by the parallel machines. Consult Chapter 3 for more discussion on this topic.

Table I.1. Resources and Representations presupposed

Resource	Chapter(s)
Thesaurus	6
Bilingual dictionary	5, 6, 10, 12, 14, 15
Lexical Semantics	7
POS-tagging	5, 7, 8, 12
Morphology	6, 7, 9, 11, 12, 13
Lexeme/lemmatization	5, 9, 12, 13
Monolingual chunking	7, 12, 13
Dependency trees	13, 14, 15
Aligned LFG-treebanks	16

2.2 Translation Templates vs. Translation Patterns

The words **translation-template** and **translation-pattern** (**pattern pairs** and **equivalence class** may also be seen) are used synonymously in the different papers in this volume. These words denote generalizations of translation examples where translated subsequences (e.g. translations of words or sequences of words) are replaced by linked variables.

A translation template (or pattern) is a pre-compiled — often recursive — transfer rule, similar to a transfer rule in a transfer-based MT system. These translation templates are inferred from example translations and are stored in a database to be reused at a later stage in the translation process. For a similar definition and an example, see Chapter 9, page 257, or Chapter 11, page 310.

Depending on the richness of the system, the variables can be annotated with morphosyntactic and/or semantic constraints, or may even represent entire derivation trees.

The extracted translations of words or sequences of words which contain no variables may be referred to as an **atomic translation template**, **lexical translation template** or (more widely) as the **sur-**

face string. Translation templates are also known more generically as **transfer rules** or **transfer mappings**. Sets of lexical and structural translation templates are also known as **translation grammars**.

2.3 Induction, Acquisition and Extraction

The words **Induction**, **Extraction** and **Acquisition** are largely used synonymously and are investigated at various levels of correspondences from words to chunks, templates, derivation trees and logical forms. As Yamamoto and Matsumoto (cf. Chapter 13, section 13.2) point out, there is a difference between **Alignment** and **Extraction**: while the former term implies completeness, the latter focuses on precision. Accordingly, alignment of words, chunks or nodes in pairs of derivation trees is usually a prerequisite for extracting translation patterns, chunk pairs or transfer mappings.

2.4 Fragments, Sequences and Chunks

These terms are also often used synonymously and denote coherent pieces of (monolingual) text. Some authors use the term **fragment** to refer to parsed representations (e.g. Chapters 14 and 16) while others (e.g. Chapter 11) use this to denote sequences of surface word-forms. The term **sequence** itself occurs in a wide variety of variants: sequence of words, sequence of characters, sequence of lemmas; morphemes or simply as match sequence (e.g. Chapter 9), while **chunk** is most often used to denote a segment of surface words.

3. Overview of the Book

We have separated this volume into four parts: the first part, *Foundations of EBMT*, assembles four papers which ground EBMT in a historical and technological context. These papers attempt to explore the rationale of EBMT, to find common characteristics and possible future developments of the translation paradigm. The remaining three parts of the volume describe the different approaches to EBMT. The papers assembled here reflect a general progression from approaches which are least rule-based (the first papers in part II) to those which are most rule- (or constraint-)based, i.e. the latter contributions in part IV.

Part II groups together run-time approaches to EBMT. The contributions in this part have in common that sub-sentential alignment of the input sentence and their mapping on the translation examples in an aligned corpus is computed dynamically at run-time. Notice that here the translation knowledge is left implicit in the bilingual corpus (cf. Chapter 2).

Parts III and IV present compiled approaches to EBMT. We use the bifurcation 'template-driven' versus approaches based on 'derivation trees' in this book. These methods assume that the sub-sentential translation knowledge implicit in the bilingual corpus can be extracted and/or aligned in advance and thus made explicit. Consequently, these approaches distinguish two separate modules: a learning module to acquire and extract implicit knowledge from the bilingual corpus, and a working module which applies this knowledge in the translation phase. While extraction of translation knowledge is at best a side effect in runtime approaches, this is an important processing step in compiled EBMT approaches.

Chapters 2, 3, 4, 10, 11, 12, 15 and 16 are based on papers presented at the workshop in Santiago de Compostela. In addition, a number of authors were invited to complete the volume with Chapters 1, 5, 6, 7, 8, 9, 13 and 14.

3.1 Part I: Foundations of EBMT

The first paper in this section is *An Overview of EBMT*, a revised reprint of an article by Harold Somers which previously appeared in the journal *Machine Translation*. The paper reviews various research efforts within the EBMT paradigm and gives a historical background to TM and EBMT technology. Like RBMT systems, the author claims that EBMT systems also comprise three phases: matching, alignment and recombination. Accordingly, Somers examines how translation examples are stored, matched, retrieved and adapted for new translations in EBMT. Even though examples may be used for different purposes, for Somers, "EBMT means that the main knowledge-base stems from examples" (p.45).

With the aim of approaching a definition of EBMT, Davide Turcato & Fred Popowich argue in Chapter 2, *What is Example-Based Machine Translation?*, that linguistically principled approaches to EBMT significantly overlap with other linguistically principled approaches which are not example-based. In order to find common characteristics in different MT paradigms, the authors examine the declarative knowledge represented in MT systems. Two approaches, they claim, can be regarded as synonynous if they use the same knowledge in the same way. Turcato and Popowich conclude that — in contrast to other approaches — the most characteristic technique in EBMT is translation by analogy.

In Chapter 3, *Example-Based Machine Translation in a Controlled Environment*, Reinhard Schäler, Andy Way & Michael Carl investigate the limits of conventional TM technology. As an extension, the authors propose the idea of the linguistically principled phrasal lexicon (PL), which is learned in a controlled way from a bilingual reference text. TMs, like every corpus-based MT system (including the PL), is necessarily bound to the type of domain from which the translation units are learned. In contrast to TMs, the PL is characterized by an exact match of sub-sentential translation units. The authors suggest that the phrasal lexicon represents a controlled translation device which might be a bridge between TMs and general purpose MT in a multi-engine environment.

Bróna Collins & Harold Somers investigate the view that EBMT is a special case of Case-Based Reasoning (CBR) in Chapter 4. The idea they explore in their contribution, *EBMT Seen as Case-Based Reasoning*, is whether this firmly established AI technique is able to provide the relatively newer EBMT paradigm with novel insights into the solution of the problems of translation. The authors point out that CBR subsumes a number of methods, such as memory-based reasoning, instance-based reasoning, exemplar-based reasoning and analogy-based reasoning. These CBR methods differ in the way examples are stored, how they are represented and how they are used. Although EBMT and CBR have largely developed independently, Collins & Somers find that there is a considerable overlap between components in CBR and components in EBMT and that both can mutually profit from their respective findings.

Within the EBMT community, there is a wide variety of ways that the three phases of matching, alignment and recombination are realized, as shown in Table I.2. There is a wide variety in the resources that different EBMT approaches presuppose (as we showed in Table I.1). While all EBMT approaches require at least a bilingual, sentence-aligned corpus, there is some controversy within the EBMT paradigm (cf. Chapter 2) as to whether the knowledge implicit in the bilingual corpus can be dynamically acquired only at run-time or whether it may be extractable in advance. Parts II, III and IV are structured according to these differences of approach. While Part II presents run-time methods, Parts III and IV present approaches to compiled EBMT which extract translation knowledge in a pre-processing step.

Table I.2. Phases in the Translation Process

Chapter	Author	extraction	translation
Part II			
Chapter 5	Planas & Furuse	—	*
Chapter 6	Sumita	—	*
Chapter 7	Bond & Shirai	—	*
Chapter 8	Andriamanankasina *et al.*	—	*
Part III			
Chapter 9	Cicekli & Güvenir	*	*
Chapter 10	Brown	*	*
Chapter 11	McTait	*	*
Chapter 12	Carl	*	—
Part IV			
Chapter 13	Yamamoto & Matsumoto	*	—
Chapter 14	Watanabe *et al.*	*	—
Chapter 15	Menezes & Richardson	*	*
Chapter 16	Way	—	*

3.2 Part II: Run-time Approaches to EBMT

Part II presents approaches which determine translation units at run-time. Mapping rules are dispensed with in favour of a procedure which involves matching against stored example translations. A similarity measure determines which examples in the source side of the bilingual corpus best match the input string. Translation templates are generated on the fly which can then be filled in by word-for-word translation. As in translation memory technology, therefore, the notion of similarity becomes important with respect to degrees of 'fuzziness' of matches. The advantage of this method of EBMT is that the quality of translations improves incrementally as the example set becomes more complete without the need to update and improve detailed grammatical and lexical descriptions. Moreover, the approach can be very efficient since in the best case there is no complex rule application to perform.

In Chapter 5, *Formalizing Translation Memory*, Emmanuel Planas & Osamu Furuse give theoretical support to translation memories. Based on the TELA structure, a multi-layered lattice, the authors formally redefine the notion of 'fuzzy match' as a mathematically grounded similarity measure. The TELA structure codes the surface forms, lemmas and POS categories of the translation examples. The similarity of the input TELA structure and the TELA structures of the bilingual corpus can be mathematically computed via the 'Multi-level Similar String

Matching' algorithm. Having found the most similar examples, Planas & Furuse eliminate superfluous words in the target example and use a bilingual lexicon to replace translations of words with the appropriate correspondences in the input sentence.

In Chapter 6, *An Example-based Machine Translation System Using DP-Matching Between Word Sequences*, Eiichiro Sumita proposes an EBMT system which retrieves closely matched examples via the similarity of the semantic classes they share. Translation patterns are generated on the fly by generalizing differences. These patterns are temporary structures which are not stored or reused at a later point in the translation process. The approach presupposes knowledge of semantic similarity between words, a thesaurus and a bilingual dictionary. The thesaurus and knowledge of a word's semantics are needed for selecting an appropriate example and for generating an interim template, while the bilingual dictionary is used to translate the differences in the generated template. The author shows that his approach is robust, achieves higher quality than previous approaches and can be extended to multilingual translation.

Francis Bond & Satoshi Shirai propose *A Hybrid Rule and Example-based Method for Machine Translation* in Chapter 7. The authors seek to combine the strengths of the rule-based approach — i.e. information can be obtained by inspection and analysis — and example-based methods which permit translation correspondences to be extracted from raw data. The hybrid approach makes the most of their strengths while compensating as much as possible for the weaknesses of each approach. Inspired by an 'adaptation-guided retrieval' approach (cf. Chapter 4), the example-based approach is used to select the most appropriate translation examples. Translation templates are generated in a similar manner to those in Chapter 6. A rule-based translation method is used to translate differing parts in these templates and to detect and replace their corresponding parts in the target template.

Tantely Andriamanankasina, Kenji Araki & Koji Tochinai propose *EBMT of POS-Tagged Sentences by Recursive Division via Inductive Learning* in Chapter 8. Unlike the approaches in Chapters 5, 6 and 7, Andriamanankasina *et al.* store sub-sententially aligned and POS-tagged examples in a database. Sub-sentential translations can be extracted from the context of the stored examples, thereby avoiding the need for a bilingual lexicon at run-time. The induction of the corresponding sub-sentential source–target parts is based on case-based reasoning. The translations produced can be manually corrected and dynamically added to the database. Andriamanankasina *et al.* show that this learning cycle — a CBR cycle in the terminology of Chapter 4 — leads to better translation results.

3.3 Part III: Template-Driven EBMT

Part III discusses template-driven EBMT systems. EBMT based on the extraction and recombination of translation templates (or translation patterns, cf. page xxi) can be placed somewhere between those EBMT approaches described in Part I of this volume — where the target equivalents of the partial source matches are dynamically computed and recombined — and those EBMT approaches using patterns that bear more resemblance to structural transfer rules, as described in Part IV in this book.

The approaches presented in Part III differ with respect to the resources presupposed. Ilyas Cicekli & Altay Güvenir assume morphologically tagged and lemmatized examples in Chapter 9. Ralf Brown proposes a 'pure' EBMT approach in Chapter 10 where all knowledge (apart from a bilingual dictionary) is extracted from the bilingual corpus. Kevin McTait (Chapter 11) makes use of a POS-tagger and Michael Carl (Chapter 12) presupposes bracketed alignments. Table I.1 on page xxii summarizes the resources assumed for these approaches. While chapters 9, 10 and 11 examine how the induced translation templates are used in the translation process, Chapter 12 is concerned only with the inference of a translation grammar.

Language-neutral techniques for extracting translation patterns are described in chapters 9, 10 and 11. The general principle applied is that given two sentence pairs in a corpus, the orthographically similar parts of the two source language (SL) sentences correspond to the orthographically similar parts of the two target language (TL) sentences. Similarly, the differing parts of the two SL sentences correspond to the differing parts of the TL sentences. The differences are replaced by variables to generalize the sentence pair. Highly inflective (or worse, agglutinative) languages require an amount of linguistic pre-processing.

In the case of Turkish, Cicekli & Güvenir use morphological analysis to alleviate orthographical differences. In their contribution *Learning Translation Templates from Bilingual Translation Examples*, Chapter 9, Cicekli & Güvenir propose the use of analogical reasoning for the learning of lexical correspondences and translation templates from translation examples. Translation templates are learned by generalizing similarities and differences in pairs of translation examples. Generalizations are expressed by means of variables on both source and target language sides of a translation template. These variables replace subsequences in the translation example that can be compositionally translated. Each source variable has a 1-to-1 link to a target variable. The extracted knowledge — lexical correspondences and translation templates — is stored in a database and used at a later stage for the translation of new sentences.

The contribution of Ralf Brown in Chapter 10, *Clustered Transfer-Rule Induction for Example-Based Translation*, represents an instance of a 'pure' EBMT system which extracts translation templates from a bilingual corpus using a conventional and statistical dictionary. While in a previous study the author replaced certain strings denoting numbers, weekdays, country names etc. by an equivalence-class name, he now uses clustering techniques to determine equivalence classes. He combines two techniques from previous work, namely the induction of grammars from (monolingual and bilingual) unlabelled text as well as the use of clustering techniques in EBMT. Translation templates are generated in a similar fashion to the techniques described in Chapter 9. Brown shows in a preliminary experiment that the amount of training text required to translate from French to English can be reduced by a factor of 12 and that the level of abstraction or generalization has consequences for coverage and accuracy.

Kevin McTait discusses *Translation Patterns, Linguistic Knowledge and Complexity in an Approach to EBMT* in Chapter 11. In a similar manner to chapters 9, 10 and 12, he presents an approach to EBMT that extracts translation patterns from aligned bilingual corpora. McTait permits variables in translation patterns to have more than one link in the other language. In this way, he caters for the fact that translation phenomena are not always bijective and that translation relations of a nature other than 1:1 exist. In this way, he is also able to translate non-contiguous constituents. McTait compares three versions of his approach, which vary in the amount of linguistic knowledge incorporated. He concludes that despite the increase in the translation quality achieved, the "cost ... of adding linguistic knowledge sources may not be justified, since they affect portability to new language pairs and domains."

In Chapter 12, *Inducing Translation Grammars from Bracketed Alignments*, Michael Carl presents a knowledge-rich(er) approach to find bilingual correspondences at the phrase-structure level. Aligned structures are replaced by variables to produce translation patterns which are annotated with morphosyntactic information. Carl claims that three properties of translation grammars are desirable: homomorphy, invertibility and compositionality. The author presents an algorithm to generate and filter such a translation grammar from alignments. Carl assumes a seed dictionary, together with morphologically tagged, lemmatized and bracketed alignments, and shows that the induction of such grammars can disambiguate meanings as well as correct bracketing errors.

3.4 Part IV: EBMT and Derivation Trees

Part IV of this volume also examines compilation-time approaches to EBMT. As in part III, the approaches presented here assume that translation knowledge can be extracted from a bilingual corpus (i.e. made explicit) and stored separately with restricted context. Unlike the approaches in Part III, the approaches here deal with structured representations. Kaoru Yamamoto & Yuji Matsumoto (Chapter 13), Hideo Watanabe, Sadao Kurohashi & Eiji Aramaki (Chapter 14) and Arul Menezes & Stephen Richardson (Chapter 15) presuppose dependency trees, while Andy Way (Chapter 16) requires aligned Lexical-Functional Grammar (LFG) treebanks.

The contribution of Kaoru Yamamoto & Yuji Matsomoto, *Extracting Translation Knowledge from Parallel Corpora*, Chapter 13, examines the possibilities of extracting word and phrase translations using different resources. First, the authors investigate how far statistically probable dependency relations are efficient for this end. Using a publicly available dependency parser, they achieve 90% precision despite the fact that statistical parsers are prone to errors. Secondly, they investigate the extent to which linguistic clues obtained using Natural Language Processing tools can be fruitfully exploited to extract translation units. Three methods are compared: bounded-length n-gram, chunk-bounded n-gram and dependency-linked n-gram. The authors find that bounded-length n-gram performs worst while the chunk-bounded n-gram method yields best results in terms of accuracy and coverage. The chunk-bounded n-gram seems to achieve better results because the shallow parser produces more reliable results than the dependency parser. The authors conclude that chunk boundaries seem useful for building an initial lexicon, while for domain-specific or idiomatic expressions the partial use of dependency links is desirable.

The aim of Hideo Watanabe, Sadao Kurohashi & Eiji Aramaki in *Finding Translation Patterns from Paired Source and Target Dependency Structures*, Chapter 14, is to find structural correspondences from pairs of dependency trees which will be re-used in a corpus-based MT system. Their approach first tries to find word correspondences by consulting a bilingual dictionary. Based on these word correspondences, phrasal correspondences are retrieved which cover all elements of the paired dependency trees. As with the dependency parser in Chapter 13, the approach of Watanabe *et al.* suffers in a similar manner from parse errors. In order to overcome this shortcoming, parse errors can be manually corrected via a separate tool. Any such manually corrected word and phrase correspondences are still efficiently reused even if the parser is updated.

Arul Menezes & Stephen Richardson propose *A Best-First Alignment Algorithm for Automatic Extraction of Transfer Mappings from Bilingual Corpora* in Chapter 15. Their approach presupposes a parsed bilingual corpus, inflectional morphology, lemmatization and the semantic labelling of relations between words. The transfer mappings are pairs of logical forms which abstract away from language-specific aspects and which are automatically acquired by using a small alignment grammar. In this way, the authors combine rule-based analysis and generation with example-based transfer. The paper outlines how transfer rules are acquired, post-processed and applied in the translation process. Four different variants of the alignment algorithm are compared and evaluated. The best-first algorithm is shown to improve the quality of the mappings as more contextual information is encoded.

Finally, in Chapter 16, *Translating with Examples: The LFG-DOT Models of Translation*, Andy Way discusses four hybrid EBMT models based on a combination of Data-Oriented Parsing (DOP) and LFG. All models translate new strings on the basis of linked source–target fragments. The two fundamental problems of 'boundary definition' and 'boundary friction' in EBMT are discussed in the light of these models. Way shows that a model of translation harnessing LFG and DOP — unlike many other approaches to EBMT — does not suffer from the problem of boundary friction thanks to the presence of the additional syntactic information present in the f-structures.

References

Brown, P., J. Cocke, S. Della Pietra, F. Jelinek, V. Della Pietra, J. Lafferty, R. Mercer and P. Rossin. 1990. A Statistical Approach to Machine Translation. *Computational Linguistics* **16**:79–85.

Nagao, M.A. 1984. Framework of a Mechanical Translation between Japanese and English by Analogy Principle. In A. Elithorn and R Banerji (eds.) *Artificial and Human Intelligence*, Amsterdam: North-Holland, pp.173–180.

I

FOUNDATIONS OF EXAMPLE-BASED MACHINE TRANSLATION

Chapter 1

AN OVERVIEW OF EBMT

Harold Somers
Harold.Somers@umist.ac.uk

Abstract In the last ten to fifteen years there has been a significant amount of research in Machine Translation within a 'new' paradigm of empirical approaches, often labelled collectively as 'Example-based' approaches. The first manifestation of this approach caused some surprise and hostility among observers more used to different ways of working, but the techniques were quickly adopted and adapted by many researchers, often creating hybrid systems. This paper reviews the various research efforts within this paradigm reported to date, and attempts a categorisation of different manifestations of the general approach.

This paper first appeared in 1999 in *Machine Translation* **14**:113–157. It has been updated with a small number of revisions, and references to more recent work.

Keywords: translation memory, example-based storage, example-based matching, example-based adaptation, example-based transfer, example-based recombination, example-based evaluation

1. Introduction

In 1988, at the Second *TMI* conference at Carnegie Mellon University, IBM's Peter Brown shocked the audience by presenting an approach to Machine Translation (MT) which was quite unlike anything that most of the audience had ever seen or even dreamed of before (Brown *et al.*, 1988). IBM's 'purely statistical' approach, which was inspired by successes in speech processing, and characterized by the infamous statement "Every time I fire a linguist, my system's performance improves", flew in the face of all the received wisdom about how to do MT at that time,

M. Carl and A. Way (eds.), Recent Advances in Example-Based Machine Translation, 3–57.

eschewing the rationalist linguistic approach in favour of an empirical corpus-based one.

There followed something of a flood of 'new' approaches to MT, few as overtly statistical as the IBM approach, but all having in common the use of a corpus of translation examples rather than linguistic rules as a significant component. This apparent difference was often seen as a confrontation, especially for example at the 1992 *TMI* conference in Montreal, which had the explicit theme 'Empiricist vs. Rationalist Methods in MT' (TMI, 1992), though already by that date most researchers were developing hybrid solutions using both corpus-based and theory-based techniques.

The heat has largely evaporated from the debate, so that now the 'new' approaches are considered mainstream, in contrast though not in conflict with the older rule-based approaches.

In this paper, we will review the achievements of a range of approaches to corpus-based MT which we will consider variants of EBMT, although individual authors have used alternative names, perhaps wanting to bring out some key difference that distinguishes their own approach. Among the terms that have been used are: 'analogy-based', 'memory-based', 'case-based' and 'experience-guided'. These approaches all have in common the use of a corpus or database of already translated examples, and involve a process of matching a new input against this database to extract suitable examples which are then recombined in an analogical manner to determine the correct translation.

There is an obvious affinity between EBMT and Machine Learning techniques such as Exemplar-Based Learning (Medin & Schaffer, 1978), Memory-Based Reasoning (Stanfill & Waltz, 1986), Derivational Analogy (Carbonell, 1986), Case-Based Reasoning (Riesbeck & Schank, 1989), Analogical Modelling (Skousen, 1989), and so on, though interestingly this connection is only rarely made in EBMT articles, and there has been no explicit attempt to relate the extensive literature on this approach to Machine Learning to the specific task of translation, a notable exception being Collins' 1998 PhD thesis (see also Chapter 4, this volume).

One major variant of the 'new paradigm' is the purely statistical approach already mentioned, and usually identified with the IBM group's *Candide* system (Brown *et al.*, 1990; Brown *et al.*, 1993), though the approach has also been taken up by a number of other researchers, e.g. (Vogel *et al.*, 1996; Chen & Chen, 1995; Wang & Waibel, 1997). The statistical approach is clearly example-based in that it depends on a bilingual corpus, but the matching and recombination stages that characterize EBMT are implemented in quite a different way in these approaches; more significant is that the important issues for the statistical approach are somewhat different, focusing, as one might expect, on the mathematical aspects of estimation of statistical parameters for the language models. Nevertheless, we will try to include these approaches in our overview.

2. EBMT and Translation Memory

EBMT is often linked with the related technique of 'Translation Memory' (TM). This link is strengthened by the fact that the two gained wide publicity at roughly the same time, and also by the (thankfully short-lived) use of the term 'memory-based translation' as a synonym for EBMT. Some commentators regard EBMT and TM as basically the same thing, while others — the present author included — believe there is an essential difference between the two, rather like the difference between computer-aided (human) translation and MT proper. Although they have in common the idea of reuse of examples of already existing translations, they differ in that TM is an interactive tool for the *human* translator, while EBMT is an essentially *automatic* translation technique or methodology. They share the common problems of storing and accessing a large corpus of examples, and of matching an input phrase or sentence against this corpus; but having located a (set of) relevant example(s), the TM leaves it to the human to decide what, if anything, to do next, whereas this is only the start of the process for EBMT. Recently, Simard & Langlais, 2001 have started to bridge the gap between TM and EBMT with their TM system that takes sub-sentential matches and tries to integrate them into proposals for the target text.

2.1 History of TM

One other thing that EBMT and TM have in common is the long period of time which elapsed between the first mention of the underlying idea and the development of systems exploiting the ideas. It is interesting, briefly, to consider this historical perspective. The original idea for TM is usually attributed to Martin Kay's well-known 'Proper Place' paper (1980), although the details are only hinted at obliquely:

> " ... the translator might start by issuing a command causing the system to display anything in the store that might be relevant to [the text to be translated] ... Before going on, he can examine past and future fragments of text that contain similar material." (Kay, 1980:19)

Interestingly, Kay was pessimistic about any of his ideas for what he called a 'Translator's Amanuensis' ever actually being implemented. But Kay's observations are predated by the suggestion by Peter Arthern, 1978[1] that translators can benefit from on-line access to similar, already translated documents, and in a follow-up article, Arthern's proposals quite clearly describe what we now call TMs:

> "It must in fact be possible to produce a programme [sic] which would enable the word processor to 'remember' whether any part of a new text typed into it had already been translated, and to fetch this part, together with the translation which had already been translated, ... Any new text would be typed into a word processing station, and as it was being typed, the system would check this text against the earlier texts stored in its memory, together with its translation into all the other official languages [of the European Community]. ... One advantage over machine translation proper would be that all the passages so retrieved would be grammatically correct. In effect, we should be operating an electronic 'cut and stick' process which would, according to my calculations, save at least 15 per cent of the time which translators now employ in effectively producing translations." (Arthern, 1981:318).

Melby, 1995:225f. suggests that the idea might have originated with his group at Brigham Young University (BYU) in the 1970s. What is certain is that the idea was incorporated, in a very limited way, from about 1981 in *ALPS*, one of the first commercially available MT systems, developed by personnel from BYU. This tool was called 'Repetitions Processing', and was limited to finding exact matches *modulo* alphanumeric strings. The much more inventive name of 'translation memory' does not seem to have come into use until much later.

The first TMs that were actually implemented, apart from the largely inflexible *ALPS* tool, appear to have been Sumita & Tsutsumi's, 1988 *ETOC* ('Easy TO Consult'), and Sadler & Vendelman's, 1990 'Bilingual Knowledge Bank', predating work on corpus alignment which, according to Hutchins, 1998 was the prerequisite for effective implementations of the TM idea.

2.2 History of EBMT

The idea for EBMT dates from about the same time, though the paper presented by Makoto Nagao at a 1981 conference was not published until three years later (Nagao, 1984). The essence of EBMT, called "machine

[1] I am indebted to John Hutchins for bringing this article to my attention. Early proposals for a TM, and other aspects of the idea of a Translator's Workstation are described in (Hutchins, 1998).

translation by example-guided inference, or machine translation by the analogy principle" by Nagao, is succinctly captured by his much quoted statement:

> "Man does not translate a simple sentence by doing deep linguistic analysis, rather, man does translation, first, by properly decomposing an input sentence into certain fragmental phrases, ... then by translating these phrases into other language phrases, and finally by properly composing these fragmental translations into one long sentence. The translation of each fragmental phrase will be done by the analogy translation principle with proper examples as its reference." (Nagao, 1984:178f.)

Nagao correctly identified the three main components of EBMT, namely (i) matching fragments against a database of real examples, (ii) identifying the corresponding translation fragments, and (iii) recombining these to give the target text. Clearly EBMT involves two important and difficult steps beyond the matching task which it shares with TM.

To illustrate, we can take Sato & Nagao's, 1990 example in which the translation of (1) can be arrived at by taking the appropriate fragments from (2a,b) to give us (3).[2] How these fragments are identified as being the appropriate ones and how they are reassembled varies widely in the different approaches that we discuss below.

(1) He buys a book on international politics.

(2) a. He buys a notebook.
Kare wa nōto o kau.
HE topic NOTEBOOK obj BUY.

b. I read a book on international politics.
Watashi wa kokusai seiji nitsuite kakareta hon o yomu.
I topic INTERNATIONAL POLITICS ABOUT CONCERNED BOOK obj READ.

(3) Kare wa kokusai seiji nitsuite kakareta hon o kau.

It is perhaps instructive to take the familiar pyramid diagram, probably first used by Vauquois, 1968, and superimpose the tasks of EBMT (Figure 1.1). The source-text analysis in conventional MT is replaced by the **matching** of the input against the example set (see 'Matching',

[2]In this and subsequent Japanese examples, the widely used Hepburn transcription (Hepburn, 1872) is adopted. This is a phonetic rather than phonemic or literal transcription, and differs from the transcription often used by Japanese authors — sometimes referred to as *wâpurō* 'word-processor' transcription — in several respects, including the transcription of the topic and object particles as *wa* and *o*, rather than *ha* and *wo*, respectively.

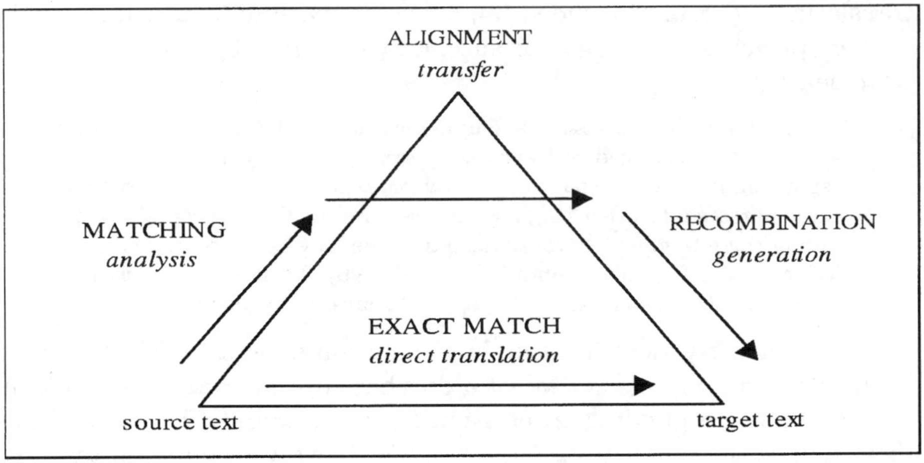

Figure 1.1. The 'Vauquois pyramid' adopted for EBMT. The traditional labels are shown in *italics*; those for EBMT are in CAPITALS.

section 3.6). Once the relevant example or examples have been selected, the corresponding fragments in the target text must be selected. This has been termed **alignment** or **adaptation** and, like transfer in conventional MT, involves contrastive comparison of both languages (see 'Adaptability and recombination', section 3.7). Once the appropriate fragments have been selected, they must be **combined** to form a legal target text, just as the generation stage of conventional MT puts the finishing touches to the output. The parallel with conventional MT is reinforced by the fact that both the matching and recombination stages can, in some implementations, use techniques very similar (or even identical in hybrid systems — see 'Example-based transfer', section 4.4) to analysis and generation in conventional MT. One aspect in which the pyramid diagram does not really work for EBMT is in relating 'direct translation' to 'exact match'. In one sense, the two are alike in that they entail the least analysis; but in another sense, since the exact match represents a perfect representation, requiring no adaptation at all, one could locate it at the top of the pyramid instead.

To complete our history of EBMT, mention should also be made of the work of the DLT group in Utrecht, often ignored in discussions of

EBMT, but dating from about the same time as (and probably without knowledge of) Nagao's work. The matching technique suggested by Nagao involves measuring the semantic proximity of the words, using a thesaurus. A similar idea is found in DLT's 'Linguistic Knowledge Bank' of example phrases described in Pappegaaij *et al.*, 1986a, Pappegaaij *et al.*, 1986b and Schubert, 1986:137f. — see also Hutchins & Somers, 1992:305ff. The 'Bilingual Knowledge Bank' of Sadler, 1991 clearly lies within the EBMT paradigm.

3. Underlying Problems

In this section we will review some of the general problems underlying example-based approaches to MT. Starting with the need for a database of examples, i.e. parallel corpora, we then discuss how to choose appropriate examples for the database, how they should be stored, various methods for matching new inputs against this database, what to do with the examples once they have been selected, and finally, some general computational problems regarding speed and efficiency.

3.1 Parallel corpora

Since EBMT is corpus-based MT, the first thing that is needed is a parallel aligned corpus.[3] Machine-readable parallel corpora in this sense are quite easy to come by: EBMT systems are often felt to be best suited to a sublanguage approach, and an existing corpus of translations can often serve to define implicitly the sublanguage which the system can handle. Researchers may build up their own parallel corpus or may locate such corpora in the public domain. The Canadian and Hong Kong parliaments both provide huge bilingual corpora in the form of their parliamentary proceedings, the European Union is a good source of multilingual documents, while of course many World Wide Web pages are available in two or more languages (Resnik, 1998). Not all these resources necessarily meet the sublanguage criterion, of course.

Once a suitable corpus has been located, there remains the problem of aligning it, i.e. identifying at a finer granularity which segments (typically sentences) correspond to each other. There is a rapidly growing

[3]By 'parallel' we mean a text together with its translation. By 'aligned', we mean that the two texts have been analysed into corresponding segments; the size of these segments may vary, but typically corresponds to sentences. It is of interest to note that for some corpus linguists, the term 'translation corpus' is used to indicate that the texts are mutual translations, while 'parallel corpus' refers to any collection of multilingual texts of a similar genre. Other researchers prefer the term 'comparable corpus', (McEnery & Wilson, 1996:60).

literature on this problem (Fung & McKeown, 1997, includes a reasonable overview and bibliography; see also Somers, 1998) which can range from relatively straightforward for 'well behaved' parallel corpora, to quite difficult, especially for typologically different languages and/or those which do not share the same writing system.

The alignment problem can of course be circumvented by building the example database manually, as is sometimes done for TMs, when sentences and their translations are added to the memory as they are typed in by the translator.

3.2 Granularity of examples

As Nirenburg *et al.*, 1993 point out, the task of locating appropriate matches as the first step in EBMT involves a trade-off between length and similarity. As they put it:

> "The longer the matched passages, the lower the probability of a complete match ... The shorter the passages, the greater the probability of ambiguity (one and the same S' can correspond to more than one passage T') and the greater the danger that the resulting translation will be of low quality, due to passage boundary friction and incorrect chunking." (Nirenburg *et al.*, 1993:48)

The obvious and intuitive 'grain-size' for examples, at least to judge from most implementations, seems to be the sentence, though evidence from translation studies suggests that human translators work with smaller units (Gerloff, 1987). Furthermore, although the sentence as a unit appears to offer some obvious practical advantages — sentence boundaries are for the most part easy to determine, and in experimental systems and in certain domains, sentences are simple, often monoclausal — in the real world, the sentence provides a grain-size which is too big for practical purposes, and the matching and recombination process needs to be able to extract smaller 'chunks' from the examples and yet work with them in an appropriate manner. We will return to this question under 'Adaptability and recombination' below.

Cranias *et al.*, 1994, make the same point: "the potential of EBMT lies [i]n the exploitation of fragments of text smaller than sentences" (Cranias *et al.*, 1994:100) and, in a later paper, suggest that what is needed is a "procedure for determining the best 'cover' of an input text" (Cranias *et al.*, 1997:256). This in turn suggests a need for parallel text alignment at a subsentence level, or that examples are represented in a structured fashion (see 'How are examples stored?', section 3.5).

3.3 How many examples

There is also the question of the *size* of the example database: how many examples are needed? Not all reports give any details of this important aspect. Table 1.1 shows the size of the database of those EBMT systems for which the information is available.

When considering the vast range of example database sizes in Table 1.1, it should be remembered that some of the systems are more experimental than others. One should also bear in mind that the way the examples are stored and used may significantly affect the number needed. Some of the systems listed in the table are not MT systems as such, but may use examples as part of a translation process, e.g. to create transfer rules.

One experiment, reported by Mima *et al.*, 1998 showed how the quality of translation improved as more examples were added to the database: testing cases of the Japanese adnominal particle construction (*A no B*), they loaded the database with 774 examples in increments of 100. Translation accuracy rose steadily from about 30% with 100 examples to about 65% with the full set. A similar, though less striking result was found with another construction, rising from about 75% with 100 examples to nearly 100% with all 689 examples. Sumita & Iida, 1991 and Sato, 1993 also suggest that adding examples improves performance. Although in both cases reported by Mima the improvement was more or less linear, it is assumed that there is some limit after which further examples do not improve the quality. Indeed, as we discuss in the next section, there may be cases where performance starts to decrease as examples are added.

Considering the size of the example data base, it is worth mentioning here Grefenstette's (1999) experiment, in which the entire World Wide Web was used as a virtual corpus in order to select the best (i.e. most frequently occurring) translation of some ambiguous noun compounds in German–English and Spanish–English.

3.4 Suitability of examples

The assumption that an aligned parallel corpus can serve as an example database is not universally made. Several EBMT systems work from a manually constructed database of examples, or from a carefully filtered set of 'real' examples.

There are several reasons for this. A large corpus of naturally occurring text will contain overlapping examples of two sorts: some examples will mutually reinforce each other, either by being identical, or by exemplifying the same translation phenomenon. But other examples will

Table 1.1. Table 1. Size of example database in EBMT systems

System	Reference(s)	Language Pair	Size
PanLite	Frederking & Brown (1996)	Eng → Spa	726 406
PanEBMT	Brown (1997)	Spa → Eng	685 000
MSR-MT	Richardson *et al.* (2001)	Spa → Eng	161 606
MSR-MT	Richardson *et al.* (2001)	Eng → Spa	138 280
TDMT	Sumita *et al.* (1994)	Jap → Eng	100 000
CTM	Sato (1992)	Eng → Jap	67 619
Candide	Brown *et al.* (1990)	Eng → Fre	40 000
no name	Murata *et al.* (1999)	Jap → Eng	36 617
PanLite	Frederking & Brown (1996)	Eng → SCr	34 000
TDMT	Oi *et al.* (1994)	Jap → Eng	12 500
TDMT	Mima *et al.* (1998)	Jap → Eng	10 000
no name	Matsumoto & Kitamura (1997)	Jap → Eng	9 804
TDMT	Mima *et al.* (1998)	Eng → Jap	8 000
MBT3	Sato (1993)	Jap → Eng	7 057
no name	Brown (1999)	Spa → Eng	5 397
no name	Brown (1999)	Fre → Eng	4 188
no name	McTait &Trujillo (1999)	Eng → Spa	3 000
ATR	Sumita *et al.* (1990), Sumita & Iida	Jap → Eng	2 550
no name	Andriamanankasina *et al.* (1999)	Fre → Jap	2 500
Gaijin	Veale & Way (1997)	Eng → Ger	1 836
no name	Sumita *et al.* (1993)	Jap → Eng	1 000
TDMT	Sobashima *et al.* (1994), Sumita & Iida (1995)	Jap → Eng	825
TTL	Güvenir & Cicekli (1998)	Eng → Tur	747
TSMT	Sobashima *et al.* (1994)	Eng → Jap	607
TDMT	Furuse & Iida (1992a,b, 1994)	Jap → Eng	500
TTL	Öz & Cicekli (1998)	Eng → Tur	488
TDMT	Furuse & Iida (1994)	Eng → Jap	350
EDGAR	Carl & Hansen (1999)	Ger → Eng	303
ReVerb	Collins *et al.* (1996), Collins & Cunningham (1997), Collins (1998)	Eng → Ger	214
ReVerb	Collins (1998)	Irish → Eng	120
METLA-1	Juola (1994, 1997)	Eng → Fre	29
METLA-1	Juola (1994, 1997)	Eng → Urdu	7

Key to languages — Eng: English, Fre: French, Ger: German, Jap: Japanese, SCr: Serbo-Croatian, Spa: Spanish, Tur: Turkish be in conflict: the same or similar phrase in one language may have two different translations for no other reason than inconsistency (cf. Carl & Hansen, 1999:619).

Where the examples reinforce each other, this may or may not be useful. Some systems (e.g. Somers *et al.*, 1994; Öz & Cicekli, 1998; Murata, *et al.*, 1999) involve a similarity metric which is sensitive to frequency, so that a large number of similar examples will increase the score given to certain matches. But if no such weighting is used, then multiple similar or identical examples are just extra baggage, and in the worst case may present the system with a choice — a kind of 'ambiguity' — which is simply not relevant: in such systems, the examples can be seen as surrogate 'rules', so that, just as in a traditional rule-based MT system, having multiple examples (rules) covering the same phenomenon leads to overgeneration.

Nomiyama, 1992 introduces the notion of 'exceptional examples', while Watanabe, 1994 goes further in proposing an algorithm for identifying examples such as the sentences in (4) and (5a).[4]

(4) a. *Watashi wa kompyūtā o kyōyōsuru.*
I topic COMPUTER obj SHARE-USE.
'I share the use of a computer.'

b. *Watashi wa kuruma o tsukau.*
I topic CAR obj USE.
'I use a car.'

(5) *Watashi wa dentaku o shiyōsuru.*
I topic CALCULATOR obj USE.
a. 'I share the use of a calculator.'
b. 'I use a calculator.'

Given the input in (5), the system might incorrectly choose (5a) as the translation because of the closer similarity of *dentaku* 'calculator' to *kompyūtā* 'computer' than to *kuruma* 'car' (the three words for 'use' being considered synonyms; see 'Word-based matching', section 3.6.2), whereas (5b) is the correct translation. So (4a) is an exceptional example because it introduces the unrepresentative element of 'share'. The situation can be rectified by removing example (4a) and/or by supplementing it with an unexceptional example.

[4]I have adapted Watanabe's transcription here, and corrected an obvious misprint in (5a).

Distinguishing exceptional and general examples is one of a number of means by which the example-based approach is made to behave more like the traditional rule-based approach. Although it means that 'example interference' can be minimized, EBMT purists might object that this undermines the empirical nature of the example-based method.

3.5 How are examples stored?

EBMT systems differ quite widely in how the translation examples themselves are actually stored. Obviously, the storage issue is closely related to the problem of searching for matches, discussed in the next section.

In the simplest case, the examples may be stored as pairs of strings, with no additional information associated with them. Sometimes, indexing techniques borrowed from Information Retrieval (IR) can be used: this is often necessary where the example database is very large, but there is an added advantage that it may be possible to make use of a wider context in judging the suitability of an example. Imagine, for instance, an example-based dialogue translation system, wishing to translate the simple utterance *OK*. The Japanese translation for this might be *wakarimashita* 'I understand', *iidesu yo* 'I agree', or *ijō desu* 'let's change the subject', depending on the context.[5] It may be necessary to consider the immediately preceding utterance both in the input and in the example database. So the system could broaden the context of its search until it found enough evidence to make the decision about the correct translation.

Of course if this kind of information was expected to be relevant on a regular basis, the examples might actually be stored with some kind of contextual marker already attached. This was the approach taken in the *MEG* system (Somers & Jones, 1992).

3.5.1 Annotated tree structures. Early attempts at EBMT — where the technique was often integrated into a more conventional rule-based system — stored the examples as fully annotated tree structures with explicit links. Figure 1.2 (from Watanabe, 1992) shows how the Japanese example in (6) and its English translation is represented. Similar ideas are found in Sato & Nagao, 1990, Sadler, 1991, Matsumoto *et al.*, 1993, Sato, 1995, Matsumoto & Kitamura, 1995; Meyers *et al.*, 1998 and Watanabe *et al.*, Chapter 14 this volume.

[5]Examples are from Somers *et al.*, 1990:274.

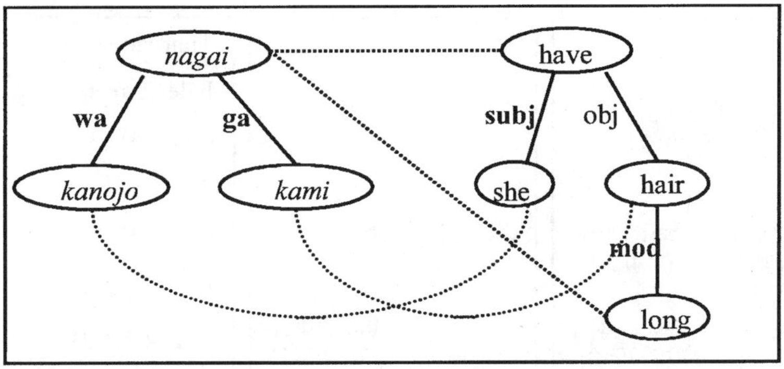

Figure 1.2. Representation Scheme for (6). (Watanabe, 1992)

(6) *Kanojo wa kami ga nagai.*
SHE topic HAIR subj IS-LONG
'She has long hair.'

More recently a similar approach has been used by Poutsma, 1998 and Way, 1999 (cf. Chapter 16, this volume): here, the source text is parsed using Bod's, 1992 DOP (data-oriented parsing) technique, which is itself a kind of example-based approach, then matching subtrees are combined in a compositional manner.

In the system of Al-Adhaileh & Tang, 1999, examples are represented as dependency structures with links at the structural and lexical level expressed by indexes. Figure 1.3 shows the representation for the English–Malay pair in (7).

(7) a. He picks the ball up.
b. *Dia kutip bola itu*
HE PICK-UP BALL THE

The nodes in the trees are indexed to show the lexical head and the span of the tree of which that item is the head: so for example the node labelled 'ball(1)[n](3-4/2-4)' indicates that the subtree headed by *ball*, which is the word spanning nodes 3 to 4 (i.e. the fourth word) is the head of the subtree spanning nodes 2 to 4, i.e. *the ball.* The box labelled 'Translation units' gives the links between the two trees, divided into 'Stree' links, identifying subtree correspondences (e.g. the English subtree 2-4 *the ball* corresponds to the Malay subtree 2-4 *bola itu*) and

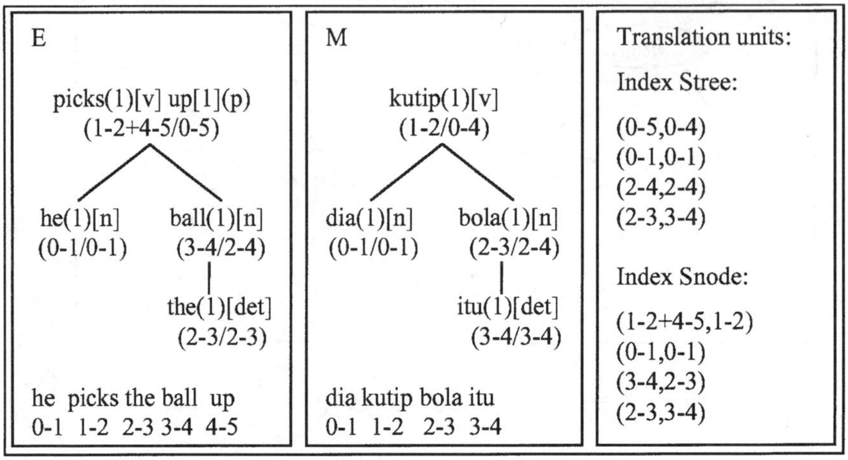

Figure 1.3. Representation scheme for (7). (Al-Adhaileh & Tang, 1999:247)

'Snode' links, identifying lexical correspondences (e.g. English word 3-4 *ball* corresponds to Malay word 2-3 *bola*).

Planas & Furuse, 1999 (see Chapter 5, this volume) represent examples as a multi-level lattice, combining typographic, orthographic, lexical, syntactic and other information. Although their proposal is aimed at TMs, the approach is also suitable for EBMT. Zhao & Tsujii, 1999 propose a multi-dimensional feature graph, with information about speech acts, semantic roles, syntactic categories and functions and so on.

Other systems annotate the examples more superficially. In Jones, 1996 the examples are POS-tagged, carry a Functional Grammar predicate frame and an indication of the sample's rhetorical function. In the *ReVerb* system (Collins & Cunningham, 1995; Collins, 1998), the examples are tagged, carry information about syntactic function, and explicit links between 'chunks' (see Figure 1.5, p.28). Andriamanankasina *et al.*, 1999 (see also Chapter 8, this volume) have POS tags and explicit lexical links between the two languages. Kitano's, 1993 'segment map' is a set of lexical links between the lemmatized words of the examples. In Somers *et al.*, 1994 the words are POS-tagged but not explicitly linked.

3.5.2 Generalized examples. In some systems, similar examples are combined and stored as a single 'generalized' example. Brown, 1999 (and Chapter 10, this volume) for instance tokenizes the examples to show equivalence classes such as 'person's name', 'date', 'city name', and also linguistic information such as gender and number. In this approach, phrases in the examples are *replaced* by these tokens, thereby making the examples more general. For example, (8a) can be generalized as (8b), or, further as (8c). If we then have an input like (8d), this can be matched quite easily with (8c) which can then be used as a template, whereas a match with the original text (8a) would be more difficult because of superficial differences.

(8) a. John Miller flew to Frankfurt on December 3rd.

b. <1stname> <lastname> flew to <city> on <month> <ord>.

c. <person-m> flew to <city> on <date> .

d. Dr Howard Johnson flew to Ithaca on 7 April 1997.

This idea is adopted in a number of other systems where general rules are derived from examples, as detailed in 'Example-based transfer' below. Collins & Cunningham, 1995:97f. show how examples can be generalized for the purposes of retrieval, but with a corresponding precision–recall trade-off.

The idea is taken to its extreme in the proposal of Furuse & Iida, 1992a and Furuse & Iida, 1992b, where examples are stored in one of three ways: (a) literal examples, (b) 'pattern examples' with variables instead of words, and (c) 'grammar examples' expressed as context-sensitive rewrite rules, using sets of words which are concrete instances of each category. Each type is exemplified in (9–11), respectively.

(9) *Sochira ni okeru* → We will send it to you.
Sochira wa jimukyoku desu → This is the office.

(10) *X o onegai shimasu* → may I speak to the X′
(X = *jimukyoku* 'office', ...)
X o onegai shimasu → please give me the X′
(X = *bangō* 'number', ...)

(11) *N*1 *N*2 *N*3 → the N3′ of the N1′
(N1 = *kaigi* 'meeting', N2 = *kaisai* 'opening', N3 = *kikan* 'time')

$N1\ N2\ N3 \quad \rightarrow$ N2′ N3′ for N1′

(N1 = *sanka* ‘participation’, N2 = *mōshikomi* ‘application’, N3 = *yōshi* ‘form’)

As in previous systems, the appropriate template is chosen on the basis of distance in a thesaurus, so the more appropriate translation is chosen as shown in (12).

(12) a. *jinjika o onegai shimasu* (*jinjika* = ‘personnel section’) → may I speak to the personnel section

b. *kenkyukai kaisai kikan* (*kenkyukai* = ‘workshop’) → the time of the workshop

c. *happyō mōshikomi yōshi* (*happyō* = ‘presentation’) → application form for presentation

What is clear is the hybrid nature of this approach, where the type (a) (literal) examples are pure strings, type (c) (‘grammar examples’) are effectively ‘transfer rules’ of the traditional kind, with type (b) (‘pattern examples’) half-way between the two. A similar idea is found in Kitano & Higuchi, 1991a, Kitano & Higuchi, 1991b, who distinguish ‘specific cases’ and ‘generalized cases’, with a ‘unification grammar’ in place for anything not covered by these, though it should be added that their ‘memory-based’ approach lacks many other features usually found in EBMT systems, such as similarity-based matching, adaptation, realignment and so on.

Several other approaches in which the examples are reduced to a more general form are reported together with details of how these generalizations are established in ‘Deriving transfer rules from examples’, section 4.5.

3.5.3 Statistical approaches. At this point we might also mention the way examples are ‘stored’ in the statistical approaches. In fact, in these systems, the examples are not stored at all, except inasmuch as they occur in the corpus on which the system is based. What is stored is the precomputed statistical parameters which give the probabilities for bilingual word pairings, the ‘translation model’. The ‘language model’ which gives the probabilites of target word strings being well-formed is also precomputed, and the translation process consists of a search for the target-language string which optimizes the product of the two sets of probabilities, given the source-language string.

3.6 Matching

The first task in an EBMT system is to take the source-language string to be translated and to find the example (or set of examples) which most closely match it. This is also the essential task facing a TM system. This search problem depends of course on the way the examples are stored. In the case of the statistical approach, the problem is the essentially mathematical one of maximising a huge number of statistical probabilities. In more conventional EBMT systems, the matching process may be more or less linguistically motivated.

3.6.1 Character-based matching. All matching processes necessarily involve a distance or similarity measure. In the most simple case, where the examples are stored as strings, the measure may be a traditional character-based pattern-matching one. In the earliest TM systems as mentioned above (*ALPS*' 'Repetitions Processing', cf. Weaver, 1988), only exact matches, *modulo* alphanumeric strings, were possible: (13a) would be matched with (13b), but the match in (14) would be missed because the system has no way of knowing that *small* and *large* are similar.

(13) a. This is shown as A in the diagram.
b. This is shown as B in the diagram.

(14) a. The large paper tray holds up to 400 sheets of A3 paper.
b. The small paper tray holds up to 300 sheets of A4 paper.

There is an obvious connection to be made here with the well-known problem of sequence comparison in spell-checking (the 'string-correction' or 'string-edit' problem, cf. Wagner & Fischer, 1974), file comparison, speech processing, and other applications, see (Kruskal, 1983). Interestingly, few commentators make the connection explicitly, despite the significant wealth of literature on the subject.[6]

In the case of Japanese–English translation, which many EBMT systems focus on, the notion of character-matching can be modified to take account of the fact that certain 'characters' (in the orthographic sense: each Japanese character is represented by two bytes) are more discriminatory than others (e.g. Sato, 1992). This introduces a simple linguistic dimension to the matching process, and is akin to the well-known device in IR, where only keywords are considered.

[6]Exceptions include Kitano, 1993 and Somers *et al.*, 1994, both of which make reference to Dynamic Programming, and McLean, 1992 who proposes a connectionist model.

3.6.2 Word-based matching. Perhaps the 'classical' similarity measure, suggested by Nagao, 1984 and used in many early EBMT systems, is the use of a thesaurus or similar means of identifying word similarity on the basis of meaning or usage. Here, matches are permitted when words in the input string are replaced by near synonyms (as measured by relative distance in a hierarchically structured vocabulary, or by collocation scores such as mutual information) in the example sentences. This measure is particularly effective in choosing between competing examples, as in Nagao's examples, where, given (15a,b) as models, we choose the correct translation of *eat* in (16a) as *taberu* 'eat (food)', and in (16b) as *okasu* 'erode', on the basis of the relative distance from *he* to *man* and *acid*, and from *potatoes* to *vegetables* and *metal.*

(15) a. A man eats vegetables. *Hito wa yasai o taberu.*

b. Acid eats metal. *San wa kinzoku o okasu.*

(16) a. He eats potatoes. *Kare wa jagaimo o taberu.*

b. Sulphuric acid eats iron. *Ryūsan wa tetsu o okasu.*

Another nice illustration of this idea is provided by Sumita *et al.*, 1990 and Sumita & Iida, 1991 who proposed EBMT as a method of addressing the notorious problem of translating Japanese adnominal particle constructions (*A no B*), where the default or structure-preserving translation (*B of A*) is wrong 80% of the time, and where capturing the wide varieties of alternative translation patterns — a small selection of which is shown in (17) — with semantic features, as had been proposed in more traditional approaches to MT, is cumbersome and error-prone. Note that the Japanese is also underspecified for determiners and number, as well as the basic structure.

(17) a. *yōka no gogo*
8TH-DAY adn AFTERNOON
the afternoon of the 8th

b. *kaigi no mokuteki*
CONFERENCE adn SUBJECT
the subject of the conference

c. *kaigi no sankaryō*
CONFERENCE adn APPLICATION-FEE
the application fee for the conference

d. *kyōto-de no kaigi*
KYOTO-IN adn CONFERENCE
a conference in Kyoto

e. *kyōto-e no densha*
KYOTO-TO adn TRAIN
the Kyoto train

f. *isshukan no kyuka*
ONE-WEEK adn HOLIDAY
one week's holiday

g. *mittsu no hoteru*
THREE adn HOTEL
three hotels

Once again, a thesaurus is used to compare the similarity of the substituted items in a partial match, so that in (18)[7] we get the appropriate translations due to the similarity of *Kyōto* and *Tōkyō* (both place names), *kaigi* 'conference' and *kenkyukai* 'workshop', and *densha* 'train' and *shinkansen* 'bullet train'.

(18) a. *tōkyō-de no kenkyukai*
a workshop in Tokyo

b. *tōkyō-e no shinkansen*
the Tokyo bullet-train

Examples (15)–(18) show how the idea can be used to resolve both lexical and structural transfer ambiguity.

3.6.3 Carroll's 'angle of similarity'. In a little-known research report, Carroll, 1990 suggests a trigonometric similarity measure based on both the relative length and relative contents of the strings to be matched. The basic measure, like others developed later, compares the given sentence with examples in the database looking for similar words and taking account of deletions, insertions and substitutions. The relevance of particular mismatches is reflected as a 'cost', and the cost can be programmed to reflect linguistic generalizations. For example, a missing comma may incur a lesser cost than a missing adjective or noun. And a substitution of like for like — e.g. two dissimilar alphanumerics as in (13) above, or a singular for a plural — costs less than a

[7] The examples have been adapted slightly.

more significant replacement. The grammatical assignment implied by this was effected by a simple stem analysis coupled with a stop-word list: no dictionary as such was needed (though a re-implementation of this nowadays might, for example, use a tagger of the kind that was not available to Carroll in 1990). This gives a kind of 'linguistic distance' measure which we shall refer to below as δ.

In addition to this is a feature which takes into account, unlike many other such similarity measures, the important fact illustrated by the four sentences in (19): if we take (19a) as the given sentence, which of (19b–d) is the better match?

(19) a. Select 'Symbol' in the Insert menu.

b. Select 'Symbol' in the Insert menu to enter a character from the symbol set.

c. Select 'Paste' in the Edit menu.

d. Select 'Paste' in the Edit menu to enter some text from the clip board.

Most similarity metrics will choose (19c) as the better match for (19a) since they differ by only two words, while (19b) has eight additional words. But intuitively, (19b) is a better match since it entirely includes the text of (19a). Further, (19b) and (19d) are more similar than (19a) and (19c). Carroll captures this with his notion of the **angle of similarity**: the distance δ between two sentences is seen as one side of a triangle, with the 'sizes' of the two sentences as the other two sides. These sizes are calculated using the same distance measure, δ, but comparing the sentence to the null sentence, which we represent as $\emptyset$. To arrive at the 'angle of similarity' between two sentences x and y, we construct a triangle with sides of length $\delta(x,\emptyset)$ (the size of x), $\delta(y,\emptyset)$ (the size of y) and $\delta(x,y)$ (the difference between x and y). We can now calculate the angle θ_{xy} between the two sentences using the 'half-sine' formula in (20).[8]

(20) $$\sin\frac{\theta_{xy}}{2} = \frac{\delta(x,y) - |\delta(x,\emptyset) - \delta(y,\emptyset)|}{2\times\min\{\delta(x,\emptyset),\delta(y,\emptyset)\}}$$

We can illustrate this by assuming some values for the δ measure applied to the example sentences in (19), as shown in Table 1.2. The

[8]This formula is preferred over the simpler cosine formula to overcome a small problem to do with the fact that the Euclidean hypothesis implicit in the use of the cosine formula does not in fact hold for our problem. See Carroll, 1990 for details.

angle of 0° in the first row shows that the difference between (19a) and (19b) is entirely due to length differences, that is, a quantitative difference but no qualitative difference. Similarly, the second and third rows show that there is both a qualitative and quantitative difference between the sentences, but the difference between (19b) and (19d) is less than that between (19a) and (19c).

Table 1.2. Half-sine differences between sentences in (19).

Sentence pair		Distance	Size x	Size y	Angle
x	y	δ(x,y)	δ(x,$\emptyset$)	δ (y,$\emptyset$)	θ_{xy}
(19a)	(19b)	125	113	238	0°
(19a)	(19c)	103	113	125	47°
(19b)	(19d)	103	238	250	22°

3.6.4 Annotated word-based matching. The availability to the similarity measure of information about syntactic classes implies some sort of analysis of both the input and the examples. Cranias *et al.*, 1994, Cranias *et al.*, 1997 describe a measure that takes function words into account, and makes use of POS tags. The idea of 'constituent boundary parsing', Furuse & Iida, 1994, is not dissimilar. Here, parsing is simplified by recognizing certain function words as typically indicating a boundary between major constituents. Other major constituents are recognized as part-of-speech bigrams.

Veale & Way, 1997 similarly use sets of closed-class words to segment the examples. Their approach is based on the 'Marker hypothesis' from psycholinguistics (Green, 1979) — the basis also for the EBMT experiments of Juola, 1994, Juola, 1997 — which states that all natural languages have a closed set of specific words or morphemes which appear in a limited set of grammatical contexts and which signal that context.

In the multi-engine *Pangloss* system, the matching process successively 'relaxes' its requirements until a match is found (Nirenburg *et al.*, 1993; Nirenburg *et al.*, 1994): the process begins by looking for exact matches, then allows some deletions or insertions, then word-order differences, then morphological variants, and finally POS-tag differences, each relaxation incurring an increasing penalty.

Chatterjee, 2001 proposes an evaluation scheme where a number of different features, differentially weighted, combine to give a score which reflects similarity at various levels: lexical, morphological, syntactic, semantic, pragmatic. The strength of EBMT, especially for dissimilar language-pairs, is in using examples with a similar meaning, rather than a similar structure, so that the semantic and pragmatic features, which can still be captured by simple morphosyntactic features (e.g. whether the subject of the verb is animate), are weighted heavily.

3.6.5 Structure-based matching. Earlier proposals for EB-MT, and proposals where EBMT is integrated within a more traditional approach, assumed that the examples would be stored as structured objects, so the process involves a rather more complex tree-matching (e.g. Maruyama & Watanabe,1992, Matsumoto *et al.*, 1993, Watanabe, 1995, Al-Adhaileh & Tang, 1999), though there is generally not much discussion of how to do this (Maruyama & Watanabe,1992, Al-Adhaileh & Tang, 1998), and there is certainly a considerable computational cost involved. Indeed, there is a not insignificant literature on tree comparison, the 'tree edit distance' (Noetzel & Selkow, 1983, Zhang & Shasha, 1997; see also Meyers *et al.*, 1996, Meyers *et al.*, 1998) which would obviously be of relevance.

Utsuro *et al.*, 1994 attempt to reduce the computational cost of matching by taking advantage of the surface structure of Japanese, in particular its case-frame-like structure (NPs with overt case-marking). They develop a similarity measure based on a thesaurus for the head nouns. Their method unfortunately relies on the verbs matching exactly, and also seems limited to Japanese or similarly structured languages.

3.6.6 Partial matching for coverage. In most of the techniques mentioned so far, it has been assumed that the aim of the matching process is to find a single example or a set of individual examples that provide the best match for the input. An alternative approach is found in Nirenburg *et al.*, 1993 (see also Brown, 1997), Somers *et al.*, 1994, and Collins, 1998. Here, the matching function decomposes the cases, and makes a collection of — using these authors' respective terminology — 'substrings', 'fragments' or 'chunks' of matched material. Figure 1.4 illustrates the idea.

Jones, 1992 likens this process to 'cloning', suggesting that the recombination process needed for generating the target text (see 'Adaptability and recombination', section 3.7) is also applicable to the matching task:

> "If the dataset of examples is regarded as not a static set of discrete entities but a permutable and flexible interactive set of process modules, we can envisage a control architecture where each process (example) attempts to clone itself with respect to (parts of) the input." (Jones, 1992:165)

```
danger/NN0 of/PRP NN0 < > above/PRP
danger/NN0 of/PRP
of/PRP NN0 < > above/PRP
above/PRP CRD m/NP0
there/PNP is/VVV a/AT0
avalanche/NN0 < > above/PRP
there/PNP is/VVV
is/VVV a/AT0
danger/NN0 of/PRP avalanche/NN0
avalanche/NN0 above/PRP CRD m/NP0
avalanche/NN0 above/PRP
of/PRP avalanche/NN0
there/PNP is/VVV < > a/AT0
is/VVV < > a/AT0
there/PNP is/VVV a/AT0 < > danger/NN0 < > of/PRP
there/PNP
is/VVV < > danger/NN0 < > of/PRP
there/PNP is/VVV a/AT0 < > danger/NN0
a/AT0 < > danger/NN0
there/PNP is/VVV < > danger/NN0
```

Figure 1.4. Fragments extracted for the input ***there is a danger of avalanche above 2000m***. The individual words are tagged; the matcher can also match tags only, and can skip unmatched words, shown as $\langle\ \rangle$. The fragments are scored for relevance and frequency, which determines the order of presentation. From Somers *et al.* 1994.

In the case of Collins, the source-language chunks are explicitly linked to their corresponding translations, but in the other two cases, this linking has to be done at run-time, as is the case for systems where the matcher collects whole examples. We will consider this problem in the next section.

3.7 Adaptability and recombination

Having matched and retrieved a set of examples, with associated translations, the next step is to extract from the translations the appropriate fragments (**alignment** or **adaptation**), and to combine these so as to produce a grammatical target output (**recombination**). This is arguably the most difficult step in the EBMT process: its difficulty can be gauged by imagining a source-language monolingual trying to use a TM system to compose a target text. The problem is twofold: (a) identifying which portion of the associated translation corresponds to the matched portions of the source text, and (b) recombining these portions in an appropriate manner. Compared to the other issues in EBMT, they have received considerably less attention.

We can illustrate the problem by considering again the first example we saw in (1), reproduced here (slightly simplified) as (21):

(21) a. He buys a notebook ⟹ *Kare wa nōto o kau.*

b. I read a book on politics ⟹ *Watashi wa seiji nitsuite kakareta hon o yomu.*

c. He buys a book on politics ⟹ *Kare wa seiji nitsuite kakareta hon o kau.*

To understand how the relevant elements of (21a,b) are combined to give (21c), we must assume that there are several minimally different examples such as those in (22a,b), and a mechanism to extract from them the common elements (underlined here), which are assumed to correspond. Then, we have to make the further assumption that they can be simply pasted together as in (21a), and that this recombination will be appropriate and grammatical. Notice for example how the English word *a* and the Japanese word *o* are both common to all the examples: we might assume (wrongly as it happens) that they are mutual translations. More significantly, a simple pasting of the fragments would actually produce (22c), so there must be some additional mechanism to prevent this.

(22) a. <u>He buys</u> a pen ⟹ <u>*Kare wa*</u> *pen* <u>*o kau.*</u>

b. She wrote <u>a book on politics</u> ⟹
Kanojo <u>*wa seiji nitsuite kakareta hon o*</u> *kaita.*

c. * *Kare wa wa seiji nitsuite kakareta hon o o kau.*

In some approaches, where the examples are stored as tree structures, with the correspondences between the fragments explicitly labeled (cf. Figure 1.2, page 15), the problem effectively disappears. For example, in Sato, 1995, the recombination stage is a kind of tree unification, familiar in computational linguistics. Watanabe, 1992 and Watanabe, 1995 adapt a process called 'gluing' from Graph Grammars, which is a flexible kind of graph unification. Al-Adhaileh & Tang, 1999 state that the process is "analogous to top-down parsing" (p. 249).

Even if the examples are not annotated with the relevant information, in many systems the underlying linguistic knowledge includes information about correspondence at word or chunk level. This may be because the system makes use of a bilingual dictionary (e.g. Kaji *et al.*, 1992;

Matsumoto *et al.*, 1993) or existing MT lexicon, as in the cases where EBMT has been incorporated into an existing rule-based architecture, e.g. Sumita *et al.*, 1990; Frederking & Nirenburg, 1994. Alternatively some systems extract automatically from the example corpus information about probable word alignments, e.g. Somers *et al.*, 1994; Brown, 1997; Veale & Way, 1997; Collins, 1998.

3.7.1 Boundary friction. The problem is also eased, in the case of languages like Japanese and English, by the fact that there is little or no grammatical inflection to indicate syntactic function. So for example the translation associated with *the handsome boy* extracted, say, from (23), is equally reusable in either of the sentences in (24). This, however, is not the case for a language like German (and of course many others), where the form of the determiner, adjective and noun can all carry inflections to indicate grammatical case, as in the translations of (24a,b), shown in (25).

(23) The handsome boy entered the room.

(24) a. The handsome boy ate his breakfast.
b. I saw the handsome boy.

(25) a. *Der schöne Junge aß seinen Frühstück.*
b. *Ich sah den schönen Jungen.*

This is the problem sometimes referred to as 'boundary friction', e.g. Nirenburg *et al.*, 1993:48, Collins, 1998:22 (see also Chapters 14 and 16, this volume). One solution, in a hybrid system, would be to have a grammar of the target language, which could take the results of the gluing process and somehow smooth them over. Where the examples are stored as more than simple text strings, one can see how this might be possible. There is however no report of this approach having been implemented, as far as we know.

Somers *et al.*, 1994 make use of the fact that the fragments have been extracted from real text, and so there is some information about contexts in which the fragment is known to have occurred:

> "'Hooks' are attached to each fragment which enable them to be connected together and their credibility assessed. The most credible combination, i.e. the one with the highest score, *should* be the best translation." Somers *et al.*, 1994:8; emphasis original)

The hooks indicate the words and POS tags that can occur before and after the fragment, with a weighting reflecting the frequency of

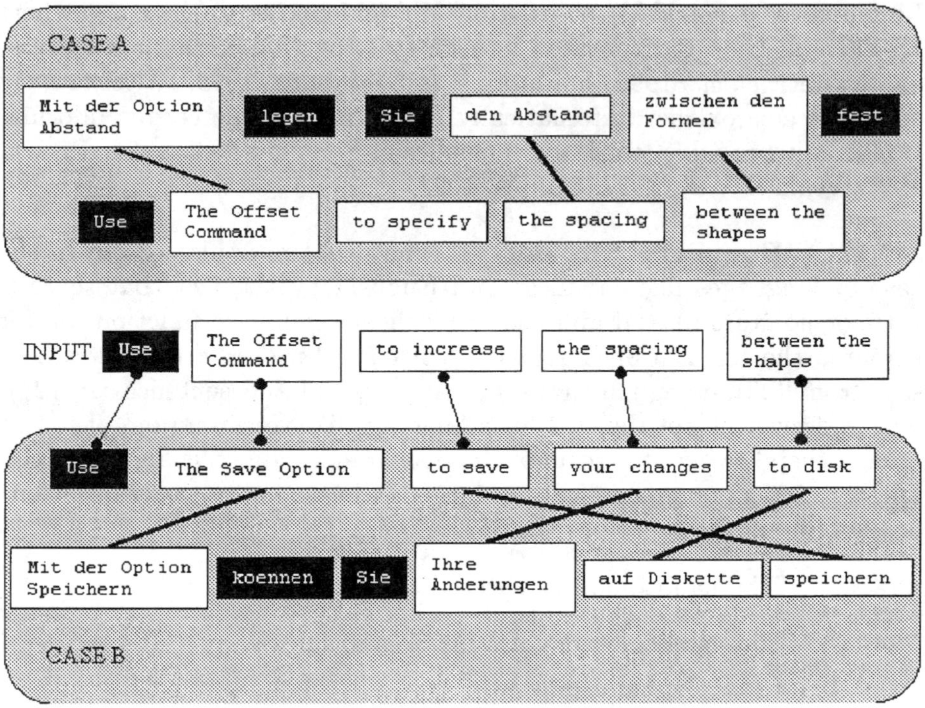

Figure 1.5. Adaptability versus similarity in retrieval (Collins, 1998:81)

this context in the corpus. Competing proposals for target text can be further evaluated by a process the authors call 'disalignment', a kind of back-translation which partly reverses the process: if the proposed target text can be easily matched with the target-language part of the example database, this might be seen as evidence of its grammaticality.

3.7.2 Adaptability. Collins & Cunningham, 1996, Collins & Cunningham, 1997, and Collins, 1998 stress the question of whether all examples are equally reusable with their notion of 'adaptability'. Their example-retrieval process includes a measure of adaptability which indicates the similarity of the example not only in its internal structure, but also in its external context. The notion of 'adaptation-guided retrieval' has been developed in Case-Based Reasoning (CBR) (Smyth & Keane, 1993, Leake, 1995; see also Chapter 4 in this volume): here, when cases are retrieved from the example-base, it is not only their similarity with the given input, but also the extent to which they represent a good model for the desired output, i.e. to which they can be adapted, that determines whether they are chosen. Collins, 1998:31 gives the example of a robot using a restaurant script to get food at *McDonald's*, when buying a stamp at the post-office might actually be a more appropriate, i.e. adaptable, model (cf. Chapter 4, page 141, this volume). Their EBMT system, *ReVerb*, stores the examples together with a functional annotation, cross-linked to indicate both lexical and functional equivalence. This means that example-retrieval can be scored on two counts: (a) the closeness of the match between the input text and the example, and (b) the adaptability of the example, on the basis of the relationship between the representations of the example and its translation. Obviously, good scores on both (a) and (b) give the best combination of retrievability and adaptability, but we might also find examples which are easy to retrieve but difficult to adapt (and are therefore bad examples), or the converse, in which case the good adaptability should compensate for the high retrieval cost. As the following example (from Collins, 1998:81) shows, (26) has a good similarity score with both (27a) and (28a), but the better adaptability of (28b), illustrated in Figure 1.5, makes it a more suitable case.

(26) Use the Offset Command to increase the spacing between the shapes.

(27) a. Use the Offset Command to specify the spacing between the shapes.

b. *Mit der Option Abstand legen Sie den Abstand*
WITH THE OFFSET COMMAND MAKE YOU THE SPACING
zwischen den Formen fest.
BETWEEN THE SHAPES FIRM

(28) a. Use the Save Option to save your changes to disk.

b. *Mit der Option Speichern können Sie ihre Anderungen auf Diskette speichern*
WITH THE SAVE OPTION CAN YOU YOUR CHANGES TO DISK SAVE

3.7.3 Statistical modelling. One other approach to recombination is that taken in the purely statistical system: like the matching problem, recombination is expressed as a statistical modelling problem, the parameters having been precomputed. This time, it is the 'language model' that is invoked, with which the system tries to maximize the product of the word-sequence probabilities.

This approach suggests another way in which 'recombined' target-language proposals could be verified: the frequency of co-occurrence of sequences of 2, 3 or more words (n-grams) can be extracted from corpora. If the target-language corpus (which need not necessarily be made up only of the aligned translations of the examples) is big enough, then appropriate statistics about the probable 'correctness' of the proposed translation could be achieved. There are well-known techniques for calculating the probability of n-gram sequences, and a similar idea is found in the experiment run by Grefenstette, 1999, mentioned above, in which alternative translations of ambiguous noun compounds are verified by using them as search terms on the World Wide Web.

By way of example, consider again (24b) above, and its translation into German, (25b), repeated here as (29a). Suppose that an alternative translation (29b), using the substring from (25a), was proposed. In an informal experiment with *AltaVista*, we used 'Ich sah den' and 'Ich sah der' as search terms, stipulating German web pages. The former gave 341 hits while the latter only 17. With ich rather than Ich in either case, the hits were 467 and 28 respectively. Other search engines produced similar or better results.

(29) a. *Ich sah den schönen Jungen.*

b. * *Ich sah der schöne Junge.*

3.8 Computational problems

All the approaches mentioned so far of course have to be implemented as computer programs, and significant computational factors influence many of them. One criticism to be made of the approaches which store the examples as complex annotated structures is the huge computational cost in terms of creation, storage and matching/retrieval algorithms. This is particularly problematic if such resources are difficult to obtain for one (or both) of the languages, as Güvenir & Cicekli, 1998 report, relating to earlier work by Güvenir & Tunç, 1996 on Turkish. Sumita & Iida, 1995 is one of the few papers to address this issue explicitly, turning to parallel processing for help, a solution also adopted by Kitano, 1994 and Sato, 1995. The approach of Utsuro *et al.*, 1994 has been described in 'Structure-based matching' above.

A further criticism is that the complexities involved detract from some of the alleged advantages of EBMT, particularly the idea that the system's linguistic knowledge can be extended 'simply' by increasing the size of the example-set, cf. Sato & Nagao, 1990:252: adding more examples involves a significant overhead if these examples must be parsed, and the resulting representations possibly checked by a human. In the same vein, another advantage of the EBMT approach is said to be the ability to develop systems despite a lack of resources such as parsers, lexicons and so on, a key difference between the so-called rationalist and empiricist approaches to MT: a good example of this is the corpus-based Portuguese–Chinese MT system developed by Li *et al.*, 1999, a language pair whose development is enabled (and, in a circular manner, made necessary) by the particular situation in Macao.

One important computational issue is speed, especially for those of the EBMT systems that are used for real-time speech translation. Sumita *et al.*, 1993 address this problem with the use of 'massively parallel processors'. With a small example base (1,000 cases) they achieved processing speeds almost 13 times faster than a more conventional architecture. For a more significant database, say 64,000 examples, the improvement would be 832 times. They warn, however, that speed advantages can be lost if the communication between the parallel processors and other processors is inefficient. It is understandable that some researchers are looking at ways of maximising the effect of the examples by identifying and making explicit significant generalizations. In this way the hybrid system has emerged, assuming the advantages of both the example-based and rule-based approaches.

4. Flavours of EBMT

So far we have looked at various solutions to the individual problems which make up EBMT. In this section, we prefer to take a wider view, to consider the various different contexts in which EBMT has been proposed. In many cases, EBMT is used as a component in an MT system which also has more traditional elements: EBMT may be used in parallel with these other 'engines', or just for certain classes of problems, or when some other component cannot deliver a result. Also, EBMT methods may be better suited to some kinds of applications than others. And finally, it may not be obvious any more what exactly is the dividing line between EBMT and so-called 'traditional' rule-based approaches (cf. Chapter 2, this volume). As the second paragraph of this paper suggests, EBMT was once seen as a bitter rival to the existing paradigm, but there now seems to be a much more comfortable coexistence.

4.1 Suitable translation problems

Let us consider first the range of translation problems for which EBMT is best suited. Certainly, EBMT is closely allied to *sublanguage* translation, not least because of EBMT's reliance on a real corpus of real examples: at least implicitly, a corpus can go a long way towards defining a sublanguage. On the other hand, nearly all research nowadays in MT is focused on a specific domain or task, so perhaps all MT is sublanguage MT.

More significant is that EBMT is often proposed as an antidote to the problem of 'structure-preserving translation as first choice', cf. Somers, 1987:84, inherent in MT systems which proceed on the basis of structural analysis. Because many EBMT systems do not compute structure, it follows that the source-language structure cannot be imposed on the target language. Indeed, some of the early systems in which EBMT is integrated into a more traditional approach explicitly use EBMT for such cases:

> "When one of the following conditions holds true for a linguistic phenomenon, [rule-based] MT is less suitable than EBMT.
>
> a Translation rule formation is difficult.
>
> b The general rule cannot accurately describe [the] phenomen[on] because it represents a special case.
>
> c Translation cannot be made in a compositional way from target words." (Sumita & Iida, 1991:186)

One obvious question is whether any particular language pairs are more or less well suited to EBMT. Certainly, a large number of EBMT systems have been developed for Japanese–English (or vice versa) — cf. Table 1.1 — and it is sometimes claimed that the EBMT methodology favours typologically distinct languages, in that it distances itself from the structure-preserving approach that serves such language pairs so badly. But the fact that this language-pair is well represented could of course just be an accident of the fact that much of the research has been done in Japan. The availability of corpus material is also a factor, enabling for example an otherwise unlikely (for commercial reasons) language pair such as Portuguese–Chinese to be developed (Li *et al.*, 1999). In fact, the range of languages for which EBMT systems — albeit experimental — have been developed is quite extensive.

4.2 Pure EBMT

Very few research efforts have taken an explicitly 'purist' approach to EBMT. One exception is our own effort (Somers *et al.*, 1994), where we wanted to push to the limits a 'purely non-symbolic approach' in the face of, we felt, a premature acceptance that hybrids were the best solution. Not incorporating any linguistic information that could not be derived automatically from the corpus became a kind of dogma.

The other non-linguistic approach is of course the purely statistical one of Brown *et al.*, 1988, Brown *et al.*, 1990 and Brown *et al.*, 1993. In fact, their aspirations were much less dogmatic, and in the face of mediocre results, they were soon resorting to linguistic knowledge (Brown *et al.*, 1992); not long afterwards the group broke up, though other groups have taken up the mantle of statistics-based MT (Vogel *et al.*, 1996; Wang & Waibel, 1997).

Other approaches, as we have seen above, while remaining more or less true to the case-based (rather than theory-based) approach of EBMT, accept the necessity to incorporate linguistic knowledge either in the representation of the examples, and/or in the matching and recombination processes. This represents one kind of hybridity of approach; but in this section we will look at hybrids in another dimension, where the EBMT approach is integrated into a more conventional system.

4.3 EBMT for special cases

One of the first uses envisaged for the EBMT approach was where the rule-based approach was too difficult. The classical case of this, as was shown above, example (16), was the translation of Japanese adnominal particle constructions. In the *ATR* system (Sumita *et al.*, 1990; Sumita & Iida, 1991), a traditional rule-based system, the EBMT module was invoked just for this kind of example (and a number of other similarly difficult cases). In a similar way, Katoh & Aizawa, 1994 describe how only 'parameterizable fixed phrases' in economics news stories are translated on the basis of examples, in a way very reminiscent of TM systems. Yamabana *et al.*, 1997 integrate rule-based MT with a corpus-based statistical model for lexical selection, and an example-based method for structures such as compound nouns and noun phrases, which have a simple (and therefore sometimes syntactically and semantically idiosyncratic) structure, and also idiomatic expressions.

4.4 Example-based transfer

One can describe a number of systems where examples are stored as trees or other complex structures as 'example-based transfer' systems. Such systems are described in Chapters 14, 15 and 16 in this volume, but see also Sato & Nagao, 1990, Sato, 1992, Sadler, 1991, Watanabe, 1992,

Watanabe, 1993, Watanabe, 1994, Watanabe, 1995, Matsumoto *et al.*, 1993, Jain *et al.*, 1995, Jain *et al.*, 2001, Matsumoto & Kitamura, 1995, Meyers *et al.*, 1998, Al-Adhaileh & Tang, 1998, Al-Adhaileh & Tang, 1999, Zhao & Tsujii, 1999, Richardson *et al.*, 2001. In these systems, source-language input strings are analysed into structured representations in a conventional manner, only transfer is on the basis of examples rather than rules, and then generation of the target-language output is again done in a traditional way.

Watanabe, 1993 (cf. Chapter 14, this volume), provides a detailed description of how 'translation patterns' are actually extracted from examples. Crucial to the process is the comparison of incorrect translations produced by the normal structure-preserving technique with the correct translation, as illustrated in (30).

(30) a. *Kare wa kuruma o kuji de ateru.*
HE topic CAR obj LOTTERY inst STRIKES
Lit. 'He strikes a car with the lottery.'
He wins a car as a prize in the lottery.

b. *Watashi no seibutsugaku no chishiki wa hinjaku da.*
I adn BIOLOGY adn KNOWLEDGE topic WEAK IS
Lit. 'My knowledge of biology is weak.'
I have little knowledge of biology.

Taking the case of (30a), Figure 1.6 shows (a) the translation produced by existing rules or patterns, and (b) the correct translation. The parts of (b) which are different from (a) are highlighted, and provide the new pattern (c).

4.5 Deriving transfer rules from examples

Some researchers take this scenario a step further, using EBMT as a research technique to build the rule base rather than a translation technique *per se*. We can see this in the distinction made by Furuse & Iida, 1992a, Furuse & Iida, 1992b, of the three types of 'example' (9)–(11) above: they refer to 'string-level', 'pattern-level' and 'grammar-level' transfer knowledge, and it seems that the more abstract representations are derived from examples by a process of generalization. The authors do not go into detail about how these generalized rules are constructed, though they *do* give some indication of how and where they are distributed (p. 146): from an analysis of the corpus on which their system is based, they have about 500 string-level rules covering the 50

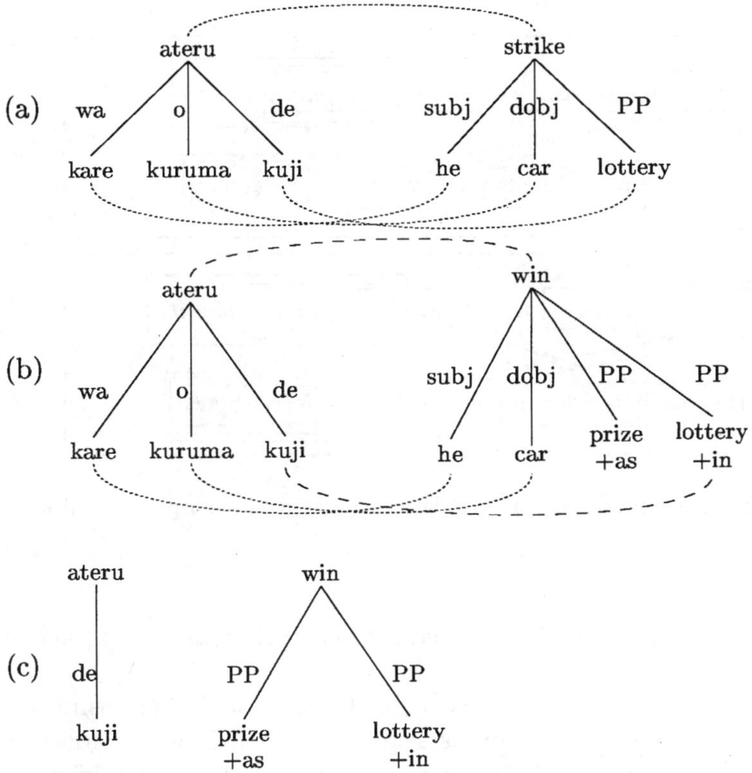

Figure 1.6. Extraction of translation pattern from example. (Watanabe, 1993:293)

most frequent sentences, frequent compound nouns, and single lexical items. About 300 pattern-level rules cover "frequent sentence patterns" and "A particle B patterns such as *A no B*", while there are about 20 grammar-level rules covering "continuation of nouns" (this term is not further explained). Remaining translation problems are handled in the traditional manner.

4.5.1 Generalization by syntactic category. Kaji *et al.*, 1992 describe their 'two phase' EBMT methodology, the first phase involving 'learning' of templates (i.e. transfer rules) from a corpus. Each template is a 'bilingual pair of pseudo sentences', i.e. example sentences containing variables. The translation templates are generated from the corpus first by parsing the translation pairs and then aligning the syntactic units with the help of a bilingual dictionary, resulting in a translation template as in Figure 1.7a. This can then be generalized by replacing

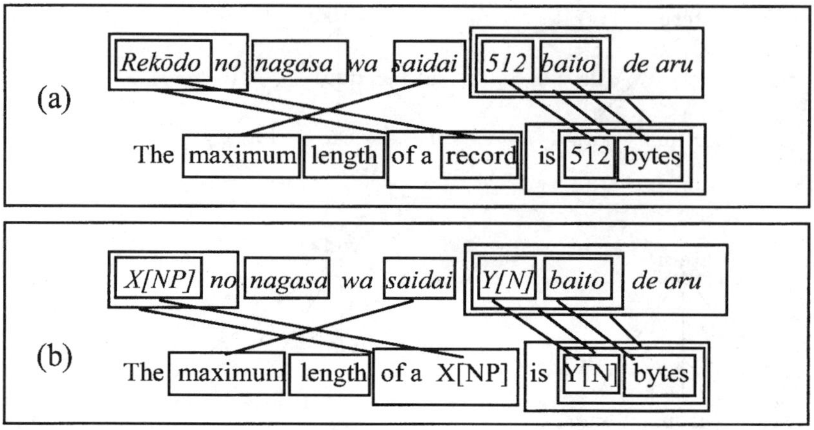

Figure 1.7. Generation of translation templates from aligned example. (Kaji *et al.*, 1992:673)

the coupled units with variables marked for syntactic category, as shown in Figure 1.7b.

Kaji *et al.*, 1992 do not make explicit the criteria for choosing the units: any coupled unit pair can be replaced by variables. However, they do discuss the need to eliminate or refine templates which give rise to a conflict, as in (31–32).

(31) a. play baseball → *yakyu o suru*
b. play tennis → *tenisu o suru*
c. play X[NP] → *X[NP] o suru*

(32) a. play the piano → *piano o hiku*
b. play the violin → *baiorin o hiku*
c. play X[NP] → *X[NP] o hiku*

If possible, the template is 'refined' by the addition of 'semantic categories' which are "extracted from the original translation examples and attached to variables in the template", as shown in (33). The features are apparently determined manually.

(33) a. play X[NP/sport] → *X[NP] o suru*
b. play X[NP/instrument] → *X[NP] o hiku*

Carl, 1999 similarly refines examples to give generalizations based on syntactic categories and morphological features. Likewise, Langé *et al.*, 1997 describe their 'skeleton-sentences' approach to TMs, where candidates for generalization are term pairs or 'transwords' (roughly, alphanumerics and proper names which are not translated). Jain *et al.*, 1995 report a similar approach.

4.5.2 Generalization by semantic features. Matsumoto & Kitamura, 1995 describe how acquisition of general rules centres on individual words. A word must first be chosen explicitly as a possible source of translation rules. Then examples of the word in use are found in the corpus, these being then parsed with 'LFG-like grammars' into dependency structures. From these, matching subgraphs are extracted. If the graphs consist just of a single word, then a word-level rule is generated. Otherwise, it is regarded as a 'phrasal expression'. The elements that differ are generalized according to similarities as determined by thesauri. Matsumoto & Kitamura, 1995 work through an example with the Japanese verb *ataeru*. The most frequent translation found was *give*, when the subject is in one of the semantic classes [substance], [school], [store] or [difference], the direct object one of [difference], [unit], [chance], [feeling], [number] or [start end], and so on. A number of phrasal rules are also identified, as shown in (34), where the number of occurrences in the corpus is also indicated. It is not clear from the text how a rule can be generalized from a single occurrence, as in the last two cases.

(34) a. A[store, school] *ga* B[store, school, cause, ...] *ni eikyō o ataeru*} (17) ↔ A affect B

b. A[store, school] *ga* B[store, school] *ni hōshū o ataeru* (2) ↔ A compensate B

c. A[store, school] *ga* B[store, school] *ni doi o ataeru* (2) ↔ A assent to B

d. A[store] *ga* B[store] *ni shōnin o ataeru* (1) ↔ A authorize B

e. A[store] *ga* B[store] *ni* C[substance] *no hitsuyōryō o ataeru* (1) ↔ A furnish B with C

The authors note that "the quality of the translation rules depends on the quality of the thesaurus" (Matsumoto & Kitamura, 1995:415), and also note that their method works best with non-idiomatic text. Furthermore, their method is restricted to simple active declarative sentences.

Nomiyama, 1992 similarly describes how examples ('cases') can be generalized into rules by combining them when similar segments occur in similar environments, this similarity being based on semantic proximity as given by a hierarchical thesaurus.

Almuallim *et al.*, 1994 and Akiba *et al.*, 1995 report much the same idea, though they are more formal in their description of how the process is implemented, citing the use of two algorithms from Machine Learning. Interestingly, these authors make no claim that their system is therefore 'example-based'. Also, many of the examples that they use to induce the transfer rules are artificially constructed. Watanabe & Takeda, 1998 come to much the same position from the other direction: their 'pattern-based MT' is essentially a variant of the traditional transfer-rule approach, but they propose extending the rule set by incorporating more specific rules (i.e. with fewer variables), and by treating existing rules as if they were examples, so that the rule used to translate a phrase like *take a bus* can be used, in the familiar manner, to translate *take a taxi.*

Malavazos & Piperidis, 2000 present a general scheme based on the Analogical Modelling technique described in Skousen, 1989. Generalizations are automatically learned from the results of attempting to unify similar examples: the similarities between the examples, expressed in terms of linguistic annotations, provide 'supracontexts' in Skousen's terms, i.e. translation *patterns*, while the differences identify translation *units.*

4.5.3 Aligned parse trees. Grishman, 1994, Meyers *et al.*, 1996 and Meyers *et al.*, 1998 are also quite formal in their description of how transfer rules are derived from aligned parse trees. Their representation is very similar to the dependency structures seen in many EBMT papers, though they restrict themselves to "alignments which preserve the dominance relationship" (unlike, for example, the well-known *long hair* example shown in Figure 1.3 above), stating that they see no need to consider violations of this constraint as "there are [none] in our corpus and many hypothetical cases can be avoided by adopting the appropriate grammar" (Meyers *et al.*, 1998:843).

4.5.4 Automatic generalization. A simpler approach, requiring less initial analysis of the corpora is described by Cicekli & Güvenir, 1996, Güvenir & Tunç, 1996 and Güvenir & Cicekli, 1998 for Turkish–English (cf. Chapter 9, this volume); and by McTait *et al.*, 1999, McTait & Trujillo, 1999 (cf. also Chapter 11, this volume) for English–Spanish. Similar examples of translation sentence pairs are discovered and then combined into more general rules in the following way. Consider the pairs of sentences in (35) or (36):

(35) a. I took a ticket from Mary ↔ *Mary'den bir bilet aldım*
b. I took a pen from Mary ↔ *Mary'den bir kalem aldım*

(36) a. The Commission gave the plan up ↔ *La Comisión abandonó el plan*
b. Our Government gave all laws up ↔ *Nuestro Govierno abandonó todas las leyes*

From the sentence pairs can be identified the common elements, which are supposed to be mutual translations (37).

(37) a. I took a ... from Mary ↔ *Mary'den bir ... aldım*
b. ... gave ... up ↔ *abandonó*

This generalization can be stored as a translation 'template'. For Turkish, an agglutinative language, many such generalizations can be missed if examples are considered in their surface form. Therefore, the examples are subjected to a simple morphological analysis. This permits pairs like (38a) to be matched, with lexical representations as in (38b), where *H* is a morphophonemic representation capturing the Turkish vowel harmony.

(38) a. I am coming ↔ *geliyorum*
I am going ↔ *gidiyorum*
b. I am come+ing ↔ *gel+Hyor+yHm*
I am go+ing ↔ *gid+Hyor+yHm*

In both the approaches, the complementary elements in the matched sentences can be supposed to correspond as shown in (39).

(39) a. ticket ↔ *bilet*; pen ↔ *kalem*
b. The Commission ... the plan ↔ *La Comisión ... el plan*;
Our Government ... all laws ↔ *Nuestro Govierno ... todas las leyes*

While the Turkish examples shown here involve a single correspondence, the Spanish examples leave more work to be done, since it is not obvious which of *La Comisión* and *el plan* correspond to *The Commission* and *the plan* (notwithstanding knowledge of Spanish, or recognition of cognates, which is not part of this approach). Güvenir & Cicekli, 1998 (cf. Chapter 9, this volume) also face this problem, which they refer to as a 'Corresponding Difference Pair' (CDP), as in (40), where, taking morphological alternation into account, the common, corresponding, elements are underlined, leaving non-unique CDPs.

(40) a. I gave the book ↔ *Kitabi verdim*

b. You gave the pen ↔ *Kalemi verdin*

Güvenir & Cicekli, 1998 solve this problem by looking for further evidence in the corpus. For example, the pair already seen as (35) suggests that *kalem* corresponds to *pen*. McTait & Trujillo, 1999 suggest an alternative method in which the elements of the 'complement of collocation' are aligned according to their relative string lengths, as in the corpus alignment technique described in Gale & Church, 1993.

A further refinement is added by Öz & Cicekli, 1998, who associate with each translation template derived in the above manner a 'confidence factor' or weight based on the amount of evidence for any rule found in the corpus.

4.6 EBMT as part of a multi-engine system

One other scenario for EBMT is exemplified by the *Pangloss* system, where EBMT operates in parallel with two other techniques: knowledge-based MT and a simpler lexical transfer engine (Frederking & Nirenburg, 1994; Frederking *et al.*, 1994). Nirenburg *et al.*, 1994 and Brown, 1996 describe the EBMT aspect of this work in most detail. Frederking & Brown, 1996 describe the *PanLite* implementation which covers four language pairs: English–Spanish, English–Serbo-Croatian and the inverse. What is most interesting is the extent to which the different approaches often mutually confirm each other's proposed translations, and the comparative evidence that the multi-engine approach offers. Yamabana *et al.*, 1997 also propose a multi-engine system, combining EBMT with rule-based and corpus-based approaches. An important feature of this system is its interactive nature: working bottom up, the system uses a rule-based approach to attempt to derive the syntactic structure, and proposes translations for the structures so determined. These translations are determined in parallel by the different modules of the system, i.e. rule-based transfer, statistics-based lexical selection, and an example-based module. These are then presented to the user who can modify the result of the analysis, intervene in the choice of translation, or directly edit the output.

Chen & Chen, 1995 offer a combination of rule-based and statistical translation. Their approach differs from the previous two in that the translation method chosen is determined by the translation problem, whereas in the other two typically all the different engines will be activated in all cases, and their results compared.

5. Evaluation

An important feature of MT research in recent years has been evaluation, and this is no less the case for EBMT systems. A number of papers report usually small-scale evaluations of their proposals. As with all evaluations, there are the usual questions of what to evaluate and how. Nowhere in the literature so far, as far as we can ascertain, is there a paper exclusively reporting an evaluation of EBMT: so the evaluations that have been reported are usually added on as parts of papers describing the authors' approach. Some papers describe an entire EBMT translation system and so the evaluation section addresses overall translation quality. Other papers describe just one part of the EBMT method, often the matching part, occasionally other aspects.

5.1 Evaluating EBMT as a whole

Where papers describe an entire EBMT translation system and include an evaluation section, this will be an evaluation of the translation quality achieved. As is well known, there are many different ways to evaluate translation quality, almost all of them beset with operational difficulties. The small-scale evaluations described as part of papers reporting broader issues are inevitably informal or impressionistic in nature.

A common theme is to use part of an available bilingual corpus for 'training' the system, and then another part of the same corpus for testing. The translations proposed by the system are then compared to the translations found in the corpus. This is the method famously used by Brown *et al.*, 1990 with their statistical MT system: having estimated parameters based on 117,000 sentences which used only the 1,000 most frequent words in the corpus, they then got the system to translate 73 sentences from elsewhere in the corpus. The results were classified as 'identical', 'alternate' (same meaning, different words), 'different' (legitimate translation but not the same meaning), 'wrong' and 'ungrammatical'. 30% of the translations came in the first two categories, with a further 18% possible but incorrect translations. This figure of 48% provided the baseline from which the authors strive to improve statistical MT until it came close to matching the performance of more traditional MT systems.

A simpler, binary, judgment was used by Sato, 1993 for his example-based technical-term translation system. His test set includes some terms which are also in the training set, though, as he points out, his method does not guarantee correct translation of known terms; nevertheless 113 out of 114 are correctly translated, with 78% accuracy for unknown terms. Using a similar right-or-wrong assessment, Andriamanankasina *et al.*, 1999 (cf. Chapter 8, this volume) initially set up an example-base of 2,500 French–Japanese examples from conversation books, and then tested their system on 400 new sentences taken from the same source. The result was 62% correct translations. In a further experiment, these translations are edited and then added to the database. The success rate rises to 68.5%, which they take to be a very promising result.

Not so rigorous is the evaluation of Furuse & Iida, 1992a and Furuse & Iida, 1992b, who claim an 89% success rate (their notion of 'correct translation' is not defined) for their *TDMT* system, though it seems possible that their evaluation is using the same material from the *ATR* corpus that was used to construct the model in the first place. This also appears to be the case with Murata, *et al.*, 1999, who use a corpus of 36,617 sentences taken from a Japanese–English dictionary for the translation of tense, aspect and modality; they then take 300 randomly selected examples from the same source and compare their system with the output of commercially available software. The problem of needing test data independent of the training data is solved by Sumita & Iida, 1991 with their 'jackknife' evaluation method: the example database of 2,550 examples is partitioned into groups of 100. One group is taken as input and the remaining examples are used as data. This is then replicated 25 times. They report success rates (on the translation of *A no B* noun phrases — see above) between 70% and 89%, with an average of 78%.

Frederking & Nirenburg, 1994 compare the translation performance of the EBMT module with that of the other translation systems in *Pangloss*, their multi-engine MT system. Their evaluation consisted of counting the number of editing key-strokes needed to convert the output into a 'canonical' human translation. The results of a test using a 2,060-character text showed the multi-engine configuration to require 1,716 key-strokes, compared to 1,829 for simple dictionary look-up, 1,876 for EBMT and 1,883 for KBMT, with phrasal glossary look-up worst at 1,973 key-strokes. The authors admit that there are many flaws in this method of evaluation, both in the use of a single model translation (a human translator's version differed from the model by 1,542 key-strokes), and in the way that key-strokes are counted. The evaluation in Brown, 1996 focuses on the usefulness of the proposals made by the EBMT engine, rather than their accuracy. He talks of 70% 'coverage', meaning that useful translation chunks are identified by the matcher, and 84% for which some translation is produced.[9]

Carl & Hansen, 1999 compare translation performance of three types of EBMT system: a string-based TM, a lexeme-based TM and their structure-based EBMT system, *EDGAR*. Each of the systems is trained on a 303-sentence corpus and then tested on 265 examples taken from similar material. The evaluation metric involves comparison of the proposed translation with a manually produced 'ideal', and measures the number of content words in common, apparently taking no account of word-order or grammatical correctness. The evaluation leads to the following conclusions:

> "[T]he least generalizing system ... achieved higher translation precision when near matches can be found in the data base. However, if the reference corpus does not contain any similar translation example, *EDGAR* performed better. We therefore conclude that the more an MT system is able to decompose and generalize the translation sentences, translate parts or single words of it and to recompose it into a target language sentence, the broader is its coverage and the more it loses translation precision." (Carl & Hansen, 1999:623)

5.2 Evaluating the matcher

Some papers on EBMT concentrate on the matching function of their system, a feature which is obviously of relevance also for TM systems. In each case, an attempt is made to quantify not only the number of examples retrieved, but also their usefulness for the translator in the case of a TM, or the effort needed by the next part of the translation process in the case of EBMT. Most evaluations exclude from the test suite any exact matches with the database, since identifying these is recognized as trivial.

Some evaluations involve rating the matches proposed. Both Sato & Nagao, 1990 and Cranias *et al.*, 1994 use 4-point scales. Sato's 'grades' are glossed as follows: (A) exact match, (B) "the example provides

[9]The text is garbled at this point, so we cannot be sure what was meant.

enough information about the translation of the whole input", (C) "the example provides information about the translation of the whole input", (F) "the example provides almost no information about the translation of the whole input". Sato apparently made the judgments himself, and so was presumably able to distinguish between the grades. More rigorously, Cranias *et al.*, 1994 asked a panel of five translators to rate matches proposed by their system on a scale ranging from "a correct (or almost) translation", "very helpful", "[it] can help" and "of no use". Of course both these evaluations could be subject to criticism regarding subjectivity and small numbers of judges.

Matsumoto *et al.*, 1993 could evaluate their structure-based matching algorithm by comparing the proposed structure with a target model. Their reported success rate of 89.8% on 82 pairs of sample sentences randomly selected from a Japanese–English dictionary conceals the fact that 23 of the examples could not be parsed, and of the remaining 59, 53 were correctly parsed. Of these 53, 47 were correctly matched by their algorithm, uniquely in the case of 34 of the examples. So this could be construed as 34 out of 82 unique correct matches: a success rate of 41.4%.

Collins, 1998 uses a classification of the errors made by the matcher to evaluate her 'adaptation-guided retrieval' scheme on 90 examples taken from an unused part of the corpus which she used to train her system.

The matching metrics described in Nirenburg *et al.*, 1993 include a self-scoring metric which can be used to evaluate matches. But an independent evaluation is also needed: they count the number of key-strokes required to convert the closest match back into the input sentence. Counting key-strokes is a useful measure because it relates to the kind of task (post-editing) that is relevant for an example-matching algorithm. As Whyman & Somers, 1999 discuss, however, arriving at this apparently simple measure is not without its difficulties, since mouse moves and clicks must also be counted, and also there are often alternative ways of achieving the same post-editing result, including simply retyping. Their proposal is a general methodology, based on variants of the standard precision and recall measures, for determining the 'fuzzy matching' rate at which a TM performs most efficiently, and is illustrated with a case study. A simpler variant on key-stroke counting is found in Planas & Furuse, 1999 (cf. Chapter 5, this volume), who evaluate their proposed retrieval mechanism for TM by comparing its performance against a leading commercial TM system. Again taking sentences from an unused part of the training corpus, they quantify the difference between the input and the matched sentence by simply counting number of words needing to be changed.

5.3 Other evaluations

Almuallim *et al.*, 1994 and Akiba *et al.*, 1995 describe how examples are used to 'learn' new transfer rules. Their approach, which is in the framework of Machine Learning, includes a 'cross-validation' evaluation of the rules proposed by their technique. The small-scale experiments described in Juola, 1994 and Juola, 1997 with 'self-organizing' MT are accompanied by detailed evaluations, both 'black-box' and 'glass-box'.

McTait & Trujillo, 1999 applied their algorithm for extracting translation patterns to a corpus of 3,000 sentence pairs, and evaluated the 'correctness' of 250 of the proposed templates by asking five bilinguals to judge them. The patterns align 0, 1 and 2 words in the source and target languages in various combinations. The 1:1 patterns, which were the most frequent (220) were 84% correct. The 146 2:2 patterns were 52% correct. 2:1 and 1:2 patterns were the next most accurate (35% of 26 and 21% of 72), while patterns involving alignments with no words (0:1, 0:2 and the converse) were frequently incorrect.

6. Conclusions

In this review, we have seen a range of applications all of which might claim to 'be' EBMT systems. So one outstanding question might be, What counts as EBMT (cf. Chapter 2, this volume)? Certainly, the use of a bilingual corpus is part of the definition, but this is not sufficient. Almost all research on MT nowadays makes use at least of a 'reference' corpus to help to define the range of vocabulary and structures that the system will cover. It must be something more, then.

EBMT means that the main knowledge-base stems from examples. However, as we have seen, examples may be used as a device to shortcut the knowledge-acquisition bottleneck in rule-based MT, the aim being to generalize the examples as much as possible. So part of the criterion might be whether the examples are used at run-time or not: but by this measure, the statistical approach would be ruled out; although the examples are not used to derive rules in the traditional sense, still at run-time there is no consultation of the database of examples.

The original idea for EBMT seems to have been couched firmly in the rule-based paradigm: examples were to be stored as tree structures, so rules must be used to analyse them: only transfer was to be done on the basis of examples, and then only for special, difficult cases. This was apparent in the reserved comments of Sumita *et al.*, 1990:

> "[I]t is not yet clear whether EBMT can/should deal with the whole process of translation. We assume that there are many kinds of phenomena: some are suitable for EBMT and others are not .... Thus, it is more acceptable ... if [rule-based] MT is first introduced as a base system which can translate totally, then its translation performance can be improved incrementally by attaching EBMT components as soon as suitable phenomena for EBMT are recognized." (Sumita *et al.*, 1990:211)

Jones, 1992 discusses the trend towards 'pure' EBMT research, which was motivated both by the comparative success of Sumita *et al.*'s approach, and also as a reaction to the apparent stagnation in research in the conventional paradigm. So the idea grew that EBMT might be a 'new' paradigm altogether, in competition with the old, even. As we have seen, this confrontational aspect has quickly died away, and in particular EBMT has been integrated into more traditional approaches (and *vice versa*, one could say) in many different ways.

We will end this article by mentioning, for the first time, some of the advantages that have been claimed for EBMT. Not all the advantages that were claimed in the early days of polemic are obviously true. But it seems that at least the following do hold, inasmuch as the system design is primarily example-based (e.g. the examples may be 'generalized', but corpus data is still the main source of linguistic knowledge):

- Examples are real language data, so their use leads to systems which cover the constructions which really occur, and ignore the ones that do not, so overgeneration is reduced.
- The linguistic knowledge of the system can be more easily enriched, simply by adding more examples.
- EBMT systems are data-driven, rather than theory-driven: since there are therefore no complex grammars devised by a team of individual linguists, the problem of rule conflict and the need to have an overview of the 'theory', and how the rules interact, is lessened. (On the other hand, as we have seen, there is the opposite problem of conflicting examples.)
- The example-based approach seems to offer some relief from the constraints of 'structure-preserving' translation.
- Depending on the way the examples are used, it is possible that an EBMT system for a new language pair can be quickly developed

on the basis of (only) an aligned parallel corpus. This is obviously attractive if we want an MT system involving a language for which resources such as parsers and dictionaries are not available.

EBMT is certainly here to stay, not as a rival to rule-based methods but as an alternative, available to enhance and, sometimes, replace it. Nor is research in the purely rule-based paradigm finished. As I mentioned in Somers, 1997:116, the problem of scaling up remains, as do a large number of interesting translation problems, especially as new uses for MT (e.g. web-page and e-mail translation) emerge. The 'new' paradigm is now approaching its teenage years: the dust has settled, and the road ahead is all clear.

References

Akiba, Y., M. Ishii, H. Almuallim and S. Kaneda. 1995. Learning English Verb Selection Rules from Hand-made Rules and Translation Examples. In *TMI* (1995), 206–220.[10]

Al-Adhaileh, M.H. and E.K. Tang. 1998. A Flexible Example-Based Parser Based on the SSTC. In *Coling-ACL* (1998), pp.687–693.

Al-Adhaileh, M.H. and E.K. Tang. 1999. Example-Based Machine Translation Based on the Synchronous SSTC Annotation Schema. In *Machine Translation Summit VII*, Singapore, pp.244–249.

Almuallim, H., Y. Akiba, T. Yamazaki, A. Yokoo and S. Kaneda. 1994. Two Methods for Learning ALT-J/E Translation Rules from Examples and a Semantic Hierarchy. In *Coling* (1994), pp.57–63.

Andriamanankasina, T., K. Araki and K. Tochinai. 1999. Example-Based Machine Translation of Part-Of-Speech Tagged Sentences by Recursive Division. In *Machine Translation Summit VII*, Singapore, pp.509–517.

Arthern, P.J. 1979. Machine Translation and Computerized Terminology Systems: A Translator's Viewpoint. In B.M. Snell (ed.) *Translating and the Computer: Proceedings of a Seminar, London*, Amsterdam: North-Holland, pp.77–108.

Arthern, P.J. 1981. Aids Unlimited: The Scope for Machine Aids in a Large Organization. *Aslib Proceedings* **33**:309–319.

Bod, R. 1992. A Computational Model of Language Performance: Data Oriented Parsing. In *Coling* (1992), pp.855–859.

[10] A large number of the papers listed here are from the Coling and TMI conference series. To avoid lengthy repetition, these are listed here separately, and cross-referenced as appropriate.

Brown, P., J. Cocke, S. Della Pietra, V. Della Pietra, F. Jelinek, R. Mercer and P. Roossin. 1988. A Statistical Approach to French/English Translation. In *TMI* (1988), [pages not numbered].

Brown, P.F., J. Cocke, S.A. Della Pietra, V.J. Della Pietra, F. Jelinek, J.D. Lafferty, R.L. Mercer and P.S. Roossin. 1990. A Statistical Approach to Machine Translation. *Computational Linguistics* **16**:79–85.

Brown, P.F., S.A. Della Pietra, V.J. Della Pietra, J.D. Lafferty and R.L. Mercer. 1992. Analysis, Statistical Transfer, and Synthesis in Machine Translation. In *TMI* (1992), pp.83–100.

Brown, P.F., S.A. Della Pietra, V.J. Della Pietra and R.L. Mercer. 1993. The Mathematics of Statistical Machine Translation: Parameter Estimation. *Computational Linguistics* **19**:263–311.

Brown, R.D. 1996. Example-Based Machine Translation in the Pangloss System. In *Coling* (1996), pp.169–174.

Brown, R.D. 1997. Automated Dictionary Extraction for 'Knowledge-Free' Example-Based Translation. In *TMI* (1997), pp.111–118.

Brown, R.D. 1999. Adding Linguistic Knowledge to a Lexical Example-based Translation System. In *TMI* (1999), pp.22–32.

Carbonell, J.G. 1986. Derivational Analogy: A Theory of Reconstructive Problem Solving and Expertise Acquisition. *Machine Learning* **2**.

Carl, M. 1999. Inducing Translation Templates for Example-Based Machine Translation. In *Machine Translation Summit VII*, Singapore, pp.250–258.

Carl, M. and S. Hansen. 1999. Linking Translation Memories with Example-Based Machine Translation. In *Machine Translation Summit VII*, Singapore, pp.617–624.

Carroll, J.J. 1990. Repetitions Processing Using a Metric Space and the Angle of Similarity. Report No. 90/3, Centre for Computational Linguistics, UMIST, Manchester, England.

Chatterjee, N. 2001. A Statistical Approach for Similarity Measurement Between Sentences for EBMT. In *STRANS-2001: Proceedings of a Symposium on Translation Support Systems*, Kanpur, India. [no page numbers]

Chen, K. and H-H. Chen. 1995. Machine Translation: An Integrated Approach. In *TMI* (1995), pp.287–294.

Cicekli, I., and H.A. Güvenir. 1996. Learning Translation Rules From A Bilingual Corpus. In *NeMLaP-2: Proceedings of the Second International Conference on New Methods in Language Processing*, Ankara, Turkey, pp.90–97.

Coling. 1986. *11th International Conference on Computational Linguistics, Proceedings of Coling '86*, Bonn, West Germany.

Coling. 1990. *COLING-90, Papers Presented to the 13th International Conference on Computational Linguistics*, Helsinki, Finland.

Coling. 1992. *Proceedings of the fifteenth [sic] International Conference on Computational Linguistics, COLING-92*, Nantes, France.

Coling. 1994. *COLING 94: The 15th International Conference on Computational Linguistics*, Kyoto, Japan.

Coling. 1996. *COLING-96: The 16th International Conference on Computational Linguistics*, Copenhagen, Denmark.

Coling-ACL. 1998. *COLING-ACL '98: 36th Annual Meeting of the Association for Computational Linguistics and 17th International Conference on Computational Linguistics*, Montreal, Quebec, Canada.

Coling. 2000. *The 18th International Conference on Computational Linguistics: COLING 2000 in Europe*, Saarbrücken, Germany.

Collins, B. 1998. *Example-Based Machine Translation: An Adaptation-Guided Retrieval Approach.* PhD thesis, Trinity College, Dublin.

Collins, B. and P. Cunningham. 1995. A Methodology for Example Based Machine Translation. In *CSNLP 1995: 4th Conference on the Cognitive Science of Natural Language Processing*, Dublin, Ireland, [pages not numbered].

Collins, B. and P. Cunningham. 1996. Adaptation-Guided Retrieval in EBMT: A Case-Based Approach to Machine Translation. In I. Smith and B. Faltings (eds.) *Advances in Case-Based Reasoning: Third European Workshop, EWCBR-96* (Lecture Notes in Computer Science 1168), Berlin: Springer, pp.91–104.

Collins, B. and P. Cunningham. 1997. Adaptation Guided Retrieval: Approaching EBMT with Caution. In *TMI* (1997), pp.119–126.

Collins, B., P. Cunningham and T. Veale. 1996. An Example-Based Approach to Machine Translation. In *Expanding MT Horizons: Proceedings of the Second Conference of the Association for Machine Translation in the Americas*, Montreal, Quebec, Canada, pp.1–13.

Cranias, L., H. Papageorgiou and S. Piperidis. 1994. A Matching Technique in Example-Based Machine Translation. In *Coling* (1994), pp.100–104.

Cranias, L., H. Papageorgiou and S. Piperidis. 1997. Example Retrieval from a Translation Memory. *Natural Language Engineering* **3**:255–277.

Farwell, D., L. Gerber and E. Hovy (eds.). 1998. *Machine Translation and the Information Soup: Third Conference of the Association for Machine Translation in the Americas, AMTA'98*, Berlin: Springer.

Frederking, R. and R. Brown. 1996. The Pangloss-Lite Machine Translation System. In *Expanding MT Horizons: Proceedings of the Second*

Conference of the Association for Machine Translation in the Americas, Montreal, Quebec, Canada, pp.268–272.

Frederking, R. and S. Nirenburg. 1994. Three Heads are Better than One. In *4th Conference on Applied Natural Language Processing*, Stuttgart, Germany, pp.95–100.

Frederking, R., S. Nirenburg, D. Farwell, S. Helmreich, E. Hovy, K. Knight, S. Beale, C. Domashnev, D. Attardo, D. Grannes and R. Brown. 1994. Integrating Translations from Multiple Sources within the Pangloss Mark III Machine Translation System. In *Technology Partnerships for Crossing the Language Barrier: Proceedings of the First Conference of the Association for Machine Translation in the Americas*, Columbia, Maryland, pp.73–80.

Fung, P. and K. McKeown. 1997. A Technical Word- and Term-Translation Aid Using Noisy Parallel Corpora across Language Groups. *Machine Translation* **12**:53–87.

Furuse, O. and H. Iida. 1992a. An Example-Based Method for Transfer-Driven Machine Translation. In *TMI* (1992), pp.139–150.

Furuse, O. and H. Iida. 1992b. Cooperation between Transfer and Analysis in Example-Based Framework. In *Coling* (1992), pp.645–651.

Furuse, O. and H. Iida. 1994. Constituent Boundary Parsing for Example-Based Machine Translation. In *Coling* (1994), pp.105–111.

Gale, W.A. and K.W. Church. 1993. A Program for Aligning Sentences in Bilingual Corpora. *Computational Linguistics* **19**:75–102.

Gerloff, P. 1987. Identifying the Unit of Analysis in Translation. In C. Færch and G. Kasper (eds.) *Introspection in Second Language Research*, Clevedon: Multilingual Matters, pp.135–158.

Green, T.R.G. 1979. The Necessity of Syntax Markers: Two Experiments with Artificial Languages. *Journal of Verbal Learning and Verbal Behavior* **18**:481–496.

Grefenstette, G. 1999. The World Wide Web as a Resource for Example-Based Machine Translation Tasks. In *Translating and the Computer 21*, London: Aslib/IMI, [pages not numbered].

Grishman, R. 1994. Iterative Alignment of Syntactic Structures for a Bilingual Corpus. In *Second Annual Workshop on Very Large Corpora (WVLC2)*, Kyoto, Japan, pp.57–68.

Güvenir, H.A. and I. Cicekli. 1998. Learning Translation Templates from Examples. *Information Systems* **23**:353–363.

Güvenir, H.A. and A. Tunç. 1996. Corpus-Based Learning of Generalized Parse Tree Rules for Translation. In G. McCalla (ed.) *Advances in Artificial Intelligence*, Berlin: Springer Verlag, pp.121–132.

Hepburn, J.C. 1872. *A Japanese-English and English-Japanese Dictionary.* Shanghai: American Prestbyterian Mission Press.

Hutchins, J. 1998. The Origins of the Translator's Workstation. *Machine Translation* **13**:287–307.

Hutchins, W.J. and H.L. Somers. 1992. *An Introduction to Machine Translation.* London: Academic.

Jain, R., R.M.K. Sinha and A. Jain. 1995. Role of Examples in Translation. In *1995 IEEE International Conference on Systems, Man and Cybernetics*, Vancouver, BC, pp.1615–1620.

Jain, R., R.M.K. Sinha and A. Jain. 2001. ANUBHARTI: Using Hybrid Example-Based Approach for Machine Translation. In *STRANS: 2001 Symposium on Translation Support Systems*, Kanpur, India, [pages not numbered].

Jones, D. 1992. Non-hybrid Example-based Machine Translation Architectures. In *TMI* (1992), pp.163–171.

Jones, D. 1996. *Analogical Natural Language Processing.* London: UCL Press.

Juola, P. 1994. A Psycholinguistic Approach to Corpus-Based Machine Translation. In *CSNLP 1994: 3rd Conference on the Cognitive Science of Natural Language Processing*, Dublin, Ireland, [pages not numbered].

Juola, P. 1997. Corpus-Based Acquisition of Transfer Functions Using Psycholinguistic Principles. In D. Jones and H. Somers (eds.) *New Methods in Language Processing*, London: UCL Press, pp.207–218.

Kaji, H., Y. Kida and Y. Morimoto. 1992. Learning Translation Templates from Bilingual Text. In *Coling* (1992), pp.672–678.

Katoh, N. and T. Aizawa. 1994. Machine Translation of Sentences with Fixed Expressions. In *4th Conference on Applied Natural Language Processing*, Stuttgart, Germany, pp.28–33.

Kay, M. 1980. The Proper Place of Men and Machines in Language Translation. Research Report CSL-80-11, Xerox PARC, Palo Alto, Calif. Reprinted in *Machine Translation* (1997) **12**:3–23.

Kitano, H. 1993. A Comprehensive and Practical Model of Memory-Based Machine Translation. In *Proceedings of the International Joint Conference on Artificial Intelligence*, Chambéry, France, pp.1276–1282.

Kitano, H. 1994. *Speech-to-Speech Translation: A Massively Parallel Memory-Based Approach.* Boston: Kluwer.

Kitano, H. and T. Higuchi. 1991a. High Performance Memory-Based Translation on IXM2 Massively Parallel Associative Memory Processor. In *AAAI-91: Proceedings Ninth National Conference on Artificial Intelligence*, Menlo Park: AAAI Press/The MIT Press, pp.149–154.

Kitano, H. and T. Higuchi. 1991b. Massive Parallel Memory-Based Parsing. In *IJCAI-91: Proceedings of the Twelfth International Conference on Artificial Intelligence*, Sydney, Australia, pp.918–924.

Kruskal, J.B. 1983. An Overview of Sequence Comparison. In Sankoff & Kruskal (eds.) (1983), pp.1–44.

Langé, J.M., É. Gaussier and B. Daille. 1997. Bricks and Skeletons: Some Ideas for the Near Future of MAHT. *Machine Translation* **12**:39–51.

Leake, D. 1995. Adaptive Similarity Assessment for Case-based Explanation. *International Journal of Expert Systems* **8**:165–194.

Li, Y., C. Pu and F. Wu. 1999. Portuguese–Chinese Machine Translation in Macao. In *Machine Translation Summit VII*, Singapore, pp.236–243.

Malavazos, C. and S. Piperidis. 2000. Application of Analogical Modelling to Example Based Machine Translation. In *Coling* (2000), pp.516–522.

Maruyama, H. and H. Watanabe. 1992. Tree Cover Search Algorithm for Example-Based Translation. In *TMI* (1992), pp.173–184.

Matsumoto, Y., H. Ishimoto and T. Utsuro. 1993. Structural Matching of Parallel Texts. In *31st Annual Meeting of the Association for Computational Linguistics*, Columbus, Ohio, pp.23–30.

Matsumoto, Y. and M. Kitamura. 1995. Acquisition of Translation Rules from Parallel Corpora. In R. Mitkov and N. Nicolov (eds.) *Recent Advances in Natural Language Processing: Selected Papers from the Conference*, Amsterdam: John Benjamins, pp.405–416.

McEnery, T. and A. Wilson. 1996. *Corpus Linguistics*. Edinburgh: Edinburgh University Press.

McLean, I.J. 1992. Example-Based Machine Translation Using Connectionist Matching. In *TMI* (1992), pp.35–43.

McTait, K., M. Olohan and A. Trujillo. 1999. A Building Blocks approach to Translation Memory', In *Translating and the Computer 21*, London: Aslib/IMI, [pages not numbered].

McTait, K. and A. Trujillo. 1999. A Language-Neutral Sparse-Data Algorithm for Extracting Translation Patterns. In *TMI* (1999), pp.98–108.

Medin, D.L. and M.M. Schaffer. 1978. Context Theory of Classification Learning. *Psychological Review* **85**:207–238.

Melby, A.K. 1995. *The Possibility of Language: A Discussion of the Nature of Language*. Amsterdam: John Benjamins.

Meyers, A., R. Yangarber and R. Grishman. 1996. Alignment of Shared Forests for Bilingual Corpora. In *Coling* (1996), pp.459–465.

Meyers, A., R. Yangarber, R. Grishman, C. Macleod and A. Moreno-Sandeval. 1998. Deriving Transfer Rules from Dominance-Preserving Alignments. In *Coling-ACL* (1998), pp.843–847.

Mima, H., H. Iida and O. Furuse. 1998. Simultaneous Interpretation Utilizing Example-based Incremental Transfer. In *Coling-ACL* (1998), pp.855–861.

Murata, M., Q. Ma, K. Uchimoto and H. Isahara. 1999. An Example-Based Approach to Japanese-to-English Translation of Tense, Aspect, and Modality. In *TMI* (1999), pp.66–76.

Nagao, M. 1984. A Framework of a Mechanical Translation between Japanese and English by Analogy Principle. In A. Elithorn and R. Banerji (eds.) *Artificial and Human Intelligence*, Amsterdam: North-Holland, pp.173–180.

Nirenburg, S., S. Beale and C. Domashnev. 1994. A Full-Text Experiment in Example-Based Machine Translation. In *International Conference on New Methods in Language Processing (NeMLaP)*, Manchester, England, pp.78–87.

Nirenburg, S., C. Domashnev and D. J. Grannes. 1993. Two Approaches to Matching in Example-Based Machine Translation. In *TMI* (1993), pp.47–57.

Noetzel, A.S. and S.M. Selkow. 1983. An Analysis of the General Tree-Editing Problem. In Sankoff & Kruskal (eds.) (1983), pp.237–252.

Nomiyama, H. 1992. Machine Translation by Case Generalization. In *Coling* (1992), pp.714–720.

Oi, K., E. Sumita, O. Furuse, H. Iida and T. Higuchi. 1994. Real-Time Spoken Language Translation Using Associative Processors', In *4th Conference on Applied Natural Language Processing*, Stuttgart, Germany, pp.101–106.

Öz, Z. and I. Cicekli. 1998. Ordering Translation Templates by Assigning Confidence Factors. In Farwell *et al.* (eds.) (1998), pp.51–61.

Pappegaaij, B.C., V. Sadler and A.P.M. Witkam (eds.). 1986a. *Word Expert Semantics: An Interlingual Knowledge-Based Approach.* Dordrecht: Reidel.

Pappegaaij, B.C., V. Sadler and A.P.M. Witkam. 1986b. Experiments with an MT-Directed Lexical Knowledge Bank. In *Coling* (1986), pp.432–434.

Planas, E. and O. Furuse. 1999. Formalizing Translation Memories. In *Machine Translation Summit VII*, Singapore, pp.331–339.

Poutsma, A. 1998. Data-Oriented Translation. In *Computational Linguistics in the Netherlands: Ninth CLIN Meeting*, Leuven, Belgium, [pages not numbered].

Resnik, P. 1998. Parallel Strands: A Preliminary Investigation into Mining the Web for Bilingual Text. In Farwell *et al.* (eds.) (1998), pp.72–82.

Richardson, S.D., W.B. Dolan, A. Menezes and J. Pinkham. 2001. Achieving Commercial-quality Translation with Example-based Methods. In *MT Summit VIII: Machine Translation in the Information Age*, Santiago de Compostela, Spain, pp.293–298.

Riesbeck, C. and R. Schank. 1989. *Inside Case-Based Reasoning.* Hillsdale, NJ: Lawrence Erlbaum.

Sadler, V. 1991. The Textual Knowledge Bank: Design, Construction, Applications. In *International Workshop on Fundamental Research for the Future Generation of Natural Language Processing (FGNLP)*, Kyoto, Japan, pp.17–32.

Sadler, V. and R. Vendelmans. 1990. Pilot Implementation of a Bilingual Knowledge Bank. In *Coling* (1990) **3**:449–451.

Sankoff, D. and J. Kruskal (eds.). 1983. *Time Warps, String Edits, and Macromolecules: The Theory and Practice of Sequence Comparison.* Reading, Mass.: Addison-Wesley; reprinted 1999 by CSLI Publications, Stanford, CA.

Sato, S. 1992. CTM: an Example-Based Translation Aid System. In *Coling* (1992), pp.1259–1363.

Sato, S. 1993. Example-Based Translation of Technical terms. In *TMI* (1993), pp.58–68.

Sato, S. 1995. MBT2: A Method for Combining Fragments of Examples in Example-Based Machine Translation. *Artificial Intelligence* **75**:31–49.

Sato, S. and M. Nagao. 1990. Toward Memory-Based Translation. In *Coling* (1990), **3**:247–252.

Schubert, K. 1986. Linguistic and Extra-Linguistic Knowledge: A Catalogue of Language-related Rules and their Computational Application in Machine Translation. *Computers and Translation* **1**:125–152.

Simard, M. and P. Langlais. 2001. Sub-sentential Exploitation of Translation Memories. In *MT Summit VIII: Machine Translation in the Information Age*, Santiago de Compostela, Spain, pp.335–339.

Skousen, R. 1989. *Analogical Modeling.* Dordrecht: Kluwer.

Smyth, B. and M. T. Keane. 1993. Retrieving Adaptable Cases. In I. Smith and B. Faltings (eds.), *Topics in Case-Based Reasoning: Proceedings of the First European Workshop on Case-Based Reasoning, EWCBR-93*, Berlin: Springer Verlag, **1**:76–82.

Sobashima, Y., O. Furuse, S. Akamine, J. Kawai and H. Iida. 1994. A Bidirectional, Transfer-driven Machine Translation System for Spoken Dialogues. In *Coling* (1994), pp.64–68.

Somers, H. 1987. Some Thoughts on Interface Structure(s). In W. Wilss and K.-D. Schmitz (eds.) *Maschinelle Übersetzung – Methoden und Werkzeuge*, Tübingen: Niemeyer, pp.81–99.

Somers, H. L. 1997. The Current State of Machine Translation. *MT Summit VI: Machine Translation Past Present Future*, San Diego, California, pp.81–99. 115–124.

Somers, H. 1998. Further Experiments in Bilingual Text Alignment. *International Journal of Corpus Linguistics* **3**:1–36.

Somers, H. L. and D. Jones. 1992. Machine Translation Seen as Interactive Multilingual Text Generation. In *Translating and the Computer 13: The Theory and Practice of Machine Translation – A Marriage of Convenience?*, London: Aslib, pp.153–165.

Somers, H., I. McLean and D. Jones. 1994. Experiments in Multilingual Example-Based Generation. In *CSNLP 1994: 3rd Conference on the Cognitive Science of Natural Language Processing*, Dublin, Ireland, [pages not numbered].

Somers, H.L., J. Tsujii and D. Jones. 1990. Machine Translation without a Source Text. In *Coling* (1990) **3**:271–276.

Stanfill, C. and D. Waltz. 1986. Toward Memory-Based Reasoning. *Communications of the ACM* **29**:185–192.

Sumita, E. and H. Iida. 1991. Experiments and Prospects of Example-Based Machine Translation. In *29th Annual Meeting of the Association for Computational Linguistics*, Berkeley, California, pp.185–192.

Sumita, E. and H. Iida. 1995. Heterogeneous Computing for Example-Based Translation of Spoken Language. In *TMI* (1995), pp.273–286.

Sumita, E., H. Iida and H. Kohyama. 1990. Translating with Examples: A New Approach to Machine Translation. In *TMI* (1990), pp.203–212.

Sumita, E., N. Nisiyama and H. Iida. 1994. The Relationship Between Architectures and Example-Retrieval Times. In *AAAI-94: Proceedings of the Twelfth National Conference on Artificial Intelligence*, Menlo Park: AAAI Press, pp.478–483.

Sumita, E., K. Oi, O. Furuse, H. Iida, T. Higuchi, N. Takahashi and H. Kitano. 1993. Example-Based Machine Translation on Massively Parallel Processors. In *Proceedings of the Thirteenth International Joint Conference on Artificial Intelligence*, Chambéry, France, pp.1283–1288.

Sumita, E. and Y. Tsutsumi. 1988. A Translation Aid System Using Flexible Text Retrieval Based on Syntax-Matching. In *TMI* (1988), Proceedings Supplement, [pages not numbered].

TMI. 1988. *Second International Conference on Theoretical and Methodological Issues in Machine Translation of Natural Languages*, Pittsburgh, Pennsylvania.

TMI. 1990. *Third International Conference on Theoretical and Methodological Issues in Machine Translation of Natural Language*, Austin, Texas.

TMI. 1992. *Fourth International Conference on Theoretical and Methodological Issues in Machine Translation: Empiricist vs. Rationalist Methods in MT TMI-92*, Montréal, Canada.

TMI. 1993. *Proceedings of the Fifth International Conference on Theoretical and Methodological Issues in Machine Translation TMI '93: MT in the Next Generation*, Kyoto, Japan.

TMI. 1995. *Proceedings of the Sixth International Conference on Theoretical and Methodological Issues in Machine Translation*, Leuven, Belgium.

TMI. 1997. *Proceedings of the 7th International Conference on Theoretical and Methodological Issues in Machine Translation*, Santa Fe, New Mexico.

TMI. 1999. *Proceedings of the 8th International Conference on Theoretical and Methodological Issues in Machine Translation (TMI 99)*, Chester, England.

Utsuro, T., K. Uchimoto, M. Matsumoto and M. Nagao. 1994. Thesaurus-Based Efficient Example Retrieval by Generating Retrieval Queries from Similarities. In *Coling* (1994), pp.1044–1048.

Vauquois, B. 1968. A Survey of Formal Grammars and Algorithms for Recognition and Transformation in Machine Translation. In *IFIP Congress-68*, Edinburgh, pp.254–260; reprinted in Ch. Boitet (ed.) *Bernard Vauquois et la TAO: Vingt-cinq Ans de Traduction Automatique – Analectes*, Grenoble (1988): Association Champollion, pp.201–213.

Veale, T. and A. Way. 1997. *Gaijin*: A Bootstrapping Approach to Example-Based Machine Translation. In *International Conference, Recent Advances in Natural Language Processing*, Tzigov Chark, Bulgaria, pp.239–244.

Vogel, S., H. Ney and C. Tillmann. 1996. HMM-Based Word Alignment in Statistical Translation. In *Coling* (1996), pp.836–841.

Wagner, R.A. and M.J. Fischer. 1974. The String-to-String Correction Problem. *Journal of the Association for Computing Machinery* **21**: 168–173.

Wang, Y-Y. and A. Waibel. 1997. Decoding Algorithm in Statistical Machine Translation. In *35th Annual Meeting of the Association for Computational Linguistics and 8th Conference of the European Chap-*

ter of the Association for Computational Linguistics, Madrid, Spain, pp.366–372.

Watanabe, H. 1992. A Similarity-Driven Transfer System. In *Coling* (1992), pp.770–776.

Watanabe, H. 1993. A Method for Extracting Translation Patterns from Translation Examples. In *TMI* (1993), pp.292–301.

Watanabe, H. 1994. A Method for Distinguishing Exceptional and General Examples in Example-Based Transfer Systems. In *Coling* (1994), pp.39–44.

Watanabe, H. 1995. A Model of a Bi-Directional Transfer Mechanism Using Rule Combinations. *Machine Translation* **10**:269–291.

Watanabe, H. and K. Takeda. 1998. A Pattern-Based Machine Translation System Extended by Example-Based Processing. In *Coling-ACL* (1998), pp.1369–1373.

Way, A. 1999. A Hybrid Architecture for Robust MT using LFG-DOP. *Journal of Experimental and Theoretical Artificial Intelligence* **11**:441–471.

Weaver, A. 1988. Two Aspects of Interactive Machine Translation. In M. Vasconcellos (ed.) *Technology as Translation Strategy*, Binghamton, NY: State University of New York at Binghamton (SUNY), pp.116–123.

Whyman, E.K. and H.L. Somers. 1999. Evaluation Metrics for a Translation Memory System. *Software–Practice and Experience* **29**:1265–1284.

Yamabana K., S. Kamei, K. Muraki, S. Doi, S. Tamura and K. Satoh. 1997. A Hybrid Approach to Interactive Machine Translation – Integrating Rule-based, Corpus-based, and example-based Method. In *Proceedings of the Fifteenth International Joint Conference on Artificial Intelligence*, Nagoya, Japan, pp.977–982.

Zhang, K. and D. Shasha. 1997. Tree Pattern Matching. In A. Apostolico and Z. Galil (eds.) *Pattern Matching Algorithms*, New York: Oxford University Press, pp.341–371.

Zhao, G. and J. Tsujii. 1999. Transfer in Experience-Guided Machine Translation. In *Machine Translation Summit VII*, Singapore, pp.501–508.

Chapter 2

WHAT IS EXAMPLE-BASED MACHINE TRANSLATION?

Davide Turcato
turk@gavagai.net

Fred Popowich
popowich@gavagai.net

Abstract We maintain that the essential feature that characterizes a Machine Translation approach and sets it apart from other approaches is the kind of knowledge it uses. From this perspective, we argue that Example-Based Machine Translation is sometimes characterized in terms of non-essential features. We show that Example-Based Machine Translation, as long as it is linguistically principled, significantly overlaps with other linguistically principled approaches to Machine Translation. We make a proposal for translation knowledge bases that make such an overlap explicit. We relate our proposal to translation by analogy, which stands out as an inherently example-based technique.

Keywords: classification of EBMT, symbolic EBMT, lexical transfer, translation by analogy, knowledge acquisition

1. Introduction

1.1 Motivation

Human translation is a complex intellectual activity and accordingly Machine Translation (MT) is a complex scientific task, involving virtually every aspect of Natural Language Processing. Many approaches to MT have been proposed, each of them inspired by some insight about translation. Each approach has its own merits, accounting for some aspect of translation better than other approaches, but typically each

M. Carl and A. Way (eds.), Recent Advances in Example-Based Machine Translation, 59–81.

approach's advantages are countered by weaknesses in other respects. The real challenge is combining different approaches and insights into a comprehensive whole. To this end it is important to analyse and classify different approaches, for two reasons:

1 It is important to see to what extent differences are substantial or notational. Sometimes different approaches look at the same subject from different viewpoints, or use different representations, but a formal analysis shows that they are equivalent. This was the case with many formal systems (categorial and phrase structure grammars, finite state machines and regular grammars, explanation-based generalization and partial evaluation, etc.). In other cases differences have been demonstrated to be matters of degree (for instance, in the field of MT, transfer and interlingua approaches).

2 It is important to see to what extent different approaches are mutually exclusive, or whether they can be integrated into one system that encompasses all of them.

In the broad and diversified panorama of MT, we believe that this definition task, far from being a pedantic exercise, is an important step towards separating essential differences among MT approaches from inessential ones. This effort may lead to uncovering overlaps between approaches that at first glance seem quite far apart, or conversely it may bring to light significant differences between approaches that are superficially similar. We believe that a better understanding of the relations among different approaches provides valuable insight that can guide MT researchers in their decisions about further directions to take.

In this chapter we provide a classification of the broad variety of MT research falling within the paradigm of Example-Based Machine Translation (EBMT), and make an attempt at capturing the essential features that make an MT system an example-based one.

1.2 EBMT Overview

This section provides a brief overview of the core ideas of EBMT. Needless to say, this overview is far from complete. It is merely intended as a historical survey describing the fundamental ideas around which the EBMT paradigm was established. More recent approaches are mentioned in parts II–IV in this volume. Some of the most recent of these approaches are not covered in the present chapter. We leave to the reader the exercise of applying the ideas expressed herein to such latest developments.

Arnold *et al.*, 1994:198 outline EBMT as follows: "The basic idea is to collect a bilingual corpus of translation pairs and then use a best match algorithm to find the closest example to the source phrase in question. This gives a translation template, which can then be filled in by word-for-word translation." Given a corpus we can find example translations, which we then adapt based on our current translation needs. Of course, one then needs to address the issue of what constitutes the best match, for there may be many possible near matches in a corpus. This then raises the issue of what kind of processing is done to the corpora to facilitate this matching process.

The paradigm of *translation by analogy* was first introduced by Nagao, 1984. In that paper Nagao advocates the use of raw, unanalysed bilingual data, claiming that linguistic data are more durable than linguistic theories, thus constituting a steadier ground for MT systems. He proposes the use of an unannotated database of examples (possibly collected from a bilingual dictionary) and a set of lexical equivalences simply expressed in terms of word pairs (except for verb equivalences, which are expressed in terms of case frames). The matching process is mainly focused on checking the semantic similarity between the lexical items in the input sentence and the corresponding items in the candidate example.

Many variations and extensions to Nagao's ideas followed, under different names and acronyms, such as Example-Based Machine Translation (EBMT, Sumita & Iida, 1991), Memory-Based Translation (MBT, Sato & Nagao, 1990), Transfer-Driven Machine Translation (TDMT, Furuse & Iida, 1992), and Case-Based Machine Translation (CBMT, Kitano, 1993). There is not always agreement about the usage of such names: for instance, some authors use EBMT and MBT interchangeably, while others keep them distinct. However, all these approaches share the basic idea described above. There are three main directions in which Nagao's original model has been extended.

First, augment the example database with linguistic annotations and, accordingly, perform some linguistic analysis on the input before the matching phase. Sato & Nagao, 1990 store examples in the form of pairs of word-dependency trees, along with a set of *correspondence links*. For instance, the English–Japanese pair of sentences in (1) is represented as the Prolog facts in (2):

(1) He eats vegetables $\Longrightarrow$ Kare ha yasai wo taberu.

(2)
```
ewd_e([e1,[eat,v]
          [e2,[he,pron]]
          [e3,[vegetable,n]]]).}

jwd_e([j1,[taberu,v]
        [j2,[ha,p]
            [j3,[kare,pron]]]
        [j4,[wo,p],
            [j5,[yasai,n]]]]).

clinks([[e1,j1],[e2,j3],[e3,j5]]).
```

Kitano, 1993 proposes the annotation of examples with morphological information for words and then suggests splitting the source and target sentences into *segments*, i.e. continuous sequences of words. He then proposes to annotate examples with a *segment map*, i.e. a correspondence between segments in the source and target sentences, in a similar fashion to what Sato & Nagao, 1990 do with word-dependency sub-trees.

A second direction in which Nagao's original model has been extended is through explicitly storing templates, rather than sentences, in the bilingual database (Kaji *et al.*, 1992). A template is a sentence where some phrases have been replaced by variables, annotated with linguistic information, as in (3):

(3) X[PRON] eats Y[NP] $\leftrightarrow$ X[PRON] ha Y[NP] wo taberu

Templates are learnt from pairs of sentences by parsing them, in order to perform correct replacement of words or phrases with annotated variables, and to obtain cross-linguistic variable-sharing.

Furuse & Iida, 1992 propose encoding different kinds of bilingual correspondences in the database: string-level correspondences (i.e. plain phrase pairs), pattern-level correspondences (pairs of templates containing variables), and grammar-level correspondences (pairs of templates containing variable annotated with syntactic categories, like those proposed by Kaji *et al.*, 1992). Moreover, they associate a source expression with several target expressions, each of which is provided with a set of examples that show the contexts in which each target expression can be correctly used, as in (4):

(4) X wo o-negaishimasu ↔
may I speak to X′ ((jimukyoku{office}), ...)
please give me X′ ((bangou{number}), ...)

where X′ is the translation of X and each (X{X′}) pair in parentheses is an instantiation of such a translation pair.

A third direction in which Nagao's approach has been extended is to obtain the translation of a complete sentence by utilizing more than one translation example and combine some fragments of them. For instance, Sato & Nagao, 1990 show how to obtain the translation (5), given the examples (6) and (7).

(5) He buys a book on international politics ↔
Kare ha kokusaiseiji nitsuite kakareta hon wo kau

(6) **He buys** a notebook ↔
Kare ha nouto **wo kau**

(7) I read **a book on international politics**↔
Watashi ha **kokusaiseiji nitsuite kakareta hon** wo yomu

For an input sentence, they construct a *matching expression*, i.e. a pointer to a *translation unit.* A translation unit is a word-dependency sub-tree to be found in the example database (the $\mathsf{e}_1, \ldots, \mathsf{e}_n, \mathsf{j}_1, \ldots, \mathsf{j}_m$ of example (2)). Such pointers can be optionally followed by a list of commands for deletion/replacement/adjunctions of nodes dominated by the node pointed to. The replaced or adjoined elements are other matching expressions. For instance, given (2), a matching expression for the sentence (8) might be (9).

(8) He eats mashed potatoes.

(9) $\text{e1,[r,e3,[e}_x\text{]]]}$

which represents the tree obtained by replacing (r for *replace*) e3 with e_x in e1. In turn, e_x is a pointer to a sub-tree for *mashed potatoes* in some other example.

As several matching expressions can be candidates for the same input sentence, Sato & Nagao define a scoring system for competing translation units, based on their length (the longer, the better) and the semantic similarity between their contexts, i.e. the input sentence and the example from which the translation unit is taken (the more similar, the better).

1.3 Outline

In the remainder of this paper, we will take a close look at specific classification criteria used in defining EBMT. We will focus on the distinction between implicit and explicit knowledge in the knowledge sources, and in the use of multiple knowledge sources. We will then reassess the traditional definition of EBMT, looking at some non-symbolic (statistical) and symbolic approaches to EBMT. This will result in classification criteria that focus on the kind of linguistic knowledge used by a system.

2. Classification Criteria

In his apparently provisional conclusions about a definition of EBMT, Somers, 1999 (cf. Chapter 1, this volume) discusses three increasingly specific criteria for defining EBMT:

1 EBMT uses a bilingual corpus.

2 EBMT uses a bilingual corpus as its main knowledge base.

3 EBMT uses a bilingual corpus as its main knowledge base, at runtime.

Somers states that the first two criteria are too broad, but he argues that the third criterion may be too strict, as it rules out, for instance, statistical MT, where all the corpus-driven probabilities are computed in advance. While agreeing with Somers on the inadequacy of the first two criteria, we would like to suggest that the third criterion might also be too broad (disregarding here whether it is at the same time too strict for the reasons put forward by Somers). In the following sub-sections we discuss the proposed criteria.

2.1 Implicit vs. Explicit Knowledge

One of Somers' criteria is that an example database be used at runtime. As far as we can see, there are two reasons why a corpus is used at run-time in an MT system:

1 The system uses knowledge that can only be dynamically acquired at run-time by accessing an entire corpus, or sections of it whose extent cannot be determined in advance.

2 The system uses knowledge that could be extracted in advance, but is instead left implicit in the corpus, and extracted as needed at run-time.

We argue that only the former case is relevant to the above-mentioned criterion for characterizing EBMT. We adopt here the software engineering perspective of separating processes from data, and we focus on data. Obviously, there may be reasons for preferring to leave knowledge implicit rather than making it explicit (in terms of efficiency, memory requirements, time/space trade-off, etc.). However, from the point of view of characterizing an approach to MT, such as is taken here, what we regard as essential is ascertaining what kind of knowledge a given approach uses, as opposed to whether the same body of knowledge is explicitly or implicitly encoded.

Analogously, once a body of knowledge is explicitly encoded, we regard the source from which it was acquired as secondary, for classification purposes. Of course, we do not intend to overlook the issue of knowledge acquisition, both in terms of cost-effectiveness and system coverage. However, we maintain that this issue is not crucial in classifying an MT system. To give an example coming from direct experience, in our English–Spanish lexicalist transfer system (Popowich *et al.*, 1997; Popowich *et al.*, 2000) we initially handcrafted our bilingual lexicon. Subsequently, we developed tools for the automatic acquisition of relevant terms from corpora and for the automatic or semi-automatic generation of bilingual lexicons (Turcato *et al.*, 2000a and references therein). Although we obviously considered this a major achievement, nevertheless we did not feel that this made our MT system more example-based than it was before.

2.2 Single vs. Multiple Knowledge Sources

Another criterion stated by Somers is that the example database be the main knowledge base used by a system. This is a point often emphasized in the EBMT literature. One of its corollaries is that a system's accuracy can be increased by simply adding more examples.

One preliminary remark is that accounts of EBMT systems tend sometimes to overlook or understate the use they make of other resources, besides an example database. For example, most EBMT systems assume the existence of a bilingual lexicon to perform substitutions in examples.

To give another example, one of the most characteristic operations performed in EBMT, the *similarity comparison*, is usually driven by a thesaurus. Of course, the availability of thesauri does not make an MT approach more data-driven or knowledge-free than if a thesaurus had to be specifically developed by hand. Moreover, such resources do not readily lend themselves to the porting of an MT system to a specific domain. Work on semantic databases like *WordNet* has shown that much of their information can be misleading in specific domains. For example, an MT system dealing with weather reports would have serious problems using a thesaurus where very frequent words like *snow* and *C* (for *Celsius*) were considered semantically similar because they are both synonyms for *cocaine* (Turcato *et al.*, 2000b).

Finally, several other kinds of linguistic processing are performed in EBMT, ranging from named entity recognition (Brown, 1999), morphological analysis, and tagging to full parsing. In other words, most of the linguistic processing techniques used in conventional MT systems have been proposed in EBMT systems. Each of these processes requires some sort of linguistic resource.

A further and perhaps more crucial remark is that EBMT approaches tend to use the same resource (i.e. an example database) for different purposes, while traditional MT systems tend to use different resources. For instance, target sentences are used as sentence templates for the recombination task via some kind of substitution. The recombination task parallels generation, for which many other systems used specific target grammars. Analogously to what is argued about the implicit vs. explicit encoding of knowledge, we maintain that what is relevant here is to ascertain what kind of knowledge is used for the recombination/generation task. Again, there may be practical arguments for preferring a single resource to separate resources, or vice versa. However, what affects the output of a system is the knowledge used for a task, not the integration vs. segregation of this knowledge with respect to other knowledge sources.

2.3 A Declarative Classification Criterion

To sum up, in classifying an MT approach, we believe it is useful to ask the following three distinct questions:

1 *What* linguistic information is used?

2 *Where* is linguistic information acquired from?

3 *When* is linguistic information acquired?

We claim that only the first question should be the primary focus of a classification, while the differences in terms of the other two questions should be regarded as secondary. In other words, we suggest a declarative criterion that looks at the knowledge being used, rather than at the processes used to obtain that knowledge.

We illustrate this point with an example. In presenting their *Gaijin* EBMT system, Veale & Way, 1997:239 claim that "the only linguistics employed by *Gaijin* is a psycholinguistic constraint — the marker hypothesis". However, in describing the system they explain that they use a bilingual lexicon, statistically constructed by corpus word alignment. They also explain that "*Gaijin* employs corpus-based statistics not as a translation strategy in themselves, but as a basis for inferring symbolic transfer rules" (Veale & Way, 1997:240). So, in answering our first question, we would say that *Gaijin* uses a bilingual lexicon and a set of symbolic transfer rules, besides knowledge about phrase markers. In addition, one might question whether the mere fact that *Gaijin* acquires its linguistic information from a corpus makes it an EBMT system.

Arguably, two approaches can be regarded as one and the same approach if they use the same knowledge in the same way, regardless of whether such knowledge is extracted in advance or at run-time, from a corpus or from other resources, or whether it is distributed over one or several resources. All variants ultimately behave in the same way.

To look at the same issue from a slightly different perspective, we tend to consider two systems that perform full syntactic analysis more similar among themselves, regardless of whether this information is encoded in a grammar or a treebank, than each of them is to a system that only performs, say, morphological analysis.

3. EBMT Reassessment

Equipped with this criterion that prioritizes the knowledge content of a system over the way knowledge is expressed or acquired, we turn to a tentative review of EBMT based on this criterion. Our goal is not so much to give an absolute definition of what 'true' EBMT is, but rather to assess the proximity of approaches that look superficially distant, or conversely to assess the distance between systems that look superficially similar. We will draw a comparison between linguistically principled EBMT systems and other linguistically principled approaches to MT. Our comparison places a special emphasis on a specific transfer approach, the lexicalist variant, particularly when the discussion concerns translation selection. This preference is contingently motivated by the fact that lexicalist transfer is the symbolic approach we are most familiar with. However, we think that such a comparison bears a general significance, for the following reasons:

1 Lexicalist transfer, in its turn, considerably overlaps with other symbolic approaches, not limited to the class of transfer approaches.

2 If we show that EBMT (or a subclass of it) is equivalent to (or significantly overlaps with) a symbolic approach that is customarily characterized in terms that make no reference to example bases, then we are led to either:

   (a) draw the somewhat paradoxical conclusion that EBMT can be characterized in terms that make no reference to example bases; or

   (b) conclude that the characterisation of example-based approaches rests more upon knowledge acquisition aspects than upon knowledge usage aspects.

So example-based characterisation could be viewed as orthogonal to the distinction between data-driven vs. theory-driven approaches, cutting across multiple linguistically principled approaches, rather than being a separate approach on par with the others. So, one could imagine *data-driven lexicalist transfer* vs. *theory-driven lexicalist transfer*, or say *data-driven structural transfer* vs. *theory-driven structural transfer*, depending on how knowledge is acquired.

We finally note that in our review we leave out systems that are explicitly claimed to be hybrid by their authors, narrowing down our scope to systems that are claimed to be variants of the EBMT approach.

3.1 Non-Symbolic EBMT

A fundamental distinction exists between systems that use linguistic knowledge and systems that do not. Statistical MT falls in the latter class. We leave open the issue whether statistical MT is a kind of EBMT. In any case, it is clear that the methods of such approaches set them apart as much from linguistically principled EBMT as from other kinds of linguistically principled MT.

We illustrate this point by discussing a sample statistical MT system, the French–English system *Candide* (Berger *et al.*, 1994). *Candide* is described in terms of three components resembling the traditional partition of transfer MT: analysis, transfer, and synthesis. Analysis maps source French sentences onto what the authors call “intermediate French”, i.e. normalized representations of sentences. Normalisation consists of case and spelling correction, name and number detection, segmentation, morphological analysis and word reordering. Conversely, synthesis maps “intermediate English” representations onto target sentences. Although these components do use some linguistic knowledge, the knowledge they use is low-level. Their task is to normalize the input and the output, rather than to add any linguistic knowledge to be used in transfer. The input and the output of transfer are just strings, and transfer is purely statistical. Its task is described as decoding an English sentence that was transmitted over a noisy communication channel, which "corrupted" it to a French sentence.

Transfer uses two knowledge sources: a *language model* of English, and a *translation model*. A language model is used to assign probabilities to English sequences of words, and it simply consists of a set of trigrams (i.e. triples of English words), with associated probabilities (i.e. numeric values). No other knowledge about words is used. A translation model is used to compute the conditional probability of an English sentence, given a French sentence and an alignment (an exhaustive mapping of word positions between two sentences). Several translation models are proposed. The simplest consists of a set of word translation probabilities (i.e. pairs of English and French words, to which numeric values are assigned). The other translation models are more refined in terms of more sophisticated parameter estimations, but none of them makes use of any additional linguistic knowledge.

Summing up, besides the result of alignment, which can be considered a word-based probabilistic bilingual lexicon (analogously to what was previously discussed for the *Gaijin* system), it can be seen here that transfer uses none of the other linguistic knowledge sources (either monolingual or bilingual) used by linguistically principled EBMT or other symbolic approaches.

3.2 Symbolic EBMT

The present section expands and generalizes some remarks we made in Turcato *et al.*, 1999, where we attempted a comparison of different kinds of EBMT systems with lexicalist transfer MT. In that paper we remarked, as also mentioned above, that an EBMT example database is used for different purposes at the same time: as a source of sentence frame pairs, and as a source of sub-sentential translation pairs. Accordingly, Somers, 1999 (cf. Chapter 1, this volume) points out that EBMT comprises three phases (*matching*, *alignment*, and *recombination*), and draws a parallel with analogous phases in traditional transfer MT systems (*analysis*, *transfer*, and *generation*). Sentence frames are used in matching and recombination as aligned basic sentence structures to be combined with aligned sub-sentential translation pairs. In the next section we provide a preliminary comparison between EBMT and lexicalist transfer MT, based on their respective theoretical guidelines. In the following two sections we comparatively re-examine the two key operations of EBMT, *sentence decomposition* and *translation selection*, in the light of our knowledge-oriented classification criterion. The last section applies the same criterion to translation by analogy.

3.2.1 EBMT and Lexicalist Transfer: A Preliminary Comparison. Lexicalist MT is a variant of the transfer approach to MT. In lexicalist MT transfer is a mapping between bags of lexical items, instead of trees (Whitelock, 1994).

The first step of the translation process is the analysis of an input sentence. Such analysis is performed on a purely monolingual basis, independently from considerations of translation direction and language pair. The same kind of declarative grammars are used for parsing and generation. Moreover, grammars tend to follow a lexicalist, sign-based approach (Pollard & Sag, 1994). Grammar rules are reduced to a small number of general rule schemata. Lexical items are multi-dimensional signs containing all the information about their modes of combination (subcategorization, head-modifier relations, etc.) As a result of parsing, lexical items are instantiated with indices expressing their interdependencies with other lexical items in the sentence.

Transfer is a mapping from a bag of instantiated source lexical items resulting from parsing to a corresponding bag of target lexical items. Bilingual knowledge is reduced to a bilingual lexicon, augmented with cross-linguistic correspondences in the form of equated variables. Transfer is performed by finding a set of bilingual entries that covers the source bag. The target bag is comprised of the target sides of the selected bilingual entries. Phrasal and idiomatic expressions are accounted for by multi-word bilingual entries, where lexical items on either side have no inherent order and can be discontinuous in the input or output sentence. A schematic bilingual entry is shown below, where subscripts represent indices encoding word dependencies.

(10) $\text{eat:v}_{a,b,c} \leftrightarrow \text{taberu:v}_{a,d,e}\ \&\ \text{ha:p}_{d,b}\ \&\ \text{wo:p}_{e,c}$

Generation orders the target lexical items into a grammatical sentence, according to a target grammar and to the constraints expressed by the indices instantiated on target lexical items as a result of transfer.

It is interesting to note that the introduction of both EBMT and lexicalist MT was motivated by the rejection of structural transfer, due to its inadequacy to cope with structurally divergent languages like English and Japanese (Nagao, 1984:179; Whitelock, 1994:343–345). However, the two approaches differ in the way they avoid the recursive traversal of an analysis tree structure in transfer.

In EBMT structural transfer is avoided by adopting the following guidelines:

1 Sentence-level correspondences are covered via an explicit stipulation of all such possible correspondences in the bilingual knowledge base. Therefore EBMT advocates a bilingual knowledge base stating equivalences between the maximal translation units, i.e. sentences (or sentence templates).

2 Given such flat structure of the bilingual database, no deep linguistic analysis is required. Transfer is performed by looking up the bilingual database for a suitable match to the input sentence. Linguistic analysis is only performed to the extent it is necessary to effectively perform the template matching.

In lexicalist MT the following guidelines are adopted:

1 A full linguistic analysis is performed on input sentences. As a result of the lexicalist, sign-based approach to parsing and the use of indices to represent dependencies among lexical items, individual lexical items contain all the information about their structural relationships with the other lexical items.

2 Given that all the information about a sentence structure is stored in lexical items, transfer can be reduced to a mapping of a bag of source lexical items onto a bag of target lexical items. Therefore lexicalist MT advocates a bilingual knowledge base stating equivalences between the minimal translation units, i.e. lexical items. Information about word order is also dropped from transfer, as it is considered a monolingual issue, accounted for by the linear precedence constraints expressed in grammar rules. The dependencies expressed by indices are the only information that must be necessarily transferred from source to target lexical items.

As one can see, the two architectures seem somehow antithetic. However, in the next two sections we show how the two paradigms tend to converge.

3.2.2 Sentence Decomposition. Given the obvious fact that exact match would be too strict a requirement, a match between dissimilar sentences is generally obtained by decomposing them into some kind of constituents, in order to perform a partial match, in which dissimilar parts are substituted.

Proposals about how to decompose examples vary considerably. In most cases, some sort of linguistic analysis is used. The range of proposed techniques includes, just to name a few: segmenting sentences using markers as segment boundaries (Veale & Way, 1997), performing named entity recognition to obtain more abstract examples (Brown, 1999), using morphologically analyzed segments (Kitano, 1993), using tagged sequences as fragments (Somers *et al.*, 1994), parsing sentences into dependency trees (Sato & Nagao, 1990). In brief, the whole range of available linguistic techniques is used for this purpose. In some cases it is proposed to explicitly store generalized examples (Furuse & Iida, 1992), in other cases examples are decomposed on-the-fly. In any case, the idea behind all proposals is that examples can be decomposed into smaller constituents to be processed independently.

While there is obviously a remarkable difference in analyzing power between performing a simple detection of segment boundaries or morphological analysis and performing full parsing, the common idea of decomposing sentences into constituents resembles the idea that underlies grammars. In fact, each of the proposed techniques for decomposing sentences parallels some corresponding kind of grammar in a conventional MT system. In each case, the knowledge used for decomposition could be explicitly stored as a separate set of rules. For example, in Toole *et al.*, 1999 we describe a grammar in terms of a flat list of tag sequences, used to cover a segmented input sentence.

In brief, we would like to argue that some of the techniques used in EBMT for sentence decomposition are farther apart from each other than each of them is from the corresponding technique used (or usable) in a conventional transfer system. This latter similarity would stand out more clearly if sentence templates were separately stored, as proposed in some EBMT systems, instead of being extracted on-the-fly. It is not apparent that there is any compelling reason ruling out this option.

We make a final remark about the advantage of easily handling structural mismatches, ascribed to EBMT. Although this is certainly true of EBMT, since no recursive transfer is performed, this is a property that EBMT shares with several other proposals not only in transfer approaches, such as lexicalist MT or semantic transfer (Dorna *et al.*, 1998), but also in the interlingua approach, such as proposed by Traum & Habash, 2000.

3.2.3 Translation Selection. Given that exact match of complete examples is the exception rather than the rule, and translation is usually done by decomposing a sentence into constituents, two questions arise: (i) to what extent the availability of complete examples is needed in translating constituents? (ii) how does EBMT translation of constituents differ from other symbolic approaches to MT (e.g. lexicalist transfer)? We discuss the two issues by putting forward a proposal for a translation knowledge base, then discussing how such a knowledge base would suit EBMT.

Paraphrasing the definition of grammars as descriptions of infinite sets of sentences by finite means, we can analogously define the translation task as the description of an infinite set of equivalences by means of a finite set of equivalences.

The translation task can be defined in terms of two fundamental properties:

1 Translation is *compositional.* The translation of an expression is a function of the translation of its constituents. E.g. the Spanish translation of *business trip* (*viaje de negocios*) is a function of the translations of *business* (*negocios*) and *trip* (*viaje*), when these appear in isolation. In turn, the translation of *a long business trip* (*un viaje de negocios largo*) is a function of the translations of *a* (*un*), *long* (*largo*) and *business trip.*

2 Translation is *non-monotonic.* In specific context, compositionality holding for narrower contexts is reversed. E.g. the Spanish translation of *field trip* (*viaje de estudio*) is not a function of the translations of *field* (*campo*) and *trip*, when these appear in isolation. However, the translation of *a long field trip* (*un viaje de estudio largo*) is indeed a function of the translations of *a* (*un*), *long* (*largo*) and *field trip.*

Accordingly, the knowledge that a bilingual knowledge base should contain can be declaratively stated as follows:

1 A repository of basic translation equivalences, i.e. a bilingual lexicon of word-to-word equivalences. This bilingual lexicon would define the base step in a recursive, compositional translation process. E.g. *business* $\leftrightarrow$ *negocios, viaje* $\leftrightarrow$ *trip, field* $\leftrightarrow$ *campo, long* $\leftrightarrow$ *largo.*

2 A repository of phrases that do not translate compositionally. This repository would define all and only translation 'turning points',

which violate the monotonicity of compositional translation. E.g. *field trip* ↔ *viaje de estudio.* Note that the phrases in this repository could in turn be part of a compositional translation.

This proposed distinction resembles the distinction between *general examples* and *exceptional examples* proposed by Nomyiama, 1992, cited by Somers, 1999 (cf. Chapter 1, this volume). The sum of the two knowledge bases would account for any possible translation. In other words, it would be a finite set of equivalences that account for an infinite set of translations.

The repository of non-monotonic contexts would serve one of the main purposes of example databases, i.e. identifying the appropriate translation of a particular word or phrase, based on its context. However, it would be more specific and explicit in two ways:

1 It would specify minimal contexts, i.e. just enough context as necessary to trigger a non-compositional translation. Consider an example database like the following: *I read an article about your business trip* ↔ *Leí un artículo sobre tu viaje de negocios; I gave up my field trip* ↔ *Renuncié a mi viaje de estudio.* An input sentences like *I read an article about your field trip* would probably match the first example, because of irrelevant context, and wrongly replace the translation of *business* with the translation of *field.*

2 It would eliminate redundancies (or, in EBMT terms, *example interference).* Each context would be specified only once.

Of course, one might argue that a knowledge base of this kind is a significant departure from an example database, and requires extra work. This may well be true. However, the point we are trying to make is that there is no inherent reason why example decomposition could not be done off-line and explicitly expressed in the knowledge base. If an example database defines a finite set of equivalences, then this set of equivalences can be explicitly stated (with each equivalence stated only once).

A knowledge base as we propose would be compatible with different approaches to MT. It would equally be equivalent to an EBMT example database (under some specified conditions), and to a lexicalist transfer bilingual lexicon. Declaratively stated, the linguistic information used by EBMT is indistinguishable from the information used by lexicalist

MT. The evidence explicitly stated in a knowledge base is the same for the two approaches. The same knowledge base can be used by both.

Where would EBMT and lexicalist MT differ then? If their knowledge base was complete, they would not differ. Where the two perspectives would differ is in dealing with incompleteness. A lexicalist, bottom up approach emphasizes compositionality, while an example-based, top down approach emphasizes non-monotonicity. The former is more likely to miss relevant contexts that override compositionality. The latter is more likely to miss lexical generalizations that hold across different contexts. However, the evidence provided by the way either approach deals with incompleteness is a much weaker argument than the evidence either approach could put forward if they used different kinds of knowledge.

3.2.4 Translation by Analogy. We have intentionally postponed the discussion of translation by analogy until after the proposal put forward in the previous section. A classical example of translation by analogy is the one discussed by Nagao (1984). As briefly illustrated in Section 1.2, Nagao shows a method for translating new sentences, based on their semantic similarity with available examples. Similarity is measured by the distance of words in a thesaurus (although other methods could be devised). For instance, Nagao shows how the two English–Japanese examples in (11):

(11) a. A man eats vegetables $\leftrightarrow$ Hito wa yasai o taberu.

b. Acid eats metal $\leftrightarrow$ San wa kinzoku o okasu.

can be used to translate the new sentence in (12):

(12) He eats potatoes.

provided that a bilingual lexicon at the word level is available. The problem here is to choose one of two competing translations for *eat* (*taberu* vs. *okasu*). In Nagao's approach, the translation *taberu* is correctly selected, based on the greater semantic similarity of *he* and *potatoes* with *man* and *vegetables*, respectively, than with *acid* and *metal.* Conversely, the occurrence of *eat* in (13):

(13) Sulfuric acid eats iron.

is correctly translated by *okasu*, based on the greater semantic similarity of *sulfuric acid* and *iron* with *acid* and *metal*, respectively, than with *man* and *vegetables.*

If we rephrase the translation selection problem in the terms described in the previous section, assuming one of the two translations as the "default" translation for *eat* (most likely *taberu*, which translates the more literal sense), the task is to identify the non-monotonic contexts that require a different translation from the default one. In doing this, it would be desirable to find the minimal context that triggers a given translation, so as to use it in a broader range of cases. It turns out that things stand differently, depending on whether exact match of contexts or match by analogy is performed.

When exact match of contexts is performed, an example (e.g. *a man eats vegetables*) only accounts for itself, i.e. it is only used when the same example, or a part of it, is input (e.g. *a man eats* ... or ... *eats vegetables*). In other words, given a set of examples, it is known in advance what input sentences they can be useful for. In this situation it is conceivable to use a contrastive method to reduce a set of overlapping examples to a set of minimal local contexts accounting for different translations of the same term. For instance, the set of examples in (14):

(14) a. A man eats vegetables ↔ Hito wa yasai o taberu.

b. Acid eats metal ↔ San wa kinzoku o okasu.

c. He eats potatoes ↔ Kare wa jagaimo o taberu.

d. Sulfuric acid eats iron ↔ Ryūsan wa tetsu o okasu.

could be reduced to the set of minimal contexts (omitting function words for simplicity) in (15):

(15) a. man & eat ↔ hito & taberu

b. acid & eat ↔ san & okasu

c. he & eat ↔ kare & taberu

d. sulfuric acid & eat ↔ ryūsan & okasu

This would be done on the basis of a generalization that ascribes the selection of one or the other translation of *eat* to its subject (alternatively, one could choose to generalize over the objects, or perhaps to do no generalization). The set of contexts can be further reduced by identifying a default translation for *eat* and only explicitly encoding non-monotonic contexts, as in (16):

(16) a. eat ↔ taberu

b. acid & eat ↔ san & okasu

c. sulfuric acid & eat ↔ ryūsan & okasu

When contexts are matched by analogy, a given example (e.g. *a man eats vegetables*) may account not only for itself, but also for previously unseen contexts (e.g. *he eats potatoes*). Conversely to that discussed for exact matches, given a set of examples, it is not known in advance what input sentences the examples can be useful for. In principle, an example might be used for an input sentence with no words in common, as long as there is a term-to-term semantic similarity between the example and the input sentence. Given an example like *a man eats vegetables*, how does one determine in advance what is the relevant context for an unforeseen translation? *A man eats* or *eats vegetables*? Or the two together? Because of the incompleteness assumption, extracting local contexts from examples becomes problematic. Given a set of examples, one can know what local contexts would adequately cover the examples at hand, but one cannot know whether such contexts would be adequate for all possibly relevant sentences. For instance, a sentence like *moths eat holes in clothes* may require that a larger context be taken into account, for a more informed similarity assessment. Therefore, it is advisable to have the largest possible contexts available (i.e. entire examples), so as to be able to use different portions of them depending on the input sentence to be translated.

A traditional counterpart of this selection mechanism would be to abstractly encode contexts by means of some sort of semantic features that would act as selectional restrictions. For instance, the distinction between the two senses of *eat* (respectively translated by *taberu* and *okasu*) might be captured by a [+/- animate] feature, which would select the appropriate subject. This approach would make a database of explicit contexts superfluous, and would also lend itself to a similarity-based approach, if selectional restrictions were used as preferences rather than hard constraints. However, this approach would be labor-intensive and, as Somers, 1999 (cf. Chapter 1, this volume) points out, it would be "cumbersome and error-prone".

From this informal discussion it appears that translation by analogy, which is the most characteristic technique of EBMT, is also the one where the use of entire examples is most motivated. As a final remark, we note only that an example database for the purpose of translating by analogy can be an additional resource to whatever other resources are used, along the lines discussed above. In principle, translation by analogy could also be an extension to a traditional transfer MT system, to solve cases of lexical ambiguity for which no direct evidence is found in a translation database.

4. Conclusions

Classifications of EBMT systems often tend to bring to the foreground the fact that such systems use a bilingual corpus as the source of their linguistic knowledge, relegating to the background the assessment of what linguistic knowledge a system actually uses.

We propose a classification criterion that reverses the terms of the question, focusing primarily on the linguistic knowledge used by a system, and considering the source of this knowledge or the format in which it is represented as secondary. Accordingly, we make a distinction between the use of a corpus as: (i) a mere source for knowledge acquisition; (ii) a mere way of storing knowledge in a compact form; (iii) a genuine repository of knowledge that the system needs to access, and that could not be easily stored in other forms. A preliminary application of this criterion to linguistically principled EBMT approaches shows that:

- An example database is usually only one of the resources used by an EBMT system.
- The allegedly holistic approach of EBMT can be equivalently decomposed in a series of distinct knowledge sources and related tasks.
- The amount of linguistic knowledge required for any given component varies considerably for different approaches, ranging from low-level information like part of speech to full syntactic information.
- For most components a counterpart can be found in more conventional approaches to MT that performs an equivalent task without the need to access a database of full examples.
- The original idea of translation by analogy stands out as truly example-based.

We feel that clarifying the linguistic knowledge required by an MT approach and making the overlap with other approaches explicit is important. MT is a complex task that requires a vast amount of knowledge, linguistic and possibly extra-linguistic, to be performed adequately. We feel there is no shortcut to overcome this requirement. Hence it is important for MT practitioners to emphasize commonalities among different approaches, and put some effort towards integrating and sharing resources.

References

Arnold, D., L. Balkan, R.L. Humphreys, S. Meijer and L. Sadler. 1994. *Machine Translation: An Introductory Guide.* NCC Blackwell, Manchester/Oxford, England.

Berger, A.L., P.F. Brown, S.A. Della Pietra, V.J. Della Pietra, J.R. Gillett, G.D. Lafferty, R.L. Mercer, H. Printz, and L. Ureš. 1994. The *Candide* System for Machine Translation. In *Proceedings of the 1994 ARPA Workshop on Human Language Technology.* Plainsboro, NJ.

Brown, R.D. 1999. Adding Linguistic Knowledge to a Lexical Example-based Translation System. In *Proceedings of the 8th International Conference on Theoretical and Methodological Issues in Machine Translation (TMI 99).* Chester, England, pp.22—32.

Dorna, M., A. Frank, J. van Genabith and M.C. Emele. 1998. Syntactic and Semantic Transfer with F-Structures. In *The 36th Annual Meeting of the Association for Computational Linguistics and 17th International Conference on Computational Linguistics.* Montréal, Canada, pp.341–347.

Furuse, O. and H. Iida. 1992. Cooperation between transfer and analysis in example-based framework. In *Proceedings of the fifteenth [sic] International Conference on Computational Linguistics, COLING-92.* Nantes, France, pp. 645–651.

Kaji. H., Y. Kida & Y. Morimoto 1992. Learning Translation Templates from Bilingual Text. In *Proceedings of the fifteenth [sic] International Conference on Computational Linguistics, COLING-92.* Nantes, France, pp. 672–678.

Kitano, H. 1993. A comprehensive and practical model of memory-based Machine Translation. In *Proceedings of the Thirteenth International Joint Conference on Artificial Intelligence.* Chambéry, France, pp. 1276–1282.

Nagao, M. 1984. A Framework of a Mechanical Translation between Japanese and English by Analogy Principle. In A. Elithorn and R. Banerji (eds.) *Artificial and Human Intelligence*, Amsterdam: North-Holland, The Netherlands, pp.173–180.

Nomyiama, H. 1992. Machine Translation by Case Generalization. In *Proceedings of the fifteenth [sic] International Conference on Computational Linguistics, COLING-92.* Nantes, France, pp.714—720.

Pollard, C. and I. Sag. 1994. *Head-driven Phrase Structure Grammar.* CSLI, Stanford, CA.

Popowich, F., D. Turcato, O. Laurens, P. McFetridge, J.D. Nicholson, P. McGivern, M. Corzo-Pena, L. Pidruchney and S. McDonald. 1997. A Lexicalist Approach to the Translation of Colloquial Text. In *Proceedings of the 7th International Conference on Theoretical and Methodological Issues in Machine Translation.* Santa Fe, NM., pp.76–86.

Popowich, F., P. McFetridge, D. Turcato and J. Toole. 2000. Machine Translation of Closed Captions. *Machine Translation* **15**(4):311–341.

Sato, S. and M. Nagao. 1990. Toward memory-based translation. In *COLING-90, Papers Presented to the 13th International Conference on Computational Linguistics.* Helsinki, Finland, **3**:247–252.

Somers, H., I. McLean and D. Jones. 1994. Experiments in Multilingual Example-Based Generation. In *CSNLP-94: 3rd Conference on the Cognitive Science of Natural Language Processing.* Dublin, Ireland, [no page numbers].

Somers, H. 1999. Review Article: Example-based Machine Translation. *Machine Translation* **14**(2):113–157 (cf. Chapter 1, this volume).

Sumita, E. and H. Iida. 1991. Experiments and prospects of example-based Machine Translation. In *29th Annual Meeting of the Association for Computational Linguistics.* Berkeley, CA., pp.185–192.

Toole, J., F. Popowich, D. Nicholson, D. Turcato and P. McFetridge. 1999. Explanation-Based Learning for Machine Translation. In *Proceedings of the 8th International Conference on Theoretical and Methodological Issues in Machine Translation (TMI-99).* Chester, England, pp.161–171.

Traum, D. and N. Habash. 2000. Generation from Lexical Conceptual Structures. In *Proceedings of the Third Workshop on Interlinguas and Interlingual Approaches, NAACL/ANLP-2000.* Seattle, WA., pp.34–41.

Turcato, D., P. McFetridge, F. Popowich and J. Toole 1999. A Unified Example-Based and Lexicalist Approach to Machine Translation. In *Proceedings of the 8th International Conference on Theoretical and Methodological Issues in Machine Translation (TMI 99).* Chester, England, pp.33–43.

Turcato, D., F. Popowich, P. McFetridge and J. Toole. 2000a. Creating high-quality, large-scale bilingual knowledge bases using minimal resources. In *Proceedings of the LREC-2000 Workshop on 'Developing*

Language Resources for Minority Languages: Reusability and Strategic Priorities'. Athens, Greece, pp.92–99.

Turcato, D., F. Popowich, J. Toole, D. Fass, D. Nicholson and G. Tisher. 2000b. Adapting a synonym database to specific domains. In *Proceedings of the ACL-2000 Workshop on Recent Advances in Natural Language Processing and Information Retrieval.* Hong Kong, pp.1–11.

Veale, T. and A. Way. 1997. *Gaijin*: A Bootstrapping Approach to Example-Based Machine Translation. In *International Conference, Recent Advances in Natural Language Processing.* Tzigov Chark, Bulgaria, pp.239–244.

Whitelock, P. 1994. Shake and bake translation. In C.J. Rupp, M.A. Rosner and R.L. Johnson (eds.) *Constraints, Language and Computation.* Academic Press, London, pp.339–359.

Chapter 3

EBMT IN A CONTROLLED ENVIRONMENT

Reinhard Schäler
Reinhard.Schaler@ul.ie

Andy Way
away@computing.dcu.ie

Michael Carl
carl@iai.uni-sb.de

Abstract One key to the success of EBMT is the removal of the boundaries limiting the potential of translation memories (TMs). We discuss a linguistically enhanced TM system, a *Phrasal Lexicon* (PL), which takes advantage of the huge, underused resources available in existing translation aids. We claim that PL and EBMT systems can provide valuable translation solutions for restricted domains, especially where controlled language restrictions are imposed. When integrated into a hybrid and/or multi-engine MT environment, the PL will yield significant improvements in translation quality. We establish a future model of translation usage and anticipate that EBMT and the PL will have a central place in future hybrid integrated translation platforms.

Keywords: translation memory, phrasal lexicon, controlled translation, hybrid MT

1. Introduction

It is right for the wider MT community to acknowledge that there have been a number of success stories where rule-based MT (RBMT) systems have provided a general solution to the problems of translation. Examples include the *Météo* system (Chandioux, 1976) and *PAHO*'s

M. Carl and A. Way (eds.), Recent Advances in Example-Based Machine Translation, 83–114.

ENGSPAN and *SPANAM* (Vasconcellos & León, 1985) systems, to name but two.

However, at the same time it is generally agreed that the overall quality of today's MT systems is somewhat short of what might be desired. Nevertheless, translators remain wary that MT software might pose a considerable threat to well established work practices, despite clear evidence to the contrary. Indeed, it is hard to know how such entrenched views may be overcome, despite the best efforts of MT educators and researchers to level the playing field in this emotive issue. It is clear that RBMT *can* be a solution: the problem is in knowing in what circumstances. We will address this issue in more depth later in the paper.

Despite the widespread view that RBMT will never be good enough to warrant serious consideration as systems capable of high quality general purpose translation, research and development in RBMT systems continues to this day. Furthermore, their deployment, especially in limited domains, cf. *PaTrans* (Ørsnes *et al.*, 1996), is growing, and real savings are being made where business professionals are prepared to keep an open mind and take the time to see where RBMT can be of use, and where it (probably) cannot.

At the same time, Translation Memory (TM) systems have rapidly come to be regarded as an extremely useful tool in the translator's armoury. Notwithstanding the widespread acceptance of such tools, the emergence of TM applications have continued to keep some translators on their guard. This is even harder to understand: TM systems do *not* translate. All they do is find close matches for the input string in their database of previously seen translations and display these matches together with their translations for the translator himself to manipulate into the final, output translation. At all stages in the translation process, the translator is the integral figure: he is free to accept or reject any suggested matches, and may or may not insert any suggested translations into the target document and the TM itself wherever he deems this to be appropriate.

In the view of some researchers, TM technology may be considered as some sort of sophisticated search-and-replace engine. For example, Macklovitch & Russell, 2000 liken TM systems to information retrieval tools, in that all the translator does in effect is search for 'documents' (aligned sentence pairs) which may help translate a given sentence. The TM system formulates the query itself from the input string to be translated, i.e. in most cases, the query *is* the source language sentence, while the retrieval process tries to match the query as closely as possible to existing examples in the system database.

A *sine qua non* for TM (and Example-based Machine Translation (EBMT)) applications is an aligned parallel corpus. The translator may be presented with a pre-aligned TM, but may also be a central figure in its construction: using a tool such as Trados *WinAlign*, for instance, the translator may manually overwrite some of the decisions made by the aligner by linking ⟨source, target⟩ sentence pairs using the graphical interface provided.

However, the potential of TM technology to facilitate the task of the translator still further is limited by the fact that the fragments contained in the TM are linked only at sentential level. If sub-sentential alignment could be integrated into the TM databases, more useful fragments could be put at the disposal of the translator. If a more radical view were to be taken, once sub-sententially aligned chunks exist, then automatic translation via EBMT could be made available reasonably straightforwardly.

Although EBMT as a paradigm has been described in research papers as far back as the mid 1980's (Nagao, 1984) and although it has managed to capture the interest and enthusiasm of many researchers, it has — so far — not reached the level where it could be transformed from a research topic into a technology used to build a new generation of machine translation engines — and new approaches, technologies and applications are badly needed in MT.

We believe that the time is ripe for the transformation of EBMT into demonstrators and, eventually, commercially viable products. We see the niche area for EBMT as being somewhere between RBMT and TMs. In this paper we shall claim that EBMT — like all corpus-based approaches to MT, be it human-assisted or fully automatic — may successfully be applied only for restricted domain, special purpose translations. We investigate the relation of controlled language and translation more precisely and come to the conclusion that EBMT is a paradigm especially suited to controlled translation. We develop a model for the future of translation technology, and propose an integrated hybrid environment for translation mining, management and scheduling. We believe that example-based translation technologies will play a central role in such a hybrid translation environment, as they are by their very nature dynamic, have the ability to learn, are extensible and scalable to new, large sublanguage domains.

In section 2 we argue for using phrases (and not just words) as basic translation units in any MT system and contrast our approach to mainstream MT research. We examine TMs as a possible application for a phrasal lexicon in section 3 and point to their structural limitations. As a consequence we require in section 4 that TMs are enhanced with more sophisticated processing devices. Here we investigate the impact of controlled language and MT. Our conclusion is that EBMT is especially suited to obtaining translations in restricted domains, as they are easy to adapt and able to produce high quality translations. We then investigate multi-engine and hybrid system architectures in section 5, and develop a model for the future use of translation technology in section 6. We anticipate a hybrid integrated translation platform which, as a kernel, contains an example-based component capable of adapting quickly to different user needs and which is complemented by linguistic, statistical and rule-based technologies.

2. EBMT and the Phrasal Lexicon

EBMT has been proposed as an alternative methodology capable of replacing RBMT, initially by Nagao, 1984, followed by extensions reported in Sato & Nagao, 1990 and Sadler & Vendelmans, 1990. EBMT has also been proposed as a solution to specific translation problems, as reported in Sumita & Iida, 1991, and culminating in the current volume.

There is an enormous variety of approaches to the use of examples in natural language processing (NLP), with different areas of focus and with different motivations. In the area of automatic translation, this provides a strong testimony to the high level of interest in EBMT. Taking existing parallel texts as their starting point, some of the areas that researchers have worked on include:

- Word-sense disambiguation;
- Translation ambiguity resolution;
- Lexicography;
- Extraction of bilingual collocations or translation patterns from parallel corpora;
- Translation Quality Measures;
- Extensions to and variations on the basic idea of EBMT.

One idea which precedes all of the approaches mentioned and which, surprisingly, has not until recently been taken up by researchers to any significant degree (cf. Simard & Langlais, 2001), is that of the 'Phrasal

Lexicon', described first by Becker, 1975, and applied by Schäler (1996, 2001).[1]

Becker's model was radically different from the mainstream linguistic theories prevalent in the mid-1970's: instead of considering language production as the process of combining units the size of words or morphemes to form utterances, he identified phrases consisting of more than one word as the building blocks for the formation of utterances.

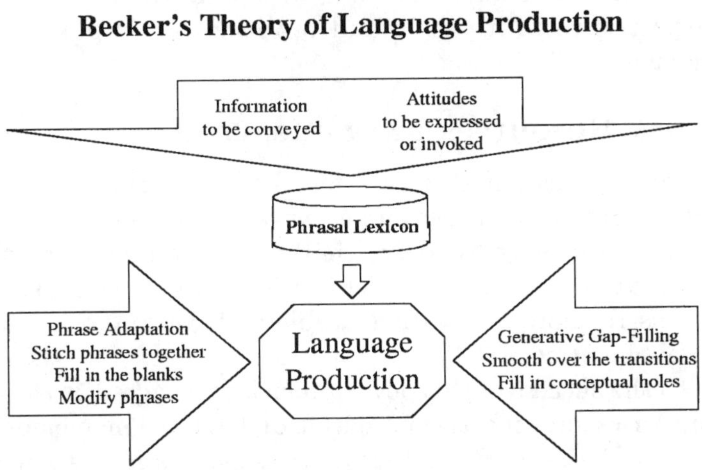

Figure 3.1. Becker's Theory of Language Production

For Becker, language generation is compositional[2] in the way illustrated in Figure 3.1 (cf. Schäler, 1996, Schäler, 2001). The phrasal lexicon provides patterns that can provide (at least some of) the expressions needed to convey a message in a certain 'tone'. These phrases are then stitched together, blanks filled in and phrases modified where necessary. If this is not sufficient to generate the utterance, new phrases are generated to smooth over transitions and fill in conceptual holes.

[1] For a discussion of some of the underlying problems of the technical implementation of this model, see Ramsay & Schäler, 1997.

[2] Becker's notion of 'compositionality' is different from that used in the context of semantics or, in fact, that used in rule-based MT (RBMT), i.e. that a target structure can be ***generated*** in a compositional manner following a detailed analysis of the source structure and the establishment of correspondences between grammatical descriptions of the source and the target structures.

It is not difficult to see that the notion of language generation as envisaged by Becker is in exactly the same spirit as many approaches to EBMT. With respect to TM technology, translations cannot be produced automatically (except in the case of exact matches) as sub-sentential ⟨source, target⟩ chunks are not identified by the system: the translator himself has to use his knowledge of how the source language relates to the target, extract the relevant parts of any close matches suggested by the TM system and stitch them together himself to produce the final translation. If there are any 'gaps' or 'conceptual holes', the translator uses his expertise to fill these in and produce the output text in the target language.

2.1 TM Resources are underused

We believe that the time is ripe for the transformation of EBMT into demonstrators, technologies and eventually commercially viable MT engines along the lines suggested by Schäler, 1996 and Macklovitch, 2000, both of which are based on the belief that existing translations contain more solutions to more translation problems than any other available resource (Isabelle *et al.*, 1993).

The key to the success of this development, we suggest, is the removal of the boundaries limiting the potential of translation memories. To bring EBMT to fruition, researchers and developers have to go beyond the self-imposed limitations of what is now traditional — in computing terms almost old fashioned — TM technology.

In Translation Memory systems, two intellectually challenging problems have to be addressed which cannot just be solved by clever engineering:

1 **Contents of the TM (alignment).**
The first problem occurs when translators want to create *translation memories* by aligning previous translations with their source equivalents on a segment-by-segment basis in order to import these aligned segments into a TM and then use this for the translation of a new version of the same source material. Developers generally offer alignment tools which work in either interactive or fully automatic mode.

2 **Retrieving similar entries.**
The other is the decision of how to deal with cases where no exact matches can be found. Developers generally opt to search for similar matches and to calculate a ranking of identified 'fuzzy' matches

which are then offered to the translator as a possible basis for the translation of the new segment.

Current TM systems do not have to carry out any significant amount of linguistic processing. They need to know practically nothing about the target language as the processing (matching, calculation of fuzziness, identification of changes etc.) is performed on the source language only.

While the latter problem still remains to be solved both in theory and in practice (the work of Planas & Furuse, 1999 is a significant step in this direction, cf. Chapter 5, this volume), the former has often been claimed to be solved to a large extent. However, we will show that there is still considerable work to be done if TM technology is to go beyond its current limitations.

2.1.1 Contents of the Translation Memory. The availability of alignment tools linked with the now widespread use of translation memory systems has led to the creation of massive bilingual and multilingual parallel corpora aligned at sentence level, the smallest segment level currently accessible by TM systems. However, matching segments at sentence level unnecessarily restricts the potential and the usefulness of translation memories as extremely valuable linguistic resources. Thus, translation knowledge at a phrasal or sub-sentential level is lost if alignment and matching only works on a sentence level.[3]

A second shortcoming in current TM technology is the unavailability of tools to control and/or cross-check the extracted segments. Furthermore, there is no easy way to control the quality of the segments and their translation. For instance, it is possible (in principle at any rate) to map any source sentence onto the same target expression. Given a real reference text, this is, of course, an extremely unlikely case. Nevertheless, any TM system is likely to store redundant, ambiguous or wrong translations in the TM with no possibility of reducing or avoiding such entries other than manually checking the entire database.

Inconsistent translation segments are likely to be produced during initial alignment. They can also be produced when multiple users share a TM in real-time, adding different translations for the same sentence. This is usually controlled using meta-data fields such as <user>, <date>,

[3]Segments currently used by TM systems can be defined to a certain degree by users of TM systems and can also include text strings defined in documents such as headers or members of lists. Segments, however, can never be defined using linguistic criteria. The only counterexample to this that we are aware of is Multi*Corpora*, cf. `http://www.multicorpora.ca`, which permits segmentation at levels other than the sentence.

etc., but unless the process for sharing TMs is properly controlled, this can still add to the inconsistencies present in the TM. While in some cases such inconsistencies might be required, in other cases it is undesirable.

Furthermore, last minute changes are frequently made to translated documents *outside* the TM environment. If the process of using TMs is controlled properly, these changes will be added to the TM. However, this does not happen on a frequent basis and leads to gaps between the reference text and the new translations, which reduces the precision of the TM and increases the amount of fuzzy matching required when the TM is used for a new translation.

2.1.2 Retrieving similar entries. If a TM system cannot find an exact match in a TM, it can only propose fuzzy matches. Ideally, a TM system should find a segment (or a set of segments) in its database which is similar in meaning to the new sentence in the hope that their translations will be similar as well. However, given that there is no known algorithm to compute the meaning of arbitrary sentences and to quantify their similarity, this approach seems not to be feasible (cf. Reinke, 1999 for an in-depth discussion on similarity of meaning).

Fuzzy matching can be a highly complex operation: in fact, it may prove so cumbersome that translators often opt out of the fuzzy match proposal operation by setting the percentage threshold of the fuzzy match component so high that high percentage matches which could contain matching phrases are hidden away from them. Instead, they prefer to translate the new source document without the support of the TM system in order to save time. In the language of statistical NLP, they impose a high Precision threshold, but low Recall, for this matching process. The consequence, of course, is that potentially valuable matches at sub-sentence level are lost. Adding a facility capable of providing ⟨source, target⟩ chunks at the phrasal level will overcome this shortcoming.

2.1.3 Recombination of Target Segments. TMs are usually fed with domain-specific reference material in order to achieve maximum precision for translating specialized texts and their segments. However, TMs have little or no capacity to check that such reference texts are consistent. Thus, if the reference text contains two (or more) different translations for the same source language segment, the user is asked which of the translations, if any, he prefers in the given context, without the TM learning from this decision. If the same sentence were to be translated later, exactly the same scenario would arise. Adding more reference translations to the TM increases the chance of adding more ambiguous translations.

The way translations are produced in TM systems is, therefore, *descriptive*, since retrieved and proposed translations reflect the quality of the reference translations and their alignment functions. As the quality of translations available in the TM decreases and the new text or sentence differs from reference examples in the TM, the quality of proposed segment translations decreases in a corresponding manner.

3. The Phrasal Lexicon and EBMT

While we discussed in section 3.2.1.1 some other possible ways in which the translation process in a TM system may be distorted, there remain two main factors which may adversely affect the way in which the TM is used:

- the way entries are retrieved from the TM (i.e. fuzzy matching);
- inconsistencies in the contents of the TM.

Both factors may cause translation quality to deteriorate, especially where these two problematic factors cooccur. The Phrasal Lexicon avoids these shortcomings by permitting exact phrasal matches together with a manner of controlling the contents of the memory.

3.1 Phrasal Matching

In the phrasal lexicon, exact matches are performed at a phrasal level, so the problem of fuzzy matching disappears (or at any rate, is considerably reduced). The probability of exact matches at a lower phrasal level (e.g. at NP, VP or PP level) is significantly higher than the probability of exact matches at the sentence level, the level at TM segments are currently provided.

Phrasal units are looked up in a phrasal lexicon and translated by combining already translated phrases stored in the phrasal lexicon, very much along the lines proposed originally by Becker, and applied by

Schäler (1996, 2001). As an example, let us assume a TM containing the two entries in (1):

(1) a. EN: The bullets move to the new paragraph.
DE: Die Blickfangpunkte rücken in den neuen Abschnitt.

b. EN: The title moves to the centre of the slide.
DE: Der Titel rückt in die Mitte des Dias.

Despite the fact that the TM entries in (1) are good matches for the new sentence in (2), it would not be translated automatically by the TM system:

(2) The bullets move to the centre of the slide.

At most, the system would be capable of identifying one (or both) of the two source sentences in the TM in (1) as fuzzy matches. If so, these would be displayed together with their translations, which would then have to be adapted by a translator to generate the final output string in (3):[4]

(3) Die Blickfangpunkte rücken in die Mitte des Dias.

Note, however, that depending on how fuzzy matching is calculated in the TM, and at what percentage level fuzzy matching is set by the user, the useful translation pairs in (1) may not be presented at all to the translator: if we compare the source strings in (1) with the new input in (2), observe that 5 out of 7 (71%) of the words in (1a) match those in (2) exactly, while 6 out of 9 (67%) of the words in (1b) match those in (2) exactly. If we were to set our level of fuzzy matching at 75% (say), neither candidate would be accessible by the translator.[5]

If, however, we produced a phrasal lexicon capable of providing translation units at the phrase level, and wrote a procedure to combine them so that a correct translation of the new sentence were produced automatically, then we would have built an EBMT system. Notwithstanding this, if a phrasal lexicon (cf. Figure 3.2, Schäler (1996, 2001)) were to be integrated into a TM system, then translators would be able to avail themselves of many of the advantages of a TM, principally those of consistency and savings in terms of time and cost.

---

[4]One point of interest is that while many evaluations of EBMT systems exist, we are unaware of any research into the accuracy of translations where multiple phrases are combined to form one translated segment in the TM environment.

[5]Fuzzy matching may also be calculated in terms of characters, of course, or by means of some more sophisticated algorithm.

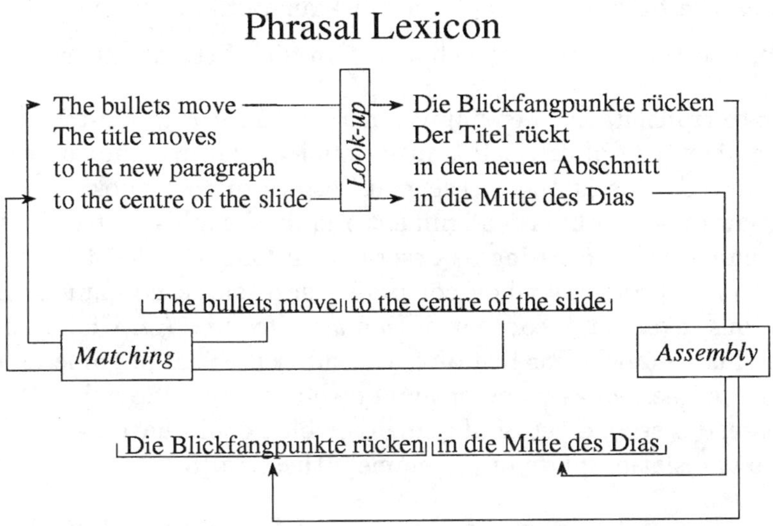

Figure 3.2. Overview of the Phrasal Lexicon

Storing, matching and proposing segments at the phrasal level has a number of advantages, including:

- Translators will be offered a higher percentage of exact matches from TMs.
- The quality of proposed translation segments will improve.
- The use of information stored in TMs will increase; matching phrases in otherwise fuzzy matching sentences will no longer fall below the match percentage threshold set by most translators.
- TM systems will be able to translate larger amounts of source text automatically without the need to manually adapt fuzzy matches.

3.2 More sophisticated processing devices

Since the PL is based on smaller translation units, it can potentially identify more exact matches than sentence-based TM systems — but at a price. In contrast to a TM, a PL would need to know — at the very least — enough about the source *and* the target language to identify phrases and describe the linguistic characteristics of their constituent parts. For instance, while the translator may be able to pick out the appropriate sub-sentential alignments from (1), namely:

(4) a. the bullets move $\Longrightarrow$ die Blickfangpunkte rücken

b. to the centre of the slide $\Longrightarrow$ in die Mitte des Dias

in order to translate the new input string in (2), it is a non-trivial problem as to how to obtain such translationally relevant chunks automatically. Indeed, this is one of the main topics of this book: automatic or semi-automatic phrasal alignment requires sophisticated linguistic and/or numerical processing as described in Chapters 9–14 in this volume. Typical problems when combining sub-sentential chunks in new translations involve the concept of *boundary friction* (cf. Chapters 1, 14 and 16, this volume). For instance, the sub-sentential alignments in (4) have been chosen so as to be optimal given the new input in (2). Consider instead a second set of alignments which could have been selected from the translation pairs in (1), namely those in (5):

(5) a. the bullets move to the $\Longrightarrow$ die Blickfangpunkte rücken in den

b. centre of the slide $\Longrightarrow$ Mitte des Dias

Combining these translation chunks would result in the mistranslation of (2), namely *Die Blickfangpunkte rücken in den Mitte des Dias*. Here we note in the target PP a masculine accusative determiner *den* together with a feminine singular noun *Mitte*. In the correct translation (3), meanwhile, we see that determiner-noun agreement has been maintained within the NP.

Dependent on the language pair, further restrictions such as the addition of case or semantic markers, or other linguistic information, have to be imposed on the entries in the PL and treated accordingly when recombining target phrases (cf. Carl *et al.*, 2001). For example, Way, 2001 (Chapter 16, this volume) incorporates the syntactic functions of LFG (Kaplan & Bresnan, 1982) into an EBMT system based on aligned ⟨source, target⟩ tree pairs. Way notes that the ill-formed string *John swim* cannot be translated by LFG-MT (Kaplan *et al.*, 1989), as the constraints that the subject NP must be singular and the verb plural cannot be resolved by the LFG constraint solver. In his LFG-DOT system, Way *op cit.* shows that this string may be translated by relaxing these constraints, and, importantly, that the system *knows* that the input string and the translation formed are ungrammatical, unlike other EBMT systems. Perhaps more significantly, this research shows that one needs less than the full target language grammar in order to obtain translations: in RBMT, it is far from clear (a) that a translation could be obtained at all in this situation, and (b) if it could, arguably the whole target grammar would be involved in enabling some translation. In contrast, in a 'linguistics-rich' EBMT system such as LFG-DOT, all that is required is to relax one feature on the NP and on the VP for a translation to ensue. This demonstrates a clear advantage of EBMT systems over their rule-based counterparts.

More questions arise with respect to the quality of the translations in the PL. According to Collins and Somers (Chapter 4, this volume), the EBMT literature has little to offer regarding the question as to how best to store cases in relation to each other, as well as how to decide on the organisation of the memory. It is very likely that for the PL in Figure 3.2, a phrase like *The bullets move* would be translated differently if the alignments were taken from a text on wars. While the co-occurrence of *bullet* and *paragraph* in the original alignment implies a high probability that the segment was taken from a software localisation context, this information is lost in the PL. However, the translation *bullet* $\Longrightarrow$ *Blickfangpunkt* cannot be understood in a text tackling wars.

Therefore, a number of methods have been proposed for human-assisted or fully automatic alignment in order to store non-ambiguous translation pairs in the PL. To achieve an accuracy of more than 90% for automatically generated phrase translations, Watanabe *et al.* (Chapter 14, this volume) use a graphical interface where users confirm alignment proposals of the system. Menezes & Richardson (Chapter 15, this volume) use a fully automatic device to filter out translation ambiguities in a post-processing step and Carl (Chapter 12, this volume) investigates the induction of invertible translation grammars from reference translations.

The motivation of the investigation in this chapter is to extract and store high quality translation units according to a number of criteria in order to enable the database to be scaled up in a controlled manner. Consequently, it is unrealistic to think that a corpus-based MT system can succeed as a general solution to the problems of translation. In contemplating such issues, it is clear that the notions of controlled translation and controlled language will play a role. In the next section, we investigate these matters further, and recommend that EBMT systems incorporating a phrasal lexicon might be optimally suited to controlled translation.

4. Controlled Language and MT

Controlled languages define a writing standard for domain-specific documents. Linguistic expressions in texts are restricted to a subset of natural language. They are characterized by simplified grammars and style rules, a simplified and controlled vocabulary with well defined meanings, and a thesaurus of frequently occurring terms. Controlled languages are used to enhance the clarity, usability, transferability, retrievability, extractability, and translatability of documents.

According to Lehrndorfer & Schachtl, 1998:8, "the concept of controlled language is a mental offspring of machine translation". That is, one of the main *raisons d'être* of controlled language was to facilitate automatic translation of documents. A number of companies (e.g. *Boeing, British Airways, Air Canada,* and *Caterpillar*) use controlled language in their writing environment. Nor is this trend restricted to English: *Siemens* use controlled German (*Dokumentationsdeutsch*: Schachtl, 1996; Lehrndorfer & Schachtl, 1998), *Aérospatiale* use controlled French (*GIFAS Rationalised French*: Lux & Dauphin, 1996; Barthe, 1998), while *Scania* use controlled Swedish (*ScaniaSwedish*: Almqvist & Sågvall Hein, 1996), for example.

4.1 Controlled Language and RBMT

By definition, therefore, controlled languages are characterized by simplified grammars and vocabulary, a consistent syntax and terminology to which the MT system has to be adjusted. Controlled languages have been developed for restricted domains, such as technical documentation for repair, maintenance and service documents in large companies (e.g. *Boeing, Siemens, Scania, GM* etc.).[6]

Caterpillar's 'Caterpillar Technical English', for instance, defines monolingual constraints on the lexicon, constraints on the complexity of sentences, and the use of generalized markup language. However, when using this controlled language for translation in the *KANT* RBMT system (Mitamura & Nyberg, 1995), it was found that "[terms] that don't

[6]Note, however, that *GM* have since abandoned the use of their Controlled Automotive Service Language (CASL) English. From an objective point of view, this seems hard to understand given that Godden (personal communication, cited in Bernth & Gdaniec, 2001) reports on a contrastive experiment designed to test the translations obtained from a set of texts rewritten to conform to 30 CASL rules against those obtained from the original texts. These were rated by both a translator and an expert bilingual automotive technician. Godden reports "a *very* significant increase in percentage of correct translations for the pre-edited version over the original version, as well as a *very* significant decrease in percentage of incorrect translations" (Bernth & Gdaniec, 2001:207).

appear to be ambiguous during superficial review turned out to have several context- specific translations in different target languages" (Kamprath *et al.*, 1998).

Van der Eijk *et al.*, 1996 state that "an approach based on fine-tuning a general system for unrestricted texts to derive specific applications would be unnecessarily complex and expensive to develop". Later work in *METAL* applications refers to there being "limits to fine-tuning big grammars to handle semi-grammatical or otherwise badly written sentences. The degree of complexity added to an already complex NLP grammar tends to lead to a deterioration of overall translation quality and (where relevant) speed" (Adriens & Schreurs, 1992:595). Despite this, from 1994, *General Motors* used *METAL* for controlled authoring and MT (Means & Godden, 1996). Furthermore, attempts at redesigning the *Météo* system (Chandioux, 1976), probably the biggest success story in the history of MT, to make it suitable for another domain (aviation) proved unsuccessful.

Controlled translation, therefore, involves more than just the translation of a controlled language. Passing a source language text through a controlled language tool is not sufficient for achieving high quality translation. Large general purpose (rule-based) MT systems can be converted only with considerable difficulties to produce controlled translations. Controlling the translation process in a conventional transfer-based MT system involves controlling three processing steps:

- the segmentation and parsing of the source text (analysis);
- the lexical and structural mapping of the source segments into the target language (transfer);
- the recombination and ordering of the target language segments according to the target language grammar (generation).

As the resources of each of these steps require independent knowledge resources, adjusting a conventional RBMT system to a new controlled language is non-trivial.

4.2 Controlled Language and Corpus-based MT

Using traditional rule-based systems for the translation of controlled languages leads to the well known 'knowledge-acquisition bottleneck'. This may take several forms, including:

- Lack of *coverage*: knowledge is restricted to (theoretically interesting) interactions of linguistic phenomena;

- Lack of *robustness*: 'toy' grammars and lexica do not scale up;

- Lack of *consistency*: translation data is often invented in an *ad hoc* manner.

In addition, several knowledge resources have to be adjusted and homogenized. An often heard claim is that corpus-based MT systems can overcome this bottleneck given that available translations can be exploited. In contrast to traditional approaches, corpus-based MT systems induce the knowledge required for transfer from a reference text. To date, corpus-based MT technologies have yet to tackle controlled languages: they have not supported the acquisition of controlled translation knowledge, nor have they provided an appropriate environment for controlled translation.

This is extremely surprising: the quality of corpus-based translation systems depends on the quality of the reference translations from which the translation knowledge is learned. The more a reference text is consistent, the better the expected quality of the translations produced by the system. By contrast, therefore, translation knowledge extracted from noisy corpora has an obvious adverse impact on the overall translation quality. The only research we are aware of which attempts to detect omissions (but not *other* errors) in translations is Chen, 1996 and Melamed, 2001. However, in the context of corpus-based MT, such methods have not been used to date to eliminate noisy or mistranslated parts of the reference text, nor to enhance the quality and consistency of the extracted translation units.

If EBMT is to make the leap from research topic to industrial applications, we contend that the niche for EBMT may well be found somewhere between RBMT and TM systems. That is, there is a need for a controlled, domain-specific, easily adaptable MT engine, one which proposes translation candidates *and* recombines them in a controlled manner.

Conventional TM systems are not suitable for this task. Within the *Tetris-IAI* project (TETRIS, 1999), an experiment was undertaken whereby controlled language was fed into a TM. It was found that controlling the source language without controlling the reference material does not increase the hit-rate of the TM and thus does not increase the likelihood of high quality translations — from a company's point of view, the bottom line is that the translation cost is not lowered. Methods for preparing and modifying reference texts to achieve better consistency on both terminological and syntactic levels have, therefore, been proposed (e.g. Somers, 1993) and could also be a feasible way forward for TMs.

Furthermore, statistics-based MT (e.g. Brown *et al.*, 1990) is not an appropriate candidate for controlled translation. One cannot usually expect consistent reference translations in statistics-based MT, owing to the huge size of the reference texts required. In many cases, texts from different domains are necessarily merged together to compute word translation probabilities for a language pair in various contexts owing to sparse data: there is not enough textual material in one sublanguage domain to compute accurate, robust language and translation models. Of course, how words and phrases are used in different domains can differ greatly. In order to achieve high translation accuracy, therefore, it is unwise to calculate one's statistical language and translation models on corpora merged from different sublanguage areas, but this is often a prerequisite in statistical MT. It is clear from the methodology adopted so far that the implicit goal in statistical MT has been general purpose translation.

In our view, the main potential of EBMT lies in the possibility to easily generate special purpose MT systems. The more restricted the purpose, the better defined such restrictions and the greater the availability of high quality reference translations, so the potential of EBMT to produce high quality translations increases. Brown (Chapter 10, this volume) shows that coverage can be increased by a factor of 10 or thereabouts if templates are used, but it would be fanciful to think that this would scale up to domain-independent translation. Even if EBMT systems were augmented with large amounts of syntactic information (Chapters 15 and 16, this volume), they would in all probability stop short of becoming solutions to the problems of translating general language. Even though a number of techniques are described to select and control segmentation, transfer and recombination, EBMT has not been seen as suited for controlled translation until now. It is our contention that EBMT systems may be able to generate controlled, domain-specific translations given a certain amount of built-in linguistic knowledge together with some preparation of the aligned corpus. This translation knowledge may, we contend, be reused to produce controlled, example-based translations of high quality.

Controlling the translation process in EBMT implies the careful selection of a set of translation examples which are 'similar' to the input. That is, segmentation, transfer and recombination of target segments is largely determined by the set of retrieved examples. Given that only retrieved examples are recombined, the task of controlling EBMT systems essentially consists of controlling the retrieval of appropriate analogous examples from the database. This process, in turn, is triggered by the segmentation of the input sentence, which is why this procedure is perhaps the most crucial in any EBMT system, and why, therefore, system descriptions examine this point most carefully and thoroughly.

We will now take a broader view of machine translation to see in which context EBMT might be a suitable component. We examine the role of EBMT in variations of a multi-engine approach, as well as an integral component of a hybrid architecture. We compare the two basic approaches, and give our view as to how an EBMT system in such an environment might best be located and used.

5. EBMT in a Multi-Engine Environment

It is widely accepted that different MT paradigms have different advantages and shortcomings. TMs are fed with domain-specific reference translations and are widely used as tools for translators in the area of Computer Assisted Translation (CAT). TMs, however, do not provide sufficient control mechanisms to enable a more sophisticated translation environment. In contrast, rule-based MT systems may automatically provide high quality translations in limited domains (cf. *Météo* , Chandioux, 1976), but are more usually designed for general purpose translations. As a consequence, RBMT systems are difficult to adjust to specialized types of texts and consequently suffer from limited portability. EBMT systems have more sophisticated processing devices at their disposal than TMs. In addition, they make better use of available resources than TMs do. This, we have argued, gives EBMT systems the unique possibility to generate controlled translations.

Given the different advantages and shortcomings of each approach, multi-engine MT systems have been designed as an attempt to integrate the advantages of different systems without accumulating their shortcomings. We shall now describe and compare a number of different architectures which have been proposed whereby a number of different MT systems and techniques may be integrated.

5.1 Parallel vs. Sequential Linkage

In order to describe these systems and attempt some classification of them, one distinction can be made along the lines of whether entire translation engines are triggered in parallel or sequentially. In a parallel multi-engine scenario, each system is fed with the source text and generates an independent translation. The candidate translations output by each system are then collected and (manually or automatically) recombined to give the 'best' translation.

There are a number of projects which incorporate different MT components in parallel in a multi-engine system. The most notable of these are *VerbMobil* (Wahlster, 1993; Wahlster, 2000) and *Pangloss* (Frederking & Nirenburg, 1994).

VerbMobil integrates the complementary strengths of various MT approaches in one framework, i.e. deep analysis, shallow dialogue act-based approach and simple TM technology. Nübel, 1997 shows that the performance of the integrated system outperforms each individual system. *Pangloss* uses EBMT (Brown 1996, cf. also Chapter 10, this volume) in conjunction with KBMT — the mainline *Pangloss* engine — and a transfer-based engine.

While there is an element of redundancy in such approaches given that more than one engine may produce the correct translation (cf. Way, 2001:23) one might also treat the various output translations as comparative evidence in favour of the best, overall translation. Somers, 1999 observes that "what is most interesting is the extent to which the different approaches mutually confirm each other's proposed translations" (see Chapter 1, section 1.4.6, p.40, this volume).

In a sequential multi-engine approach, two or more MT components are triggered on different sections of the same source text. The output of the different systems is then concatenated without the need for further processing. This dynamic interaction is monitored by one system — usually the most reliable amongst the available systems. The reasoning behind this approach is that if one knows the properties of the translation components involved, reliable translations can be produced by using fewer resources than in a parallel multi-engine approach.

Integration of a TM with a rule-based component is a common strategy in commercial translation. A dynamic sequential interaction between a TM (*Trados*) and an MT system (*Logos*) is described in Heyn, 1996. In the case where only poorly matching reference translations are available in the *Trados* TM, the input sentence is passed to the *Logos* MT system for regular translation. The user is then notified which of the systems has processed the translation, since the *Logos* system is less likely to produce reliable results.[7]

A similar scenario is described in Carl & Hansen, 1999, where a TM is linked with an EBMT system. This research shows that the quality

[7]Note that compared to translations produced by humans, any translations derived via MT which are inserted into the TM are automatically penalized by *Trados* and other TM systems.

of translations is likely to be higher for EBMT translation than for TM translation, in cases where the fuzzy match score of the TM falls below 80%.

The OTELO[8] project is another example of how both local and remote translation resources such as MT, TM, and other NLP applications may be integrated. In OTELO, two MT systems, *Logos* and *IBM LMT*, were combined with the *IBM* TranslationManager and OTELO's HyperLink Translator.

5.2 Hybrid MT Systems

In each example multi-engine MT system discussed in the previous section, each module in the integrated environment has its own resources and data structures. In a strong integration of two or more MT techniques, however, the same data structures are shared by the different components. Some of the components of such hybrid systems may, therefore, modify or adjust certain processing resources of another component in order to bring about an improvement in coverage or translation quality.

Coupling statistical data and RBMT often leads to a strong integration to improve translation quality. In some hybrid systems, statistical data is added to the lexical resources of the RBMT system, which judge different translation candidates as more or less felicitous for a given textual or thematic context. In particular, it has been shown that statistically enriched RBMT systems can handle collocational phenomena (for example, establishing the most likely translation match in the context of a particular word). The statistical data are drawn from monolingual corpora (Nomiyama, 1991) or independent corpora of source and target language (Doi & Muraki, 1992).

Rayner & Bouillon, 1995 describe an application of statistical data during the rule-based transfer phase. Statistical data are derived by manually scoring translation variants produced by the system. Since

---

Thus an exact match of the input string against a source string whose translation was obtained automatically would not be deemed an 100% match.

In this context, note that *Trados* offers a special filter to permit translations input from *Systran*, which is complemented by *Systran*'s special import format for *Trados*. *SDLX* offers MT functionality (via *Transcend*) within the TM environment itself. Of course, in principle any TM tool may be combined with any MT engine if the user is sufficiently patient to manipulate input and output files using the Translation Memory Exchange (TMX) format (Shuttleworth, 2002).

[8] `http://www.hltcentral.org/projects/detail.php?acronym=otelo` [last consulted: March 1st, 2003].

the training is based on texts belonging to one specific subject field, typical mistakes made by the system can be corrected. The probability of a transfer candidate is calculated via the transfer probability and the probability of the resulting target structure. As such a multiplication of probabilities requires large amounts of data in order to be effective, such an approach is applicable only to very restricted subject fields where only a few examples may suffice in order to produce reliable data. In such cases, translation quality is traded for improved coverage.

In a hybrid stratificational integration of example-based and rule-based techniques, some processing steps are carried out by the rule-based component while for others examples are used.

Menezes & Richardson (Chapter 15, this volume) combine rule-based analysis and generation components with example-based transfer. Bond & Shirai (Chapter 7, this volume) generate translation templates for new sentences on the fly from a set of alignments. The differing sections in the source template and the input sentence are identified and translated by a rule-based noun-phrase translation system. Carl *et al.*, 2001 use EBMT as a front and backend to a RBMT system for translation of simple phrases and multi-word units.

All these approaches attempt to make the most of the strengths of the hybrid approach while compensating for the weaknesses of each as much as is possible. The main idea is to integrate a significant share of human translation experience (as accumulated in Translation Memories and Term Banks) with the rule-based paradigm.

Even a very large TM or EBMT system is unlikely to be able to translate a completely new sentence correctly, let alone an entire new text. However, such systems are able to 'learn' in that new examples can be added to the system database, so that subsequent encounters with previously unknown source strings will be translated successfully. In RBMT systems there is no such analogous process. That is, they do not store translation results for later reuse, so that all post-editing effort is wasted: RBMT systems will deal with the same input in exactly the same way in perpetuity.

A hybrid system, in contrast, will be able to learn and adapt itself easily to new types of text. In addition, the rule-based component provides sophisticated language models to a hybrid set up. Consequently, one can envisage that even if none of the individual engines can translate a given sentence correctly, the overall system may be able to do so if the engines are allowed to interact. Even if the individual components improve, the integrated system should always outperform the individual systems with respect to either the quality of the translation, the performance, or the tunability of the system.

6. A Model for the Use of MT

So far in this chapter, we have discussed the Phrasal Lexicon as a link between TM and MT systems. We have focussed specifically on the role of the PL, TM and EBMT in multi-engine and hybrid MT environments. We recommended that the best role for EBMT is in providing high quality translations in restricted domains written with controlled language rules very much in mind.

We will now bring this chapter to a close by presenting a future model for the use of MT and CAT which has been developed in a recent study (Schäler, 1999; cf. also Carl *et al.*, 2002) following discussions with localisation and translation technology experts. This, we propose, will provide an effective basis for an MT environment in a number of different future situations. The model is based on the assumption that information can be categorised into three types. The intended translation model visualises translation in the form of a pyramid, as in Figure 3.3.

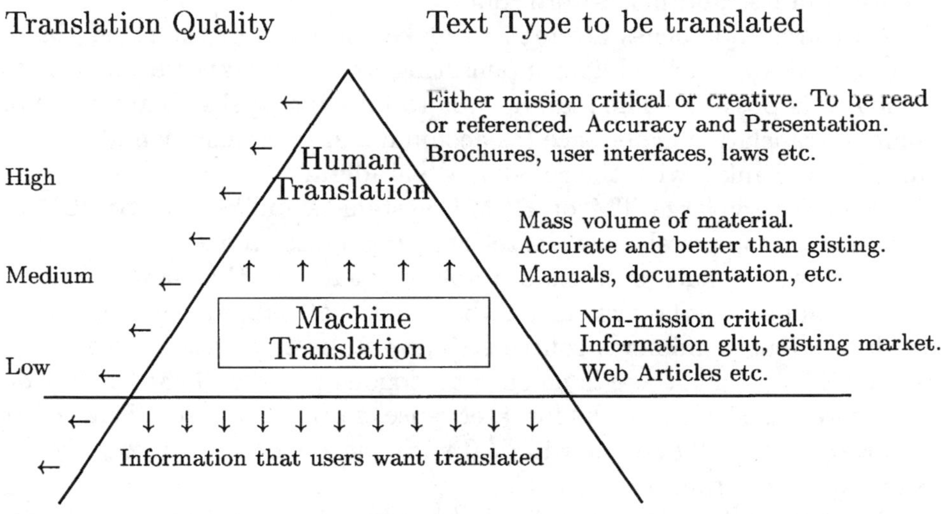

Figure 3.3. A Model for the Future Use of Translation Technology

At the bottom of this pyramid, we see 'non-mission-critical' information, known more widely as the 'gisting' market. An example of this type of information might be an on-line article about Napoleon written in French and published on a web site in France, of which a Spanish speaker with no knowledge of French but interested in Napoleon wants a rough and ready translation at minimal cost. We view this as the ideal application scenario to facilitate the widest usage of MT. Indeed, this is currently the biggest growth area of MT: people are translating web pages or communicating with one another in their own languages via email, using on-line MT systems as the translation engine.

In the middle of the pyramid, we see large amounts of material that must be translated accurately; here gisting is simply unacceptable. Examples of this type of information are product manuals or other technical documentation. Most examples of this type of translation are domain-specific. While MT is currently being used at this level, it is more the exception than the rule. However, we have argued that it is in this area of translation that EBMT has the capability to play a central role.

At the top of the pyramid, we see small amounts of mission-critical or creative material where accuracy and presentation are of paramount importance. Examples of this are marketing material, laws, user interfaces and creative literature. These are all areas which are not especially suited to MT, unless expert post-editing is available.

The model presumes (i) that the pyramid is expanding in two directions and (ii) that improvements in translation technology (MT in its widest sense) will open up new markets for developers of MT systems. We began this chapter by discussing how unnerved some translators continue to be by the availability of MT systems. We noted in the general case that the MT systems of today are simply not capable of generating translations of sufficiently high quality to justify this wariness of MT technology. However, one area where MT has met a demand for translation that up to now was not being met is in the continuous updating of webpages and their translations. Thus MT has provided a solution to this new area of demand, and is not replacing translators at all, as human translation in this area and on this scale simply cannot be envisaged.

The expansion of the pyramid will be driven by two factors:

- a growing demand for translated material given the further trend towards globalisation of the economy (horizontal expansion);

- the increasing availability and accessibility of information in a variety of languages to end-users on the web (vertical expansion).

At the same time, research and development in the area of translation technology will allow MT to push its way up the pyramid and be used for higher quality translation. Translation service providers will offer a variety of on-line translation facilities, from high quality human translation to low-end, cheaper MT, with a range of mixed options in between. These options will include human-edited MT using specialised, fine-tuned lexical and semantic databases, TM-based translation combined with MT, and alignment and maintenance of previously translated legacy material.

We anticipate a hybrid MT platform which integrates in one environment a wide range of applications, techniques and resources, including (but not limited to):

- multilingual alignment,
- terminology mining,
- automatic and computer-assisted terminology structuring, management and control,
- automatic or semi-automatic induction of grammars and translation templates,
- automatic consistency checks etc.

We foresee that such a hybrid MT platform will also integrate a number of different techniques and resources such as example-based, statistics-based and rule-based approaches to translation, as well as a variety of linguistic resources and corpora.

Some researchers have given some thought to the suitability of texts for MT. We are all aware of MT systems being confronted with texts that pose unfair demands on them as some texts should *never* be translated automatically, but as Kenny & Way, 2001:13 observe:

> "Those of us who have developed MT systems in the past and demonstrated them in various fora can only hope that the days of someone typing in a 50-word sentence consisting of strings of auxiliaries, prepositional phrases and containing ellipses, and the system either keeling over or else coming up with a hopeless 'translation' after some minutes, followed by our system tester uttering 'MT is not for me!', are long gone".

Despite the importance of this topic, the work that we are aware of regarding translatability and MT focuses only on what texts should be sent to *rule*-based MT systems. One possible translatability indicator for the use of MT in general is the identification of (sets of) phenomena which are likely to cause problems for MT systems (e.g. Gdaniec, 1994 with respect to the *Logos* MT system; Bernth & Gdaniec, 2001). Based on their work with the *PaTrans* system (Ørsnes *et al.*, 1996), a descendant of the *Eurotra* system, Underwood & Jongejan, 2001 provide a definition of translatability:

> "the notion of translatability is based on so-called 'translatability indicators' where the occurrence of such an indicator in the text is considered to have a negative effect on the quality of machine translation. The fewer translatability indicators, the better suited the text is to translation using MT" (Underwood & Jongejan, 2001:363).

In an integrated translation environment, these definitions would have to be widened considerably. Future translatability indicators will have to be more fine-grained. MT systems will have to have the capacity to adapt to such indicators and learn from them if progress in this area is to be made. Translatability indicators will have to give specific reasons as to why any text might not (yet) be suitable for automatic translation. If this can be achieved, a tool would be triggered to incrementally modify such texts and/or the system's resources in order to render the text suitable for automatic translation. That is, a hybrid integrated translation environment has to provide a means of separating the translatable parts from the non-translatable parts of a source text in a much more sophisticated manner than TMs currently do. In order to improve translation quality, one would have to estimate:

- the expected quality of the translation;
- the cost (both in terms of human effort as well as price in real terms) of upgrading the system's resources;
- the cost of amending the source text to make it suitable for processing by an MT system.

Furthermore, and perhaps more ambitiously, the integrated system would have to be aware of gaps in the source text which it cannot tackle and provide intelligent inference mechanisms to generate solutions for bridging these gaps.

Translations will be routed through the available translation options according to criteria such as the type of text at hand, the value of the information to be translated, the quality requirements of the customer, and the resources in terms of time and money available to them. Finally, it is important that customers receive accurate information on the quality, pricing and time implications of their choice prior to selecting their preferred translation option.[9]

[9]This problem area has been investigated within the *EU*-funded *Transrouter* project, cf. Schäler, 2000.

7. Summary

On various occasions in recent decades, MT companies have claimed that the linguistic technology developed by them has made human translation redundant. These claims have so far not had a significant impact on the reality of translation as a profession and as a business. The only impact such hype has really had is in unrealistically raising the expectation of users as to the quality of such systems, only to disappoint them when they actually interact with MT and turn them away from the undoubted benefits to be made.

The one technology that has had a considerable impact on translation has been TM — it has changed the way translators work, as can be seen when examining the impact it had in the localization industry, one of the largest employers of technical translators. Ironically, TM technology works without any of the sophisticated linguistic technologies developed over decades by MT developers — it is little more than a sophisticated search and replace engine.

Because of the enormous success of TM systems, large amounts of aligned, bilingual material are now available — exactly how many can only be estimated: individual products, which are frequently translated into 30 languages and more, can easily contain up to one million words. However, the highly successful approach taken by TM developers is also the cause of the inherent restrictions and limitations in TMs.

In order to try and overcome these, we have proposed an implementation of EBMT based on the idea of a phrasal lexicon, a linguistically enhanced version of a TM system working at phrasal level. We propose that EBMT should be viewed as a solution where the requirement is special purpose, high quality translation. Accordingly, we recommend that such systems be restricted to using texts which are suitable for translation in the domain in question. Such texts should be written according to controlled language guidelines in identifiable sublanguage domains. If phrasal lexicons and EBMT systems are used according to such guidelines, we are confident that as more is known about these relatively new fields, the PL will come to play a central role and provide substantial support for special purpose MT. This will bring about a paradigm shift from TM to EBMT via the PL: given their attitude towards such technology, adding an automated translation facility to today's TM environment is likely to raise the hackles of many translators. Rather, our envisaged scenario will demonstrate clearly to translators the benefit of having phrasal alignments made available to them, and once they are happy with this additional mode of operation, it is a reasonably short step to enabling an automated solution via the recombination element of EBMT systems such as those described in this volume.

If EBMT is to find a niche amongst the different MT paradigms, we believe it has to offer the potential to easily adapt to new domains in a more controlled manner than TMs do. The adaptation process differs from TM technology with respect to how translation knowledge is stored, what kind of such knowledge is stored, how it is retrieved and how it is recomposed to build a new translation. This requires sophisticated processing based on linguistic resources and/or advanced numerical processing. We have developed a model for the future use of translation technology which is intended to be a valuable aid to translators, capable of generating descriptive, controlled or general translations according to the needs of the user and the effort he is willing to invest. Finally, the setting we propose is a hybrid translation environment which integrates together a number of MT technologies, linguistic and processing resources in harmony with the actual translator, the latter remaining *the* most valuable resource in the translation chain.

Acknowledgments

Schäler's initial research on the Phrasal Lexicon and its implementation in a prototype was conducted at University College Dublin under Allan Ramsay. It was part-funded by the Irish Industrial Development Agency.

Thanks also to Sharon O'Brien (*DCU*) for bringing one of the authors up to speed on recent developments in the area of translatability, as well as providing many useful comments on an early draft of this paper.

References

Adriens, G. and D. Schreurs. 1992. From Cogram to Alcogram: toward a controlled English grammar checker. In *Proceedings of the fifteenth [sic] International Conference on Computational Linguistics, COLING-92*, Nantes, France, pp.595–601.

Almqvist, I. and A. Sågvall Hein. 1996. Defining ScaniaSwedish — a Controlled Language for Truck Maintenance. In *CLAW 96: Proceedings of the First International Workshop on Controlled Language Applications*, Leuven, Belgium, pp.159–164.

Barthe, K. 1998. GIFAS Rationalised French: Designing one Controlled Language to Match Another. In *CLAW98: Proceedings of the Second International Workshop on Controlled Language Applications*, Pittsburgh, PA., pp.87–102.

Becker, J.D. 1975. The Phrasal Lexicon. In *Proceedings of Theoretical Issues in Natural Language Processing*, Cambridge, MA., pp.70–73.

Bernth, A. and C. Gdaniec. 2001. MTranslatability. *Machine Translation* **16**(3):175–218.

Brown, P., J. Cocke, S. Della Pietra, F. Jelinek, V. Della Pietra, J. Lafferty, R. Mercer and P. Rossin. 1990. A Statistical Approach to Machine Translation. *Computational Linguistics* **16**:79–85.

Brown, R. 1996. Example-Based Machine Translation in the Pangloss System. In *COLING-96: Proceedings of the 16th International Conference on Computational Linguistics*, Copenhagen, Denmark, pp.169–174.

Carl, M. and S. Hansen. 1999. Linking Translation Memories with Example-Based Machine Translation. In *Machine Translation Summit VII*, Singapore, pp.617–624.

Carl, M., L. Iomdin, C. Pease and O. Streiter. 2001. Towards a Dynamic Linkage of Example-Based and Rule-Based Machine Translation. *Machine Translation* **15**(3):223-257.

Carl, M., A. Way and R. Schäler. 2002. Toward a Hybrid, Integrated Translation Environment. In S. Richardson (ed.) *Machine Translation: From Research to Real Users*, LNAI 2499, Berlin/New York: Springer, pp.11–20.

Chandioux, J. 1976. MÉTÉO: un système opérationel pour la traduction automatique des bulletins météorologiques destinés au grand public. *META* **21**:127–133.

Chen, S. 1996. *Building Probabilistic Models for Natural Language*. PhD Thesis, Harvard University, Cambridge, MA.

Doi, S. and K. Muraki. 1992. Translation ambiguity resolution based on text corpora of source and target language. In *Proceedings of the fifteenth [sic] International Conference on Computational Linguistics, COLING-92*, Nantes, France, pp.525–531.

Frederking, R. and S. Nirenburg. 1994. Three Heads are better than one. In *ANLP-94: 4th Conference on Applied Natural Language Processing*, Stuttgart, Germany, pp.95–100.

Gale, W.A. and K.W. Church. 1991. A program for aligning sentences in bilingual corpora. In *29th Annual Meeting of the Association for Computational Linguistics*, Berkeley, CA., pp.177–184.

Gdaniec, C. 1994. The Logos Translatability Index. In *Proceedings of the First Conference for Machine Translation in the Americas*, Columbia, MD., pp.97–105.

Heyn, M. 1996. Integrating machine translation into translation memory systems In *TKE 96: Proceedings of the First Workshop of the*

European Association for Machine Translation: Language Resources, Terminology, Economics, and User Needs, Vienna, Austria, pp.113–126.

Isabelle, P., M. Dymetman, G.Foster, J-M. Jutras, E. Macklovitch, F. Perrault, X. Ren and M. Simard. 1993. Translation Analysis and Translation Automation. In *Proceedings of the Fifth International Conference on Theoretical and Methodological Issues in Machine Translation TMI '93: MT in the Next Generation*, Kyoto, Japan.

Kamprath, C., E. Adolphson, T. Mitamura and E. Nyberg. 1998. Controlled Language Multilingual Document Production: Experience with Caterpillar Technical English. In *CLAW98: Proceedings of the Second International Workshop on Controlled Language Applications*, Pittsburgh, PA., pp.51–61.

Kaplan, R. and J. Bresnan. 1982. Lexical Functional Grammar: A Formal System for Grammatical Representation. In J. Bresnan (ed.) *The Mental Representation of Grammatical Relations*, MIT Press, Cambridge, MA., pp.173–281.

Kaplan, R., K. Netter, J. Wedekind and A. Zaenen. 1989. Translation by Structural Correspondences. In *Fourth Conference of the European Chapter of the Association for Computational Linguistics*, Manchester, England, pp.272–281.

Kenny, D. and A. Way. 2001. Teaching Machine Translation and Translation Technology: A Contrastive Study. In M. Forcada, J-A. Pérez-Ortiz and D. Lewis (eds.) *Proceedings of the Workshop on Teaching Machine Translation, MT Summit VIII*, Santiago de Compostela, Spain, pp.13–17.

Lehrndorfer, A. and S. Schachtl. 1998. Controlled Siemens Documentary German and TopTrans. In *TC-FORUM*, Stuttgart, Germany.

Lux, V. and E. Dauphin. 1996. Corpus Studies: a Contribution to the Definition of a Controlled Language. In *CLAW 96: Proceedings of the First International Workshop on Controlled Language Applications*, Leuven, Belgium, pp.193–204.

Macklovitch, E. 2000. Two types of Translation Memory. In *Translating and the Computer, Proceedings of the 22nd ASLIB Conference, Translation and the Computer*, London.

Macklovitch, E. and G. Russell. 2000. What's Been Forgotten in Translation Memory. In J.S. White (ed.) *Envisioning Machine Translation in the Information Future: Proceedings of the 4th Conference of the Association for Machine translation in the Americas (AMTA 2000)* (Lecture Notes in Artificial Intelligence Vol. 1934), Berlin/New York: Springer, pp.137–146

Means, L. and K. Godden. 1996. The Controlled Automotive Service Language (CASL) Project. In *CLAW 96: Proceedings of the First International Workshop on Controlled Language Applications*, Leuven, Belgium, pp.106–114.

Melamed, D.I. 2001. *Empirical Methods for Exploiting Parallel Texts.* MIT Press, Cambridge, MA.

Mitamura, T. and E. Nyberg. 1995. Controlled English for Knowledge Based MT: Experience with the KANT System. In *Proceedings of Sixth International Conference on Theoretical and Methodological Issues in Machine Translation*, Leuven, Belgium, pp.158–172.

Nagao, M. 1984. A framework of a mechanical translation between Japanese and English by analogy principle. In A. Elithorn and R. Banerji (eds.) *Artificial and Human Intelligence*, North Holland, Amsterdam, pp.173–180.

Nomiyama, H. 1991. Lexical selection mechanism using target language knowledge and its learning ability. In *Proceedings of the Semi-Annual Meeting of the Information Processing Society of Japan*, NL86-8 (in Japanese, cited in [Doi and Maraki, 1992]), Tokyo, Japan.

Nübel R. 1997. End-to-end evaluation in VerbMobil I. In *Machine Translation Summit VI*, San Diego, CA., pp.232–240.

Ørsnes, B., B. Music and B. Maegaard. 1996. PaTrans — A Patent Translation System. In *COLING-96: Proceedings of the 16th International Conference on Computational Linguistics*, Copenhagen, Denmark, pp. 1115–1118.

Planas, E. and Furuse O. 1999. Formalizing Translation Memories. In *Machine Translation Summit VII*, Singapore, pp.331–339.

Rayner, M. and P. Bouillon. 1995. Hybrid Transfer in an English-French Spoken Language Translator. In *IA'95: Proceedings of the Fifth International Conference*, Montpellier, France, pp.153–162.

Ramsay, A. and R. Schäler. 1997. Case and Word Order in English and German. In R. Mitkov and N. Nicolov (eds.) *Recent Advances in Natural Language Processing: Selected Papers from RANLP'95* (Current Issues in Linguistic Theory, Volume 136), John Benjamins, Amsterdam/Philadelphia, pp.15–34.

Reinke, U. 1999. Evaluierung der linguistischen Leistungsfähigkeit von Translation Memory-Systemen — Ein Erfahrungsbericht. In *LDV-Forum. Forum der Gesellschaft für Linguistische Datenverarbeitung*, Vol. **1-2**.

Sadler, V. and R. Vendelmans. 1990. Pilot Implementation of a Bilingual Knowledge Bank. In *COLING-90, Papers Presented to the 13th Inter-*

national Conference on Computational Linguistics, Helsinki, Finland, pp.449–451.

Sato, S. and M. Nagao. 1990. Toward Memory-based Translation. In *COLING-90, Papers Presented to the 13th International Conference on Computational Linguistics*, Helsinki, Finland, 1990, pp.247–252.

Schachtl, S. 1996. Requirements for Controlled German in Industrial Applications. In *CLAW 96: Proceedings of the First International Workshop on Controlled Language Applications*, Leuven, Belgium, pp.143–149.

Schäler, R. 1996. Machine translation, translation memories and the phrasal lexicon: the localisation perspective. *TKE 96: Proceedings of the First Workshop of the European Association for Machine Translation: Language Resources, Terminology, Economics, and User Needs*, Vienna, Austria, pp.21–33.

Schäler, R. 1999. *New Media Localisation*—a Linglink Report for the European Commission DGXIII, Luxembourg, `www.hltcentral.org/usr_docs/studies/Localisation.pdf`.

Schäler, R. 2000. The EU LE4 Transrouter Project. In *Proceedings of the 22nd ASLIB Conference, Translation and the Computer*, London.

Schäler, R. 2001. Beyong Translation Memories. In M. Carl and A. Way (eds.) *Proceedings of the Workshop on Example-Based Machine Translation, MT Summit VIII*, Santiago de Compostela, Spain, pp.49–55.

Simard, M. and P. Langlais. 2001. Sub-sentential Exploitation of Translation Memories. In *Machine Translation Summit VIII*, Santiago de Compostela, Spain, pp.335–339.

Shuttleworth, M. 2002. Combining MT and TM on a Technology-oriented Translation Masters: Aims and Perspectives. In *Proceedings of 6th EAMT Workshop on Teaching Machine Translation*, Manchester, UK, pp.123–129.

Somers, H.L. 1993. The Current State of Machine Translation. In *Machine Translation Summit IV*, Kobe, Japan, pp.115–124.

Somers, H.L. 1999. Review Article: Example-based Machine Translation. *Machine Translation* **14**(2):113–157 (also Chapter 1, this volume).

Sumita, E. and H. Iida. 1991. Experiments and Prospects of Example-based Machine Translation. In *29th Annual Meeting of the Association for Computational Linguistics*, Berkeley, CA., pp.185–192.

TETRIS 1999. Technologie-Transfer intelligenter Sprachtechnologie. IAI, Saarbrücken, Germany.

Underwood, N. and B. Jongejan. 2001. Translatability Checker: A Tool to Help Decide Whether to Use MT. In *Machine Translation Summit VIII*, Santiago de Compostela, Spain, pp.363–368.

Van der Eijk, P., M. de Koning and G. van der Steen. 1996. Controlled language correction and translation. In *CLAW 96: Proceedings of the First International Workshop on Controlled Language Applications*, Leuven, Belgium, pp.64–73.

Vasconcellos, M. and M. León. 1985. SPANAM and ENGSPAN: Machine Translation at the Pan American Health Organization. *Machine Translation* **11**(2-3):122–136.

Wahlster, W. 1993. *VerbMobil*–Translation of Face-to-Face Dialogs. In *Machine Translation Summit IV*, Kobe, Japan, pp.127–135.

Wahlster, W. 2000. *VerbMobil: foundations of speech-to-speech translation.* Berlin/New York: Springer.

Way, A. 2001. *LFG-DOT: A Hybrid Architecture for Robust MT.* PhD Thesis, University of Essex, Colchester, UK (cf. Chapter 16, this volume).

Chapter 4

EBMT SEEN AS CASE-BASED REASONING

Bróna Collins
Brona.Collins@ireland.com

Harold Somers
Harold.Somers@umist.ac.uk

Abstract This paper looks at EBMT from the perspective of the Case-based Reasoning (CBR) paradigm. We attempt to describe the task of machine translation seen as a potential application of CBR, and attempt to describe MT in standard CBR terms. The aim is to see if other applications of CBR can suggest better ways to approach EBMT.

Keywords: case-based reasoning, case-based representation, case-based retrieval, case-based adaptation

1. Introduction

Case-based reasoning (CBR) is a well-established paradigm for problem solving which emerged in the 1980s as an alternative to rule-based expert systems. Instead of rules, CBR represents expertise in the form of past 'cases', and new problems are solved by finding the most similar case in the case-base, and using this as a model for the new solution through a process of 'adaptation'.

EBMT is a reasonably well-established paradigm for machine translation (MT) which emerged in the 1990s as an alternative to rule-based MT systems. Instead of rules, EBMT represents its linguistic knowledge in the form of 'examples' of previous translations, and new translations are made by finding the most similar example in the example-base, and

M. Carl and A. Way (eds.), Recent Advances in Example-Based Machine Translation, 115–153.

using this as a model for the new translation through a process of 're-combination'.

The parallel between CBR and EBMT is so obvious that one would think it perhaps unnecessary to make it. But, despite the earlier establishment of CBR as a problem-solving paradigm, very few papers on EBMT make the connection explicit, and if they do, it is only as a passing comment. With one notable exception, reference to CBR pays only lip service: no attempt is made to take what has been said about CBR to see if it applies to the problem of MT. The major exception is the work of Collins and her colleagues (Collins & Cunningham, 1995; Collins & Cunningham, 1996; Collins et. al., 1996; Collins & Cunningham, 1997; Collins, 1998): this work was explicitly in the paradigm of CBR, since it was carried out from within a Computer Science department specialising in CBR. As for the rest of the EBMT literature, Somers, 1999 (see Chapter 1, this volume) has attempted a very thorough survey of articles on EBMT: of about 130 articles collected and read, less than 10% even mentioned CBR or related paradigms, by name.

The purpose of this paper is to look at MT from the perspective of CBR, that is, to consider the CBR approach to problem solving, to see how (or whether) CBR terminology and ideas fit the particular problem of MT, and to see if we can gain any insights from this exercise. The basic assumption of this paper is that EBMT does indeed come within the general paradigm of CBR-based systems. For the purposes of discussion, however, we will use the terms 'EBMT' and 'CBR' distinctively: the former in its normal meaning, the latter to imply CBR seen as a generic problem-solving method.

2. CBR: The Paradigm

CBR emerged in the 1980s as an approach to problem solving which offered an alternative to the rule-based approach typical of 'expert systems' up until that time. CBR offered a more intuitive approach, based on the way humans appear to solve problems, namely by finding previous similar examples as precedents, and using common-sense reasoning and extrapolation to adapt the precedent to the current problem. This mode of operation is extremely widespread, and can be applied to almost any imaginable human problem. As Leake, 1996:3f. states, the CBR approach is based on two tenets about the nature of the world: first, "similar problems have similar solutions", and second, "future problems are likely to be similar to current problems". Psychological reality is claimed for CBR as a model of human cognition: "[E]xperts solve problems by applying their experience, whilst only novices attempt to solve problems by applying rules they have recently acquired." (Watson & Marir, 1994:348)

Riesbeck & Schank, 1989 suggest a trade-off between the rule-based and case-based approaches to problem solving:

> "A rule-based system will be flexible and produce nearly optimal answers, but it will be slow and prone to error. A case-based system will be restricted to variations on known situations and produce approximate answers, but it will be quick and its answers will be grounded in actual experience. In very limited domains, the tradeoffs favor the rule-based reasoner, but the balance changes as domains become more realistically complex." (Riesbeck & Schank, 1989:26)

This methodology applies to a variety of distinct areas of reasoning, and is widely acknowledged as closely modelling human reasoning strategies. In particular, it closely resembles the way human *translators* tend to handle a new text to be translated (Wilss, 1998), which in turn explains the huge popularity among translators of Translation Memory (TM) tools, which are of course a cousin of EBMT (in sharp contrast to the reception that other results of MT research have so far had in that community).

CBR is generally acknowledged to have its roots in the work done by Schank & Abelson, 1977 on scripts, along with the 'Exemplar-based Learning' of Medin & Schaffer, 1978, the 'Memory-based Reasoning' of Stanfill & Waltz, 1986 and the 'Derivational Analogy' of Carbonell, 1986, while the term itself is probably due to Kolodner & Riesbeck, 1986. Other trails into the CBR field have come from the study of analogical reasoning (Gentner, 1983), and — further back — from theories of concept formation, problem solving and experiential learning within philosophy and psychology (e.g. Wittgenstein, 1953:31ff.; Tulving, 1972).

CBR is often contrasted with rule-based reasoning, in that rules are replaced by cases. By 'case' we mean a "contextualized piece of knowledge representing an experience that teaches a lesson fundamental to achieving the goals of the reasoner" (Kolodner, 1993:13). In fact, cases can be seen as very specific rules, that is, rules which apply to distinct situations. So CBR is a special kind of rule-based reasoning because the rules have to be interpreted 'on the fly', and the same rule may be used differently from one situation to another. Thus far, the same can be said of EBMT.

Typical examples of CBR are: a system which tries to find a suitable menu given some ingredients and diners' preferences and constraints (Hammond, 1986), a medical diagnosis system (Koton, 1988), or an

```
Problem:
   (include tofu)
   (taste hot)
   (style stir-fry)
Solution:
  (ingredients
ingr1 (tofu lb .5)
ingr2 (soy-sauce tablespoon 2)
ingr3 (rice-wine spoon 1)
ingr4 (cornstarch tablespoon .5)
ingr5 (sugar spoon 1)
ingr6 (broccoli lb 1)
ingr7 (r-pepper piece 6))
  (actions
    act1 (chop object (ingr1) size (chunk))
    act2 (marinate object (result act1)
    in (& (ingr2)(ingr3)(ingr4) (ingr5)) time (20))
    act3 (chop object (ingr6) size (chunk))
    act4 (stir-fry object (& (result act2)(ingr7)) time
          (1))
    act5 (add object (result act3) to (result act4))
    act6 (stir-fry object (result act5) time (2)))
  (style stir-fry)
```

Figure 4.1. Example of a case, cited in Kolodner, 1993

agony aunt (Domeshek, 1991). The vocabulary of problem solving permeates the CBR literature: "Cases can be represented in a variety of forms using the full range of AI representational formalisms, including frames, objects, predicates, semantic nets and rules — the frame/object presentation currently being used by the majority of CBR software." (Watson & Marir, 1994:331). Figure 4.1 shows an example.

Here already we see a difference between CBR and EBMT: many CBR systems address 'problems' which have 'solutions' which involve a sequence of **goals** to achieve, and 'outcomes' or changes to the state of the 'world' after the case has been invoked. In contrast, in EBMT the examples are of input–output mappings, and the means of getting from one to the other is rarely made explicit, except inasmuch as elements in the input pattern may be linked to corresponding elements in the output pattern. We will see consequences of this difference at almost every stage.

One of the claimed advantages of CBR is that it overcomes the 'knowledge-acquisition bottleneck' (Hayes-Roth *et al.*, 1983) of hand-coding a great number of rules, and verifying how they interact with each other. The complexity of real-world domains, according to Riesbeck & Schank, 1989:26, makes it "impossible or impractical to specify fully all the rules involved." In CBR, when the existing 'rules' do not work (i.e. there is no suitable case in the case-base), one simply adds a new one. Such claims have been made for CBR and related 'lazy learning' techniques (e.g. Watson & Marir, 1994:348) as well as for EBMT itself (e.g. Sato & Nagao, 1990). However, these approaches eventually have to deal with the issue of case-base size as will be discussed below.

3. Crucial Elements of CBR

CBR thus favours learning from experience, since it is arguably easier to learn by retaining a concrete problem-solving experience than it is to generalize from it. Nevertheless, effective learning in CBR requires a well-established set of methods in order to extract the relevant knowledge from a given experience, integrate a case into the existing knowledge structure, and to index the case for later matching with similar cases. These are presented in the following sections.

The CBR paradigm covers a range of different methods for organizing, retrieving, utilizing and indexing the knowledge retained in past cases. In fact, 'case-based' reasoning is just one of a set of terms used to refer to artificial reasoning systems of this nature. This has led to some confusion, particularly since 'case-based reasoning' is used both as an umbrella term (similar to analogical reasoning) for several types of approaches, as well as for one particular type of approach. Aamodt & Plaza, 1994 distinguish the following types:

- Exemplar-based reasoning
- Instance-based reasoning
- Memory-based reasoning
- Case-based reasoning
- Analogy-based reasoning

This list presents a continuum of approaches, ranging from those which attempt only to *classify* new examples (exemplar- and instance-based) to those approaches where previous knowledge is used to actually solve new problems (memory- and case-based reasoning) and finally to analogy-based reasoning, which could be described as a method for solving new problems based on past cases from a *different* domain. As we are concerned with problem solving in a single domain, we will limit the discussion to memory-based and case-based reasoning here.

3.1 Memory-based reasoning (MBR)

Characteristic of this approach is a large collection of cases in the memory, and reasoning as a data-driven process of accessing and searching in this memory rather than employment of knowledge-inference techniques. The retrieval and storage methods are often based on parallel architectures and tend to rely on purely syntactic/structural criteria, as in the *MBR-Talk* system (Stanfill & Waltz, 1988). Some do attempt to utilize general domain knowledge, e.g. the EBMT systems built on massively parallel processors (Kitano & Higuchi, 1991; Kitano, 1993). As we will see, EBMT systems have tended to gravitate more towards MBR than CBR because of the sheer case-base sizes required in translation, and the relatively easy manner in which huge case bases can be created for EBMT from parallel corpora.

3.2 Case Based Reasoning

The typically assumed features of CBR methods are, firstly, that a case has a certain degree of richness of information, and complexity in its internal organization. In contrast, a feature vector with a set of corresponding values and an associated class, as typical in classification-based techniques, would *not* be considered a typical case description.

Secondly, CBR methods are crucially able to modify, or adapt, a retrieved solution when applied in a different problem-solving scenario. Some case-based methods also utilize general background knowledge (see section 7 on adaptation) — although there is a great deal of variation in how this is done.

4. The CBR Cycle

Most texts discussing CBR are agreed on the essential elements that make up a CBR system, namely the database of 'cases', of course, and the accompanying design format consisting of the classic 'CBR cycle', as illustrated in Figure 4.2.

The initial description or **indexing** of a problem defines a new or 'input' case. This new case is used to **retrieve** a case from the collection of previous cases. This retrieved case is then combined with the new case — through **reuse** or **adaptation** — to produce a **solved case**, i.e. a proposed solution to the initial problem. This solution is then feasibility

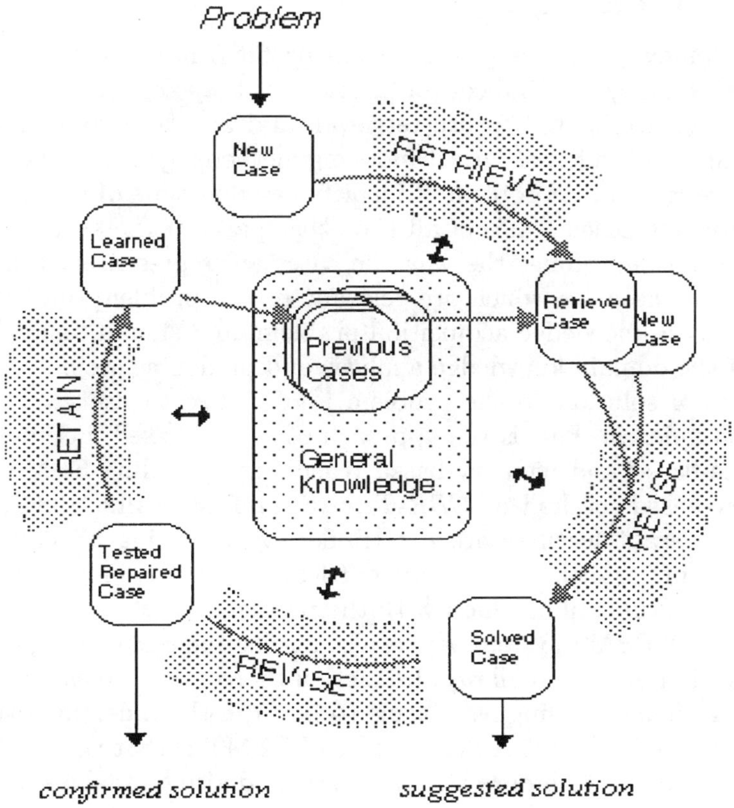

Figure 4.2. The CBR cycle (based on Aamodt & Plaza, 1994)

tested during **retain**, e.g. by being applied to the real-world environment or evaluated by a teacher, and repaired if failed.

During the **retain** phase, useful experience is retained for future reuse, perhaps after the solution is again **tested** and the case base is updated by a new **learned** case, or by modification of some existing cases. General knowledge can play a part in this cycle, by supporting the CBR processes.

This support may range from very weak (or none) to very strong, depending on the type of CBR method. General knowledge should be understood as domain-dependent knowledge, as opposed to the specific knowledge contained in the cases.

In the following sections we will take each of these elements in turn to see how they relate to EBMT.

4.1 Indexing

The 'indexing problem' is a central problem in CBR. It amounts to deciding what type of indices (or 'indexes' as they are commonly known) to use for current and future retrieval, and also how to structure the search space of indexes. Direct indexing methods ignore the latter issue, but there is still the problem of identifying what type of indexes to use. The indexing scheme affects all the other parts of the system, since it reflects and determines the way the cases are represented, that is, the aspects of the cases which are relevant to the problem domain. This is actually a knowledge acquisition problem, and should be analysed as part of the domain knowledge analysis and modelling step.

A trivial solution to the problem is of course to use *all* input features as indexes. This is the approach of syntax-based methods within instance-based and memory-based reasoning, including EBMT. In the memory-based method of *CBR-Talk* (Stanfill & Waltz, 1986), for example, relevant features are determined by matching all cases in the case-base in parallel, and filtering out features that belong to cases that have few features in common with the problem case.

Nearly all EBMT system papers also discuss indexing. Here, the entire input sentence, or a (shallow) abstraction thereof, is used as the basis for indexing. Some use linguistic tools to perform the indexing, others use the case-base itself. One of the ironies of EBMT is that the mechanisms used to produce the indexes for the cases, and also to analyse a new case into the appropriate format, are usually the same as, or very similar to, the rules found in the rule-based systems they are supposed to replace. However, this is far from making the claim that EBMT as an entire methodology is therefore a subset of, or equivalent to, such rule-based MT systems. As we will see, there is a lot more to EBMT than the indexing problem.

5. Case Storage and Representation

The content of the cases is distinguished in the literature from the indexing scheme used to retrieve cases.

The representation problem in CBR is essentially that of

- deciding what should be stored in a case,
- finding an appropriate structure for describing case contents, and
- deciding how the case memory should be organized and indexed for effective retrieval and reuse.

An additional problem is how to integrate the case memory structure into a model of general domain knowledge, to the extent that the approach is attempting to represent such knowledge, although as we discuss below, this is almost never attempted in EBMT.

The EBMT literature has a tendency to focus on the first two points above, in particular the linguistic methods employed to create the source language (SL)–target language (TL) links and the design of the resulting template structures, whereas the equally crucial question of global memory organization, i.e. how best to store these cases in relation to each other to enable efficient retrieval and storage, is only given whatever scant room is left after the justifications for a certain level of linguistic processing have been dispensed with. By attempting to view EBMT from the broader point of view of CBR, we choose to side-step the debate of how linguistic knowledge is gathered (and whether EBMT is therefore traditional MT in disguise or not), and to focus on the issues of efficient case storage, retrieval, reuse and case-base maintenance. Interestingly, CBR researchers never debate the 'CBR-ness' of a given system simply because some first-principles knowledge engineering tools may have been employed in order to create the cases. According to Aamodt & Plaza, 1994, "If cognitive plausibility is a guiding principle, an architecture for intelligence where the reuse of cases is at the centre, should also incorporate other and more general types of knowledge in one form or another".

5.1 The CBR case-base size

A striking feature from the point of view of EBMT is the small size of the case-base in many of the earliest reported CBR systems. As case-base sizes grew, however, CBR researchers noted that system efficiency did not automatically or monotonically increase as a result (Smyth, 1996). Smyth & Cunningham, 1996 cite the example of a case-base size 1,000 from the housing-pricing domain that generated solutions within 90% of their optimum while the addition of a further 1,000 cases improved the accuracy by only 4%. In EBMT, an example set of under 1,000 examples would be considered small, and the bigger systems might have as many as three-quarters of a million examples (cf. Chapter 1, this volume). However, the fact still remains that in every EBMT system also, there will be a theoretical optimum case-base size, and once this is reached, there will be a trade-off between case-base size and efficiency. This levelling off of the retrieval efficiency curve is referred to as the 'utility problem' in AI literature. Smyth & Keane, 1995b describe a strategy of coping with the CBR utility problem, a strategy of 'remembering to forget' using deletion techniques that preserve system efficiency, solution quality and target coverage. Case-base maintenance issues are rarely mentioned in the EBMT literature which is strange seeing as generalization and templatization are major issues in the design of the cases themselves.

5.2 Case Memory Organisation

The basic tenet of CBR is to favour learning from experience, since it is usually easier to learn by retaining a concrete problem-solving experience than it is to generalise from it. Still, effective learning in CBR requires a well worked-out set of methods in order to extract relevant knowledge from the experience, integrate a case into an existing knowledge structure, and index the case for later matching with similar cases. All this ironically means that the case memory should be organized and indexed for both effective and time-efficient retrieval and reuse, which entails some degree of generalization or classification of the knowledge contained within.

Two influential models for case memory are the Dynamic Memory model proposed by Schank, 1982 and Kolodner, 1983, and the Category-Exemplar model of Porter & Bareiss, 1986.

In the Dynamic Memory model, the case memory is a hierarchical structure of so-called 'episodic memory organization packets' (E-MOPs, Kolodner, 1993) also known as 'generalized episodes' (Koton, 1989). This model was developed from Schank's more general MOP theory. The basic idea is to organize specific cases which share similar properties under a more general structure (a generalized episode).

A generalized episode (GE) contains three different types of objects: *Norms*, *cases* and *indexes*. Norms are features *common* to all cases indexed under a GE, whereas indexes are features which *discriminate* between a GE's cases. Norms contain abstract general information that characterize the cases organized below the episode in question. An index may point to a more specific GE, or directly to a concrete case. When a new case description is given, the best match is searched for, and the input case structure is 'pushed down' the network structure, starting at the root node. If — during the storage of a case — two cases (or two GEs) end up under the same index, a new GE is automatically created. Hence, the memory structure is *dynamic* in the sense that similar parts of two case descriptions are dynamically generalized into a GE, and the cases are indexed under this GE by their difference features. A case is retrieved by finding the GE with most norms in common with the problem description. Since the index structure is a discrimination network, a case (or pointer to a case) is stored under each index that discriminates it from other cases. This may easily lead to an explosive growth of indexes with an increased number of cases. Most systems using this indexing scheme therefore put some limits to the choice of indices for the cases.

The *PROTOS* system (Porter & Bareiss, 1986; Bareiss, 1989; Porter *et al.*, 1990) embodies an alternative proposal for organizing cases in a case memory, inspired by ideas from concept classification. Cases are also referred to as *exemplars.* Different features are assigned different significances, or weights, in describing a case's membership to a category. Unlike with the Dynamic Memory model above, generalization of a set of cases is done with caution. Within this memory organization, categories are interlinked within a semantic network which also contains the features and intermediate states (e.g. subclasses of goal concepts) referred to by other terms. This network represents a background of general domain knowledge, which provides explanatory support to some of the CBR tasks. Case matching or 'knowledge-based pattern matching' is done by combining the input features of a problem case into a pointer to the case or category that shares most of the features.

Riesbeck & Schank, 1989:36ff. describe the dynamic formation of "new abstractions ... when a number of cases are discovered to share some common set of features", and Branting, 1989 describes a system which integrates generalizations into a CBR system. Hammond, 1987 similarly suggests that abstract cases can be created where common sets of features are shared. Bergmann & Wilke, 1996 explore the idea further. On the other hand, Kolodner, 1993:7 suggests that generalization, although possible, is not a significant feature of CBR systems hinting perhaps that general rules are in some way the antithesis of the CBR philosophy.

5.3 Case Memory Organisation in EBMT

A feature of recent EBMT research has been the tendency to take similar examples and store them as a single generalized example, sometimes so much so that they resemble traditional transfer rules (Kitano & Higuchi, 1991; Brown, 1999). Many researchers report procedures for automatically discovering generalized patterns such as in Chapter 9 (see also Cicekli & Güvenir, 1996, Güvenir & Tunç, 1996, Güvenir &

Cicekli, 1998) and Chapter 11 (McTait & Trujillo, 1999) in this volume. While nearly all EBMT system papers discuss such generalized indexing schemes, rather less is said about the way in which the generalized templates or patterns are then stored *relative* to each other, i.e. the structuring of the set of cases that is actually being indexed into. EBMT case-bases on the whole tend not to be structured according to any concept classification or discriminatory indexing schemes of the types described in the previous section and it is therefore difficult to see how a newly solved problem can be re-entered into the system (the **retain** function) in order to allow the system to learn. General domain knowledge (e.g. knowledge of linguistic rules; the translation domain) is also rarely used to assist in the categorization/generalization of cases.

An example of a structured case memory for EBMT is the *ReVerb* system (Collins, 1998) where cases are stored as separate frames in a frame-representation language called *Krell*. This allows the definition of typical feature–value frame structures and their subsequent organization in a semantic net-type memory. Facilities include a choice of inheritance mechanisms between concepts and 'demon' programs that lie dormant until some precondition is satisfied (e.g. a new word is being entered into the system), whereupon the system updates all the relevant concepts and pointers in order to keep track of the new information and maintain a consistent case base.

The memory structure of *ReVerb* assumes only a very shallow concept hierarchy, no deeper than two. However the inheritance mechanisms and marker-passing facilities between all lexical items and their containing chunks in the cases mean that cases can, in theory, be classified into generalized 'metacase' groupings according to any chosen criteria, e.g. presence of a particular group of words, parts of speech, syntactic functions, degree of mismatch between SL and TL, etc. The deliberately flexible memory schema is currently arranged as follows.

A case, which represents one sentence pair, contains a list of 'chunks' which contain a pair of SL–TL strings, or a single SL string or TL string (depending on how bijective the mapping between the two languages was judged to be). Cases are not directly connected to each other. However, every word instance that is present in any case has an explicit link back to a mother concept for that word. This WORD concept in turn links to all case-chunks that contain an instance of the word type (this applies for both the SL and TL) — see Figure 4.3. Other information in the chunk

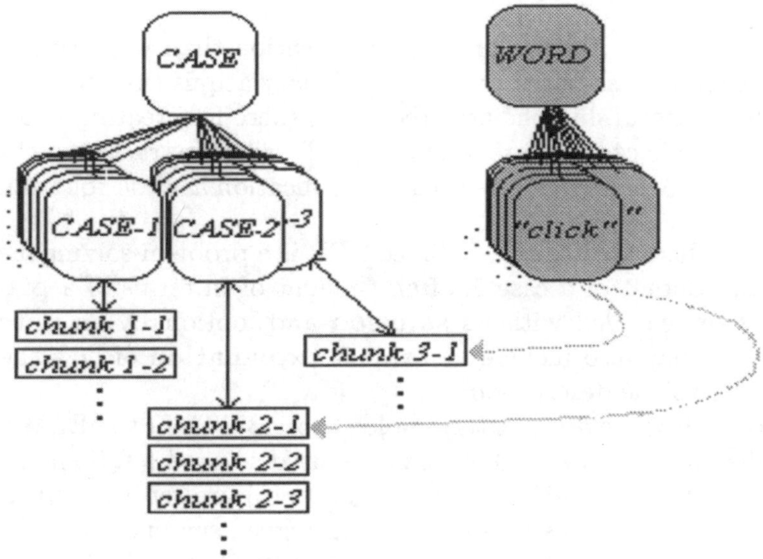

Figure 4.3. The shallow case memory organisation scheme in the *ReVerb* EBMT system (Collins, 1998). The WORD concept keeps track of all chunks (and hence, cases) that contain an instance of it.

provides the context of the word occurrence (part of speech, syntactic function, TL equivalent, etc).

Every time a new case is being created (i.e. during a problem solving episode), the WORD and CASE concepts are updated. This simply means updating the list of chunk-IDs that are listed under the WORD concept for that particular word, or, if the word is new to the system, creating a new WORD concept. This applies equally to SL and TL. The CASE concept is similarly updated to contain a new pointer to the new case-ID. As we shall see in the Retrieval section, this type of memory organization facilitates retrieval (using a method called 'spreading activation'). Also, the system dictionary is easily constructed on the principle that pairs of SL–TL WORDs that co-occur in several translation examples (have similar lists of chunk-IDs) are likely to be genuine translation fragments. A similar idea is described in McTait, 2001 (cf. Chapter 11, this volume), where each lexical item is linked to a sentence ID and the size of the intersection set of two lexical items' sentence IDs is indicative of the plausibility of the items being translations of each other.

ReVerb went no further in case classification than was necessary for the functions of case-based parsing, dictionary acquisition, template creation and retrieval, but the architecture is there for creating potentially deeper semantic case hierarchies for EBMT using abstraction techniques like Dynamic Memory or Exemplar Classification as described earlier.

5.3.1 Case Content. Since CBR is a problem-solving methodology, the content of a case is often thought of in terms of a **problem description** coupled with its **solution** and, optionally an **outcome**. Some cases may also include an explicit **explanation** of how the solution relates to the description.

So how can we relate this terminology to EBMT? In the EBMT literature, the nature of the case base is widely discussed (cf. Somers, 1999; Chapter 1, this volume). The cases (examples) are represented in a variety of formats, such as lexically aligned tagged sentences (e.g. Kitano, 1993), tree structures (e.g. Sato & Nagao, 1990; Al-Adhaileh & Tang, 1999), multi-level lattices (e.g. Planas & Furuse, 1999, see also Chapter 5 this volume), and so on. Theoretically the cases could 'speak for themselves' and be stored as unanalysed pairs of strings, though no EBMT system is reported to take this extreme step. This *is* the case with TMs, a special case of EBMT which, in CBR terms, has the retrieval and storage functions, but leaves adaptation to the human user.

6. Representation and Retrieval

The Retrieve task starts with a (partial) problem description, and ends when a best-matching previous case has been found. Its subtasks are referred to as **identify features**, **initially match**, **search**, and **select**, executed in that order. The identification task basically comes up with a set of relevant problem descriptors. The goal of the matching task is to return a set of cases that are sufficiently similar to the new case — given a similarity threshold of some kind, and the selection task works on this set of cases and chooses the best match (or at least a first case to try out).

While some case-based approaches and practically all EBMT approaches retrieve a previous case largely based on superficial, syntactic similarities among problem descriptors — see the section on Similarity Assessment, section 6.5 (e.g. *CYRUS* (Kolodner, 1983), *PATDEX-1* (Richter & Weiss, 1991)) — some approaches attempt to retrieve cases based on features that have deeper, semantic similarities (e.g. *PROTOS* (Bareiss, 1989), *CASEY* (Koton, 1989), and *MMA* (Plaza & Arcos, 1993)).

6.1 Identify Features

To identify a problem may involve simply noticing its input descriptors, but often — and particularly for knowledge-intensive methods — a more elaborate approach is taken, in which an attempt is made to 'understand' the problem within its context.

6.2 Initial Match

The task of finding a good match is typically split into two subtasks: an initial matching process which retrieves a set of plausible candidates, and then a more elaborate process of selecting the best one among these. The latter is the **select** task, described below. Finding a set of matching cases is done by using the problem descriptors (input features) as indexes to the case memory in a direct or indirect way. There are in principle three ways of retrieving a case or a set of cases: by following direct index pointers from problem features, by searching an index structure, or by searching in a model of general domain knowledge.

Dynamic Memory-based systems take the second approach, but general domain knowledge may be used in combination with search in the discrimination network.

In the *ReVerb* system the **initial match** is restricted to the search to the space of cases which contain n words in common with the problem input sentence. The Retriever then tries to find a matching case by unification of the parsed representation of the input sentence with the SL side of all cases. Cases are stored off-line in a hash table using their most general, parsed template as a key, so all cases that share the same flat syntactic structure will have the same hash-table key. If this fails to retrieve a match, then the Retriever uses the input template as a basis for 'spreading activation' in the shallow semantic network. Each cell of the new case activates all cases in the network whose chunks match it in syntactic functionality and relative sentence position. These are ranked in parallel according to their lexical content. No case will match exactly on a syntactic structural basis (for otherwise it would have unified in the first pass) but many near matches could exist. This pattern-matching scheme is flexible enough to allow gaps of arbitrary length between syntactic functions in the input and the current case but these, and other discontinuities (crossovers) are penalized (see Collins, 1998).

6.3 Select

From the set of similar cases, a best match is chosen. This may have been done during the initial match process, but more commonly a set of cases is returned from that task. The best-matching case is usually determined by evaluating the degree of initial match more closely. This is done by an attempt to generate explanations to justify non-identical features, based on the knowledge in the semantic network. If a match turns out not to be strong enough, an attempt to find a better match by following difference links to closely related cases is made. This subtask is usually a more elaborate one than the retrieval task, although the distinction between retrieval and elaborate matching is not distinct in all systems.

For example, in the **select** phase of *ReVerb*, the n-best matches from the initial match phase (described above) are matched in more detail for adaptability and given an explicit score. Once the final best case is chosen, this is then used as the new solution case whose TL contents will have to be adapted to take account of differences between the input sentence and the sentence represented by the SL side of the case. If the best match is very poor, then the end translation result may be no better than stitching fragments of cases together, but at least there is an explicit case structure available before and after the adaptation stage for the user to monitor what case was used as a solution and what part of it did not get adapted correctly, and why.

6.4 Fragmentation

While many CBR and EBMT systems try to retrieve the single best match, or at least to supply a ranking to a set of matches, some systems permit multiple retrievals, the idea being that the correct solution will result from taking the best bits of each of them. These might also be described as partial retrievals, where the cases are decomposed, making a collection of 'substrings' (Nirenburg *et al.*, 1993; Brown, 1997), 'fragments' (Somers *et al.*, 1994) or 'chunks' (Cunningham *et al.*, 1994; Collins, 1998) of matched material. Figure 4.4 illustrates this idea. There is a heavy focus on the resolution of the boundary friction problems that are associated with the recombination of fragments from different cases. In the *ReVerb* system (Collins & Cunningham, 1995), the Retriever tries to avoid recombination problems by first striving to choose

```
danger/NN0 of/PRP NN0 < > above/PRP
danger/NN0 of/PRP
of/PRP NN0 < > above/PRP
above/PRP CRD m/NP0
there/PNP is/VVV a/AT0
avalanche/NN0 < > above/PRP
there/PNP is/VVV
is/VVV a/AT0
danger/NN0 of/PRP avalanche/NN0
avalanche/NN0 above/PRP CRD m/NP0
avalanche/NN0 above/PRP
of/PRP avalanche/NN0
there/PNP is/VVV < > a/AT0
is/VVV < > a/AT0
there/PNP is/VVV a/AT0 < > danger/NN0 < > of/PRP
there/PNP is/VVV < > danger/NN0 < > of/PRP
there/PNP is/VVV a/AT0 < > danger/NN0
a/AT0 < > danger/NN0
there/PNP is/VVV < > danger/NN0
```

Figure 4.4. Fragments extracted for the input *there is a danger of avalanche above 2000m.* The individual words are tagged; the matcher can also match tags only, and can skip unmatched words, shown as ⟨ ⟩. The fragments are scored for relevance and frequency, which determines the order of presentation. From Somers et al., 1994

a single case to base the solution on. Cases make explicit any areas of a TL sentence that may be difficult to adapt (non-isomorphic mappings between SL and TL) so the system chooses candidate cases where the items to be adapted are all in 'safe' positions — see section 7.3 on adaptation-guided retrieval. The template structure is variabilised only in safe areas where SL and TL correspond, an idea also present in the system of Kaji *et al.*, 1992.

The idea of using fragments of cases is found in a number of CBR systems, including that of Redmond, 1990, who describes how especially more complex problems can be addressed by looking at subgoals individually, and correspondingly storing cases in 'snippets'. Smyth, 1996 presents a scheme of hierarchical case-based reasoning, combining subsolutions to solve a global problem. Marir & Watson, 1995 describe a system to estimate building and refurbishment costs, where the complex problems and solutions are all broken down into 'subcases': the context information becomes all important in this case, since superficially similar solutions can be quite inappropriate if the underlying situation is different.

6.5 Similarity Assessment

The way the cases are represented ('indexed') is of course intimately related to the method of selecting cases which are similar to the given input. Similarity assessment involves a similarity metric which is used to rank the cases retrieved, together with a search algorithm.

A much used **similarity metric** in CBR is expressed as in (1), where w_i is the importance ('weight') of feature f_i and s is a similarity function for the individual features, I and R indicating input and retrieved cases, respectively.

$$(1) \qquad S(I,R) = \frac{\sum_{i=1}^{n} w_i \times s(f^I{}_i, f^R_i)}{\sum_{i=1}^{n} w_i}$$

There are obviously three elements to this: identification of the primitive similarity function(s) s, determination of the weights w associated with each feature, and an algorithm for finding the case for which the equation in (1) gives the best value.

The **primitive similarity functions** depend on the choice of features and in particular their complexity. Where features map in an obvious way onto scalar ranges, s can involve simple arithmetic. If the features are more complex then correspondingly more complex functions have to be invoked.

More problematic is the assignment of **weights**. One method is simply to ask human experts to do this (or to weight all features equally). More adventurous systems include a component which learns which features are the most predictive of case differences, or which features are more or less likely to be adapted, and adjusts the relative weights accordingly.

Many CBR systems reportedly use a quite simple **search algorithm** which exhaustively applies the similarity function to all the cases in the case-base. Retrieval time increases linearly with the size of the case-base. One obvious way to overcome this is to organize the search-space so that the higher-weighted features are compared first.

For EBMT in general, these do not appear to be important issues. Even in early systems where examples are stored as tree structures, little detail is given concerning how tree structures are compared. A similarity metric which makes use of linear distance in a hierarchical thesaurus is widely used for quantifying word similarity (e.g. Nagao, 1984). For the most part, in EBMT the examples have very simple structures, typically sequences of words (this is the case with TMs), or word-tag pairs. The string-edit distance algorithm (Levenshtein, 1966) is widely used, sometimes effectively weighting certain words or categories favourably (e.g. Furuse & Iida, 1994; Cranias *et al.*, 1997; Veale & Way, 1997).

7. Reuse and Adaptation

The reuse of the retrieved case solution in the context of the new case focuses on two aspects, firstly the differences between the past and the current case and secondly, what part of a retrieved case can be transferred to the new case.

7.1 Copy

In simple classification tasks, the differences are abstracted away (they are optimistically considered to be non-relevant while similarities are relevant) and the solution contained in the retrieved case is transferred to the new case as its solution. This is a trivial type of reuse — also see section 7.2.1 on Null Adaptation. However, other systems have to take into account differences between the past and the current case and so the reused part cannot be directly transferred to the new case but will require an adaptation process that takes into account those differences.

7.2 Adapt

In more complex tasks, past cases can be reused in two ways: (a) reuse the past case solution (structural or transformational reuse), and (b) reuse the past method that constructed the solution (derivational reuse). Overviews (e.g. Riesbeck & Schank, 1989:43; Kolodner, 1993:395ff.; Watson & Marir, 1994:334) list up to a dozen types of adaptation, broadly divided between **structural** and **derivational** adaptation techniques. In the former, rules are applied to (a copy of) the case selected as the best match. In the latter, the algorithms, methods or rules which generated the original solution are reused to generate a new solution. Because of differing terminology, it is not always clear whether differently named methods are really distinct.

New Case: Enter a prefix to be attached to the dimension text here.
Example Source [CASE-92]: Enter a suffix to be attached to the dimension text here.
Example Target [CASE-92]: Geben sie hier ein Suffix ein das dem Dimensionstext angehängt werden soll.

Translate:

Direct: GEBEN
Direct: SIE
Direct: HIER
Direct: EIN
Adapt: (**lookup** (A PREFIX, OBJ) **:was** (A SUFFIX, OBJ)) = (EIN PRAEFIX)
:quality 1.0
Direct: EIN
Direct: DAS
Direct: DEM DIMENSIONSTEXT
Direct: ANGEHÄNGT
Direct: WERDEN
Direct: SOLL

Translating case [CASE-93] ...

Solution Target [GERMAN]: Geben sie hier ein Praefix ein das dem Dimensionstext angehängt werden soll

Figure 4.5. Operator Adapt in *ReVerb* performing a 'safe' dictionary lookup (Collins, 1998) where replacing an SL word has a clear consequence in the TL. Direct is a null-adaptation operator applying where the input SL and retrieved SL are identical.

In 'transformational reuse', the past case solution is not directly a solution for the new case but there exists some knowledge in the form of transformational operators such that when applied to the old solution they transform it into a solution for the new case. One way to organize these operators is to index them around the differences detected among the retrieved and current cases. Transformations in EBMT generally amount to adding, deleting and replacing strings (via dictionary lookups) for TL words that are not in the new case. Figure 4.5 shows one transformational operator (of a possible 8) called 'Adapt' in *ReVerb.*

For many, this adaptive aspect is the heart and soul of CBR. Riesbeck & Schank, 1989 refer to it as "the ultimate task of a case-based reasoner" (p. 41). It is important because it not only permits the reuse of existing solutions, but it also contributes to the creation of new solutions and hence to the *learning* capability of CBR.

Despite its importance, adaptation is sometimes omitted from CBR systems, or replaced with human intervention. Watson & Marir, 1994 comment that "it should not be viewed as a weakness of CBR that it encourages human collaboration in decision support" (1994:330). In *CLAVIER* (Mark, 1989), an early commercial CBR system, it is reported by Mark *et al.*, 1996 that, as the case-base grew through usage, adaptation and maintenance became more difficult, and eventually the designers decided to replace the adaptation component with an interactive module.

The EBMT equivalent of a system which consists essentially of a retrieval mechanism whose output is then passed to a human is a TM system; Somers, 1999:114 (cf. Chapter 1, this volume) has explicitly tried to distinguish EBMT and TMs on precisely these grounds: what makes EBMT an interesting process is the extent to which the 'hard' part is automated! Similarly, CBR can hardly be considered 'reasoning' if its performance amounts to copying and pasting.

The CBR literature is in agreement that adaptation is the most taxing aspect of the paradigm. Hanney & Keane, 1997 for example refer to the 'adaptation knowledge bottleneck' suggesting that it is difficult to derive any knowledge about how adaptation should be conducted from the cases alone. In an earlier attempt to do just that (Hanney & Keane, 1996), they proposed to compute all feature differences in the case base, prune them, and examine how those differences relate to differences in case solutions in order to learn automatically a set of adaptation rules. The implicit assumption is that the differences that occur between cases in the case-base are representative of the differences that will occur between future problems and the case-base. They later concluded that what is needed is some prior domain knowledge which serves to contextualize the cases; and this domain knowledge is necessarily expressed as general *rules*. In this way, hybrid case- and rule-based systems are developed.

We can see this approach in some EBMT systems, where the cases are 'generalized', as described above, sometimes to such an extent that they really end up as rules.

The adaptation step in EBMT is usually termed **recombination**, though this term is more specifically applicable in systems where the matching process retrieves multiple, sometimes partial, solutions, a strategy not widely used in CBR as discussed earlier.

The simplest of the CBR adaptation methods is null adaptation; then there are substitution methods (reinstantiation, parameter adjustment, abstraction and respecialization, case-based substitution, specialized search), transformation methods (commonsense transformation and model-guided repair) and finally derivational replay.

7.2.1 Null adaptation. The first method in reality involves no adaptation at all. Clearly it is used when the new problem exactly matches an existing case, or it may be used when the new problem is sufficiently close to the matched case that no adaptation is necessary (bearing in mind the existence of a revision stage). In EBMT, null adaptation occurs when an exact match is found, which may be more or less common depending on the application, but for null adaptation to apply when the match is not exact would involve the system 'knowing' that the differences between the input and the match were insignificant. One can imagine ways of doing this.

7.2.2 Reinstantiation. In reinstantiation, the old and new problems are structurally similar, but differ in the values of elements. Reinstantiation involves replacing the old values with new. This is a method often found in EBMT: for instance (2) could be used as a model for the translation of (3) by replacing *she* with *he*, *big* with *blue* and *feet* with *eyes* to give (4).

(2) *Kanojo wa ashi ga ōkii.*
SHE topic FOOT subj BIG
She has big feet.

(3) *Kare wa me ga aoi.*
HE topic EYE subj BLUE

(4) He has blue eyes.

In reinstantiation we have to know the correspondences between the elements that we are exchanging, but we also have to be sure that the simple substitution is permitted. In CBR terms, if there are implicit relationships between the slots, reinstantiating one might have repercussions. This can be easily illustrated in the case of EBMT: if we want to use (5) as a model for the translation of (6), we cannot simply replace *man–homme* with *woman–femme* (7a), but we must also change some of other words in the sentence (7b).

(5) That old man has died.
Ce vieil homme est mort.

(6) That old woman has died.

(7) a. **Ce vieil femme est mort.*

b. *Cette vieille femme est morte.*

This problem is referred to in the EBMT literature as **boundary friction** (cf. Nirenburg *et al.*, 1993:48; Collins, 1998:22; Somers, 1999:133; cf. Chapters 14 and 16, this volume). One solution to this problem in CBR terms might be to treat it as a case for parameter adjustment, which we discuss in the next section.

7.2.3 Parameter adjustment. This is a structural adaptation technique in which specific parameters of the retrieved and new cases differ. A key element seems to be the use of 'specialized adjustment heuristics' to cope with the problem (Kolodner, 1993:404). A possible interpretation of this in EBMT terms is if in (5) the representation of the French translation included an indication of the agreement requirements, so that the substitution of *man* with *woman* in (6) would trigger specific agreement rules to adapt the other words. MT experts might call such a specialized adjustment heuristic a 'transfer rule'.

7.2.4 Abstraction and respecialization. This technique, also termed 'local search', is a type of substitution that allows a novel solution to be generated from an example which differs only in a small part. The idea is to take the piece of the solution that does not fit, look for abstractions of that piece, and then try other specializations of the abstraction in the current situation. This technique obviously depends on there being a hierarchically structured knowledge base behind the case base, and is very well illustrated for EBMT by the system developed by Sumita & Iida, 1991, which translates Japanese adnominal particle constructions (*A no B*) with the help of a thesaurus.

7.2.5 Case-based substitution. This adaptation technique comes into play when parts of a solution have to be found in additional cases.

Papaioannou, 2000 adopted this as a solution to the boundary friction problem in a simulated English–Greek EBMT system. Because Greek is a highly inflected language, there is a danger of recombining inappropriately inflected fragments. The examples in Papaioannou's system are tagged and lemmatised to show appropriate morphological information, as in Figure 4.6.

I saw the new prime-minister.

Είδα τον νέο πρωθυπουργό.

```
<s>
  <gw cat="V" attrs="Act Pst Ind Sng 1st"
   lemma="blepw/see">Eida</gw>
  <gw cat="Art" attrs="Msc Sng Acc" lemma="o/the">ton</gw>
  <gw cat="Adj" attrs="Msc Sng Acc"
   lemma="neos/new">neo</gw>
  <gw cat="N" attrs="Msc Sng Acc" lemma="prw8upourgos/prime
   minister">prw8upourgo</gw>
  <punc>.</punc>
```

Figure 4.6. An example from Papaioannou, 2000

The recombination stage 'knows' that certain attributes have to match up (agreement of Art, Adj and N, for instance), so when the system retrieves examples for a new input, it notes the particular details of any discrepancies and specifically searches the rest of the example-base for the missing item(s). For instance, the sentence in (8) matches the example in Figure 4.6 perfectly, except for the last lemma and surface word. In order to adapt the example, the system searches the example-base for another case that contains exactly the configuration in (9), and, if it is found can generate the appropriate form *πρόεδρο*.

(8) I saw the new president.

(9) `⟨gw cat=''N'' attrs=''Msc Sng Acc'' lemma=''???/president''⟩ ??? ⟨/gw⟩`

If we now give the input (10), there are several mismatches. Two of the words have the wrong attributes, and the third word also has the wrong lemma. So the system has to search for the three items in (10).

(10) I saw the new delegates.

(11) a. `⟨gw cat=''Art'' attrs=''Msc Plr Acc'' lemma=''o/the''⟩ ??? ⟨/gw⟩`

b. `⟨gw cat=''Adj'' attrs=''Msc Plr Acc'' lemma=''neos/new''⟩ ??? ⟨/gw⟩`

c. `⟨gw cat=''N'' attrs=''Msc Plr Acc'' lemma=''???/delegate''⟩ ??? ⟨/gw⟩`

Supposing there is no 'evidence' in the case-base for one of these new combinations. If the missing case is (11c), where we do not know the lemma, there is not much we can do. In the case of (11b), we may be able to generate the appropriate form of the adjective by looking at other masculine plural adjectives, and comparing the lemma and the surface form, though this would be a further complexity for the adaptation phase. This might be termed 'specialized search' (Kolodner, 1993:411).

7.2.6 Common-sense transformation. Kolodner, 1993 describes two types of adaptation involving 'transformations'. Transformation in general involves making deletions or insertions either to the solution as a whole or to some part of it. The first of these is common-sense transformation, which makes use of "a small set of heuristics that use knowledge about the relative importance of different components of an item to determine whether deletions or substitutions should be done" (pp.420f.). To be able to do this, the system must of course identify the component needing to be changed, but the representations need to indicate which components are susceptible to this kind of manipulation. In particular, the internal relationships between the components must be maintained after the transformation has taken place.

How might this be implemented in an EBMT system? The idea of deleting or inserting components is widespread in EBMT systems, and is very intuitive. If we have the Malay–English examples in (12), it is not difficult to construct the correct translations of sentences like those in (13).

(12) a. *Dia nak pĕrgi k kĕdai bĕli roti.*
She is going to go to the shops to buy bread.

b. *Dia pĕrgi kĕ pasar nak bĕli baju.*
She went to the market to buy a shirt.

c. *Mĕreka pĕrgi kĕ kampung nak bĕli kereta.*
They went to the village to buy a car.

(13) a. She went to the village to buy bread.

b. They are going to the market.

In fact as humans we bring to bear a certain amount of generic (common-sense) knowledge about how languages work to do this. The work — mentioned above — to extract patterns fully automatically (Cicekli & Güvenir, 1996, Güvenir & Tunç, 1996, Güvenir & Cicekli, 1998, cf. Chapter 9, this volume; McTait & Trujillo, 1999, cf. Chapter 11, this volume) needs minimal pairs and would not be able to extract as much as humans can from the examples in (12).

This kind of activity does have its limitations though. Kolodner, 1993 notes that internal relationships between elements must be maintained, and here we meet again the 'boundary friction' problem already illustrated in (5)–(7). A further problem is that language is not always logical: you might guess from the examples in (14)

(14) *stryd fawr*–big street
stryd fach–small street
tŷ mawr–big house
??? – small house

that the Welsh for 'small house' is *tŷ mach* ... unfortunately though you would be wrong (it should be *bach*)!

7.2.7 Model-guided repair. For these reasons, model-guided repair might be a better way of implementing adaptation. As its name suggests, the transformations are guided by some knowledge of the domain, rather than just common sense. In EBMT terms, this would mean verifying that the proposed adaptation is legitimate by submitting it to some kind of analysis. As we will see below, most CBR systems involve an evaluation step where this kind of verification is done, but it could be regarded as part of the adaptation procedure. An obvious way to verify a proposed translation is to try to parse it, though this step would require a grammar of the target language which, perhaps, would undermine the reason for adopting the example-based approach in the first place.

Somers *et al.*, 1994 proposed 'disalignment': the proposed output was checked by rerunning the matching algorithm that had been used on the input, this time comparing the proposed output against the target side of the examples. The ease with which the proposed output could be matched was felt to be an indication of its well-formedness.

7.2.8 Derivational replay. Kolodner, 1993 describes 'derivational replay' as follows:

> "Each of the adaptation methods described up to now fixes an old solution to fit a new solution. Sometimes, however, it is more appropriate to recompute a new solution or partial solution using the same means by which the old solution was computed." (p. 435)

A problem with seeing how this technique could apply to EBMT is that there is an underlying assumption that solutions are 'computed', whereas in EBMT the solutions are usually just 'given'. Where solutions (i.e. translations) *are* computed, this is usually in the traditional rule-based manner. So we could regard the hybrid systems that have been described in this light. In the early days of EBMT it was sometimes suggested that this method could be used just for special problem cases (cf. Sumita *et al.*, 1990).

7.3 Adaptation-guided retrieval

An implicit assumption in many CBR systems is that the most similar case in the case-base is also the most adaptable. This is not always the case, as Smyth & Keane, 1993, Smyth & Keane, 1995a, Leake, 1995, Rousen & Aarts, 1996 and others have noted. The notion of 'adaptation-guided retrieval' has been developed whereby the retrieval of cases is based not only on their similarity with the given input, but also the extent to which they represent a good model for the desired output, i.e. to which they can be adapted, that determines whether they are chosen. Collins, 1998:31 gives the example of a robot using a restaurant script to get food at *McDonald's*, when buying a stamp at the post-office might actually be a more appropriate, i.e. adaptable, model. Collins et al.'s EBMT system, *ReVerb*, stores the examples together with a functional annotation, cross-linked to indicate both lexical and functional equivalence. This means that example-retrieval can be scored on two counts: (a) the closeness of the match between the input text and the example, and (b) the adaptability of the example, on the basis of the relationship between the representations of the example and its translation. Obviously, good scores on both (a) and (b) give the best combination of retrievability and adaptability, but we might also find examples which are easy to retrieve but difficult to adapt (and are therefore bad examples), or the converse, in which case the good adaptability should compensate for the high retrieval cost.

8. Evaluation and Repair

When a case solution generated by the reuse phase is not correct, an opportunity for learning from failure arises. In CBR, this phase is called **case revision** and consists of two tasks: (a) evaluating the case solution generated by reuse, and, if successful, learning from the success (case retainment, see next section), (b) otherwise repairing the case solution using domain-specific knowledge.

8.1 Evaluate solution

The evaluation task takes the result from applying the solution in the real environment (asking a teacher/monitor or performing the task in the real world). This normally entails stepping outside the CBR system because it involves the application of a suggested solution to the real problem. The results from applying the solution may take some time to appear, depending on the type of application. In a medical decision-support system, the success or failure of a treatment may take from a few hours up to several months. The case may still be learned, and be available in the case-base in the intermediate period, but it has to be marked as a non-evaluated case. A solution may also be applied to a simulation program that is able to generate a correct solution. This is used in the CBR system *CHEF* (Kolodner, 1993), where a solution (i.e. a cooking recipe) is applied to an internal model assumed to be strong enough to give the necessary feedback for solution repair.

An important part of this is the explanation, whereby the reasoner gives the reasons for the failure of the solution. The system thus needs somehow to be aware that it has failed to provide a correct solution — the 'Revise' phase shown in Figure 4.2.

The language in which these ideas are expressed, for example in Riesbeck & Schank, 1989, once again reflects the problem-solving scenario that so strongly influences researchers' ideas in CBR. They suggest that two sorts of failures are possible: "Goals specified in the input are simply not achieved ... [or] implicit goals, not specified in the input, are violated" (p. 52). Nevertheless, it quickly emerges from study of the literature that any 'evaluation' of the system's output will be done by human intervention. Any alternative introduces a familiar vicious circle: if the system knew that it had got the wrong answer, it would not have got the wrong answer.

The best example is perhaps the *CHEF* system, mentioned above, where causal knowledge is used to generate an explanation of why certain goals of the solution plan were not achieved. *CHEF* learns the general situations that give rise to failures using an explanation-based learning technique. These are included into a 'failure memory' which is used in the Reuse phase to predict possible shortcomings of plans. This form of learning implies that errors can be systematically predicted, handled and avoided.

In an EBMT situation it is comparatively easy to evaluate a translation manually straightaway and one can imagine automatic evaluation methods using standard MT engines to give the feedback. Many EBMT and all statistical MT systems generate a score for the translation (plausibility of recombined elements), but because there is no case-memory structure it is impossible to index this knowledge for reuse.

8.2 Repair fault

A related task is the solution repair task. Here, the failure explanations are used to modify the solution so that failures do not re-occur. For instance, the failed plan in the *CHEF* system is modified by a repair module that inserts extra steps into the plan which ensure that the causes of the errors will not arise. The repair module has access to general causal knowledge and domain knowledge about how to disable or compensate causes of errors in the domain. The revised plan is retained directly if the revision phase judges it to be correct or it is evaluated and repaired again.

One of the advantages of empirical approaches (as opposed to rule-based approaches) is the role that stochastic processing can play. Empirical methods can deliver a 'certainty rating' along with any result, inasmuch as the result is based on probabilities. Thus, it is claimed, an EBMT system for example not only tells you what it thinks the translation is, but how sure it is of that answer, what its second and third choice solutions might be, and how far behind they are in the ranking.

One area that is important in the CBR community, but which seems to be lacking in EBMT, is **explanation**. Originally thought of as a step in the CBR cycle to facilitate repair of faulty solutions prior to learning, it has developed into a major field of its own (cf. Schank *et al.*, 1994) related to AI tasks such as story understanding.

All in all, however, it seems that for EBMT, with its shallow representation of cases, and typically uncomplicated 'reasoning', there is not much on offer here.

9. Learning for Reuse

The final step in CBR is to store accepted solutions in the case-base for later use. This is the process of incorporating what is useful to retain from the new problem-solving episode into the existing knowledge. The learning from success or failure of the proposed solution is triggered by the outcome of the evaluation and possible repair. It involves selecting which information from the case to retain, in what form to retain it, how to index the case for later retrieval from similar problems, and how to integrate the new case in the memory structure.

In the same way, an approved translation can be added to the example-base. This is normal practice in the case of TMs, where the whole process is supervised by a human user. Descriptions of EBMT systems do not generally mention this possibility, nor is it ruled out.

The main issue here is the need for human quality control, though, conversely, some TM systems allow examples to be stored with an annotation identifying whether their source is human translation or MT (including EBMT).

Kolodner, 1993:566 briefly discusses some of the issues in case-based learning. She notes that new cases can be added by the system itself, as well as (of course) manually. She also suggests that storing failures, i.e. cases where the system could not come up with the correct solution, can be beneficial: a system can learn from its mistakes as well as from its successes, especially if the failed case is annotated to show where it went wrong. There may be something in this for EBMT.

A second issue is the effect on the case-base of storing multiple similar or even identical examples. As Kolodner, 1993 states, "Some cases added to a case library might add to the library without adding to the capabilities of a system. Such cases might or might not affect the efficiency of retrieval, depending on the retrieval algorithm." (p. 567) This levelling off of the retrieval efficiency curve is referred to as the 'utility problem' in CBR literature as mentioned in the section on case-base size earlier, and methods have been proposed (Smyth & Keane, 1995b) to contain it

A similar point can be made with regard to EBMT (see Somers, 1999:121 and Chapter 1, this volume). If we construct the example-base from a corpus, there will be repetition and overlap. Some examples will mutually reinforce each other, being identical, or exemplifying the same translation phenomenon. But other examples will be in conflict: the same or similar phrase in one language may have two different translations for no other reason than inconsistency (e.g. Carl & Hansen, 1999:619).

Where examples reinforce each other this may or may not be useful. Some systems (e.g. Somers *et al.*, 1994; Öz & Cicekli, 1998; Murata, *et al.*, 1999) involve a similarity metric which is sensitive to frequency. But if no such weighting is used, multiple similar or identical examples are just extra baggage, introducing a kind of spurious ambiguity because there seem to be multiple alternative solutions to the same problem.

10. Integrated Approaches

Most CBR systems make some use of general domain knowledge alongside the knowledge inherent in the cases. The representation and use of such domain knowledge entails that case-based methods are integrated with other methods and representations of problem solving, like rule-based expert systems or deeper models, like causal reasoning. According to Aamodt & Plaza, 1994 "the overall architecture of the CBR system has to determine the interactions and control regime between the CBR method and the other components". For instance, the *CASEY* system integrates a model-based causal reasoning program to diagnose heart diseases. When the case-based method fails to provide a correct solution *CASEY* executes the model-based method to solve the problem and stores the solution as a new case for future use. In many CBR systems the adaptation stage is rule-based (Leake, 1996:11), while some systems have a rule-based component as a back-up if no relevant cases are available (e.g. Koton, 1988; Goel *et al.*, 1994).

Usually the domain knowledge used in a CBR system is acquired in traditional AI manner for knowledge-based systems. As already discussed, the knowledge can be extrapolated from the cases themselves either in a case-based fashion (Hanney & Keane, 1997) or by induction, as explored in the *INRECA* project (Manago *et al.*, 1993).

Many of the earliest EBMT systems were indeed hybrids, using the example-based method for only a part of the process (e.g. Sato & Nagao, 1990; Watanabe, 1992; and several others) or for certain problems (e.g. Sumita *et al.*, 1990). The CBR component often fall backs on more traditional MT architectures if no match is found, e.g. in the *CAT-2* system (Carl *et al.*, 2001) and the *Pangloss* system (Frederking *et al.*,1994) but very little EBMT research has been done on truly integrating different types of knowledge in a symbiotic relationship to the extent that it is explored in CBR systems.

11. Conclusions

The aim of this paper was to see if the similarity between EBMT and CBR was anything more than skin-deep. The hope was to find some inspiration in the CBR literature to push EBMT forward.

We have shown that in many respects EBMT can be described using CBR terminology, but that certain aspects of the standard process-cycle description for CBR seem to be underrepresented in EBMT literature.

One main reason seems to be the discrepancy in the complexity of representation of examples in CBR compared to EBMT. The latter, being more inclined towards an MBR-like MT model, rarely sets out to search for one optimal case to mimic, which is the holy grail of CBR, giving rise to such careful retrieval, reuse and revision techniques in the first place. Instead, EBMT researchers grapple with thorny issues of linguistic knowledge representation, such as how to link discontinuous SL–TL sentence elements for indexing, and how to recombine TL fragments in the face of boundary friction.

We think the most fruitful areas for further consideration are at least those where CBR techniques are already well established, for example in the area of adaptation, especially the way it might interact with retrieval, as the Dublin group (Collins and colleagues) have already shown us. But EBMT might also be a perfect vehicle for exploring the less established CBR issues of learning adaptation rules automatically and integration of domain knowledge into the CBR cycle, as well as repair and retainment strategies.

All this will require that researchers be willing to focus on designing richer EBMT cases, or at least better structured case-memory schemas to support smart indexing and case storage. Perhaps there could also be a shift towards the lesser explored area of retrieving single-case solutions and using sophisticated adaptation knowledge gleaned from the case base itself, to produce good translation solutions.

References

Aamodt, A. and E. Plaza. 1994. Case-based Reasoning: Foundational issues, methodologiocal variations and system approaches. *AI Communications* **7**:39–59.

Al-Adhaileh, M.H. and E.K. Tang. 1999. Example-based machine translation based on the synchronous SSTC annotation schema. In *Machine Translation Summit VII*, Singapore, pp.244–249.

Bareiss, R. 1989. *Exemplar-Based Knowledge Acquisition*, San Diego, California: Academic Press.

Bareiss, E.R, B.W. Porter and C.C. Weir. 1990. Protos: An Exemplar-Based Learning Apprentice. In Y. Kodratoff and R. S. Michalski (eds.) *Machine Learning: An Artificial Intelligence Approach (Volume III)*, San Mateo, CA: Morgan Kaufmann, pp.112–139.

Bergmann, R. and W. Wilke. 1996. On the role of abstraction in case-based reasoning. In *EWCBR-96*, pp.28–43.

Branting, L.K. 1989. Integrating generalizations with exemplar-based reasoning. In *Case-Based Reasoning: Proceedings of a Workshop on Case-Based Reasoning*, Pensacola Beach, Florida, pp.224–229.

Brown, R.D. 1997. Automated dictionary extraction for 'knowledge-free' example-based translation. In *Proceedings of the 7th International Conference on Theoretical and Methodological Issues in Machine Translation*, Santa Fe, NM., pp.111–118.

Brown, R.D. 1999. Adding linguistic knowledge to a lexical example-based translation system. In *Proceedings of the 8th International Conference on Theoretical and Methodological Issues in Machine Translation (TMI 99)*, Chester, England, pp.22–32.

Carbonell, J.G. 1986. Derivational analogy: A theory of reconstructive problem solving and expertise acquisition. In R. Michalski, J. Carbonell and T. Mitchell (eds.) *Machine Learning: An Artificial Intelligence Approach*, Vol. 2, Los Altos, CA.: Morgan Kaufmann, pp.371–392.

Carl, M., L. Iomdin, C. Pease and O. Streiter. 2001. Towards a Dynamic Linkage of Example-Based and Rule-Based Machine Translation. *Machine Translation* **15**:223-257.

Carl, M. and S. Hansen. 1999. Linking translation memories with example-based machine translation. In *Machine Translation Summit VII*, Singapore, pp.617–624.

Cicekli, I., and H.A. Güvenir. 1996. Learning translation rules from a bilingual corpus. In *NeMLaP-2: Proceedings of the Second International Conference on New Methods in Language Processing*, Ankara, Turkey, pp.90–97.

Collins, B. 1998. *Example-based Machine Translation: an adaptation-guided retrieval approach.* PhD thesis, Trinity College, Dublin, Ireland.

Collins, B. and P. Cunningham. 1995. A methodology for example-based machine translation. In *CSNLP 1995: 4th Conference on the Cognitive Science of Natural Language Processing*, Dublin, Ireland, [no page numbers].

Collins, B. and P. Cunningham. 1996. Adaptation-guided retrieval in EBMT: A case-based approach to machine translation. In *EWCBR-96*, pp.91–104.

Collins, B. and P. Cunningham. 1997. Adaptation guided retrieval: Approaching EBMT with caution. In *Proceedings of the Seventh International Conference on Theoretical and Methodological Issues in Machine Translation*, Santa Fe, NM., pp.119–126.

Collins, B., P. Cunningham and T. Veale. 1996. An example-based approach to machine translation. In *Expanding MT Horizons: Proceedings of the Second Conference of the Association for Machine Translation in the Americas*, Montreal, Quebec, Canada, pp.1–13.

Cranias, L., H. Papageorgiou and S. Piperidis. 1997. Example retrieval from a translation memory. *Natural Language Engineering* **3**:255–277.

Cunningham, P., B. Smyth and T. Veale. 1994. On the limitations of memory based reasoning. In *EWCBR-94*, pp.75–86.

Daengdej, J., D. Lukose, E. Tsui, P. Beinat and L. Prophet. 1996. Dynamically creating indices for two million cases: a real world problem. In *EWCBR-96*, pp.195–119.

Domeshek, E.A. 1991. What Abby cares about. *Proceedings of the Case-Based Reasoning Workshop*, Washington, D.C., pp.13–24.

EWCBR-93. S. Wess, K.-D. Althoff and M.M. Richter (eds.), *Topics in Case-Based Reasoning: First European Workshop, EWCBR-93, Kaiserslautern, Germany* (Lecture Notes in Computer Science 837), Berlin: Springer.

EWCBR-94. J.-P. Haton, M. Keane and M. Manago (eds.) *Advances in Case-Based Reasoning: Second European Workshop, EWCBR-94, Chantilly, France* (Lecture Notes in Computer Science 984), Berlin: Springer.

EWCBR-96. I. Smith and B. Faltings (eds.), *Advances in Case-Based Reasoning: Third European Workshop, EWCBR-96, Lausanne, Switzerland* (Lecture Notes in Computer Science 1168), Berlin: Springer.

Frederking, R., S. Nirenburg, D. Farwell, S. Helmreich, E. Hovy, K. Knight, S. Beale, C. Domashnev, D. Attardo, D. Grannes and R. Brown. 1994. Integrating translations from multiple sources within the Pangloss Mark III machine translation system. In *Technology Partnerships for Crossing the Language Barrier: Proceedings of the First Conference of the Association for Machine Translation in the Americas*, Columbia, Maryland, pp.73–80.

Furuse, O. and H. Iida. 1992. An example-based method for transfer-driven machine translation. In *Fourth International Conference on Theoretical and Methodological Issues in Machine Translation (TMI-92)*, Montréal, Canada, pp.139–150.

Furuse, O. and H. Iida. 1994. Constituent boundary parsing for example-based machine translation. In *COLING-94: The 15th International Conference on Computational Linguistics*, Kyoto, Japan, pp.105–111.

Gentner, D. 1983. Structure mapping – a theoretical framework for analogy. *Cognitive Science* **7**:155–170.

Goel, A., K. Ali, M. Donnellan, A. Garza and T. Callantine. 1994. Multistrategy adaptive navigational path planning. *IEEE Expert* **9**(6):57–65.

Güvenir, H.A. and I. Cicekli. 1998. Learning translation templates from examples. *Information Systems* **23**:353–363.

Güvenir, H.A. and A. Tunç. 1996. Corpus-Based Learning of Generalized Parse Tree Rules for Translation. In G. McCalla (ed.) *Advances in Artificial Intelligence*, Berlin: Springer Verlag, pp.121–132.

Hammond, K.J. 1986. CHEF: a model of case-based planning. In *Proceedings AAAI-86: Fifth National Conference on Artificial Intelligence*, Philadelphia, PA., pp.267–271.

Hammond, K.J. 1987. On functionally motivated vocabularies: an apologia. In *Proceedings of the International Joint Conference on Artificial Intelligence*, Milan, Italy.

Hanney, K. and M.T. Keane. 1996. Learning Adaptation Rules from a case base. In *EWCBR-96*, pp.179–192.

Hanney, K. and M.T. Keane. 1997. The adaptation knowledge bottleneck: How to ease it by learning from cases. In *ICCBR-97*, pp.359–370.

Hayes-Roth, F., D. Waterman and D. Lenat (eds.) 1983. *Building Expert Systems*. Reading, MA.: Addison Wesley.

ICCBR-95. M. Veloso and A. Aamodt (eds.), *Case-Based Reasoning Research and Development: First International Conference on Case-Based Reasoning, ICCBR-95, Sesimbra, Portugal*, (Lecture Notes in Computer Science 1010), Berlin: Springer.

ICCBR-97. D.B. Leake and E. Plaza (eds.), *Case-Based Reasoning Research and Development: Second International Conference on Case-Based Reasoning, ICCBR-97, Providence, RI*, (Lecture Notes in Computer Science 1266), Berlin: Springer.

Kaji, H., Y. Kida and Y. Morimoto. 1992. Learning translation templates from bilingual text. In *Proceedings of the fifteenth [sic] International Conference on Computational Linguistics, COLING-92*, Nantes, France, pp.672–678.

Kitano, H. 1993. A comprehensive and practical model of memory-based machine translation. In *Proceedings of the International Joint Conference on Artificial Intelligence*, Chambéry, France, pp.1276–1282.

Kitano, H. and T. Higuchi. 1991. High performance memory-based translation on IXM2 massively parallel associative memory processor. In *AAAI-91 Proceedings Ninth National Conference on Artificial Intelligence*, Menlo Park, CA.: AAAI Press/The MIT Press, pp.149–154.

Kolodner, J. 1983. Maintaining organization in a dynamic long-term memory. *Cognitive Science* **7**:243–280.

Kolodner, J. 1988. Retrieving events from case memory: A parallel implementation. In *Proceedings from the DARPA Case-based Reasoning Workshop*, Clearwater Beach, Florida, pp.233–249.

Kolodner, J. 1993. *Case-Based Reasoning*, San Mateo, CA: Morgan Kaufmann.

Kolodner, J.L. and D.B. Leake. 1996. A tutorial introduction to case-based reasoning. In Leake (ed.) (1996), pp.31–65.

Kolodner, J.L. and C.K. Riesbeck. 1986. *Experience, Memory and Reasoning*, Hillsdale, New Jersey: Laurence Erlbaum.

Koton, P. 1988. Reasoning about evidence in causal explanation. In *AAAI 88: The Seventh National Conference on Artificial Intelligence*, St Paul, Minnesota.

Koton, P. 1989. Using experience in learning and problem solving. *Technical Report*, Massachusetts Institute of Technology, Laboratory of Computer Science MIT/LCS/TR-441.

Leake, D. 1995. Adaptive similarity assessment for case-based explanation. *International Journal of Expert Systems* **8**:165–194.

Leake, D.B. (ed.) 1996. *Case-based Reasoning – Experiences, Lessons & Future Directions.* Menlo Park, California: AAAI Press/MIT Press.

Levenshtein, V.I. 1966. Binary codes capable of correcting deletions, insertions, and reversals. *Cybernetics and Control Theory*, **10**:707–710.

Manago, M., K.D. Althoff, E. Auriol, R. Traphoner, S. Wess, N. Conruyt, and F. Maurer. Induction and reasoning from cases. In *EWCBR-93*, pp.313–318.

Marir, F. and I. Watson. 1995. Representing and indexing building refurbishment cases for multiple retrieval of adaptable pieces of cases. In *ICCBR-95*, pp.55–66.

Mark, W.S. 1989. Case-based reasoning for autoclave management. In *Case-Based Reasoning: Proceedings of a Workshop on Case-Based Reasoning*, Pensacola Beach, Florida, pp.176–180.

Mark, W.S., E. Simoudis and D. Hinkle. 1996. Case-based reasoning: expectations and results. In Leake (ed.) (1996), pp.267–294.

McTait, K. and A. Trujillo. 1999. A language-neutral sparse-data algorithm for extracting translation patterns. In *Proceedings of the 8th International Conference on Theoretical and Methodological Issues in Machine Translation (TMI 99)*, Chester, England, pp.98–108.

McTait, K. 2001. Linguistic knowledge and complexity in an EBMT system based on Translation Patterns. In *Proceedings of the Workshop on Example-Based Machine Translation*, Santiago de Compostela, Spain, pp.23–34 (see Chapter 11, this volume).

Medin, D.L. and M.M. Schaffer. 1978. Context theory of classification learning. *Psychological Review* **85**:207–238.

Murata, M., Q. Ma, K. Uchimoto and H. Isahara. 1999. An example-based approach to Japanese-to-English translation of tense, aspect, and modality. In *Proceedings of the 8th International Conference on*

Theoretical and Methodological Issues in Machine Translation (TMI 99), Chester, England, pp.66–76.

Nagao, M. 1984. A Framework of a Mechanical Translation between Japanese and English by Analogy Principle. In A. Elithorn & R. Banerji (eds.), *Artificial and Human Intelligence*, Amsterdam: North-Holland, pp.173–180.

Nirenburg, S., C. Domashnev and D.J. Grannes. 1993. Two approaches to matching in example-based machine translation. In *Fifth International Conference on Theoretical and Methodological Issues in Machine Translation TMI '93: MT in the Next Generation*, Kyoto, Japan, pp.47–57.

Öz, Z. and I. Cicekli. 1998. Ordering translation templates by assigning confidence factors. In D. Farwell, L. Gerber and E. Hovy (eds.) *Machine Translation and the Information Soup: Third Conference of the Association for Machine Translation in the Americas*, (Lecture Notes in Artificial Intelligence 1529), Berlin: Springer, pp.51–61.

Papaioannou, V. 2000. *Recombination in Example-based MT: A Case-Based Reasoning approach.* MSc dissertation, Department of Language Engineering, UMIST, Manchester, UK.

Planas, E. and O. Furuse. 1999. Formalizing translation memories. In *Machine Translation Summit VII*, Singapore, pp.331–339.

Plaza, E. and J. L. Arcos. 1993. Reflection and Analogy in Memory-based Learning. In *EWCBR-93*, pp.42–49.

Porter, B. and R. Bareiss. 1986. PROTOS: An experiment in knowledge acquisition for heuristic classification tasks. In *Proceedings of the First International Meeting on Advances in Learning (IMAL)*, Les Arcs, France, pp.159–174.

Porter, B., R. Bareiss, and R. Holte. 1990. Concept learning and heuristic classification in weak theory domains. *Artificial Intelligence* **45**:229–263.

Redmond, M. 1990. Distributed cases for case-based reasoning; facilitating use of multiple cases. In *AAAI-90 Proceedings Eighth National Conference on Artificial Intelligence*, Menlo Park, CA.: AAAI Press/The MIT Press, pp.304–309.

Richter, A.M., and S. Weiss. 1991. Similarity, uncertainty and case-based reasoning in PATDEX. In R.S. Boyer (ed.), *Automated reasoning, Essays in honour of Woody Bledsoe*, Dordrecht: Kluwer, pp.249–265.

Riesbeck, C.K. and R.C. Schank. 1989. *Inside Case-based Reasoning.* Hillsdale, New Jersey: Lawrence Erlbaum.

Rousen, J. and R.J. Aarts. 1996. Adaptation cost as a criterion for solution evaluation. In *EWCBR-96*, pp.354–361.

Sato, S. and M. Nagao. 1990. Toward memory-based translation. In *COLING-90, Papers presented to the 13th International Conference on Computational Linguistics*, Helsinki, Finland, **3**:247–252.

Schank, R.C. and R.P. Abelson. 1977. *Scripts, Plans, Goals and Understanding*, Hillsdale, New Jersey: Lawrence Erlbaum.

Schank, R.C. 1982. *Dynamic memory; a theory of reminding and learning in computers and people.* Cambridge: Cambridge University Press.

Schank, R.C., A. Kass and C.K. Riesbeck. 1994. *Inside Case-Based Explanation.* Hillsdale, New Jersey: Lawrence Erlbaum.

Smyth, B. 1996. *Case Based Design.* PhD Thesis, Trinity College Dublin, Ireland.

Smyth, B. and M.T. Keane. 1993. Retrieving adaptable cases. In *EWCBR-93*, pp.209–220.

Smyth, B. and M.T. Keane. 1995a. Experiments on adaptation-guided retrieval in case-based design. In *ICCBR-95*, pp.313–324.

Smyth, B. and M.T. Keane. 1995b. Remembering to forget: A competence preserving deletion policy for CBR systems. In *Proceedings of the 14th International Joint Conference on Artificial Intelligence (IJCAI-95)*, San Mateo, CA: Morgan Kaufmann, pp.377–383.

Smyth, B. and P. Cunningham. 1996. The Utility Problem analysed: A case-based reasoning perspective. In *EWCBR-96*, pp.392–399.

Somers, H. 1999. Review article: Example-based Machine Translation. *Machine Translation* **14**:113–157 (see Chapter 1, this volume).

Somers, H., I. McLean and D. Jones. 1994. Experiments in multilingual example-based generation. In *CSNLP 1994: 3rd Conference on the Cognitive Science of Natural Language Processing*, Dublin, Ireland, [no page numbers].

Stanfill, C. and D. Waltz. 1988. The memory based reasoning paradigm. In *Case-Based Reasoning: Proceedings from a Workshop*, San Mateo, CA: Morgan Kaufmann, pp.414–424.

Stanfill, C. and D. Waltz. 1986. Toward memory-based reasoning, *Communications of the ACM* **29**:185–192.

Sumita, E. and H. Iida. 1991. Experiments and prospects of example-based machine translation. In *29th Annual Meeting of the Association for Computational Linguistics*, Berkeley, CA., pp.185–192.

Sumita, E., H. Iida and H. Kohyama. 1990. Translating with examples: a new approach to machine translation. In *The Third International Conference on Theoretical and Methodological Issues in Machine Translation of Natural Language*, Austin, TX., pp.203–212.

Tulving, E. 1972. Episodic and semantic memory. In E. Tulving and W. Donaldson (eds.) *Organization of Memory*, New York: Academic Press, pp.381–403.

Veale, T. and A. Way. 1997. *Gaijin*: A Bootstrapping Approach to Example-Based Machine Translation. In *International Conference, Recent Advances in Natural Language Processing*, Tzigov Chark, Bulgaria, pp.239–244.

Watanabe, H. 1992. A similarity-driven transfer system. In *Proceedings of the fifteenth [sic] International Conference on Computational Linguistics, COLING-92*, Nantes, France, pp.770–776.

Watson, I. and F. Marir. 1994. Case-based reasoning: A review. *The Knowledge Engineering Review* **9**:327–354.

Wilss, W. 1998. Decision making in translation. In M. Baker (ed.) *Routledge Encyclopedia of Translation Studies*, London: Routledge, pp.57–60.

Wittgenstein, L. 1953. *Philosophical Investigations.* Oxford: Blackwell.

II

RUN-TIME EXAMPLE-BASED MACHINE TRANSLATION

Chapter 5

FORMALIZING TRANSLATION MEMORY

Emmanuel Planas
emmanuel.planas@imag.fr

Osamu Furuse
furuse.osamu@lab.ntt.co.jp

Abstract The TELA structure — a set of layered and linked lattices — the notion of similarity between TELA structures based on the notion of Edit Distance, and the MSSM algorithm based on dynamic programming techniques are all introduced in order to formalize Translation Memories (TM). We show how this approach leads to a real gain in recall and precision, and allows the extension of TM towards rudimentary, yet useful Example-Based Machine Translation (EBMT) that we call 'Shallow Translation'.

Keywords: translation memory, edit distance, multi-level similar segment matching

1. Introduction

This paper describes what could be considered a pioneering step towards a theoretical approach to Translation Memories (TM). Our purpose is to set up a coherent enough framework so that it becomes the norm that EBMT techniques, rather than just TM technology, could be used in the translation and localization processes. In this respect, it is close to the discussion of Chapter 3 in this book. Note that we do not speak here about sub-segment units (cf. Planas, 2000 for more information on this). Instead, we show which structures could help in the handling of documents so that EBMT techniques as described in this book could be applied. The 'Multi-level Similar String Matching' (MSSM) algorithm described here is a way of comparing two chunks of

M. Carl and A. Way (eds.), Recent Advances in Example-Based Machine Translation, 157–188.

text. In this way, it is close to other comparison processes that may be seen in other contributions of this book (e.g. Bond & Shirai, Chapter 7; Brown, Chapter 10; McTait, Chapter 11).

There are two phases in the use of TM. The first consists of accumulating translation units (TU). A TU is simply a source sentence (source TU) and its corresponding translation, also called the target sentence (target TU), as the human translator has translated it. In the second phase, given an input source sentence (INPUT), the TM retrieves the most similar source TU and proposes the corresponding target TU as the 'best' translation of the input sentence INPUT.

The first issue we want to address is how sentences are represented in the TM. Does a linear string of characters suffice? In considering this question, one has to address the question as to whether characters are the only entities involved in the representation of sentences extracted from current editing tools like *Adobe* Frame Maker, Interleaf, or *Microsoft* Word. Section 2, 'Structures', proposes some answers to such questions.

Another important question is what does it mean to be 'the most similar sentence'? Does it involve the number of different characters between INPUT and source TU? In this case, in the example below, is sentence (1) closest to sentence (2), as there are only four different letters, or to sentence (3), where nine letters differ?

(1) The wild child is destroying his new toy.

(2) The wild chi*ef* is destroying his new to*ol*.

(3) The wild child*ren are* destroying *their* new toy.

Furthermore, how are we to cope with non-literal data such as index marks and layout attributes that are inevitably found in today's edited documents? Section 3, 'Similarity', deals with these points.

We have built a prototype implementing our proposals for the issues of structures and similarity. We use a special algorithm for retrieving the similarity between two segments. This algorithm is described in detail in Section 4.

Section 5 shows that this leads to a real improvement in TM efficiency. This section also introduces the notion of 'Shallow Translation' as a natural extension of TM, and we give some example responses from our prototype.

2. Structures

2.1 Markup in Real Documents

Let us take the following example sentence:

(4) Click a color and press ENTER.

Figure 5.1 displays the typical layout of this sentence in classical word processors.

Click a **color** *[IMAGE]* and press **ENTER**

Figure 5.1. Sentence (4) as displayed in Word Processors

Let us suppose that there is also an index mark on 'press'. In typical internal code used in word processor formats (*Microsoft* RTF in the example below), this might look like Figure 5.2.

```
{{\lang1033Click_a_}    {\b\lang1033color}    {\lang1033_and_}
{\xe\b\lang1033press}} _ENTER}
```

Figure 5.2. Sentence (4) as coded in Word Processors

Current TM tools[1] often represent this sentence internally in an SGML-like way with some variations according to each tool. Figure 5.3 shows an XML-like representation of our example sentence.

```
<s>Click_a_<em>color_</em></IMG ttr=I.jpg>and_<idx
attrib=01>press</idx>_ENTER</s>
```

Figure 5.3. Sentence (4) as coded in a TM system

This is a necessary step in TM for encoding, in a standard way, documents whose formats are as different as *Adobe* Frame Maker and *Corel* WordPerfect, for instance. Otherwise, a memory built from such a formatted document could not be immediately applicable to another kind

[1] *Trados* Workbench, *IBM* Translation Manager, and *Star* Transit are the current leaders in the TM tools market. To this list, we must include today's challengers such as *Xerox* XMS, *Atril* DéjàVu, and *SDL* XSDL.

of formatted document. One has to realize that this involves non-trivial filtering problems, since the approaches that word processors adopt to text representations are quite different. In addition, some format definitions change rapidly, so filters which exist today may become obsolete quite quickly.

2.2 Using XML as Exchange Standard

We looked for such a basic level standard representation that could cope with the following conditions:

- This standard should be able to handle commercial editing file formats.
- It should also be able to cope with first generation TM formats.
- It should be able to integrate linguistic data.
- It should be exchangeable on the Internet.
- We did not want to reimplement a new standard.

We came to the conclusion that the XML standard is the basic representation we were looking for. The basic document unit is the 'segment'. A segment corresponds to the source or target part of the TU. This is generally a sentence, but not always ('Recommendations for the authors', for example, can be such a segment). We use beginning and ending tags (we call such a set a 'content tag') for delimiting groups of elements such as emphasis groups, indexed words or revision marks and empty tags for isolated elements such as hyperlinks buttons or images.[2]

2.3 The TELA Structure: Separating Data into Different Layers

When trying to match a new input sentence with a similar sentence in its memory, a first generation TM system applies its matching algorithm to a heterogeneous flow of linear data such as that shown in Figure 5.3. This approach leads to errors:

- A modification in the layout will have an influence on the retrieval process.

[2]See Planas, 1998a for an extended description of the reasons for this choice, and Thurmair, 1997 for an overview of existing exchange formats.

- The kind of phenomena shown in the introduction with sentences (1)–(3) cannot be handled.
- Transferring the non-literal data to the target sentence is not possible, unless it has been previously recorded in the memory (and then only the old recorded layout can be transferred).
- The application of external modules or tools to this representation is difficult: one can imagine, for example, how a morphological analyzer or even a spelling checker would behave on such a heterogeneous segment!

If the first use of such a heterogeneous kind of representation is necessary for standardization and exchange matters, and we recommend the use of the XML standard, it does not suffice as the above points show.

We propose two improvements:

- The separation of the document data into a 'layered' structure, that contains only one kind of data by level.
- The inclusion of linguistic data in supplementary layers.

Hence, rather than a flat heterogeneous structure, we propose a multi-level structure, with each level containing homogeneous information. We call these levels 'layers' and the whole structure TELA[3].

This structure can have as many layers as necessary. Each layer is a lattice whose bottom row is less important than all other elements of the layer, and whose top row is more important than all these elements. The natural order induced by the sequence of elements in the XML segment can be maintained through the partial order borne by the lattices. Other orders can be specified by what we call a 'linear measure scale', i.e. a mapping M from each element of the lattice to the Cartesian square of a numerical set. We propose eight basic layers:

1 *Text Characters*: this layer contains all relevant characters involved in the text to be displayed by the document. The XML notation makes it easy to distinguish between attributes and real text. The first 'path' (from bottom to top) of the lattice contains all the sequences of such characters, as found in the XML segment. These characters can be converted to a relevant coding for subsequent processes. Each time a rewriting rule is applied on characters,

[3]TELA is a French acronym for 'Treillis Etagés et Liés pour le traitement Automatique', i.e. 'Floored and Linked Lattices for Automatic Processing'.

the result constitutes a new path, and a 'link relation' indicates the relation between old and new nodes. Imagine for example that a French extended ASCII *é* is represented by the '&eacute' string. If we use a French parser, it is more likely that the input sentence should be written in extended ASCII. Figure 5.4 shows how TELA can express such a rewriting operation. Note that similar operations can be applied at all layers.

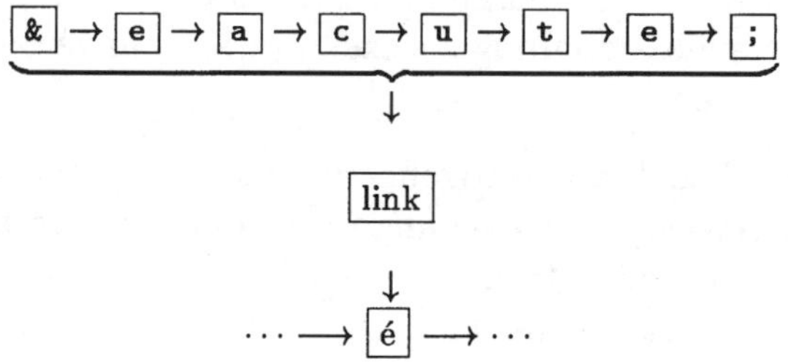

Figure 5.4. Creating a new node for a different coding of *é* in French

2 *Words*: this layer simply consists of the surface forms of the words of the sentence. Tokenizing the string of characters into separate words requires the use of an analyzer for languages for which the words are not separated by blanks in the sentence (Japanese, Chinese, Thai, ancient Latin etc.).

3 *Lemmas (Basic forms)*: For precise processing of sentences, there is a need for (at least) a superficial linguistic analysis. The lemmas are output as the result of this shallow parsing process.

4 *Parts of Speech (POS)*: This also comes from the shallow parsing phase. The 'O' part of speech qualifies terms found in the glossary (not in the parse dictionary), such as *hit the ENTER key.*

5 *XML content tags*: these tags represent where to apply layout attributes in the original XML segment.

6 *XML empty tags*: these tags cope with objects (such as images) inserted in the flow of text of the XML segment. They are represented on a separate layer.

7 *Glossary entries*: they specify some terminology information for the current context. It is important to bear in mind that almost all translation work uses contextual terminology. This may differ even

between companies in the same sublanguage area, e.g. Renault terminology differs from that of Citroen.

8 *Linguistic analysis structures*: this level depends on how deep one's linguistic analyzer can process. This layer could, for example, contain light structural approaches such as the Constituent Boundary Analysis in the approach to EBMT of Furuse & Iida, 1994, or templates such as those in Takeda, 1996 or Argamon *et al.*, 1998. We propose the notion of 'pivot schema' as a light structure analysis. A pivot schema is simply a pattern composed of variables and pivot keywords (such as *and*), plus links. Such a pivot schema is shown on Figure 5.5. A target pivot pattern corresponds to the source one, to which it is linked.

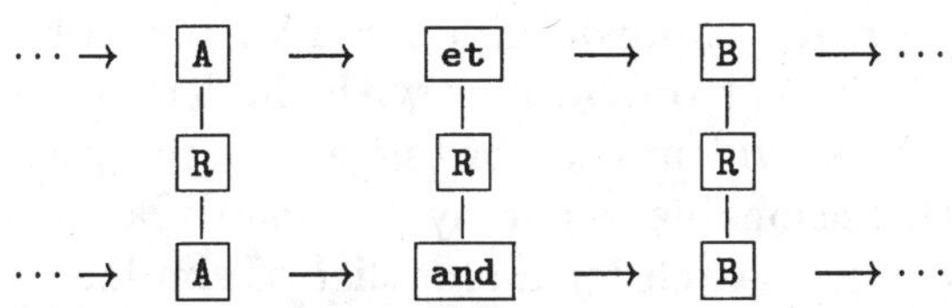

Figure 5.5. A French-English pivot expression with source and target parts

Given all 8 layers, we show in Figure 5.6 a TELA structure for sentence (4), with most of the links omitted for sake of clarity.

3. Similarity

In this section we describe how similar source translation units may be discovered by searching for keywords together with the use of a matching algorithm. We go on to explain how two sentences may be matched using TELA structures, and how the layout attributes may be transferred from the source to the target sentences.

3.1 Using Key Words Plus a Matching Algorithm

First generation TM tools generally use a key word index-based engine for retrieving a similar source TU from the memory. This is a fast and efficient technology, allowing the manipulation of memories containing a large number of TUs. This works rather well: in order to obtain a shortlist of matching sentences, the human translator will be able to judge their reusability, but this is not optimal in terms of precision and recall, as the experiments in Section 5 confirm.

Furthermore, when we want to automatically process some operations such as layout transfer on the retrieved TU, we have no idea where to start from, because the best this kind of retrieval can offer is a general score of how many keywords have been found in the source part of the candidate TU. We claim that in order to perform such operations, we need to know something about the structures of the INPUT, the source TU, and its target TU.

A first option could be to perform a deep analysis of these sentences that would give us the syntactic and perhaps also the logical structure of the sentence. For each language to be taken into consideration, this requires a classical analyzer that takes a long time to be build, whose accuracy is never satisfactory, and the application of which would take many seconds to run, or even longer for some sentences. Therefore, we regard such an approach as unsuitable for TM. Instead, we propose to use a shallow analysis that provides us with the lemma and the POS of every word, a task for which a lot of taggers or morphological parsers are available with reasonable accuracy for many languages. We propose, therefore, to first search for a shortlist of similar sentences in the database of examples via an index-based technique, and to refine the selection with a precise matching algorithm to be applied between the

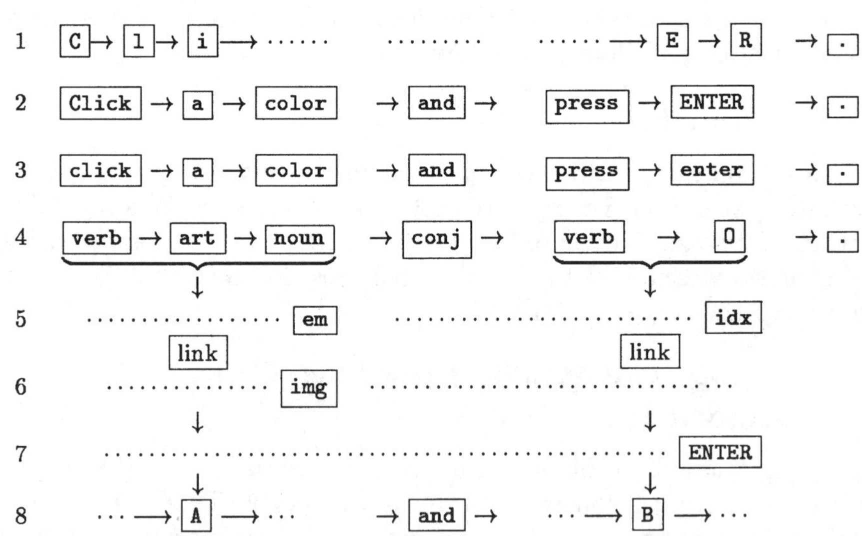

Figure 5.6. A TELA Structure representing sentence (4)

TELA representation of each sentence in the shortlist which includes this shallow analysis, and of the INPUT. We show in the next section how the similarity between the structure of INPUT and the source TU may be interpreted as an editing operation involving the different available layers of the TELA structure.

Table 5.1. T4, a simplified TELA structure for sentence (4)

	1	*2*	*3*	*4*	*5*	*6*
2	*click*	**a**	**color**	*and*	**press**	*enter*
3	**click**	a	color	*and*	press	*enter*
4	verb	art	noun	**conj**	verb	**O**
5			em		idx	
7						ENTER

3.2 Matching Two Sentences: the Principle

For the sake of simplicity, we will now represent TELA structures as stacked sequences of items in an array. In our example, we will consider five layers: words (layer 2), lemmas (layer 3), parts of speech (layer 4), content tags, i.e. no empty tags (layer 5), and glossary entries (layer 7). Let us consider sentence (4) as the input sentence. Sentence (4) is represented by its related TELA structure T4 in Table 5.1.

Suppose that we want to estimate the similarity of sentence (4) to sentence (5):

(5) He clicks on a color, then presses OK.

We show the encoding of sentence (5) in the TM in Figure 5.7.

```
<s>He_ clicks_ on_ a_ <em>color,_ </em>then_
<idx attrib=01> presses</idx>_ OK</s>
```

Figure 5.7. Sentence (5) as coded in a TM system

This sentence is represented by T5 in Table 5.2. Because the TELA structure is a set of layered lattices, for each layer, there always exists a path from the bottom (left) to the top (right) node. We only take the path resulting from the last rewriting process. Now that we are dealing only with sequences, we reduce the comparison of two TELA structures to the comparison of a set of linear sequences of items that are presented in Arrays T4 and T5 in Table 5.1 and Table 5.2 respectively.

Table 5.2. T5, a simplified TELA structure for sentence (5)

	1	*2*	*3*	*4*	5	*6*	*7*	*8*	*9*
2	*He*	*clicks*	*on*	**a**	**color**	,	*then*	*presses*	*OK*
3	*he*	**click**	*on*	a	color	,	*then*	**press**	*OK*
4	*pp*	verb	*prep*	art	noun	,	**conj**	verb	**O**
5				em				idx	
7									*OK*

We consider the matching of two sentences as a global process involving all layers. We use five layers in our example, but we could also include more layers (by adding a semantic one, for example), or fewer layers (e.g. when no layout or non-textual objects would be considered).

Starting from the first represented layer (layer 2: the words) and ending with the fifth (layer 7: the words from a glossary), we try to match each item of T5, the retrieved example, onto corresponding items of T4, the pattern searched for. In our example, *He* does not correspond to item *click* so we try to match it at a higher level. As it does not match any item, at any level, it is then considered as a deletion when editing (5) into (4). The next word *clicks* is not equal to surface form *click*, so we look up a layer to see if lemma *click* matches with lemma *click*. It does, so we keep this match, and try to match the following word *on* in sentence (5) with the following word *a* in sentence (4). We continue this process for every word of (5). Finally the matching words are indicated in bold (cf. Arrays T4 and T5). The word *and* is in (4), but not in (5), so this is considered to be an insertion.

We consider that two sentences match if and only if there exists a matching word for each of the words of the INPUT. We do not accept strict substitutions so that we are sure that the two sentences really match. A match that includes an insertion in INPUT is useful for the human translator, but it is useless for the machine because it does not have enough linguistic knowledge to know where to insert the word in the target segment.

3.3 The Match as an Edit Operation

3.3.1 Edit Distance. The above matching process is based on the notion of Edit Distance. Edit Distances have been developed

for matching the characters of two words, so that corrections could be performed on spelling errors (see Wagner & Fischer, 1974). Given a level f and two sentences 1 and 2, we consider the layers of TELA structures T1 and T2 as sequences of items
$s_1^f = (s_{1i}^f)_{1<i<n_1^f}$, $s_2^f = (s_{2j}^f)_{1<j<n_2^f}$, where $n_1^f <= n_2^f$. Here n_1^f and n_2^f represent the number of items of the layer f of T1 and T2. The edit distance between layers s_1^f and s_2^f is the total cost of the sequence of elementary operations transforming s_1^f into s_2^f that minimizes this total cost. Here are the classical elementary operations:

- Equality (cost 0)
- Deletion (cost 1)
- Insertion (cost 1)

As an example, the distance between layers 3 in arrays T5 and T4 (s_4^3 and s_3^3) is 7 because, apart from equalities, one insertion (*and*), and six deletions (*he*, *on*, ',', *then*, *enter* and *OK*) are involved.

We do not consider strict substitutions as Wagner & Fischer did because we are looking for a complete match, not a fuzzy match. This is essential so that we can use this match for subsequent transfer operations. What we are interested in is similarity, which is the opposite of distance, so instead of counting differences, we count equalities. We will factor deletions into our counts as negative numbers.

3.3.2 Similarity Between two TELA Structures.

For matching TELA structures, we consider the following editing operations between the layers of T1 and T2:

- Layer 1 equality (score 1)
- ...
- Layer F equality (score 1)
- Deletion for all layers (score 1)
- Insertion for all layers (score 1)

Let $sum_1^{12}, \ldots, sum_F^{12}; sum_-^{12}, sum_+^{12}$ be the sequence of the number of these elementary operations for editing S2 into S1. For example the editing of T5 into T4 has the following sequence: (2, 4, 5, 2, 1; 4, 1).

We insert a semicolon between the equality scores and the deletion and insertion scores because they play a (geometrically) opposite role

in the comparison between S1 and S2 than equality scores do. The similarity between S1 and S2 is defined as the following vector: $\alpha = (\frac{sum_1^{12}}{n_1^1}, \ldots, \frac{sum_F^{12}}{n_1^F}, 1 - \frac{sum_-^{12}}{n_2^2}, 1 - \frac{sum_+^{12}}{n_1^2})$ For example n_1^2 is the number of surface words in S1, and n_2^5 is the number of content tags in S2. Sentences (4) and (5) have, therefore, the following similarity:
$\alpha_{34} = (\frac{2}{6}, \frac{4}{6}, \frac{5}{6}, \frac{2}{2}, 1 - \frac{4}{9}, 1 - \frac{1}{6}) = (\frac{2}{6}, \frac{4}{6}, \frac{5}{6}, \frac{2}{2}, \frac{5}{9}, \frac{5}{6})$

Let S0 be an input sentence, with S1 and S2 two candidate matches. Let α_{01} and α_{02} be the corresponding similarities between T0 and T1, and T0 and T2 respectively. S0 and S1 are said to be closer than S0 and S2 if $\alpha_{01} > \alpha_{02}$, where the $>$ notation stands for the classical partial order defined on vectors:

$$(2, 4, 5) > (1, 4, 5) \text{ and } (2, 4, 5) > (2, 4, 4).$$

Now let us consider sentence (6):

(6) Click on a color and press OK.

<s> Click_ on _a _<em> color_ </em> and_ <idx attrib=01> press </idx> _OK </s>

Figure 5.8. Sentence (6): *Click on a color and press OK*

We represent the encoding of sentence (6) in the TM in Figure 5.8. Its corresponding Array T6 is given in Table 5.3.

Table 5.3. T5, a simplified TELA structure for sentence (6)

	1	*2*	*3*	*4*	*5*	*6*	*7*
2	**click**	*on*	**a**	**color**	**and**	**press**	*OK*
3	click	*on*	a	color	and	press	*OK*
4	verb	*prep*	art	noun	conj	verb	**O**
5				em		idx	
6							OK

If we now compare all three sentences via their TELA structures, we have:

$\alpha_{35} = (\frac{5}{6}, \frac{5}{6}, \frac{6}{6}, 1, \frac{6}{7}, 1)$, then $\alpha_{35} > \alpha_{34}$.

(6) is considered to be closer to (4) than (5). Note that we choose to give priority to the least analyzed level, namely the surface word level. This could be redefined according to the availability of data and the linguistic analyzers, as well as the strategy employed. This current choice is not exact according to linguistic criteria. There could, for example, be a match for two sentences bearing some surface form belonging to two different base forms (e.g. the 3rd person singular verb *tables* as well as the plural noun). There are, however, two reasons for this choice. The first is that we want our matching operation to be robust: as we do not require the parser to know the lemma and part of speech of every word, it may happen that we do know the surface form but neither lemma nor POS. In this case, the match would be possible at the surface level layer, but not at other ones. Beginning at the surface words layer allows a response even when the analyzer cannot parse the word. This means that the recall is increased. The second reason is that we intend to use TM on similar sentences from the shortlist (see Section 3.1), and there are good reasons to hope (and the experiments confirm it) that the sentences to be compared are close and use related vocabulary. In such cases, the precision is only slightly altered.

3.3.3 Matching Algorithm. Our matching procedure gives the similarity between two multi-sequences of items. This notion of similarity is precise because it involves a clear, constructive procedure based on located correspondences between the items of the two compared sentences. This is a new approach, different from the classical one that relies on the retrieval of a bag of common key words, indexed on their characters and gives a global similarity score called 'fuzzy matching'. Our approach is near to symbolic matching in the sense that the operands of the basic editing operations are any kind of item that match (or not) in a Boolean manner.

The advantage of this procedure is that it not only provides us with the similarity between the two chains, but it also gives the correspondence between matching words, in a 'trace'. This concept has been introduced by Wagner & Fischer, 1974. The matching trace for sentences (4) and (5), is:

(1 0 −) (2 1 3) (3 0 −) (4 2 2) (5 3 2) (0 4 +) (6 0 −) (7 0 −) (8 5 3) (9 6 4)

This indicates, for example, that word #4 of sentence (4) has to be inserted (0 4 +), word #7 of sentence (5) has to be deleted (7 0 −), and word #8 of sentence (5) matches with word #5 of sentence (4), on the 3rd layer (8 5 3).

We have constructed a specific matching algorithm using Dynamic Programming for this purpose— the MSSM algorithm. It is fast since it has a linear behavior for sentences of comparative lengths, but in other cases it is sub-quadratic at any rate. This algorithm is an adaptation of ideas that can be found in the algorithms of Wagner & Fischer, 1974, Ukkonen, 1985 and Lepage, 1998. A related approach can be found in Cranias *et al.* 1997, without the notion of trace. Details of our algorithm are given in section 4.

3.4 Transfer of Layout

Now we have a structure able to interrelate lemmas, surface forms, and layout containers. All we need to do is add a dictionary to be able to transfer the layout attributes from the source to the target sentence. In Figure 5.9, the 'dictionary' links represent bilingual correspondence found in a dictionary, 'glossary' links come from a correspondence found in a glossary, and 'links' links are inherited from the XML segment structure. From the layout recipient node 'em' (*emphasis* being linked to *color* on the source TELA structure), and the bilingual dictionary showing that English *color* corresponds to French *couleur*, we deduce that an 'em' node can be assigned to the French word *couleur* of the TELA structure for the French sentence. The same operation can be performed if the link between *ENTER* and *ENTRÉE* is found in a glossary. Note that as the English word *enter* is a verb, and French *entrée* is a noun, a dictionary would not give a correspondence between the two words, but this would be considered a translation in classical software products. Note also that the classical ambiguity problem that prevents us from such an easy transfer in MT does not apply here. The reason is that we do not look for the target word, as we have it already. We only need to look for a bilingual correspondence between a word in the source segment and a word in the target segment. A brute force method looking for all possible corresponding translations for the source word in a dictionary and a glossary would, of course, do the job too: we would, however, only rarely find different corresponding target words in the same sentence.

4. Details of the MSSM Algorithm

4.1 Introduction

Retrieving the best matching TU in the memory involves a two-step retrieval procedure. The first step uses a rapid and rough index-based

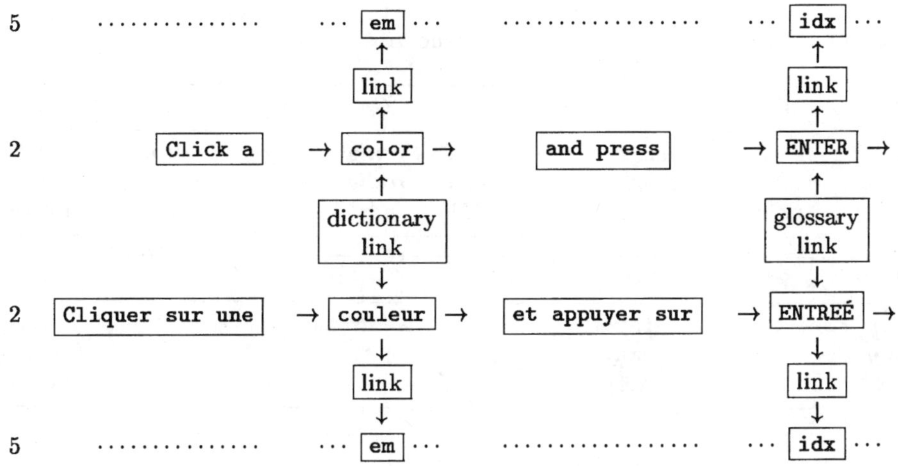

Figure 5.9. Transferring layout attributes

search to give a shortlist of example candidates. The second step uses refined matching to select the best candidate(s) from this list. We describe here the Multi-level Similar Segment Matching (MSSM) algorithm on which the second step of the retrieval procedure is based.

This algorithm not only gives the distance between the input and the example source segments, but also indicates which words match together. It uses F different levels of data (surface words, lemmas, parts of speech etc.) in a combined and uniform way. The computation of the worst case requires $F*m*(n-m+2)$ operations, where m and n are respectively the lengths of the input and the candidate ($m \leq n$). This leads to a linear behavior when m and n have similar lengths, which is often the case for TM segments. Furthermore, because this algorithm gives the exact matching links (along with the level of match) between all of the words of the input and the candidate sentence, it prepares the transfer stage of an evolution of TM that we call Shallow Translation. This involves the substitution of some words in the example target segment by translation of words of the sentence to be translated, provided that the input and the candidate are 'similar enough'.

The similarity is considered as a vector whose coordinates refer to the levels of analysis of the segments. This algorithm is extremely efficient for retrieving the best example in Translation Memory systems. As the calculus is constructive, it also gives the correspondences between the words of the two segments. This allows the extension of Translation Memory systems towards Example-based Machine Translation.

Table 5.4. Example of matching TELA structures

C_1	C_2	C_3	C_4	C_5	C_6	C_7	C_8	C_9
Nikkei	*Journal*	*reported*	*that*	*NTT*	*really*	**stayed**	*strong*	*Monday*
nikkei	*journal*	*report*	*that*	*NTT*	*really*	stay	**strong**	*Monday*
PN	*noun*	*verb*	*conj*	**PN**	*adv*	verb	adj	**noun**

I_1	I_2	I_3	I_4
Sony	**stayed**	*stronger*	*Tuesday*
Sony	stay	**strong**	*Tuesday*
PN	verb	adj	**noun**

4.2 Matching Principle

4.2.1 The TELA Structure. The purpose of this algorithm is to match two segments of words, the input I and candidate match C. Both of these can be any sequence of words: phrases, sentences, or paragraphs, for example. Let us consider input I of length m, not as a single segment of surface words, but rather as a group of F parallel layered segments $I^f_{(1 \leq f \leq F)}$, each bearing m tokens, which is a degraded version of a TELA structure. On each layer f, the i-th token corresponds to one of the paradigms of the i-th word of input I. In our implementation, we use a shallow analyzer that gives three paradigms ($F = 3$) for each surface word of the segments: the surface word itself ($f = 1$), its lemma ($f = 2$), and its POS tag ($f = 3$). Because we do not need a syntactic analyzer, the time required for this analysis is not a major disadvantage. Moreover, such parsers are available for many languages. Let C be a candidate segment of length n, for matching input I of length m ($n \geq m$). The basic problem involves matching the elements of the set $(C^f_i)_{f \leq F, i \leq n}$ to those of $(I^f_j)_{f \leq F, j \leq m}$. Only three layers are shown in the following examples but other types of layers, such as a semantic layer, or even non-linguistic information such as layout features can be considered, as in Planas, 1998a. Our algorithm is written for the general case (F layers).

4.2.2 Edit Distance-Based Similarity. As introduced in Section 3.3.1, a match from C to I is an edit distance process (Wagner & Fischer, 1974). Here, we do not consider six basic operations as in Gale & Church, 1993, but only deletions and equalities (i.e. equal substitutions), making $F+1$ basic operations in total. One equality corresponds to each of the F layers, and a deletion affects all layers at once. In Table 5.4, the items in bold match each other, and the ones in italics have to be deleted. The editing of C into I involves five deletions (*Nikkei*, *journal*, *reported*, *that*, *really*), one equality at layer 1 (*stayed*), two at layer 2 (*stay*, *strong*), and four at layer 3 ('PN', 'verb', 'adj', 'noun'). At the Word level, the similarity between the two segments is considered to be the relative number of words of the input segment that are matched by some word of the candidate segment in the 'matching zone' (from *NTT* to *Monday* in our example), namely $\frac{1}{4}$. The same similarity can be considered at different levels. Here, the lemma similarity is $\frac{2}{4}$, and the POS similarity is $\frac{4}{4}$. We consider the total similarity as a vector involving all layer equalities, plus deletions: $(C, I) = (\frac{1}{4}, \frac{2}{4}, \frac{4}{4}, 1-\frac{1}{4}, 1-\frac{5}{9})$. The fourth coordinate counts the complementary proportion of deletions in the matching zone of the candidate C. The last coordinate counts the same proportion, relatively to the whole candidate. We take the complement to be 1, because the more deletions there are, the smaller the similarity becomes. When different C_i candidates are possible for matching I, we establish the best match as follows: assume two vector matches $V_1 = a_1, a_2, a_3, a_4, a_5$ and $V_2 = b_1, b_2, b_3, b_4, b_5$, then the best match is determined by the greater partial order, i.e. if $a_1 > b_1$, then $V_1 > V_2$, else if $a_1 < b_1$, then $V_1 < V_2$, else $a_2 > b_2$, then $V_1 > V_2$, etc.

4.3 Matching Strategy

4.3.1 Basics. We try to match each word C_i of candidate C, to a word I_j of input I. C_i matches I_j if one of the paradigms of C_i equals one of the paradigms of I_j at the same level f, i.e. if C_i^f and I_j^f are equal. When a failure to match two words with their paradigms C_i^f to I_j^f occurs at a given level f, we try to match the words at the next upper level $f+1$, i.e. C_i^{f+1} and I_j^{f+1}. When all of the possible layers of the two words have been tried without success, we try to match the next word C_{i+1} to the same I_j. If C_i does not match any word of I at any level, we consider that it has to be deleted. All words of I have to be matched by some word of C: no insertion is allowed.

4.3.2 Lazy Match. With TM tools, if some useful candidates are found, they usually utilize words similar to the input words because translation memories are applied within very similar documents, most of the time between older and newer versions of a document. When the priority is speed (rather than non-ambiguity), we can consider that a match is reached as soon as a word of C and a word of I match at a certain layer f. It is not necessary to look at the upper levels, for they should match because of the expected similarity between the input and the candidate. The previous example illustrates this. As upper levels are not tested, this allows a gain in the number of iterations of the algorithm. The experiments in Section 5 confirm this to be a correct strategy for TM.

Table 5.5. Lemma ambiguity

$C2^1$	**Sony**	*stay*	*ended*	**Tuesday**
$C2^2$	**Sony**	**stay**	*end*	**Tuesday**
$C2^3$	**PN**	*noun*	*verb*	**noun**
I^1	**Sony**	*stayed*	*stronger*	**Tuesday**
I^2	**Sony**	**stay**	*strong*	**Tuesday**
I^3	**PN**	*verb*	*adj*	**noun**

4.3.3 Exhaustive Match. In the most general case, ambiguity problems prevent us from employing the lazy match strategy, and a correct match requires that whenever two items C_i^f and I_j^f match at a certain level f, they should match at upper levels. Table 5.5 is an example. In $C2$, the lemma *stay* of surface word *stay* matches the lemma *stay* of surface word *stayed* of I, but they do not match at the POS level (noun and verb). The algorithm should go to this level to find that there is no match. Once again, however, because this algorithm has been built for TM systems, such ambiguities hardly occur.

4.3.4 Insertion. If some items in I are not matched by any item of C, the match involves an insertion.

- *Case of Translation Memories:* if the candidate sentences are to be used by human translators, they will be able to insert the missing word at the right place. Accordingly, a match with insertion can be used for pure TM.
- *Case of Shallow Translation (EBMT):* in the EBMT system we are targetting, we plan to use the matching substring of C for adaptation to I without syntactic rules. Accordingly, we consider that we do not know where to insert the non-matching item: in

this case, we force the algorithm to stop if an insertion is needed to match C and I. From now on, we will follow this position.

4.3.5 Trace. It is desirable to have the algorithm output a list of triplets $(C_i^f, I_j^f, op)_{1 \leq i \leq n}$ (called a 'trace') where C_i^f matches to I_j^f through the 'op' operation. We note op='f' an equality at level f, and op='0' a deletion. For Table 4, the trace should be:

(1 0 0) (2 0 0) (3 0 0) (4 0 0) (5 1 3) (6 0 0) (7 2 1) (8 3 2) (9 4 3)

4.4 Adapting the Algorithms of Wagner & Fischer, and Sellers

4.4.1 Algorithm Principle. The Wagner & Fischer (W&F) dynamic programming algorithm, displayed in Figure 5.10, gives the edit distance between C and I. The distance is obtained in $m * n$ operations, by building an $[m+1, n+1]$ array, as shown in Table 5.6.

In addition, Wagner & Fischer, 1974 proposed a backtracking procedure, shown in Figure 5.11, that scans backwards this array to give a 'trace' of the match between C and I (i.e. it prints the position of the matching words), in $(m+n)$ operations. The trace is then obtained in $(mn+m+n)$ operations in total. This algorithm was previously used in Planas, 1998a at each layer of a TELA structure to give a trace by layer. The data from the traces of the different layers were combined afterwards for the purposes of TM and EBMT. However, this procedure is not optimal for at least two reasons. First, the layers are compared in an independent way, leading to a waste of time in the case of TM, because the lazy match phenomenon is not used. Second, the combination of the results was processed after the algorithm had run, and this required a supplementary process. One can imagine that processing all the data in the flow of the instructions of the algorithm would be more efficient.

4.4.2 Minimization Based on Two Operations. If we look at the W&F algorithm in Figure 5.10, the part in bold represents the code involved in the calculus of the nearest local distance $d[i, j]$. It tests which of the four basic edit operations (deletion, insertion, equality or strict substitution) gives the lowest partial distance. Nevertheless, we have shown that only deletions and equalities interest us. We therefore reduce the test in the algorithm to that shown in Figure 5.12. Furthermore, we initiate the columns of the array with infinite values (huge values in practice) to show that initial insertions are not possible, and

```
For j=0 to m   {d[j, 0]=j }                    (initiating the columns)
For i=1 to n   {d[0, i]=i }                       (initiating the rows)
For i=1 to n {
  For j=1 to m {
    if(I[j]=C[i])   {d=d[i-1, j-1]}                          (equality)
    else   {d=d[i-1, j-1]+1}                             (substitution)
    d[j,i]=min(d[i-1, j]+1, d[i, j-1]+1, d)
  }
}
Print d[n, m]
```

Figure 5.10. The Wagner & Fischer (1974) algorithm

```
i = 0;   j = m;
while ((i > 0) and (j > 0)) {
  if (d[i, j] = d[i-1, j]+1)   {i = i-1 }                    (deletion)
  else if (d[i, j] = d[i, j-1]+1)   {j = j-1 }              (insertion)
  else {                             (equality or substitution )
    print (i, j)
    i = i-1; j = j-1
  }
}
```

Figure 5.11. The Wagner & Fischer backtracking algorithm

the rows to '0' to count the deletions relatively to input I (cf. Sellers, 1980 for an explanation).

An example of the successive scores calculated with this algorithm are shown in Table 5.6. The total distance (equal to 1) between C and I appears in the lowest right cell. The fact that only two operations are used eradicates the ambiguity that appears in selecting the next cell in the W&F algorithm backtracking procedure with four operations. In our algorithm, either there is an equality (cost 0), or a deletion (cost

```
if(I[j]=C[i])   {d=d[i-1, j-1]}                    (equal: no cost)
else   {d=inf}                 (big integer, in theory infinite)
d[j,i] = min (d[i-1, j]+1, d)                (deletion or equal ?)
```

Figure 5.12. Matching with deletions and equalities

Table 5.6. Successive scores produced by the adapted Wagner & Fischer (1974) algorithm

		I_j	I^1_1	I^1_2	I^1_3	I^1_4	I^1_5
			First	**press**	**the**	**red**	**button**
C^1_i		*0*	inf	inf	inf	inf	inf
C^1_1	**First**	*0*	**0**	inf	inf	inf	inf
C^1_2	**press**	*0*	1	**0**	inf	inf	inf
C^1_3	*only*	*0*	2	**1**	inf	inf	inf
C^1_4	**the**	*0*	3	2	**1**	inf	inf
C^1_5	**red**	*0*	4	3	2	**1**	inf
C^1_6	**button**	*0*	5	4	3	2	**[1]**

1). The possibility of having the same cost 1 for insertions, deletions, or strict substitutions has been eliminated.

4.4.3 Introducing One Equality per Level.

As mentioned previously, we need to match items at different layers. We introduce here two new points to deal with this:

- In order to keep the score for each equality and deletion, $d[i,j]$ is a vector instead of a number:

$$d[i,j] = [score_1, ..., score_F, score_{--}]$$

- In this vector, $score_1$ through $score_F$ store the number of equalities for each layer f, and $score_{--}$ records the number of deletions, as in W&F (underlined in the arrays).

Table 5.7 shows an example of different score vectors involved in such a match. To calculate the successive $d[i,j]$, we use the algorithm adapted for F levels in Figure 5.13.

We first try to get the maximum number of equalities and then the minimum number of deletions. Each time we find a new match in the

Table 5.7. Introducing a vector of deletion and layer equalities

			I_j^f	0	I_1	I_2	I_3	I_4
			I^1	*word*	Sony	stays	strong	Tuesday
			I^2	*lem*	Sony	stay	strong	Tuesday
C_i^f	C^1	C^2	$\frac{C^3}{I^3}$	*pos*	PN	verb	adj	PN
0	*word*	*lem*	*pos*	*0000*	*000inf*	*000inf*	*000inf*	*000inf*
C_1	**Sony**	Sony	PN	*0000*	**1000**	000inf	000inf	000inf
C_2	reported	report	**verb**	*0000*	1001	**1010**	000inf	000inf
C_3	*that*	*that*	*conj*	*0000*	1002	1011	000inf	000inf
C_4	*NTT*	*NTT*	**PN**	*0000*	**0010**	1012	000inf	000inf
C_5	*stayed*	**stay**	verb	*0000*	0011	**0110**	000inf	000inf
C_6	*stronger*	**strong**	adj	*0000*	0012	0111	**0210**	000inf
C_7	**Tuesday**	Tuesday	PN	*0000*	0010	0112	0211	**1210**
C_8	morning	morning	noun	*0000*	0011	0113	0212	**1211**

if $(I^f[j] = C^f[i])$ {

$$d_e = [d^1[i-1, j-1], ..., d^f[i-1, j-1] + 1,$$
$$d^{f+1}[i-1, j-1], ..., d^F[i-1, j-1], d^-[i-1, j-1]]$$

}

else $\{d_e = [0, ..., 0, inf]\}$

$$d_d = [d^1[i-1, j], ..., d^f[i-1, j], ..., d^F[i-1, j], d^-[i-1, j] + 1]$$

$$d[i, j] = max(d_e, d_d) \qquad \text{(equality or deletion)}$$

Figure 5.13. Adapting the algorithm to F levels

first column, we start a new path (see I_1 matching with C_1, C_4 and C_7 in Table 5.7). If one of the vectors of the last column of the array is such that $\sum(score_f)_{1 \le f \le F} = m$, there is a matching substring of C in which there is a matching word for each of the words of I, in which case this constitutes a solution. In our example, cell (7, 4), with score 1210 shows that there is a sub-chain of the candidate that matches the input with 1, 2, and 1 matches at the word, lemma, and POS levels and 0 deletions. Cell (8, 4) indicates a similar match, but with 1 deletion (*morning*). The best path ends therefore at cell (7,4). Starting from this cell, we can retrieve the full solution using the W&F backtracking algorithm adapted to F levels. This approach allows us to choose as compact a string as possible. When there are several possible paths, as in Table 5.8,

Table 5.8. Selecting the best concurrent sub-segment

			I^f_j	0	I_1	I_2	I_3	I_4
			I^1	*word*	Sony	stays	strong	Tuesday
			I^2	*lem*	Sony	stay	strong	Tuesday
C^f_i	C^1	C^2	$\frac{C^3}{I^3}$	*pos*	PN	verb	adj	PN
0	*word*	*lem*	*pos*	*0000*	*000inf*	*000inf*	*000inf*	*000inf*
C_1	**Sony**	Sony	PN	*0000*	**1000**	000inf	000inf	000inf
C_2	*stayed*	**stay**	verb	*0000*	1001	**1100**	000inf	000inf
C_3	*stronger*	**strong**	adj	*0000*	1002	1101	**1200**	000inf
C_4	**Tuesday**	Tuesday	PN	*0000*	1000	1102	1201	**2200**
C_5	*and*	*and*	*conj*	*0000*	1001	1103	1202	**2201**
C_6	NTT	NTT	**PN**	*0000*	**0010**	1104	1203	2202
C_7	*stayed*	**stay**	verb	*0000*	0011	**0110**	1204	2203
C_8	**strong**	strong	adj	*0000*	0012	0111	**0210**	2204
C_9	**Tuesday**	Tuesday	PN	*0000*	0010	0112	0211	**1210**
C_{10}	*morning*	*morning*	*noun*	*0000*	0011	0113	0212	**1211**

the algorithm is able to choose the best matching substring. If we first look for a similarity involving surface word matches, and then lemmas and parts of speech, then cell (4,4) with score 2200 will be chosen. This strategy can be adapted to particular needs: it suffices to change the order of the scores in the vectors.

4.5 Optimizing

4.5.1 Triangularization of the Array. In this algorithm, for each I_j, there must be at least one possible matching C_i. Hence, in a valid path, there are at least m matches. As a match between C_i and I_j occurs when 'stepping across a diagonal', the $(m-1)$ first diagonals (from the lower left corner of the array) cannot give rise to a valid path. Therefore, we do not calculate $d[i,j]$ across these small diagonals. Symmetrically, the small diagonals after the last full one (in the upper right corner) cannot give rise to a valid path. We therefore eliminate these $(m-1)$ last diagonals. This gives a reduced matrix as shown in the new example in Table 5.9. The computed cells are then situated in a parallelogram of dimensions $(n-m+1)$ and m. This implies that only $m(n-m+1)$ cells have to be computed. Instead of initiating the first row 0 to 'inf', we initiate the cells of the diagonal just before the last full top diagonal (between cell (0,1) and cell (3,4) in Table 5.9) to '000inf' to be sure that no insertion is possible.

Table 5.9. Eliminating left and right small diagonals

			I_j^f	0	I_1	I_2	I_3	I_4
			I^1	*word*	Sony	stays	strong	Tuesday
			I^2	*lem*	Sony	stay	strong	Tuesday
C_i^f	C^1	C^2	$\frac{C^3}{I^3}$	*pos*	PN	verb	adj	PN
0	*word*	*lem*	*pos*	*0000*	*000inf*			
C_1	**Sony**	Sony	PN	*0000*	**1000**	000inf		
C_2	*reported*	*report*	**verb**	*0000*	1001	**1010**	000inf	
C_3	*that*	*that*	*conj*	*0000*	1002	1011	000inf	000inf
C_4	*NTT*	*NTT*	**PN**	*0000*	**0010**	1012	000inf	000inf
C_5	*stayed*	**stay**	verb	*0000*	0011	**0110**	000inf	000inf
C_6	*stronger*	**strong**	adj	*0000*		0111	**0210**	000inf
C_7	**Tuesday**	Tuesday	PN	*0000*			0211	**1210**
C_8	*morning*	*morning*	*noun*	*0000*				**1211**

4.5.2 Complexity. The worst time complexity of this algorithm is F-proportional to the number of cells in the computed array, which is $m * (n - m + 1)$. With the lazy match strategy, it is often the case that all F levels are not visited. As the number of cells computed by the W&F algorithm is $m * n$, our algorithm always runs faster. The backtracking algorithm takes $m + n$ operations in the W&F algorithm, as in our algorithm. In total, this leads to $m(n - m + 2) + n$ operations in the MSSM algorithm, and $m(n + 1) + n$ operations in the W&F algorithm. The general complexity is then sub-quadratic. When the lengths of both segments to be compared are similar (as often happens in TMs), the complexity is close to linear. The two graphs in Figure 5.14 and 5.15 show two interesting particular cases ($m = n$ and m running from 1 to $n = 10$), comparing W&F and our algorithm. For strings of similar lengths, the longer they are, the more the MSSM algorithm becomes interesting. When n is fixed, the MSSM algorithm is more interesting for extreme values of the length of I: small and similar to n.

4.5.3 Conclusions. The first contribution of this algorithm is to provide TM and EBMT systems with a precise and quick way to compare segments of words with a similarity vector. This leads to an almost complete eradication of noise for the matter of retrieving similar sentences in TM systems (97% 'reusability' in our prototype, as shown in the next section, 'Experiments'). The second is to offer an unambiguous word to word matching procedure via the 'trace'. This last point opens the way to the use of Shallow Translation.

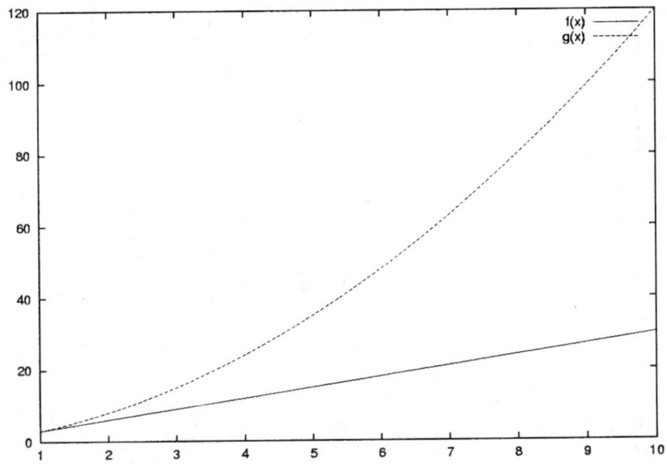

Figure 5.14. Compared number of loops for MSSM (plain) and W&F (dashed) complexities when m=n

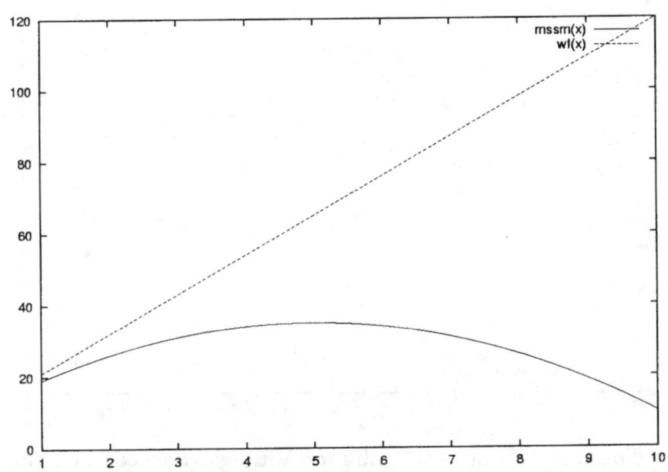

Figure 5.15. compared number of loops for MSSM (plain) and W&F (dashed) complexities when n=10 and 0< m <11

5. Experiments

We now present now two experiments based on the use of the TELA structure and the notion of similarity that we have described above.

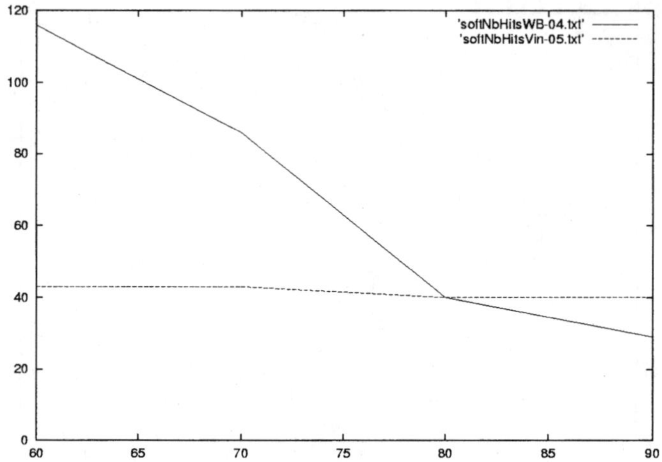

Figure 5.16. Compared no. of hits for Vintage (dashed) and the market TM leader (plain) performances on a software corpus

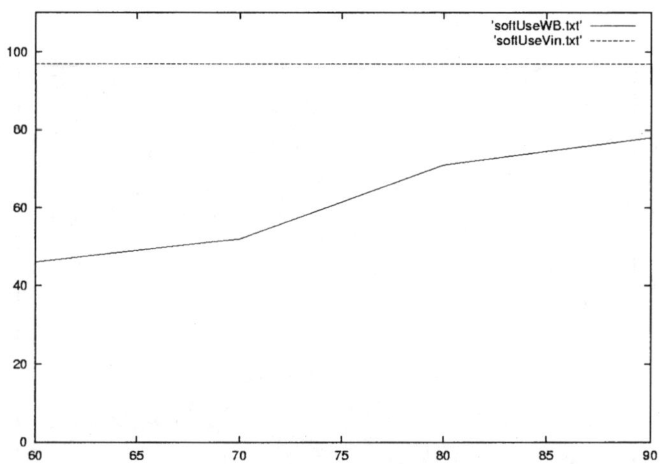

Figure 5.17. Compared % of usable hits for Vintage (dashed) and the market TM leader (plain) performances on a software corpus

5.1 Retrieving Similar Translations

The aim of this experiment is to compare our prototype ('Vintage') retrieval performances against the leader in the TM tools market. The source language is English, the target languages are French and Japanese. The nature of the target language does not influence the results of this first experiment since all operations are conducted on the source side. The source language analyzer we used to generate the lemmas and the parts of speech is the *Apple Pie* parser[4], from New York City University. We used two corpora. The first one is a list of strings used in an online English–French Help package. It has 7192 sentences that have been stored in the memory, and we used the first 50 sentences as a test set. The second corpus we used is a collection of brief online economic news items. Originally, it had 31,526 source Japanese sentences totalling 447,772 words, aligned with a similar number of English sentences. We used the English sentences as the source, and the Japanese as the target. We took the first 75 sentences of this second corpus as a test set. For both corpora, we looked for similar sentences in the original corpus. We collected only non-identical sentences. The number of total sentences that each system retrieved for both tools is illustrated in each of the left-hand graphs in Figure 5.16 and 5.18. The X axis represents the percentage of matching lemmas in the sentence. For example, in Figure 5.16, if we want 90% of the lemmas to match between the retrieved examples and the input sentences, we get 40 proposals for all of the 75 input sentences with Vintage, and 29 with the market TM leader.

We then estimated how many of these sentences could be used by a translator according to the following criteria: if for a retrieved sentence, less than half the words need be edited to get the input sentence, we considered the sentence usable. Figure 5.17 and Figure 5.19 show the percentage of usable hits.

It is clear from the graphs in Figure 5.16 and Figure 5.18 that our system offers a better recall for higher similarity thresholds, which are the ones used for retrieving reasonable proposals. When the threshold decreases, the quality of the sentences our prototype proposes is almost constant, while with the market TM leader numerous proposals diverge with respect to precision. Note that the notion of similarity is different in the market TM leader (based on the number of similar characters), so the comparison should be considered as a relative one.

For lower thresholds, a translator using our prototype would be presented with fewer noisy sentences, and more really similar ones, so less time will be spent evaluating which is the best to be used. For higher thresholds, he will be given more sentences. It is worth noticing that the precision we obtained never goes below 97% (for these tests), whereas precision in classical TM systems would be badly affected when the

[4]`http://cs.nyu.edu/cs/projects/pro-teus/app/`

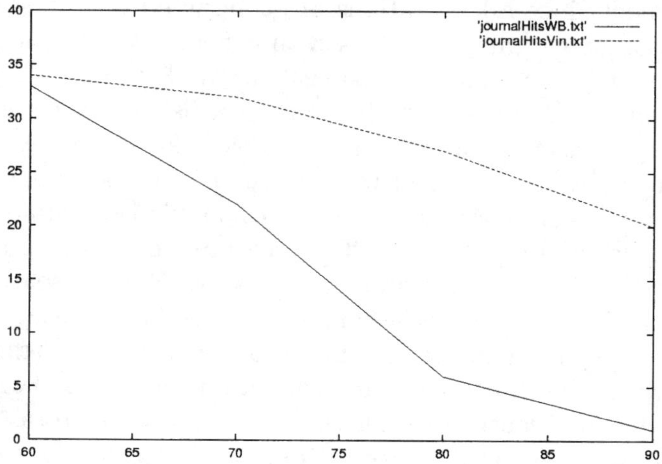

Figure 5.18. Compared Vintage (dashed) and the market TM leader (plain) performances on a journal corpus: no. of hits

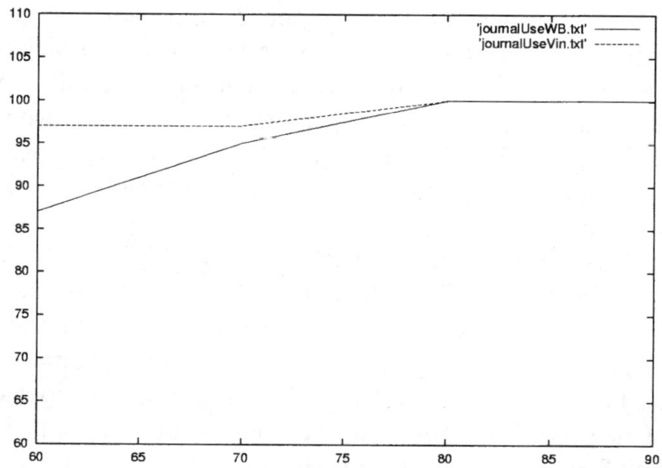

Figure 5.19. Compared Vintage (dashed) and the market TM leader (plain) performances on a journal corpus: % of usable hits

threshold similarity decreases, because of the retrieval process they use which is almost exclusively index-based.

In Planas, 1999b and Planas, 1999c, we checked to see that other classical TM systems from the market show similar behavior, while the *Xerox* XMS Translation Manager, which uses linguistic data, is closest to our results. It is worth noting that these TM software tools are well designed, and allow everyday translation companies to save time and money. Our prototype is only a research program that has been built for testing the core behavior of TM systems. It does not include all the useful features that commercial TM software offers.

5.2 Shallow Translation

Previous research studies such as Collins & Cunningham, 1997 and Veale & Way, 1997 have shown that approaching translation as a transfer problem using TUs as 'surface patterns' can lead to interesting results for some specific situations: around 30% of 'adaptable' Translation Units in software manuals for the first reference, and 63% for sentences that did have correspondences, for the second. We thought it could be interesting to try to obtain similar evidence where TUs are used as surface patterns with substitutable words for translating similar sentences, without the use of any syntactic structures in the case of English to Japanese translation.

We have developed a specific algorithm that matches only equalities and deletions (we do not know where to insert words, and only longer example sentences are usable for translating a shorter input sentence), and have applied it after a retrieval phase, as in the previous experiment. The target language parser was the *NTT* ALT-JAWS parser[5] for the Japanese language, provided by our colleagues from the Translation Group of *NTT* Communication Science labs. The French parser was built *ad hoc* for this experiment. Using a dictionary look-up procedure, we then replaced the corresponding target words in the target part of the TU, and eliminated superfluous words to obtain a translation for the input sentence. This approach is really basic and does not take into consideration important problems such as the correct choice of the target word (lexical and semantic ambiguity), or of the correct syntactic structure (syntactic ambiguity). Moreover, in the examples below, we do not give the final inflected sentence, but only the sequence of lemmas. We intend to tackle such non-trivial issues in further research. However, when used for technical manuals or software translation (localization), it seems to us that these results may be of some help. In (7) we show some input English sentences (I), the corresponding closest TU

[5] `http://www.kecl.ntt.co.jp/icl/mtg/resources/altjaws.html`

retrieved from the database (TU has a source part (S) and a target part (T)), and the French translation solution (R) proposed by the prototype.

(7) I: Press on the red button.
S: Press on the green window
T: Appuyez sur la fenêtre verte
R: (Appuyer) (sur) (le) (bouton) (rouge)

I: Select 'Open' and click 'OK'
S: Select 'Now' and click 'Done'
T: Choisissez 'Maintenant' et cliquez sur 'Fini'
R: Choisissez 'Ouvrir' et cliquez sur 'OK'

This last example requires a translation glossary of preferred terms to have been loaded into the system, in order to apply the conventions of a particular company. According to these conventions, 'Open' should be translated into 'Ouvrir' and 'Done' into 'Fini'.

6. Conclusions and Perspectives

We have designed a structure (TELA) for representing data for use in Translation Memory tools. Using this multi-level structure, we have proposed a notion of similarity based on Edit Distance. We have also presented the MSSM algorithm which gives us a means to obtain this distance together with the exact trace of the match between two segments. We have shown in experiments that this approach gives better results than techniques used in Translation Memories currently used in the market. Notably, we have increased the recall for higher similarity thresholds, and reduced the worst precision to 97% in the tested corpora. Finally we have outlined a proposal which extends TM towards Machine Translation via Shallow Translation, together with some initial results.

Acknowledgments

The whole *NTT* team should be thanked here for its constant support: Mr. Ikeda who provided the support for the ALT-JAWS and Apple Pie parsers, Mr. Adachi who provided the test files, Francis Bond who kindly agreed to review this article, and Mr. Ooyama. Thanks also to Prof. Christian Boitet of Université Joseph Fourier (Grenoble, France) who supervised the Ph.D. thesis that led to most of the results presented here.

References

Argamon, S., I. Dagan and Y. Krymolowski. 1998. A Memory-Based Approach to Learning Shallow Natural Language Patterns. In *36th Annual Meeting of the Association for Computational Linguistics and 17th International Conference on Computational Linguistics*, Montreal, Quebec, Canada, **1**:67–73.

Collins, B. and P. Cunningham. 1997. Adaptation Guided Retrieval: Approaching EBMT with Caution. In *Proceedings of the 7th International Conference on Theoretical and Methodological issues in Machine Translation*, Santa Fe, NM., pp.119–126.

Cranias, L., H. Papageorgiou and S. Piperidis. 1997. Example retrieval from a Translation Memory. *Natural Language Engineering* **3**(4):255–277.

Furuse, O. and H. Iida. 1994. Constituent Boundary Parsing for Example-Based Machine Translation. In *COLING-94: Proceedings of the 15th International Conference on Computational Linguistics*, Kyoto, Japan, pp.105–111.

Gale, W. and K. Church. 1993. A Program for Aligning Sentences in Bilingual Corpora. *Computational Linguistics* **19**(1):75–102.

Lafourcade, M. 1993. LEAF ou comment garder l'Originalité de l'ambiguité, Actualité Scientifique. In *Troisièmes Journées Scientifiques Traductique-TA-TAO*, Montréal, Quebec, Canada, pp.165–185 (in French).

Lepage, Y. 1998. Solving analogies on words: an algorithm. In *36th Annual Meeting of the Association for Computational Linguistics and 17th International Conference on Computational Linguistics*, Montreal, Quebec, Canada, **1**:728–734.

Planas, E. 1998. *TELA: Structures and Algorithms for Memory-Based Machine Translation.* PhD thesis, University Joseph Fourier, Grenoble, France (in French).

Planas, E. 1999a. Towards Second Generation Translation Memories. In *LISA Newsletter 1999* **8**(2):7–11.

Planas, E. 1999b. Translation Memory Tools: Comparative studies of Star, Trados, IBM TM2 and Shallow Translation. In *Proceedings of the LISA Asia Forum Workshop*, Shanghai, China.

Planas, E. 2000. Extending Translation Memories. In *Proceedings of the Fifth EAMT Workshop, Harvesting Existing Resources*, Ljubljana, Slovenia, [no page numbers], `http://www.eamt.org/archive/ljubljana/Planas.htm`.

Sellers, P.H. 1980. The theory and computation of evolutionary distances: pattern recognition. *Journal of Algorithms* **127**:359–373

Takeda, K. 1996. Pattern-Based Machine Translation. In *COLING-96: Proceedings of the 16th International Conference on Computational Linguistics*, Copenhagen, Denmark, pp.1155–1158.

Thompson, H. and C. Brew. 1996. Automatic Evaluation of Computer Generated text: Final Report on the TextEval Project. *HCRC Working Paper*, Human Communication Research Centre, University of Edinburgh, UK.

Thurmair, G. 1997. Exchange Interfaces for Translation Tools. In *Machine Translation Summit VI*, San Diego, CA., pp.74–93.

Ukkonen, E. 1985. Algorithms for Approximate String Matching. *Information and Control* **64**:100–118.

Veale, T. and A. Way. 1997. *Gaijin*: A Bootstrapping, Template-Driven Approach to Example-Based MT. In *International Conference, Recent Advances in Natural Language Processing*, Tzigov Chark, Bulgaria, pp.239–244.

Wagner, A. and M. Fischer. 1974. The String-to-String Correction Problem. *Journal of the ACM* **21**(1):168–173.

Chapter 6

AN EXAMPLE-BASED MACHINE TRANSLATION SYSTEM USING DP-MATCHING BETWEEN WORD SEQUENCES

Eiichiro Sumita
eiichiro.sumita@atr.co.jp

Abstract We propose a new approach to the example-based machine translation paradigm. First, the proposed approach retrieves the most similar example by carrying out DP-matching of the input sentence and source sentences in an example database while measuring the semantic distances of the words. Second, the approach adjusts the gap between the input and the most similar example by using a bilingual dictionary. We demonstrate its high coverage and accuracy through a computational experiment for a limited domain.

Keywords: DP-matching, semantic distance, example-based retrieval

1. The Proposed Method

1.1 Overview

This paper proposes a new approach to EBMT featuring dynamic-programming (DP) matching between word sequences. Hereafter, we call our approach D^3 (Dp-match Driven transDucer). We first explain the algorithm. Section 2 reports experimental results, and Section 3 presents implications and prospects.

As shown in Figure 6.1, our language resources are (1) a bilingual corpus, in which sentences are aligned beforehand; (2) a bilingual dictionary, which is used for generating target sentences; and (3) thesauri of

M. Carl and A. Way (eds.), Recent Advances in Example-Based Machine Translation, 189–209.

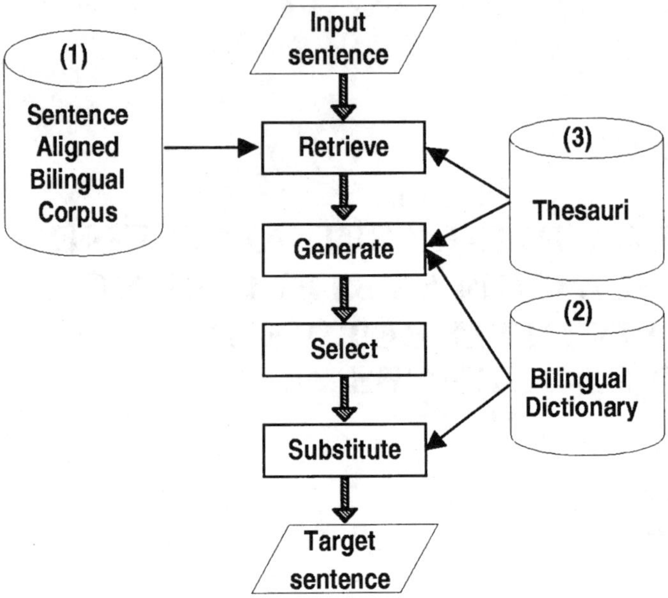

Figure 6.1. System Configuration

both languages, which are used for incorporating the semantic distance between words into the distance between word sequences (see Section 1.2.1). Furthermore, (2) and (3) are also used for word alignment.

The characteristics of D^3 are different from previous EBMT studies. Firstly, most EBMT proposals assume syntactic parsing and bilingual treebanks, but D^3 does not. Secondly, most EBMT proposals divide the translation process in two, i.e. learning of translation patterns in advance followed by application of the translation patterns learned, but D^3 generates translation patterns on the fly according to the input and the retrieved translation examples when they are needed.

1.2 Algorithm

The translation process consists of four steps:

1 **Retrieve** the most similar translation example;

2 **Generate** translation patterns;

3 **Select** the best translation pattern;

4 **Substitute** the target words for the unmatched input words.

Here, we illustrate the algorithm step-by-step using translation from Japanese to English.

1.2.1 Retrieval. This step scans the source parts of all example sentences in the bilingual corpus. By measuring the distance (*dist* shown below) between the word sequences of the input and example sentences, the process retrieves the examples with the minimum distance, provided that the distance is smaller than the given threshold. Otherwise, the entire translation *fails* with no output.

According to equation (1), *dist* is calculated as follows. The counts of the Insertion (I), Deletion (D), and Substitution operations are summed and the total is normalized by the sum of the length of the input and example sequences.

$$(1) \qquad dist = \frac{I+D+2\sum SEMDIST}{L_{input}+L_{example}}$$

Substitution considers the semantic distance between two substituted words and is called *SEMDIST*. *SEMDIST* is defined as the division of *K* (the level of the *most specific common abstraction* in the thesaurus of two words) by *N* (the height of the thesaurus) according to equation (2), taken from Sumita & Iida, 1991. It ranges from 0 to 1.

$$(2) \qquad SEMDIST = \frac{K}{N}$$

Figure 6.2 illustrates the *SEMDIST* calculation between *potato* and *beef*. The *most specific common abstraction* of the two words is *ingredients* as shown in boldface. The *SEMDIST* is the *K* divided by *N* in the figure.

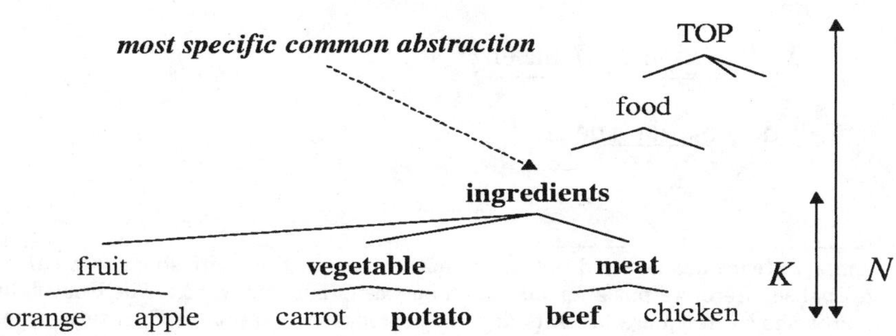

Figure 6.2. Semantic distance: *K* is the 'most common abstraction' of two words in the Thesaurus, and *N* is its overall 'height'

Let us consider the following two sentences, (3) the input and (4) the source sentence of the translation example, where the italicised parts represent the differences between the two sentences.[1]

(3) *iro*/ga/ki/ni/iri/masen (input sentence)
[*color*/SUB/favor/OBJ/enter/POLITE-NOT]
{I do not care for the *color.*}

(4) *dezain*/ga/ki/ni/iri/masen (translation example)
[*design*/SUB/favor/OBJ/enter/POLITE-NOT]
{I do not care for the *design.*}

Because *iro* and *dezain* are completely dissimilar in the thesaurus used in the experiment, *SEMDIST* is 1, and therefore, the *dist* between them is (0+0+2*1) / (6+6) = 0.167. The *dist* is calculated efficiently by the so-called *DP-matching* algorithm, which is often used in speech recognition research (cf. Cormen *et al.*, 1989).

1.2.2 Pattern Generation. This step aligns the italicised parts of source sentence (4) of the translation example to the corresponding target sentence (5) of the translation example by using lexical resources.[2]

(5) I do not like the design.

We obtain the following translation pattern, where the variable X is used to connect source (6) and target (7) and then store instance (8) in the input sentence.

(6) X_j/<u>ga/ki/ni/iri/masen</u>

(7) <u>I do not like the</u> X_e

[1]A Japanese sentence has no word boundary marker such as the white space that surrounds words in English. Here, we put a forward slash between Japanese words. The English literal translation is shown in square brackets and the sentence translation in English is shown in curly brackets.

[2]We do not adhere to the method of word alignment. We have a free hand in selecting an appropriate alignment method out of a spectrum (Manning & Schütze, 1999, chapter 13) ranging from statistical to lexical types. In the experiment, we rely on a bilingual dictionary and thesauri in both languages.

(8) $X_j = iro$

We align the different parts only. We do not align the remaining parts, shown with underlining, word-by-word. We deal with their correspondence as a whole. This produces long canned parts in the translation pattern and reduces the chance of mixing errors or producing unnatural translations.

1.2.3 Pattern Selection. Because we may have multiple translation examples with the same *dist*, multiple translation patterns can be generated. This requires us to select the most suitable one from among these translation patterns. We use the heuristic rule below for this purpose.

- Select the most frequent translation pattern.
- If this cannot be uniquely determined, select the translation pattern with the largest sum of the word frequencies in the translation patterns.
- If this cannot be determined, select one randomly as a last resort.

1.2.4 Word Substitution. By translating[3] the source word corresponding to the variable using the bilingual dictionary and instantiating the variable within the target part of the selected translation pattern by the target word (9), we finally get a target sentence (10).

(9) $X_e = color$

(10) I do not like the color.

1.2.5 Summary. Let us review the process using the examples above. The input (3) is translated into (10) by utilizing (5) whose source (4) is similar to (3).

(3) *iro*/ga/ki/ni/iri/masen

(4) *dezain*/ga/ki/ni/iri/masen

(5) I do not like the *design*.

[3]The current implementation does not select the target word but just takes the target word from the one-to-one bilingual dictionary. Incorporating word selection will improve accuracy in the future.

(10) I do not like the *color*.

The common parts are constant and the different portions are substituted by consulting a bilingual dictionary.

2. Experiment

To see whether this rough approach actually works, we conducted a computational experiment in translating from Japanese to English. This section describes the experimental conditions and results.

2.1 Experimental Conditions

Bilingual Corpus: We built a corpus of Japanese sentences and their English translations that are typically found in phrasebooks for foreign tourists. Because the translations were made sentence by sentence, the corpus was sentence-aligned from the start. We *lemmatized and POS-tagged* both the Japanese and English sentences using our morphological analysis programs. The total sentence count was about 200 K.[4] The statistics[5] are summarized in Table 6.1.

Table 6.1. Corpus statistics

Sentences	204,108
Sentence Length	(J) 8.3 (E) 6.1
Words	(J)1,689,449 (E)1,235,747
Vocabulary	(J) 19,640 (E) 15,374

Test set: A quality evaluation was performed for 500 sentences selected randomly from the above corpus, and the remaining sentences were used as translation examples for the experiment.

Bilingual Dictionary: We also used a bilingual dictionary previously developed for another EBMT system, TDMT (Transfer-Driven MT), in the travel domain, (Sumita *et al.*, 1999). The size of the dictionary is 24,658 words.

---

[4]We call a sequence of sentences uttered by a single speaker an utterance. Our corpus is in fact aligned utterance-by-utterance. Strictly speaking, "sentence" in this paper should be replaced by "utterance."

[5]J stands for Japanese and E stands for English.

Table 6.2. Coverage and sentence length

	%	Average length
Exactly (*dist* = 0)	46.4	5.6
Approximately (0 < *dist* <= 1/3)	42.8	7.7
No output (1/3 < *dist*)	10.8	11.0
Total	100.0	7.0

Thesaurus: We used thesauri whose hierarchies are based on the Kadokawa Ruigo-shin-jiten (Ohno & Hamanishi, 1984) for distance calculation and word alignment. The size of the Japanese thesaurus is 21,608 words and that of the English thesaurus is 11,359 words.

2.2 Results

Here we show coverage, accuracy, and error analysis, with discussions on the relationship between the system performance and the influential factors, i.e. the distance, *dist*, or the sentence length. In addition, we give processing time and describe a pilot experiment with spoken language sentences.

2.2.1 Coverage.

D^3 does not produce any translation when there is no example whose *dist* is within the given threshold, which was randomly chosen as 1/3 in the experiment. D^3 covers about 90% of test sentences. As shown in Table 6.2, about one half of this 90% is matched *exactly* and the other half is matched *approximately* ($0 < dist \leq 1/3$).

The average length of *no output* sentences is much longer than that of others. D^3 is not effective with longer sentences because our algorithm has no explicit step for decomposing an input sentence into subsentences, and because the longer the sentence, the smaller the possibility that there exists a similar sentence in the example database.

2.2.2 Accuracy.

Each translation is graded into one of four ranks[6] by a bilingual human translator who is a native speaker of the target language, American English: (A) Perfect: no problems in ei-

[6]This ranking was developed for evaluation in spoken language translation. For more details, see Sumita *et al.*, 1999.

Table 6.3. Translation accuracy

	Rank	%
Good	A	41.4
	B	25.2
	C	11.8
Bad	D	10.8
No output	*Fail*	10.8

ther information or grammar; (B) Fair: easy-to-understand with some unimportant information missing or flawed grammar; (C) Acceptable: broken but understandable; (D) Nonsense: important information has been translated incorrectly.

As shown in Table 6.3, D[3] achieved a high accuracy of about 80% (i.e. total of A, B, C ranks). The sentences in the remaining 20% are divided into rank D and *Fail* (*No output*).

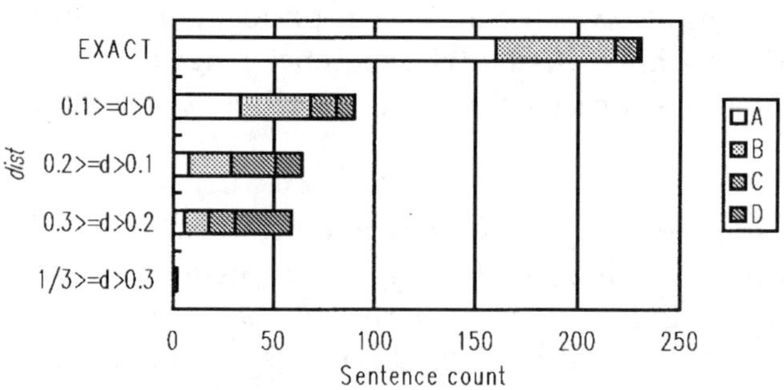

Figure 6.3. Accuracy by distance (*dist*), according to the levels of translation quality (A–D) outlined in section 2.2.2

2.2.3 Error Analysis. With respect to *distant* sentences, Figure 6.3 shows that the accuracy clearly decreases as the *dist* increases. This implies that the current algorithm has a problem in handling distant cases.

The distant cases shown in Figure 6.4 are divided into three types:

1 The input is short but the distance is large, that is, there is no similar example in the corpus;

2 The input is long, even though its parts have similar examples in the corpus;

3 The input is long and there is no similar example for its parts.

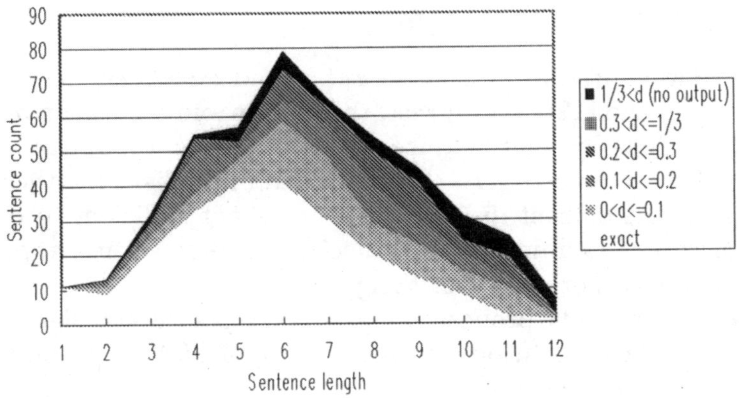

Figure 6.4. Distance vs. Length

We do not expect that we can collect such a dense corpus to cover long sentences because the variation causes combinatorial explosion. The second of these distant cases will be solved by decomposing the input sentence. We plan to incorporate the chunking of inputs and examples by using a phrase alignment (e.g. Imamura, 2001). If we add similar examples into the corpus, the first and third distant cases will be solved to a considerable degree.

As shown so far, the dominant problem is in dealing with *distant* sentences. In the following, we explain problematic cases that arise even for *similar* sentences:

Collocations: Even when the *dist* between the two sentences is small, i.e. they are quite similar in the source language, the translation can be quite different in the target language. This case is not so frequent, but is possible with *collocations* as exemplified in (11)–(13):

(11) *mizu*/o/ippai/o/negai/shi/masu
[water/OBJ/one/POLITE/want/do/POLITE]
{I'd like a **glass** of *water*, please.}

(12) *biiru*/o/ippai/o/negai/shi/masu
[beer/OBJ/one/POLITE/want/do/POLITE]
{I'd like a **glass** of *beer*, please.}

(13) *koohii*/o/ippai/o/negai/shi/masu
[coffee/OBJ/one/POLITE/want/do/POLITE]
{I'd like a **cup** of *coffee*, please.}

The replaceability between *mizu[water]* and *biiru[beer]* does hold for sentences (11) and (12). In contrast, the replaceability between *mizu[water]* and *koohii[coffee]* does not hold for sentences (11) and (13) due to different words for containers (*glass/cup*) required in English. In other words, resolution of the current distance measure is not sufficient to discriminate such cases. Refining the distance measure or adding appropriate examples into the corpus solves this problem.

Noise in data: The proposed approach accepts the translation example blindly. If the translation is *wrong* or *inappropriate*, the quality of the output will suffer. The translation examples in (14)–(15) show contextual inappropriateness. The source parts of the two examples are exactly the same, but the target part of (14) is neutral while that of (15) is specific, i.e. valid only in a special situation. This goes beyond the capability of any approach that translates sentence-by-sentence, which is what the state-of-the-art technology does. Cleaning the example database, preferably by machine, or collecting sufficiently large amounts of data could suppress the influence of noisy examples.

(14) hai/ari/masu = Yes, we do.
[yes/exist/POLITE]

(15) hai/ari/masu = Yes, we have a shuttle bus.
[yes/exist/POLITE]

2.2.4 Processing Time. Retrieval is the predominant step of the entire translation process because the time and space complexity of retrieval is proportional to corpus size, which is quite large. Moreover, we assume that more examples in the corpus result in better translation quality. With a 200K corpus, the current naïve implementation takes about 10 seconds per sentence on average and about 60 seconds per sentence in the worst case on a PC running on a 600 MHz Pentium processor with 500 MB memory.

We plan to exploit techniques developed in information retrieval research such as indexing and clustering. Accordingly, we expect to achieve a performance that is below one second per sentence on average. We do not think that processing time will be problematic.

2.2.5 Robustness for spoken language input. Spoken language is different from written language in various ways. For example, spoken language, in general, features phenomena such as *ellipsis*, *repetition*, *repair*, *insertion* and *inversion*, which are found less frequently in written language and which often go well beyond the competence of natural language processing systems dealing with written language.

Here, we focus on particles of Japanese. Particles are basic devices for sentence construction because Japanese mainly depends on particles rather than on word order. On the other hand, in spoken Japanese, these important particles are often missing (Maruyama, 1998). MT systems for spoken Japanese should, therefore, produce an appropriate target sentence when particles are missing in the input Japanese.

In order to evaluate the robustness of D^3, we conducted a simulation[7]. We produced two translations: one is the translation of an original test sentence and the other is the translation of the sentence where a particle is randomly omitted from the original test sentence. Then we compared the translation qualities by measuring the Word Error Rate (WER)[8] from the reference translation of the original test sentence.

Of our 446 test sentences that have at least one particle, 137 sentences contained altered translations after particle deletion and the translations of the remaining 309 sentences were unchanged as in (16):

(16) a. koi/koohii/**ga**/nomi/tai (original test sentence)
b. koi/koohii/nomi/tai (particle "**ga**" deleted)
c. I'd like a strong coffee (the same translation for (a) and (b))

Figure 6.5 shows changes in WER for the 10 most frequent particles[9]: *wa*, *o*, *no*, *ni*, *ga*, *de*, *ka*, *kara*, *te*, and *to*. The change depends on each particle, so some are downgraded and others are upgraded. The average

[7]We omitted the particle randomly because detecting the omission cannot be done automatically and such analysis by a human is time-consuming. This simulation is rough because it does not take into account the following two points: (i) not all kinds of particles are necessarily elided in spoken Japanese; (ii) whether a particle exits or not affects the subtle nuances of a sentence.

[8]WER is the lowest edit-distance between the reference translation and system translation. If I is the number of insertions, D is the number of deletions, S is the number of substitutions, and R is the number of words in the reference translation, then WER = (I+D+S)/R.

[9]These are divided into different types: adverbial case particles (*wa, o, ni, ga, de, kara*, and *to*), an adnominal particle (*no*), a conjunctive particle (*te*), and a sentence-final particle (*ka*).

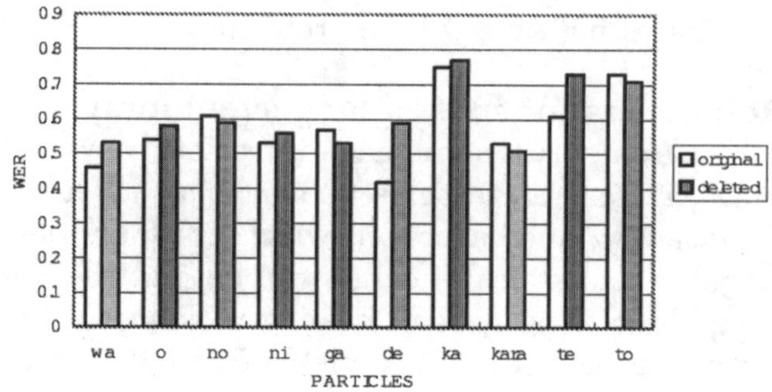

Figure 6.5. Change in translation quality by particle deletion

WER[10] of translation of the original sentences was 0.54 and that of the particle-deleted sentences increased slightly to 0.57. This suggests that the total loss caused by particle omission is not serious. Thus, we conclude that D^3 is robust for particle deletion, which is frequently found in spoken Japanese.[11]

3. Discussion

Here, we explain the implications of the experimental results: (i) confidence measure of translation; (ii) relationship between quality and generality; (iii) task; (iv) limitations; and (v) future extensions. Finally, we compare D^3 with related research efforts.

3.1 Confidence measure of translation

Many MT systems are designed to generate as many translations as possible without taking the quality of each translation into consideration. Consequently, the output is a mixture of good translations and bad translations. There is no information regarding the confidence of each translation.

In contrast, D^3 is designed to translate when the system has confidence in the translation quality. We associate the *dist* with each trans-

[10]The WER looks large because it maintains one reference translation while translation can vary in several ways. Figures of around 0.5 are usually OK in that most of these translations are acceptable by humans.

[11]No investigation has yet been undertaken on robustness with respect to recognition errors.

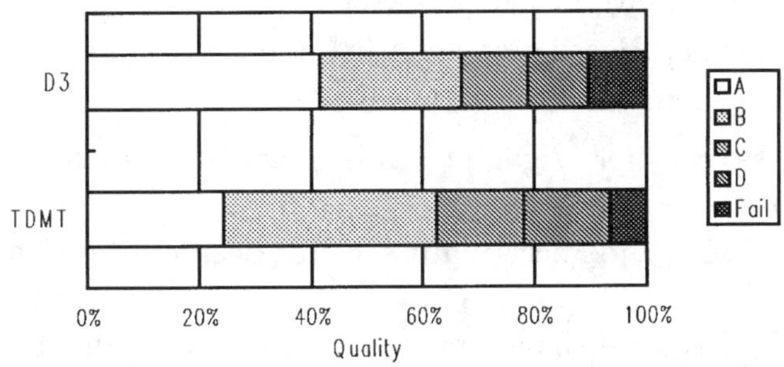

Figure 6.6. Comparison of proposed EBMT, D^3 and (a previous EBMT system) TDMT, according to the levels of translation quality (A–D) outlined in section 2.2.2

lation. The *dist* can indicate the quality of the produced translation as illustrated in Figure 6.3. The smaller the *dist*, the better the quality.

If the user wants a broader coverage, we can combine D^3 and with other MT systems with broader coverage when D^3 fails to translate, or when the confidence is not high (i.e. when the *dist* is large).

3.2 Generality vs. Quality

Figure 6.6 shows a comparison of D^3 and TDMT, our previous EBMT system that *accepts* travel conversations. The combined accuracy of ranks A, B, and C is comparable between the two systems, but D^3 excels over TDMT in the proportion of the higher ranks, A and B.

The reason behind the performance difference for this task is that TDMT uses small translation units for the sake of generality, and phrase-book sentences are not easy to translate into high-quality results in such a general way.

In (17) we show sample translations produced by the above two systems. The first sentence in each block is the input Japanese. The upper English translation was produced by TDMT and the lower English translation by D^3.

(17) a. kore/no/irochigai/wa/ari/masu/ka

[TDMT] Do you have a different color this?

[D^3] Do you have this in different colors?

b. pan/o/mou/sukoshi/kudasai
[TDMT] Please give me a little more the bread.
[D^3] Some more bread please.

c. kesa/choshoku/igai/ni/nanika/saabisu/o/ouke/ni/nari/mashi/ta/ka
[TDMT] Did I accept any services besides breakfast this morning?
[D^3] Did you have any other services besides breakfast this morning?

d. naoshidai/99doru/itadaki/masu
[TDMT] The repair charge, we require ninety-nine dollars.
[D^3] There is a ninety-nine dollar repair charge.

e. kibun/ga/sugure/masen
[TDMT] I don't feel excel.
[D^3] I'm not feeling well.

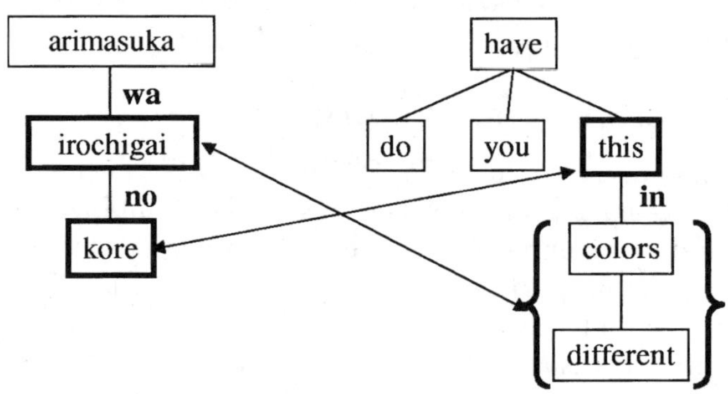

Figure 6.7. Headswitching

We will now explain the problems with the above sample translations one-by-one. In (17a), the word *irochigai* is converted the two words *different colors.* The modification-relationship in the noun phrase *kore/no/irochigai* is reversed to that in the noun phrase *this in different colors* to obtain a natural translation as shown in Figure 6.7. This is called *head-switching.* It is difficult to translate such phenomena by using small translation units, so D^3 exploits much larger translation units to succeed in generating fluent translation.

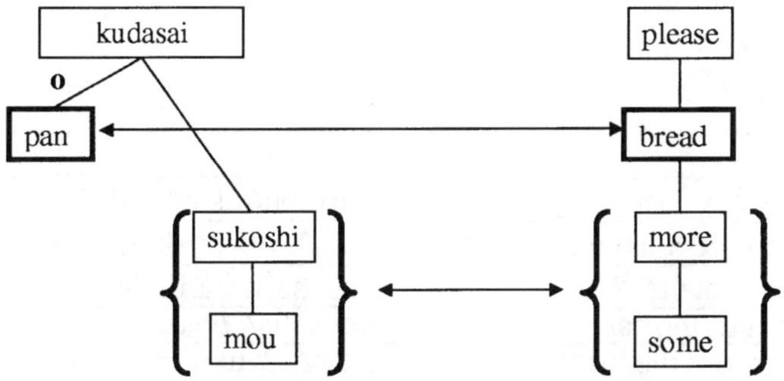

Figure 6.8. Quantifier float

Regarding the translations in (17b), in Japanese, quantifiers such as *sukoshi* float freely, unlike in English. Thus, the structure of such Japanese may be greatly varied as in Figure 6.8. If such an example exists in the corpus, D^3 translates it fluently.

In (17c), the subject of the Japanese sentence is elided. In Japanese, case elements such as subject and object are frequently elided, while many languages require such case elements to be expressed explicitly. In TDMT, a module recovers such ellipsis independently of the transfer module. In this case, such a combination of recovery and transfer fails to generate a coherent translation.

In (17d), this sentence is translated literally by TDMT, but the colloquial expression is generated by D^3. Finally, in (17e) the mistranslation comes from the mismatch of word selection for *sugure* and word selection for *kibun* in TDMT.

We freely admit that general-purpose architectures can be effective, and we do not mean to criticize them by this comparison. However, it is reasonable to suggest that general-purpose architectures are not the most suitable option for achieving high-quality translations.

3.3 Task

We are aiming at the development of a multilingual speech-to-speech translation system to be used in place of a phrasebook by foreign tourists. Phrasebooks are merely fixed lists of sentence translations. In contrast, we would like to provide an automatic translator for tourists. Table 6.4 shows some sample sentences from a Japanese-English phrasebook.

Table 6.4. Sample sentences in the phrasebook task

English	*Japanese*
I want to buy a roll of film.	fuirumu/o/kai/tai/desu
I'd like to reserve a table for eight.	8nin/bun/yoyaku/shitai/desu
Do you have some tea?	koucha/wa/ari/masu/ka
I'd like to return the car.	jidousha/o/kaeshi/tai/no/desuga
You need to cross the bridge to go there.	soko/ni/yuku/niwa/hashi/o/watara/ne /ba/nari/masen
My friend was hit by a car and badly injured.	yuujin/ga/kuruma/ni/hikare/ookega/o /shi/mashi/ta

Table 6.5. Comparison with other bilingual databases

	ATR/SLDB	ATR/phrasebook	Verbmobil
Sentences	16,110	204,108	58,332
Words	(J) 231,267 (E) 181,263	(J) 1,689,449 (E) 1,235,747	(G) 519,523 (E) 549,921
Vocabulary	(J) 4,895 (E) 4,032	(J) 19,640 (E) 15,374	(G) 7,940 (E) 4,673
Sentence Length	(J) 14.3 (E) 11.3	(J) 8.3 (E) 6.1	(G) 8.9 (E) 9.4

Table 6.5 compares our phrasebook corpus with two other spoken dialogue corpora developed by *ATR* and *VerbMobil*.[12] Our corpus has the shortest average sentence length. On the other hand, our phrasebook corpus is rich in topics and thus has the largest vocabulary. We plan to migrate from phrasebook task to tasks that include longer or more complex sentences in the near future.

[12] J stands for Japanese, E for English and G for German.

3.4 Limitations

D^3 has the following limitations.

- **Database limitation**: If a *nearest neighbor* within the threshold does not exist in the example database, we cannot produce a translation, as in the case with many other EBMT systems. One positive note is that we were able to build the necessary example database for the phrasebook task, which is far from a toy task, and D^3 covers 90% of the input strings.

- **Context limitation**: We cannot translate words which are context-dependent because contexts are often hard to embed in an example database, in the same way that state-of-the-art MT systems cannot deal with context-dependency. For example, the Japanese *konnichiwa* corresponds to *Good morning* or *Good afternoon* in English depending on the time of utterance. It is generally difficult to embed situational information into the example database.

- **Implementation limitation**: We have no method for dividing an input into chunks (such as clauses) at present, so long sentences cannot be successfully handled.

3.5 Development Cost and Its Reduction in the Future

We do not need grammars and transfer rules but we do need a bilingual corpus and lexical resources.

The applicability of D^3 to multilingual translation is promising. Because we have already succeeded in J-to-E, one of the most difficult translation pairs, we have little concern about other pairs. If we can create an n-lingual corpus, we can construct $n(n-1)$ MT systems.

To enable such a desideratum within a shorter timeframe, we have to reduce the necessary resources such as bilingual dictionaries and thesauri by automating the construction of lexical knowledge (cf. Manning & Schütze, 1999, chapter 8). We are aiming at such a cost reduction. We also want to eliminate restrictions, such as the need for sentence-aligned and morphologically tagged example databases (cf. Manning & Schütze, 1999, chapter 13). In so doing, the applicability of D^3 can be increased. A further challenging goal is to establish technology enabling the use of smaller scale corpora.

3.6 Related Research in EBMT and Phrasebook Task

Here we compare D^3 and related research under four headings: level of knowledge, application of dynamic programming, the use of thesauri, and the task.

3.6.1 Knowledge. Many studies in EBMT (e.g. Sato, 1991) assume the existence of *a bank of phrase-aligned bilingual trees* or *a set of translation patterns*. However, human construction of such knowledge banks is quite expensive. Methods for automating knowledge-building are under rapid development (Part III and IV, this volume). In contrast, D^3 does not rely on such a high-level analysis of the corpus and requires only word-level knowledge, i.e. morphological tags and dictionaries. The technology of morphological analysis has been well developed, and highly accurate programs are available for some languages. Furthermore, many dictionaries are now available on-line. Consequently, the availability of necessary resources for D^3 is greater than for other research projects.

3.6.2 Dynamic programming. Dynamic programming has been used within the EBMT paradigm for technical term translation (Sato, 1993) and for translation support (Cranias *et al.*, 1997).

Sato translates technical terms, which are usually compound nouns, while we translate sentences. He uses a corpus in which translation units of a pair of technical terms are aligned, while we do not require the alignment of translation units. He defines the matching score and we define the distance between word sequences, which are different metrics. However, both are computed by a standard dynamic programming technique.

Based on the surface structures and content words, Cranias *et al.* defined a similarity score between texts and introduced the idea of clustering the translation memory to speed up the retrieval of similar translation examples. The score is again computed by a standard dynamic programming technique, but the system of Cranias *et al.* does not provide a translation, since it is concerned only with the retrieval task.

3.6.3 Thesaurus. Brown (Chapter 10, this volume) uses *equivalence classes* to successfully improve the coverage of EBMT. He proposes a method of automatically generating equivalence classes using clustering techniques, while we use hand-coded thesauri (in the experiment). Such automation is attractive, and the author is planning to follow the approach of Brown, despite the concern that low frequency words will not be dealt with effectively by clustering techniques. Brown uses a hard condition, namely whether a word is included in an equivalence class or not, while we provide the relative distance between two words. It is not yet known which method is better for EBMT. We do not plan on sticking with the current implementation using hand-coded thesauri to the exclusion of other approaches, as we realize that further research on these open problems is indispensable.

3.6.4 Task. The phrasebook task was first advocated for the task of speech translation by Stentiford & Steer, 1987. They pointed out that when communicating within a limited domain such as *international telephone communications*, it is possible to specify nearly all of the required message concepts.

They used a *keyword-based approach* to access concepts that can overcome speech recognition errors. On the other hand, we use *DP-matching techniques* for this end. The scalability of the keyword-based approach has raised questions because enlarging a corpus directly increases the chances of conflict in identifying the concepts to be conveyed.

4. Concluding Remarks

We proposed D^3, a new approach using DP-matching for retrieving examples within the EBMT paradigm and demonstrated its high coverage and accuracy through a computational experiment in a limited domain.

The characteristics of D^3 are different from previous EBMT studies:

- It does not assume syntactic parsing and bilingual treebanks;
- It generates translation patterns on the fly when they are needed, depending on the input and the retrieved translation examples.

There are many ways in which our translation method can be further improved:

- D^3 does not cover longer sentences. We plan to incorporate the chunking of input strings and translation examples using a phrase alignment procedure such as Imamura, 2001. This will allow retrieval on a chunk-by-chunk basis, which will improve coverage.
- Techniques developed in information retrieval research such as indexing and clustering (cf. Cranias *et al.*, 1997), which will dramatically improve the efficiency of the current naïve implementation.

- We have to reduce the required resources such as bilingual dictionaries and thesauri by automating the construction of lexical knowledge (cf. Manning & Schütze, 1999, chapter 8). We are aiming at such a cost reduction, which will broaden the applicability of D^3.

Acknowledgments

First, the author's heartfelt thanks go to Kadokawa-Shoten for providing the Ruigo-Shin-Jiten. Thanks also go to Dr. Seiichi Yamamoto, Director, and Mr. Satoshi Shirai, Department Head of *ATR* Spoken Language Translation Laboratories, for providing the author with the chance to pursue this research. The research reported here was supported in part by a contract with the Telecommunications Advancement Organization of Japan entitled "A study of speech dialogue translation technology based on a large corpus".

References

Cormen, H.T., C.E. Leiserson and L.R. Rivest. 1989. *Introduction to Algorithms.* MIT Press, Cambridge, MA.

Cranias, L., H. Papageorgiou and S. Piperidis. 1997. Example-retrieval from a translation memory. *Natural Language Engineering* **15**(3):255–277.

Imamura, K. 2001. Hierarchical Phrase Alignment Harmonized with Parsing. In *Proceedings of the 6th Conference on Natural Language Processing Pacific Rim Symposium*, Tokyo, Japan, pp.377–384.

Manning, D., C. and H. Schütze. 1999. *Foundations of Statistical Natural Language Processing.* MIT Press, Cambridge, MA.

Maruyama, N. 1998. Hanashi-kotoba no shosou. In S. Doshita, Y. Niimi, S. Shirai, H. Tanaka and R. Mizoguchi (eds.) *Onsei-niyoru ningen to kikai no taiwa*, Ohmsha, pp.119–132. (in Japanese).

Ohno, S. and M. Hamanishi. 1984. Ruigo-Shin-Jiten. In Kadokawa, p.932 (in Japanese).

Sato, S. 1991. *MBT2*: A Method for Combining Fragments of Examples in Example-Based Translation. *Journal of the Japanese Society for Artificial Intelligence* **15**(6):861–871 (in Japanese).

Sato, S. 1993. Example-Based Translation of Technical Terms. In *Proceedings of the Fifth International Conference on Theoretical and Methodological Issues in Machine Translation TMI '93: MT in the Next Generation*, Kyoto, Japan, pp.58–68.

Stentiford, F.W.M. and M.G. Steer. 1987. A Speech Driven Language Translation System. In *Proceedings of European Conference on Speech Technology* **15**(2):418–421.

Sumita, E. and H.Iida. 1991. Experiments and Prospects of Example-Based Machine Translation. In *29th Annual Meeting of the Association for Computational Linguistics*, Berkeley, CA., pp.185–192.

Sumita, E., S. Yamada, K. Yamamoto, M. Paul, H. Kashioka, K. Ishikawa. and S. Shirai. 1999. Solutions to Problems Inherent in Spoken-language Translation: The ATR-MATRIX Approach. In *Machine Translation Summit VII*, Singapore, pp.229–235.

Chapter 7

A HYBRID RULE AND EXAMPLE-BASED METHOD FOR MACHINE TRANSLATION

Francis Bond
bond@cslab.kecl.ntt.co.jp

Satoshi Shirai
sat@fw.ipsj.or.jp

Abstract This paper introduces a new example-based method of machine translation in which the examples need not be direct translations. The system will weed out strange examples during translation, allowing the use of currently available sentence-aligned corpora as data. Rule-based modules are used where appropriate. A prototype Japanese-to-English system has been implemented that allows multiple users to share corpora.

Keywords: hybrid machine translation, template-guided translation, adaptation-guided retrieval

1. Introduction

Methods for machine translation can be generally classified as rule-based, example-based or statistical, and each has numerous problems which remain unsolved. Especially in Japanese-to-English translation, due to the difference in language families, current methods are far from providing satisfactory results (Narita, 1996).

EBMT, as introduced by (Nagao, 1984) assumes the existence of an aligned corpus with examples that align on a strict 1-to-1 basis as well as on appropriate tag information showing the correspondence between words and phrases (Sadler, 1989:117). However, cases of direct translation equivalents are limited in number and assessments of similarity

M. Carl and A. Way (eds.), Recent Advances in Example-Based Machine Translation, 211–224.

using a thesaurus are rarely reliable. Somers, 1999 (cf. Chapter 1, this volume) claims that parallel aligned corpora are quite easy to come by. We have not found this to be the case for Japanese and English. Even where corpora do exist for one domain, they are rarely useful in another domain; data-driven approaches may scale well, but are not portable to new domains without new data. If example-based translation systems need to have well-aligned corpora of very similar text, then they will only ever be a slight extension of translation memory, very useful for tasks such as upgrading manuals, where much of the text is reused, but not generally useful.

We found that while it was possible to produce reasonably sized aligned corpora, by, for example, aligning newspaper articles, the translations were not very direct.

Even if it were possible to secure a large volume of corresponding example sentences, the task of tagging them in a uniform and accurate manner is difficult. For example, Kaji *et al.*, 1992 make a set of templates with variable expressions from their corpus, before using it. These templates can only be as accurate as the parsers used to prepare them, and must be remade every time the parsers change. Strictly speaking, we consider systems such as those of Kaji *et al.* or Watanabe *et al.* (Chapter 14, this volume) to be rule-based, rather than example-based: it just so happens that the rules are learned from a corpus.

Cranias *et al.*, 1995 propose a matching method based on differences between function and content words. It relies crucially, however, on segmenting sentences into coherent segments and alignment at the subsentential level, both processes that are hard to automate.

Multi-engine systems use both the rule and example-based methods and then choose one of the translations. These systems take over all of the strengths and weaknesses of each method and add the fresh problem of how to decide which output to use.

Brown, 1996 is an example of an example-based system run in parallel with a rule-based (knowledge-based) system as part of the *Pangloss* system. It only translates sequences of connected words, and so fails to give one of the expected benefits of an example-based system, the production of sentences with coherent structure. Its main strength seems to be in the fact that it is easy to adapt to new languages.

This paper will attempt to make use of the strengths of both the rule and example-based methods to suggest a form of machine translation that can be built with existing technologies: Hybrid Machine Translation. It was first introduced in Shirai *et al.*, 1997 and Takahashi *et al.*, 1997.

2. A Hybrid Translation Method

The following hybrid design is an effort to produce a method that makes the most of the strengths of both rule and example-based methods and that will compensate for their weaknesses. The strengths of the rule-based method lie in the fact that information can be obtained through introspection and analysis, while those of the example-based method are that correspondences can be found from raw data. The weakness of the rule-based method is that the accuracy of the entire process is the product of the accuracies of each sub-stage. The weakness of the example-based method is the difficulty of finding appropriate examples, and the problems of adapting them.

The basic outline of our algorithm is as follows:

1 Select a set of candidate sentences which are similar to the input sentence (§7.2.2);

2 Select the most typical translation out of those corresponding to the candidates (§7.2.3);

3 Use this translation and its source as templates to translate the input sentence (§7.2.4).

The major innovation of this algorithm is in step two. Instead of simply choosing the source-target pair whose source sentence best matches the input sentence, a pair is chosen which both matches the input sentence and has a translation similar to other examples. By discarding candidates with atypical translations, the algorithm filters out free, incorrect or context-dependent translations. It is thus a kind of **adaptation-guided retrieval**, to use the case-based reasoning terminology (see Collins and Somers, Chapter 4, this volume). This means that the input corpus does not have to consist of good, context-independent sentence pairs to be useful. The only requirement is that there be *enough* translations to be able to find a typical translation.

A variety of methods could be used to determine similarity in step one, to select the most typical translation in step two, and to finally translate the sentence in step three. The methods currently being used in our system are described in the following subsections, after a brief discussion of the construction of the corpus.

We use various rule-based modules in our system, but the critical transfer stage is based on translation templates taken from an aligned corpus based on their similarity to the input sentence. It is thus an EBMT system in the sense of Turcato and Popowich (Chapter 2, this volume) as it "uses knowledge that can only be dynamically acquired at run-time by accessing an entire corpus, or sections of which whose extent cannot be determined in advance."(Chapter 2.2.1, page 64, this volume)

As all processing is done during the translation process, improvements in any of the modules will not require the entire corpus to be re-parsed.

A more detailed outline is given in Figure 7.1.

For each input sentence: S_I

1 Find candidate sentences $\{S_i$: S_i is similar to $S_I\}$ (§7.2.2)

   If there are none, translate using rule-based system to give T_I, goto step 4.

2 Select the template: S_t (§7.2.3)

   (a) Rank the candidates, S_i, by similarity to the input sentence

   (b) Cluster the translations, T_i, of the candidate sentences

   (c) Select the highest ranked pair of the best cluster (S_t, T_t)

3 Translate S_I by analogy to S_t (§7.2.4)

   For each difference d_i between input S_I and selection S_t

   (a) Find the corresponding section t_i of the selected translation T_t

   (b) Replace t_i with the translation of d_i, translated using the rule-based modules

   Adjust for number agreement and so forth

4 Output the adjusted sentence T_I

Figure 7.1. An outline of the hybrid algorithm

A practical example-based system requires a large volume of suitable data. In the case of our hybrid algorithm, for the corpus to be suitable it need only consist of sentences that are loosely aligned, not necessarily exact translations. We discuss the creation of the corpus in the next section.

2.1 Creating and Indexing a Corpus

The accuracy of an EBMT system will depend greatly on the nature of the corpus it uses. The increasingly widespread use of translation memories is beginning to create large well-aligned corpora. However, these are still comparatively rare. Much bilingual data is only loosely aligned. We feel that the utility of EBMT systems cannot be assessed without an explicit description of (1) the kind of data they are designed to handle; and (2) how sufficient quantities of that data can be obtained.

A large volume of newspaper data is currently available, for example, the *Nihon Keizai Shinbun* (a Japanese financial newspaper), much of it on CD-ROM. From Japanese publishers, there is much more Japanese data than English. Considering stock-market reports alone, we estimate that there are 1,000,000 Japanese sentences (35 characters on average) and 150,000 English sentences (13 words on average) of newspaper reports each year. The Japanese and English articles are normally not direct translations of each other, but for around half of the English sentences there are Japanese sentences that are close to being literal translations (Shirai *et al.*, 1995). The aligned sentence pairs are thus, to some extent, translation equivalents. Ideally they are sentences with equivalent meanings in the two languages; in reality many of them only contain sub-sections with equivalent meanings. For use in an EBMT system, it is not important which was originally the source and which the translation.

As our algorithm weeds out unsuitable sentences during translation, we focus on recall rather than precision when aligning our sentences, which can thus be done entirely automatically. First we align the newspaper articles, using numerical expressions and proper nouns as anchors, following the method outlined in Takahashi *et al.*, 1997. Then we align sentences within the aligned articles. We accept as aligned sentences, any sentence pair that contains even a small amount of equivalent text, so sentence level alignment can also be done automatically. Currently we adopt a method that uses both statistical and dictionary information (Haruno & Yamazaki, 1996), but any method could be used.

We have tagged the data with SGML tags, using the TEI P3 document type definition, Sperberg-McQueen & Burnard, 1994. We do not tag any elements smaller than sentences as our algorithm does not require a corpus tagged with details of the internal structure.

Each article and each sentence in the article has a unique ID. The Japanese and English data are stored in separate files. A separate file contains links showing the correspondences between the two languages.

The format is similar to that used in the **Lingua** Project (Bonhomme & Romary, 1995). As the links are in a separate file, they can easily be replaced as better alignment algorithms appear and are used.

In addition, an index of all n-grams ($n \geq 2$) that appear more than once in the Japanese data has been prepared. It is used for finding similar sentences. The n-grams are found using the method outlined in Ikehara *et al.*, 1996, which eliminates any n-grams that appear only as substrings of larger n-grams. For a language such as English, which is separated into words by default, a word index (preferably lemmatized), could also be used. We indexed the n-grams using a variety of trie index, for fast and efficient searching (Aoe *et al.*, 1992). Because indexing must be done over the entire corpus, it is essential that it is both fast and scalable.

The indexing is character-based, not word-based, so does not require any morphological analysis, unlike the method suggested by Planas & Furuse (Chapter 5, this volume). Baldwin, 2001 has shown that for Japanese at least, simple character-based indexing is superior to word-based indexing. However, like Planas, our indexing is only an initial step and is designed to give us multiple candidates. We then further filter the results, as outlined in Section 7.2.3.

We end up with the following data:

- Source Sentences S^i
- Target Sentences T^j
- links l_{i-j} (not all sentences have links)
- trie index (of all n-grams that appeared more than once in the source sentences)

To add new data to the collection, it must be aligned, then the whole collection re-indexed.

2.2 Finding Candidate Sentence Pairs

In order to translate an input sentence S_I, we first look for similar source-language sentences. To do this we extract all indexed n-grams in the input sentence. These are then used as keys to retrieve all the sentences in the corpus that contain one or more of these n-grams. We select all of the extracted sentences which are linked to English equivalents as candidate sentences.

To show how our algorithm works, we have created examples assuming an unreasonably small corpus: in reality there would be more indexed n-grams. All input sentences are actually stored using EUC encoded Japanese characters, although we show only their transliterations in this paper. For example, consider the following input sentence S_I which contains the following indexed n-grams: **nikkei, heikin, gatsu-mono-wa-zokuraku, wa-zokuraku.**

S_I	nikkei	heikin	10	gatsu	mono	wa	zokuraku	.
	Nikkei	average	10	month	thing	TOP	continue-decline	.

The Nikkei Average October contracts continued declining.

For the sake of explaining our method, we will assume it only matched the following three sentences (matching n-grams marked in bold):

S_1	**nikkei**	**heikin**	9	**gatsu**	**mono**	**wa**	**zokuraku**	.
	Nikkei	average	9	month	thing	TOP	continue-decline	.

The Nikkei Average September contracts were lower.

S_2	**nikkei**	tentoo	**heikin**	**wa**	**zokuraku**	.
	Nikkei	over-the-counter	average	TOP	continue-decline	.

The Nikkei over-the-counter average continued declining

S_3	8	**gatsu**	**mono**	**wa**	**zokuraku**	.
	8	month	thing	TOP	continue-decline	.

August contracts continued declining.

If there are no candidate sentences, the example-based part of the hybrid design method is unable to function and the sentence is translated using a rule-based translation system.

2.3 Selecting the Template

All of the matching methods in the selection step are applied to a reasonably small set of sentences returned from the indexing process. We do not use any more sophisticated analysis than a segmenter.

2.3.1 Ranking the Candidate Sentences. The input sentences and all the candidates are segmented using a morphological analyzer (the same as used by the rule-based Japanese-to-English machine translation system **ALT-J/E** (Ikehara *et al.*, 1991)).

The sentences are ranked using the similarity metric given below. The result is an ordered set of candidate sentences and their translation equivalents $S_1, \ldots S_n$. The higher ranked a sentence is, the more similar it is to the input sentence.

At this stage it would be possible to discard some lower-ranked sentences, in order to increase speed, either by discarding any with similarities below a certain threshold, or all those beyond a certain number. However, at present, speed has not been a problem, so we do not do this.

Definition of 'Similarity' The similarity metric is calculated with two components, one based on the order of shared segments (M_o), and one based only on their co-occurrence (M_c).

The two components are calculated as follows. First all segments of S_I are given a value from left to right, starting with 0, and increasing by one for each segment. Then all segments in S_i that also occur in S_I are given the same values, but differing segments are given a very high value (such as 99).

M_o and M_c are defined as follows (bubble sort values given when compared to S_I):

$$M_o(S_I, S_i) = \frac{no.\ of\ swaps\ to\ bubble\ sort\ S_i}{no.\ of\ swaps\ to\ reverse\ S_i} \tag{7.1}$$

$$M_c(S_I, S_i) = \frac{number\ of\ shared\ segments}{number\ of\ segments\ in\ S_i} \tag{7.2}$$

The combined similarity metric $M = (1 - M_o)M_c$. The first component $(1 - M_o)$ penalizes changes in order, while M_c penalizes non-matching segments. We take the final similarity as the average of $M(S_I, S_i)$ and $M(S_i, S_I)$. We make use of semantic information in our calculation.

For example, the above sentences are ranked as follows:

S_I	nikkei	heikin	10	gatsu	mono	wa	zokuraku	.
	0	1	2	3	4	5	6	7
S_1	nikkei	heikin	9	gatsu	mono	wa	zokuraku	.
	0	1	99	3	4	5	6	7
	($M(S_I, S_1) = 0.719$: 5 swaps, 7 shared segments)							

S_2	nikkei-tentoo-heikin	wa	zokuraku	.
	99	5	6	7
	($M(S_I, S_3) = 0.375$: 3 swaps, 3 shared segments)			

S_3	8	gatsu	mono	wa	zokuraku	.
	99	3	4	5	6	7
	($M(S_I, S_2) = 0.556$: 5 swaps, 5 shared segments)					

Note that *nikkei-tentoo-heikin* "the Nikkei over-the-counter average" appears as a single word in the user dictionary, and thus is analyzed as a single constituent. Therefore it does not match *nikkei* "Nikkei" or *heikin* "average", although it matched them using the initial n-gram index.

This method considers not only the number of matching characters and the number of continuous matching characters, as in Sato, 1992, but also the number of non-matching characters found in the candidates.

Because our morphological analyzer also gives POS and sense, as well as chunking the strings into phrases, we are currently investigating ways of using this additional information, for example, by comparing the number and order of case-marked noun phrases and comparing senses. However, our method is designed to work with a large corpus, so a simple fast algorithm is to be preferred.

Recently there has been a lot of work on matching similar strings for translation memories and EBMT. Baldwin, 2001 has shown that simple character-based matching does well for finding translation memory matches. Ikeda *et al.*, 2000 have proposed a matching method based on dynamic programming, which appears to give good results. Our system could switch to either of these methods without changing the overall algorithm.

2.3.2 Finding the Best Cluster. The next step is to cluster the translation equivalents $\{T_i\}$ of the candidate sentences $\{S_i\}$ into groups of similar sentences. This is done in order to find translations that are reasonably direct. In other words, we are looking for candidates that are **adaptable** (Somers, 1999, cf. Chapter 1, this volume). As all the candidate sentences are similar to the input sentence, we expect that direct translations will also be similar to each other.

We cluster the translations as follows:

1 Determine the frequency of all words in the set of translation equivalents $\{T_i\}$, ignoring any words that are in a set of stop words (mainly function words such as articles, auxiliary verbs and prepositions).

2 If there is one most common word, then the best cluster is the set of sentences that include it. Otherwise, the best cluster is the set of those with the maximum number of the most common words.

For example (frequencies given as subscripts; stop words have no subscripts):

T_1 The Nikkei_2 Average_1 September_1 contracts_2 were lower_1

T_2 August_1 contracts_2 continued_2 declining_2

T_3 The Nikkei_2 $\text{over-the-counter}_1$ average_1 continued_2 declining_2

In this case the best cluster has two members T_2 and T_3.

2.3.3 Selecting the Sentence with the most Typical Translation. The sentence pair to be used in the actual translation is the sentence pair (candidate sentence + translation equivalent) in the best cluster that has the highest similarity to the input sentence (in our example (S_2, T_2)). We call the two sentences the source template (S_t) and the target template (T_t). This sentence pair ideally (if the corpus is large enough to produce a choice of candidates) has the following properties: (1) the source template resembles the input sentence, (2) the translation template is a reasonably direct translation of the source template. This makes the sentence pair a suitable template for example-based translation by analogy.

2.4 Translating the Input using the Template as Guide

The differing sections of the input sentence and the source template are identified. Translations of these different sections in the input sentence are produced by rule-based methods and these translated sections are fitted into the translation sentence in the template. The resulting sentence is then smoothed over, by checking for agreement and inflection mismatches.

The resulting translation has the overall structure provided by the example-based template, with only individual words or phrases translated by the rule-based system. In general, rule-based systems give better results for small segments, so this gives the best of both worlds.

The input sentence and selected template are:

S_I nikkei heikin 10 gatsu mono wa zokuraku .

S_t 8 gatsu mono wa zokuraku .

T_t August contracts continued declining .

2.4.1 Finding the Differences. In order to find any differences, both the input sentence and source template are parsed, and their parses are compared. Because the sentences are similar, even if there are errors in the parse, they are likely to be *the same errors* in both sentences. Therefore the errors will have little effect on finding the differences. In this way, the algorithm will work even with imperfect parsers. We consider this one of the major strengths of our system. This is the only part of the process that requires parsing, and it is tolerant of errors, so there is no need for structural tagging in the corpus.

In this case the difference is between *nikkei heikin 10* and *8*. The parsing process however shows that *nikkei heikin 10 gatsu mono* is all one noun phrase, and so matches it with *8 gatsu mono* "August contracts"

2.4.2 Replacing the Differences. The rule-based translation of the source template is compared with the target template. Those parts of the template that correspond to the differing sections are replaced by their translations.

nikkei heikin 10 gatsu mono is translated as "The Nikkei Average October contracts", by the rule-based noun phrase translation system, which gives good results for small segments. This is slotted into T_t giving the following:

T_I The Nikkei Average October contracts continued declining.

2.4.3 Smoothing the Output. A rough surface analysis of the output sentence is used to check for boundary friction problems, such as person and number agreement.

At present we have no mechanism for identifying and deleting extraneous elements in the example-based translation, such as temporal adverbs. This is one of the major sources of errors in our system. One possible solution would be to add a filter to identify and delete such terms. As the size of our corpus increases, the step where we select the most typical translation will become more effective in filtering out candidate templates with extraneous material. Alternatively one could try to clean the corpus, as suggested by Sumita (Chapter 6, this volume), but we would like to avoid this, as material could be extraneous for one input, but necessary for another.

In their Shallow Translation, Planas & Furuse (Chapter 5, this volume) avoid this problem by only choosing candidate sentences that have more information in them than the input sentence, but then deleting all elements that are not aligned in some way. This strategy should work for extremely similar sentences. It would be more robust if there were some way of also aligning multiword expressions: for example *can* ≡ *be able to*.

2.5 System Architecture

The features of the system as it is implemented are listed below:

- The system operates as a multi-user client/server network. The server runs on UNIX and the clients on Windows-NT.
- Because the corpora are unparsed aligned sentences, users can combine their own aligned corpora with the system's, and share them amongst themselves.
- The rule-based components and dictionaries are taken from **ALT-J/E**.

The prototype was tested translating from Japanese to English, with a corpus of 5,000 sentences. It allows users to take advantage of any aligned text they may already have by adding it to the set of sentences searched by the system.

In the future, we plan to improve the individual modules in the system, in particular the similarity measure and output smoother.

3. Conclusion

The merits of using examples are: translations of expressions which are idiomatic, literal or domain dependent can all be put to use; and the system should be reversible, that is it can translate in either direction. Previously, many example-based systems assumed the existence of large word- or phrase-aligned corpora. To date, we know of no large-scale corpora accurately aligned below the sentence level. For an example-based system to be useful in the foreseeable future, it has to be able to accept loosely aligned corpora, not aligned at low levels. We have suggested a design for a system that can use such loosely aligned texts.

Acknowledgments

We would like to thank Satoru Ikehara, Yamato Takahashi, Takayuki Adachi, Toshiaki Tanabe, Masatoshi Tachibana, Hiroko Inoue, Makiko Nishigaki, Hiromi Ueda, Emmanuel Planas and Timothy Baldwin for their help and advice.

References

Aoe, J., K. Morimoto and T. Sato. 1992. An efficient implementation of trie structures. *Software Practice & Experience* **22**(9):695–721.

Baldwin, T. 2001. Low-cost, high-performance translation retrieval: Dumber is better. In *39th Annual Meeting of the Association of Com-*

putational Linguistics and 10th Conference of the European Chapter, Toulouse, France, pp.18–25.

Bonhomme, P. and L. Romary. 1995. The Lingua Parallel concordancing project: Managing multilingual texts for educational purpose. In *IA-95: Proceedings of the Fifth International Conference*, Montpellier, France.

Brown, R.D. 1996. Example-based machine translation in the Pangloss system. In *COLING-96: Proceedings of the 16th International Conference on Computational Linguistics*, Copenhagen, Denmark, pp.169–174.

Cranias, L., H. Papageorgiou and S. Piperidis. 1995. A matching technique in example-based machine translation. `http://xxx.lanl.gov/abs/cmp-lg/9508005`.

Haruno, M. and T. Yamazaki. 1996. High-performance bilingual text alignment using statistical and dictionary information. In *34th Annual Conference of the Association for Computational Linguistics*, Santa Cruz, CA., pp.131–138.

Ikeda, N., H. Uchino and O. Furuse. 2000. Yōrē-riyō-gata honyaku-no tame-no ruiji yōrē kensaku hōhō [a method to retrieve similar examples for example-based machine translation]. In *6th Annual Meeting of the Association for Natural Language Processing*, pp.43–46, JAIST, Japan. (in Japanese).

Ikehara, S., S. Shirai and H. Uchino. 1996. A statistical method for extracting uninterrrupted and interrupted collocations from very large corpora. In *COLING-96: Proceedings of the 16th International Conference on Computational Linguistics*, Copenhagen, Denmark, pp.574–579.

Ikehara, S., S. Shirai, A. Yokoo and H. Nakaiwa. 1991. Toward an MT system without pre-editing—effects of new methods in **ALT-J/E**. In *Machine Translation Summit III*, Washington DC., pp.101–106. `http://xxx.lanl.gov/abs/cmp-lg/9510008`.

Kaji, H., Y. Kida and Y. Morimoto. 1992. Learning translation templates from bilingual text. In *Proceedings of the fifteenth [sic] International Conference on Computational Linguistics, COLING-92*, Nantes, France, pp.672–678.

Nagao, M. 1984. A Framework of a Mechanical Translation between Japanese and English by Analogy Principle. In A. Elithorn and R Banerji (eds.) *Artificial and Human Intelligence*, Amsterdam: North-Holland, pp.173–180.

Narita, H. 1996. Language type and machine translation. *IPSJ SIG Notes 96-NL-114-21*, **96**(65):143–150. (in Japanese).

Sadler, V. 1989. *Working with Analogical Semantics: Disambiguation techniques in DLT*. FORIS Publications, Dordrecht, The Netherlands.

Sato, S. 1992. CTM: An example based translation aid system. In *Proceedings of the fifteenth [sic] International Conference on Computational Linguistics, COLING-92*, Nantes, France, pp.1259–1263.

Shirai, S., F. Bond and Y. Takahashi. 1997. A hybrid rule and example based method for machine translation. In *NLPRS-97: Proceedings of the Natural Language Processing Pacific Rim Symposium*, Phuket, Thailand, pp.49–54.

Shirai, S., M. Matsuo, T. Seshimo, S. Fujinami and S. Ikehara. 1995. Constructing an aligned Japanese/English corpus of newspaper articles (3) — peculiarities of the articles and sentence alignment. In *Record of the 1995 Joint Conference of Electrical and Electronics Engineers in Kyushu*, p.857. (in Japanese).

Somers, H. 1999. Review Article: Example-based Machine Translation. *Machine Translation* **14**(2):113–157 (see also Chapter 1, this volume).

Sperberg-McQueen, C.M. and L. Burnard. (eds.) 1994. *Guidelines for Electronic Text Encoding and Interchange*. Chicago, Oxford.

Takahashi, Y., S. Shirai, M. Tachibana, M. Nishigaki and S. Ikehara. 1997. Yōrē-riyō-gata nichiē kikai honyaku-no kihon sekkē [Basic Specifications for Japanese-to-English Example Based Machine Translation]. In *Proceedings of the 3rd Annual Meeting of the Association for Natural Language Processing* (in Japanese), Kyoto, Japan, pp.145–148.

Takahashi, Y., S. Shirai and F. Bond. 1997. A method of automatically aligning Japanese and English newspaper articles. In *NLPRS-97: Proceedings of the Natural Language Processing Pacific Rim Symposium*, Phuket, Thailand, pp.657–660.

Chapter 8

EBMT OF POS-TAGGED SENTENCES BY RECURSIVE DIVISION VIA INDUCTIVE LEARNING

Tantely Andriamanankasina
tantely@mx10.freecom.ne.jp

Kenji Araki
araki@media.eng.hokudai.ac.jp

Koji Tochinai
tochinai@media.eng.hokudai.ac.jp

Abstract We present an Example-Based Machine Translation approach which recursively divides the sentence to be translated, and translates each part separately. The sentence is divided according to the structure of similar examples extracted during the matching process. The approach is especially intended for languages where resources and tools are pretty much unavailable. POS taggers are the only tools utilized, and the bilingual corpus the only resource employed. In addition, the translation system contains an analogy-based sub-sentential alignment module, which predicts word correspondences between new pairs of sentences. This module causes the corpus to grow because new examples can be appended automatically. Consequently, a relatively small initial corpus is sufficient for the translation system to start. The approach has been tested on a French–Japanese corpus of spoken language and produced promising results worthy of further investigation.

Keywords: translation by recursive devision, similarity-based translation, analogy-based sub-sentential alignment

M. Carl and A. Way (eds.), Recent Advances in Example-Based Machine Translation, 225–252.

1. Introduction

Translating long sentences is one of the problems in EBMT. Long sentences can be only be translated when the input sentence is almost covered by the matching sentence. However, when such examples cannot be discovered, it is hard to translate these sentences correctly. Even for relatively short sentences, there are cases where uncovered segments cause errors. Furthermore, there are likely to be errors from mismatches appearing during the matching process. We have solved these problems by a so-called "recursive-division" translation method, which successively divides the sentence to be translated, and translates each part independently. The system predicts the position where the input sentence or a segment of the input sentence should be divided according to the links existing between the source sentence and the target sentence of the extracted translation example. This method requires a specific matching method which is almost a partial matching one, but also tries to maintain the structure of the sentence to be translated.

On the other hand, the method requires a link-included bilingual corpus. Links are word-to-word correspondences between a source sentence and a target sentence. They are especially necessary to extract translation patterns from translation examples. For example, consider the French input sentence "**je suis heureux** (I am happy)", and suppose that the sentence "**je suis malade** (I am ill)" is the best match. Its Japanese translation is "*watashi ha byouki desu*"[1]. If the link between "**malade**" and "*byouki*" can be identified, the translation result, which is "*watashi ha shiawase desu*", will easily be obtained by replacing "*byouki*" by the translation of "**heureux**", which is "*shiawase*", in the translation of the best match.

Current methods for such alignment of parallel text at word level are all based on statistics (Brown *et al.*, 1993; Melamed, 1997; Kitamura & Matsumoto, 1997). Statistical methods are not able to produce reliable results with small corpora. Furthermore, predicting links involving multiple tokens or links of a token appearing more than once in a sentence has not entirely been resolved. To solve these problems, we have proposed an analogy-based word level alignment method using a link-included set of initial translation examples (Andriamanankasina *et al.*, 1999). Experiments confirmed that with 2,400 translation examples, more than 80% of the links are extracted with a rate of accuracy of

[1]French words are presented in boldface characters, with Japanese words presented in italics.

90%. This alignment method was introduced in the translation system to predict links of new examples. This makes the translation system able to use new examples. An evaluation of the application of this alignment method in the translation system is also presented in this chapter, in addition to the description of the translation method itself.

The rest of the chapter is organized as follows. In the next section, an overview of the translation system is presented. The translation process and the structure of the bilingual corpus are then described. In section 3, the ideas behind the translation method are briefly described. In section 4, the extraction of examples (the matching process) is presented. It is divided into four parts: a description of a number of conditions required by the method, the presentation of the matching algorithm, the similarity score together with a brief discussion of other matching methods. In section 5, "Production of translation results", we describe the recursive-division approach, which is the core of the translation process. In section 6, "Predicting links of new pairs", the learning module is described. The search for similar pairs to be used in the link prediction, the prediction method itself, and the selection of correct links among the output candidates are all described. Finally, in section 7 we provide a summary together with possible future research directions.

2. Overview of the Translation System

The translation process can be divided into three steps (Figure 8.1). First, a number of sentence pairs are extracted from the translation examples, whose source sentences have similarities with the input sentence. Next, the recursive-division procedure, which is the core of the translation process, is applied to the input sentence, according to the structure of these extracted examples, and a translation result is produced. The user now checks the output of the translation: if it is not correct, he is asked to enter the correct translation result. Finally, the system predicts the links or word correspondences between the input sentence and the correct translation result, according to similar sentence pairs, which exist in the corpus. The link-included new translation example is appended to the corpus.

The extraction and use of similar examples from the system database characterizes any EBMT system. Apart from the recursive-division approach itself, the utilization of new examples is particular to EBMT. It makes the corpus grow dynamically. That is why a system which prompts the user for the correct translation when the result is wrong, as well as one which can automatically predict links of new examples, is

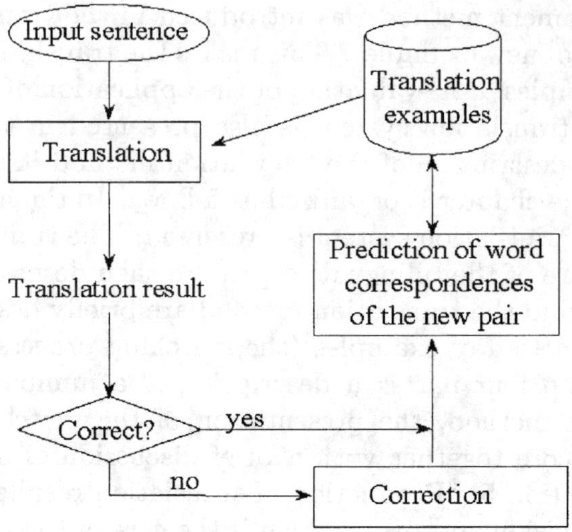

Figure 8.1. Overview of the translation system

preferred. The prediction of links is necessary as these are required in the corpus. It is also important to note that the new pair of sentences must be POS-tagged prior to the link prediction process as this is the format the system requires.

2.1 Structure of a Translation Example

Table 8.1. Structure of a translation example

French Sentence	**je**/PRV **suis**/ECJ **sans**/PREP **profession**/SBC
Japanese Sentence	*musyoku*/6 *desu*/4
Links	2/2 3,4/1

PRV: pronoun, PREP: preposition, SBC: common noun, ECJ: verb "être"
6: noun, 4: assertive

An entry in the bilingual corpus is presented in Table 8.1. It comprises:

1 the French source sentence,

2 its Japanese translation, and

3 a mapping describing links between words in both sentences.

Table 8.2. French POS tag list

Abbrev.	Tag name	Example
ABR	Abbreviation	**p., ref. , chap.**
ADJ	Adjective	**beaux, troisième**
ADJPAR	Adjective (past participle)	**coiffées, détendues**
ADV	Adverb	**trop, simplement**
VNCNT	Verb (-ant) or gerund	**souffrant**
ANCNT	"**avoir**" (to have) (-ant)	**ayant**
ENCNT	"**être**" (to be) (-ant)	**étant**
CAR	Numeral (numbers or strings)	**vingt, 30**
COO	Coordinate conjunction	**et, or, mais, donc**
DTN	Determinant (nominal group)	**le, ces, son, un**
DTC	Composed determinant	**du, au, des, aux**
FGW	Foreign words	**petto, rauchen**
VNCFF	Verb (infinitive)	**conclure**
ANCFF	"**avoir**" (infinitive)	**avoir**
ENCFF	"**être**" (infinitive)	**être**
INJ	Interjection	**oui, non**
VPAR	Verb (past-participle)	**enflée, défilé**
APAR	"**avoir**" (past-participle)	**eu**
EPAR	"**être**" (past-participle)	**été**
PFX	Prefix (detached)	**entre, mi**
PREP	Preposition	**vers, de, dans**
PRV	Pronoun (supported by the verb)	**je, on, se, elles**
PRO	Other pronoun	**moi, celui, en, siens**
PUL	Particle	**tandis, parce, afin**
REL	Relative (Pronoun or Adverb)	**dont, lesquelles, qui**
SUB	Subordinate conjunction	**comme, lorsque**
SUB$	Subordinate conj. (special case)	**que**
SBC	Common noun	**panier, grèves**
SBP	Proper noun or title	**Maheu, Monsieur**
SYM	Symbol	**%, $**
VCJ	Verb (conjuguated)	**redressaient**
ACJ	"**avoir**" (conjuguated)	**avait**
ECJ	"**être**" (conjuguated)	**était**

A token is presented with the format "token/POS tag". For the tagging operation, the *EBTI* program from the Institut National de la Langue Française (INALF) was used for the French sentences and CHASEN1.51 (Yamashita, 1996) for the Japanese sentences. EBTI is an adaptation of the Eric Brill Tagger (Brill, 1993) for French. INALF has proposed a non-definitive list of 48 POS tags for French. There are 15 punctuation marks and special characters. The remaining 33 tags are described in Table 8.2.

Table 8.3. Japanese POS tag list

Abbrev.	Tag name	Example
SC	Special characters	*., !*
V	Verbs	*konasu*
A	Adjectives	*furui*
AS	Assertives	*da*
AUX	Auxiliaries	*darou*
N	Nouns	*kyou*
D	Demonstratives	*kono, kore*
AV	Adverbs	*yoku*
P	Particles	*wa, ni*
C	Conjunctions	*shikashi*
AD	Adnominals	*taishita*
I	Interjections	*hai*
PR	Prefixes	*go-*
S	Suffixes	*-tai*

As for the Japanese language, POS tags are hierarchically classified. We consider only the highest level, which consists of 14 POS tags. They are described in Table 8.3.

A link has the form "$Wf_1, Wf_2, \ldots / Wj_1, Wj_2, \ldots$". "$Wf_i$" are word positions in the French sentence and "Wj_i" word positions in the Japanese sentence. In the example in Table 8.1, "2/2" means that the token "**suis** (am)" corresponds to "*desu*". By the same way, "3,4/1" means that "**sans profession** (jobless)" corresponds to "*musyoku*". Words or segments of words having no correspondences are not specified.

The translation method requires links composed by contiguous words. For example, to align the phrase "**ne va pas** (does not go)" with "*iki masen*", the obvious way might be aligning "**ne pas** (do not)" with "*masen*" and "**va** (go)" with "*iki*". However, since "**ne pas**" is not a contiguous segment, only one link between "**ne va pas**" and "*ikimasen*" is considered. Although "**va**" alone cannot be translated, a contiguous segment map is obtained. This requirement does not raise problems since a mapping of non-contiguous segments can always be modified to a contiguous one, by combining segments.

Building these links for the initial corpus is not always straightforward. Statistical methods can be applied for large corpora but small ones must be aligned manually. Of course, the result of any automatic alignment should be checked manually to ensure that the proposed alignment is correct. It is also important to note that during a manual check of an alignment, even an expert may still face difficulties or hesitations on some cases. The person who checks the alignment result, or who does the manual alignment must endeavour to use the same alignment technique throughout the corpus.

3. The Translation Method

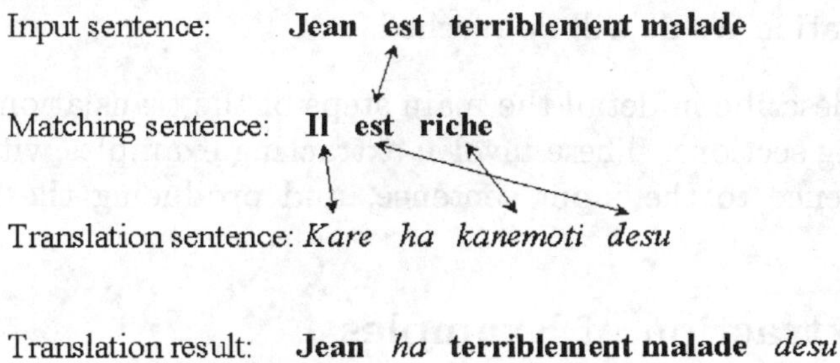

Figure 8.2. Illustration of the ideas behind the translation method

We now describe the ideas behind our translation method. A simple illustration is presented in Figure 8.2. The input sentence and matching sentence mean *Jean is seriously ill* and *He is rich*, respectively. A translation example having a source sentence matching the input sentence is extracted from the translation example. The input sentence is divided at the position of the word "**est**" (is), which is a common segment for both sentences. In the source sentence of the selected example, the segment "il" (he) is situated on the left of the common segment with "**riche**" (rich) on the right. If one observes their correspondences in the target sentence, the structure "(left side) *ha* (right side) *desu*" of the target sentence will be discovered. This structure will be applied to the input sentence which can be rewritten as "**Jean** *ha* **terriblement malade** *desu*". Using other examples, the same process will be applied recursively to any existing non-translated segments. Here, there are two non-translated segments "**Jean**" and "**terriblement malade**". "**Jean**" is a one word segment and can be translated without division. On the other hand, "**terriblement malade**" can again be divided into "**terriblement**" and "**malade**" by the same process or be translated directly if it appears somewhere in the corpus. Whether they need a division or not, appropriate examples must be selected and applied to translate them.

The present method has two important advantages.

1 First, utilization of a syntactic analyzer is unnecessary because sentences can be translated without understanding their syntactic structures.

2 Second, any sentence can always be divided. This characteristic allows us to translate long sentences. If non-translated segments can be divided at the right position at every step, the correct translation result will be reached.

We will describe in detail the main steps of the translation process in the following sections. These involve extracting examples with a similar source sentence to the input sentence, and producing the translation itself.

4. Extraction of Examples

According to our translation method, sentences having a common segment with the input sentence will be the target of the extraction. On the basis of that segment, the sentence or a segment of a sentence will be divided into independent parts. Similarity in the structure of both sentences is also an important factor because it ensures that both right hand and left hand side segments will be similar. Source sentences having both a common segment and the same structure as the input sentence will therefore be searched. That makes our matching method different from others as similarity over the whole sentence may not always be satisfied. Because of the possibility of links, common segments and unlinked segments, a number of conditions must be fulfilled during the matching process.

4.1 Matching under Different Conditions

To make the matching valid and the translation method applicable, three conditions must be fulfilled during the matching process.

1 First, in the translation example the common segment must be linked with the target sentence by a one-to-one contiguous segment link. Consider the source sentence "**nous sommes amis.**" (We are friends.) and its target sentence "*watashitachi ha tomodachi desu*". "**nous**" (we), "**sommes**" (are), "**amis**" (friends), and "**.**" correspond to "*watashitachi*", "*desu*", "*tomodachi*" and "." respectively. If "**nous sommes**" exists in the sentence to be translated, it could be a common segment. However, since the correspondents of "**nous**", namely "*watashitachi*", and "**sommes**" ("*desu*"), are

separated in the target sentence, the translation will be performed by considering only either "**nous**" or "**sommes**" as the common segment. Otherwise, the sentence could not be divided.

2 For a link involving multiple tokens, the relevant tokens in the source sentence must match exactly with their correspondents in the input sentence when they are used as the common segment. According to our translation method, the common segment is immediately translated in one step. Therefore, a mismatch existing in the common segment could generate a false translation. Consider the source sentence "**je suis sans profession.**" (I am jobless.) and its translation "*mushoku desu.*". Here the segment "**sans profession**", which is composed of two tokens, corresponds to a single token "*mushoku*". Therefore, when "**sans profession**" is used as a common segment, both tokens must match exactly with their correspondents in the input sentence.

3 In the case where a segment has no link is the common segment, it is considered to be a fixed segment and must match exactly with its correspondent. For example, consider the source sentence "**je vous remercie.**" (I thank you) and its translation "*arigatou gozaimasu.*" Here, "**remercie**" (thank) corresponds to "*arigatou*", but "**je**" (I) and "**vous**" (you) have no correspondents. Therefore, since "**je**" and "**vous**" are contiguous, not only one but both of them must exactly match with their correspondent in the input sentence when they are the common segment. This condition is set to allow any segment of the input sentence to be covered by the matching sentence. In the present example, if "**vous**" does not match exactly with its correspondent and "**je**" is taken as the common segment, the real meaning of the correspondent of "**vous**" is not transmitted. Instead, it is replaced by the 'invisible' meaning of "**vous**" since it does not have any correspondent in the other language.

Having provided an overview of the matching method, we will now describe the core algorithm of the matching process.

4.2 The Matching Algorithm

The matching algorithm is very simple:

1 For each token of the input sentence, search for the same token in the source sentence.

2 If found, from that position, start a forward and backward search for matches. The search starts with exact matches and continues with POS tag matches when a POS tag match or a non-contiguous match is encountered.

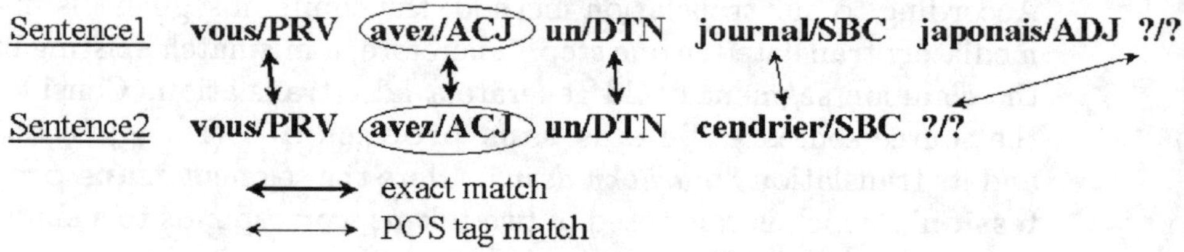

Figure 8.3. Matching in our translation method

An illustration is presented in Figure 8.3. For the token **"avez/ACJ"** in sentence 1, an exact match is detected at the second position in both sentences. A backward search produces one exact match, **"vous/PRV-vous/PRV"**, and a forward search gives one exact match, **"un/DTN-un/DTN"**. Of course, **"journal/SBC-cendrier/SBC"** is not an exact match. Therefore, from this position, only POS tags are observed. This allows **"journal/SBC"** and **"cendrier/SBC"**to be considered as a POS tag match, although it is not an exact match. We will see later in the computation of the similarity score that POS-matching is considerd in order to strengthen matches between the common segment, which are located within the exact matching segment. Here, the token **"japonais/SBC"** is skipped because a correspondent does not exist. During the forward and backward searches, if multiple matches are discovered, the match nearest to the last selected match is selected and the search continues.

We define the distance between two matches as the sum of the distance separating their respective components. Consider two sentences X and Y, written as "x_1 x_2 ... x_n" and "y_1 y_2 ... y_m" respectively, where "x_i" and "y_j" are their tokens. Let us assume that "x_i" matches with "y_j" and "x_m" with "y_n". The distance between (x_i, y_j) and (x_m, y_n) is equal to the absolute value of $(j - i) + (n - m)$. For example, the distance between **"journal/SBC-cendrier/SBC"** and **"?/?-?/?"** is 3 since they are separated by the token **"japonais/SBC"** in the first sentence and no tokens in the second sentence. For contiguous couples (x_i, y_j) and (x_{i+1}, y_{j+1}), this distance is $(i+1-i)+(j+1-j)=2$.

Since this algorithm always begins the search from an exact match, it has a subsidiary advantage that processing time can be reduced considerably by indexing the corpus on each token.

4.3 Similarity Score

To select the best matching sentences, the following similarity score is used:

$$SC = \alpha \times NE + \sum_{i=1}^{NP} \frac{2}{D_i} \tag{8.1}$$

SC is the similarity score, NE the number of exact matches, NP the number of POS tag matches and D_i the distance separating a token from the common segment, measured in number of tokens. α is set to 10, which renders the presence of exact matches located within or around the common segment more significant compared to the POS-matches. In other words, the similarity is almost entirely decided by the exact matches which compose the common segment. In the case they are equal, POS tag matches surrounding the common segment will make a difference. D_i is introduced to differentiate between matches located near the common segment from those located far further away. It is assumed that a match located far from the common segment contributes less in establishing the similarity of sentences which include the common segment. The numerator '2' in the similarity score is explained by the presence of two sentences being involved in the comparison.

It is important to note that D_i never becomes 0 because it concerns only POS tag matches. POS tag matches are located outside the exact matching segment. Consider two sentences "$x_1\ x_2 \ldots x_i\ x_{i+1}\ x_{i+2} \ldots x_m \ldots x_p$" and "$y_1\ y_2 \ldots y_j\ y_{j+1}\ y_{j+2} \ldots y_n \ldots y_q$". Let us assume that $x_i = y_j$, $x_{i+1} = y_{j+1}$ and $x_{i+2} = y_{j+2}$, i.e. there is an exact matching segment from x_1 to x_{i+2}. Let us also assume that x_m and y_n have the same POS tag. The distance between (x_{i+2}, y_{j+2}), the right bound of the exact matching segment, and (x_m, y_n), the POS tag match, is $p-(i+2)+q-(j+2)$. Since $p > i+2$ and $q > j+2$, that distance must be at least 2.

As an illustration, in Figure 8.3, there are 3 exact matches and 2 POS tag matches. The common segment is **"vous/PRV avez/ACJ un/DTN"**. As far as the sum of distances separating tokens from the common segment in both sentences is concerned, the first POS tag match are 2 tokens apart, one in each sentence, and the second by 5 tokens, 3 in the first sentence and 2 in the second. Consequently, the similarity score is as follows.

$$SC = 10 \times 3 + \frac{2}{2} + \frac{2}{5} = 31.4 \tag{8.2}$$

4.4 How many Examples are Extracted?

During the search for similar sentences, one matching sentence is extracted for each token of the input sentence. If the length of the input sentences is n tokens, n sentences should be extracted. However, according to the matching algorithm, the same sentence may be extracted for two or multiple consecutive tokens. Moreover, any sentence will not be selected for a token which has not yet been registered in the corpus. Therefore, cases are found where the number of tokens in extracted examples is fewer than the number of tokens in the input sentence. Therefore, the number of extracted sentences is at most n. As an example, in Figure 8.3, the same similarity score is obtained by any sentence containing the tokens **"vous/PRV"**, **"avez/ACJ"** and **"un/DTN"**.

4.5 Notes on Other Matching Methods

Other methods for searching similar sentences in EBMT include the length-first method (Nirenburg *et al.*, 1994), the Dynamic Programming matching (DP-Matching) method (Kitano, 1993) (cf. also Chapter 6, this volume), and a method based on the observation of functional words (Cranias *et al.*, 1994).

The length-first method searches for the longest contiguous segment match within the two strings in question. The search continues within unmatched substrings until no more matches can be discovered. This method is very effective for comparing full sentences, especially when sentences are relatively short, because if a long segment match can be discovered early, the remaining substrings become short, and finding the longest segment match within a short segment almost always results in the right match, if one exists. However, the length-first method is hardly applicable in the present case because of the presence of the common segment, which must be searched for different parts of the input sentence. In addition, there must be a match around the common segment because it determines the position of left and right-hand side segments. The first-length method does not guarantee such a condition especially for long sentences because the next match does not depend on the last discovered match. Nirenburg et al. (1994), the first to apply this method in EBMT, utilize different lexicons and a thesaurus to categorize words. Having multiple categories for a word increases the probability that the word has a matching correspondent, because if a word fails to have a correspondent via one category, it still can be matched with a different word via another. In the present case, only an exact match and a POS tag match are considered. This makes the method simple and applicable with less cost.

The DP-Matching method starts the search from one end of a sentence (or substring) and continues until the next end of segment. The search for the next match depends on those discovered previously. A predefined function with a value that is to be minimized is used to select the best match when different possibilities appear. This method is very effective for discovering local matches around the first discovered match. However, isolated matches may occur and they are not guaranteed to be a non-mismatch. In the matching method described in this chapter, the DP-Matching method is used only partially. The difference is that the search for an exact match is performed first, and when one is discovered, then the backward and forward searches, starting from the exact match position and continuing to both ends of sentences, use the DP-Matching method. We select this method since a strong correspondence around the exact match is required.

As for the method based on functional words, it mainly searches for an exact match for functional words in the string in question. Since functional words in a sentence can determine its surface structure (cf. Veale & Way, 1997), the method can be very effective to extract translation patterns by replacing non-functional words with variables. As for the applicability of the method to the present study, it can be a good method for searching a similar sentence having a functional word as a common segment. However, it is not sufficient because any similar sentences must also be searched for non-functional words. Furthermore, the definition of functional words is a separate issue to be considered because they may be combined with their functional word neighbors to form a non-disjoint set. Having described the matching method, we will look at the production of translations in the next section.

5. Production of Translation Results

The translation results are generated using the extracted examples. The process whereby results are produced is illustrated in Figure 8.4.

The sentence "**nous sommes camarades d'école**" (We are schoolmates) is the input sentence. Example 1 and example 2 mean "We are friends from long ago" and "He is my childhood friend" respectively. In example 1, "**sommes**" (are) is considered as the common segment. If one observes the correspondence of its left- and right-hand segments in the target sentence, the pattern "(left-side) *ha* (right-side) *desu*" can be extracted. An application of this pattern to the input sentence produces "**nous** *ha* **camarades d'école** *desu*". Here "*ha*" has no correspondent. However, since it is an element which is located in the middle of the right and left-hand segments, it remains.

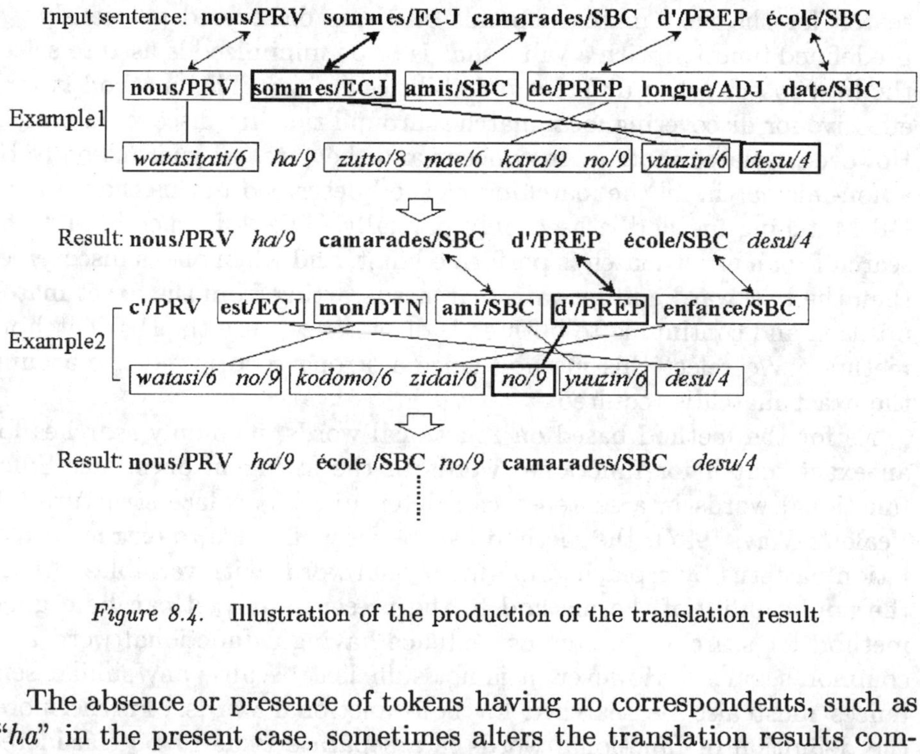

Figure 8.4. Illustration of the production of the translation result

The absence or presence of tokens having no correspondents, such as "*ha*" in the present case, sometimes alters the translation results completely. We consider two cases where segments having no correspondents are maintained:

1 They are located between the translation of the right-hand and one of the left-hand segments. This is explained by the fact that the common segment is located between the left and right-hand segments. It is assumed, therefore, that a segment which is located between the translation of the right-hand segment and one of the left-hand segments in the target sentence plays an important role

when a common segment exists, as the case of "*ha*" in the above example.

2 They are closely related to the translation segment of the common segment (prefixes, suffixes, particles). This is the most obvious case because if they depend on the translation of the common segment, they should automatically follow it. For example, for the Japanese language, there are the prefix honorifics "*o*" or "*go*", which mean "yours", and which always accompany the noun they precede. There is also the suffix "*san*", meaning "Mr." or "Mrs.", which also accompanies the noun it follows.

After the application of example 1, the output contains two non-translated segments "**nous**" and "**camarades d'école**". The recursion continues with the application of example 2 to the segment "**camarades d'école**" by the same method. Only the matching segment "**ami d'enfance**" is therefore considered. "**d'**" is the common segment. According to the position of the translations of the left-hand segment "**ami**" and right-hand segment "**enfance**", "**camarades d'école**" can be rewritten as "**école** *no* **camarades**". After the application of example 2, there still remain three non-translated segments "**nous**", "**école**" and "**camarades**". The translation process continues with the translation of these segments by the same method. Here, the case is specific because segments are each composed of one token. They can be translated directly without segment division.

There are cases where the left or right-hand segment is non-contiguous. Consider translation example 2 in Figure 8.4. The segment "**d'**" (of) is considered to be the common segment. The correspondents of its left-hand segment in the target sentence are "*watashi no*" (my), "*yuujin*" (friend) and "*desu*" (be). The right-hand segment corresponds to "*kodomo jidai*" (school days). Therefore, if this example is applied first, a pattern such as "(left side) (right side) *no* (left side)" will be extracted from the target sentence. Two "(left side)" segments appear in this pattern and the sentence cannot be divided. In that case, priority is given to the one which is closer to the common segment. Therefore "*yuujin*" is selected and the extracted pattern will be "(right side) *no* (left side)". This partially explains why a match near the common segment is given a higher weight compared to a match farther away in the similarity score.

Actually, if translation example 2 is used before translation example 1, in handling the initial input sentence, it will produce an incorrect result: "**école** *no* **nous sommes camarades**". This generates a completely different result, namely "*gakkou no watashitachi ha yuujin desu*". In short, the order of use of the extracted translation examples is very important. We propose three conditions to decide this priority order:

1 Top priority is given to examples having common segments which successfully divide the sentence without causing fragmentation of each part. Punctuation, conjunctions and so forth generally fall into this category.

2 Next, examples having common segments containing a verb are considered. This is explained by the importance of verbs in recognizing the structure of the whole sentence. It is assumed that the corpus is large enough to contain different sentences including a given verb. Otherwise, our matching method would not produce examples which have the same structure as the input sentence. The presence of the common segment is, of course, important. However, the accuracy of the translation also depends on the exactness of the match between both left- and right-hand segments.

3 For the rest, the similarity score will make a difference on condition that examples including non-functional words such as nouns, adverbs or adjectives as the common segment will be the last to be considered.

6. Predicting Links of New Pairs

Predicting links of new examples is part of the translation process in order to make new examples utilizable for further translation. It is necessary because our translation method requires link-included translation examples. Here, the input of the prediction is the pair consisting of the input sentence and the correct translation result. The output (or the link-included translation example) goes directly into the corpus.

The link prediction or word-level alignment process is based completely on case-based reasoning. To predict the link of a new pair, the system imitates links of similar pairs in the corpus. There are two steps in the alignment process:

1 The search for examples to be used for the prediction, and

2 The prediction process itself.

6.1 Searching for Similar Pairs

To predict the links between a new pair of sentences, similar pairs are required. These similar pairs are again extracted from the corpus.

Finding a similar pair is not straightforward because if two sentences are similar in one language, their translations are not necessarily similar in the other language. Therefore, during the search, similarity between segments of sentences is considered, not whole sentences. It is more likely that a similar pair of translation sentences will be discovered if short segments are observed. To cover the whole sentence, multiple similar pairs which cover different parts of the input pair are extracted.

The search for similar segments of sentences is therefore a partial matching process and is performed independently in both languages. For each similar discovered segment, one must confirm if any similarity can be found between their translations in the other language. If this is not the case, the selected segment will be rejected. The search algorithm is similar to the one described in section 4.2 except that the skip operation is not allowed and the search stops when a mismatch is encountered. It is described as follows:

1 For each token of the input sentence, search for an exact matching token in the example sentence.

2 If found, start a backward and forward comparison from the found exact match. The comparison starts by considering exact matches, continues thereafter with POS tag matches, and stops when a mismatch is encountered.

The algorithm searches for a similar segment containing at least an exact-match token of the input sentence. It is important to note that when a POS tag match is encountered, further discovered matches are all considered as POS tag matches, even though they might be exact matches. This condition is set to increase the importance of similarities near the first discovered exact match token and weaken those further away. It is assumed that such consideration is appropriate for searching for the local matching segment. The comparison stops when a mismatch is encountered because only a contiguous segment is searched. In the case of Figure 8.3, since "**japonais/ADJ**" is skipped, the link between "**?/?**" and "**?/?**" is not considered. In addition, the distance D_i is ignored and the similarity score is thus:

$$SC = 10 \times NE + NP \tag{8.3}$$

where NE is equal to the number of exact (token) matches, and NP is equal to the number of matching POS tags. For the example in Figure

8.3, since one POS tag match is rejected, there are 3 exact matches, and 1 POS tag match. The similarity score is, therefore:

$$SC = 10 \times 3 + 1 = 31 \tag{8.4}$$

The search operation is executed for each token of the input sentence. As a result, it should produce one similar segment for each token. However, it is better to select multiple similar segments because the verification of similarity between translation pairs may fail and the example will be rejected. In addition, since the algorithm always searches first for an exact-match token, similar sentences cannot be discovered for unknown words. If multiple segments are considered, it is more likely that the whole sentence will be covered because of POS tag matches. Summing the similarity scores of source and target sentences gives us the similarity score of the translation example.

It is important to mention that the number of selected segments per token may change depending on the situation. No segment is selected when any exact match for the token does not exist. Furthermore, a similar segment might be selected for different tokens. In other words, if n is the number of similar segments to be extracted for each token, n will be a maximum. At most $6 \times n$ similar segments are selected for a 6 token sentence. Since we talk of pairs of sentences, the total number of selected segments is the sum of the selected segments during the execution of the matching process in both languages. If L_s and L_t are the number of tokens in the source sentence and translation sentence respectively, the total number of selected segments will be:

$$T = (L_s + L_t) \times n \tag{8.5}$$

This number T is a maximum. It will be reduced considerably firstly given the above-mentioned reasons and especially because the other pair of sentences are likely to be dissimilar.

6.2 Illustrating the Prediction Method

Having selected similar pairs of segments, links between the new pair of sentences are predicted. The process is described in Figure 8.5. $(f1, j1)$ is the new pair of sentences. $(f2, j2)$ is a selected pair from the translation examples. Links between $f2$ and $j2$ are defined beforehand within the translation examples. Links between $f1$ and $j1$ (and $f2$ and $j2$) are determined during the matching process. The task here is

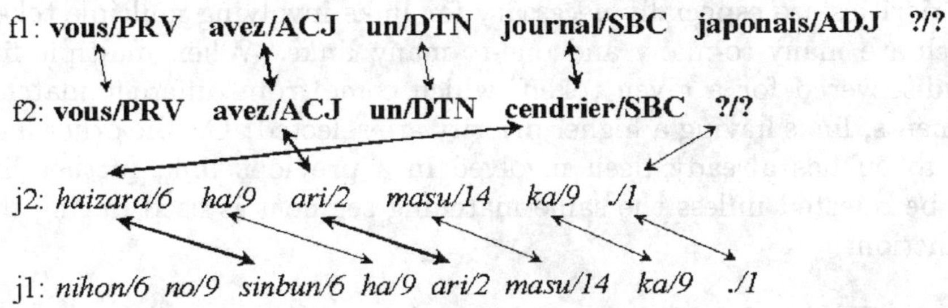

Figure 8.5. Searching for links by analogy

to find all paths starting from an element of $f1$ and reaching an element of $j1$. In this case, there are two paths, which correspond to 2 links "**avez/ACJ**-*ari/V*" and "**journal/SBC**-*shinbun/N*".

6.3 Selecting the Correct Links

Multiple segments are selected during the matching process and links between elements of the new sentence pair are predicted by executing the above-mentioned prediction process for each selected segment. Therefore, the result will be a long list of links, which probably contains repetitions and errors. Priorities must therefore be defined in order that correct links are selected. Priorities depend on the following two parameters:

1 The length l of the exact match segment inside the selected segment. For example, in Figure 8.5, the exact match segment is "**vous/PRV avez/ACJ un/DTN**". It is composed of 3 tokens. Therefore $l = 3$.

2 The distance d separating a token from the exact match segment. For example, that distance is 1 for the token "**journal/SBC**" in Figure 8.5 because it is one token away from the exact match segment. That distance will be 0 for tokens inside the exact match segment.

Having set these parameters, priorities for selecting correct links are defined as follows: top priorities are given to links where the distance d is small for both tokens. This assigns higher priority to links inside or close to the exact match segment, compared to links further away. If that distance is equal for multiple links, those arising from longer exact matching segments (defined by l) will be given a higher priority.

Priorities are especially necessary for links involving multiple tokens, which are many-to-many and one-to-many links. When multiple links are discovered for a given token, which come from different matching segments, links having a higher priority are selected. On the other hand, if a token has already been involved in a previous link, further links will be rejected unless the same matching segment is used during their prediction.

7. Experiments and Results

We now describe some experiments which have been carried out to evaluate the translation method. This includes detailed descriptions of the corpus and the input sentences. It is followed by the presentation of experimental results. It consists of a numerical result showing the correct translation rate, together with some real samples selected randomly from the output. In the last paragraph, we discuss the effectiveness of the method as well as why it fails on occasion.

7.1 Experiment Procedure

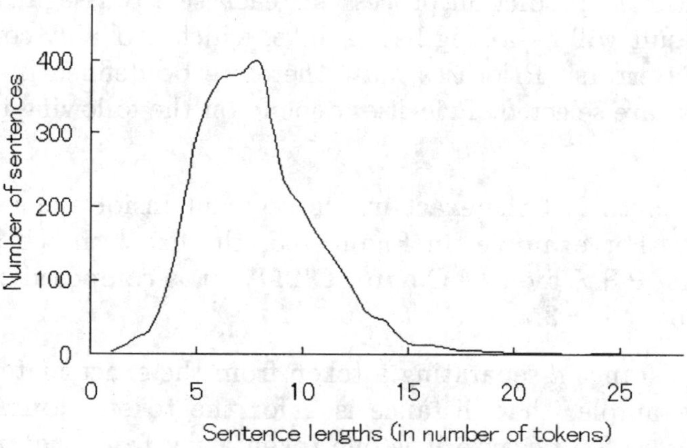

Figure 8.6. **Distribution of French sentence lengths**

The initial bilingual corpus was composed of 2,500 examples. Sentences were taken from French–Japanese conversation books (Meguro, 1987; Sato, 1990). The average length of sentences are 7.74 tokens for Japanese and 7.84 for French. To give the reader a better understanding of the data being used, the distribution of French sentence lengths is presented in Figure 8.6. 400 new French sentences, taken from the same sources, are entered one by one into the system to be translated.

Initially, as soon as a translation result is obtained, the new translation example is not appended to the corpus. The initial 2,500 examples are used to translate all 400 input sentences ("Experiment 1"). This was carried out in order to compare the result with the case where the number of examples in the corpus is increased. Next, translation results are corrected if necessary. Links between words of the new pair are predicted but not corrected manually. The new examples are appended to the corpus ("Experiment 2"). This was carried out to confirm whether 2,500 translation examples is a large enough number to produce a fully automatic translation system, without correcting the output of the link prediction procedure. To avoid a possible degradation of the whole system, newly appended examples are prevented from being involved in the prediction of links of new translation examples. They are considered only during the translation process itself. It is important to note that degradation may occur if new examples are allowed to participate in link prediction. This is because the link prediction is not 100% accurate and its result is not corrected manually during the experiment. Therefore, examples having erroneous links will gradually produce worse results.

Table 8.4. Comparison of Experiment 1 and Experiment 2

Input sentences	Length of input sentences	Correct translation rate		Difference between Exp.1 and Exp.2	Ratio of use of new examples
		Exp.1	Exp.2		
1–50	7.5	70.0%	72.0%	2.0%	1.1%
51–100	7.7	70.0%	74.0%	4.0%	2.4%
101–150	7.2	72.0%	72.0%	0.0%	2.4%
151–200	8.1	60.0%	66.0%	6.0%	5.3%
201–250	8.1	60.0%	68.0%	8.0%	6.0%
251–300	8.0	60.0%	70.0%	10.0%	13.6%
301–350	7.8	56.0%	64.0%	8.0%	15.4%
351–400	9.5	48.0%	62.0%	14.0%	24.2%
Average	8.0	62.0%	68.5%		

Since unknown words exist and a dictionary is not used, French words sometimes remain in the output translations. Evaluating such results is very difficult. We have focussed on segment position and consider the translation to be correct (i) if it has the same structure as the correct translation, and (ii) all segments are inserted in the right positions. The 400 input sentences are divided into subsets of 50 sentences and a comparative result of "Experiment 1" and "Experiment 2" is presented in

Table 8.4. "Ratio of use of new examples" in column 6 represents the ratio of the new translation examples in the extracted translation examples. In addition, sample results are selected from the output and presented in Tables 8.5, 8.6 and 8.7.

7.2 Experimental Results and Discussion

We obtain on average 62.0% correct translations in "Experiment 1". Despite the small number of translation examples and the presence of sentences which do not follow grammar rules in the spoken language, an accuracy rate of 62.0% is considered to be a very promising result. In Table 8.4, the correct translation rate rises to an average of 68.5% in "Experiment 2". The trend of the values in "Experiment 2", where the size of the corpus is increased, is for them not to rise. This can be explained partially by the difficulties in translating long sentences compared to shorter ones. Given the variation in the rate of correct translations and the variation of the average length of the input sentences, shorter sentences are translated more correctly than longer ones.

However, the difference between the correct translation rates in these two experiments in column 5 shows the effect of using new translation examples. The difference between the two experiments drops slightly at the 101st and at the 301st input sentences, but it generally increases as the number of translation examples increases. This confirms the effectiveness of the link prediction method in the translation system. It is necessary to verify whether these new translation examples are really involved during the production of these translation results. That is the purpose of the column "Ratio of use of the new translation examples". In the beginning, since the corpus does not contain any new translation examples, but is composed solely of the initial translation examples, low values of that ratio can be seen. However, the rising trend is clearly visible as the number of translation examples increases.

It may be very evident that a bigger corpus gives a better correct translation rate. However, it is important to note that the presence of the link prediction module, although not 100% perfect, did not change that trend.

Sample correct results are presented in Table 8.5. These selected results all arise from combining multiple translation examples. For example, the first sentence was translated using three examples. The first one contains the segment "**Je rappelerai**" (I will call again), the second "**dans l' après-midi**" (in the afternoon) and the third "**.**". They are translated into "*kakenaosimasu*", "*gogo ni*" and "." respectively. Here,

Table 8.5. Sample correct results

1	Input	**Je rappellerai dans l'après-midi.**
		(I will call again in the afternoon.)
	Output	*gogo ni kakenaosimasu.*
2	Input	**Y a-t-il un médecin qui parle japonais?**
		(Is there a doctor who speaks Japanese?)
	Output	*nihongo no wakaru isha ga imasuka.*
3	Input	**C'est combien pour cinq cents grammes?**
		(How much is it for five hundred grammes?)
	Output	*5 hyaku guramu ikura desuka.*
4	Input	**Je suis venu il y a trois jours.**
		(I came three days ago.)
	Output	*mikka mae ni kimashita.*
5	Input	**Quand est-ce que vous partez?**
		(When do you leave?)
	Output	*anata ha itsu o dekake desuka.*

"**Je**" (I) is translated successfully into a zero pronoun by analogy with the extracted examples. Of course, "*watashi ha gogo ni kakenaosimasu.*" would also be a valid result. However, the ability to reuse exactly the contents of the extracted examples is considered to be a good thing, because it allows us to find the right expression of the translation result in the target language. In the second sentence, "**Y a-t-il**" (Is there) could be translated into "*arimasuka*", but the more appropriate instance "*imasuka*" is selected. This explains the effectiveness of the matching algorithm. When a long segment match is discovered and POS tags are explicit, examples having the appropriate semantic information can be extracted. Explicit POS tags signify the presence of a large number of POS tags. With only a few POS tags, it is quite likely that long segment matches can be found, but their quality may leave something to be desired. In the third example, it is important to note the absence of the particle "*ha*" between "*ikura*" (how much) and "*guramu* (gramme)". This again illustrates the conversational style of the corpus.

Table 8.6 shows some correct results but which still contain untranslated French words. Input sentences are successfully divided. For example, the second input sentence "**Il m'a écrit qu'il avait neigé la veille**" is divided at the position of "**qu**'". It produces the pattern "**il avait neigé la veille** *to,* **il m'a ecrit**", which leads to the result "*zenjitsu* **(avait neigé)** *to, kare ha kaite kita*". The segment "**(avait neigé)**", which corresponds exactly to "*yuki ga futta*", could not be translated because it did not appear in the corpus. It is important to

Table 8.6. Sample exact word order results

1	Input	**Il danse avec peine.**
		(He dances with difficulty.)
	Result	*kare ha kanasi irete odorimasu.*
	Correct	*kare ha karoujite odorimasu.*
2	Input	**Il m'a écrit qu'il avait neigé la veille.**
		(He wrote me that it had snowed the previous day.)
	Result	*zenjitsu* **(avait neigé)** *to, kare ha kaita.*
	Correct	*zenjitsu ha yuki ga futta to, kare ha kaita.*

Table 8.7. Sample failure

1	Input	**Demain soir, madame S donnera un bal chez elle.**
		(Tomorrow evening, Mrs. S will give a ball at her home.)
	Result	*ashita yoru* **(bal)** *S* **(donnera)** .
	Correct	*myouban S fujin ga jitaku de dansu pa-ti wo mouyoushimasu.*
2	Input	**Laissez les moustaches comme elles sont.**
		(Leave the moustaches as they are.)
	Result	*kuchihige wo nokosite kudasai kanojora you na.*
	Correct	*hige ha sono mama ni site oite kudasai.*
3	Input	**Du coca, s' il vous plaît.**
		(Cola, please.)
	Result	*ko-ra ni wo kudasai.*
	Correct	*ko-ra wo kudasai.*

note here that "**avait**" is an auxiliary and normally is a high frequency word in the French language. Although it appeared in the corpus, it is always combined with its neighbor and the set corresponds to a past tense verb in Japanese. In short, it could not be divided since it is linked with its neighbor via its correspondent in the target language. This characteristic is important because separating such segments sometimes produces the wrong result. As an example, in the first sentence, "**avec peine**" (with difficulty), which normally corresponds to "*karoujite*", was not present in the corpus and separated. Therefore, an inappropriate expression "*kanasi irete*" was produced. We presume that such cases will be resolved as the number of translation examples increases.

Table 8.7 presents some cases of failure. In the input sentence 2, the structure of the result is completely different from the correct translation. This failure is due to applying the examples in the wrong order in trying to obtain the translation. We admit that the method still needs improvement, but the correct translation rate improves when a defined priority order is placed on the reuse of examples. A simple observation of the extracted examples confirms the fact that when an infrequent word is part of the common segment, it is less likely that a sentence will be discovered which structurally matches the input sentence. There might be an inappropriate match or no match between both left-hand segments or between both right-hand ones. This is because there are very few sentences containing that infrequent word, and the available examples were automatically extracted regardless of their structure. Giving such examples a higher priority during the generation of the translation result will probably cause errors. Extending the size of the corpus will again resolve this problem. However, further study is required regarding the order of application of the examples, as well as how to deal efficiently with infrequent words.

In contrast to the examples of Japanese zero pronoun which can be eliminated successfully, there are also cases where the translations of some words do not appear in the result, although they are required. For example, in the input sentence "**Demain soir, madame S donnera un bal chez elle**", "**madame**" and "**chez elle**" disappear but their translations are not present. These words have no correspondent in the target sentence of the selected examples. We again assume that these problems will be resolved as the number of translation examples increases.

Japanese words such as "*ha*", "*wo*" and "*ni*", which sometimes have no correspondent in the French language, sometimes provoke errors. For example, in the third input sentence, "*ko-ra ni wo*" results instead of "*ko-ra wo*". In this case, "*ni*" was assumed to depend on "*ko-ra*" and therefore follows it. As far as the correct translation rate is observed, that dependency is true in most cases. However, the decision as to whether words having no correspondent should be maintained or eliminated sometimes depends on the structure of the translation result, rather than on one of the extracted examples. The problem does not exist if both have same structure. We would like to study further the placement of words which have no correspondent in the source sentence in future work.

Placing a defined priority order for the application of examples and dealing with the placement of words having no correspondents, as proposed above, gave very promising results, but they are still not perfect since they are language-dependent. An alternative language-independent approach which considers all possible priority orders of the selected examples might also be a new direction for us to follow. In that case, a module which can select the correct result from all generated results would be needed. Placing or rejecting words having no correspondents might also be dealt with in the same way.

8. Concluding Remarks

8.1 Summary

We have described a method for EBMT based on a recursive division of the input sentence. At each step, a segment to be translated is split and a sub-segment common to both the extracted matching sentence and the input sentence is translated. An appropriate matching algorithm, which searches for a sentence which matches the structure of the input sentence and which contains an exact-matching segment, is also presented. By dividing the sentence, it becomes possible to translate sentences which are not fully covered by the matching sentence. Long sentences can also be translated and any possible mismatch between source sentence and the similar sentence can be prevented from affecting the translation result. In addition, obtaining translations without understanding the syntactic structure of a sentence is possible.

The method is designed especially for languages whose dictionaries or syntactic analyzers are unreliable or scarce. POS taggers are the only tools required. The proposed translation method is supported by the recent considerable increase in the quality of POS taggers and the availability of machine readable text.

Since the method requires word correspondences or a link-included corpus, an analogy-based link prediction module was introduced to allow the system to use new translation examples. It imitates links of similar examples to predict links for a new translation example.

During the experiments, 2,500 initial link-included translation examples were used and 400 new sentences were entered into the system to be translated. A 68.5% average correct translation rate was obtained. Despite the small number of translation examples and the presence of sentences not following grammar rules in the spoken language, this is considered to be a very promising result. We also confirmed the effectiveness of the recursive-division procedure for sentences which could not be covered by a single example, the defined priority order of the extracted examples and the way we dealt with words having no link.

Failures and errors are derived from a slight imperfection of the link prediction method, a possible inapropriateness of the priority order of the selected examples, and the wrong positioning of words which have no correspondent.

8.2 New Directions

Although we still need to look carefully at the priority order of selected examples as well as words which have no link, the recursive division method is definitely applicable in EBMT. Experiments on the application of the method in other fields of NLP strongly suggest themselves. As for the translation system, we hope to carry out experiments on larger corpora with longer sentences from different domains, not only to improve the system, but also to refine our translation method. We might also be able to adjust the similarity score with a larger corpus because the likelihood of discovering an exact match will increase. New avenues of investigation include a study of the inappropriateness of the priority order of the selected examples, the wrong placement of words having no correspondent, a special consideration of high frequency words, and a language-independent method capable of generating all possible results and selecting the correct result from the candidate translations.

Adding more tools can be expected to improve the system further. However, it should not become a burden for the system because the main goal of this study is to come up with a translation method for languages for which resources are not available.

The method is designed to be adaptable to any additional tags. Therefore, the use of any low-cost tags would be an interesting study to improve the translation system.

Acknowledgments

The authors wish to thank the "Institut National de la Langue Française" for providing the *EBTI* tagger for the French language.

References

Andriamanankasina, T., K. Araki and K. Tochinai. 1999. Sub-Sentential Alignment Method by Analogy. In *PACLIC13: Proceedings of the 13th Pacific Asia Conference on Language, Information and Computation*, Taipei, Taiwan, pp.277–284.

Araki, K., Y. Takahashi, Y. Momouchi and K. Tochinai. 1996. Non-Segmented Kana-Kanji Translation Using Inductive Learning. *Transactions of the IEICE* **J97-D-II**(4):391–402.

Brill, E. 1993. *A Corpus-Based Approach To Language Learning.* PhD Dissertation, University of Pensylvania, Philadelphia, PA.

Brown, P., S. Della Pietra, V. Della Pietra and R. Mercer. 1993. The Mathematics of Statistical Machine Translation: Parameter Estimation. *Computational Linguistics* **19**(2):263–309.

Cranias, L., H. Papageorgiou and S. Piperidis. 1994. A Matching Technique in Example-Based Machine Translation. In *COLING-94: Proceedings of 15th International Conference on Computational Linguistics*, Kyoto, Japan, pp.100-104.

Kitamura M., and Y. Matsumoto. 1997. Automatic Extraction of Translation Patterns in Parallel Corpora. *Transactions of the IPSJ* **38**(4): 727–736 (cf. Chapter 13, this volume).

Kitano, H. 1993. A Comprehensive and Practical Model of Memory-Based Machine Translation. In *Proceedings of the Thirteenth International Joint Conference on Artificial Intelligence*, Chambéry, France, pp.1276–1282.

Meguro, S. 1987. *Manuel de Conversation Française.* Hakusuisha, Tokyo, Japan.

Melamed, D. 1997. A Word-to-Word Model of Translational Equivalence. In *35th Conference of the Association for Computational Linguistics and 8th Conference of the European Chapter of the Association for Computational Linguistics*, Madrid, Spain, pp.490–497.

Nirenburg S., S. Beale and K. Domashnev. 1994. A Full-Text Experiment in Example-Based Machine Translation. In *NeMLaP: Proceedings of the International Conference on New Methodologies in Language Processing*, Manchester, UK, pp.95–103.

Nirenburg, S., D. Grannes and K. Domashnev. 1993. Two Approaches to Matching in Example-Based Machine Translation. In *Proceedings of the Fifth International Conference on Theoretical and Methodological issues in Machine Translation TMI '93: MT in the Next Generation*, Kyoto, Japan, pp.47–57.

Sato, F. 1990. *Locutions de base.* Hakusuisha, Tokyo, Japan.

Veale, T. and A. Way. 1997. *Gaijin*: A Bootstrapping Approach to Example-Based Machine Translation. In *International Conference, Recent Advances in Natural Language Processing*, Tzigov Chark, Bulgaria, pp.239–244.

Yamashita, T. 1996. ChaSen Technical Report. *Technical Report*, Nara Advanced Institute of Science and Technology, Nara, Japan.

III

TEMPLATE-DRIVEN EXAMPLE-BASED MACHINE TRANSLATION

Chapter 9

LEARNING TRANSLATION TEMPLATES FROM BILINGUAL TRANSLATION EXAMPLES

Ilyas Cicekli
ilyas@cs.bilkent.edu.tr

H. Altay Güvenir
guvenir@cs.bilkent.edu.tr

Abstract A mechanism for learning lexical correspondences between two languages from sets of translated sentence pairs is presented. These lexical level correspondences are learned using analogical reasoning between two translation examples. Given two translation examples, any similarities in the source language sentences must correspond to the similar parts of the target language sentences, while any differences in the source strings must correspond to the respective parts in the translated sentences. The correspondences between similarities and between differences are learned in the form of translation templates. A translation template is a generalized translation exemplar pair where some components are generalized by replacing them with variables in both sentences and establishing bindings between these variables. The learned translation templates are generalizations obtained by replacing differences or similarities by variables. This approach has been implemented and tested on a set of sample training datasets and produced promising results for further investigation.

Keywords: exemplar-based machine learning, difference translation templates, similarity translation templates

M. Carl and A. Way (eds.), Recent Advances in Example-Based Machine Translation, 255–286.

1. Introduction

Researchers in the Machine Learning community have widely used exemplar-based representations. The basic idea in exemplar-based learning is to use past experiences or cases to understand, plan, or learn from novel situations (Kolodner, 1988; Hammond, 1989; Ram, 1993). Collins and Somers (Chapter 4, this volume) view the EBMT approach as a special case of Case-Based Reasoning. Medin & Schaffer, 1978 were the first researchers who proposed exemplar-based learning as a model of human learning. In this chapter, we formulate the acquisition of translation rules as a machine learning problem.

Our first attempt in this direction was to construct parse trees between the example translation pairs (Güvenir & Tunç, 1996). However, the difficulty we found was the lack of reliable parsers for both languages. In later work, we have proposed a learning technique (Cicekli & Güvenir, 1996; Güvenir & Cicekli, 1998) to learn *translation templates* from translation examples and store them as *generalized exemplars*, rather than parse trees. A template is defined as an example translation pair, where some components (e.g. word stems and morphemes) are generalized by replacing them with variables in both sentences. In that earlier work, we replaced only the differing parts by variables to obtain a generalized exemplar. In this chapter, we have extended and generalized our learning algorithm by adding new heuristics to form a complete framework for EBMT. In this new framework (Cicekli, 2000; Cicekli and Güvenir, 2001), we are also able to learn generalized exemplars by replacing similar parts in the sentences. These two distinct learning heuristics are called *similarity template learning* and *difference template learning*. These algorithms are also able to learn new translation templates from examples in which the number of differing or similar components between the source and target sentences differs. We refer to this technique as *Generalized Exemplar Based Machine Translation.*

The translation template learning framework presented in this chapter is based on a heuristic to infer correspondences between the patterns in the source and target languages given two translation pairs. According to this heuristic, given two translation examples, if the sentences in the source language exhibit some similarities, then the corresponding sentences in the target language must have similar parts, and they must be translations of the similar parts of the sentences in the source language. Furthermore, the remaining differing constituents of the source sentences should also match the corresponding differences of the target sentences. However, if the sentences do not exhibit any similarities, then no correspondences are inferred.

Our learning algorithm is called *Translation Template Learner* (TTL). Given a corpus of translation pairs, TTL infers correspondences between the source and target languages in the form of templates. These templates can be used for translation in both directions. Therefore, in the rest of the chapter we will refer to these languages as L^1 and L^2. Although the examples and experiments used here are on English and Turkish, we believe the model is equally applicable to many other language pairs.

The rest of the chapter is organized as follows. Section 9.2 explains the representation in the form of translation templates. The TTL algorithm is described in Section 9.3, and some of its performance results are given in Section 9.4. Section 9.5 describes how these translation templates can be used in translation, and the general system architecture. Our system is evaluated in Section 9.6. The limitations of the learning heuristics are described in Section 9.7, and Section 9.8 concludes the chapter with pointers for further research.

2. Translation Templates

A translation template is a generalized translation exemplar pair, where some components (e.g. word stems and morphemes) are generalized by replacing them with variables in both sentences, and establishing bindings between these variables. Let us asume the example translations in (1):

(1) I will drink orange juice ↔ portakal suyu içeceğim
I will drink coffee ↔ kahve içeceğim

Given these examples, the translation templates in (2) can be learned using our first learning heuristic:

(2) I will drink X^1 ↔ X^2 içeceğim
if $X^1 \leftrightarrow X^2$
orange juice ↔ portakal suyu
coffee ↔ kahve

The first translation template is read as the sentence "I will drink X^1" in L^1 and the sentence "X^2 içeceğim" in L^2 are translations of each other, given that X^1 in L^1 and X^2 in L^2 are translations of each other. Therefore, if it has already been acquired that "tea" in L^1 and "çay" in L^2 are translations of each other, for example, i.e. "tea" ↔ "çay", then the sentence "I will drink tea" can be easily translated into L^2 as "çay içeceğim". In a similar manner, the sentence "çay içeceğim" in L^2 can be translated in L^1 as "I will drink tea". The second and third translation templates are *atomic* templates representing atomic correspondences of two strings in the languages L^1 and L^2. An *atomic translation template* does not contain any variable. The TTL algorithm also stores the given translation examples as atomic translation templates.

Since the TTL algorithm is based on finding the similarities and differences between translation examples, the representation of sentences plays an important role. As explained above, the TTL algorithm may use the sentences exactly as they are found in a regular text. That is, there is no need for grammatical information or preprocessing on the bilingual parallel corpus. Therefore, it constitutes a grammar-less extraction algorithm for phrasal translation templates from bilingual parallel texts.

For agglutinative languages such as Turkish, this surface level representation of the sentences limits the generality of the templates to be learned. For example, the translation of the sentence "they are running" into Turkish is a single word "koşuyorlar", and the translation of "they are walking" is "yürüyorlar". When a surface level representation is used, it is not possible to find a template from these translation examples. In this case, it is assumed that a sentence is a sequence of words and a word is indivisible. Therefore, we will represent a word as its lexical level representation,[1] that is, its stem and its morphemes. For example, the translation pair "They are running" $\leftrightarrow$ "koşuyorlar" will be represented as "they are run+PROG" $\leftrightarrow$ "koş+PROG+3PL". Similarly, the pair "they are walking" $\leftrightarrow$ "yürüyorlar" will be represented as "they are walk+PROG" $\leftrightarrow$ "yürü+PROG+3PL". Here, the + symbol is used to mark the beginning of a morpheme. In the English and Turkish sentences, the PROG morpheme indicates the progressive tense suffix, while 3PL indicates the third person plural agreement marker. In this case, the sentence is treated as a

[1] In the lexical level representation of Turkish words appearing in the examples, we used the following notations which are similar to the notations used in phrase structure grammar papers (Gazdar *et al.*, 1985; Pollard & Sag, 1987): 1SG, 2SG, 3SG, 1PL, 2PL and 3PL for agreement morphemes; AOR, PAST and PROG for aorist, progressive and past tense morphemes, respectively; ABL for ablative morpheme; ACC for accusative morpheme; LOC for locative morpheme; DAT for dative morpheme; P1SG, P2SG, P3SG, P1PL, P2PL, and P3PL for possessive markers; ConvNoun=DHk for a morpheme (DHk) which is used to convert a verb into a noun. The following notations are used in the lexical level representations of English words appearing in the examples: PAST and PROG for past and progressive tense morphemes (for -ed and -ing suffixes); 3SG for the third person agreement morpheme (for the -s suffix) in the verbs. The surface level realizations of these morphemes are determined according to vowel and consonant harmony rules. The surface level realization of the PAST morpheme for English verbs also depends on whether that verb is regular or irregular.

sequence of morphemes (root words and morphemes). According to this representation, these two translation pairs would be as in (3):

(3) they are run+PROG ↔ koş+PROG+3PL
they are walk+PROG ↔ yürü+PROG+3PL

Using our first heuristic, the translation templates in (4) can be learned from the two translation pairs in (3):

(4) they are X^1+PROG ↔ X^2+PROG+3PL
if $X^1 \leftrightarrow X^2$
run ↔ koş
walk ↔ yürü

This representation allows an abstraction over technicalities such as vowel and/or consonant harmony rules in Turkish, and also different realizations of the same verb according to tense in English. We assume that the generation of surface level representation of words from their lexical level representations is unproblematic.

3. Learning Translation Templates

The TTL algorithm infers translation templates using similarities and differences between two translation examples (E_a, E_b) taken from a bilingual parallel corpus. Formally, a translation example $E_a : E_a^1 \leftrightarrow E_a^2$ is composed of a pair of sentences, E_a^1 and E_a^2 that are translations of each other in L_1 and L_2, respectively.

A *similarity* between two sentences of a language is a non-empty sequence of common items (root words or morphemes) in both sentences. A *difference* between two sentences of a language is a pair of two sequences (D_1, D_2) where D_1 is a sub-sequence of the first sentence, D_2 is a sub-sequence of the second sentence, and D_1 and D_2 do not contain any common item.

Given two translation examples (E_a, E_b), we try to find similarities between the constituents of E_a and E_b. A sentence is considered as a sequence of lexical items (i.e. root words or morphemes). If no similarities can be found, then no template is learned from these examples. If similar constituents do exist, then a *match sequence* $M_{a,b}$ of the form in (5) is generated:

(5) $$S_0^1, D_0^1, S_1^1, \cdots, D_{n-1}^1, S_n^1 \leftrightarrow S_0^2, D_0^2, S_1^2, \cdots, D_{m-1}^2, S_m^2$$
for $1 \leq n, m$

Here, S_k^1 represents a similarity (a sequence of common items) between E_a^1 and E_b^1. Similarly, $D_k^1 : (D_{k,a}^1, D_{k,b}^1)$ represents a difference between

E_a^1 and E_b^1, where $D_{k,a}^1$ and $D_{k,b}^1$ are non-empty differing items between two similar constituents S_k^1 and S_{k+1}^1. Corresponding differing constituents do not contain common items. That is, for a difference D_k, $D_{k,a}$ and $D_{k,b}$ do not contain any common item. Also, no lexical item in a similarity S_i appears in any difference. Any of S_0^1, S_n^1, S_0^2 or S_m^2 can be empty, but S_i^1 for $0<i<n$ and S_j^2 for $0<j<m$ must be non-empty. Furthermore, at least one similarity on each side must be non-empty. Note that given these conditions, there exists either a unique match or no match between two example translation pairs.

For instance, let us assume that the translation examples in (6) are given:

(6) "I bought the book for Cathy" ↔ "Cathy için kitabı satın aldım"

"I bought the ring for Cathy" ↔ "Cathy için yüzüğü satın aldım".

The lexical level representations of the example pairs in (6) are shown in (7):

(7) I buy+PAST the book for Cathy ↔
Cathy için kitap+ACC satın al+PAST+1SG

I buy+PAST the ring for Cathy ↔
Cathy için yüzük+ACC satın al+PAST+1SG

For the translation examples in (7), the match sequence in (8) is obtained by our matching algorithm.

(8) I buy+PAST the (book,ring) for Cathy ↔
Cathy için (kitap,yüzük) +ACC satın al+PAST+1SG

That is, the match sequences in (9) are obtained:

(9) S_0^1 = I buy+PAST the,
D_0^1 = (book,ring),
S_1^1 = for Cathy,
S_0^2 = Cathy için,
D_0^2 = (kitap,yüzük),
S_1^2 = +ACC satın al+PAST+1SG.

After a match sequence is found for two translation examples, we use two different learning heuristics to infer translation templates from that match sequence. These two learning heuristics try to locate the corresponding differences or similarities in the match sequence, respectively. If the first heuristic can locate all corresponding differences, a new translation template can be generated by replacing all differences with variables. This translation template is called a *similarity translation template* since it contains the similarities in the match sequence. The second heuristic can infer translation templates by replacing similarities with variables, if it is able to locate corresponding similarities in the match sequence. These translation templates are called *difference translation templates* since they contain differences in the match sequence. Note that both similarity and difference translation templates contain variables.

For each pair of examples in the training set, the TTL algorithm tries to infer translation templates using these two learning heuristics. After all translation templates are learned, they are sorted according to how specific they are. Given two templates, the one that has a higher number of terminals is more specific than the other. Note that the templates are ordered according to the source language. For two-way translation, the templates are ordered once for each language as the source.

3.1 Learning Similarity Translation Templates

If there exists only a single difference in both sides of a match sequence, i.e. $n=m=1$, then these differing constituents must be translations of each other. In other words, we are able to locate the corresponding differences in the match sequence. In this case, the match sequence must be of the form in (10):

(10) $S_0^1, D_0^1, S_1^1 \leftrightarrow S_0^2, D_0^2, S_1^2$

Since D_0^1 and D_0^2 are the corresponding differences, the similarity translation template in (11) is inferred by replacing these differences with variables:

(11) $S_0^1\ X^1\ S_1^1 \leftrightarrow S_0^2\ X^2\ S_1^2$
if $X^1 \leftrightarrow X^2$

Furthermore, the two atomic translation templates in (12) are learned from the corresponding differences $(D_{0,a}^1, D_{0,b}^1)$ and $(D_{0,a}^2, D_{0,b}^2)$:

(12) $D_{0,a}^1 \leftrightarrow D_{0,a}^2 \qquad D_{0,b}^1 \leftrightarrow D_{0,b}^2$

For example, since the match sequence given in (8) contains a single difference on both sides, the similarity translation template and two additional atomic translation templates in (13) can be inferred from the corresponding differences (book,ring) and (kitap,yüzük):

(13) I buy+PAST the X^1 for Cathy $\leftrightarrow$
Cathy için X^2+ACC satın al+PAST+1SG
if $X^1 \leftrightarrow X^2$
book $\leftrightarrow$ kitap
ring $\leftrightarrow$ yüzük

On the other hand, if the number of differences are equal on both sides but greater than one, i.e. $1 < n = m$, without prior knowledge, it is impossible to determine which difference in one side corresponds to which difference on the other side. In such cases, learning depends on those translation templates acquired previously. Our similarity template learning algorithm tries to locate $n-1$ corresponding differences in the match sequence by checking previously learned translation templates. That is, the kth difference $(D^1_{k,a}, D^1_{k,b})$ on the left side corresponds to the lth difference $(D^2_{l,a}, D^2_{l,b})$ on the right side if the two translation templates in (14) have been learned earlier:

(14) $D^1_{k,a} \leftrightarrow D^2_{l,a} \qquad D^1_{k,b} \leftrightarrow D^2_{l,b}$

After finding $n-1$ corresponding differences, two unchecked differences, one on each side, should correspond to each other. Thus, for all differences in the match sequence, we determine which difference on one side corresponds to which difference on the other. Now, let us assume that the list $CDPair_1, CDPair_2, \ldots, CDPair_n$ represents the list of all corresponding differences where $CDPair_n$ is the pair of two unchecked differences, and each $CDPair_i$ is the pair of two differences in the form $(D^1_{k_i}, D^2_{l_i})$. For each $CDPair_i$, we replace $D^1_{k_i}$ with a variable X^1_i, and $D^2_{l_i}$ with a variable X^2_i in a match sequence $M_{a,b}$. Thus, we get a new match sequence $M_{a,b}WDV$ in which all differences are replaced by proper variables. As a result, the similarity translation template in (15) can be inferred:

(15) $M_{a,b}WDV$
if $X^1_1 \leftrightarrow X^2_1$ **and** $\cdots$ **and** $X^1_n \leftrightarrow X^2_n$

In addition, the atomic translation templates in (16) are learned from the last corresponding differences $(D^1_{k_n,a}, D^1_{k_n,b})$ and $(D^2_{l_n,a}, D^2_{l_n,b})$:

procedure SimilarityTTL($M_{a,b}$)
begin

- Assume that the match sequence $M_{a,b}$ for the pair of translation examples E_a and E_b is:
  $S_0^1, D_0^1, \cdots, D_{n-1}^1, S_n^1, \leftrightarrow S_0^2, D_0^2, \cdots, D_{m-1}^2, S_m^2$

if $n{=}m{=}1$ **then**

- Infer the following templates:
  $S_0^1\ X^1\ S_1^1 \leftrightarrow S_0^2\ X^2\ S_1^2$ if $X^1 \leftrightarrow X^2$
  $D_{0,a}^1 \leftrightarrow D_{0,a}^2$
  $D_{0,b}^1 \leftrightarrow D_{0,b}^2$

else if $1 < n{=}m$ **and** $n{-}1$ corresponding differences can be found in $M_{a,b}$ **then**

- Assume that the unchecked corresponding differences is $((D_{k_n,a}^1, D_{k_n,b}^1), (D_{l_n,a}^2, D_{l_n,b}^2))$.
- Assume that the list of corresponding differences is $(D_{k_1}^1, D_{l_1}^2) \cdots (D_{k_n}^1, D_{l_n}^2)$ including unchecked ones.
- For each corresponding difference $(D_{k_i}^1, D_{l_i}^2)$, replace $D_{k_i}^1$ with X_i^1 and $D_{k_i}^2$ with X_i^2 to get the new match sequence $M_{a,b}WDV$.
- Infer the following templates:
  $M_{a,b}WDV$ if $X_1^1 \leftrightarrow X_1^2$ and $\cdots$ and $X_n^1 \leftrightarrow X_n^2$
  $D_{k_n,a}^1 \leftrightarrow D_{l_n,a}^2$
  $D_{k_n,b}^1 \leftrightarrow D_{l_n,b}^2$

end

Figure 9.1. The Similarity TTL (STTL) Algorithm

(16)
$$D_{k_n,a}^1 \leftrightarrow D_{l_n,a}^2$$
$$D_{k_n,b}^1 \leftrightarrow D_{l_n,b}^2$$

For example, the translation examples in (17) have two differences on both sides:

(17) I break+PAST the window ↔ pencere+ACC kır+PAST+1SG
You break+PAST the door ↔ kapı+ACC kır+PAST+2SG

The match sequence in (18) is obtained for these examples:

(18) (i,you) break+PAST the (window,door) $\leftrightarrow$
(pencere,kapı) +ACC kır+PAST (+1SG,+2SG)

Without prior information, we cannot determine whether "i" corresponds to "pencere" or "+1SG". However, if it has already been learned that "i" corresponds to "+1SG" and "you" corresponds to "+2SG", then the similarity translation template and two additional atomic translation templates in (19) can be inferred:

(19) X_1^1 break+PAST the $X_2^1 \leftrightarrow X_2^2$+ACC kır+PAST$X_1^2$
if $X_1^1 \leftrightarrow X_1^2$ **and** $X_2^1 \leftrightarrow X_2^2$
window $\leftrightarrow$ pencere
door $\leftrightarrow$ kapı

In general, when the number of differences in both sides of a match sequences is greater than or equal to 1, i.e. $1 \leq n = m$, the similarity TTL (STTL) algorithm learns new similarity translation templates only if at least $n-1$ of the differences have already been learned. A formal description of the similarity TTL algorithm is summarized in Figure 9.1.

3.2 Learning Difference Translation Templates

If there exists only a single non-empty similarity in both sides of a match sequence $M_{a,b}$, then these similar constituents must be translations of each other. In this case, each side of the match sequence can contain one or two differences, and they may contain different number of differences. In other words, each side ($M_{a,b}^i$ where i is 1 or 2) of the match sequence $M_{a,b} : M_{a,b}^1 \leftrightarrow M_{a,b}^2$ can be one of the following:

1 S_0^i, D_0^i, S_1^i, where S_0^i is non-empty, and S_1^i is empty.

2 S_0^i, D_0^i, S_1^i where S_1^i is non-empty, and S_0^i is empty.

3 $S_0^i, D_0^i, S_1^i, D_1^i, S_2^i$, where S_1^i is non-empty, and S_0^i and S_2^i are empty.

In this case, we replace the non-empty similarity in $M_{a,b}^i$ with variable X^i, and separate difference pairs in the match sequence to obtain two match sequences with similarity variables, namely M_aWSV and M_bWSV, as shown in (20):

(20) $M_a^1WSV \leftrightarrow M_a^2WSV$
$M_b^1WSV \leftrightarrow M_b^2WSV$

For example, for the third case given above, M_a^1WSV and M_b^1WSV will be as shown in (21):

(21) $M_a^1WSV: \; D_{0,a}^1 \, X^1 \, D_{1,a}^1$
$M_b^1WSV: \; D_{0,b}^1 \, X^1 \, D_{1,b}^1$

As a result, the two difference translation templates in (22) are learned when there is a single non-empty similarity on both sides of a match sequence:

(22) M_aWSV
  if $X^1 \leftrightarrow X^2$
M_bWSV
  if $X^1 \leftrightarrow X^2$

In addition to these templates, the atomic translation template in (23) is also learned from the corresponding non-empty similarities S_k^1 in $M_{a,b}^1$ and S_l^2 in $M_{a,b}^2$:

(23) $S_k^1 \leftrightarrow S_l^2$

For example, the match sequence in (18) contains a single non-empty similarity on both sides. The two difference translation templates, and one additional atomic template in (24) are learned from the corresponding similarities "break+PAST the" and "+ACC kır+PAST", in the match sequence in (23):

(24) i X^1 window $\leftrightarrow$ pencere X^2 +1SG
  if $X^1 \leftrightarrow X^2$
you X^1 door $\leftrightarrow$ kapı X^2 +2SG
  if $X^1 \leftrightarrow X^2$
break+PAST the $\leftrightarrow$ +ACC kır+PAST

Let us assume that the number of non-empty similarities on both sides is equal to n (i.e. they are equal), and n is greater than 1. Without prior knowledge, it is impossible to determine which similarity in one side corresponds to which similarity in the other side. Our difference template learning algorithm can infer new difference translation templates if it can locate $n-1$ corresponding non-empty similarities. We say that non-empty similarity S_k^1 on the left side corresponds to non-empty similarity

S_l^2 on the right side if the translation template in (25) has been learned earlier:

(25) $S_k^1 \leftrightarrow S_l^2$

After finding n–1 corresponding similarities, there will be two unchecked similarities, one on each side. These two unchecked similarities should correspond to each other. Now, let us assume that the list $CSPair_1, CS$ $Pair_2, \ldots, CSPair_n$ represents the list of all corresponding similarities in the match sequence. In that list, each $CSPair_i$ is a pair of two non-empty similarities in the form $(S_{k_i}^1, S_{l_i}^2)$, and $CSPair_n$ is the pair of two unchecked similarities. For each $CSPair_i$, we replace $S_{k_i}^1$ with a variable X_i^1 and $S_{l_i}^2$ with a variable X_i^2 in the match sequence $M_{a,b}$. Then the resulting sequence is divided into two match sequences with similarity variables, namely M_aWSV and M_bWSV, by separating difference pairs in the match sequence. As a result, the two difference translation templates in (26) can be inferred:

(26)
$$M_aWSV \quad \textbf{if } X_1^1 \leftrightarrow X_1^2 \textbf{ and } \cdots \textbf{ and } X_n^1 \leftrightarrow X_n^2$$
$$M_bWSV \quad \textbf{if } X_1^1 \leftrightarrow X_1^2 \textbf{ and } \cdots \textbf{ and } X_n^1 \leftrightarrow X_n^2$$

In addition, the atomic translation template in (27) is learned from the last corresponding similarities:

(27) $S_{k_n}^1 \leftrightarrow S_{l_n}^2$

For instance, from the match sequence $S_0^1, D_0^1, S_1^1 \leftrightarrow S_0^2, D_0^2, S_1^2$ where all similarities are non-empty, and if the list of corresponding similarities is $(S_0^1, S_1^2), (S_1^1, S_0^2)$, the difference translation templates in (28) can be inferred:

(28)
$$X_1^1 D_{0,a}^1 X_2^1 \leftrightarrow X_2^2 D_{0,a}^2 X_1^2 \quad \textbf{if } X_1^1 \leftrightarrow X_1^2 \textbf{ and } X_2^1 \leftrightarrow X_2^2$$
$$X_1^1 D_{0,b}^1 X_2^1 \leftrightarrow X_2^2 D_{0,b}^2 X_1^2 \quad \textbf{if } X_1^1 \leftrightarrow X_1^2 \textbf{ and } X_2^1 \leftrightarrow X_2^2$$

In addition, if (S_1^1, S_0^2) is the pair of two unchecked similarities, the atomic translation template in (29) is learned:

(29) $S_1^1 \leftrightarrow S_0^2$

For example, the match sequence in (8) contains two non-empty similarities. Without prior information, we cannot determine whether "for

Cathy" corresponds to "Cathy için" or "+ACC satın al+PAST+1SG". However, if it has been already learned that "for Cathy" corresponds to "Cathy için", then the two difference translation templates and one additional translation template in (30) can be inferred:

(30) X_1^1 book $X_2^1 \leftrightarrow X_2^2$ kitap X_1^2
  if $X_1^1 \leftrightarrow X_1^2$ **and** $X_2^1 \leftrightarrow X_2^2$
X_1^1 ring $X_2^1 \leftrightarrow X_2^2$ yüzük X_1^2
  if $X_1^1 \leftrightarrow X_1^2$ **and** $X_2^1 \leftrightarrow X_2^2$
i buy+PAST the $\leftrightarrow$ +ACC satın al+PAST+1SG

In general, when the number of non-empty similarities on both sides of a match sequence is greater than or equal to 1, i.e. $1 \leq n = m$, the difference TTL (DTTL) algorithm learns new difference translation templates only if at least $n-1$ of the similarities have already been learned. A formal description of the difference TTL algorithm is summarized in Figure 9.2.

procedure DifferenceTTL($M_{a,b}$)
begin
  if $numofsim(M_{a,b}^1) = numofsim(M_{a,b}^2) = n \geq 1$
    and $n-1$ corresponding similarities can be found in $M_{a,b}$ **then**
    - Assume that the unchecked corresponding similarities is $(S_{k_n}^1, S_{l_n}^2)$.
    - Assume that the list of corresponding similarities is $(S_{k_1}^1, S_{l_1}^2) \cdots (S_{k_n}^1, S_{l_n}^2)$ including unchecked ones.
    - For each corresponding difference $(S_{k_i}^1, S_{l_i}^2)$, replace $S_{k_i}^1$ with X_i^1 and $S_{k_i}^2$ with X_i^2 to get the new match sequence $M_{a,b}WSV$.
    - Divide $M_{a,b}WSV$ into M_aWSV and M_bWSV by separating differences.
    - Infer the following templates:
      M_aWSV if $X_1^1 \leftrightarrow X_1^2$ and $\cdots$ and $X_n^1 \leftrightarrow X_n^2$
      M_bWSV if $X_1^1 \leftrightarrow X_1^2$ and $\cdots$ and $X_n^1 \leftrightarrow X_n^2$
      $S_{k_n}^1 \leftrightarrow S_{l_n}^2$

end

Figure 9.2. The Difference TTL (DTTL) Algorithm

3.3 Different Numbers of Similarities or Differences in Match Sequences

The STTL algorithm given in Section 9.3.1 can learn new translation templates only if the number of differences on both sides of a match sequence are equal. Similarly, the DTTL algorithm requires that a match sequence has to have the same number of similarities on both sides. In this section, we describe how to relax these restrictions so that the STTL and the DTTL algorithms can learn new translation templates from a match sequence with different numbers of differences or similarities, respectively. We try to make the number of differences equal on both sides of a match sequence by separating differences, before the STTL algorithm tries to learn from that match sequence. Similarly, we try to equate the number of similarities on both sides of a match sequence for the DTTL algorithm. For example, the match sequence of the two translation examples ("I came" ↔ "geldim" and "You went" ↔ "gittin") in (31) has one difference on the left side, but it has two differences on the right side:

(31) i come+PAST ↔ gel+PAST+1SG
you go+PAST ↔ git+PAST+2SG

Match Sequence:
(i come,you go) +PAST ↔ (gel,git) +PAST (+1SG,+2SG)

The STTL algorithm given in Section 9.3.1 cannot learn translation templates from this match sequence because the number of differences is not the same. Since both constituents of the difference on the left side contain two morphemes, we can separate that difference into two differences by dividing both constituents of that difference into two parts given morpheme boundaries. As a result, we obtain the match sequence in (32):

(32) (i,you) (come,go) +PAST ↔ (gel,git) +PAST (+1SG,+2SG)

Now, the match sequence in (32) has two differences on both sides. If we know that (i,you) corresponds to (+1SG,+2SG), we can learn the translation templates in (33):

(33) $X_1^1\ X_2^1$ +PAST $\leftrightarrow$ X_2^2 +PAST X_1^2
if $X_1^1 \leftrightarrow X_1^2$ **and** $X_2^1 \leftrightarrow X_2^2$
come $\leftrightarrow$ gel
go $\leftrightarrow$ git

In general, before we apply the STTL algorithm to a match sequence, we try to create an instance of that match sequence with the same number of differences on both sides by dividing a difference into several differences. A difference (D_a, D_b) can be divided into two differences (D_{a_1}, D_{b_1}), and (D_{a_2}, D_{b_2}) if the lengths of D_a and D_b are greater than 1. The reader should note that if D_{a_1}, D_{a_2}, D_{b_1} and D_{b_2} are non-empty, the equalities $D_a = D_{a_1}D_{a_2}$ and $D_b = D_{b_1}D_{b_2}$ hold. We continue to create an instance of a match sequence with the same number of differences until new translation templates can be learned from that instance, or until there is no other way to create an instance with the same number of differences. We may need to create an instance of the original match sequence even if it has the same number of differences on both sides. For example, the match sequence of the translation examples "I drank water" $\leftrightarrow$ "su içtim" and "You ate orange" $\leftrightarrow$ "portakal yedin" has two differences on both sides, as shown in (34):

(34) i drink+PAST water $\leftrightarrow$ su iç+PAST+1SG
you eat+PAST orange $\leftrightarrow$ portakal ye+PAST+2SG

Match Sequence:
(i drink,you eat) +PAST (water,orange) $\leftrightarrow$
(su iç,portakal ye) +PAST (+1SG,+2SG)

Now, let us assume that we do not know whether the difference (i drink,you eat) corresponds to (su iç,portakal ye) or (+1SG,+2SG), or whether the difference (water,orange) corresponds to (su iç,portakal ye) or (+1SG,+2SG). In fact, none of these correspondences should hold because they will all yield incorrect translation templates. However, if we divide the differences on both sides, we obtain the match sequence in (35), with three differences on both sides:

(35) (i,you) (drink,eat) +PAST (water,orange) $\leftrightarrow$
(su,portakal) (iç,ye) +PAST (+1SG,+2SG)

From this match sequence, if we know two correspondences between the differences above, such as (i,you) corresponds to (+1SG,+2SG), and (water,orange) corresponds to (su,portakal), we can learn the translation templates in (36):

(36) $X_1^1\ X_2^1$ +PAST $X_3^1 \leftrightarrow X_3^2\ X_2^2$ +PAST X_1^2
if $X_1^1 \leftrightarrow X_1^2$ **and** $X_2^1 \leftrightarrow X_2^2$ **and** $X_3^1 \leftrightarrow X_3^2$
drink ↔ iç
eat ↔ ye

For the DTTL algorithm, we divide similarities to equate the number of similarities on both sides of a match sequence. A similarity S can be divided into two non-empty similarities S_1 and S_2 in order to increase the number of similarities in one side. Before the DTTL algorithm is executed, we try to equate the number of similarities on both sides. We continue to create an instance of a match sequence with the same number of similarities until the DTTL algorithm can learn new translation templates from this instance or until there is no other way to create an instance.

For example, from the match sequence of the translation examples "I came" ↔ "geldim" and "I went" ↔ "gittim", the DTTL algorithm cannot learn new templates because it contains two similarities on the left side and one on the right side, namely those in (37):

(37) i come+PAST ↔ gel+PAST+1SG
i go+PAST ↔ git+PAST+1SG

Match Sequence:
i (come,go) +PAST ↔ (gel,git) +PAST+1SG

On the other hand, we can divide the similarity "+PAST+1SG" into two similarities "+PAST" and "+1SG" by inserting an empty difference between them. Now the new match sequence has two similarities on both sides. If the correspondence of "i" to "+1SG" is already known, the translation templates in (38) can be learned by the DTTL algorithm:

(38) X_1^1 come $X_2^1 \leftrightarrow$ gel $X_2^2\ X_1^2$
if $X_1^1 \leftrightarrow X_1^2$ **and** $X_2^1 \leftrightarrow X_2^2$
X_1^1 go $X_2^1 \leftrightarrow$ git $X_2^2\ X_1^2$
if $X_1^1 \leftrightarrow X_1^2$ **and** $X_2^1 \leftrightarrow X_2^2$
+PAST ↔ +PAST

3.4 Differences with Empty Constituents

The current matching algorithm does not allow a difference to contain an empty constituent. For this reason, the matching algorithm fails for certain translation example pairs although we may learn useful translation templates from those pairs. For example, the current matching algorithm fails for the following examples "I saw the man" ↔ "adamı gördüm" and "I saw a man" ↔ "bir adam gördüm" because "bir" and "+ACC" have to match empty strings, as shown in (39):

(39) i see+PAST the man ↔ adam+ACC gör+PAST+1SG
i see+PAST a man ↔ bir adam gör+PAST+1SG

However, if we relax this restriction in the matching algorithm by allowing a difference to have an empty constituent, then this new version of the matching algorithm will find the match sequence in (40) for the example in (39):

(40) i see+PAST (the,a) man ↔
(ϵ,bir) adam (+ACC,ϵ) gör+PAST+1SG

In this match sequence, "bir" in the difference (ϵ,bir) and "+ACC" in the difference (+ACC,ϵ) correspond to the empty string. If we apply the DTTL algorithm to this match sequence by assuming that the correspondence of "man" to "adam" is already known, the translation templates in (41) can be learned:

(41) X_1^1 the $X_2^1 \leftrightarrow X_2^2$ +ACC X_1^2
if $X_1^1 \leftrightarrow X_1^2$ **and** $X_2^1 \leftrightarrow X_2^2$
X_1^1 a $X_2^1 \leftrightarrow$ bir X_2^2 X_1^2
if $X_1^1 \leftrightarrow X_1^2$ **and** $X_2^1 \leftrightarrow X_2^2$
i see+PAST ↔ gör+PAST+1SG

We do not apply the STTL algorithm to a match sequence containing a difference with an empty constituent. If we apply the STTL algorithm to this kind of a match sequence, a translation template with one side empty can be generated. This would mean that a non-empty string in a language always corresponds to an empty string in another language. This is not a plausible situation. For this reason, we only apply the DTTL algorithm to this kind of match sequence in order to prevent the problem mentioned above. We only try to create a match sequence with a difference having an empty constituent if the original match algorithm cannot find a match sequence without differences which contains no empty constituents.

3.5 Complete Learning Examples

In this section, we describe the behavior of our learning algorithms by giving the details of algorithm steps on the two translation example pairs in (43) and (48). We assume that the two translation templates in (42) have been learned earlier:

(42) i ↔ +1SG
you ↔ +2SG

Assume the translation example pair in (43):

(43) I drank wine ↔ Şarap içtim
You drank beer ↔ Bira içtin

Since our learning algorithms work on the lexical form of sentences, the input for our algorithm will be the two translation examples in (44):

(44) i drink+PAST wine ↔ şarap iç+PAST+1SG
you drink+PAST beer ↔ bira iç+PAST+2SG

We now try to find a match sequence between these two translation examples. To do that, a match sequences between the English sentences "i drink+PAST wine" and "you drink+PAST beer" is found, and a match sequence between the Turkish sentences "şarap iç+PAST+1SG" and "bira iç+PAST+2SG" is found. As a result, the match sequence in (45) is obtained between these two translation examples:

(45) (i,you) drink+PAST (wine,beer) ↔
(şarap,bira) iç+PAST (+1SG,+2SG)

We then try to apply the STTL and DTTL algorithms to this match sequence. Since there is an equal number of differences (namely, two) on both sides, the STTL algorithm is applicable to this match sequence. The STTL algorithm can learn new translation templates from this match sequence, if it can determine the corresponding differences. Given the correspondence between (i,you) and (+1SG,+2SG), (wine,beer) should correspond to (şarap,bira). Thus, the STTL algorithm infers the three translation templates in (46) from this match sequence:

(46) X_1^1 drink+PAST X_2^1 ↔ X_2^2 iç+PAST X_1^2
if $X_1^1 \leftrightarrow X_1^2$ **and** $X_2^1 \leftrightarrow X_2^2$
wine ↔ şarap
beer ↔ bira

Since there is an equal number of similarities (namely, one) on both sides, the DTTL algorithm is also applicable to this match sequence. Since there is only one similarity on both sides, these similarities ("drink+PAST" and "iç+PAST") should correspond to each other. Thus, the DTTL algorithm infers the three translation templates in (47) from this match sequence:

(47) i X_1^1 wine ↔ şarap X_1^2 +1SG
if $X_1^1 \leftrightarrow X_1^2$
you X_1^1 beer ↔ bira X_1^2 +2SG
if $X_1^1 \leftrightarrow X_1^2$
drink+PAST ↔ iç+PAST

Let us now assume the translation example pair in (48):

(48) I drank a glass of white wine ↔ Bir bardak beyaz şarap içtim
You drank a glass of red wine ↔ Bir bardak kırmızı şarap içtin

The actual input for our algorithm will be the two translation examples in lexical form in (49):

(49) i drink+PAST a glass of white wine ↔
bir bardak beyaz şarap iç+PAST+1SG
you drink+PAST a glass of red wine ↔
bir bardak kırmızı şarap iç+PAST+2SG

Then, a match sequence between the English sentences "i drink+PAST a glass of white wine" and "you drink+PAST a glass of red wine" will be found, as will a match sequence between the Turkish sentences "bir bardak beyaz şarap iç+PAST+1SG" and "bir bardak kırmızı şarap iç+PAST+2SG". As a result, the match sequence in (50) is found between these two translation examples:

(50) (i,you) drink+PAST a glass of (white,red) wine ↔
bir bardak (beyaz,kırmızı) şarap iç+PAST (+1SG,+2SG)

We then try to apply the STTL and DTTL algorithms to this match sequence. Since there is an equal number of differences (namely, two) on both sides, the STTL algorithm is applicable to this match sequence. The STTL algorithm can learn new translation templates from this match sequence if it can determine the corresponding differences. Since a correspondence between (i,you) and (+1SG,+2SG) has been given, (white,red) should correspond to (beyaz,kırmızı). Thus, the STTL algorithm infers the three translation templates in (51) from this match sequence:

(51) X_1^1 drink+PAST a glass of X_2^1 wine $\leftrightarrow$
bir bardak X_2^2 şarap iç+PAST X_1^2
if $X_1^1 \leftrightarrow X_1^2$ **and** $X_2^1 \leftrightarrow X_2^2$
white $\leftrightarrow$ beyaz
red $\leftrightarrow$ kırmızı

Since there is an equal number of similarities (two) on both sides, the DTTL algorithm is also applicable to this match sequence, but we cannot determine the similarity correspondences in this match sequence. In other words, we cannot know whether "drink+PAST a glass of" corresponds to "bir bardak" or "şarap iç+PAST". Therefore, the DTTL algorithm cannot directly learn any new translation template from this match sequence. In this case, we look at instances of this match sequence. A suitable instance should contain an equal number of similarities on both sides, in which cases and correspondences of similarity can be determined. One of the instances of this match sequence can be obtained by separating the similarity "drink+PAST a glass of" into the similarities "drink+PAST" and "a glass of", and by separating the similarity "şarap iç+PAST" into the similarities "şarap" and "iç+PAST". Now we have three similarities on both sides in this instance of the original match sequence. From the first example, we learned the correspondence between "wine" and "şarap", and the correspondence between "drink+PAST" and "iç+PAST". Furthermore, the similarity "a glass of" should correspond to "bir bardak". Since all similarity correspondences can be determined in this instance, the three translation templates in (52) can be inferred from this instance by the DTTL algorithm:

(52) i X_1^1 X_2^1 red X_3^1 $\leftrightarrow$ X_2^2 kırmızı X_3^2 X_1^2 +1SG
if $X_1^1 \leftrightarrow X_1^2$ **and** $X_2^1 \leftrightarrow X_2^2$ **and** $X_3^1 \leftrightarrow X_3^2$
you X_1^1 X_2^1 white X_3^1 $\leftrightarrow$ X_2^2 beyaz X_3^2 X_1^2 +2SG
if $X_1^1 \leftrightarrow X_1^2$ **and** $X_2^1 \leftrightarrow X_2^2$ **and** $X_3^1 \leftrightarrow X_3^2$
a glass of $\leftrightarrow$ bir bardak

In this example, we looked at the instances of the original match sequence because we could not learn translation templates from it. In this kind of situation, we continue to generate instances of the original match sequence until a translation template can be learned, or until there are no more instances of the original match sequence. In the first example, we did not generate instances of the original match sequence because we were able to learn translation templates from the original one.

Table 9.1. Performance Results for The Training Set with 747 Training Pairs

We applied only the STTL algorithm without dividing differences in match sequences and without having match sequences with an empty difference constituent.	• In the first pass, the STTL algorithm learned 642 translation templates. • No new templates were learned in the second pass. • Each pass took about 53 seconds real time.
We applied only the DTTL algorithm without dividing similarities in match sequences and without having match sequences with an empty difference constituent.	• In the first pass, the DTTL algorithm learned 812 translation templates. • In the second pass, using the initial pairs and these new translation templates, the DTTL algorithm inferred 6 more templates. • No new templates were learned in the third pass. • Each pass took about 54 seconds real time.
We applied both the STTL and the DTTL algorithms on the training set without dividing similarities or differences in match sequences and without having match sequences with an empty difference constituent.	• In the first pass, 1239 translation templates were learned. • In the second pass, the TTL algorithms inferred 6 more templates. • No new templates were learned in the third pass. • Each pass took about 81 seconds real time.
We applied both the STTL and the DTTL algorithms on the training set with dividing similarities or differences in match sequences and without having match sequences with an empty difference constituent.	• In the first pass, 1330 translation templates were learned. • In the second pass, the TTL algorithms inferred 11 more templates. • No new templates were learned in the third pass. • Each pass took about 101 seconds real time. • By dividing similarities or differences, 8% more new templates were learned costing 25% more on the learning time.
We applied both the STTL and the DTTL algorithms on the training set with dividing similarities or differences in match sequences and with having match sequences with an empty difference constituent.	• In the first pass, 2055 translation templates were learned. • In the second pass, the TTL algorithms inferred 55 more templates. • No new templates were learned in the third pass. • Each pass took about 170 seconds real time. • By having match sequences with an empty difference constituent, 57% more new templates were learned costing 68% more on the learning time.

4. Performance Results

In order to evaluate our TTL algorithms empirically, we have implemented them in Prolog and evaluated them on medium-sized bilingual parallel texts. Our training sets are artificially collected because of the unavailiabilty of a large morphologically tagged parallel text between English and Turkish.

In each pass of the learning phase, we applied our learning algorithms for each pair of translation examples in a training set. Since the number of pairs is $\sum_{i=1}^{n-1} i$ when the number of translation examples in a training set is n, the time complexity of each pass of the learning phase is $O(n^2)$. The learning phase continues until its last pass cannot learn any new translation templates. In other words, when the number of new learned translation templates is zero in a pass, the learning process terminates. Although the maximum number of passes of the learning phase theoretically is $n-2$, the maximum number of passes which the learning phase had to do on our training sets was 4. This means that the worst case time complexity of our learning algorithm is $O(n^3)$, but in practice it remained in $O(n^2)$.

One of our training sets contained 747 training pairs, which is enough for the system to learn a small coverage of the basics of English grammar. To find the cost/gain of each portion of our learning algorithm, we applied the different portions of our algorithms to this training set. We obtained the results in Table 9.1 for this training set on a SPARC 20/61 workstation.

5. System Architecture and Translation

The templates learned by the TTL algorithm can be used directly in the translation phase. These templates are in lexical form, and they can be used for translation in both directions. The general system architecture is given in Figure 9.3. As can be seen, the input for the learning module is a set of bilingual examples in lexical form. In order to create a set of bilingual examples in lexical form, a set of bilingual examples in their surface form is created, following which all words in these examples are morphologically tagged using Turkish and English morphological analyzers. In this process, a morphological analyzer produces possible lexical forms of a word from its surface form, and the correct lexical form is selected by a human expert. Thus, a set bilingual examples in lexical form is created. Of course, if morphologically tagged sets of bilingual examples existed between English and Turkish, this step would become redundant.

From the surface form of a sentence, the lexical form of that sentence is created by replacing every word with its correct lexical form. Non-words such as punctuation markers are assumed to have the same lexical and surface form. The only exception to this is a punctuation marker depicting the end of sentences. In this case, we delete these completely from the lexical forms.

In the translation process, a given source language sentence in surface form is translated into the corresponding target language sentence in surface form. The outline of the translation process is given below:

1 First, the lexical level representation of the input sentence to be translated is derived by using the source language lexical analyzer.

2 Then any translation templates matching the input are collected. They are collected from most to least specific. For each selected template, its variables are instantiated with the corresponding values in the source sentence. Then we search for templates matching these bound values. If they are found successfully, target language variables are replaced by the values in the matching template.

3 Finally, the surface level representation of the sentence obtained in the previous step is generated by the target language morphological generator.

Note that if the sentence in the source language is ambiguous, then templates corresponding to each sense will be retrieved, and the corresponding sentences for each sense will be generated. The user can choose the right one among the possible translations according to the context. We hope that the correct answer will be among the first results generated in the translation steps by imposing the constraint that templates are to be used from most to least specific. Although this helps to obtain the correct answer among the top results, it may not be enough. We also investigated using a statistical method (Öz & Cicekli, 1998) to order our learned translation templates. In this statistical method, we assign a confidence factor to the learned translation templates, and we use these confidence factors to sort the results of translations. The training data is again used to collect this statistical information. Using this statistical method, the percentage of the correct results is increased by 50% in the top 5 results.

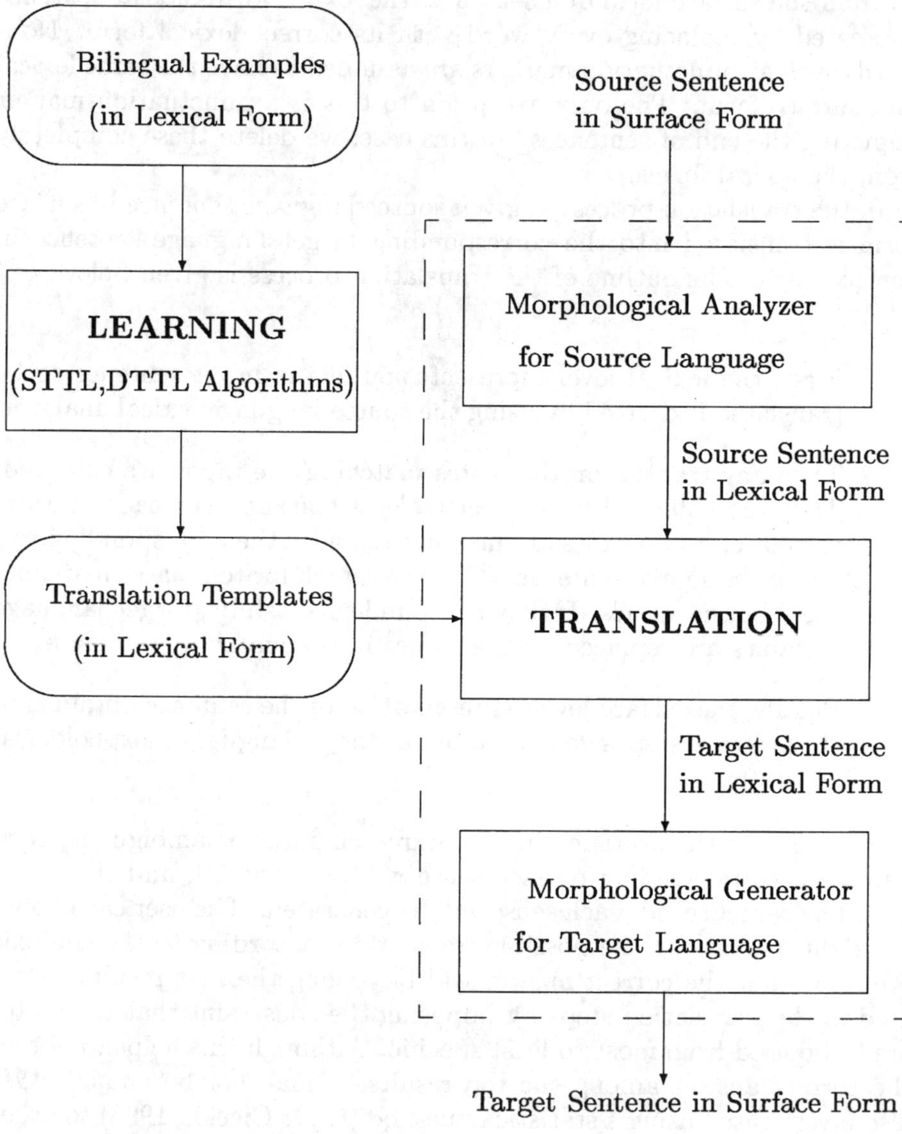

Figure 9.3. The System Architecture

6. Evaluation

Since the TTL algorithm can overspecialize, useless and incorrect templates can be learned. Given this, together with the problem of ambiguity noted above, the translation results produced by our translation algorithm can contain incorrect translations in addition to correct ones. However, our main goal is to obtain correct translations among the top-ranked results. For example, according to our results given in Öz & Cicekli, 1998, we show that the percentage of correct results among the total results is 33%. If we just use the templates according to how specific they are, the percentage of correct results is increased to 44% in the top 5 results. This means that at least 2 of the top 5 results are correct. In addition to our ordering constraint, using the statistical method described in Öz & Cicekli, 1998 increased the percentage of the correct results to 60%. In addition, we investigated whether the top results contain at least one correct translation or not. When we just use our ordering constraint, the top 5 results of 77% of all translations contained at least one correct translation. When the statistical method is used together with our ordering constraint, the percentage is increased to 91%. Thus, a human expert can choose the correct answer by just looking at the top few results.

Our algorithms are tested on training sets constructed by us and others. We only morphologically tagged the training sets prepared by others. Although these training sets are not huge by other standards, they are big enough to be treated as real corpora. One aspect of our future work will be to test our algorithms on huge, morphologically tagged bilingual corpora between other languages (unfortunately there is no huge bilingual corpus between English and Turkish, but we are trying to construct one). The next language pair that we are planning to work on is English and French.

The success of an MT system can be measured according to two criteria: coverage and correctness. Coverage is the percentage of the sentences which can be translated, and correctness is the percentage of correct translations among all translation results produced by that system. However, no MT system is able to guarantee correctness and complete coverage. That is, no MT system will always produce the correct translation for any given sentence, nor produce some translation for any given sentence. This is a direct consequence of the complexity and inherent ambiguity of natural languages. Since natural languages are dynamic, new words enter the language, or new meanings are assigned to old words in time. For the case of English, the word *Internet* is a new addition and the word *web* has a new meaning. In addition, words and sentences are interpreted differently depending on their context. The best way to cope with such issues is to have a translation system that can learn and adapt itself to the changes in the language and the context. The TTL algorithms presented in this chapter achieve this by learning new templates corresponding to the new meaning of the words and interpretation of the sentences from new translation examples.

As a whole, our system can be seen as a human-assisted EBMT system. Our system suggests possible translations which usually contain the correct translation among the top few candidates, and a human expert then chooses the correct translation just by evaluating the given results. The coverage of our system depends on the coverage of the given training sets and how much our learning algorithms learn from these training sets. When the size of training sets is increased, the coverage of our system also increases. Although we cannot say that our learning algorithms can extract all available information in training sets, they can extract most of the available information as translation templates. In measuring the correctness of our system, one needs to look at whether the top few results contain the correct translation or not. In order to increase the level of correctness, we imposed a constraint on the use of the translation templates according to how specific they were, and assigned confidence factors to them. This helps ensure that the correct translation is found among the top few results. The general performance of our system and other EBMT systems depends firstly on the quality of the bilingual corpora used, because they constitute the sole information source, and secondly as to how the available information in the corpora is used in the translation process.

7. Limitations of Learning Heuristics

The preconditions in the definition of the match sequence (see Section 9.3) may appear to be very strong, and they may restrict the practical usage of our learning algorithms. These preconditions are stated as explicitly and strongly as they could be to reduce the number of the useless translation templates which can be learned from match sequences in the expense of missing the opportunity of learning some useful translation templates.

Let us consider the 'translation' examples between American and British English in (53)–(55):

(53) The other day, the president analyzed the state of the union ↔
The other day, the president analysed the state of the union

(54) Recently, the president analyzed the state of the union ↔
Recently, the president analysed the state of the union

(55) Recently, the president analyzed the union ↔
Recently, the president analysed the union

Note that the only difference between source and target sentences here is the alternative spellings of *analyse* vs. *analyze*. Despite the very strong similarity between these sentence pairs, our learning heuristics will not learn any translation templates from these examples. The reader will notice that the lexical item "the" appears 4, 3 and 2 times in the sentences of the three examples in (53)–(55), respectively. Therefore, the lexical item "the" will try to end up in both a similarity and a difference in a match sequence of any two of these examples because the sentences in any two of these examples do not contain same number of lexical items of the form "the". Since we do not allow the same lexical item to appear in both a similarity and a difference, any pair of these examples cannot have a match sequence. Since our system will not learn any translation examples, it will not be able to 'translate' the sentence in (56):

(56) The other day, the president analyzed the union

into British English when only the examples in (53) are given.

Therefore, our learning algorithms can only learn if there is a match sequence between the examples. On the other hand, if we supply two more examples, namely those in (57)–(58):

(57) He analyzed today's situation ↔
He analysed today's situation

(58) Recently, the president analyzed today's situation ↔
Recently, the president analysed today's situation

our learning algorithms will be able learn the required translation templates from the examples (53)–(58). Some of the learned templates will be those in (59):

(59) X_1 analyzed $X_2 \leftrightarrow Y_1$ analysed Y_2
if $X_1 \leftrightarrow Y_1$ **and** $X_2 \leftrightarrow Y_2$
today's situation $\leftrightarrow$ today's situation
He analyzed $\leftrightarrow$ He analysed
Recently, the president analyzed $\leftrightarrow$ Recently, the president analysed
The other day, the president $\leftrightarrow$ The other day, the president
Recently, the president $\leftrightarrow$ Recently, the president
the union $\leftrightarrow$ the union
the state of the union $\leftrightarrow$ the state of the union
analyzed $\leftrightarrow$ analysed
He $\leftrightarrow$ He

These templates will be enough to 'translate' the sentence (55) to British English.

Let us examine the consequences of relaxing the conditions for the definition of a match sequence. If we let a lexical item appear in a similarity and a difference of a match sequence, we will no longer have a unique match sequence for any given two strings and there may be more than one match sequence for those strings. For instance, the American English sentences in the examples (54) and (55) will have the five match sequences in (60) in this case:

(60)
- Recently, the president analyzed the (state of the,ϵ) union
- Recently, the president analyzed (the state of,ϵ) the union
- Recently, (the president analyzed,ϵ) the (state of,president analyzed) the union
- Recently, (the president analyzed the state of,ϵ) the (ϵ,president analyzed the) union
- Recently, (ϵ,the president analyzed) the (president analyzed the state of the,ϵ) union

The British sentences in those examples will also have 5 match sequences. Thus, examples (54) and (55) will have 25 different match sequences because there will be five match sequences for each side of those sentences in this situation. Since only some of these match sequences will be correct, we may learn a lot of useless (wrong) templates from the rest of these match sequences. This is the main reason for insisting on such strong preconditions on the match sequences.

Nevertheless, our learning algorithms may still learn useless wrong translation templates. For example, let us consider the two examples in (61):

(61) I know hardly anybody ↔ Hemen hemen hiç kimseyi tanımam
You know almost everything ↔ Hemen hemen her şeyi bilirsin

From these examples, the correspondence of "know" and "hemen hemen" will be inferred, even though it is wrong. There are two reasons for this problem. First, Turkish differentiates two meanings of "know" as "tanımak" ("to know somebody") and "bilmek" ("to know something"). Second, English phrases "hardly" and "almost" map to the same Turkish phrase ("hemen hemen"). Of course, there can be other situations in which wrong translation templates can be inferred. In order to reduce the effect of these wrong translations, we have also incorporated the statistical methods described in Öz & Cicekli, 1998 into our system. According to these statistical methods, each translation result is associated with a computed confidence factor (a value between 0 and 1) and the translation results are sorted with respect to these computed confidence factors. Each translation template is associated with a confidence factor during the learning phase, and the confidence factor of a translation result is computed from the confidence factors of the translation templates that are used to find that translation result.

8. Conclusion

In this chapter, we have presented a model for learning translation templates between two languages. The model is based on a simple pattern matcher. We integrated this model with an EBMT system to form our Generalized Exemplar-Based Machine Translation model. We have implemented this model as the TTL (Translation Template Learner) algorithms.

The TTL algorithms are illustrated in learning translation templates between Turkish and English. We believe that the approach is applicable to many pairs of natural languages (at least for West-European languages such as English, French, and Spanish), assuming sets of morphologically tagged bilingual examples.

The major contribution of this chapter is that the proposed TTL algorithm eliminates the difficult task of manually encoding the translation templates. The TTL algorithm can work directly on the surface level representation of sentences. However, in order to generate useful translation patterns, it is helpful to use the lexical level representations. For English and Turkish, at least, it is quite trivial to obtain the lexical level representations of words.

Our main motivation was that the underlying inference mechanism is compatible with one of the ways humans learn languages, i.e. learning from examples. We believe that in everyday usage, humans learn general sentence patterns using the similarities and differences between many different example sentences that they are exposed to. This observation led us to the idea that a computer can be trained in a similar fashion, using analogy within a corpus of example translations.

The techniques presented here can be used in an incremental manner. Initially, a set of translation templates can be inferred from a set of translation examples, with extra templates learnable from another set with the help of previously learned translation templates. In other words, the templates learned from previous examples help in learning new templates from new examples, as in the case of natural language learning by humans. This incremental approach allows us to incorporate existing translation templates when new translation examples become available, instead of re-running previous sets of examples along with the new set of examples.

The learning and translation times on the small training set are quite reasonable, and that indicates the program will scale up to large, naturally occurring training corpora. Note that this algorithm is not specific to the English and Turkish languages, but should be applicable to the task of learning to translate automatically between many pairs of languages. Although the learning process on a large corpus will take a considerable amount of time, it is a task to be performed only once. Once the translation templates are learned, the translation process is fast.

The model that we have proposed in this chapter may be integrated with other systems as a natural language front-end, where a small subset of a natural language is used. This algorithm can be used to learn to translate user queries into the language of the underlying system.

This model may also be integrated with an intelligent tutoring system (ITS) for second language learning. The template representation model provides a level of information that may help in error diagnosis and student modelling tasks of an ITS. The model may also be used to tune the teaching strategy according to the needs of the student by analysing the student answers analogically with the closest cases in the corpus. Specific corpora may be designed to concentrate on certain topics that will help in the student's acquisition of the target language. The work presented in this chapter provides an opportunity to evaluate this possibility as a future research topic.

Acknowledgments

This research has been supported in part by *NATO* Science for Stability Program Grant TU-LANGUAGE and The Scientific and Technical Council of Turkey (TÜBİTAK) Grant EEEAG-244.

References

Cicekli, I. 2000. Similarities and Differences. In *SCI2000: Proceedings of the Multi-Conference on Systemics, Cybernetics and Informatics*, Orlando, FL., pp.331–337.

Cicekli, I. and H.A. Güvenir. 1996. Learning Translation Rules From A Bilingual Corpus. In *NeMLaP-2: Proceedings of the 2nd International Conference on New Methods in Language Processing*, Ankara, Turkey, pp.90–97.

Cicekli, I. and H.A. Guvenir. 2001. Learning Translation Templates from Bilingual Translation Examples. *Applied Intelligence* **15**(1):57–76.

Gazdar, G., E. Klein, G.K. Pullum, and I.A. Sag. 1985. *Generalized Phrase Structure Grammar*. Blackwell, Cambridge, MA.

Güvenir, H.A., and A. Tunç. 1996. Corpus-Based Learning of Generalized Parse Tree Rules for Translation. In Gord McCalla (ed.) *New Directions in Artificial Intelligence: Proceedings of the 11th Biennial Conference of the Canadian Society for Computational Studies of Intelligence.* Springer-Verlag, LNCS 1081, Toronto, Ontario, Canada, pp.121–131.

Güvenir, H. A, and I. Cicekli. 1998 Learning Translation Templates from Examples. *Information Systems* **23**(6):353–363.

Hammond, K.J. (ed.). 1989. *Proceedings of the DARPA Case-Based Reasoning Workshop, Pensacola Beach, Florida*, San Mateo, CA: Morgan Kaufmann.

Kolodner, J.L. (ed.). 1988. *Proceedings of the DARPA Case-Based Reasoning Workshop, Clearwater Beach, Florida*, San Mateo, CA: Morgan Kaufmann.

Medin, D.L., and M.M. Schaffer. 1978. Context Theory of Classification Learning. *Psychological Review*, **85**:207–238.

Öz, Z., and I. Cicekli. 1998. Ordering Translation Templates by Assigning Confidence Factors. In D. Farwell, L. Gerber and E. Hovy (eds.) *Machine Translation and the Information Soup: Third Conference of the Association for Machine Translation in the Americas, AMTA'98* (Lecture Notes in Computer Science 1529), Berlin: Springer, pp.51-61.

Pollard, C. and I. Sag. 1987. *Information-based Syntax and Semantics.* CSLI, Stanford, CA.

Ram, A. 1993. Indexing, Elaboration and Refinement: Incremental Learning of Explanatory Cases. In J.L. Kolodner (ed.) *Case-Based Learning*, Kluwer Academic Publishers, Dordrecht, The Netherlands.

Chapter 10

CLUSTERED TRANSFER RULE INDUCTION FOR EXAMPLE-BASED TRANSLATION

Ralf D. Brown
ralf+@cs.cmu.edu

Abstract Previous work has shown that grammars and similar structure can be induced from unlabelled text (both monolingually and bilingually), and that the performance of an example-based machine translation (EBMT) system can be substantially enhanced by using clustering techniques to determine equivalence classes of individual words which can be used interchangeably, thus converting translation examples into templates. This paper describes the combination of these two approaches to further increase the coverage (or conversely, decrease the required training text) of an EBMT system. Preliminary results show that a reduction in required training text by a factor of twelve is possible for translation from French into English.

Keywords: induction of transfer rules, clustered transfer rule, word clustering

1. Introduction

Lexicalist Example-Based Machine Translation (EBMT) systems such as those of Veale & Way, 1997 (see Chapter 16 for more recent work by Andy Way) and the author (Brown, 1999) have the advantage that they require little or no additional knowledge beyond the parallel text forming the example base, but the disadvantage that the example base must be quite large to provide good coverage of unrestricted texts. Since parallel texts of the required size are often difficult or (for lesser-used languages) even impossible to obtain, there have been various efforts to reduce the data needs by generalizing the training examples into templates and then perform template matching (see Figure 10.1), including those described

M. Carl and A. Way (eds.), Recent Advances in Example-Based Machine Translation, 287–305.

Training Input	205 delegates met in London. 200 delegates met in Paris.
String Match Template Match	delegates met in <number> delegates met in <city>.

Figure 10.1. String Match vs. Template Match

in the previous and next two chapters. Such generalization makes a portion of the knowledge which is implicit in the training corpus explicit.

Three approaches to generalization have been used: manually-generated equivalence classes, automatically-extracted equivalence classes, and transfer rule induction. The EBMT systems mentioned above both convert translation examples into templates using manually-created information, such as from a machine-readable dictionary with part-of-speech information, to replace words with tokens indicating the class of word which may occur in a particular location. More recently, the author added automatically-generated equivalence classes using word-level clustering (Brown, 2000) and Cicekli & Güvenir, 2001 (cf. Chapter 9, this volume) have implemented transfer-rule induction from parallel text.

We report here the results of combining the latter two approaches, using transfer rule induction followed by word-level clustering to find not only single words but also transfer rules which can be combined into equivalence classes.

2. Transfer Rule Induction

To induce a set of grammar rules from a parallel corpus, we make the same assumption used by Cicekli and Güvenir (see Chapter 9, this volume) and van Zaanen, 2000: when two sentence pairs in the corpus have some part in common but differ in some other part, the similar and dissimilar parts each correspond to some coherent constituent. Note that such a "constituent" need not be a traditional constituent as used by linguists, such as a noun phrase or prepositional phrase; for our purposes, it suffices that the groupings which are found can be used interchangeably.

Initially, the system only searches for pairs of training instances where the source-language halves show the pattern $S_1\ D\ S_2$, where S_1 and S_2 are the same in both instances (at most one of these may be the empty string) and D differs between the two training instances, but may contain common subsequences. The algorithm is outlined in Figure 10.2 and described in detail below. Naturally, such a simple pattern will

1 read the corpus into memory, creating a rough bitext mapping for each bilingual sentence pair

2 sort the corpus alphabetically by source-language sentence

3 for each F, find all sequences of sentence pairs which share the same first F words in the source language

4 for each sequence, create a subcorpus and:

   (a) sort the subcorpus alphabetically by **reversed** source-language sentence

   (b) for each L, find all sequences of sentence pairs which share the same last L words in the source language

   (c) for each sequence, create another subcorpus and:

      i perform a pairwise comparison between sentence pairs, adding the differences to a new equivalence class and to the corpus. The bitext map is used to discard those differences which do not appear to match between source- and target-language sentences.

      ii if sufficiently long, add the common initial/final strings to the corpus

5 apply the learned rewriting rules to the corpus, except to sentence pairs where doing so would generate a single token

6 repeat steps 2 through 5 until no more new equivalence classes are added or the number of iterations reaches a preset maximum

Figure 10.2. The Induction Process

not capture all interesting phenomena; future work will address more complex patterns.

A recursive method is used to find sets of training instances with common word sequences at beginning or end ("initial string" and "final string" or "prefix" and "suffix"). After sorting the sentence pairs by their source-language sentences, one can simply perform a linear scan of the collection for runs of training instances with at least I words in common. Each run found determines a subcorpus on which one can search for runs with at least $I + 1$ words in common. At each level in

Input:

1 nous regardons la production de acier .
we are watching steel production .

2 nous regardons les approvisionnements en énergie .
we are watching energy supplies .

3 nous regardons les approvisionnements en engrais .
we are watching fertilizer supplies .

4 nous regardons les approvisionnements en matériel .
we are watching equipment supplies .

5 nous regardons les produits chimiques agricoles .
we are watching agricultural chemicals .

Rewritten Corpus:

- nous regardons la production de acier .
  we are watching steel production .
- nous regardons les $\langle cl_2 \rangle$.
  we are watching $\langle cl_2 \rangle$.
- nous regardons
  we are watching

Induced Rules – $\langle CL_2 \rangle$:

- approvisionnements en $\langle CL_0 \rangle$
  $\langle CL_0 \rangle$ supplies
- produits chimiques agricoles
  agricultural chemicals

Induced Rules – $\langle CL_0 \rangle$:

- engrais
  fertilizer
- matériel
  equipment
- énergie
  energy

Figure 10.3. Sample Induction

1. find bilingual word pairs which uniquely correspond to each other according to a bitext mapping generated with a bilingual dictionary
2. accumulate counts for the words in the immediate vicinity of each occurrence of a word pair, as well as the frequency of the word pair itself
3. convert the word counts into weighted term vectors, and generate an initial cluster for each vector; associate the word pair's frequency with the term vector
4. repeatedly find the two most similar clusters whose similarity is above the threshold value for the lesser of their frequency values and merge them (adding the associated frequencies), until no pair of clusters is above threshold or only two clusters remain
5. if the number of clusters is still above 2500, relax the clustering by allowing those clusters with frequency values of 5 or less to merge regardless of the clustering threshold for their frequency (if necessary, repeat for frequencies of 10, 15, etc.)
6. output the clusters with more than one member, recovering the word pair with which each vector in a cluster is associated

Figure 10.4. Clustering Algorithm

the recursion, sorting the training instances as though the order of their words were reversed allows the same type of scan to find runs of training instances with a common final string of specified length.

Consider the small set of example sentence pairs in Figure 10.3. These all share the common initial string "nous regardons" and final string "."; further, all but the first one share the initial string "nous regardons les", and instances 2-4 share the initial string "nous regardons les approvisionnements en". We will first process the smallest set (instances 2-4), then the intermediate set (instances 2-5), and finally the complete set (instances 1-5).

Thus, for each combination of initial-string length and final-string length, a set of training instances has been defined by the above scans, whose differences may be assigned to an equivalence class. These instances are then compared pair-wise to determine the differences between them. For each pair, the target-language halves are compared, and segmented into a common initial string, dissimilar central portion, and common final string. To ensure that the dissimilar center does in fact correspond to the difference on the source-language side, a bitext mapping is used. The bitext mapping is generated for each training instance from a bilingual dictionary, indicating which words in the target-language half potentially correspond with each source-language word. If, for either of the two training instances, the bitext map rules out any part of the target-language difference, neither instance is added to the current equivalence class (one or both of the instances may eventually have its center portion added when compared against other sentence pairs in the corpus).

Should a pair of instances pass the bitext-map test, the portions which differ between the two are added to the training corpus as new (but shorter) training instances, and are added to the equivalence class of all instances having the same initial and final strings. After the pair-wise comparison between each pair in the set of instances with that common prefix and suffix is complete, the initial and final strings themselves are also added to the corpus as two additional training instances provided that they are sufficiently long (currently, at least two words each).

Once the corpus has been completely processed, the result is a corpus augmented by various sentence fragments which are assumed to be constituents of some kind. We now apply the learned equivalence classes interpreted as a set of rewriting rules or a context free grammar, replacing each instance of a class member by the class name. The replacements may occur anywhere in a sentence pair, including the portions which had been used as common prefix or suffix strings during the learning phase. An exception is made if the end result of applying the grammar to a training instance is a single class name; in this case, the training instance is left unchanged. The rationale for applying rewriting rules in this manner is to increase the similarity of the items in the corpus to permit more matches on the next iteration, e.g. two instances which previously had different initial segments may have the same initial segment after rewriting rules are applied, because the differing phrases are both members of the same equivalence class.

At this point, if any changes were made, the entire process repeats using the updated corpus, until no more equivalence classes can be created. To forestall an extremely lengthy execution time should a large number of iterations be required, the program can also terminate learning after a specified number of iterations.

After the induction completes, it can optionally be re-run in the reverse direction, comparing target-language sentences with each other.

This feature can increase the yield of equivalence classes by 50% or more, since the target-language sentences will show different patterns of similarities with each other which were not captured during the first pass.

Figure 10.3 shows the result of this process. The pairwise comparison between instances 2 through 4 yields the single-word differences which have been added to equivalence class $\langle CL_0 \rangle$. The further comparisons between instances 2 through 5 yield the equivalences in $\langle CL_2 \rangle$; after applying the rewriting rules created by $\langle CL_0 \rangle$, three of its members collapse into a single rule containing an equivalence-class marker.

The output of the induction phase is a set of parallel rewriting rules which form the transfer-rule grammar (see Figure 10.5 for a few examples from actual runs), and optionally an updated parallel corpus with the rewriting rules added and already applied. The updated corpus which is already present in the computer's memory can then be used as input to the word-clustering phase.

3. Word Clustering

To cluster words into equivalence classes, the approach of (Brown, 2000) (outlined in Figure 10.4) was used. The main feature of this approach is a transformation step which converts the word-clustering problem into a document-clustering problem.

The first step in word clustering is to determine *which* words should be clustered. Since it is also necessary to cluster bilingually, a dictionary is used to generate a rough bitext mapping between the source and target halves of each sentence pair in the training corpus. Whenever the bitext map indicates a unique correspondence between a word in the source-language sentence and some word in the target-language sentence, a word pair is formed from the source- and target-language words and is treated as an indivisible unit. These word pairs are what will be clustered.

For each occurrence of a word pair, add the source-language words immediately surrounding its occurrence (for these experiments, the three words preceding and the three words following) to a term vector which tallies all neighbouring words across all occurrences of the word pair. This converts the problem into one of finding which term vectors cluster together, a standard document-clustering approach.

Next, the term vectors are clustered using bottom-up agglomerative clustering. Initially, one cluster is created for each vector; next, the two clusters with the highest similarity measure are merged, and the process is repeated until no more clusters have sufficiently high similarity with

$\langle CL_{18} \rangle$:
plutôt ridicule
rather ridiculous

peut-être le condamner avec de fausses louanges , mais je ne y puis rien
If it is damning him with feint praise , I cannot help

$\langle cl_{847} \rangle$ monsieur l'Orateur
$\langle cl_{847} \rangle$ Mr . Speaker

bien pour Toronto
lucky in Toronto

...

$\langle CL_{119} \rangle$:
question # 2 est oui
part two is yes

question # 2601 de la première session de la 29e législature ne tenait pas compte de les travaux de construction entrepris en 1973 - 1974 à la résidence de le premier ministre à Ottawa
question No . 2,601 of the First Session of the twenty-ninth Parliament did not list construction work carried out in the year 1973 - 74 at the Prime Minister's Ottawa residence

$\langle CL_{122} \rangle$:
, confié à la garde de un service de sécurité , fut transporté par tout le pays à bord de un avion de la Défense nationale et un exemplaire en a été remis à toutes les capitales provinciales au moment même où je prenais la parole à la Chambre
was sent under security guard in national defence aircraft right across the country , and copies were released in all provincial capitals simultaneously with my rising in the House

que $\langle cl_{644} \rangle$
that the $\langle cl_{644} \rangle$

Figure 10.5. Sample Replacement Rules

Cluster	French	English
507	NE	NOT
	NE	NO
568	CETTE	THIS
	CETTE	THAT
575	PROCHAIN	NEXT
	DERNIER	LAST
659	UNE	THE
	UNE	AN
	UNE	A
	UN	THE
	UN	A
	LE	THE
	LE	OF
	LE	IT
	LE	IN
	LE	A
	LA	THE
	LA	OF
	LA	IN
678	VALEUR	VALUE
	SÉCURITÉ	SECURITY
	PRODUCTION	PRODUCTION
	PLUS	MORE
	NÉCESSITÉ	NEED
	LIVRAISON	DELIVERY
	FA CON	WAY
	DATE	DATE
	CROISSANCE	GROWTH
	CONSTRUCTION	CONSTRUCTION
	COMMERCIALISATION	MARKETING
1085	POINTS	POINTS
	LIVRES	POUNDS
	ANS	YEARS
1196	MILLIONS	MILLION
	MILLIARDS	BILLION
1776	ABSURDE	NONSENSE
	$\langle CL_{18} \rangle$	$\langle CL_{18} \rangle$
2158	PÊCHEURS	FISHERIES
	PÉNURIES	SHORTAGES
	OFFICIERS	OFFICERS
2609	$\langle CL_{54} \rangle$	$\langle CL_{54} \rangle$
	$\langle CL_{98} \rangle$	$\langle CL_{98} \rangle$
	$\langle CL_{375} \rangle$	$\langle CL_{375} \rangle$
	$\langle CL_{458} \rangle$	$\langle CL_{458} \rangle$
	$\langle CL_{462} \rangle$	$\langle CL_{462} \rangle$
	...6 more...	

Figure 10.6. Sample Clusters from 107,000 words

any other clusters. The similarity metric used is a term-weighted cosine similarity measure, e.g. the normalized inner product of the two vectors:

$$cos(\vec{u}, \vec{v}) = \frac{\vec{u} \cdot \vec{v}}{||\vec{u}|| \times ||\vec{v}||}$$

The selected threshold for clustering proved to be excessively conservative for larger training sets, leaving a majority of word pairs in single-element clusters, so a back-off scheme was added to force the total number of final clusters closer to a target of 2500 clusters. If more than the target number of clusters remain when the first clustering pass terminates, clusters with frequency values (the sum of term frequencies for all word pairs included in the cluster) of five or less may merge regardless of the selected threshold. If necessary, further iterations will allow clusters with frequencies of up to 10, 15, 20, etc. to merge. This approach was selected to avoid the need for tuning the thresholds for each individual training set size, which would be impractical at best.

Once the vectors have been clustered, the clusters are output. For every cluster, the word pair to which each vector in the cluster corresponds is recovered and is written to the results file along with the name of the cluster. The results file becomes input to the EBMT system when it indexes the training corpus, allowing it to convert the parallel text into templates using the cluster names as class markers. Figure 10.6 shows a sample of the clusters produced from 107,000 words of parallel training text. The clustering process produced a total of 1178 clusters containing 3187 word pairs after discarding clusters containing only a single word pair (as such singletons are not useful).

4. Combining Induction and Clustering

The induction process produces a large number of usually small equivalence classes, which limits the amount of generalization that can be produced. Hence, we would like to merge different classes of rewriting rules which are used in similar contexts, in the same manner as individual words are clustered.

A by-product of the induction algorithm is an updated corpus with all replacement rules already applied, leaving single-word markers in place of the phrases found by transfer rule induction. Applying the clustering process to the modified corpus allows both words and replacement rules to cluster together. While replacement-rule non-terminals tend to cluster with other non-terminals, many clusters contain both words and non-terminals (see Figure 10.6).

5. Experimental Design

To gauge the effect of the different approaches, various combinations of method and training size were run and evaluated.

Four conditions were compared: simple string matching against the corpus (see Figure 10.1), matching templates formed using single-word clustering alone, templates formed using transfer-rule induction alone, and templates formed with the combination of clustering and induction. For French–English, the training data in each case consisted of a subset (up to 1.1 million words in 19730 sentence pairs) of the *Hansard* corpus made available by the Linguistic Data Consortium (Linguistic Data Consortium, 1997) and a bilingual dictionary formed by combining the ARTFL French–English dictionary (ARTFL Project, 1998) with a probabilistic dictionary extracted from the *Hansard* corpus. The test data consisted of 45,320 words of French text from a disjoint portion of the *Hansard* corpus.

The data for the Spanish–English experiments consisted of up to one million words of parallel text drawn primarily from the *UN* Multilingual Corpus (Graff & Finch, 1994) available from the Linguistic Data Consortium and a bilingual dictionary derived from the *Collins* Spanish–English dictionary and statistically extracted from the *UN* corpus and other parallel text. The test data consisted of 9,059 words of Spanish test from a disjoint portion of the *UN* Multilingual Corpus.

The input to the actual EBMT system consisted of the bilingual dictionary (for word-level alignment) plus the original parallel text, and (as appropriate) the output of the clustering and/or induction phases. When the clustering algorithm was applied in isolation, the single-word rewriting rules found through clustering were supplied to EBMT. When the transfer rule induction was used, the induced transfer rules were supplied to EBMT.

The transfer rule induction was limited to twelve iterations in each direction. During development it was found that the process lárgely converged after six iterations, even though total convergence may require fifteen or more iterations, with the last several iterations each adding only a few new equivalence classes with a handful of members.

The performance measure used to determine the effectiveness of the various methods is the coverage of the test text, i.e. the percentage of the total words in the test input for which the EBMT system could generate at least one candidate translation. Although this metric does not measure quality, the design of the EBMT system generally enforces some minimum level of translation quality — the translation software will not output translations when the word-level alignment for the retrieved training example fails or is deemed too poor[1]. Recent manual judgements on a Mandarin Chinese–English version of the EBMT system (Zhang *et al.*, 2001) have confirmed that increased coverage indeed correlates with improved translation quality.

Figure 10.7 shows some sample output, which will be discussed in more detail in Section 10.7; for the moment, it is important to note that the score shown is a penalty – 0.0 is considered a perfect alignment, while matches for which the penalty exceeds five times the number of words are not output at all.

6. Computational Complexity

Each iteration of the induction algorithm takes time $O(n^2)$, where n is the number of words of training text, since ultimately each sentence pair must be compared against every other sentence pair (subdividing the problem into shorter sequences does not increase the time complexity, and sorting is $O(n \, log \, n)$). The number of iterations required to run the induction to completion is potentially $O(n)$, but appears in practice to be somewhat less than $O(log \, n)$; there is a three- to four-fold increase between a 50,000-word corpus and a twenty times larger million-word corpus. More experimentation with larger corpora (several to tens of millions of words) will be required to determine the actual value.

In practice, the first iteration takes the longest time, by a factor of two or more, and subsequent iterations complete more quickly. Per-iteration execution times generally continue to decrease until the fifth iteration, after which they tend to vary both up and down but stay relatively constant. Two factors are probably at work here: on each succeeding iteration, there are fewer and smaller runs of sentences, reducing the quadratic pair-wise comparison; and the individual training instances are shorter, either because they are fragments of an older instance or due to replacement of phrases by single tokens.

The clustering algorithm is also $O(n^2)$, but here n is the number of term vectors, i.e. the number of distinct bilingual word pairs, which grows more slowly than the number of words in the training text. Thus, the execution time for the complete process of induction plus clustering is slightly worse than quadratic in the size of the input.

[1]In fact, if all corpus matches yielded good alignments, coverage would be in excess of 90% instead of 80.14% for two million words of French-English training text using just string matching.

Il me semble qu'il conviendrait maintenant de reprendre le débat.
I think it would be proper at this time for the debate to continue.

String Match, 1.1 million words:

Match	Sc	Translation
il me semble qu'il	0	it seems to me that
il me semble que	0	It seems to me that
il me semble	0	It seems to me
il me	0	Let me
il me	0	me explore
me semble	0.3	seems to me
me semble	0	I think
semble que il	0	it seems this
semble que	0	seems that
que il	0	well as
maintenant de	2.5	now the
de reprendre	0	to resume
le débat .	1	in debate .
le débat .	0	the debate .
le débat	0	in debate
le débat	0	debate in
débat .	0	debate .

Induction+Clustering, 1.1 million words:

Match	Sc	Translation
il me semble qu'il	17	it seems to me that
semble qu'il	0	it seems this
qu'il	0	that he
il conviendrait	0	IT APPROPRIATE
maintenant	0	NOW
de reprendre	0	to resume
le débat .	0	THE DEBATE .
le débat .	1	in DEBATE .
débat .	0	DEBATE .

Figure 10.7. Sample Translation 1

7. Results

As shown in Figure 10.8, clustering and transfer rule induction each outperformed simple string matching, and the combination substantially outperformed both. In fact, the combined algorithm exceeds the coverage of string matching trained on two million words of French–

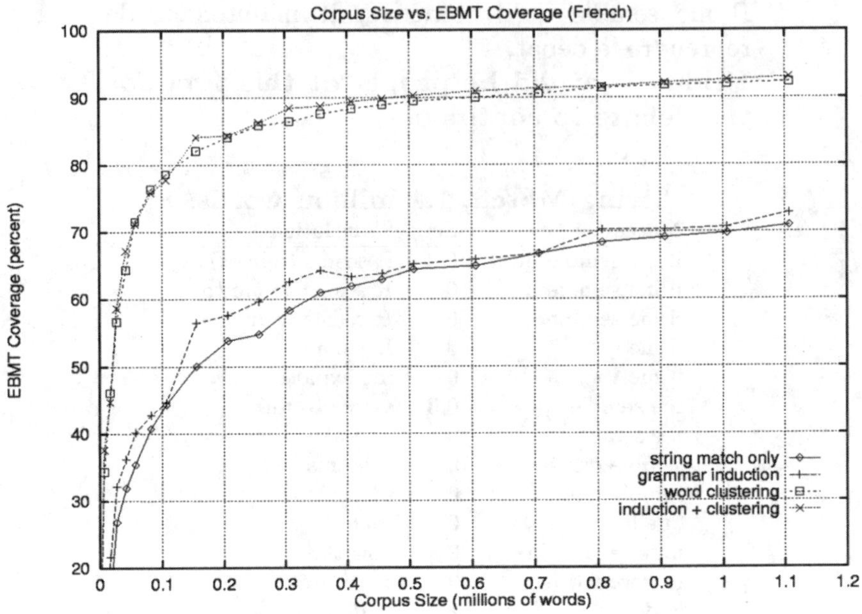

Corpus Size (words)	String Match Only	Clusters	Induction	Clust+Induc
107,000	44.35%	78.62%	44.66%	77.77%
207,000	53.81%	84.09%	57.61%	84.38%
307,000	58.31%	86.46%	62.56%	88.48%
1,107,000	70.92%	92.32%	72.79%	93.01%

Figure 10.8. Performance Comparison (French)

English parallel text with only 157,000 words of training data, more than a twelve-fold reduction in training data with no additional knowledge sources. For comparison, the best results (Brown, 1999) achieved using manually-created generalization information consisting of a large part-of-speech tagged bilingual dictionary and several hundred bilingual production rules based on those tags are shown in the graph as well. The automatic algorithms very nearly match the performance of the manual

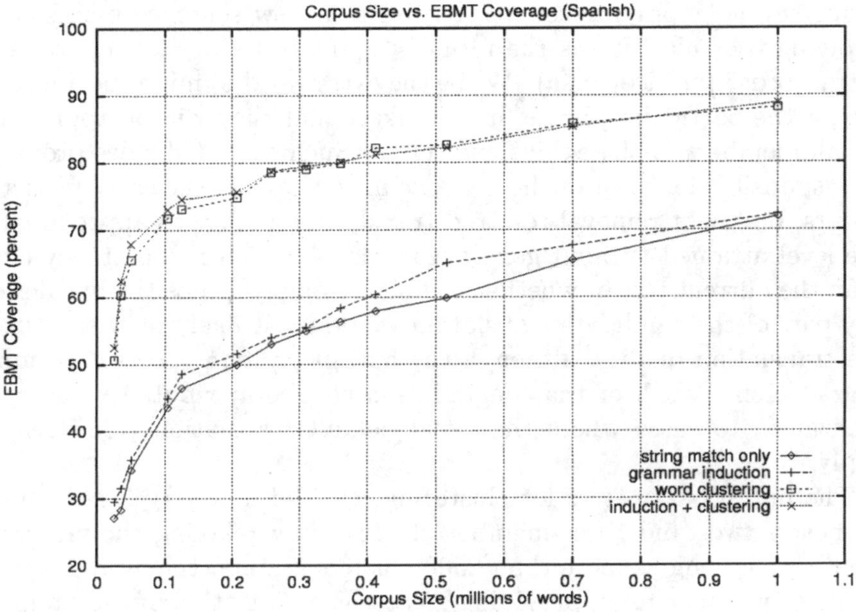

Corpus Size (words)	String Match Only	Induction	Clusters	Clust+Induc
104,000	43.53%	44.95%	71.80%	73.07%
207,000	49.94%	51.61%	74.85%	75.63%
310,000	54.95%	55.50%	79.02%	79.49%
1,000,000	71.94%	72.33%	88.19%	88.85%

Figure 10.9. Performance Comparison (Spanish)

approach, without the quarter-million words of additional data in the dictionary and grammar rules used by manual generalization.

Similar results were obtained for Spanish-English (see Figure 10.9), where the combined algorithm had greater coverage with 104,000 words of training data than string matching on a one-million-word corpus.

Early results showed that the transfer rule induction yielded nearly as great an improvement as clustering and that the two methods had great synergy. Examination of the results, however, indicated that the induction was too aggressive (resulting in much lower translation quality) and that clustering was less aggressive than it could be. In particular, most of the degradation was due to misalignments, where the translation found by the system included extraneous words or omitted a portion of the true translation. The most egregious case was fairly easy to avert, simply by not applying rewriting rules to a new sentence pair if, after applying the rules, it has the form "<equivclass>" == "<equivclass> extra words" (or vice-versa). While the extra word(s) might be appropriate for the particular phrase, it is unlikely that they will be appropriate for all members of the equivalence class. Such excluded rules proved to be responsible for most of the increase in coverage in the early induction results, but their removal restored translation quality to approximately the level attained without generalizations. A stricter consistency check than the current test of whether the bitext mapping positively rules out any part of the candidate translation would most likely further improve the translation quality, although the current system shows only minor degradation. Much of that degradation can be attributed to overgeneralization to cases where the usual default translation rule does not apply.

The initial parameters for clustering resulted in a very large number of mostly two- and three-member clusters. By relaxing the clustering threshold so long as more than 2500 clusters remain, the average size of a cluster was increased, providing greater generalization of the examples in the training corpus. With this change, performance of clustering alone substantially increased, and the performance of the combination of induction and clustering coincidentally remained virtually unchanged from the flawed initial runs.

Now that performance of clustering alone is so much closer to the performance of the combined algorithm, it becomes clear that the changes in the corpus produced by grammar induction can interfere somewhat with clustering. With certain training sets, the combined algorithm actually fares marginally worse than clustering alone. However, the induction process is using only the simplest form of inter-example differences, and a more sophisticated version may fare better.

Some examples of the EBMT output are shown in Figures 10.7 and 10.10; the reference translation from the *Hansard* corpus is given for each. Figure 10.10 includes a very terse form of the output due to the limited space available; all matches which are contained within some longer match (from another example in the corpus) have been excluded, and only the best-scoring match from among those covering a particular phrase is shown. The actual output is several times longer, and includes some translations with better quality than the maximal matches actually shown. For each match, the alignment score (lower is better) and the translation are shown. Words in all-capital letters indicate where a single word matched an equivalence class generated by clustering, rather than the surface string. The sentence in Figure 10.7 was randomly selected

Comme il est 2 heures 03, la Chambre s'ajourne à 11 heures aujourd'hui, conformément au paragraphe 24(1) du Règlement.
It being 2.03 a.m., this House stands adjourned until later this day at ll a.m., pursuant to Standing Order 24(1).

String-Match Only, 1.1 million words:

Match	Score	Translation
comme il	1	He just a couple of
il est 2	1.275	it is 2
est 2 heures	1.275	is 2 o'clock
03 , la chambre	1	03 , the House
, la chambre se	1	, the House will
à 11 heures	0	at 11 a.m.
hui , conformément	1	today , pursuant
paragraphe 24 (1) de le règlement .	41.15	subsection 24 (1) of the rule .

Induction+Clustering, 1.1 million words:

Match	Score	Translation
comme	0	LIKE
il est 2 heures	1.825	IT IS 2 o'clock
03 , la chambre	0.75	03 , THE HOUSE
à 11 heures	1.11	to 11 a.m.
hui , conformément	1	today , pursuant
conformément au paragraphe 24 (1) de	2.65	ACCORDANCE TO SUBSECTION 24 (1) of
paragraphe 24 (1) de le règlement .	1.55	subsection 24 (1) OF STANDING .

Figure 10.10. Sample Translation 2

from among the shorter sentences in the test set, while Figure 10.10 is the very last sentence in the test set.

8. Conclusion and Future Work

Experimental results indicate that combining transfer rule induction in the style of (Cicekli, 2000) with the author's prior work on single-word clustering is beneficial, resulting in a system that outperforms either method used in isolation and overall resulting in a dramatic reduction in the amount of parallel training text required for a broad-coverage EBMT system. Coverage for a given amount of training text is increased with little or no impact on translation quality.

The transfer rule induction used in this system can certainly be enhanced, and the previous chapter describes the full-blown, more sophisticated method of which only the simplest portion was used here.

The word clustering parameters need to be tuned. Currently, the same parameters are used in conjunction with transfer rule induction and in isolation. There is no *a priori* reason for the optimal settings in one case to be optimal for the other. In addition, the target of 2500 clusters was chosen arbitrarily and should be tuned for the best trade-off between quality and coverage.

The interference between transfer rule induction and clustering noted during the most recent experimental runs should be isolated and, if possible, mitigated.

Finally, there is the possibility that adding a small amount of seed knowledge to the grammar induction process (similar to what was previously done with single-word clustering) could substantially improve performance.

9. Acknowledgements

This research was supported primarily by the National Science Foundation's STIMULATE program (grant number 9618941).

References

ARTFL Project. 1998. *ARTFL Project: French-English Dictionary*. Project for American and French Research on the Treasury of the French Language, University of Chicago, Chicago, IL. `http://humanities.uchicago.edu/ARTFL.html`.

Brown, R.D. 1999. Adding Linguistic Knowledge to a Lexical Example-Based Translation System. In *Proceedings of the Eighth International Conference on Theoretical and Methodological Issues in Machine Translation (TMI 99)*, Chester, England, pp.22–32. `http://www.cs.cmu.edu/~ralf/papers.html`.

Brown, R.D. 2000. Automated Generalization of Translation Examples. In *Proceedings of the Eighteenth International Conference on Computational Linguistics: COLING 2000 in Europe*, Saarbrücken, Germany, pp.125–131.

Cicekli, I. 2000. Similarities and Differences. In *SCI2000: Proceedings of the Multi-Conference on Systemics, Cybernetics and Informatics*, Orlando, FL., pp.331–337. `http://www.cs.bilkent.edu.tr/~ilyas/pubs.html`.

Cicekli, I. and H.A. Güvenir. 2001. Learning Translation Templates from Bilingual Translation Examples. *Applied Intelligence* **15**(1):57–76 (see Chapter 9, this volume).

Graff, D. and R. Finch. 1994. Multilingual Text Resources at the Linguistic Data Consortium. In *Proceedings of the 1994 ARPA Human Language Technology Workshop*, Plainsboro, NJ., Morgan Kaufmann.

Linguistic Data Consortium. 1997. *Hansard Corpus of Parallel English and French.* Linguistic Data Consortium, University of Pennsylvania, Philadelphia, PA. `http://www.ldc.upenn.edu/`.

Veale, T. and A. Way. 1997. *Gaijin*: A Bootstrapping Approach to Example-Based Machine Translation. *International Conference, Recent Advances in Natural Language Processing*, Tzigov Chark, Bulgaria, pp.239–244.

van Zaanen, M. 2000. ABL: Alignment-Based Learning. In *Proceedings of the Eighteenth International Conference on Computational Linguistics: COLING 2000 in Europe*, Saarbrücken, Germany, pp.961–967. `http://www.comp.leeds.ac.uk/menno/docs/`.

Zhang, Y., R.D. Brown and R.E. Frederking. 2001. Adapting an Example-Based Translation System to Chinese. In J. Allan (ed.) *Proceedings of HLT 2001: First International Conference on Human Language Technology Research*, Morgan Kaufmann, San Francisco, CA., pp.7–10.

Chapter 11

TRANSLATION PATTERNS, LINGUISTIC KNOWLEDGE AND COMPLEXITY IN AN APPROACH TO EBMT

Kevin McTait
mctait@limsi.fr

Abstract An approach to Example-Based Machine Translation is presented which operates by extracting translation patterns from a bilingual corpus aligned at the level of the sentence. This is carried out using a language-neutral recursive machine-learning algorithm based on the principle of similar distributions of strings. The translation patterns extracted represent generalisations of sentences that are translations of each other and, to some extent, resemble transfer rules but with fewer constraints. The strings and variables, of which translations patterns are composed, are aligned in order to provide a more refined bilingual knowledge source, necessary for the recombination phase. A non-structural approach based on surface forms is error-prone and liable to produce translation patterns that are false translations. Such errors are highlighted and solutions are proposed by the addition of external linguistic resources, namely morphological analysis and part-of-speech tagging. The amount of linguistic resources added has consequences for computational complexity and portability.

Keywords: extraction of translation patterns, non-bijective alignment, language-neutral similarity distribution

1. Introduction

A number of example-based machine translation (EBMT) systems operate by extracting and recombining translation patterns or templates from bilingual texts (Kaji *et al.*, 1992; Güvenir & Cicekli, 1998, Chapter 9, this volume; Brown, 1999, cf. Chapter 10, this volume; Carl, 1999, cf. Chapter 12, this volume; McTait & Trujillo, 1999). Translation patterns

M. Carl and A. Way (eds.), Recent Advances in Example-Based Machine Translation, 307–338.

represent generalisations of sentences that are translations of each other in that various sequences of one or more words are replaced by variables, possibly with the alignments between word sequences and/or variables made explicit.

In this approach, which builds upon and improves that of McTait & Trujillo, 1999, translation patterns are extracted from a bilingual corpus aligned at the level of the sentence. They are extracted by means of a language-neutral recursive machine-learning algorithm based on the principle of similar distributions of strings: source language (SL) and target language (TL) strings that co-occur in the same 2 (or more) sentence pairs of a bilingual corpus are likely to be translations of each other. The SL and TL strings that make up the translation patterns are aligned so that they provide not only sentential patterns of translation, but also a more refined bilingual knowledge source representing word / phrasal translations, necessary for the recombination phase, where TL translations are produced. Since the variables also represent strings, they too are aligned. Figure 11.1 is an example of a simple translation pattern indicating how a sentence in English containing *give ... up* may be translated by a sentence in French containing *abandonner*.

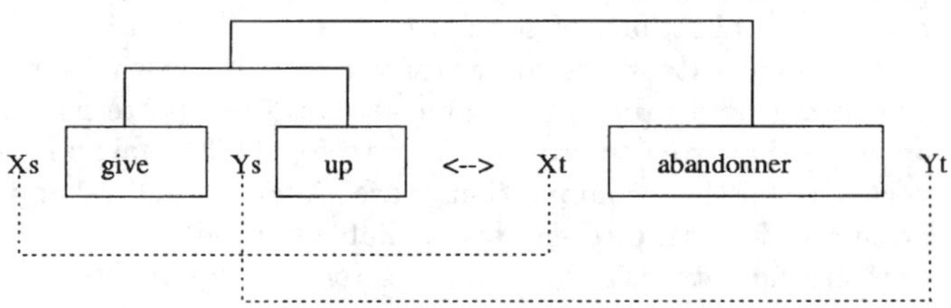

Figure 11.1. A Simple Translation Pattern

The translation pattern in Figure 11.1 contains not only simple bijective or 1:1 alignments between text fragments or variables, but also non-bijective alignment types, such as the 2:1 alignment between *give ... up* and *abandonner*. The ability to efficiently compute bijective and non-bijective alignments, as well as long-distance dependencies, is conducive to more accurately describing translation phenomena. Furthermore, it is possible to extract translation patterns and align the text fragments of which they are composed when the data is sparse, since strings only need to co-occur in a minimum of 2 sentence pairs. Furthermore, language-neutral techniques, such as cognates and bilingual lexical distribution,

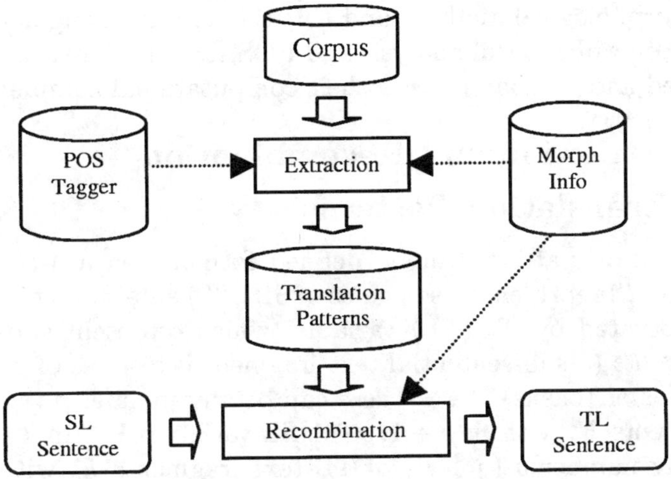

Figure 11.2. System Architecture

are used to align the strings or text fragments of which the patterns are composed.

The translation patterns extracted resemble, to some extent, transfer rules within a Rule-Based Machine Translation (RBMT) system, but with fewer constraints. A linear approach based on the distributions of surface forms within a corpus is liable to the extraction of translation patterns that are false translations. Solutions to this phenomenon are proposed by the addition of external linguistic knowledge sources such as morphological analysis and part-of-speech (POS) tagging. Figure 11.2 depicts the system architecture. The dotted lines indicate that the use of the knowledge sources is optional.

The addition of linguistic resources is intended to improve both accuracy and recall. However, their addition has consequences for portability and computational complexity. The more resources required, the less portable and the more complex the system.

This paper outlines the translation pattern extraction algorithm along with the corresponding recombination step where, given SL input sentences, TL translations are produced. The problems associated with a non-structural language-neutral approach are highlighted with solutions proposed involving the addition of external linguistic knowledge sources. Three variants of this approach are then ready for comparison, each with varying amounts of linguistic knowledge incorporated: (i) the language-neutral approach based on surface forms, (ii) the approach augmented to include morphological analysis and (iii) the approach augmented to include both morphological analysis and POS tagging. Their performance is evaluated and compared, as is their computational complexity.

2. Extraction and Recombination

2.1 Translation Patterns

A translation pattern can be defined formally as a 4-tuple $\{S,\ T,\ A_f, A_v\}$. S (T) represents a sequence of SL (TL) sub-sentential text fragments, separated by SL (TL) variables which represent sub-sentential text fragments (a sub-sentential text fragment is a series of one or more lexical items or tokens). In S, there can be any number p ($p > 0$) of SL text fragments F_p with p, $p+1, p-1$ SL variables V_p. In T, there can also be any number q ($q > 0$) of TL text fragments F_q with q, $q+1$, $q-1$ TL variables V_q. One possible configuration is depicted in (1):

(1) $$F_1, V_1, F_2, V_2 \ldots F_p, V_q \leftrightarrow F_1, V_1, F_2, V_2 \ldots F_q, V_q$$

A_f represents the global alignment of text fragments between S and T, while A_v represents the global alignment of variables between S and T. The global alignment of the text fragments is represented as a set of local alignments $\{\langle A, B\rangle_1, \langle A, B\rangle_2\ \ldots\ \langle A, B\rangle_k\}$, where each local alignment is represented as a pair $\langle A, B\rangle$. $A(B)$ represents pointers to zero or more SL (TL) text fragments according to the local alignment patterns stipulated by the sequence comparison algorithm (section 2.2.3). The global alignment of the variables A_v is represented analogously.

2.2 Extracting Translation Patterns

The input to the translation-pattern extraction phase is a bilingual corpus aligned at the level of the sentence. The output is a set of translation patterns. The algorithm is language-neutral in nature and operates on the simple principle of string co-occurrence and frequency thresholds: possibly discontinuous pairs of SL and TL strings that co-occur in a minimum of 2 translation examples are likely to be translations of each other. Since strings are only required to co-occur a minimum of twice (frequency threshold), the algorithm is useful in instances of sparse data. However, the frequency threshold can be increased to improve the accuracy of the patterns (McTait & Trujillo, 1999). This section provides a highly simplified example, using the corpus sample[1] in (2).

(2) a. The commission **gave** the plan **up** ↔ La commission **abandonna** le plan

b. Our government **gave** all laws **up** ↔ Notre gouvernement **abandonna** toutes les lois

2.2.1 Monolingual Phase. This stage is applied independently to the SL and TL sentences of the corpus (2). Lexical items (tokens) that occur in a minimum of 2 sentences are retrieved, together with a record of the sentences in which they were found: (3a) for the SL and (3b) for the TL.

(3) a. *(gave)[1,2], (up)[1,2]*

b. *(abandonna) [1,2]*

The lexical items are allowed to combine to form longer word combinations (or *collocations*) constrained only by the sentences from which they were retrieved. The lexical items combine recursively to form a tree-like data structure of collocations. Each lexical item is tested for combination with the daughters of the root node and if so, recursively with each subsequent daughter, as long as there is an intersection of at least 2 sentence IDs (this enforces string co-occurrence in 2 or more sentences). The result is a tree of collocations of increasing length but decreasing frequency. The leaves become the most informative parts of the tree and are collected at the end of this phase. The longest provide more context and hence there is less chance of ambiguity.

As an example (Figure 11.3), the SL lexical item *gave* is added to the root node (the integers denote the sentence IDs). The lexical item *up* is tested to see if it can combine with it since it is now a daughter of the root node. Since *gave* and *up* have an intersection of two sentence IDs, they are allowed to combine and form a new collocation node (*gave/up*). The TL lexical item is added to a separate tree and remains as in (3b) since there are no further TL lexical items with which it can combine.

2.2.2 Bilingual Phase. SL and TL collocations are equated by simple co-occurrence criteria to form translation patterns: SL collocations that have exactly the same sentence IDs as TL collocations

[1]The term ***corpus sample*** denotes the sentence pairs of a corpus which constitute all the relevant lexical information to form the translation pattern (as if the sample were the entire corpus).

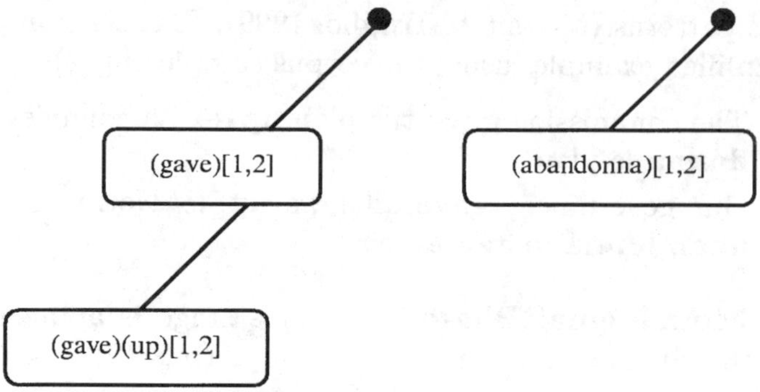

Figure 11.3. Collocation Trees

are considered to be translations of each other. This ensures that the patterns contain lexical items retrieved from the same sentences. The leaf-node collocations in Figure 11.3 are equated to form the translation pattern (4). A translation pattern is formed from lexical items in 2 (or more) sentences. Therefore, its word order is determined from either of those sentences in the corpus. The discontinuities between the strings in (4) are represented as ellipses and denote variables.

(4) (...) gave (...) up $\leftrightarrow$ (...) abandonna (...)

Translation patterns are not formed from the inner leaves of the collocation trees since they would form patterns that are subsets of patterns from the leaf nodes. This would make them spurious. They also introduce ambiguity in that the effectiveness of EBMT lies in the retrieval of the longest possible matching segments. Furthermore, they would frequently be inaccurate. For example, if the non-terminal node *gave[1,2]* were equated with *abandonna[1,2]* an incorrect pattern would be produced.

It is intuitive that if the text fragments — F in equation (1) — that make up the translation patterns are translations of each other, then the discontinuities or variables — V in (1) — that occur between them must also be translations. Since translation patterns are made up of lexical items from at least two translation examples, at least two *complement* translation patterns (5a) and (5b) are formed. They are created simply as the inverse of regular translation patterns and may contain lexical items that occur only once in the corpus.

(5) a. The commission (...) the plan (...) $\leftrightarrow$ La commission (...) le plan

b. Our government (...) all laws (...) $\leftrightarrow$ Notre gouvernement (...) toutes les lois

The text fragments form the fundamental units of translation patterns such as (4) and (5)and are not broken down further. The distinction into text fragments and variables, despite the formation of complement patterns, is a convenient representation for fragment alignment (section 2.2.3) and template matching (section 2.3).

2.2.3 Alignment of Text Fragments and Variables. Aligning the text fragments and variables of which translation patterns are composed produces translation patterns that are flexible enough for the recombination phase. In so doing, a more refined bilingual knowledge source (bilingual lexicon or "phrasicon") is produced. Aligning text fragments and variables is analogous to aligning words, phrases, terms or even sentences as in conventional bilingual alignment and involves similar problems.

Given that a translation pattern contains a SL and a TL sequence of one or more sub-sentential text fragments (separated by variables which also represent a separate series of sub-sentential text fragments), the problem may be viewed as bilingual sequence alignment or computing the optimal or most probable alignment between two sequences of text fragments in two languages. The two sequences of variables are aligned analogously by considering the text fragments that the variables represent, as defined by the corpus, as a separate series of text fragments. The solution to the alignment problem involves a sequence-comparison algorithm and a bilingual similarity (distance) metric.

The bilingual similarity metric *BS* is language-neutral in nature and is a combined score based on bilingual lexical distribution of the text fragments *BLD* and the number of cognates the text fragments share, as in (6):

(6) $$BS = \frac{BLD + |Cognates|}{1 + |Cognates|}$$

The bilingual lexical distribution score (a real value between 0 and 1) is computed by Dice's co-efficient (Dice, 1945) and cognates are determined by computing the Levenshtein Distance (Levenshtein, 1966) between SL and TL strings. The Levenshtein Distance is normalised over the maximum distance between the two strings, returning a similarity score or probability that the two strings are cognates. If the

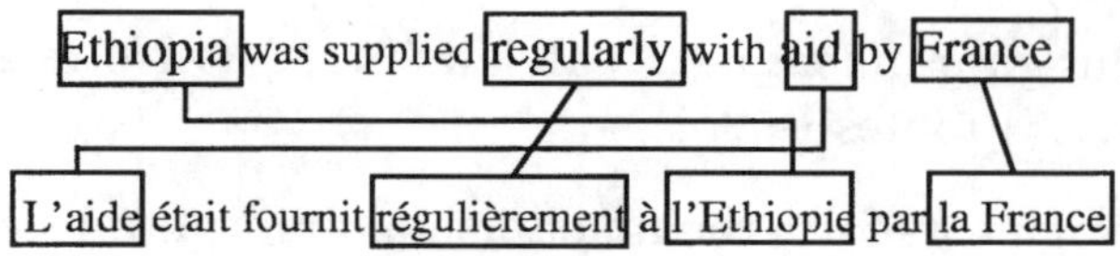

Figure 11.4. Pattern with Non-Adjacent Alignments

similarity score is above an experimentally determined threshold, the two strings are considered to be cognates. Bilingual lexical distribution suffers from well-known problems such as data sparseness, the identification of translingual collocates as opposed to true translations and the varying distributions of morphological variants of words. The inclusion of cognates into the distance metric addresses, to some extent, the problem of low frequency words and provides an alternative score.

The alignment of closed class words is particularly problematic. They are of such high frequency that they are unable to be aligned by lexical distribution. They are also not subject to cognate matching. Solutions to this problem include the non-alignment of text fragments composed uniquely of closed class words. An additional method is to 'fill in' the variable positions between text fragments where the variable is uniquely composed of closed class words. For instance *independent states (...) former Soviet Union* becomes *independent states of the former Soviet Union.* However, neither provides a satisfactory solution.

The sequence-comparison algorithm needs to be able to compute alignments denoting translation relations of a more complex variety than simple 1:1 relationships, i.e. 2:1, 1:0, etc. It must also compute alignments between adjacent and non-adjacent text fragments (long-distance dependencies) to allow for structural divergences between languages (Figure 11.4).[2] Finally, it needs to execute in a practicable asymptotic running time, therefore excluding an exhaustive search algorithm.

One solution to the problem of sequence alignment is the Dynamic Programming (DP) framework (equation (7); cf. also Chapter 6, this volume). While the problem of sentence alignment is suited to the DP al-

[2]The text between the boxed text would appear in the translation patterns as variables. It is included here to make sense of the example.

gorithm in that the order of sentences between languages is often similar (Gale & Church, 1993), sub-sentential fragment alignment must include a search for non-adjacent alignments or long-distance dependencies — a crucial task which DP is inherently unable to perform.

$$D(i,j) = min \begin{cases} D(i, j-1) + d(0, y_j) \\ D(i-1, j) + d(x_i, 0) \\ D(i-1, j-1) + d(x_i, y_j) \\ D(i-1, j-2) + d(x_i, \{y_{j-1}, y_j\}) \\ D(i-2, j-1) + d(\{x_{i-1}, x_i\}, y_j) \\ D(i-2, j-2) + d(x_i, y_{j-1}) + d(x_{i-1}, y_j) \\ D(i-1, j-3) + d(x_i, \{y_{j-2}, y_{j-1}, y_j\}) \\ D(i-3, j-1) + d(\{x_{i-2}, x_{i-1}, x_i\}, y_j) \end{cases} \tag{7}$$

An algorithm is proposed that performs the alignment in two passes: the first pass, for which DP is ideally suited, takes into account substitutions (1:1), insertions (0:1), deletions (1:0), compression (2:1, 3:1), expansion (1:2, 1:3) and *swaps* of adjacent fragments (Lowrance & Wagner, 1975), assuming all local alignments are adjacent. The second-pass algorithm computes the (possibly empty) set of non-adjacent alignments of a 1:1 nature. If any are found that improve the initial global alignment computed by DP, they are recorded and removed from the two sequences, while the remaining text fragments are re-fed into the DP algorithm. The final global alignment is then a concatenation of the non-adjacent alignments and the results of the second application of the DP algorithm. The same bilingual similarity metric is used for both passes.

```
for i = 1 to m
  for j = 1 to n
    if Score(xi,yj) > Threshold & abs(i-j) > 1
      add {xi,yj, Score(xi,yj)} to list of candidate non-adjacent alignments
```

Figure 11.5. Finding Candidate Non-Adjacent Alignments

The second-pass algorithm is summarised as follows: given two sequences x and y of lengths m and n respectively, each element x_i for $1 \leq i \leq m$ is compared with each element y_j for $1 \leq j \leq n$. For each potential alignment $\langle x_i, y_j \rangle$, the similarity score $Score(x_i,y_j)$ is computed. If $Score(x_i,y_j)$ satisfies two conditions, the text fragments x_i and y_j along with $Score(x_i, y_j)$ are recorded as a triple and added to the list of candidate non-adjacent alignments (Figure 11.5). The first condition states that the alignment must be high-scoring (above a threshold) and the second states that the alignment must be non-adjacent, i.e. the absolute difference between i and j must be greater than 1.

Once a list of triples representing candidate non-adjacent alignments has been collected $\{(\alpha, \beta \text{ Score}(\alpha, \beta)), \ldots \}$, for each triple, three conditions are applied before the alignment is declared a valid non-adjacent alignment. First, if the SL (TL) text fragment α (β) of the proposed non-adjacent alignment $\langle \alpha, \beta \rangle$ has been used elsewhere in a *non*-adjacent alignment, it cannot be used to form a subsequent one. Second, if the alignment $\langle \alpha, \beta \rangle$ is a subset of an adjacent alignment $\langle A, B \rangle$ that has previously been computed by DP (where A and B represent a series of SL and TL text fragments respectively and where $\alpha \in A$ and $\beta \in B$), they cannot be considered further. The reason for this is simply that the DP algorithm has found that an alignment other than a 1:1 type is more probable, thus the proposed alignment is not likely to improve the likelihood of the final global alignment.

$$
\begin{aligned}
&Score(\alpha, \beta) > Score(\langle A, B \rangle_p)\,\& \\
&Score(\alpha, \beta) > Score(\langle A, B \rangle_q), \\
&\alpha \in A_p, \beta \in B_q, 1 \le p \le k, 1 \le q \le k, p \ne q
\end{aligned}
$$

Figure 11.6. Non-adjacent Alignment

Finally, the score of the proposed non-adjacent alignment $\langle \alpha, \beta \rangle$ is tested to see whether it is greater than both the two individual scores of the two alignments computed by DP of which α and β are a member. In more detail, each adjacent alignment computed by DP is represented as a pair $\langle A, B \rangle$, where A and B represent a series of SL and TL fragments according to the alignment patterns stipulated by the DP equation. The initial global alignment computed solely by DP is a set containing one or more of these alignments, $\{\langle A, B \rangle_1, \ldots, \langle A, B \rangle_k\}$. The proposed non-adjacent alignment can also be represented by a pair $\langle \alpha, \beta \rangle$ where α and β represent one SL and TL text fragment respectively. This condition is summarised in Figure 11.6, which stipulates that the bilingual similarity score of the non-adjacent alignment must be greater than both of the two adjacent alignments which subsume it, which means that the addition of the proposed non-adjacent alignment would *improve* the overall global alignment.[3]

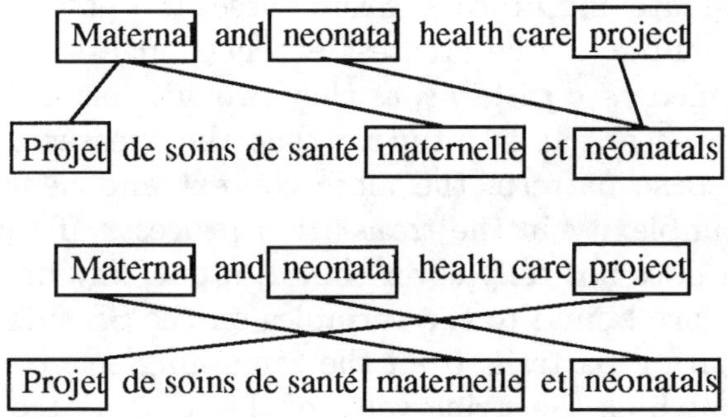

Figure 11.7. Before and After Second Pass Algorithm

To illustrate the second pass algorithm, the translation pattern in Figure 11.7 is first aligned using only the DP algorithm. The alignment of the text fragments (boxed text) is incorrect. After the application of the second pass algorithm, a non-adjacent alignment (*project-projet*) is computed. Subsequent application of the DP algorithm produces the correct correspondences *maternal-maternelle*, and *neonatal-néonatals.*

Only non-adjacent alignments of a 1:1 nature are considered to ensure that the alignment process executes in a practical asymptotic running time. The second-pass algorithm therefore runs with a worst-case complexity of $O(mn)$, as does DP.

2.3 Recombination

In the case of EBMT systems where examples are stored as tree structures with the correspondences between the fragments explicitly labelled, the recombination problem is a matter of tree traversal (Sato, 1995; Watanabe, 1995). In this approach, the input to the recombination phase is an SL input sentence and a set of translation patterns with their constituent text fragments and variables aligned. The output is

[3]The notation A_p in Figure 11.6 is shorthand for "the A in $\langle A, B\rangle_p$".

one or more TL translations which can be ranked best first according to confidence.

Given an SL input sentence, translation patterns that share lexical items with the SL input and partially (or fully) cover it are retrieved in a pattern-matching process. From these, the patterns whose SL side cover the SL input to the greatest extent (longest cover) are selected. They are termed *base patterns*, as they provide sentential context in the translation process. It is intuitive that the greater the extent of the cover of the base pattern, the more context and hence the less ambiguity and complexity in the translation process. If the SL side of the base pattern does not fully cover the SL input, any unmatched parts of the SL input are bound to the variables on the SL side of the base pattern. Translation patterns from the remaining set, containing SL text fragments matching the string value of the instantiated variables on the SL side of the base pattern, are retrieved. Since the text fragments and variables in translation patterns are aligned, their TL equivalents are easily retrieved and bound to the relevant TL variables in the TL side of the base pattern.

The following is a simple example: given the SL input in (8), suppose the longest covering base pattern is (9). To complete the match between (8) and the SL side of (9), a translation pattern containing the text fragment *Ethiopia* is required (10). The TL translation (11) is generated by recombining the text fragments: *Ethiopia* and *Etiopía* are aligned in (10) as are the variables in the base pattern (9). Since *Ethiopia* and *Etiopía* are aligned on a 1:1 basis and so are the variables in the base pattern (9), the TL text fragment *Etiopía* is bound to the variable on the TL side of (9) to produce (11). It is clearer to think of the algorithm proceeding in terms of matching successive alignments of the variables in the base pattern, rather than successive variables on the SL side of the base pattern. This is because it is not only text fragments that are matched but also the alignment type. As pointed out in section 2.2.3, alignments between fragments may be non-bijective.

(8) AIDS control programme for Ethiopia

(9) AIDS control programme for (...) ↔ programa contra el SIDA para (...)

(10) (...) Ethiopia ↔ (...) Etiopía

(11) programa contra el SIDA para Etiopía

2.3.1 Translation Confidence. On account of translation ambiguity, there may be more than one translation per SL input. The list of competing translations is ranked best-first according to a score of translation confidence (12). The score is based on three components. The first is a score based on a bigram model of the TL formed from the TL side of the corpus *BG*. The model is used as a test of the "grammaticality" of the TL sentence. The second is a score that measures boundary friction *BF* by checking the extent of the overlap of the inserted TL text fragments. The third is a score reflecting the bilingual similarity *BS* between translated text fragments. Finally a penalty p is applied if any TL variables in the base pattern remain uninstantiated.

(12) $$Confidence = (\omega_1(BG) + \omega_2(BF) + \omega_3(BS))(1 - p)$$

The TL bigram model is computed from the TL side of the corpus. It is easily improved by adding more TL text. The strength of association between the words in the bigrams is computed by Dice's co-efficient. For each TL sentence produced of length n, BG in equation (12) is computed by taking the average score of each bigram within it, or each word pair $\langle w_i, w_{i+1}\rangle$. This is summarised in (13): For each bigram in the TL sentence, its frequency in the TL corpus is divided by the sum of the frequencies of either word in the corpus and multiplied by 2. This score is added to a running total. The total is then divided by the number of bigrams in the sentence or $n - 1$.

(13) $$BG = \frac{\sum_{i=1}^{n-1} 2\left(\frac{|w_i, w_{i+1}|}{|w_i| + |w_{i+1}|}\right)}{n-1}$$

The term *BF* in equation (12) makes use of the fact that the text fragments have been extracted from real texts and so there is information about the contexts in which the fragments are known to have occurred. The idea is borrowed from Somers *et al.*, 1994, who use the image of hooks being attached before and after the text fragment, indicating the words (and POS tags) that can occur before and after it. A window of five words before and after the text fragment bound to each TL variable of the base pattern is considered. If the same sequence of up to 5 words or less preceding and subsequent to the inserted text fragment is found in the TL side of the corpus, a score reflecting the extent of the overlap between the two sequences is returned. Where multiple match sequences are found, the maximum overlap value is returned. As an example, when the TL text fragment *Etiopía* is inserted into the TL base variable in (9), the word sequence [*programa*, *contra*, *el*, *SIDA*, *para*] is looked for in the corpus preceding *Etiopía*. Starting from *Etiopía*, the extent of the overlap is determined. If only *para* appears before *Etiopía* in the corpus, the overlap score returned would be $1/5 = 0.2$. If there were a match sequence subsequent to *Etiopía*, the average of the previous and the subsequent overlap would be returned. The formula is given in equation (14): For each base pattern with $n (n > 0)$ TL variable positions, the average overlap score between the text fragment F_i and the previous F_{prev} and subsequent fragments F_{subsqt} is returned. The final overlap score is the average overlap score for each F_i. If F_i occurs at a sentence boundary, only one of the previous or subsequent overlap scores is considered. The overlap window size is given by N.

(14) $$BF = \frac{1}{n} \sum_{i=1}^{n} \left(\frac{Overlap(F_i, F_{prev}) + Overlap(F_i, F_{subsqt})}{2N} \right)$$

For each variable alignment, the bilingual similarity score, BS in (12), is calculated between the SL text fragments bound to the SL variables of the base pattern and their TL equivalents using equation (6) in the alignment process (section 2.2.3). The average score for each alignment is returned.

Finally a penalty p is applied if there are any variables on the TL side of the base pattern that have not been instantiated on account of *partial* matches between the SL input and the SL side of the base pattern. Partial matches occur when not all variables on the SL side of the base pattern can be matched by SL text fragments in the remaining set of translation patterns. For example, if there were no translation pattern containing the text fragment *Ethiopia*, the TL variable would not be instantiated, resulting in the partial translation: *programa contra el SIDA para (...)*. The penalty p is simply the number of unfilled variables on the TL side of the base pattern over the total number of variables on the TL side of the base pattern. In the case where $p = 1$, i.e. when all TL variables remain unfilled, p is scaled by 0.9 to avoid $(1 - p)$ becoming zero.

The three terms BG, BF and BS return a real value between 0 and 1.0. To ensure that the sum of the three terms remains between 0 and 1.0, $\omega_1 + \omega_2 + \omega_3 = 1.0$. In the experiments undertaken, $\omega_1 = \omega_2 = \omega_3 = 1/3$, thus providing equal weighting to all terms. The term containing the penalty $(1 - p)$ returns a value between 0.1 and 1.0, ensuring that the entire score remains a real value no greater than 1.0.

3. Adding Linguistic Knowledge

An approach based on the distributions of surface forms is error-prone and liable to the production of translation patterns that are false translations. Linguistic knowledge, in the form of morphological analysis and POS tagging, is added in an attempt to increase the accuracy of the translation patterns and coverage. This results in three variants of this approach to EBMT: The first variant, outlined in section 2, is based on surface forms and requires no significant external linguistic knowledge, apart from the sentence-aligned parallel corpus. However, in order to remove obvious errors a very small amount of (optional) minor linguistic information is added in the form of stop lists of closed-class words and information for tokenisation, which compromises, to a certain extent, language-neutrality and portability. We believe this information to be obtainable in a few person-hours. The second variant is augmented with morphological information in the form of a set of two-level morphological rules, a list of lemmas and a finite state transducer (*PC-Kimmo*, Koskenniemi, 1983). The corpus is lemmatised so that translation patterns composed of lemmas and translation patterns on the morphological level are extracted. Furthermore, clitics such as the French *des*, *du* etc. are expanded in an effort to increase coverage and reduce boundary friction. TL surface forms are generated by reversing the direction of the transducer, combing TL lemmas with TL morphological suffixes. Since no POS information nor word grammar is used, the surface forms are validated by means of a list of TL surface forms (a spelling dictionary in this case). The third variant is extended even further to include POS annotation, using *TreeTagger* (Schmid, 1994).

As more linguistic knowledge sources are added to a system, portability generally decreases. In this case, the linguistic knowledge added is deliberately kept to a minimum and to the sort of knowledge sources that are reasonably widely available, at least for European languages. Even if they are not, it is not too difficult nor time-consuming to produce a list of stems and a set of two-level spelling rules. POS taggers such as *TreeTagger* and Brill's tagger (Brill, 1992) are also easily trained for new languages if they do not already exist.

3.1 Morphological Analysis

The principal source of errors is the phenomenon where SL words that are orthographically identical (homographs, polysemes, orthographically identical variants of the same lemma) have different TL equivalents. This can be corrected, to a certain extent, by the addition of morphological analysis and POS tagging to distinguish them. Consider the corpus sample in (15) where the morphological variants of *give* are orthographically identical, but their TL equivalents are not. This results in an incorrect or *false* translation pattern (16).

(15) He **gave the** job **up** ↔ Il abandonna **le** poste
They **gave the** plan **up** ↔ Ils abandonnèrent **le** plan

(16) (...) gave the (...) up ↔ (...) le (...)

Lemmatising the corpus, as in (17), produces a more accurate, if more general, translation pattern (18) composed of lemmas.

(17) He **give the** job **up** ↔ Il **abandonner le** poste
They **give the** plan **up** ↔ Ils **abandonner le** plan

(18) (...) give the (...) up ↔ (...) abandonner le (...)

Furthermore, abstracting all morphological variants to their root form increases the chance of string co-occurrence and collocation formation, resulting in a greater number of translation patterns with the potential to increase coverage.

3.2 Part-of-Speech Tagging

A further case is SL homographs that are of different parts-of-speech and are consequently different 'words' relating to different concepts. It is very likely that in such cases each individual homograph will have a different TL translation. Consider *chair* as a noun and a verb in the corpus sample (19) and the resulting false translation pattern (20) caused by such category ambiguity.

(19) He **chairs** a committee on **the** judiciary ↔ Il préside un comité sur **le** judiciaire
My **chairs** are in **the** cellar ↔ Mes chaises sont dans **le** placard

(20) (...) chair (...) the (...) ↔ (...) le (...)

Lemmatisation is not a solution since both forms of *chairs* abstract to the (orthographically) same root. The solution lies in POS tagging the corpus and modifying the string co-occurrence algorithm for extracting patterns to include the POS tag as a feature. In such a case, the two forms of *chair* would not 'co-occur' to form a collocation, since their respective POS tags would distinguish one form of *chair* from the other and consider them as different words.

3.3 Semantic Tagging

The solution to the false translation problem in this approach appears to lie distinguishing different 'words' from each other, on criteria deeper than just their orthography. Distinguishing different 'words', i.e. strings of characters that relate to different concepts, is not entirely possible by morphological analysis and POS tagging alone. Consider the corpus in (21) where the two senses of the polysemous verb *mark* occur with identical orthographies and POS tag, but different translations, to produce (22). While the two meanings of *mark* may or not have been historically related, they are clearly separate and consequently have different translations. In theory, the solution appears to lie in effective semantic tagging, if it were feasible, and including that tag as part of a feature structure in the co-occurrence algorithm. Again this would enable the different semantic forms of a verb such as *mark* to be distinguished and prevented from forming collocations.

(21) She **marked the** paper ↔ Elle corrigea **la** copie
He **marked the** table ↔ Il tacha **la** table

(22) (...) mark the (...) ↔ (...) le (...)

3.4 Other Sources of Error

The fact that translation patterns are formed using an algorithm based on the distribution of strings in a corpus means that there are fewer constraints than in a traditional rule-based system or system that generalizes translation examples by morphological, syntactic or even semantic means. The patterns do not contain any restrictions on the morphology, number, gender or syntactic category of the text fragment that binds to the variables in the base pattern. Furthermore, adding external knowledge sources is no guarantee of increasing the accuracy (or coverage) of a system. Taggers, parsers and other analysers are prone to a certain degree of error themselves.

4. Complexity Issues

4.1 Translation Pattern Extraction

The translation pattern extraction algorithm, in particular the construction of the collocation trees (section 2.2.1) is a notable source of complexity. As each lexical item occurring in two or more sentences is added, the tree increases in size. Since each lexical item may be added to the daughter(s) of the root node and any subsequent node, the trees grow to become very much larger than the corpus itself. On account of their high frequency, closed class words are particularly problematic in that they dramatically increase the size of the trees.

In this instance, space becomes an issue. As the size of the corpus increases, the collocation trees become very large, in effect, placing a restriction on extensibility. Figure 11.8 shows how the size of the collocation trees for a corpus of French (measured in megabytes) increases in relation to the size of the corpus (measured in sentence pairs). The straight line indicates the extrapolation of the data. Although the relationship appears to be linear, the trees take a substantial portion of memory and the limit on corpus size is dictated by the memory of a particular machine (unless hard-drive space is efficiently utilised). The size of the collocation trees is the greatest obstacle to scaling up this approach. The solution lies in reducing the space required by the trees, in particular, reducing the number of levels. This may be achieved by adding the longest substrings that appear in two or more sentence pairs to the trees instead of individual word tokens.

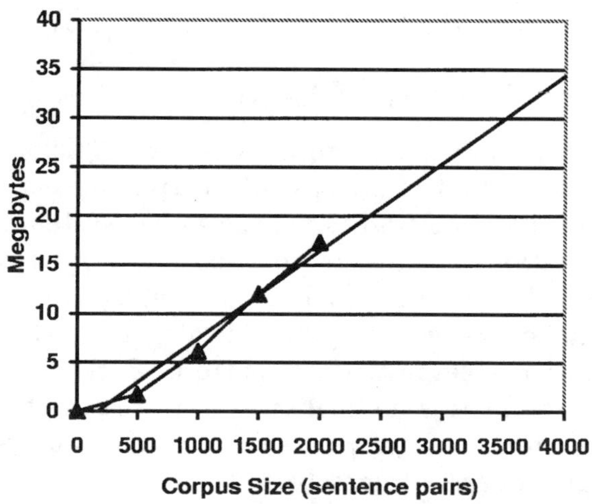

Figure 11.8. Corpus Size vs. Size of Collocation Trees

The polynomial two-pass alignment algorithm outlined in section 2.2.3 is also a notable source of complexity. In fact it is the part of the extraction algorithm that incurs the largest time processing overhead The well-known DP algorithm consists of two embedded loops and is clearly of a time and space complexity of $O(mn)$, where m and n are the lengths of the two sequences to be aligned. DP is practical in terms of time and space, but not fast. In this application, the values of m and n are rarely large.

The grain-size of the local alignment types is also pertinent. Further text fragment alignment patterns such as 2:3, 3:2 and even 2:4 could easily be included as terms in the DP equation. More terms entails a larger processing overhead, and as grain-size increases, the problem of long-distance dependencies becomes less of an issue as their likelihood diminishes. Moreover, the granularity of the alignment types involves the classic trade-off between accuracy and flexibility. While matches with longer fragments reduce ambiguity, flexibility suffers since there is a lower probability of a match. Matches with shorter segment involve a greater amount of translation ambiguity, passage and boundary friction (Nirenburg *et al.*, 1993). Fine as opposed to coarse-grained local alignment types have been favoured in this approach in order to maintain flexibility and recall.

4.2 Recombination

The core recombination algorithm is an area where the amount of entropy incurred by translation ambiguity and the lack of constraints in the translation patterns produce the most notable source of computational complexity. Since any one SL fragment can have more than one TL equivalent and there is no information present to favour one fragment over another, all possible TL fragments are considered. This results in (possibly) numerous translations per base pattern which are ranked by the translation confidence score (12).

The complex nature of the core recombination algorithm is clear. If a base pattern contains n local alignments between the SL and TL variables to cover the SL input, and there are T_i TL equivalents per alignment, such that $1 \leq i \leq n$, then the number of operations required to produce all translation solutions is the series $T_i * T_{i+1} \ldots T_n$, or (23), presuming that TL equivalents are retrieved using an efficient method of indexing, such as hashing.

$$(23) \qquad Solutions = \prod_{i=1}^{n} T_i$$

The complexity is increased if recursive matches are incorporated. In the examples (8)–(11), the string values bound to the variables on the SL side of the base pattern are matched against *single* SL text fragments in the remaining translation patterns (direct matches). If no direct matches are found, a recursive matching algorithm is invoked. The algorithm matches a single text fragment by attempting to recursively match successively shorter portions of it against several of the remaining SL text fragments in the translation patterns. The TL equivalents are concatenated naïvely according to the order of the matches with the SL fragments. Increased complexity comes about since each SL fragment that forms a subpart of the entire match can have more than one TL equivalent, each of which has to be taken into account. Therefore, there may be many more translation equivalents for the original SL fragment than if it were matched against a single SL fragment. It is this extra parameter that increases complexity.

The similarity between the core recombination and recursive matching algorithms enables the complexity of the recursive matching process to be deduced as above. If an SL fragment is partitioned k times, and there are t_j TL equivalents for each portion of the SL fragment at j, where $1 \leq j \leq k$, then the number of operations required to produce all TL equivalents of the original SL fragment is the series $t_j * t_{j+1} \dots t_k$, or (24). Where no direct match is possible and a recursive match is successful, occurring at variable position i, T_i in (23) is replaced by the equation in (24):

(24) $$Equivalents = \prod_{j=1}^{k} t_i$$

Hence, the complexity or maximum number of operations in recombination is increased to that shown in (25:

(25) $$Recombination = \prod_{i=1}^{n} \prod_{j=1}^{k} T_{i,j}$$

The addition of knowledge sources has consequences for the complexity of the recombination phase. The second variant of this approach, which is augmented to include morphological analysis involves the extraction of not only translation patterns composed of lemmas, but translation patterns composed of morphological suffixes, termed *morphological,patterns.* They are analogous to regular translation patterns (section 2.1) except that the 'text fragments' are composed of morphological suffixes instead of lexical items.

Morphological patterns are formed trivially by the replacement of lemmas in regular translation patterns extracted with the corresponding morphological suffixes computed during lemmatisation of the corpus. The tags represent (inflectional) morphological change from the lemma or root lexical form. The alignment between the sequences of fragments (composed of suffixes) and variables in a morphological pattern is also carried out trivially by transposing the alignments from the regular translation pattern from which it was formed.

The corpus (26) is lemmatised to form (27), from which translation pattern (28) is extracted (among others). By replacing the lemmas with the corresponding morphological tags from (27), the morphological patterns (29) and (30) are formed. The empty parentheses denote cases of no morphological change from the root lexical form. The fragments and variables in (29) and (30) are aligned according to alignment of the fragments in the regular translation pattern (28). The extraction of morphological patterns does not add significantly to the processing overhead of the learning phase.

(26) The telephones worked ↔ Les téléphones fonctionnaient
The telephone failed ↔ Le téléphone échouait

(27) **The telephone**+*s* work+*ed* ↔
Le+*s* **téléphone**+*s* fonctionner+*aient*
The telephone fail+*ed* ↔ **Le téléphone** échouer+*ait*

(28) The telephone (...) ↔ Le téléphone (...)

(29) [] +s (...) ↔ +s +s (...)

(30) [] [] (...) ↔ [] [] (...)

The recombination algorithm is updated to operate with translation patterns composed of lemmas and morphological patterns. First, the SL input is lemmatised and recombination proceeds in exactly the same manner as described in section 2.3, except that matching takes place on the lexical level and the result is a set of one or more sequences of TL lemmas. Morphological patterns are retrieved and recombined analogously to cover the sequence of SL morphological suffixes computed when the SL input is lemmatised. This results in a set of one or more sequences of TL morphological suffixes. TL sentences are produced by layering the sequences of TL lemmas and suffixes, generating sequences of surface forms. As an example, the sequence of lemmas (31) is layered with the sequence of suffixes (32) to produce (33).

(31) ⟨Programme, contre, le, maladie, diarrhéique⟩

(32) ⟨[], [], +s, +s, +si⟩

(33) Programme contre les maladies diarrhéiques

It is intuitive that recombination that takes place on more than one level increases the processing overhead. In this case, recombination takes place on both the lexical and morphological levels, the outputs of which are layered: each sequence of lemmas is layered with each sequence of morphological suffixes. The layering algorithm is unique to the variants of this approach that make use of external linguistic knowledge, namely morphological analysis.

One further complexity issue is ambiguity of analysis. When a surface form is lemmatised using just a list of lemmas and a set of two-level spelling rules, as in the second variant of this approach, there may be ambiguity about the lemma to which it belongs and consequently ambiguity of the morphological suffix. In the absence of a word grammar, POS annotation or other disambiguation device, the layering algorithm takes into account all alternative analyses, thus adding a further parameter, increasing the complexity of the algorithm. Given the list of all sequences of lemmas and suffixes produced by recombination on the lexical and morphological levels, for each sequence, all possible sequences of lemmas and suffixes must be returned, where each alternative analysis of any ambiguous case is specified.

Suppose that recombination on the lexical level produces a list containing m sequences of lemmas and recombination on the morphological level produces a list containing n sequence of morphological suffixes and where each sequence in either list may contain ambiguous analyses. For each sequence of lemmas seq_i where $1 \leq i \leq m$, each sequence of lemmas, where each alternative analysis is specified, is constructed. This is repeated for each sequence of morphological suffixes seq_j for $1 \leq j \leq n$. Assuming that the length (number of lemmas) of each sequence seq_i is given by p_i, and that there is a maximum of k analyses per surface form, then the maximum number of sequences of lemmas in seq_i with each ambiguous case specified is given by k^{p_i}. Similarly, given that the length of each sequence of suffixes seq_j is given by q_j, for each sequence of suffixes seq_j, the maximum number of sequences of suffixes with each ambiguous case specified is given by k^{q_j}. Therefore, if a list of m sequences of lemmas is returned by recombination on the lexical level, the maximum number of sequences of lemmas with each ambiguous case specified is given by (34):

(34) $$Sequences_{lemmas} = \sum_{i=1}^{m} k^{p_i}$$

Similarly, given a list of n sequences of suffixes returned by recombination on the morphological level, the maximum number of sequences of suffixes with each ambiguous case specified is given by (35):

(35) $$Sequences_{suffixes} = \sum_{j=1}^{n} k^{q_j}$$

In the experiments undertaken (section 5), $k = 2$, denoting a maximum of 2 analyses per surface form.

As each sequence of lemmas is layered and combined with each sequence of suffixes, the maximum number of combinations in the layering algorithm is given as the product of (34) and (35), calculated as (36):

(36) $$Combinations = \sum_{i=1}^{m} k^{p_i} \sum_{j=1}^{n} k^{q_j}$$

However, the theoretical maximum number of combinations is never reached as not all lexical items contained in any sequence of p lemmas and q suffixes are ambiguous.

The exponential nature of (34) and (35) introduces the greatest amount of complexity in the layering algorithm. However, adding a POS tagger, as in the third variant of this approach, eliminates the possibility of ambiguous cases occurring in the lists of sequences of lemmas and suffixes returned by recombination. As a result, $k = 1$, so the lengths of the sequences p and q are removed from the equation. Consequently, there are a maximum of mn combinations, reducing the complexity of the layering algorithm from an exponential worst case to polynomial.

5. Experiments

Using the first of the three variants — the one based on surface forms — translation patterns were extracted from a 3,000-sentence-pair sample of the *World Health Organisation AFI* corpus of 4,858 French and English titles.[4] From the remaining set of 1,858 sentence pairs, 1,000 were randomly selected and used as a test set of unseen SL input. 36 SL sentences in the test set occurred in the training set. Furthermore, 728 SL sentences in the test set were entirely composed of lexical items found in

[4]`http://www.who.int/pll/cat/cat_resources.html`

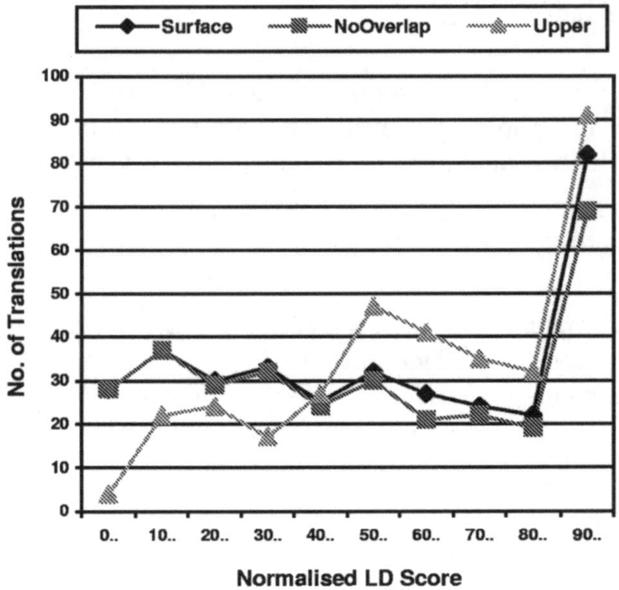

Figure 11.9. Distributions of Results

the training set, leaving 272 that contained one or more unseen words. 10,767 patterns were extracted and the most frequent values of p and q (cf. equation (1)) were 2 or 3.

For each SL input, one or more translation solutions were produced. The best translation among this set *TR* was selected according to the translation confidence score (equation (12)). The correctness of the translation was determined automatically by comparing it with the reference translation given in the corpus *RT*. The Levenshtein Distance *LD* between the translation *TR* and the reference translation *RT* was normalised to account for the maximum distance between the two strings (maximum string length), returning a "percentage of similarity" score (37).

(37) $$Similarity = 1 + \frac{LD(TR,\ RT)}{Longest(TR,\ RT)}$$

Figure 11.9 shows the distributions of the results. Only full translations were considered. The line depicted by 'Surface' indicates the results for the test set of 1,000 SL sentences. 340 SL sentences were successfully translated. Recall — the number of SL sentences translated

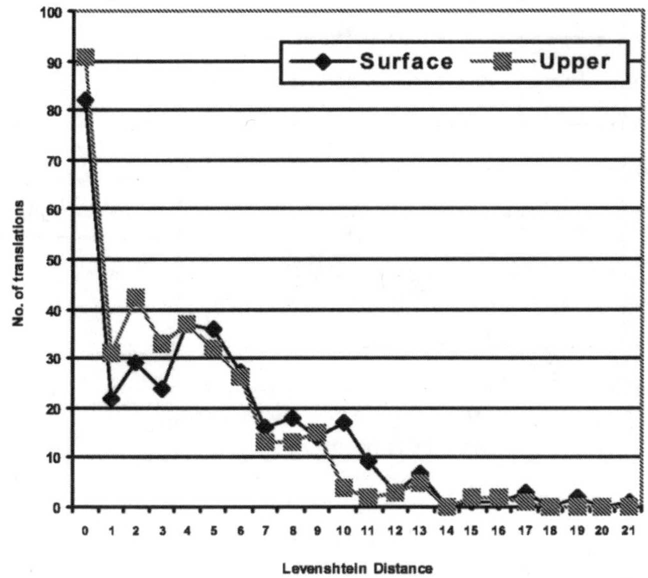

Figure 11.10. Word Error Rate

divided by the number of sentences in the test set — stands at 340/1000 = 34%. Maximal recall is obtained by dividing 340 by 728 (47%), i.e. the number of SL sentences in the test set uniquely composed of lexical items found in the training set. 82 of the 340 translations (24%) were 90–100% accurate. Moreover, 73 translations (21.5%) were 100% correct. Accurate translations were largely produced by base patterns whose SL side substantially covered the SL input. Moreover, such patterns, of which (8) is typical, represent frequently occurring phenomena in the corpus.

The line depicted by 'NoOverlap' shows the results for the test set with the 36 sentences which occur in the training set removed. Although no direct matches between the SL inputs and the SL sentences in the training set are sought (only the EBMT mechanism is evaluated), 10 of the 100% accurate translations are no longer present and there are fewer high-scoring translations generally. The line depicted by 'Upper' represents the theoretical upper bound of the system. For each SL input, the best possible translation solution — the one which returns the highest percentage of similarity score (cf. equation (37)) among the set of all translation solutions — was selected, irrespective of its translation

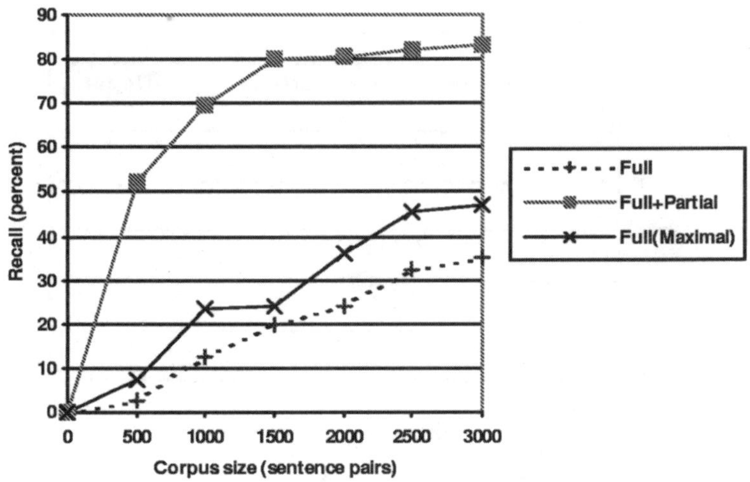

Figure 11.11. Recall vs. Corpus Size

confidence score (cf. equation (12)). This line shows that fewer low-scoring translations and more high-scoring translations are produced. The upper bound is not reached due to the inefficacy of the translation confidence score, i.e. it does not always assign the best translation with the highest score.

Figure 11.10 shows, for the same test set of 1,000 sentences, the distribution of word errors. For each translation solution, the error rate is calculated as the plain Levenshtein distance, as opposed to normalised Levenshtein Distance (cf. equation (37)). In this case, the Levenshtein Distance represents the number of insertions, deletions or substitutions required to transform the translation string into the reference translation given in the corpus. The line 'Surface' represents the errors of the translation solutions selected according to equation (12) and the line 'Upper' represents the errors of the upper bound translations. In each case, the number of translations with zero errors is equal to the number of translations that were 100% accurate in Figure 11.9.

Figure 11.11 shows increasing rates of recall as corpus size, measured in sentence pairs, increases. A test set of 500 unseen SL input sentences was used in each case. The line 'Full' represents recall calculated by dividing the number of SL sentences fully translated by the number of SL sentences in the test set. The line 'Full+Partial' represents not only SL sentences that were fully translated, but includes those that

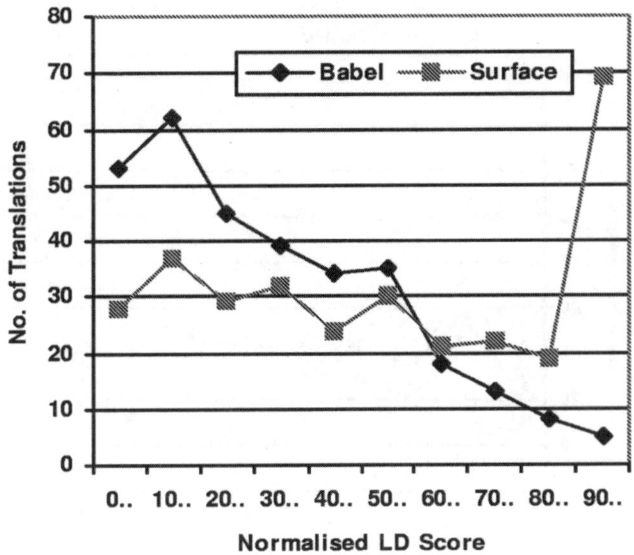

Figure 11.12. Comparison with *Babelfish*

were only partially matched against the translation patterns. The line 'Full(Maximal)' represents recall calculated by dividing the number of SL sentences fully translated by the number of SL sentences in the test set that are uniquely composed of lexical items found in the training set. The rates of recall rise fairly slowly if only full matches are considered, indicating the need for larger training sets. However, high rates of recall are rapidly achieved if incomplete or partial translations are considered. Including partial translations results in many more low-scoring than high-scoring translations.

In order to compare this approach with a commercial MT system, the same test set of 1,000 SL input sentences was translated using the *BabelFish/Systran* translation facility[5]. *BabelFish* is robust enough to achieve 100% recall for the test set of SL input sentences, far outperforming this approach.

However, in order to compare the rates of *precision*, Figure 11.12 only depicts the distributions of results for the sentences that this approach was able to translate fully. To make the test fairer, the 36 SL sentences

[5] `http://babelfish.altavista.com/`

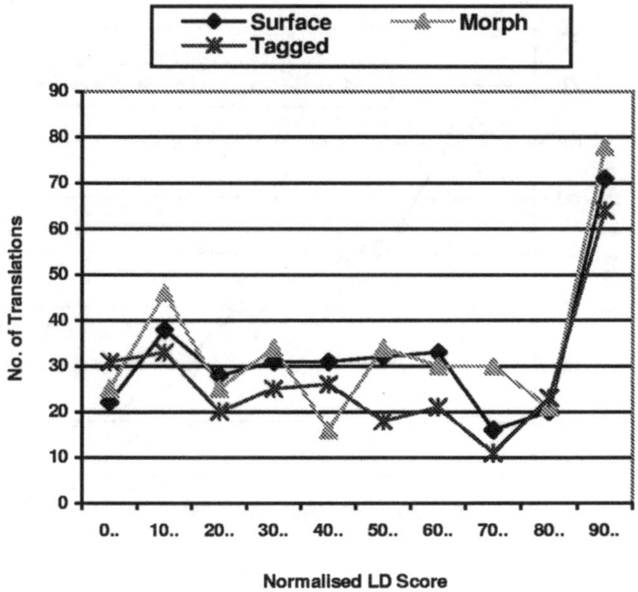

Figure 11.13. Comparison of Distributions of each Variant

in the test set that occur in the training set were removed. The graph clearly shows that for that test set, this approach (marked as 'Surface', indicating that no external knowledge sources were used) outperformed *BabelFish*. This is to be expected since this approach is tuned to the text type.

In order to test the hypothesis that adding linguistic knowledge improves accuracy and coverage (section 3), a comparison of the distributions of results of each of the three variants of this approach is shown in Figure 11.13. For each variant, translation patterns were extracted from the same 2,500-sentence-pair sample in order to make a fair test. Complexity issues (as outlined in section 4) prevented the use of a larger training set. The variant based on surface forms extracted 9,327 patterns, the variant including morphological information extracted 9,610 while the variant augmented further with POS information extracted only 7,237 patterns. The same test set of 1,000 unseen input sentences from the previous experiments was used. Only full translations were considered. The results are summarised in Table 11.1.

The distributions of the three variants are largely similar. The salient differences between them are established in terms of recall and the num-

Table 11.1. Comparison of Three Variants

	Surface	Morph	Tagged
Patterns	9,327	9,610	7,237
Translations	322	339	272
Recall	32.2%	33.9%	27.2%
Max recall	44.2%	46.5%	37.3%
Accurate	71	78	64
100% correct	61	68	53

ber of high-scoring translations produced. The morphological variant translated more SL sentences than the variant based on surface forms. Furthermore, it produced a greater number of accurate (defined as 90–100% correct) or 100% correct translations. The variant including POS information performed less well than the variant based on surface forms. Fewer translation patterns were produced, resulting in a lower number of SL sentences translated and a lower number of high-scoring translations. The reasons for the poor performance of this variant include tagger errors and the fact that more constraints operate in the translation pattern extraction phase (section 4), resulting in fewer translation patterns.

Since the evaluation method utilised in these experiments is automatic, it is possible that some of the lower scoring translations may be "correct" or useful by some other criteria, i.e. acceptability to a post-editor as raw MT output. Its usefulness could be evaluated by the amount of time or effort required to revise it to the required standard, as in Minnis, 1994 and Whyman & Somers, 1999. Alternatively, one could use any of the various methodologies in the MT evaluation literature based on human observations and scales of correctness.

6. Discussion

The addition of morphological information to the approach based on surface forms increased recall, if only slightly, and returned a slightly higher number of translations that are 100% accurate or very nearly so. There are numerous possibilities as to why there is only a slight improvement. First, only a relatively small amount of linguistic information is added. Second, the nature of the corpus (titles) is such that there are few morphological variants per root form. There tends to be a higher density of root forms in titles than in 'ordinary' texts. Third, the recursive matching algorithm in recombination (section 5) adds an amount of noise to an already noisy channel. This has the effect of blurring the improvements made by adding morphological information. Finally, and more importantly, more training data is required.

The results of the variant where POS information is included are disappointing and do not improve upon the variant based on surface forms. Given the results as they stand, the variant augmented uniquely with morphological information performs only slightly better than the variant based on surface forms. Therefore, the effort or cost (financial and computational) of adding linguistic knowledge sources may not be justified, since they affect portability to new language pairs and domains.

The rates of recall are currently low. This can only be attributed to the fact that there is simply not enough data in the corpus of the size reported. The approach must be scaled up to include corpora of millions of words. However, this requirement is in contrast to the observations in Figure 11.8 where the size of the collocation trees severely limits corpus size (unless hard-drive space is efficiently utilised). Therefore, scalability is problematic. On the other hand, if one considers the satisfactory rates of recall when partial matches are included (Figure 11.11), one has to consider whether this methodology is of more use as a flexible translation memory system (Langé *et al.*, 1997; Planas & Furuse, 1999, cf. Chapter 5, this volume; McTait *et al.*, 1999) where information from more than one translation example can be used to create new TL suggestions.

References

Brill, E. 1992. A Simple Rule-based Part-of-Speech Tagger. In *Proceedings of the Third Conference on Applied Natural Language Processing*, Trento, Italy, pp.152–155.

Brown, R.D. 1999. Adding Linguistic Knowledge to a Lexical Example-based Translation System. In *Proceedings of the 8th International Conference on Theoretical and Methodological Issues in Machine Translation (TMI 99)*, Chester, England, pp. 22–32.

Carl, M. 1999. Inducing Translation Templates for Example-Based Machine Translation. In *Machine Translation Summit VII*, Singapore, pp.617–624.

Dice, L.R. 1945. Measures of the Amount of Ecological Association Between Species. *Geology* **26**:297–302.

Gale, W.A. and K.W. Church. 1993. A Program for Aligning Sentences in Bilingual Corpora. *Computational Linguistics* **19**:75–102.

Güvenir, H.A. and I. Cicekli. 1998. Learning Translation Templates from Examples. *Information Systems* **23**:353–363.

Kaji, H., Y. Kida and Y. Morimoto. 1992. Learning Translation Templates from Bilingual Text. In *Proceedings of the fifteenth [sic] International Conference on Computational Linguistics, COLING-92*, Nantes, France, pp.672–678.

Koskenniemi, K. 1983. Two-Level Model for Morphological Analysis. In *Proceedings of the 8th International Joint Conference on Artificial Intelligence*, Karlsruhe, Germany, pp.683–685.

Langé, J-M, E. Gaussier and B. Daille. 1997. Bricks and Skeletons: Some Ideas for the Near Future of MAHT. *Machine Translation* **12**:75–102.

Levenshtein, V.I. 1966. Binary Codes Capable of Correcting Deletions, Insertions, and Reversals. *Cybernetics and Control Theory* **10**:707–710.

Lowrance, R. and R.A. Wagner. 1975. An Extension of the String-to-String Correction Problem. *Journal of the Association for Computing Machinery* **22**:177–183.

McTait, K. and A. Trujillo 1999. A Language-Neutral Sparse-Data Algorithm for Extracting Translation Patterns. In *Proceedings of the 8th International Conference on Theoretical and Methodological Issues in Machine Translation (TMI 99)*, Chester, England, pp.98–108.

McTait, K., M. Olohan and A. Trujillo 1999. A Building Blocks Approach to Translation Memory. In *Proceedings of the 21st Aslib International Conference on Translating and the Computer*, London, England.

Minnis, S. 1994. A Simple and Practical Method for Evaluating Machine Translation Quality. *Machine Translation* **9**:133–149.

Planas, E. and O. Furuse 1999. Formalizing Translation Memories. In *Machine Translation Summit VII*, Singapore, pp.331–339.

Nirenburg, S., C. Domashnev and D.J. Grannes 1993. Two Approaches to Matching in Example-Based Machine Translation. In *Fifth International Conference on Theoretical and Methodological Issues in Machine Translation TMI '93: MT in the Next Generation*, Kyoto, Japan, pp.47–57.

Sato, S. 1995. MBT2: A Method for Combining Fragments of Examples in Example Based Machine Translation. *Artificial Intelligence* **75**:31–49.

Schmid, H. 1994. Probabilistic Part-of-Speech Tagging Using Decision Trees. In *NeMLaP: Proceedings of the International Conference on New Methods in Language Processing*, Manchester, UK, pp.44–49.

Somers, H.L., I. McLean and D. Jones 1994. Experiments in Multilingual Example-Based Generation. In *CSNLP-94: 3rd Conference on the Cognitive Science of Natural Language Processing*, Dublin, Ireland, [no page numbers].

Somers, H. L. 1998. Further Experiments in Bilingual Text Alignment. In *International Journal of Corpus Linguistics* **3**:115–150.

Watanabe, H. 1992. A Similarity-Driven Transfer System. In *Proceedings of the fifteenth [sic] International Conference on Computational Linguistics, COLING-92*, Nantes, France, pp.770–776.

Watanabe, H. 1995. A Model of a Bi-Directional Transfer Mechanism Using Rule Combinations. *Machine Translation* **10**:269–291.

Whyman, E.K. and H.L. Somers 1999. Evaluation Metrics for a Translation Memory System. *Software-Practice and Experience* **29**:1265–1284.

Chapter 12

INDUCING TRANSLATION GRAMMARS FROM BRACKETED ALIGNMENTS

Michael Carl
carl@iai.uni-sb.de

Abstract This chapter presents a method for generating and filtering translation grammars from bilingually aligned and linguistically bracketed texts. Three desirable properties of translation grammars are discussed in detail. Homomorphic translation grammars enable a 1-to-1 mapping from the source language to the target language. Invertible translation grammars produce exactly one target language expression for each source language derivation tree. Compositional translation grammars recursively decompose the source language expression into segments which are translated independently of their context.

An algorithm is presented which computes weights of sub-sentential translation equivalences to generate and filter a homomorphic, invertible and compositional translation grammar from sets of bilingual aligned and linguistically bracketed texts. The algorithm is implemented and tested on a set of sample alignments. It is shown that the induction of homomorphic and invertible translation grammars can lead to the disambiguation of meaning and correction of bracketing errors.

Keywords: induction of isomorphic translation grammars, invertible translation grammar, homomorphic transfer rules,

1. Introduction

Grammar induction from sets of monolingual examples has been studied since the 1960s. As early as 1967, Gold showed that even regular grammars cannot be exactly identified from positive examples alone. This insight is based on the fact that there will always be at least two possible candidate hypotheses, (1) the language contains all possible sentences over a set of symbols and (2) the language corresponds to the set

M. Carl and A. Way (eds.), Recent Advances in Example-Based Machine Translation, 339–361.

of provided examples alone. While (1) is the most compact and general hypothesis about the nature of the underlying grammar, (2) is the most complex and least general hypothesis. Similar hypotheses underlie the induction of *translation grammars* from aligned texts: (1) each symbol in the target language side of an alignment is a possible translation of every symbol on the source language side, and (2) the translation grammar corresponds to the set of alignments alone. Neither of these hypotheses seems attractive and so it is desirable to find a compromise between the size of the hypothesis description and its generality.

In this chapter, we suggest looking for frequent collocations on the left-hand side (LHS) and right-hand side (RHS) of the alignments and assuming that these collocations are translated compositionally. We proposes an algorithm which generates and filters a translation grammar (i.e. a set of context-free transfer rules) from aligned and bracketed pieces of text. The transfer rules in this grammar are similar to Takeda's "Translation Pattern" (Takeda, 1996; Watanabe & Takeda, 1998) and also show similarities to other work in this volume (e.g. Cicekli & Güvenir, Chapter 9, this volume).

Using translation grammars in an EBMT system has the advantage of enhanced modularity, since translation grammars can be induced offline, thus reducing computation time in the working phase of the system. Furthermore, the consistency of the induced grammar can be checked and handled in a separate processing step. Accordingly, we investigate a number of properties of translation grammars, namely compositionality, homomorphy and invertibility, and show how these properties relate to the quality of the induced transfer rules. These properties provide a formal means of controlling the contents of the translation grammar and of producing high quality translations. In section 4 below we present examples of such translation grammars. For a wider prospective on controlled translation see Chapter 3 in this volume.

One of the major problems in NLP is the ambiguity of natural languages. In MT, there are essentially two different sources of ambiguity which also affect the quality of the translation: (1) how to segment the source language string into translation units and — as a consequence of this — which derivation tree to produce; and (2) how to translate the segments or subtrees into the target language. Statistical models yield answers for both types of ambiguity by ranking alternatives: different derivations of one expression can be ranked, for instance, with the inside-outside probability (Charniak, 1993; Manning & Schütze, 1999);

the most likely translations can be found by an n-gram language model.

In EBMT, this issues are handled under the label *boundary friction* and *boundary definition* (cf. Chapters 1, 14 and 16 in this volume). Boundary definition refers to the problem of how to segment the input sentence into fragments and how to define their well-formedness. Boundary friction addresses the question of how to append and smooth the translated fragments to form a correct target language sentence. The best translation is considered to be the one where the problems related to boundary definition and boundary friction are minimized.

Clearly, the two problems are related to the content of the translation grammar: while there is a large amount of literature on how to find criteria to measure the quality of automatic translations, no methods have been described until now which are capable of quantifying the quality of an automatically induced translation grammar.[1]

In this chapter we show that the induction of compositional, homomorphic and invertible translation grammars provides a control mechanism for boundary definition and boundary friction. Homomorphic, invertible translation grammars reduce the degree of ambiguity and thus enable deterministic translation, while compositionality increases its coverage. We shall show in an experiment that high quality transfer rules can be obtained following this approach.

We first examine different methods of inducing translation grammars from aligned texts and discuss properties of translation grammars in general terms. We then present an algorithm which assumes sub-sequences in the LHS and RHS of the alignment to be bracketed. The brackets are considered potential candidates for compositional translation. From the bracketed sequences, the algorithm extracts hypotheses of transfer rules, generates translation templates and filters a translation grammar.

The algorithm is applied to German–English alignments. We shall show how the meaning of ambiguous sentences can be disambiguated by assuming structural analogy (i.e. isomoprhy) of both language sides. We also show how bracketing errors are corrected.

[1]There are, however, efforts to evaluate monolingual parsers and grammars within the PARSEVAL-project, see e.g. `http://www.lrec-conf.org/lrec2002/lrec/wksh/parseval.html`

2. Approaches to Translation Grammars

A translation grammar consists of lexical transfer rules and translation templates. Lexical transfer rules consist only of lexical tokens, while translation templates also contain variables.

With respect to the way translation templates are computed one can distinguish between (1) methods which generalize chunk translations in alignments (e.g. Boström, 1999; Block, 2000 and this present approach), and (2) methods which generalize differences and similarities in sets of alignments (e.g. Cicekli & Güvenir, Chapter 9; Brown, Chapter 10, and McTait, Chapter 11).

The system of Cicekli & Güvenir searches for pairs of alignments where the LHS and the RHS show similarities and differences. The differences are then substituted by variables while the identical subsequences remain as non-reduced tokens in the translation templates. Similarities in alignments are generalized as a complement to generalizing differences. McTait generalizes alignments in a similar way. In contrast to Cicekli & Güvenir, the approach of McTait also allows $m : n$ mappings.

Alignment:
das ist was Sie wollen am Mittwoch morgen zurückzukommen
↔ which is what you were wanting to come back Wednesday morning

After Statistical Word Alignment:

das	ist	was	Sie	···	Mittwoch	morgen	zurückzukommen
↕	↕	↕	↕		↕	↕	
which	is	what	you	···	Wednesday	morning	

Chunk Pairs			Pattern Pairs		
das	↔	which			
ist	↔	is			
das ist	↔	which is	V ist	↔	V is
			das V	↔	which V
ist was	↔	is what	V was	↔	V what
			ist V	↔	is V
das ist was	↔	which is what	V ist was	↔	V is what
			das V was	↔	which V what
ist was Sie	↔	is what you	V was Sie	↔	V what you
			ist V Sie	↔	is V you
⋮		⋮	⋮		⋮

Figure 12.1. Generalization of Chunk Pairs in Alignments according to Block (2000)

A different approach is taken by Block, 2000. In his approach, word translations in alignments are assigned probabilities based on a statistical word alignment tool. Statistical word alignments are indicated by vertical arrows ($\updownarrow$) in Figure 12.1. Based on this statistical word translation information, so-called *chunk pairs* are extracted. Subsequently, translation templates (i.e. *pattern pairs*) are generated for each chunk pair. This is achieved by replacing a chunk pair in another chunk pair by a variable if the former is a substring in the latter. An example is given in Figure 12.1. The chunk pairs *das ist* $\leftrightarrow$ *which is* and *das* $\leftrightarrow$ *which* have been extracted from the alignment. The pattern pair *V ist* $\leftrightarrow$ *V is* was obtained by replacing the shorter chunk pair by the variable V. As a last step, Block filters trivial pattern pairs from the set of pattern pairs.

In section 3, we shall present an approach to induce translation grammars similar to the one of Block, 2000. In the remainder of this section we shall investigate more closely a number of properties inherent in translation grammars.

2.1 Homomorphic Translation Grammars

According to Huijsen, 1997, an MT system is *expression-complete* if and only if for all expressions which are correct according to the source language grammar, at least one translation in the target language is generated. The system is *syntactic-complete* if for each syntactic derivation tree of each well-formed source language expression, the system yields at least one well-formed target language expression.

Every transfer rule in a translation grammar has a list of arguments where the arity of a rule is equal to the number of variables in the rule's argument list[2]. A translation grammar is homomorphic if every rule has the same arity in its LHS and RHS and there exists a mutual functional correspondence, i.e. a 1-to-1 link, between the variables in the LHS and the variables in the RHS. Homomorphic translation grammars generate isomorphic derivation trees; Huijsen, 1997 calls such translation grammars *translation equivalent.*

For instance, assume that a, b, c and m, n, o are terminal tokens (e.g. words), while X^i and Y^j are variables in the LHS and RHS respectively. The lexical transfer rule (1) in Figure 12.2 has an arity of 0 — it is a ba-

[2]In Huijsen, 1997, arity is defined by the number of 'categories' in the rule's argument list. In the present context, it seems appropriate to define arity by the number of variables which occur in either language side of a translation template, not counting the number of terminal tokens which it might contain.

	Transfer Rule		
1	abc	$\leftrightarrow$	mno
2	aX^1bX^2c	$\leftrightarrow$	mY^2nY^1o
3	X^1abcX^2	$\leftrightarrow$	mY^1Y^2n
4	aX^1b	$\leftrightarrow$	mY^2nY^1o
5	aX^1bX^3c	$\leftrightarrow$	mY^1nY^2o

Figure 12.2. Transfer Rules of Different Arity

sic expression[3] according to Huijsen, 1997 — since only terminal tokens occur in the argument list. The homomorphic translation templates (2) and (3) have an arity of 2. Each language side of these templates contains two variables which have a 1-to-1 link into the other language side expressed by their indices. Translation templates (4) and (5) also have an arity of 2 but they are not homomorphic since the variables Y^2 and X^3 have no corresponding variables in the other language side.

2.2 Invertible Translation Grammars

According to Daelemans, 1998, a distinction can be made between systems which generalize and systems which perform abstractions. When generalizing, the original data is kept in the system and further data-driven generalizations are added. In abstracting systems, the reference text only serves as a basis to generate internal representations. Abstracting systems do not consider the original data in the working phase, but rather rely only on the generated internal representations. In this light, many EBMT systems can be seen as generalizing systems: the original data is segmented, either dynamically and on-line, or in a pre-processing step as proposed here. Since exceptions are not abstracted, generalizing systems can usually better regenerate the reference translations which makes these systems highly reliable.

Reliability, however, can only be maintained if sufficient context is provided in each translation such that it is unambiguous. If, for instance, the same expression in an identical context is differently translated in two reference alignments, the system cannot be expected to induce a reliable translation grammar from this expression. Translations produced from ambiguous translation grammars are unpredictable, if no means are provided to solve these ambiguities in later processing steps.

---

[3] Or atomic translation template in the terminology of Cicekli & Güvenir, Chapter 9, this volume.

Thus, in order to achieve high reliability of a translation grammar, transfer rules should be unique. For this reason, Menezes (2002, for instance, includes sufficient context to distinguish competing mappings during translation (see also Chapter 15, this volume). We shall say that a translation grammar is invertible, if and only if both language sides of the transfer rules are unique.

Alignments a_1, a_2, a_3 and a_4			
a_1:	*(business trip)*$_{\text{noun}}$	$\leftrightarrow$	*(viaje de negocios)*$_{\text{noun}}$
a_2:	*(field trip)*$_{\text{noun}}$	$\leftrightarrow$	*(viaje de estudio)*$_{\text{noun}}$
a_3:	*(long field trip)*$_{\text{noun}}$	$\leftrightarrow$	*(viaje de estudio largo)*$_{\text{noun}}$
a_4	*(field work)*$_{\text{noun}}$	$\leftrightarrow$	*(trabajo de campo)*$_{\text{noun}}$
Trivial Translation Grammar G_0			
r_1	*(business trip)*$_{\text{noun}}$	$\leftrightarrow$	*(viaje de negocios)*$_{\text{noun}}$
r_2	*(field trip)*$_{\text{noun}}$	$\leftrightarrow$	*(viaje de estudio)*$_{\text{noun}}$
r_3	*(long field trip)*$_{\text{noun}}$	$\leftrightarrow$	*(viaje de estudio largo)*$_{\text{noun}}$
r_4	*(field work)*$_{\text{noun}}$	$\leftrightarrow$	*(trabajo de campo)*$_{\text{noun}}$

Figure 12.3. Alignments and a Trivial Invertible Translation Grammar

As an example, consider the set of English $\leftrightarrow$ Spanish alignments shown in Figure 12.3. The trivial translation grammar G_0 contains for each alignment $a_i : LHS_i \leftrightarrow RHS_i$ a corresponding transfer rule $r_i : LHS_i \leftrightarrow RHS_i$. The translation grammar G_0 is homomorphic, because each of the transfer rules has an arity of 0. It is also syntactic-complete with respect to the reference text since each known syntactic-complete expression can be translated into the target language. G_0 is also invertible since each LHS_i and RHS_j string occurs exactly once. G_0 produces exactly one derivation tree for each source expression which is translated into exactly one target expression. This property of a translation grammar which produces exactly one target expression for any derivation tree is referred to as *invertible.*

To achieve high coverage, further translation templates need be generated and added to that grammar. As with the transfer rules in G_0, we require that each translation template is unique. That is, each string in either language has exactly one translation in the other language, or in other terms, each translation template contains sufficient context to disambiguate it and make it unique in the grammar.

Compositional Translation Grammar G_1

r_1	*(business trip)*$_{\text{noun}}$	$\leftrightarrow$	*(viaje de negocios)*$_{\text{noun}}$
r_5	*(business)*$_{\text{noun}}$	$\leftrightarrow$	*(negocios)*$_{\text{noun}}$
r_6	*(trip)*$_{\text{noun}}$	$\leftrightarrow$	*(viaje)*$_{\text{noun}}$
r_9	$(\{\texttt{noun}\}^1\ \{\texttt{noun}\}^2)_{\text{noun}}$	$\leftrightarrow$	$(\{\texttt{noun}\}^2\ de\ \{\texttt{noun}\}^1)_{\text{noun}}$

Compositional Translation Grammar G_2

r_2	*(field trip)*$_{\text{noun}}$	$\leftrightarrow$	*(viaje de estudio)*$_{\text{noun}}$
r_6	*(trip)*$_{\text{noun}}$	$\leftrightarrow$	*(viaje)*$_{\text{noun}}$
r_7	*(field)*$_{\text{noun}}$	$\leftrightarrow$	*(estudio)*$_{\text{noun}}$
r_9	$(\{\texttt{noun}\}^1\ \{\texttt{noun}\}^2)_{\text{noun}}$	$\leftrightarrow$	$(\{\texttt{noun}\}^2\ de\ \{\texttt{noun}\}^1)_{\text{noun}}$

Compositional Translation Grammar G_3

r_3	*(long field trip)*$_{\text{noun}}$	$\leftrightarrow$	*(viaje de estudio largo)*$_{\text{noun}}$
r_6	*(trip)*$_{\text{noun}}$	$\leftrightarrow$	*(viaje)*$_{\text{noun}}$
r_7	*(field)*$_{\text{noun}}$	$\leftrightarrow$	*(estudio)*$_{\text{noun}}$
r_8	*(long)*$_{\text{adj}}$	$\leftrightarrow$	*(largo)*$_{\text{adj}}$
r_9	$(\{\texttt{noun}\}^1\ \{\texttt{noun}\}^2)_{\text{noun}}$	$\leftrightarrow$	$(\{\texttt{noun}\}^2\ de\ \{\texttt{noun}\}^1)_{\text{noun}}$
r_{10}	$(\{\texttt{adj}\}^1\ \{\texttt{noun}\}^2)_{\text{noun}}$	$\leftrightarrow$	$(\{\texttt{noun}\}^2\ \{\texttt{adj}\}^1)_{\text{noun}}$

Compositional Translation Grammar G_4

r_4	*(field work)*$_{\text{noun}}$	$\leftrightarrow$	*(trabajo de campo)*$_{\text{noun}}$
r_{7a}	*(field)*$_{\text{noun}}$	$\leftrightarrow$	*(campo)*$_{\text{noun}}$
r_{11}	*(work)*$_{\text{noun}}$	$\leftrightarrow$	*(trabajo)*$_{\text{noun}}$
r_9	$(\{\texttt{noun}\}^1\ \{\texttt{noun}\}^2)_{\text{noun}}$	$\leftrightarrow$	$(\{\texttt{noun}\}^2\ de\ \{\texttt{noun}\}^1)_{\text{noun}}$

Figure 12.4. Compositional Translation Grammars

2.3 Compositional Translation Grammars

In a compositional translation grammar, subsequences of complex expressions are translated in a similar way independent of the context in which they occur. The trivial translation grammar G_0 (in Figure 12.3) is not compositional and can only be used to translate the four alignments given in the reference text. To achieve higher coverage, it is desirable to induce a more compositional translation grammar. Each transfer rule $r_i \in G_0$ can be decomposed into a set of homomorphic and compositional transfer rules G_i as shown in Figure 12.4. Note that the translation grammars $G_1, \ldots G_4$ in Figure 12.4 contain redundant transfer rules which reflect analogies between different alignments.[4] In-

[4]According to Lepage, 1998, analogies are characterized as: "X^1 is to Y^1 what X^2 is to Y^2". In a similar way, transfer rule r_9, for instance, expresses an analogy of all four alignments: 'LHS_i is to RHS_i what LHS_j is to LHS_j'.

ducing compositional translation grammars thus unravels analogies in translations.

As Turcato & Popowich (Chapter 2, this volume) note, a translation is compositional if a complex translation is the translation of its parts. They also note that some parts may be compositional while other parts are not. In this case the translation is non-monotonic.

Translating alignment a_4 in Figure 12.4 compositionally and analogously to alignments a_1 and a_2 requires ambiguous transfer rules r_7 and r_{7a}. Adding ambiguous transfer rules to a translation grammar increases its coverage as there are more analogies by which a source expression can be translated. However, with rules r_7 and r_{7a} in one translation grammar, it becomes difficult or even impossible to choose the correct Spanish translation *trabajo de estudio* vs. *trabajo de campo* and *viaje de estudio* vs. *viaje de campo*. There is thus a trade-off between non-monotonicity and ambiguity, between reliability and coverage of a translation grammar.

The invertibility condition requires the inclusion of a minimal context such that each transfer rule is unique in the grammar. An invertible grammar thus buys non-monotonic and reliable translations for higher coverage. To obtain an invertible translation grammar, we filter from the union $\bigcup G_i$ only one of r_7 or r_{7a}. The coverage of an invertible translation grammar decreases compared to ambiguous translation grammars. However, generating the target language expression from a source derivation tree becomes deterministic and the choice of the appropriate translation is a matter of computing the appropriate derivation tree from the source expression.

In the example above — due to a higher frequency of transfer rule r_7 — it is likely that an induction algorithm will discard (the correct) transfer rule r_{7a} from the invertible grammar if no further knowledge is provided. In the next section we shall therefore present an algorithm capable of integrating different knowledge resources when inducing translation grammars.

3. Inducing Translation Grammars

The algorithm we present in this section is similar to the approach taken by Block, 2000. First, chunk pairs (i.e. lexical transfer rules) are extracted from each alignment. Then translation templates are computed from the extracted transfer rules and from the alignments. Finally, an invertible translation grammar is filtered. In contrast to Block, 2000, the present algorithm does not use a statistical word alignment tool. Instead, constituents in both language sides of the alignments are bracketed. Hypotheses of lexical transfer rules are extracted by combining each *LHS*-bracket with each *RHS*-bracket. That is, only the bracketed expressions are considered for generation of lexical transfer rules. We currently use an extended version of the partial parser *KURD* (Carl & Schmidt-Wigger, 1998) for bracketing, although knowledge-poor methods could also be used as described in van Zaanen, 2000, for instance.

The generalization process works in a manner similar to the model described in Block, 2000, but more than one pattern pair can be replaced in a translation template which results in an arity ≥ 1. In addition, scores and weights are assigned to each of these rules.

In this section, we describe how transfer rules are extracted from bracketed alignments and how scores and weights are assigned. Then we describe how a set of invertible transfer rules is filtered. In section 4, we give examples for inducing German–English translation grammars and discuss the potential of the algorithm.

3.1 Complexity of Generalization

The program assumes a bilingual text $\mathcal{A}$ which consists of n alignments $a_1 \ldots a_n$. Each alignment a_i consists of a left-hand side (*LHS*) and a right-hand side (*RHS*). By means of a (partial) parser, both language sides are independently bracketed (i.e. parsed), resulting in a representation similar to the one shown in Figure 12.5[5].

$$a_1 : (a)\ b\ (c(d(e))) \leftrightarrow (((a')b')c')\ d'\ (e')$$

$t_1 : a \leftrightarrow e'$	$t_5 : e \leftrightarrow e'$	$t_9 : de \leftrightarrow e'$	$t_{13} : cde \leftrightarrow e'$
$t_2 : a \leftrightarrow a'$	$t_6 : e \leftrightarrow a'$	$t_{10} : de \leftrightarrow a'$	$t_{14} : cde \leftrightarrow a'$
$t_3 : a \leftrightarrow a'b'$	$t_7 : e \leftrightarrow a'b'$	$t_{11} : de \leftrightarrow a'b'$	$t_{15} : cde \leftrightarrow a'b'$
$t_4 : a \leftrightarrow a'b'c'$	$t_8 : e \leftrightarrow a'b'c'$	$t_{12} : de \leftrightarrow a'b'c'$	$t_{16} : cde \leftrightarrow a'b'c'$

Figure 12.5. Set of 16 lexical transfer rules $\mathcal{T}_{a_1}$ extracted from alignment a_1

Without further knowledge, one cannot know which of the *LHS*-brackets translate into which *RHS*-bracket or whether a *LHS*-bracket has a *RHS* translation at all. Since we assume a homomorphic transla-

[5]The letters "*abcde*" represent lemmas in the *LHS*; the letters "$a'b'c'd'e'$" lemmas in the *RHS*. The brackets are also annotated with a phrasal tag and morphosyntactic information. For the sake of simplicity, we will consider this information only in the last two sections.

tion grammar, we know, however, that if a LHS bracket has a translation in RHS then it translates into exactly one RHS-bracket. As we have no knowledge of which brackets align, we must assume that any RHS bracket is a possible translation of each LHS-bracket and *vice versa.* For an alignment a_i, we can therefore extract $p \times q$ lexical transfer rules $\mathcal{T}_{a_i} : \{t_1 \dots t_{p*q}\}$, where p is the number of LHS-brackets and q is the number of RHS-brackets. The set $\mathcal{T}_{a_1}$ extracted from a_1 is shown in Figure 12.5.

In a second step, translation templates are induced from the alignments and from the extracted lexical transfer rules $t_1 \dots t_{p*q}$. While a lexical transfer rule consists only of terminal symbols, a translation template contains variables (or reductions) in places where a shorter transfer rule matches a sub-sequence in the LHS and in the RHS. A translation template thus has at least one reduction in each language side and—due to homomorphy—it has an equal number of linked reductions in the LHS and the RHS.

Consider the set $\mathcal{T}_{a_1}$ in Figure 12.6. From the transfer rule t_{16}, for instance, 4 different translation templates can be generated, while only one translation template can be generated from transfer rule t_{11}. These templates are shown in Figure 12.6. From the alignment a_1, 25 translation templates can be generated by substituting one or more transfer rules $t_1 \dots t_{16}$.

More generally, from a transfer rule t_j which has p brackets in its LHS and q brackets in its RHS, an exponential number of translation templates $\#\mathcal{G}_{t_j}$ can be generated:

$$\#\mathcal{G}_{t_j} = \sum_{i=0}^{p} \binom{p}{i} * \binom{q}{i} = \binom{p+q}{p}$$

For instance, if we assume both p and q to be 10 and none of the 10 brackets in either language side are included in another bracket (i.e. all brackets are top-level brackets), more than 180,000 different translation templates can be generated. This is a number far too large to be computed, as 10 brackets (i.e. constituents in the parsed sentence) is not an overly large number. Therefore, a number of heuristics are proposed for generating only those templates achieving the highest weight from the set of possible translation templates.

3.2 Weighting Transfer Rules

The heuristics for inducing and filtering a translation grammar are based on weights and scores assigned to each transfer rule. We will

$\mathcal{G}_{t_i}$	Induced Translation Template	$w(g_k)$
$\mathcal{G}_{t_{11}}$:	$\{\ g_1 : \ dX^1 \leftrightarrow Y^1 b'$	0.5
$\mathcal{G}_{t_{16}}$:	$g_2 : \ cdX^1 \leftrightarrow Y^1 b'c'$	0.5
	$g_3 : \ cdX^1 \leftrightarrow Y^1 c'$	0.5
	$g_4 : \ cX^1 \leftrightarrow Y^1 b'c'$	0.5
	$g_5 : \ cX^1 \leftrightarrow Y^1 c'$	0.75

Figure 12.6. Set of translation templates $\mathcal{G}_{t_{11}}$ and $\mathcal{G}_{t_{16}}$ induced from transfer rules t_{11} and t_{16}

make a distinction between alignments a_i, lexical transfer rules t_j and translation templates (generalizations) g_k.

While inducing the translation grammar, each alignment a_i, each lexical transfer rule t_j and each translation template g_k, is linked to two sets.

$$\begin{aligned} a_i &\Rightarrow \{\mathcal{G}_{a_i}, \mathcal{T}_{a_i}\} \\ t_j &\Rightarrow \{\mathcal{G}_{t_j}, \mathcal{A}_{t_j}\} \\ g_k &\Rightarrow \{\mathcal{R}_{g_k}, \mathcal{T}_{g_k}\} \end{aligned}$$

Alignments a_i are associated with a set of lexical transfer rules $\mathcal{T}_{a_i}$ and a set of translation templates $\mathcal{G}_{a_i}$. The lexical transfer rules in $\mathcal{T}_{a_i}$ have been extracted from alignment a_i while $\mathcal{G}_{a_i}$ contains translation templates for a_i. Each lexical transfer rule t_j is associated with a set $\mathcal{A}_{t_j}$ of alignments from which t_j has been extracted, and a set of translation templates $\mathcal{G}_{t_j}$ which have been generated from t_j. Finally, each translation template g_k is associated with a set of lexical transfer rules $\mathcal{T}_{g_k}$ which have been replaced in the translation template (i.e. the daughters of the template g_k), and a set of references $\mathcal{R}_{g_k}$. Since translation templates are generated from alignments as well as from the extracted lexical transfer rules, the set of references $\mathcal{R}_{g_k}$ may consist of alignments a_i and/or transfer rules t_j. Each reference $r_i \in \mathcal{R}_{g_k}$ selects a different subset of daughters $\mathcal{T}_{g_{k,i}}$; for every i, the template g_k is generalized when substituting the daughters $\mathcal{T}_{g_{k,i}}$ in r_i.

Each of the transfer rules, ai_i, t_j, is assigned a *score* and a *weight*. The scores of alignments and transfer rules $r_i : LHS_i \leftrightarrow RHS_i \in \{\mathcal{A} \cup \mathcal{T}\}$ is calculated according to Dice's Coefficient:

$$s(r_i) = \frac{2 * f(LHS_i \leftrightarrow RHS_i)}{f(LHS_i) + f(RHS_i)} \qquad (12.1)$$

Based on the scores, a weight is computed for each a_i, t_j and g_k. The weight $w(r_j)$ of a lexical transfer rule or an alignment is equal to the maximum weight of the template that has been generated from it.

$$w(r_i) = max\{w(g \in \mathcal{G}_{r_i})\} \qquad (12.2)$$

In case no template can be generated from a lexical transfer rule or an alignment, the weight equals its score: $w(r_i) = s(r_i)$.

The weight of a translation template g_k is equal to the maximum of the score of its reference $r_i \in \mathcal{R}_{g_k}$ plus the sum of the weights of the lexical transfer rules which have been replaced in r_i to generate g_k. The set $\mathcal{T}_{g_{k,i}}$ in equation 12.3 contains daughters $t_{i_1 \ldots i_n}$ which generate g_k when substituted in r_i.

$$w(g_k) = max\{s(r_i \in \mathcal{R}_{g_k}) + \sum_{t_i \in \mathcal{T}_{g_{k,i}}} w(t_i)\} \qquad (12.3)$$

Translation templates have higher weights if they contain more reductions or if the reductions are more compositional. As an example for achieving higher weights for more compositional translation templates, consider the 16 lexical transfer rules extracted from alignment a_1 as shown in Figure 12.5. Each transfer rule is extracted exactly once, each LHS and each RHS occurs four times, so that according to equation 12.1, each of the rules in Figure 12.5 has a score of 0.25. A sub-sequence in $t_{11} : de \leftrightarrow a'b'$ can be substituted by rule $t_6 : e \leftrightarrow a'$. This substitution yields translation template g_1, as shown in Figure 12.6. The translation template g_1 is assigned the weight 0.5 (cf. equation 12.3). The same weight is assigned to the transfer rule t_{11} (cf. equation 12.2). Subsequently, when generalizing the transfer rule $t_{16} : cde \leftrightarrow a'b'c'$, a set of four translation templates $\mathcal{G}_{t_{16}}$ is generated. The translation template g_5 is assigned the highest weight due to the compositional nature of the replaced daughter $t_{11} : (de) \leftrightarrow (a'b')$.

3.3 Generating Transfer Rules

A translation grammar is generated as shown in the procedure **GenerateGrammar**(). An aligned text $\mathcal{A} : \{a_1 \ldots a_n\}$ consists of $n \geq 1$ alignments. For all a_i, the $\sum_{i=1}^{n} p_i * q_i$ lexical transfer rules are first extracted from the brackets and stored in the set $\mathcal{T}$. In practice, there will be fewer than $n * p * q$ transfer rules extracted from $\mathcal{A}$, due to (i) redundancies in the text and (ii) usage of further knowledge resources as discussed below. In addition, the strings of both language sides are stored independently such that there will be at most $n*p+n*q$ indexes in the database.

GenerateGrammar()
begin
  extract lexical transfer rules $\mathcal{T}$ from all $a \in \mathcal{A}$.
  assign scores to $r \in \{\mathcal{T} \cup \mathcal{A}\}$. // see Eq. 12.1
  sort rules $\{\mathcal{T} \cup \mathcal{A}\}$ by length of shorter LHS or RHS.
  for each $r_i \in \{\mathcal{T} \cup \mathcal{A}\}$ starting with shortest r_i:
    find set of daughters $\mathcal{D} \in \mathcal{T}$ for r_i.
    sort members in $\mathcal{D}$ by weight.
    GeneralizeRule($r_i, \mathcal{D}$).
    $w(r_i) = max\{w(g \in \mathcal{G}_{r_i})\}$ // see Eq. 12.3.
  end;
end;

Transfer rules $\{\mathcal{T} \cup \mathcal{A}\}$ are assigned scores as discussed in equation 12.1. Then translation templates are generated from the set of extracted lexical transfer rules and from the alignments. The union $\{\mathcal{T} \cup \mathcal{A}\}$ is sorted by the length of the shorter string on either LHS or RHS. Transfer rules in $\{\mathcal{T} \cup \mathcal{A}\}$ are then generalized starting with the shortest rule. Generating the set of all possible translation templates $\mathcal{G}_{r_i}$ from every transfer rule r_i is exponential in the number as shown above. In order to tackle this problem, a version of the A* algorithm generates only a limited number of the highest weighted translation templates.

For each reference $r_i : LHS_i \leftrightarrow RHS_i \in \{\mathcal{T} \cup \mathcal{A}\}$, first a set of daughters $\mathcal{D} \in \mathcal{T}$ is retrieved. Each daughter $t_j : LHS_j \leftrightarrow RHS_j \in \mathcal{D}$ is such that LHS_j is a substring of LHS_i and RHS_j is a substring of RHS_i. The set $\mathcal{D}$ is sorted by the weight of the daughters t_j. The procedure

GeneralizeRule$(r_i, \mathcal{D})$ generates a set of translation templates with the highest weights from r_i. Highest weighted daughters are substituted in r_i until either no new translation templates g_k can be produced or the maximum number of templates (*MaxTemplate*) for reference r_i are generated. The number of generated translation templates for r_i are stored in $\#\mathcal{G}_{r_i}$.

GeneralizeRule$(g_k, \mathcal{D})$
begin
  for all $t_j \in \mathcal{D}$:
    if($\#\mathcal{G}_{r_i} \geq MaxTemplate$): return.
    if(t_j is daughter of g_k):
      g_k = substitute t_j in g_k.
      add t_j to $\mathcal{T}_{g_k,i}$.
       GeneralizeRule$(g_k, \mathcal{D} \setminus t_j)$.
    end.
  end.
  add g_k to $\mathcal{G}_{r_i}$.
end.

In this way the complexity of generating the translation templates with the highest weights is reduced to $O(k * d)$ where k is the maximum number of translation templates to be generated from r_i and d is the number of daughters in $\mathcal{D}$. In addition to this, a number of parameters can be set to reduce the number of extracted transfer rules and translation templates:

- Transfer rules are only extracted if the difference in the number of words in the LHS and RHS does not exceed a certain threshold. This constraint reflects the fact that generally the same number of (content) words appear on both sides of a translation.
- By the same token, transfer rules are weighted by the difference in the number of words in LHS and RHS.
- By means of a bilingual lexicon, transfer rules may be assigned (high) *a priori* weights.
- Only a limited number of transfer rules with the highest weights is generated.

- A translation template can have a maximum number of reductions.

3.4 Filtering Invertible Translation Grammars

From the set of alignments $\mathcal{A} : \{a_1, \ldots, a_n\}$ and their associated sets of translation templates $\mathcal{G}_{a_1}, \ldots, \mathcal{G}_{a_n}$, an invertible translation grammar is filtered in a top-down fashion. The aim here is to find a compositional set of transfer rules capable of reproducing the aligned text in a most complete manner. To achieve this goal, translation ambiguities in the resulting grammar are avoided by including the smallest possible context which disambiguates each transfer rule. As discussed in section 2, a translation grammar is invertible if and only if it does not contain ambiguous transfer rules. In an invertible translation grammar, therefore, each *LHS*-string and each *RHS*-string occurs exactly once. Note that an invertible translation grammar is not deterministic. More than one translation can be generated from a source language string by differently bracketing the source string. However, each bracket has exactly one translation.

FilterGrammar(r_i)
begin
  print r_i : $lhs_i \leftrightarrow rhs_i$.
  for all rules t_m : $lhs_m \leftrightarrow rhs_m \in \{\mathcal{A} \cup \mathcal{T}\}$:
    if(($lhs_m = lhs_i$) or ($rhs_m = rhs_i$)): delete t_m.
  if($\mathcal{G}_{r_i}$ not empty):
   g_k : $lhs_k \leftrightarrow rhs_k = max\{w(\mathcal{G}_{r_i})\}$.
   print translation template g_k.
   for all g_n : $lhs_n \leftrightarrow rhs_n \in \mathcal{G}$:
    if(($lhs_n = lhs_k$) or ($rhs_n = rhs_k$)): delete g_n.
   for all $t_j \in \mathcal{T}_{g_k}$: **FilterGrammar**($t_j$).
  end.
end.

In order to extract first the higher wieghted transfer rules, the alignments $a_i \in \mathcal{A}$ are sorted by their weights. For each alignment, starting with the highest weighted one, the function **FilterGrammar**(a_i) is called. The procedure **FilterGrammar**(a_i) prints the alignment a_i and deletes all ambiguous translation rules from the search space. It then searches the highest weighted translation template g_k in $\mathcal{G}_{a_i}$ and recursively prints out their daughters. Less frequent rules (i.e. lower weighted rules) are likely to appear with more context. Note that only one translation template is printed for each alignment.

Without prior knowledge of translation equivalences, the algorithm filters the most compositional homomorphic translation grammar. Since ambiguous translation rules are deleted from the search space, the filtered grammar is also invertible. A maximally compositional translation grammar generated and filtered from alignment a_1 (cf. Figure 12.5) is shown on the left hand side in Figure 12.7. However, if the program is fed with prior knowledge of translation equivalences which do not (or only partially) support the structural equivalence of the bracketed alignments, a different translation grammar might be generated. Thus, the translation grammar on the right hand side of Figure 12.7 is generated when providing the transfer rule $a \leftrightarrow a'$ with a prior weight of $w(a \leftrightarrow a') = 0.5$. Instead of the 16 lexical transfer rules in Figure 12.5, only 10 transfer rules are extracted from alignment a_1 as $\{t_1, t_3, t_4, t_6, t_{10}, t_{14}\}$ are not consistent with the prior knowledge. The program tries to take this knowledge into account by filtering the most compositional translation grammar which is consistent with the data.

4. Results

In the remaining part of this paper we investigate a few implications of the algorithm when applied to German–English alignments. In section 4.1 we show that the meaning of an alignment can be disambiguated by filtering an invertible, compositional and homomorphic translation grammar. In section 4.2 we show that the algorithm can also correct wrong brackets in alignments.

Default Translation Grammar

			$w(\cdot)$
e	$\leftrightarrow$	a'	0.25
a	$\leftrightarrow$	e'	0.25
dX^1	$\leftrightarrow$	Y^1b'	0.50
cX^1	$\leftrightarrow$	Y^1c'	0.75
X^1bX^2	$\leftrightarrow$	$Y^2d'Y^1$	2.0

Using Prior Lexical Knowledge

prior transfer rule $w(a \leftrightarrow a') = 0.5$

			$w(\cdot)$
a	$\leftrightarrow$	a'	0.50
e	$\leftrightarrow$	e'	0.33
X^1bcdX^2	$\leftrightarrow$	$X^1b'c'd'Y^2$	1.83

Figure 12.7. Translation Grammar induced from alignment a_1 in Figure 12.5

Bracketed and Tagged Alignment

(Hans)$_{\mathrm{noun}}$	*stellt*	*((den Klotz)*$_{\mathrm{dp}}$	*in*	*(der Kiste)*$_{\mathrm{dp}}$*)*$_{\mathrm{dp}}$	*auf*	*(den Tisch)*$_{\mathrm{dp}}$
		↔				
(John)$_{\mathrm{noun}}$	*puts*	*((the block)*$_{\mathrm{dp}}$	*in*	*(the box)*$_{\mathrm{dp}}$*)*$_{\mathrm{dp}}$	*on*	*(the table)*$_{\mathrm{dp}}$
(John)$_{\mathrm{noun}}$	*puts*	*(the block)*$_{\mathrm{dp}}$	*in*	*((the box)*$_{\mathrm{dp}}$	*on*	*(the table)*$_{\mathrm{dp}}$*)*$_{\mathrm{dp}}$

Filtered Translation Grammar			$w(\cdot)$
Hans stellen art Klotz in art Kiste auf art Tisch	↔	John put the block in the box on the table	3.00
{**noun**}^{1} stellen {**dp**}^{2} auf {**dp**}^{3}	↔	{**noun**}^{1} put {**dp**}^{2} on {**dp**}^{3}	3.00
(art Klotz in art Kiste)$_{\mathrm{noun}}$	↔	(the block in the box)$_{\mathrm{noun}}$	1.30
({**dp**}^{1} in {**dp**}^{2})$_{\mathrm{noun}}$	↔	({**dp**}^{1} in {**dp**}^{2})$_{\mathrm{noun}}$	1.30
(art Tisch)$_{\mathrm{dp}}$	↔	(the table)$_{\mathrm{dp}}$	0.60
(art Kiste)$_{\mathrm{dp}}$	↔	(the box)$_{\mathrm{dp}}$	0.60
(art Klotz)$_{\mathrm{dp}}$	↔	(the block)$_{\mathrm{dp}}$	0.60
(art {**noun**}^{1})$_{\mathrm{dp}}$	↔	(the {**noun**}^{1})$_{\mathrm{dp}}$	0.60
(Tisch)$_{\mathrm{noun}}$	↔	(table)$_{\mathrm{noun}}$	0.50
(Kiste)$_{\mathrm{noun}}$	↔	(box)$_{\mathrm{noun}}$	0.10
(Klotz)$_{\mathrm{noun}}$	↔	(block)$_{\mathrm{noun}}$	0.10
(Hans)$_{\mathrm{noun}}$	↔	(John)$_{\mathrm{noun}}$	0.10

Figure 12.8. Disambiguation of PP-attachment

4.1 Disambiguating Meaning

Consider the German–English alignment in Figure 12.8. While there is only one non-overlapping sequence of brackets in the German *LHS*, the English translation has two interpretations. From the English sentence one cannot know whether *the block* is in *the box* or whether *the box* is on *the table.* Accordingly, two ambiguous brackets are generated: *(the block in the box)* and *(the box on the table)* which express these two interpretations. In the German translation, the relations of the phrases (i.e. the attachment of the PPs) are clarified by their cases. The dative *in der Kiste* expresses the location of the *Klotz*, while the accusative *auf den Tisch* expresses the direction where the *Klotz* is placed. Assuming the same meaning of the German and the English sentences, *the block* is, thus, in *the box* and John puts *the block on the table.*

As discussed in section 2, the algorithm filters homomorphic, invertible transfer rules from isomorphic brackets of English and German alignments. The filtered translation grammar in Figure 12.8 is disambiguated in the English PP-attachment. The meaning of the English sentence is thus disambiguated according to the German translation. The algorithm takes advantage of an observation by Melamed, 2001, namely that "the translation of a text into another language can be viewed as a detailed annotation of what that text means".

Note that the translation $(Tisch)_{\mathbf{noun}} \leftrightarrow (table)_{\mathbf{noun}}$ was provided with a prior weight of 0.5. The curly brackets in the translation grammar represent reductions previously marked by the capital letters X^i and Y^j. The features[6] {noun} and {dp} are phrasal tags of the transfer rules and brackets which also appear in reductions of translation templates. The superscripts 1, 2 and 3 in the *LHS* and *RHS* reductions denote the linking of the reductions. Note also that the algorithm works on sequences of lemmas, rather than on the surface forms of the words. The lemma *art* in the German side of the transfer rule represents the surface forms of the articles *der, die, das, dem, den, des.*

This disambiguation of meanings through structural analogy (i.e. isomorphy) does not work in cases where both language sides are equally ambiguous as, for instance, in the example:

	Hans sieht den Mann mit dem Fernglas			$\leftrightarrow$	*John sees the man with the binoculars*		
1.	$(\{\mathbf{noun}\}^1$	sieht	$\{\mathbf{dp}\}^2)$	$\leftrightarrow$	$(\{\mathbf{noun}\}^1$	sees	$\{\mathbf{dp}\}^2)$
2.	$(\{\mathbf{noun}\}^1$	sieht	$\{\mathbf{dp}\}^2\ \{\mathbf{pp}\}^3)$	$\leftrightarrow$	$(\{\mathbf{noun}\}^1$	sees	$\{\mathbf{dp}\}^2\ \{\mathbf{pp}\}^3)$

Given that the alignment is appropriately bracketed, at least two top-level translation templates are generated. If there is no conflicting evidence in the aligned text, the program is likely to filter the more compositional translation template 1 which assumes an attachment of the PPs to the nearest object rather than an attachment to the subject as in translation template 2.

4.2 Correcting Bracketing Errors

The meaning of sentences and their corresponding brackets can be ambiguous as shown above. Bracketing can also be misguided or wrong. However, if most of the brackets in a set of alignments are correct, the algorithm is likely to extract a correct translation grammar. Wrong brackets in alignments are ignored when filtering a compositional, homomorphic translation grammar from the alignments.

In the alignments in Figure 12.9, only nouns and adjective-noun combinations {noun} as well as simple and complex determiner phrases {dp} are bracketed. While most of the brackets are correct, some of them are linguistically not justified.

---

[6]Nouns and adjective-noun combinations are marked **noun**, with simple and complex determiner phrases marked **dp**.

A1 *((Peter)*$_{noun}$ *(der (Wolf)*$_{noun}$*)*$_{dp}$*)*$_{noun}$ *hält (ein (Referendum)*$_{noun}$*)*$_{dp}$ *für überflüssig.*
↔ *((Peter)*$_{noun}$ *(the (wolf)*$_{noun}$*)*$_{dp}$*)*$_{noun}$ *thinks (a (referendum)*$_{noun}$*)*$_{dp}$ *unnecessary.*

$\{\mathbf{noun}\}^1$ hält $\{\mathbf{dp}\}^2$ für überflüssig.	↔	$\{\mathbf{noun}\}^1$ thinks $\{\mathbf{dp}\}^2$ unnecessary.
(ein $\{\mathbf{noun}\}^1$)$_{dp}$	↔	(a $\{\mathbf{noun}\}^1$)$_{dp}$
(Referendum)$_{noun}$	↔	(referendum)$_{noun}$
($\{\mathbf{noun}\}^1$ $\{\mathbf{dp}\}^2$)$_{noun}$	↔	($\{\mathbf{noun}\}^1$ $\{\mathbf{dp}\}^2$)$_{noun}$
(art $\{\mathbf{noun}\}^1$)$_{dp}$	↔	(the $\{\mathbf{noun}\}^1$)$_{dp}$
(Wolf)$_{noun}$	↔	(wolf)$_{noun}$
(Peter)$_{noun}$	↔	(Peter)$_{noun}$

A2 *Von (Peter)*$_{noun}$ *wird erwartet, dass er mit*
((den (Gesetzen)$_{noun}$*)*$_{dp}$ *(seines (eigenen (Landes)*$_{noun}$*)*$_{noun}$*)*$_{dp}$*)*$_{dp}$ *vertraut ist.*
(Peter)$_{noun}$ *is supposed to know ((the (laws)*$_{noun}$*)*$_{dp}$ *of (his (own (country)*$_{noun}$*)*$_{noun}$*)*$_{dp}$*)*$_{dp}$.

Von $\{\mathbf{noun}\}^1$ wird erwartet, dass er mit $\{\mathbf{dp}\}^2$ vertraut ist.	↔	$\{\mathbf{noun}\}^1$ is supposed to know $\{\mathbf{dp}\}^2$.
($\{\mathbf{dp}\}^1$ $\{\mathbf{dp}\}^2$)$_{dp}$	↔	($\{\mathbf{dp}\}^1$ of $\{\mathbf{dp}\}^2$)$_{dp}$
(Gesetz)$_{noun}$	↔	(law)$_{noun}$
(sein $\{\mathbf{noun}^1\}$)$_{dp}$	↔	(his $\{\mathbf{noun}^1\}$)$_{dp}$
(eigen $\{\mathbf{noun}\}^1$)$_{noun}$	↔	(own $\{\mathbf{noun}\}^1$)$_{noun}$
(Land)$_{noun}$	↔	(country)$_{noun}$

A3 *Man hat ((Peter)*$_{noun}$ *in (das (Haus)*$_{noun}$*)*$_{dp}$*)*$_{noun}$ *gehen sehen.*
↔ *(Peter)*$_{noun}$ *was seen to enter (the (house)*$_{noun}$*)*$_{dp}$.

Man hat $\{\mathbf{noun}\}^1$ in $\{\mathbf{dp}\}^2$ gehen sehen.	↔	$\{\mathbf{noun}\}^1$ was seen to enter $\{\mathbf{dp}\}^2$.
(Haus)$_{noun}$	↔	(house)$_{noun}$

A4 *Man hat ((Peter)*$_{noun}$ *(das (Rad)*$_{noun}$*)*$_{dp}$*)*$_{noun}$ *wechseln sehen.*
↔ *(Peter)*$_{noun}$ *was seen changing (the (wheel)*$_{noun}$*)*$_{dp}$.

Man hat $\{\mathbf{noun}\}^1$ $\{\mathbf{dp}\}^2$ wechseln sehen.	↔	$\{\mathbf{noun}\}^1$ was seen changing $\{\mathbf{dp}\}^2$.
(Rad)$_{noun}$	↔	(wheel)$_{noun}$

A5 *(Peter)*$_{noun}$ *lässt (das (Haus)*$_{noun}$*)*$_{dp}$ *ungern unbewohnt.*
↔ *(Peter)*$_{noun}$ *doesn't like (the (house)*$_{noun}$*)*$_{dp}$ *to be left empty.*

$\{\mathbf{noun}\}^1$ lässt $\{\mathbf{dp}\}^2$ ungern unbewohnt.	↔	$\{\mathbf{noun}\}^1$ doesn't like $\{\mathbf{dp}\}^2$ to be left empty.

A6 *Es ist bekannt, dass ((Peter)*$_{noun}$ *(ein (Lügner)*$_{noun}$*)*$_{dp}$*)*$_{noun}$ *ist.*
↔ *(Peter)*$_{noun}$ *is known to be (a (liar)*$_{noun}$*)*$_{dp}$.

Es ist bekannt, dass $\{\mathbf{noun}\}^1$ $\{\mathbf{dp}\}^2$ ist.	↔	$\{\mathbf{noun}\}^1$ is known to be $\{\mathbf{dp}\}^2$.
(Lügner)$_{noun}$	↔	(liar)$_{noun}$

Figure 12.9. Wrong Brackets in Alignments and Correct Translation Grammar

In alignments A1, A2 and A5 all brackets in the German and English sides are correct. Alignment A5 has a bracketed noun and one simple determiner phrase on either language side, while in alignment A1 and A2, complex embedded phrases are bracketed.

In alignment A4, the bracket *(Peter das Rad)* is wrong as *Peter* is the object of the verb *sehen* and in the same time the subject of *wechseln*, while *das Rad* is the accusative object of *wechseln*. The problem here is that *das Rad* is ambiguous with respect to nominative or accusative case. Similar brackets in alignment A1 *(Peter der Wolf)* are correct as the nominative *der Wolf* modifies the subject *Peter*.

The distinction between these two cases is difficult to determine for a partial parser as it requires knowledge about valency of verbs and the type of the sentence (i.e. verb middle or verb final) being dealt with. However, if we look at the English brackets of these alignments, one sees that *(Peter)* and *(the wheel)* are not contiguous in alignment A4, while the bracket *(Peter the wolf)* in alignment A1 displays the same structure as German *(Peter der Wolf)*. Since the algorithm tries to filter a compositional, homomorphic translation grammar, the wrong German bracket in alignment A4 is disregarded. A translation template is filtered for alignment A4 such that *(Peter)* ↔ *(Peter)* and *(das Rad)* ↔ *(the wheel)* are reduced to two distinct reductions and another translation template is generated for alignment A1 where *(Peter der Wolf)* ↔ *(Peter the wolf)* is reduced to one reduction.

Hence, while correct brackets in one language might sometimes be difficult to determine, the brackets of the translation can be helpful to find their mutual analogous interpretation.

Two similar cases are shown in alignments A3 and A6. Here, the brackets *(Peter in das Haus)* and *(Peter ein Lügner)* are wrong. The algorithm overrules the wrong German brackets since their English translations are discontiguous. Instead, a structurally analogous translation grammar is filtered taking into consideration the brackets of the set of alignments as a whole and their sequences of aligned lexemes.

5. Conclusion

This Chapter presents an algorithm for the induction of translation grammars from alignments. The algorithm assumes both language sides of the alignment to be tagged and bracketed. From the brackets, hypotheses of lexical transfer rules are extracted and a set of translation templates is generated. Transfer rules are scored based on Dice's Coefficient and their weights increase as transfer rules become more compositional. A greedy algorithm, then, searches isomorphic and compositional bracketed structures with the highest weights from which a set of homomorphic and invertible transfer rules is extracted.

The implications and potential of the approach are examined on a general level and some non-trivial German–English translation problems are presented in more detail.

The results show that (1) homomorphic translation grammars can be induced in reasonable time; (2) inducing compositional and invertible translation grammars provides a means of controlling the quality of the extracted transfer knowledge from alignments and (3) the proposed algorithm is scalable for the integration of additional knowledge resources (such as a bilingual lexicon, monolingual parser, etc.) which is likely to further enhance the quality of the induced grammar.

References

Block, H.U. 2000. Example-Based Incremental Synchronous Interpretation. In W. Wahlster (ed.) *Verbmobil: Foundations of Speech-to-Speech Translation*, Springer, Heidelberg, pp.411–417.

Boström, H. 1999. Induction of Recursive Transfer Rules. In *Proceedings of the Learning Language in Logic (LLL) Workshop*, Bled, Slovenia, pp.52–62.

Carl, M. and A. Schmidt-Wigger. 1998. Shallow Postmorphological Processing with KURD. In *NeMLaP: Proceedings of the Third International Conference on New Methods in Language Processing*, Sydney, Australia, pp.257–265.

Charniak, E. 1993. *Statistical Language Learning.* MIT Press, Cambridge, MA./London, England.

Daelemans, W. 1998. Abstraction is Harmful in Language Learning. In *NeMLaP: Proceedings of the Third International Conference on New Methods in Language Processing*, pp.1–2, Sydney, Australia.

Gold, E.M. 1967. Language identification in the limit. *Information and Control* **10**:447–474.

Huijsen, W-O. 1997. Translation completeness for context-free grammars. In *WEB-SLS, The European Student Journal of Language and Speech.* `www.essex.ac.uk/web-sls/papers/97-04/97-04.html`

Lepage, Y. 1998. Solving Analogies On Words: An Algorithm. In *36th Annual Meeting of the Association for Computational Linguistics and 17th International Conference on Computational Linguistics*, Montreal, Quebec, Canada, Vol. **I**:728–735.

Manning, C. and H. Schütze. 1999. *Foundations of Statistical Natural Language Processing.* MIT Press, Cambridge, MA.

Melamed, D.I. 2001. *Empirical Methods for Exploiting Parallel Texts.* MIT Press, Cambridge, MA.

Menezes, A. 2002. Better contextual translation using machine learning. In S. Richardson (ed.) *Machine Translation: from Research to Real Users*, LNAI 2499, Berlin/New York: Springer, pp.124–134.

Takeda, K. 1996. Pattern-Based Machine Translation. In *COLING-96: Proceedings of 16th International Conference on Computational Linguistics*, Copenhagen, Denmark, pp.1155–1158.

Watanabe, H. and K. Takeda. 1998. A Pattern-based Machine Translation System Extended by Example-based Processing. In *36th Annual Meeting of the Association for Computational Linguistics and 17th International Conference on Computational Linguistics*, Montreal, Quebec, Canada, Vol. **2**:1369–1373.

van Zaanen, M. 2000. ABL: Alignment-Based Learning. In *Proceedings of the Eighteenth International Conference on Computational Linguistics: COLING 2000 in Europe*, Saarbrücken, Germany, pp.961–967.

IV

EBMT USING DERIVATION TREES

Chapter 13

EXTRACTING TRANSLATION KNOWLEDGE FROM PARALLEL CORPORA

Kaoru Yamamoto
kaoru-ya@is.aist-nara.ac.jp

Yuji Matsumoto
matsu@is.aist-nara.ac.jp

Abstract

This chapter describes two studies concerning automatic extraction of translation knowledge from parallel corpora. In the first study, we use statistically probable dependency relations to acquire word and phrasal correspondences. We obtained 90% precision using an English–Japanese parallel corpus of 9268 sentences in the business domain. The result showed that statistically probable dependency relations are effective in translation knowledge acquisition even for language pairs with different word ordering.

The second study compares three models of translation units, each of which uses different linguistic information: word segmentation, chunk boundaries, and word dependencies. The study investigates the relationship between the linguistic clues applied and translation knowledge extracted. We found that chunk boundaries are useful linguistic clues in extracting compound NPs which will be effective for extracting bilingual lexicons in the new domain. Furthermore, word dependencies are also useful for longer translation pairs such as idiomatic expressions. We demonstrate that using statistical NLP tools, in particular, statistical dependency parsers, offers robustness to the approach as well as valuable linguistic clues that work effectively in extracting translation knowledge from parallel corpora of languages from different families.

M. Carl and A. Way (eds.), Recent Advances in Example-Based Machine Translation, 365–395.

Keywords: parallel corpora, lexical knowledge acquisition, models of translation units

1. Introduction

Recent advances in natural language processing (NLP) owe a lot to corpus-based or statistical approaches. In the 1990s, large-scale machine-readable linguistic resources became available and computational power increased. These factors allowed us to process a huge amount of linguistic data using computationally expensive statistical methods that could not have been employed before. We are now in the 21st century, and corpus-based NLP can be seen in every aspect of NLP, including POS tagging and parsing.

Machine translation (MT) is no exception to the above trend, with data-driven approaches to MT exemplified by Statistical MT (SMT) and Example-based MT (EBMT). The important assumption in these paradigms is that lexicons and rules for translation are somehow acquired from corpora which can then be compiled into an MT engine. As the translation process becomes more complicated, manual preparation of translation lexicons and rules becomes too cumbersome, so that it is desirable to extract translation knowledge automatically.

This chapter focuses on extracting translation knowledge from parallel corpora. Figure 13.1 illustrates how our work is placed in the view of EBMT.

Our work takes as input *parallel corpora*, in which sentences are paired so that they are translations of each other. Parallel corpora can be prepared manually or can be obtained from parallel texts using sentence alignment methods such as Haruno & Yamazaki, 1996.

The output of our work is *translation knowledge* expressed in word- or phrase-equivalent units. Bilingual lexicographers can check the output before using them for MT systems. The workload of preparing a bilingual lexicon will be reduced dramatically.

This chapter reports two research efforts conducted by the authors in the recent past with different objectives in mind. The first study uses statistically probable dependency relations obtained from parsers to acquire word and phrasal correspondences. The objective is to examine the use of dependency relations in translation knowledge acquisition even for language pairs with different word orders. The second study compares three models of translation units, each of which uses different linguistic information: one with only word segmentation, one with chunk boundaries, and finally one with word dependencies. It aims to investi-

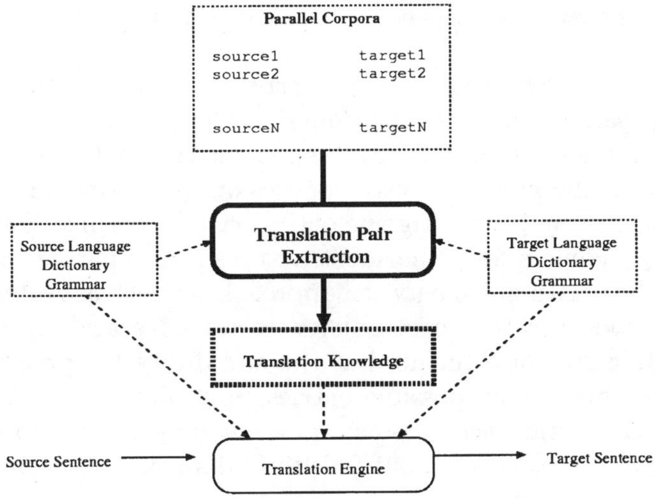

Figure 13.1. EBMT and Translation Knowledge Acquisition

gate the relationship between the linguistic clues applied and translation knowledge extracted.

From these pieces of research, we demonstrate automatic extraction of translation knowledge from parallel corpora by effective use of linguistic clues that the state-of-the-art statistical NLP tools offer.

The outline of this chapter is as follows. In Section 13.2, we review previous work that uses parallel corpora to acquire translation knowledge and describe our approach to the problem. Then, we present research aiming to acquire knowledge of phrasal correspondence using dependency relations in Section 13.3 followed by a comparative study of translation units in Section 13.4. Our motivations, descriptions of the approaches taken, along with experimental results obtained are given in both sections. In Section 13.5, we compare our research with related work. Finally, in Section 13.6, we end this chapter with concluding remarks.

2. Background

There are two distinct approaches to acquiring translation knowledge from sentence-aligned parallel corpora. One is alignment and the other is extraction. Both aim to find correspondences of smaller components in the sentences that may take the form of words, noun phrases, collocations or constituents.

Alignment is the process by which correspondences of sub-components within the paired sentences are found. The goal is to find as many correspondences as possible for *some* substructures in the parallel corpus. Extraction, as the name suggests, focuses on extracting subcomponents that correspond by processing the entire parallel corpus. The goal is to find correspondences for *some* substructures in the parallel corpus.

It is vital to distinguish between approaches which are often confused. Alignment concentrates on completeness (or coverage) by aligning all corresponding subcomponents, but the suitability (or precision) of the resultant alignments as possible entries in a bilingual lexicon is compromised. Extraction acquires as many meaningful correspondences as possible with high precision, but fails to find all such correspondences in the entire parallel corpora.

Below, we review previous approaches taken in alignment and in extraction. Based on these observations, we describe our approach to finding translational correspondences from parallel corpora.

2.1 Alignment

Alignment has been investigated at word level as well as at structural levels. Historically, word alignment was seen as a natural extension to sentence alignment. Such a view was shared by Dagan *et al.*, 1993 who employed a dynamic programming formulation similar to that of sentence alignment with finer granularity and with different slope constraints. Dagan *et al.* reported that for a 160,000-word excerpt of the Canadian *Hansards*, an alignment was produced in which about 55% of the words were correctly aligned, 73% were within one word of the correct position, and 84% were within three words of the correct position.

A structural alignment produces an alignment between constituents (or sentence substructures) within the sentence pairs of parallel corpora. The task is usually conducted in a parse-parse-match manner, in that each half of the paired sentences is parsed independently in advance with the algorithm finding matching constituents by measuring similarities. Much research has been reported in this area, including Kaji *et al.*, 1992, Matsumoto *et al.*, 1993, Grishman, 1994, Matsumoto & Kitamura, 1995 and Meyers *et al.*, , 1996. These methods not only acquire more linguistically interesting alignments but also resolve ambiguity which arises from monolingual parsing. Wu, 1995 employed a bi-parsing approach based on generative transduction grammar.

Although research results show some promise, there are some problems associated with alignment. First of all, word alignment is robust but exploits positional heuristics which do not provide good approximates to languages with relaxed word ordering constraints such as Japanese. On the other hand, structural alignment finds meaningful correspondences that can be used as translation rules in EBMT. However, these methods are often hampered by the performance of parsers used in both languages. Most methods use rule-based parsers which often fail to handle complex sentences that include subordinate clauses and conjunctions, thereby sacrificing robustness.

2.2 Extraction

As with alignment, extraction has been investigated at various levels of correspondence from words to collocations. In early work, word correspondences were searched for (e.g. Gale & Church, 1991; Melamed, 1995). However, as texts are not translated literally, there is an obvious shortcoming in word-for-word models. These methods fail to account for compounding nouns, collocations or idiomatic expressions typically found in technical documents. In order to overcome this, some research has been conducted to extract longer correspondences than words.

Kupiec, 1993 extracted English–French noun phrase (NP) correspondences. The method used an HMM-based POS tagger and a finite-state NP recognizer to extract NPs in each language and apply an EM-like algorithm to find correspondences. Kumano & Hirakara, 1994 also find NP correspondences between English and Japanese.

Smadja *et al.*, 1996 extracted English–French collocations with their *Champollion* system, which is based on the *Xtract* system (Smadja, 1993). The system uses a statistical method to successfully extract rigid collocations as well as flexible ones. First, it identifies English collocations and then gradually expands French translation words that statistically co-occur with the English collocations. The method reports that 78% of the French translations of valid English collocations were judged to be good by three evaluators. The problem with this approach is that French collocations are not found exhaustively.

Kitamura & Matsumoto, 1996 extracted rigid collocations of unrestricted length from English–Japanese parallel corpora. Translation units are strings of content words (e.g. nouns, adjectives, verbs, adverbs) in both languages. The method was tested with three different domains, achieving over 90% precision. The problem with this approach is that flexible collocations are not addressed.

Despite higher precision and robustness compared with alignment, translation knowledge by extraction does not exploit linguistic information, in particular the structural dependencies which are embedded in sentences.

2.3 Our Approach

Our work uses extraction, but pays special attention to linguistic clues obtainable from statistical NLP tools. Figure 13.2 shows the framework of our approach to translation knowledge extraction. It consists of a monolingual step and a bilingual step. In the monolingual step, we generate possible translation units using linguistic clues for each half of the paired sentences. These translation units are collected into candidate sets at the end of the monolingual step. Pair extractions then take two candidate sets from each language and correspondences based on co-occurrences in the parallel corpora are found.

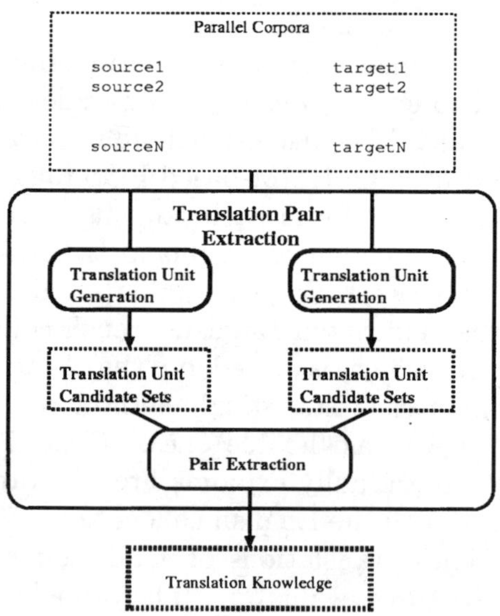

Figure 13.2. Overview of Translation Knowledge Extraction

The distinct characteristics of our approach are twofold: First, we use statistical NLP for preprocessing parallel corpora to obtain linguistic clues, thereby maintaining a high level of robustness that statistical NLP approaches enjoy. Second, we apply linguistically meaningful clues (namely chunk boundaries and word dependencies) to automatic extraction of translation knowledge. Phrasal correspondences as well as word correspondences can be extracted with our approach.

Our goal is to achieve the robustness of the extraction method while incorporating the linguistic notions used in structural alignment.

3. Phrasal Correspondence Acquisition Using Dependency Relations

This section describes a method to acquire phrase correspondences from sentence-aligned parallel corpora using statistically probable *dependency relations*, i.e. modifier-modifiee relations in a sentence.

The organisation of this section is as follows: in Section 13.3.1, we explain our rationale of applying dependency relations obtained from statistical parsers to the task of translation knowledge acquisition. In Section 13.3.2, we present how translation units are generated using dependency relations. Then, the pair extraction algorithm is described in Section 13.3.3 and experimental results are given in Section 13.3.4. Finally, we discuss the effectiveness of using dependency relations for the acquisition of phrase correspondences.

3.1 Support for Statistically Probable Dependency Relations

There are two reasons for using dependency structures estimated from statistical parsers. One is a linguistic requirement: dependency relations seem an appropriate level of abstraction for language pairs where the two languages belong to different language families. The other concerns technical advancement: recent developments in statistical parsing have led to performance accuracy of over 90%, rendering such techniques practical. Below, we describe our justification of adopting statistically probable dependency relations in translation knowledge extraction.

3.1.1 Linguistic Requirement. Melamed, 1995 conducted a comprehensive experiment on use of word position, alignment and cognates as linguistic heuristics for the extraction of bilingual lexicons. However, some heuristics such as cognate and alignment are not applicable to our language pairs. Even for word position heuristics, the effectiveness is limited to compound nouns as in "Natural/*shizen* Language/*gengo* Processing/*syori*".

Matsumoto *et al.*, 1993 argue that dependency structures are preferable to phrase structures, as they abstract away from the vagaries of word order. Japanese accomodates relatively free word ordering. For example, two sentences *kaigi-ga 2-ka nara-de kaisai-sareru* and *nara-de 2-ka kaigi-ga kaisai-sareru* convey the identical meaning of *The conference is held on the second in Nara.* The surface word orders are different, but they share the same dependency relations as illustrated in Figure 13.3.

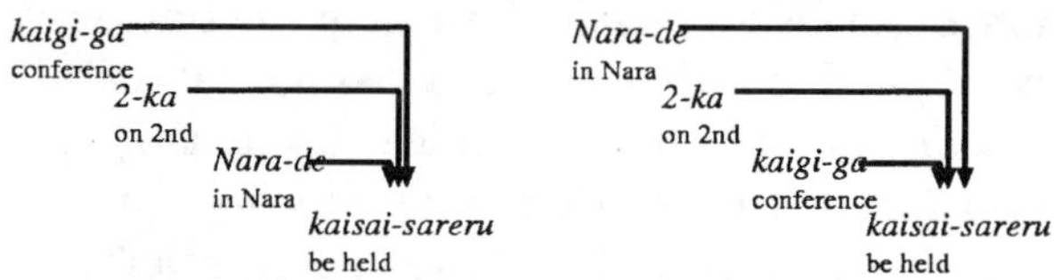

Figure 13.3. Different Word Orders, but Same Dependency Relations

Our justification for employing dependency relations as linguistic clues stems from the observation that the relative positions of source and target words may not necessarily coincide between the two languages, but the dependency structures between such words will (often) be preserved. We believe that dependency relations offer structural linguistic clues (syntactic information) and are effective for language pairs with different word ordering constraints.

3.1.2 Technical Advancement. The other reason for using statistically probable dependency relations is due to recent advances in statistical parsing. Recently, many statistical parsing models have been proposed for English, including Collins, 1997, Ratnaparkhi, 1997, Charniak, 2000 and likewise for Japanese, including Fujio & Matsumoto, 1998 and Kudoh & Matsumoto, 2002. Statistical parsing has an advantage over its rule-based counterparts owing to its wider coverage and reduced workload for grammar maintenance. More importantly, however, it produces an output with some probabilistic confidence even for long or complex sentences.

Although statistical techniques cannot always provide a complete and correct parse for a sentence, they nevertheless produce many valid partial parsing results which are useful for acquiring phrase correspondences. With the use of statistical dependency parsers, we can handle sentences that are rejected by rule-based parsers, and use partial dependency trees of those sentences to acquire phrase correspondences.

As a consequence, by using statistically probable dependency relations in the generation of translation units, our approach uses richer linguistic clues and improves coverage and robustness over previous methods.

3.2 Translation Unit Generation Using Dependency Relations

The process of generating translation units in each language is shown in Figure 13.4. The source half of the paired sentences in the parallel corpus is fed into the *morphological analysis* component to tokenize into words each annotated with its corresponding part-of-speech tag. The word-segmented sentence proceeds to the *chunking* phase. Either a set of rules or a statistical model is used to determine whether or not a group of words are chunked into a segment. The chunked sentence is passed on to the *dependency analysis* phase so that a dependency tree of the sentence may be constructed. Finally, the *subtree generation* component produces a set of subtrees of the dependency tree, each of which corresponds to a translation unit where dependencies are preserved. The process is repeated for every sentence, and all the generated subtrees form a translation unit candidate set of the language.

We use a maximum likelihood model proposed in Fujio & Matsumoto, 1998 as the basis for a statistical dependency parser. The model calculates the dependency probability between segments based on their cooccurrence and distance.

As the parser works for dependency relations between segments, we treat the following as segments in chunking:

- English
  - a base NP: none of its child consituents are NP;
  - an NP with any preceding preposition or conjunction (e.g. ([with/IN] [an/DT example/NN]) is regarded as a chunk);
  - main verbs with preceding auxiliary verbs.
- Japanese
  - a bunsetsu: one or more content words optionally followed by function words

The goal of subtree generation is to generate meaningful translation units from a dependency tree. However, dependency analysis faces the

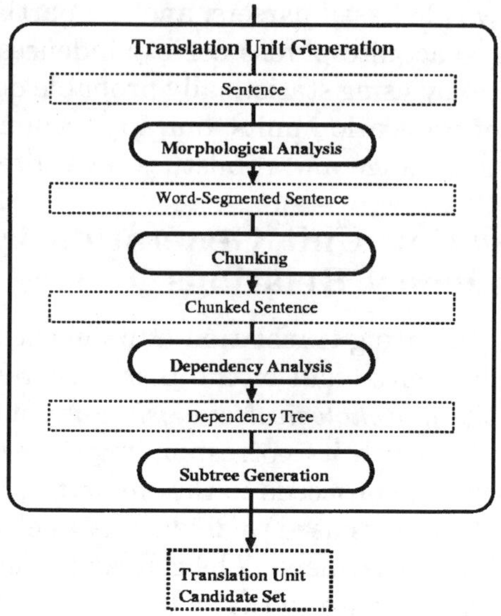

Figure 13.4. Translation Unit Generation

problem of ambiguity in that the correct dependency relation for every segment may not be determined. Even with state-of-the-art statistical parsers, sentence precision is only 50%.

However, in our problem setting, we do not require completely correct parses for all paired sentences, unlike the case with structural alignment. Rather, we want to generate as many correct partial subtrees as possible from parallel corpora. Hence, we deliberately supply multiple parsings for ambiguous dependency relations. This will hopefully increase the number of partially correct subtrees in the set of candidate translation units.

We generate translation units using the three models described below. We apply statistically probable dependency relations to translation unit generation and examine to what extent statistically probable relations are useful.

3.2.1 Model A: Best-one. The best-one model uses only the most likely (statistically best) dependency relations. At most one dependency is allowed for each segment. Translation units generated by the best-one model correspond to subtrees in sentences.

3.2.2 Model B: Ambiguous. The ambiguous model uses dependency relations above a certain confidence score. Figure 13.5 shows translation units generated by the ambiguous model. Dependency relations for *with a telescope* are ambiguous and both probable parses are considered in the generation of translation units. For translation units comprising 3 segments, two different subtrees may be generated. In order to distinguish an isomorphic subtree from a non-isomorphic one, different labels ("<T>" and "<L>") are annotated (cf. Figure 13.5).

size 1) {I, saw, girl, telescope}

size 2) {I_saw, girl_saw, **with-telescope_saw**, **with-telescope_girl**}

size 3) {I_girl_saw<T>, I_with-telescope_saw<T>, girl_**with-telescope_saw**<T>, **with-telescope_girl**_saw<L>}

Figure 13.5. Ambiguous Model

The $(k+1)$th dependency relation for $k \geq 1$ (i.e. statistically non-best dependency relation) is also included if

$$\frac{\texttt{prob(kth ranked dependency)}}{\texttt{prob((k + 1)th ranked dependency)}} \leq 2$$

The parameter 2 is chosen arbitarily. Multiple dependencies may be considered for each segment. Translation units generated by the ambiguous model also correspond to subtrees in sentences. In fact, the ambiguous model is a superset of the best-one model.

In this model, more likely dependency relations will appear more frequently in a large corpus, which, in turn, has the effect of boosting the correlation score in translation pair extraction. The purpose of this model is to examine whether ambiguity in dependency analysis will be resolved in pair extraction by supplying alternative parses.

3.2.3 Model C: Adjacent. The adjacent model uses only adjacency relations between segments, i.e. all segments are adjacent to the previous segment. Unlike the previous two models, translation units generated by the adjacent model correspond to substrings of sentences. Here, structural clues are ignored and word ordering constraints are the dominant influencing factor by far. This model is taken as the baseline case and is included for comparison purposes.

The sets of translation unit candidates thus generated become the input for the pair matching phase of our approach, which is described in the next subsection.

3.3 Pair Extraction Algorithm

Our strategy is to allow positive overlaps where ambiguity exists in sets of translation unit candidates. This is balanced by a rather more conservative discovery of correspondences in the pair extraction algorithm.

The pair extraction algorithm is based on Kitamura & Matsumoto, 1996. Pair matching of translation units in candidate sets is a combinatorial problem. The algorithm is controlled by a threshold. It first collects translation units from candidate sets that occur more often than the threshold. Then, it calculates the correlation of all combinations in the given candidate sets and extracts statistically correlated pairs. When no more pairs are found, the threshold is lowered to gradually expand the number of translation units under consideration. The same extraction process is repeated until the minimum threshold is reached. The full algorithm is stated below:

---

1 For each translation unit p_e in the English candidate set, store sentence positions in which the unit p_e is found. Delete any translation unit that appear less than the predefined minimum threshold f_{min}.

2 Apply the above operation for each translation unit p_j in Japanese candidate set.

3 Repeat the following until the current threshold f_{curr} reaches the predefined minimum threshold f_{min}.

   (a) Collect translation units that appear at least f_{curr} times in English candidate sets and in Japanese candidate sets and extract the corresponding pairs as follows:

      - For an English translation unit p_e, obtain the plausible candidate set PJ = $\{ p_{j1}, p_{j2}, ..., p_{jn} \}$ such that sim(p_e,p_{jk}) > $log_2\ f_{curr}$ for all k. Find a Japanese translation unit p_j in PJ whose correlation score is the maximum $sim(p_e, p_{jk})$ in PJ.

$$p_j \in \arg\max_{p_{jk} \in PJ} \ sim(p_e, p_{jk})$$

- For the Japanese translation unit p_j, obtain the plausible candidate set PE = { p_{e1}, p_{e2}, ..., p_{en} } such that sim(p_{ek},p_j) > $log_2\ f_{curr}$ for all k. Find an English translation unit p'_e in PE whose correlation score is the maximum $sim(p_{ek}, p_j)$ in PE.

$$p'_e \in \arg\max_{p_{ek} \in PE} \ sim(p_{ek}, p_j)$$

- Extract (p_e,p_j) as a translation pair if p_e is equal to p'_e. The correlation score of (p_e, p_j) is the highest among PJ for p_e and PE for p_j.

(b) For the translation pair p_e, p_j, and their overlapping translation units, filter out the sentence positions where both p_e and p_j appear in parallel corpora.

(c) Lower f_{curr} if no more pairs are found.

Several techniques are incorporated to overcome the problem of combinatorial explosion. First, we employ a greedy algorithm which means that a translation pair determined in the early stage of the algorithm will never be considered again. With a stepwise lowering of the threshold, the algorithm extracts translation pairs from higher scores to lower scores.

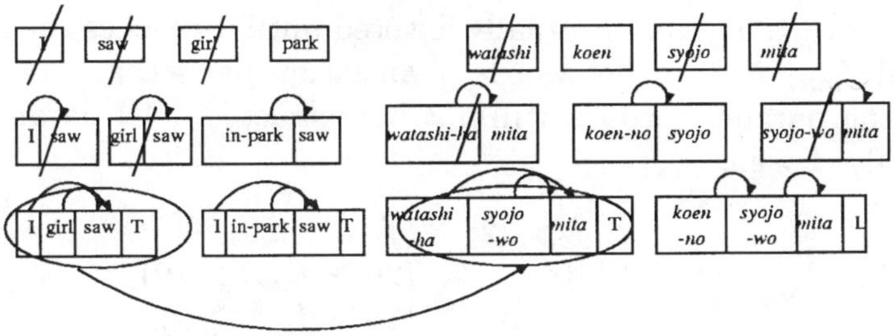

Figure 13.6. Filtering: (I,watashi),(saw,mi-ta),(girl,syojyo),(park,koen)

Secondly, filtering for competing translation units is incorporated in step (b) of the algorithm. Figure 13.6 illustrates filtering for a sentence pair "I saw a girl in the park/*watashi-ha syojyo-wo koen-de mita*". A set of translation units derived from English is depicted on the left, with the Japanese equivalents depicted on the right. Once a pair "I_girl_saw(T)/ *watashi_syojyo-wo_mita*(T)" is determined as a translation pair, the algorithm assumes that "*watashi_syojyo-wo_mita*(T)" will not be paired with translation units that are overlapped with "I_girl_saw(T)" (cancelled by the diagonal lines in Figure 13.6) for the sentence pair. The operation effectively discards the found pairs and causes correlation scores in the preceding iterations to be recalculated.

The algorithm effectively extracts translation pairs from overlapping sets of candidates.

3.4 Experimental Results

We use 9268 paired sentences of English–Japanese business letter samples (Nikkei, 1999). The NLP tools used to obtain candidates are summarised in Table 13.1.

Table 13.1. NLP tools used in this experiment

preprocessing	tool	
POS(E)	ChaSen2.0	96% precision
POS(J)	ChaSen2.0	97% precision
chunking(E)	SNPlex1.0	rule-based
chunking(J)	Unit	rule-based
dependency(E)	edep	trial system
dependency(J)	jdep	85–87 % precision

Parameter setting is performed as follows: the threshold of occurrence is adjusted according to the equations below. The threshold f_{curr} is initially set to 100 and is gradually lowered until it reaches the minimum threshold f_{min} 2. In other words, translation pairs that co-occur only once in the parallel corpora will not be extracted. All parameters are empirically chosen.

$$f_{curr} = \begin{cases} f_{curr}/2 & (f_{curr} > 20) \\ 10 & (20 \geq f_{curr} > 10) \\ f_{curr} - 1 & (10 \geq f_{curr} \geq 2) \end{cases}$$

Results are evaluated in terms of precision. The correctness of the acquired phrase correspondences is judged by a bilingual speaker of En-

Table 13.2. Precision: best-one model(top), ambigious model(middle), adjacent model(below); **e** is the number of extracted phrase correspondences found at f_{curr}. **c** is the number of correct correspondences found at f_{curr}. **acc** is the ratio of correct ones to extracted ones at f_{curr}. The accumulated results for **e**, **c**, and **acc** are indicated by $'$.

f_{curr}	**e**	**c**	**acc**	**e**$'$	**c**$'$	**acc**$'$
25	6	6	100.00	6	6	100.00
12	7	7	100.00	13	13	95.00
10	7	6	85.71	20	19	95.83
9	4	4	100.00	24	23	92.30
8	13	13	100.00	37	36	97.29
7	13	10	76.92	50	46	92.00
6	20	19	95.00	70	65	92.85
5	29	29	100.00	99	94	94.94
4	72	67	93.05	171	161	94.15
3	164	150	91.46	335	311	92.83
2	461	414	89.80	796	725	**91.08**
(*2	474	264	55.69	1270	989	77.93)

f_{curr}	**e**	**c**	**acc**	**e**$'$	**c**$'$	**acc**$'$
25	6	6	100.00	6	6	100.00
12	7	7	100.00	13	13	100.00
10	7	6	85.71	20	19	95.00
9	4	4	100.00	24	23	95.83
8	13	13	100.00	37	36	97.29
7	13	11	84.61	50	47	94.00
6	19	18	94.73	69	65	94.20
5	29	29	100.00	98	94	95.91
4	73	68	93.15	171	162	94.73
3	126	118	93.65	297	280	94.27
2	468	432	91.50	765	712	**93.07**
(*2	759	256	33.72	1524	968	63.51)

f_{curr}	**e**	**c**	**acc**	**e**$'$	**c**$'$	**acc**$'$
25	6	6	100.00	6	6	100.00
12	7	7	100.00	13	13	100.00
10	7	6	85.71	20	19	95.00
9	4	4	100.00	24	23	95.83
8	13	13	100.00	37	36	97.29
7	13	10	84.61	50	46	92.00
6	19	18	94.73	69	64	92.75
5	29	29	100.00	98	93	94.89
4	73	68	93.15	171	161	94.15
3	126	114	93.65	297	275	92.59
2	484	419	86.57	781	694	**88.86**
(*2	496	280	56.45	1277	974	76.27)

Table 13.3. Random samples of correct translation patterns in best–one model.

English	Japanese
thank+you	*arigatou*
consultations+include	*kyogi_ni_ha+fukmeru*
apply+for_the_position	*syoku_ni+ouho_itasu*
thank+you+in_advance	*mae-motte+onegai+moushi-ageru*
not+hesitate+to_contact	*enryo-naku+go-renraku*
be+enclosed+a_copy	*1_bu_doufu_itasu*
be_writing+to_let+know	*syojyo_wo-motte+oshirase_itasu*
applications+include	*yoto_ni_ha+aru*
upcoming_board+of_director_s′_meeting	*jikai_no+torishimari-yaku_kai*
will_have+to_cancel	*chushi_se_zaru_wo+e_naku+naru*
have+high_hope	*ooini+kitai_suru*
business+is_expanded	*syobai_ha+hatten_suru*
we+have_learned+from_your_fax	*ki_fakkusu_de+shiru*
leaving+in+about_ten_days	*yaku_10_nichi_go+syuppatsu*
get+you+in_close_business_relationship	*kinmitsu_na+torihiki_kankei_wo+kizuku*
we+are_inquiring+regarding	*ni-kanshi+otazune_itasu*
pay+special_attention	*tokubetsu_no+chui_wo+harau*

glish and Japanese (Japanese native). Precision for each model is summarised in Table 13.2. f_{curr} stands for the threshold. **e** is the number of extracted phrase correspondences found at f_{curr}. **c** is the number of correct correspondences found at f_{curr}. **acc** is the ratio of correct ones to extracted ones at f_{curr}. The accumulated results for **e**, **c**, and **acc** are indicated by primes (′).

To examine the characteristics of each model, we expand correspondence candidate sets PE and PJ so that translation units with the correlation score $\geq log_2\ 2$ (≥ 1) are also considered (Note, frequency for those translation units are $f_{ej} = f_e = f_j = f_{min} = 2$). These are marked by asterisks in the Tables.

3.5 Discussion

Table 13.2 shows that both the best-one and the ambiguous models achieve better performance than the adjacent (baseline) model. This implies that applying statistically probable dependency relations to the generation of translation units (subtrees) is effective in this task. Our goal of extracting phrasal correspondences without losing robustness has been achieved by the effective use of statistical dependency parsers.

However, our method did not fulfil the expectation that ambiguity in dependency analysis will be resolved in pair extraction by supplying alternative parses. The number of extracted translation pairs decreased

Table 13.4. Random samples of near-correct translation patterns where score is 1.00.

English	Japanese
(have_been_pleased)+to_serve+as_their_main_banker	*syuryoku_ginkou_to+naru*
[be_held]+at_hotel_new_ohtani	*hoteru_nyuohtani_de+kaisai_suru*
assets_position+(in_good_shape)	*shisan_jyotai*
(have_been_placed)+into_our_file	*watashidomo_no+fairu*
(put)+one_month_limit	*1_kagetsu_no+kigen*
[passed]+on_past_tuesday	*kayobi_ni+nakunara_reru*

in the ambiguous model from the best-one model, despite the fact that candidate sets in the ambiguous model constitute a superset of those in the best-one model.

The expected effect in the ambiguous model is that more partially correct subtrees are generated in candidate sets which will boost the correlation score in our pair extraction algorithm. In reality, allowing redundant parsing introduces a rapid increase in the number of translation units. For example, the number of English translation units jumped from 10892 in the best-one model to 26333 in the ambiguous model, of which 72% of translation units appear only twice in the parallel corpora. Allowing redundant parses leads to an increase of new translation units comprised of ambiguous dependency relations. The net result is that the size of candidate sets drastically increases at low thresholds, finding correspondences becomes more difficult, and the number of extracted translation pairs is reduced.

This section used statistically probable dependency relations to extract word and phrasal correspondences. With 9268 paired sentences, we achieved nearly 90% precision. The experiment shows that although statistical parsers are prone to errors, dependency relations serve as effective linguistic clues in translation knowledge extraction. Although we allow aggressive overlaps in translation unit candidate sets where ambiguity exists, this was not effectively balanced by the conservative discovery of correspondences in the pair extraction algorithm.

4. A Comparative Study of Translation Units

Parallel corpora do not have any other linguistic information than the sentences being aligned. We used NLP tools to annotate linguistic clues from which translation units can be generated.

This section compares three models of translation units, each of which uses different linguistic information: one with only word segmentation, one with chunk boundaries, and one with word dependencies. We use NLP tools to annotate such linguistic information. Table 13.5 shows some publicly available robust NLP tools, most of which use statistical techniques that are trained directly from annotated corpora. For English, *TnT* is developed by Brants, 2000, *MXPOST* by Ratnaparkhi, 1996, Collins parser by Collins, 1997 and Charniak parser by Charniak, 2000. For Japanese, *ChaSen* is developed at NAIST, Japan, *Jdep* is develped by Fujio & Matsumoto, 1998. *YamCha* and *CaboCha* are developed by Kudoh & Matsumoto, 2001, Kudoh & Matsumoto, 2002.

Although state-of-the-art NLP tools do not offer 100% precision, they enable many partially correct answers to be found.

Table 13.5. Preprocessing Tools

tool	usage	language	technique	performance
TnT	POS tagging	English	HMM	97 %
MXPOST	POS tagging	English	ME	96 %
ChaSen	POS tagging	Japanese	HMM	98 %
YamCha	chunker	English	SVM	94 %
YamCha	chunker	Japanese	SVM	96 %
Collins	parser	English	probabilistic	86 %
Charniak	parser	English	ME-like	90 %
Jdep	parser	Japanese	probabilistic	86 %
CaboCha	parser	Japanese	SVM	90 %

The purpose of this study is to examine the effectiveness of linguistic clues obtainable from NLP tools, and to investigate the relationship between the linguistic clues applied and translation knowledge extracted.

The organization of this section is as follows: in Section 13.4.1, we describe three models used to generate translation units. In Section 13.4.3, we present our experimental results. Finally, Section 13.4.4 analyzes the characteristics of each model.

4.1 Linguistic Heuristics for Translation Units

In this work, we focus on three kinds of linguistic clues obtainable from NLP tools, namely word segmentation (spaces), chunk boundaries (square brackets), and word dependencies (arrows), as shown in Figure 13.7.

NLP tools have reached a level where they have become practical, but they never guarantee 100% precision. Moreover, they propagate ambiguities or errors to translation unit generation. For example, a

```
Pierre Vinken , 61 years old , will join the board
as a nonexecutive director Nov. 29 .

[Pierre Vinken] , [61 years] [old] , [will join] [the board]
[as] [a nonexecutive director] [Nov. 29] .
```

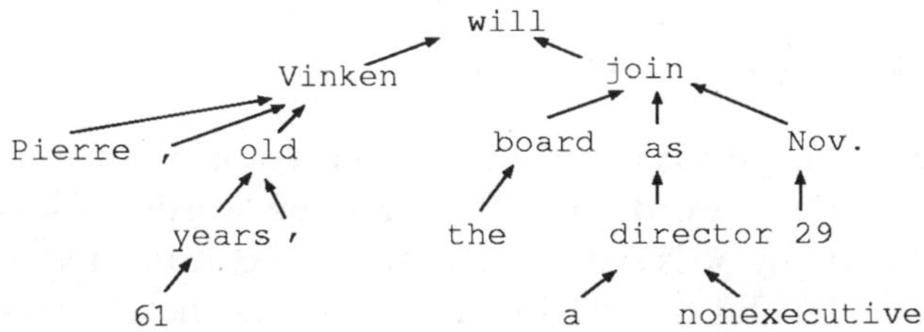

Figure 13.7. Linguistic Clues: Word Segmentation (top), Chunk Boundary (middle) and Word Dependency (bottom)

morphological analyzer may produce an inconsistent word segmentation or a dependency parser may give unintended parses. In the next section, we propose three generative models of translation units that allow overlaps which arise from real ambiguity, but which eliminate impossible overlaps.

4.2 Models of Translation Units

Three n-gram models of generating translation units, namely Plain n-gram, Chunk-bound n-gram, and Dependency-linked n-gram are compared. In the Plain n-gram and Chunk-bound n-gram models, translation units are built using only content (open-class) words. This is because functional (closed-class) words such as prepositions alone will usually act as noise and so they are filtered out in advance.

A word is classified as a functional word if it matches one of the following conditions. (The Penn Treebank, 1991 part-of-speech tag set is used for English, whereas the IpaDic, 2001 part-of-speech tag set is used for Japanese.)

part-of-speech(J) "*meishi-daimeishi*" (noun-pronoun), "*meishi-kazu*" (noun-number), "*meishi-hijiritu*" (noun-dependent), "*meishi-tokusyu*" (noun-specific), "*meishi-setsubi-jyodoshigokan*" (noun-suffix-postparticle), "*meishi-setsubi-fukushikano*" (noun-suffix-adverbial), "*meishi-setsubi-jyodoshi*" (noun-suffix-model), "*settoushi*" (prefix), "*doushi-setsubi*" (verb-suffix), "*doushi-hijiritsu*" (verb-dependent), "*jyoshi*" (postposition), "*jyodoshi*" (postparticle), "*keiyoshi-hijiritsu*" (adjective-dependent), "*keiyoshi-setsubi*" (adjective-suffix), "*kigo*" (symbol)

part-of-speech(E) "CC", "CD", "DT", "EX", "FW", "IN", "LS", "MD", "PDT", "PR", "PRS", "TO", "WDT", "WD", "WP"

stemmed-form(E) "be"

symbols punctuations and brackets

In the Dependency-linked n-gram model, translation units are built not only with content words but also function words. This is because inclusion of function words seems natural when considering word dependency. However, invalid translation units such as those consisting solely of function words are eliminated in advance.

4.2.1 Model 1: Plain n-gram. The Plain n-gram model was first proposed in Kitamura & Matsumoto, 1996. The translation units generated in this model are word sequences from unigram to a given n-gram. Linguistic information used in this model is kept to a minimum, and is used as the baseline model in our work. The upper bound for N is fixed to 5 in our experiment.

4.2.2 Model 2: Chunk-bound n-gram. The Chunk-bound n-gram model assumes prior knowledge of chunk boundaries. The definition of "chunk" has room for discussion. In our experiment, the definition for the English chunking task complies with the CoNLL-2000 text chunking task,[1] while the definition of Japanese chunks is based on "bunsetsu" in the Kyoto University Corpus (1997).[2]

Unlike the Plain n-gram model, the Chunk-bound n-gram model will not extend beyond the chunk boundaries. N varies depending on the number of words in a chunk.[3]

4.2.3 Model 3: Dependency-linked n-gram. In the Dependency-linked n-gram model, a sentence is parsed into a word dependency tree. Since there was only a marginal advantage of the ambiguous model over the best-one model (See Section 3), we only use the statistically best parse in the Dependency-linked n-gram model. We treat each branch of the word dependency tree as word sequences, and generate translation units from unigrams to n-grams where N is the number of

---

[1] `http://lcg-www.uia.ac.be/conll2000/chunking/`

[2] `http://www-lab25.kuee.kyoto-u.ac.jp/nl-resource/corpus.html`

[3] The average number of words in English and Japanese chunks are 2.1 and 3.4 respectively for our parallel corpus.

words in each branch of the word dependency tree. In our experiment, we used the probabilistically best parse result generated from the parser.

The Dependency-linked n-gram model is distinct from our previous work. The granularity of translation units in the Dependency-linked n-gram model is finer, since it is based on word dependencies rather than phrase dependencies. We conjecture that the data sparseness problem will be resolved by focusing on word dependency.

Furthermore, the Dependency-linked n-gram model can generate 'non-contiguous' n-grams which cannot be generated by the Plain n-gram model for any N. Figure 13.8 shows a set of n-grams generated from a branch of a dependency tree in Figure 13.7. Bolded n-grams are ones that cannot be generated by the Plain n-gram model.

nonexecutive
nonexecutive-director
nonexecutive-director-as
nonexecutive-director-as-join
nonexecutive-director-as-join-will
director
director-as
director-as-join
director-as-join-will
as-join
as-join-will
join
join-will

Figure 13.8. Our Dependency-linked n-gram Model

4.3 Experimental Results

We apply the same pair extraction algorithm described in the previous section with the same threshold lowering schedule, since our aim was to examine the effectiveness of each model in the extraction process.

We used a corpus of 5000 aligned sentences consisting of English–Japanese business expressions. 4000 sentences pairs are used for training and the remaining 1000 sentences are used for evaluation.

The NLP tools used in this experiment are *ChaSen, YamCha, CaboCha* for Japanese text processing and *TnT, YamCha*, and Collins' parsers for English text processing. The choice of NLP tools was made based on performance criteria (greater than 85% accuracy) as well as ease of use.

Translation units that appear at least twice are considered to be in the candidate sets for the translation pair extraction algorithm. Table

13.6 shows the number of translation units found in each model. Note that translation units are counted not by token but by type.

Table 13.6. Number of Translation Units

model	English	Japanese
Plain	4286	5817
Chunk-bound	2942	3526
Dependency-linked	15888	10229

The result is evaluated in terms of accuracy and coverage. Accuracy is the number of correct translation pairs over the extracted translation pairs in the algorithm. This is calculated by type. Coverage measures applicability of the correct translation pairs for unseen test data. It is measured by the number of tokens matched by the correct translation pairs over the number of tokens in the unseen test data. Accuracy and coverage roughly correspond to precision and percentage correct respectively in Melamed, 1995. Accuracy is calculated manually on the training data (4000 sentences), whereas coverage is calculated automatically on the test data (1000 sentences).

The stepwise accuracy for each model is listed in Table 13.7. "f_{curr}" indicates the threshold, i.e. stages in the algorithm. "e" is the number of translation pairs found at stage "f_{curr}", and "c" is the number of correct ones found at stage "f_{curr}", as judged by an English–Japanese bilingual speaker. "acc" lists accuracy, namely the fraction of correct ones over extracted ones by type. The accumulated results for "e", "c" and "acc" are indicated by primes ($'$).

The stepwise coverage for each model is listed in Table 13.8. As before, "f_{curr}" indicates the threshold. The brackets indicate language: "E" for English and "J" for Japanese. "fnd" is the number of content tokens matched with correct translation pairs. "idl" is the upper bound of content tokens that may be found by the algorithm; it is the total number of content tokens in the translation units whose co-occurrence frequency is at least "f_{curr}" times in the original parallel corpora.[4] "cvr" indicates coverage. The prefix "i_" is the fraction of found tokens over ideal tokens and the prefix "t_" is the fraction of found tokens over the total number of both content and functional tokens in the data.

[4]The Plain n-gram and Chunk-bound n-gram models have content words only, while the Dependency-linked n-gram model also includes function words. The reason for calculating "idl" is that it is unfair to evaluate coverage of content-words-only models where function words are counted.

Table 13.7. Precision: Plain n-gram (top), Chunk-bound n-gram (middle), Dependency-linked n-gram (bottom)

f_{curr}	e	c	acc	e′	c′	acc′
100.0	0	0	n/a	0	0	n/a
50.0	0	0	n/a	0	0	n/a
25.0	1	1	1.000	1	1	**1.000**
12.0	2	2	1.000	3	3	**1.000**
10.0	5	5	1.000	8	8	**1.000**
9.0	4	4	1.000	12	12	**1.000**
8.0	3	3	1.000	15	15	**1.000**
7.0	6	6	1.000	21	21	**1.000**
6.0	9	9	1.000	30	30	**1.000**
5.0	17	16	0.941	47	46	**0.979**
4.0	31	31	1.000	78	77	**0.988**
3.0	64	64	1.000	142	141	**0.993**
2.0	349	256	0.733	491	397	**0.809**

f_{curr}	e	c	acc	e′	c′	acc′
100.0	2	2	1.000	2	2	**1.000**
50.0	2	2	1.000	4	4	**1.000**
25.0	10	10	1.000	14	14	**1.000**
12.0	32	32	1.000	46	46	**1.000**
10.0	9	9	1.000	55	55	**1.000**
9.0	14	14	1.000	69	69	**1.000**
8.0	21	21	1.000	90	90	**1.000**
7.0	17	16	0.941	107	106	**0.991**
6.0	18	16	0.888	125	122	**0.976**
5.0	38	35	0.921	163	157	**0.963**
4.0	93	91	0.978	256	248	**0.969**
3.0	138	134	0.971	394	382	**0.967**
2.0	547	518	0.946	941	900	**0.956**

f_{curr}	e	c	acc	e′	c′	acc′
100.0	1	1	1.000	1	1	**1.000**
50.0	5	5	1.000	6	6	**1.000**
25.0	11	10	0.909	17	16	**0.941**
12.0	27	26	0.962	44	42	**0.955**
10.0	17	15	0.882	61	57	**0.934**
9.0	12	12	0.882	73	69	**0.945**
8.0	25	25	1.000	98	94	**0.959**
7.0	35	34	0.971	133	128	**0.962**
6.0	32	31	0.968	165	159	**0.964**
5.0	49	48	0.979	214	207	**0.967**
4.0	96	92	0.958	310	299	**0.965**
3.0	189	184	0.973	499	483	**0.968**
2.0	1003	818	0.815	1502	1301	**0.866**

For a test set of 1000 parallel sentences, there are 14422 tokens in the English half and 18998 tokens in the Japanese half. "idl" increases as the threshold is lowered, while the total remains consistent.

4.4 Discussion

The Chunk-bound n-gram and Dependency-linked n-gram models obtained better results than the baseline Plain n-gram model. The result indicates that chunk boundaries and word dependencies are useful linguistic clues in the task of translation knowledge extraction.

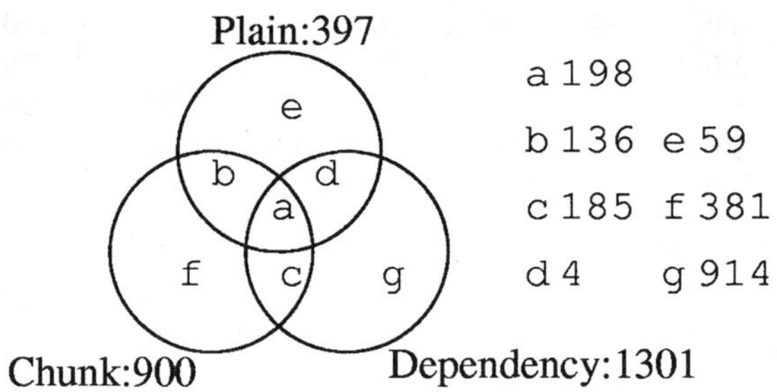

Figure 13.9. Distribution of Extracted Translation Pairs

Translation pairs extracted from Chunk-bound n-grams and those extracted from Dependency-linked n-grams seem to be in complementary relation. Chunk-bound n-grams extract locally contiguous translation pairs (rigid compounding words) with high precision, while Dependency-linked n-grams extract longer, sometimes non-contiguous, translation pairs where functional words are included.

Figure 13.9 shows the Venn diagram of translation pairs extracted by each model. An interesting observation can be made in the distribution of the Plain n-gram model. 84% of the translation pairs extracted by the Plain n-gram model can also be extracted by the Chunk-bound n-gram model. If we ignore the intersection of all three models, 34% of the units in the Plain n-gram model are shared by the Chunk-bound n-gram model. In contrast, only 1% of the translations of the Plain n-gram model are common to the Dependency-linked n-gram with, not including the intersection of all three models. Translation pairs extracted only by the Plain n-gram model account for just 14% of the total found. From these, we could conclude that translation pairs extracted by the Plain n-gram model can nearly be found by the Chunk-bound n-gram model.

Table 13.8. Coverage: Plain n-gram (top), Chunk-bound n-gram (middle), Dependency-linked n-gram (bottom). See section 4.3 for explanation.

f_{curr}	fnd(E)	idl(E)	i_cvr(E)	t_cvr(E)	fnd(J)	idl(J)	i_cvr(J)	t_cvr(J)
100.0	0	445	0	0	0	486	0	0
50.0	0	1182	0	0	0	1274	0	0
25.0	46	2562	0.018	0.0015	46	2564	0.018	0.0011
12.0	156	4275	0.036	0.0051	146	4407	0.033	0.0037
10.0	344	4743	0.073	0.0113	334	4935	0.068	0.0086
9.0	465	4952	0.094	0.0153	455	5247	0.087	0.0117
8.0	511	5242	0.097	0.0168	501	5593	0.090	0.0129
7.0	577	5590	0.103	0.0190	567	5991	0.095	0.0146
6.0	744	5944	0.125	0.0245	734	6398	0.115	0.0189
5.0	899	6350	0.142	0.0297	891	6894	0.129	0.0229
4.0	1193	6865	0.174	0.0394	1195	7477	0.160	0.0307
3.0	1547	7418	0.209	0.0511	1549	8257	0.188	0.0398
2.0	2594	8128	0.319	0.0857	2617	9249	0.283	0.0674

f_{curr}	fnd(E)	idl(E)	i_cvr(E)	t_cvr(E)	fnd(J)	idl(J)	i_cvr(J)	t_cvr(J)
100.0	92	253	0.364	0.0072	92	328	0.280	0.0092
50.0	122	764	0.160	0.0095	122	746	0.164	0.0122
25.0	243	1510	0.161	0.0191	236	1423	0.166	0.0236
12.0	439	2590	0.169	0.0345	432	2515	0.172	0.0432
10.0	483	2829	0.171	0.0379	472	2739	0.172	0.0472
9.0	540	3009	0.179	0.0424	526	2911	0.181	0.0526
8.0	629	3168	0.199	0.0494	623	3086	0.202	0.0623
7.0	687	3348	0.205	0.0540	681	3256	0.209	0.0681
6.0	760	3539	0.213	0.0597	754	3464	0.218	0.0754
5.0	871	3803	0.229	0.0685	864	3748	0.231	0.0864
4.0	1076	4091	0.263	0.0846	1070	4059	0.264	0.1070
3.0	1402	4409	0.318	0.1102	1391	4423	0.314	0.1391
2.0	2007	4803	0.418	0.1578	2004	4865	0.412	0.2004

f_{curr}	fnd(E)	idl(E)	i_cvr(E)	t_cvr(E)	fnd(J)	idl(J)	i_cvr(J)	t_cvr(J)
100.0	78	1454	0.054	0.0061	78	1957	0.040	0.0078
50.0	170	2495	0.068	0.0133	170	2715	0.063	0.0170
25.0	264	3787	0.070	0.0207	278	3606	0.077	0.0278
12.0	394	5470	0.072	0.0309	408	4465	0.091	0.0408
10.0	503	5947	0.085	0.0395	515	4709	0.109	0.0515
9.0	558	6192	0.090	0.0438	570	4837	0.118	0.0570
8.0	665	6456	0.103	0.0523	680	4967	0.137	0.0680
7.0	801	6788	0.118	0.0629	814	5123	0.159	0.0814
6.0	900	7110	0.127	0.0707	911	5274	0.173	0.0911
5.0	1043	7520	0.139	0.0820	1065	5449	0.195	0.1065
4.0	1249	8055	0.155	0.0982	1274	5674	0.225	0.1274
3.0	1690	8690	0.194	0.1329	1686	5992	0.281	0.1686
2.0	2665	9664	0.276	0.2095	2703	6531	0.414	0.2703

Table 13.9. Correct translation pairs

model	English	Japanese
Plain	U.S.-Japan	*nichibei*
Plain	look forward (to) visiting	*homon(-wo-)tanoshimi*
Plain	give information	*shiryo-teikyo*
Chunk	Hong Kong	*honkon*
Chunk	San Diego	*sandiego*
Dependency	apply for position	*syoku-ni-obo-suru*
Dependency	be at your service	*yomei-ni-shitagai-masu*
Dependency	checking into matter	*ken-wo-chosa*
Dependency	tell about matter	*ken-nitsuite-oshirase*
Dependency	free of charge	*muryo*
Dependency	out of question	*mondai-gai*
Dependency	out of print	*zeppan*

Table 13.9 lists samples of correct translation pairs that are unique to each model. The Plain n-gram model seems to extract longer translation pairs that co-occur coincidently. For example, the data contains many instances where 'look forward to visiting' and '*homon-wo-tanoshimi*' co-occur. The Plain n-gram model generates sequences of content words, such as 'look_forward_visit' and '*homon_tanoshimi*', and all instances are counted for calculating similarity. As for the Chunk-bound n-gram model, the translation pair will not be extracted due to the presence of the function words 'to' and '*wo*'. In the Dependency-linked n-gram model, 'look forward/*tanoshimi*' and 'visit/*houmon*' were extracted separately. A close examination of parsed results reveals that, in some sentences, 'look forward' and 'to' were not dependency-linked.

The Chunk-bound n-gram model mostly extracts compound NPs (including named entities) that are in one-to-one correspondence. This result complies with our intuition, as translation units are enclosed by chunk boundaries. A reason why the other two models failed to extract those candidates shown in the table is due to unnecessary generation of overlapping candidates. The filtering process in the extraction algorithm may not work effectively if too many overlapping candidates are generated.

The Dependency-linked n-gram model managed to extract translation pairs which are useful for structural disambiguation (e.g. 'checking **into** matter/*ken*-**wo**-*chosa*' and 'tell **about** matter/*ken*-**nitsuite**-*oshirase*') Such extractions become possible mainly because function words are included in translation units in the Dependency-linked n-gram model.

From the above discussion, we see that chunk boundaries are useful linguistic clues especially in extracting compound NPs. This will be effective in preparing a bilingual lexicon for a new domain. However, if we aim for longer translation pairs requiring syntactic disambiguation, word dependency plays an important role.

5. Related Work

Our view on EBMT is close to advocates of Template-driven EMBT in this volume, where phrase-equivalent correspondences seem to be an agreed unit of correspondences for transfer rules. Our first piece of research focused exclusively on extraction of phrasal correspondences which closely matches the aims of Template-driven EBMT.

Support for dependency trees as a starting point to acquire translation correspondences is also shared by Hideo Watanabe *et al.* (cf. Chapter 14) and Arul Menezes and Steven Richardson (cf. Chapter 15). Both works are noteworthy in that they demonstrate not only acquiring transfer rules by means of structural alignment but also applying these rules directly to EBMT.

Confining our discussion to the acquisition phase, our work is still unique in a number of ways. First, Watanabe *et al.* and Menezes & Richardson use alignment while our work involves extraction by our classification in Section 13.2. Second, we employ publicly available statistical dependency parsers, not in-house parsers. This not only ensures that we are able to take advantage of the robustness that statistical parsers offer, but also that our approach is portable. Finally, but most important of all, we do not require a seed bilingual dictionary to find phrasal correspondences. Moreover, the algorithm does not distinguish word correspondences from phrasal correspondences, but rather they are uniformly treated as translation units in the pair extraction algorithm. This means that bilingual resources can be incorporated into our method without modification thanks to the incremental nature of our greedy algorithm. Word correspondences that we can be sure of from bilingual dictionaries can be safely eliminated from sets of translation candidates before the pair extraction algorithm operates, and the same procedure can be taken to find further phrasal correspondences.

6. Conclusion

This chapter described two pieces of research concerning automatic extraction of translation knowledge from parallel corpora.

The first piece of research, "Phrasal Correspondence Acquisition Using Dependency Relations" (Yamamoto & Matsumoto, 2000) applied statistically probable dependency relations to extract word and phrasal correspondences. We achieved nearly 90% precision with experiments of 9268 paired sentences. The experiments show that although statistical parsers are prone to error, dependency relations serve as effective linguistic clues in translation knowledge extraction even for language pairs with different word ordering constraints. The unaccomplished goal is structural disambiguation arising from dependency analysis. We allow aggressive overlaps in translation unit candidate sets where ambiguity exists. However, this was not sufficiently balanced by a conservative discovery of correspondences in the pair extraction algorithm. Although the ambiguous model is a superset of the best-one model, it is not the optimal superset where only the real syntactic ambiguities for the parser used are considered. The problem of syntactic disambiguation still remains in our research agenda.

The second work, "A Comparative Study on Translation Units" (Yamamoto *et al.*, 2001) compares three models of translation units, each of which uses different linguistic information: one with word segmentation only, one with chunk boundaries, and one with word dependencies. We use NLP tools to annotate such linguistic information which never guarantee 100% precision. Instead, we apply partially correct results that NLP tools give to generate meaningful translation units. Translation units with chunk boundaries or with word dependencies outperformed the previous baseline model, namely one with word segmentation only. Further analysis reveals that chunk boundaries are useful linguistic clues especially in extracting compound NPs. This will be effective in preparing bilingual lexicons for a new domain. However, longer translation pairs such as idiomatic expressions are better handled by word dependency.

Throughout the two studies, we pose two questions: what are possible translation units between language pairs from different families, and how can they be extracted effectively. We believe that translation units are longer than just word-for-word. We share this idea with EBMT. For this reason, our interests lie in exploiting syntactic dependency for the extraction of translation knowledge. The first work showed that statistically probable dependency relations achieve good precision. However, this was not sufficient to explain why and under which circumstances the dependency offers an advantage. This motivates us for the second study, closely investigating different kinds of linguistic information for the extraction task. The result confirms that dependency relations are crucial for longer phrasal translation pairs.

Our work shows not only the usefulness of syntactic dependency for translation knowledge extraction, but also it sheds light on an interplay between linguistic clues from the statistical NLP tools and the outcome of our extraction method. We describe methods that extract translation knowledge from word-level to phrase-level in a robust manner. The result will be useful for EBMT, but the lesson learned in the first study concerning syntactic disambiguation will also be useful for further development of statistical dependency parsers.

Acknowledgement We thank Mihoko Kitamura for fruitful discussion. We also thank *Nikkei Shimbun* for providing us with a pre-aligned parallel corpus. Furthermore, we thank Masakazu Fujio, Taku Kudo, the *ChaSen* members, Michael Collins, and Thorsten Brants for making their NLP tools publicly available.

References

Brants, T. 2000. *TnT* – A Statistical Part-of-Speech Tagger. In *NAACL-00: Proceedings of the 1st Meeting of the North American Chapter of the Association for Computational Linguistics*, Seattle, WA., pp.224–231.

Charniak, E. 2000. A Maximum Entropy Inspired Parser. In *NAACL-00: Proceedings of the 1st Meeting of the North American Chapter of the Association for Computational Linguistics*, Seattle, WA., pp.132–139.

ChaSen and IPADIC Users Manual. 2001. `http://chasen.aist-nara.ac.jp/`

Collins, M. 1997. Three Generative Lexicalised Models for Statistical Parsing. In *35th Annual Meeting of the Association for Computational Linguistics and the 8th Conference of the European Chapter*, Madrid, Spain, pp.16–23.

Dagan, I., K.W. Church and W.A. Gale. 1993. Robust bilingual word alignment for machine aided translation. In *Proceedings of the Workshop on Very Large Corpora, Academic and Industrial Perspectives*, Columbus OH., pp.1–8.

Fujio, M. and Y. Matsumoto. 1998. Japanese Dependency Structure Analysis based on Lexicalized Statistics. In *Proceedings of the 3rd Conference of Empirical Methods in Natural Language Processing*, Granada, Spain, pp.88-96.

Gale, W. and K. Church. 1991. Identifying Word Correspondences in Parallel Texts. In *Proceedings of the 4th DARPA Speech and Natural Language Workshop*, Pacific Grove, CA., pp.152–157.

Grishman, R. 1994. Iterative alignment of syntactic structures for a bilingual corpus. In *Proceedings of the 2nd Annual Workshop on Very Large Corpora*, Kyoto, Japan, pp.57–68.

Haruno, M. and T. Yamazaki. 1996. High-performance bilingual text alignement using statistical and dictionary information. In *34th Annual Meeting of the Association for Compuational Linguistics*, Santa Cruz, CA., pp.131–138.

Kaji, H., Y. Kida and Y. Morimoto. 1992. Learning translation templates from bilingual text. In *Proceedings of the fifteenth [sic] International Conference on Computational Linguistics, COLING-92*, Nantes, France, pp.672–678.

Kitamura, M. and Y. Matsumoto. 1996. Automatic Extraction of Word Sequence Correspondences in Parallel Corpora. In *Proceedings of the 4th Annual Workshop on Very Large Corpora*, Copenhagen, Denmark, pp.79–87.

Kudo, T. and Y. Matsumoto. 2001. Chunking with Support Vector Machines. In *NAACL-01: Proceedings of the 2nd Meeting of the North American Chapter of the Association for Computational Linguistics*, Pittsburgh, PA., pp.192–199.

Kudo, T. and Y. Matsumoto. 2002. Japanese Dependency Analysis using Cascaded Chunking. In *CoNLL-2002: Proceedings of the Sixth Conference on Natural Language Learning*, Taiwan, pp.63–69.

Kumano, A. and H. Hirakawa. 1994. Building an MT dictionary from parallel texts based on linguistic and statistical information. In *COLING-94: Proceedings of the 15th International Conference on Computational Linguistics*, Kyoto, Japan, pp.76–81.

Kupiec, J. 1993. An Algorithm for Finding Noun Phrase Correspondences in Bilingual Corpora. In *31st Annual Meeting of the Association for Computational Linguistics*, Columbus, OH., pp.17–22.

Matsumoto, Y., H. Ishimoto and T. Utsuro. 1993. Structural Matching of Parallel Texts. In *31st Annual Meeting of the Association for Computational Linguistics*, Columbus, OH., pp.23–30.

Matsumoto, Y. and M. Kitamura. 1995. Acquisition of Translation Rules from Parallel Corpora. In *International Conference, Recent Advances in Natural Language Processing*, Tzigov Chark, Bulgaria, pp.406–416.

Melamed, I.D. 1995. Automatic Evaluation and Uniform Filter Cascades for Inducing N-best translation lexicons. In *Proceedings of the*

Third Annual Workshop on Very Large Corpora, Cambridge, England, pp.184–198.

Meyers, A., R. Yangarber and R. Grishman. 1996. Alignment of Shared Forests for Bilingual Corpora. In *COLING-96: Proceedings of the 16th International Conference on Computational Linguistics*, Copenhagen, Denmark, pp.460–465.

Takubo, K. and M. Hashimoto. 1999. *A Dictionary of English Business Letter Expressions*, Nihon Keizai Shimbun, Inc., Tokyo, Japan.

Santorini, B. 1991. Part-of-Speech Tagging Guidelines for the Penn Treebank Project. *Linguistic Data Consortium*, University of Pennsylvania, Philadelphia, PA.

Smadja, F. 1993. Retrieving collocation from text: Xtract. *Computational Linguistics* **19**(1):143–177.

Smadja, F., K.R. McKeown and V. Hatzivassiloglou. 1996. Translating Collocations for Bilingual Lexicons: A Statistical Approach. *Computational Linguistics* **22**(1):1–38.

Ratnaparkhi, A. 1996. A Maximum Entropy Model for Part-Of-Speech Tagging. In *Proceedings of the 1st Conference on Empirical Methods in Natural Language Processing*, Philadelphia, PA., pp.133–142.

Ratnaparkhi, A. 1997. A linear observed time statistical parser based on maximum entropy models. In *Proceedings of the 2nd Conference on Empirical Methods in Natural Language Processing*, Providence, RI., pp.1–10.

Wu, D. 1995. An algorithm for simultaneously bracketing parallel texts by aligning words. In *33rd Annual Meeting of the Association for Computational Linguistics*, Cambridge, MA., pp.244-251.

Yamamoto, K. and Y. Matsumoto. 2000. Acquisition of phrase-level bilingual correspondence using dependency relations. In *Proceedings of the 18th International Conference on Computational Linguistics: COLING 2000 in Europe*, Saarbrücken, Germany, **2**:933–939.

Yamamoto, K. Y. Matsumoto and M. Kitamura. 2001. A Comparative Study on Translation Units for Bilingual Lexicon Extraction. In *Proceedings of the Workshop on Data-driven Machine Translation, 39th Annual Meeting and 10th Conference of the European Chapter of the Association for Computational Linguistics*, Toulouse, France, pp.87–95.

Chapter 14

FINDING TRANSLATION PATTERNS FROM PAIRED SOURCE AND TARGET DEPENDENCY STRUCTURES

Hideo Watanabe
hiwat@jp.ibm.com

Sadao Kurohashi
kuro@kc.t.u-tokyo.ac.jp

Eiji Aramaki
aramaki@pine.kuee.kyoto-u.ac.jp

Abstract Example-based machine translation systems use a large set of translation patterns. It is a time-consuming task to generate these translation patterns manually. Therefore, extracting translation patterns automatically from a bilingual corpus is very important for a realistic task. This paper describes a method for extracting translation patterns from bilingual corpus and another method to generate translation pattern by checking the difference between the MT result and its manually post-edited version. Although these two methods seem to be different, they share several common technologies.

Keywords: extraction of translation patterns, phrasal correspondences, comparison of MT and human translation

1. Introduction

A number of methodologies and systems for machine translation using large corpora have been exploited, since Nagao, 1984 proposed the idea of

M. Carl and A. Way (eds.), Recent Advances in Example-Based Machine Translation, 397–420.

translation by analogy. Some example-based approaches (Takeda, 1996a; Takeda, 1996b; Watanabe & Takeda, 1998) use a large set of translation patterns, each of which is a pair of parse structures of a source-language fragment and its target-language translation fragment. Figure 14.1 shows an example of translation by an example-based method, in which translation patterns (p1) and (p2) are selected as similar to a (left hand side) Japanese dependency structure, and a (right hand side) English dependency structure is constructed by merging the target parts of these translation patterns.[1]

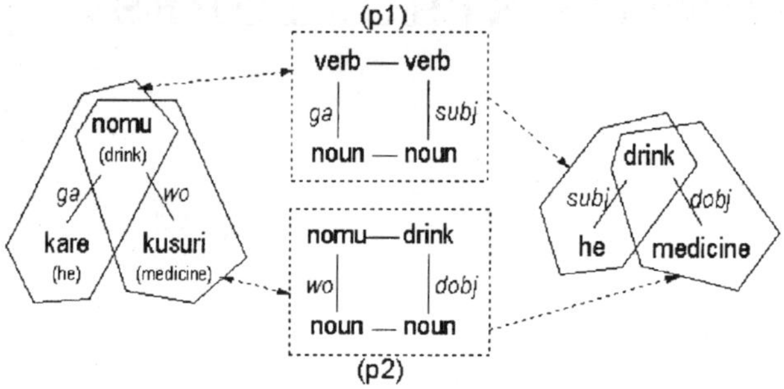

Figure 14.1. Translating via EBMT with pairs of dependency structures

In this kind of system, it is very important to collect a large set of translation patterns easily and efficiently. Collecting a large volume of such patterns is a difficult and time-consuming task, and previous systems have collected such translation patterns mostly by hand. A method for automatically collecting translation patterns is, therefore, badly needed.

Considering the human task of acquiring translation patterns, we noticed that there are at least two different approaches: one is to find translation patterns by observing many translation examples, and another is to find translation patterns by comparing a wrong translation and its correction.

Figure 14.2 shows an example of the former type of task, that is, extracting structural correspondences (or translation patterns) from a bilingual corpus. In this figure, the left tree is a Japanese dependency tree, the right tree is a dependency tree of its English translation, dotted arrows represent word correspondences, and a pair of boxes connected by

[1]Words in parentheses on the nodes in the Japanese dependency structure are representative English translations for explanatory purposes only.

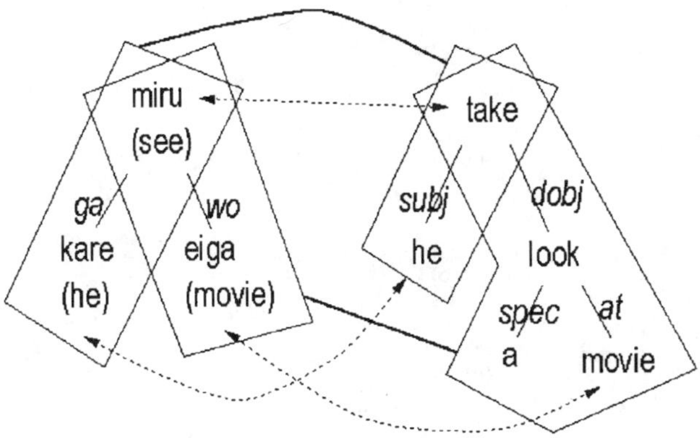

Figure 14.2. An Example of Finding Structural Correspondences

a solid line represent a phrasal correspondence. We can find translation patterns at the phrasal level by carefully inspecting a pair of source-target sentence structures.

Figure 14.3 shows an example of the latter type of task, that is, finding translation patterns by comparing an MT result and its post-edited, corrected version. In this figure, (a) is the dependency structure of an input Japanese sentence, (r1), (r2), and (r3) are given translation patterns, and (b) is the English dependency structure produced by these patterns. Clearly, (b) is not a correct translation of (a), whereas (c) is. Therefore, by comparing the current output (b) and a correct output (c), we can find a translation pattern (r4).

Several studies (Kaji *et al.*, 1992; Utsuro *et al.*, 1992; Utsuro *et al.*, 1993; Matsumoto *et al.*, 1993; Ishimoto *et al.*, 1993; Watanabe, 1993; Grishman, 1994; Meyers *et al.*, 1996) and (Yamamoto & Matsumoto, 2000, cf. Chapter 13, this volume) have followed the former approach. As well as outlining a method for this type of acquiring translation patterns, this paper describes a method for acquiring translation patterns by the latter type of process. In what follows, we will describe details of these procedures for finding translation patterns.

This paper is based on the different two papers Watanabe, 1993 and Watanabe *et al.*, 2000 which describe techniques for acquiring translation patterns from a pair of dependency structures. Section 14.2 is based on Watanabe *et al.*, 2000 and Section 14.3 is based on Watanabe, 1993, respectively. In Section 14.3, some procedures which are the same as ones in Section 14.2 are not described. These procedures in Watanabe *et al.*, 2000 are updated version of ones described in Watanabe, 1993.

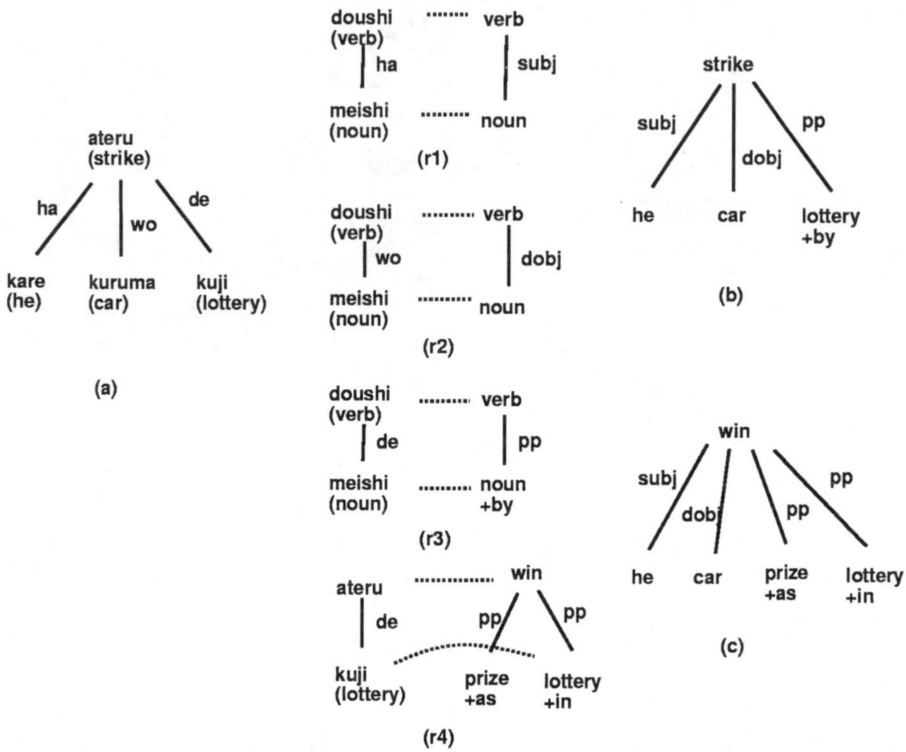

Figure 14.3. An Example of Comparing an MT result and its post-edited, corrected version

In addition, please refer to Aramaki *et al.*, 2001 for some research which further develops that of Watanabe *et al.*, 2000.

2. Finding Structural Correspondences from a Bilingual Parsed Corpus

This section describes a method for extracting structural correspondences from a pair of source–target parse trees.

2.1 Data Structure

Before going into the details of how we find structural correspondences, we describe the data format of a dependency structure. A dependency structure as used in this paper is a tree consisting of nodes and links (or arcs), where a node represents a content word, and a link represents a functional word or a relation between content words. For instance, as shown in Figure 14.2, a preposition *at* is represented as a link in English.

2.2 Finding Word Correspondences

The first task in finding structural correspondences is to find word correspondences between the nodes of a source parse tree and the nodes of a target parse tree.

Word correspondences are found by consulting a bilingual dictionary. Most words can find a unique translation candidate in a target tree, but there are cases where more than one translation candidate exists in a target parse tree for a given source word. Therefore, the main task of finding word correspondences is to determine the most plausible translation among candidate target words. We call a pair of a source word and its translation candidate word in a target tree a *word correspondence candidate* denoted by $WC(s,t)$, where s is a source word and t is a target word. If $WC(s,t)$ is a word correspondence candidate such that there is no other WC originating from s, then it is called a word correspondence of type WA.

The basic idea behing choosing the most plausible word correspondence candidate is to select a candidate which is near to another word correspondence whose source is also near to the source word in question. Suppose a source word s has multiple candidate translation target words t_i $(i = 1, \ldots, n)$. That is, there are multiple WCs originating from s. We denote these multiple word correspondence candidates by $WC(s,t_i)$. For each WC of s, this procedure finds the neighbor WA correspondence whose distance to WC is below a threshold. The distance between $WC(s_1,t_1)$ and $WA(s_2,t_2)$ is defined as the distance between s_1 and s_2 plus the distance between s_2 and t_2, where a distance between two nodes is defined as the number of nodes in the path whose ends are the two nodes. Among WCs of s for which neighbor WA is found, the one with the smallest distance is chosen as the word correspondence of s, and WCs which are not chosen are invalidated (or deleted). We call a word correspondence found by this procedure WX. We currently use 3 as the distance threshold of the above procedure. This procedure is applied to all source nodes which have multiple WCs. Figure 14.4 shows an example of WX word correspondence. In this example, since the Japanese word *ki* has two English translation word candidates *time* and *period*, there are two WCs (WC_1 and WC_2). The direct parent node *yuuryo* of *ki* has a WA correspondence (WA_1) to *concern*, and the direct child node *ikou* has also a WA correspondence (WA_2) to *transition*. In this case, since the distance between WC_2 and WA_2 is smaller than the distance between WC_1 and WA_1, WC_2 is changed to a WX, and WC_1 is adandoned.

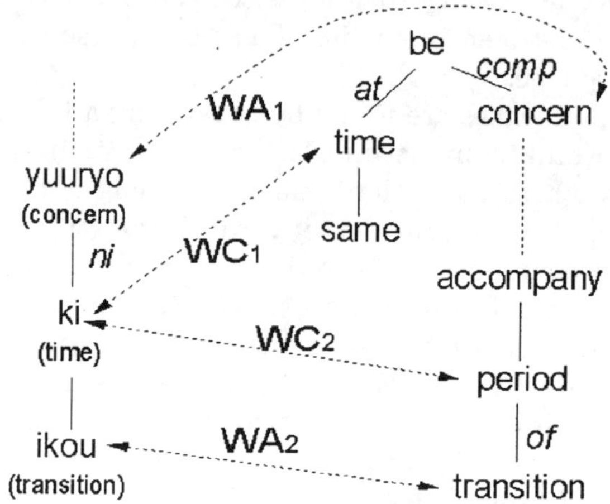

Figure 14.4. An Example of WX Word Correspondence

In addition to such WX correspondences, we consider a special case, such that given a word correspondence $W(s,t)$, if s has only one child node which is a leaf and t has also only one child node which is a leaf, then we construct a new word correspondence WS from these two leaf nodes. This WS procedure is applied to all word correspondences. Note that the purpose of this procedure is not to select one of the candidates, but rather to find a new way of finding word correspondences by utilizing a special structure. For instance, in Figure 14.4, if there is a word correspondence between *ki* and *period* and there is no word correspondence between *ikou* and *transition*, then $WS(ikou, transition)$ will be found by this procedure.

These WX and WS procedures are continuously applied until no new word correspondences are found. After applying the above WX and WS procedures, some target words t exist such that t is a destination of a $WC(s,t)$ and there is no other WC whose destination is t. In this case, the $WC(s,t)$ correspondence candidate is chosen as a valid word correspondence between s and t, and it is called a WZ word correspondence.

```
Procedure find_word_correspondences(TreeS,TreeT) {
  // TreeS ... a source dependency tree
  // TreeT ... a target dependency tree
  wrdcrs ← φ;
  for s in nodes of TreeS begin
    find candidate translation nodes t_i in TreeT;
    for each t_i, make WC(s,t_i) and add it to wrdcrs;
  end
  for s in nodes of TreeS begin
    if there is only one WC originating from s in wrdcrs, then change the WC to WA;
  end
  flag ← true;
  while (flag=true) begin
    flag ← false;
    for s in nodes of TreeS begin
      wps ← φ;
      for each WC originating from s in wrdcrs
        add a neighbor WA of WC to wps;
      if wps ≠ φ, then begin
        change WC having the smallest distance to its neighbor WA in wps to WX;
        delete all WCs whose source is s from wrdcrs;
        flag ← true;
      end
    end
    for each W(s,t) other than WC in wrdcrs begin
      if s has only one child s' which is a leaf and t has only one child t' which is a leaf,
      then begin
        make WS(s',t') and add it to wrdcrs;
        flag ← true;
      end
    end
  end
  for t in nodes of TreeT begin
    if there is only one WC whose target is t, then change the WC to WZ;
  end
  return wrdcrs;
}
```

Figure 14.5. Procedure for finding word correspondences

We call a source node or a target node of a word correspondence an *anchor node* in what follows. Figure 14.5 shows the procedure for finding word correspondences.

2.3 Finding Phrasal Correspondences

The next step is to find phrasal correspondences based on word correspondences found by the procedures described in the previous section. What we would like to retrieve here is a set of phrasal correspondences which covers all elements of a paired dependency tree.

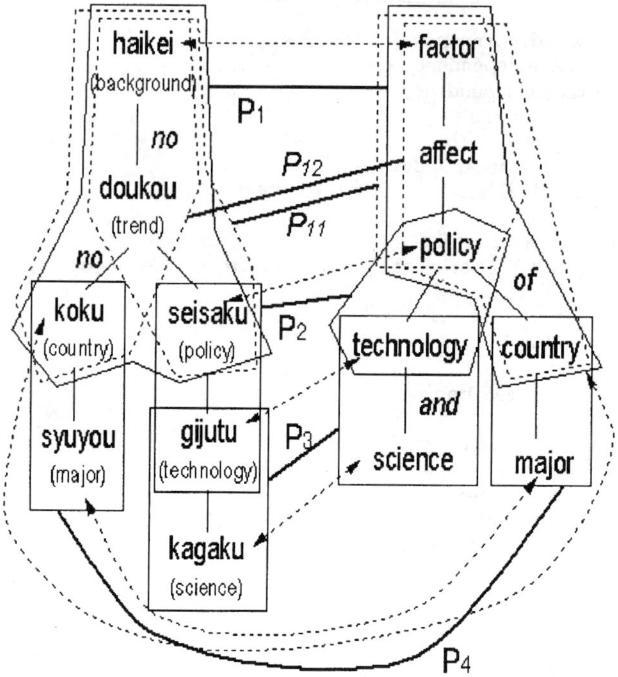

Figure 14.6. An Example of Finding Phrasal Correspondences

In what follows, we call a portion of a tree which consists of nodes in a path from a node n_1 to another node n_2 which is a descendant of n_1 a *linear tree* denoted by $T_L(n_1, n_2)$, and we denote a minimal subtree including specified nodes $n_1, \ldots, n_x$ by $T_M(n_1, \ldots, n_x)$. For instance, in the English tree structure (the right tree) in Figure 14.6, T_L(technology, science) is a rectangular area covering *technology*, and *science*, and T_M(factor,country) is a polygonal area covering *factor*, *affect*, *policy*, and *country*.

The first step is to find a pair of word correspondences $W_1(s_1, t_1)$ and $W_2(s_2, t_2)$ such that s_1 and s_2 constructs a linear tree $T_L(s_1, s_2)$ and there is no anchor node in the path from s_1 to s_2 other than s_1 and s_2, where W_1 and W_2 denote any type of word correspondences[2] and we assume there is a word correspondence between roots of source and target trees by default. We construct a phrasal correspondence from

[2]Since WC is not a word correspondence (it is a candidate for a word correspondence), it is not considered here.

source nodes in $T_L(s_1, s_2)$ and target nodes in $T_M(t_1, t_2)$, denoted by $P(T_L(s_1, s_2), T_M(t_1, t_2))$. For instance, in Figure 14.6, P_{11}, P_{12}, P_2, P_3 and P_4 are phrasal correspondences found in this step.

```
Procedure find_phrasal_correspondences(TreeS,TreeT,WrdCrs) {
// TreeS ... a source dependency tree, TreeT ... a target dependency tree
// WrdCrs = {w(s,t)|s ∈ TreeS and t ∈ TreeT}
p1set ← φ; p2set ← φ; p3set ← φ
for every pair w1(s1,t1) and w2(s2,t2) in WrdCrs begin
    if s1 is an ancestor of s2, and TL(s1,s2) have no anchor node other than s1 and s2 begin
        p ← make_a_phrasal_corresp(TL(s1,s2),TM(t1,t2))
        add p into p1set
    end
end
while (p1set ≠ φ) begin
    p ← remove_the_first_element(p1set)
    if p is open then
        for p' in p1set begin
            if p' has open nodes of p then begin
                remove p' from p1set
                p ← make_a_phrasal_corresp(p,p')
            end
        end
    end
    add p into p2set
end
while (p2set ≠ φ) begin
    p ← remove_the_first_element(p2set)
    for p' in p2set begin
        if there are any nodes other than anchor nodes which are shared in both p and p'
        then begin
            remove p' from p2set
            p ← make_a_phrasal_corresp(p,p')
        end
    end
    add p into p3set
end
openpathlist ← open paths of TreeS and TreeT
while (openpathlist ≠ φ) begin
    op ← remove_the_first_element(openpathlist)
    if the root of op is not an anchor then
        merge op into a phrasal corresp. in p3set having the root
    else begin
        op' ← an open path in openpathlist which has the opposite side node of a word corresp.
of the root
        if op' exists then begin
            remove op' from openpathlist
            op'' ← make_a_phrasal_corresp(op, op')
            add op'' into p3set
        end
        else merge op into a phrasal corresp. in p3set having the root;
    end
end
return p3set;
}
```

Figure 14.7. Procedure for finding phrasal correspondences

Here, a node in a phrasal correspondence (P) which has a word correspondence whose source or target node is not included in P is called an *open node*, otherwise it is called a *closed node*. The next step checks, for each P, whether all anchor nodes of word correspondences are closed nodes. If a phrasal correspondence satisfies this condition, then it is called *closed*, otherwise it is called *open*. If a P is open, then it is merged with other phrasal correspondences having open nodes of P so that the merged phrasal correspondence becomes closed.

Next, each P_x is checked to see whether there is another P_y which shares any nodes other than anchor nodes with P_x. If this is the case, these P_x and P_y are merged into one phrasal correspondence. In Figure 14.6, phrasal correspondences P_{11} and P_{12} are merged into P_1, since their source portions T_L(haikei,koku) and T_L(haikei,seisaku) share *doukou* which is not an anchor node.

Finally, any path whose nodes other than the root are not included in any Ps but where the root node is included in a P, is searched for. This procedure is applied to both source and target trees. A path found by this procedure is called an *open path*, and its root node is called a *pivot*. If such an open path is found, it is processed as follows: for each pivot node, (a) if the pivot is not an anchor node, then open paths originating from the pivot are merged into a P having the pivot; (b) if the pivot is an anchor node, then a new phrasal correspondence is created from open paths originating from the anchor nodes of the word correspondence.

In Figure 14.6, we get finally four phrasal correspondences P_1, P_2, P_3, and P_4, where P_1 is a correspondence between *koku no seisaku doukou no haikei* and *factor affecting policy of country*, P_2 is a correspondence between *gijutu seisaku* and *technology policy*, P_3 is a correspondence between *kagaku gijutu* and *science and technology*, and P_4 is a correspondence between *syuyou koku* and *major country*. Figure 14.7 shows the procedure for finding phrasal correspondences.

2.4 Experiments

2.4.1 Corpus and Dictionary. We used documents from White Papers on Science and Technology (1994 to 1996) published by the Science and Technology Agency (*STA*) of the Japanese government. The *STA* published these White Papers in both Japanese and English. The alignment of Japanese sentences and their corresponding English sentences of this corpus was performed by *JEITA* (Japan Electronics and Information Technology Industries Association), and this corpus was released as a part of *JEITA* Japanese-English Aligned Bilingual Corpora (Isahara & Haruno, 2000). Based on this data, we made a bilingual aligned corpus consisting of parsed dependency structures by using the *KNP* Japanese parser (Kurohashi & Nagao, 1994, developed by Kyoto University) for Japanese sentences and the *ESG* English parser (McCord, 1980, developed by *IBM* Watson Research Center) for English sentences.

We made about 500 sentence pairs, each of which has a one-to-one sentence correspondence, from the raw data of the White Papers, and selected randomly about 130 sentence pairs for experiments. However, since a parser does not always produce correct parse trees, we excluded some sentence pairs which have severe parse errors, and finally obtained 115 sentence pairs as a test set.

We needed a bilingual word dictionary between Japanese and English. First we used one containing more than 100,000 entries, but we found that there were still some word correspondences not covered in this dictionary. Therefore, we merged entries from this E-to-J translation dictionary in order to get much broader coverage. In so doing, the total number of entries increased to more than 150,000.

2.4.2 Experimental Results. Table 14.1 shows the result of the experiment for finding word correspondences. A row with ALL in the type column shows the total accuracy of word correspondences and other rows show the accuracy of each type. It is clear that WA correspondences have a very high accuracy. Other word correspondences also have a relatively high accuracy.

Table 14.1. Experimental Results of Finding Word Correspondences

type	no. found correspondences	no. correct correspondences	success ratio (%)
ALL	771	745	96.63
WA	612	600	98.03
WX	131	118	90.07
WS	13	12	92.3
WZ	15	15	100

Table 14.2 shows the result of experiments for finding phrasal correspondences. The row with ALL in the type column shows the total accuracy of phrasal correspondences found by the proposed procedure. This accuracy level is not very promising and it is not useful for later processes since it needs human checking and correction. Therefore, we subcategorize each class of phrasal correspondence, and check accuracy for each subcategory.

We consider the following subcategories for phrasal correspondences:

MIN ... The minimal phrasal correspondence, $P(T_L(s_1, s_2), T_L(t_1, t_2))$, such that there are word correspondences $W(s_1, t_1)$ and $W(s_2, t_2)$, s_2 is a direct child of s_1 and t_2 is a direct child of t_1.

LTX ... $P(T_L(s_1, s_2), T_L(t_1, t_2))$, such that all nodes other than s_2 and t_2 have only one child node.

LTY ... $P(T_L(s_1, s_2), T_L(t_1, t_2))$, such that all nodes other than s_1, s_2, t_1 and t_2 have only one child node.

LTX is a special case of LTY, since s_1 and t_1 of LTX must have only one child node; on the other hand, those in LTY may have more than two child nodes. A sub-category test for a phrasal correspondence is performed in the above order. Examples of these sub-categories are shown in Figure 14.8.

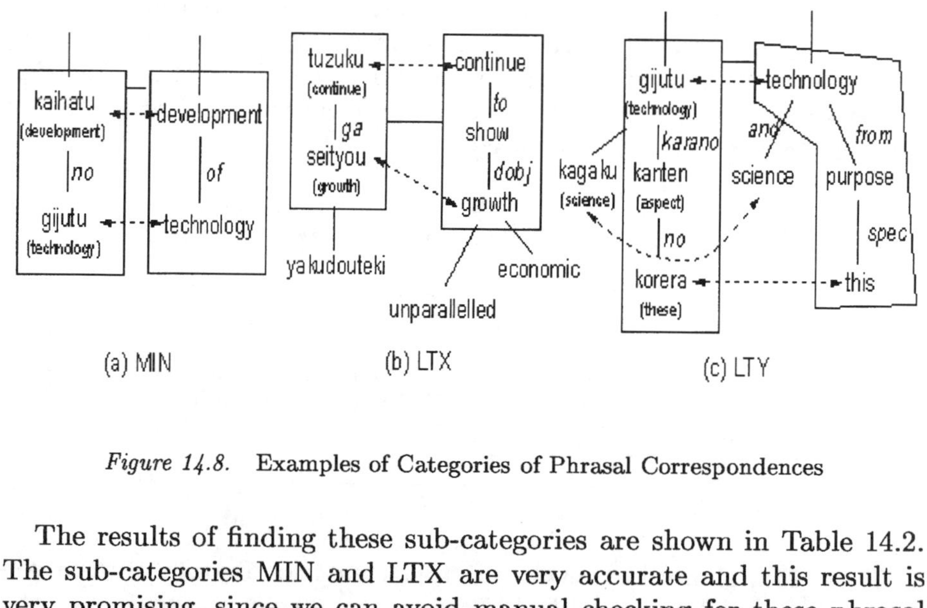

Figure 14.8. Examples of Categories of Phrasal Correspondences

The results of finding these sub-categories are shown in Table 14.2. The sub-categories MIN and LTX are very accurate and this result is very promising, since we can avoid manual checking for these phrasal correspondences.

As stated earlier, since we removed only sentences with severe parsing errors from the test set, note that the above numbers of experimental results are calculated for a bilingual parsed corpus including parsing errors.

Table 14.2. Experimental Results of Finding Phrasal Correspondences

type	A: num. of found corresp.	B: num. of correct corresp.	C: success ratio B/A (%)	D: num. of nodes covered by A	E: num. of nodes covered by B	F: success ratio E/D (%)
ALL	678	431	63.56	7248	4278	59.02
MIN	223	215	96.41	1234	1194	96.76
LTX	17	17	100	153	153	100
LTY	27	20	74.07	253	191	75.49

3. Finding Translation Patterns by Comparing an MT Result and its Correction

This section describes a method of extracting translation patterns by comparing an MT result and its correction.

Given an input string S_s, let S_t be an output string produced by our example-based translation system TS, and let S_c be a correct translation of S_s. The purpose of the proposed method in this section is to obtain translation patterns that produce the correct translation string S_c. We can break down this process of obtaining translation patterns into the following two sub-tasks:

- Making a word mapping M_c from D_s to D_c,
- Finding translation patterns by comparing $\langle D_s, M_t, D_t\rangle$ with $\langle D_s, M_c, D_c\rangle$

where D_s is a dependency structure of an input string S_s, D_t is a dependency structure produced by an example-based translation system, D_c is a dependency structure of S_c, and M_t is a word mapping from D_s to D_t which is easily extracted from a set of translation patterns T_p used in constructing D_t by means of TS. Furthermore, a word mapping M consists of ($M\uparrow$,$M\downarrow$) where $M\downarrow$ is called a *downward mapping* which roughly corresponds to a word-to-word correspondence described in the previous section, and $M\uparrow$ is called an *upward mapping* which represents a word-to-word correspondence whose source and target nodes are not a downward mapping, but rather sub-structures headed by these nodes construct a phrasal correspondence. Therefore, a word-to-word correspondence found by the procedure described in the previous section is usually considered as both a downward mapping and an upward mapping, but if either a source node or a target node of a word-to-word correspondence is the root node of a phrasal correspondence and there is no word-to-word correspondence between the root nodes of the source structure and the target structure of the phrasal correspondence, then the word-to-word correspondence is considered as a downward mapping, and an upward mapping is created between the source root node and the target root node of the phrasal correspondence.

If we consider a manual correction of an MT result, we can obtain two pairs of a source sentence and its translation; one is a source sentence and its translation by an MT system, and the other is a pair consisting of a source sentence and its translation corrected by a user. Phrasal correspondences for the former pair are apparent since an MT system already knows them. On the other hand, phrasal correspondences (with word correspondences) are unknown for the latter pair, but they can be found by using the methods described in the previous section.

In what follows in this section, we describe a method of extracting new translation patterns (or phrasal correspondences) from an MT result and its manual correction.

3.1 Finding New Translation Patterns

The basic idea behind finding new translation patterns (or phrasal correspondences) is to check whether each translation pattern used in MT is the same as the corresponding translation pattern found in a corrected pair. If it is not the same, then it should be adopted as a new translation pattern. Therefore, we must construct a translation pattern corresponding to the correct translation for each translation pattern used in MT. Since the source dependency structure is the same, we must identify the target part in the correct target dependency tree corresponding to a translation pattern.

Suppose that we are given translation patterns $Pt_i = (Ds_i, Mt_i, Dt_i)$ for an MT result pair. By using procedures in the previous section, we can obtain a word mapping (or word-to-word correspondences) between D_s and D_c. Then, for each Ds_i of Pt_i, we can obtain Mc_i whose source nodes are nodes in Ds_i, and Dc_i which is the minimal subgraph including all target nodes of Mc_i. (We call the minimal subgraph determined by a word mapping a *projected subgraph.*) Therefore, for each Pt_i, we can construct a $Pc_i = (Ds_i, Mc_i, Dc_i)$.

Then the equality of the two translation patterns must be checked. Given two translation patterns $P_i = \langle S_i, M_i, T_i \rangle$ and $P_j = \langle S_j, M_j, T_j \rangle$, P_i is identical to P_j if and only if the following conditions are all satisfied:

1 P_i and P_j are structurally identical.[3]

2 S_i and S_j are identical.[4]

3 For each node s_i of S_i and its corresponding node s_j in S_j, let the node projected by $M \uparrow_i (s_i)$ be tu_i, let the node projected by $M \downarrow_i (s_i)$ be td_i, let the node projected by $M \uparrow_j (s_j)$ be tu_j, and let the node projected by $M \downarrow_j (s_j)$ be td_j; then tu_i subsumes tu_j and td_i subsumes td_j.[5]

When p_t and p_c are compared, they are the same if they are structurally isomorphic. A p_t node n_t and a p_c node n_c are the same, (i) if parts-of-speech are equal when n_t is a non-lexical node, or (ii) if both lexical forms and parts-of-speech are equal when n_t is a lexical node.

An algorithm for finding translation patterns is shown in Figure 14.9. For each translation pattern p used to make D_t, lines 2–9 check whether the corresponding translation pattern p' is the same as p or not. If p' is not identical to p, then it is stored in the new translation pattern list; otherwise, it is stored in the same translation pattern list. After that, the translation patterns in the new translation pattern list are merged if they share any common nodes (lines 10–15). Further, for each subgraph g of D_c that is included in neither the new translation pattern list nor the same translation pattern list, the minimum subgraph g' such that g' contains both g and any leaf node of p_c in the new translation pattern list is found, and g' is merged with p_c (lines 17–21).

3.2 Example

This section gives an example of finding new translation patterns by using this method. In Figure 14.10, D_s is a dependency structure of the Japanese sentence *watashi no seibutugaku no tishiki ha hinjyakuda* (I have little knowledge of biology), and D_t is a dependency structure produced by TS as an output by using translation patterns pt_1, pt_2, and pt_3. Dotted lines denote mappings between two structures. For convenience, an unmarked dotted line is equivalent to a line marked both

[3]This means that node contents are ignored but arc labels must be checked.

[4]In this case, node contents are checked, but which features should be checked depends on the application. In our system, the lexical form and part-of-speech are checked.

[5]Since a node consists of several features, the subsumption relations on feature structures are used.

```
Procedure find-trnpat(D_s,D_t,D_c,M_t,M_c,T_p) begin
    New ← φ, Same ← φ
    for each pattern p in T_p begin
        p_s ← source part of p
        p_t ← target part of p
        m_t ← mappings between p_s and p_t
        p_c ← projected subgraph of p_s in D_c
        m_c ← mappings between p_s and p_c
        if identical(⟨p_s, m_t, p_t⟩, ⟨p_s, m_c, p_c⟩)
            then add (p_s,p_c) to Same
            else add (p_s,p_c) to New
    end
    for each node n in D_s begin
        P ← {(p_s,p_c)|(p_s,p_c) ∈ New ∧ n ∈ p_s}
        remove P from New
        (p'_s, p'_c) ← merge(P)
        add (p'_s, p'_c) to New
    end
    D'_c ← merge(all p_cs in New and Same)
    for each disconnected subgraph g in D_c − D'_c begin
        g' ← minimum subgraph of D_c that contains g and any leaf node x of p_c in New
        remove (p_s,p_c) from New
        add (p_s,merge(p_c, g')) to New
    end
    return New
end
```

Figure 14.9. Algorithm for finding translation patterns

$M\uparrow$and $M\downarrow$. As before, a word in parentheses is an English translation of the above Japanese word for the purpose of explanation only.

Suppose that D_c in Figure 14.11 is a correct English translation of D_s. Then the first step is to find mappings from D_s to D_c. By using a procedure described in Section 14.2, the mappings expressed by dotted lines are obtained. In these mappings, note that the Japanese word *hinjyaku* (*poor*) is related to the English word *have* even though it is not a translation word. This relationship can be established by the procedure which relates both the root nodes of the source and target structures, and this mapping is used as an upward mapping.

The next step is to find structural differences between the translation patterns for $\langle D_s, D_t\rangle$ and for $\langle D_s, D_c\rangle$. The translation patterns corresponding to pt_1, pt_2, and pt_3 are shown as pt'_1, pt'_2, and pt'_3 in Figure 14.11. Comparison of these corresponding translation patterns shows that pt'_1 and pt'_2 are different, and they are stored in the new translation

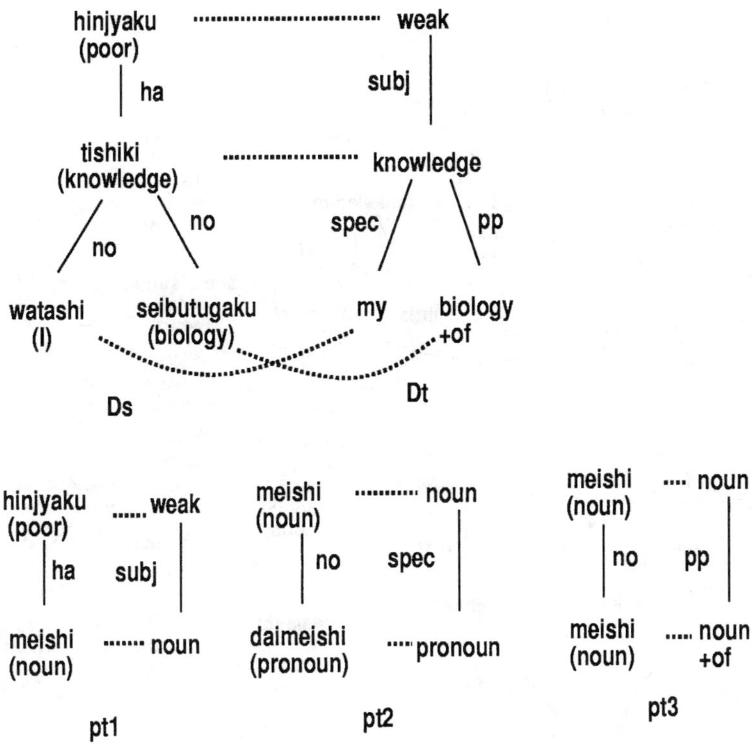

Figure 14.10. Translation patterns and dependency structures of input and translation by our EBMT system *TS*

pattern list. D_c contains a segment *little (mod)* that is not covered by the translation patterns pt'_1, pt'_2, and pt'_3. This segment is attached to pt'_1, and becomes pt''_1 in Figure 14.11. Finally, a new translation pattern pt_4 is obtained by merging pt''_1 and pt'_2 in the new translation pattern list.

4. Discussion

Strong recent interest in corpus-based processing has produced some results concerning the extraction of relevant information from bilingual corpora. There has been quite a lot of research on finding correspondences between translation pair sentences, and extracting translation patterns from them, e.g. Kaji *et al.*, 1992, Utsuro *et al.*, 1992, Utsuro *et al.*, 1993, Matsumoto *et al.*, 1993, Ishimoto *et al.*, 1993, Watanabe,

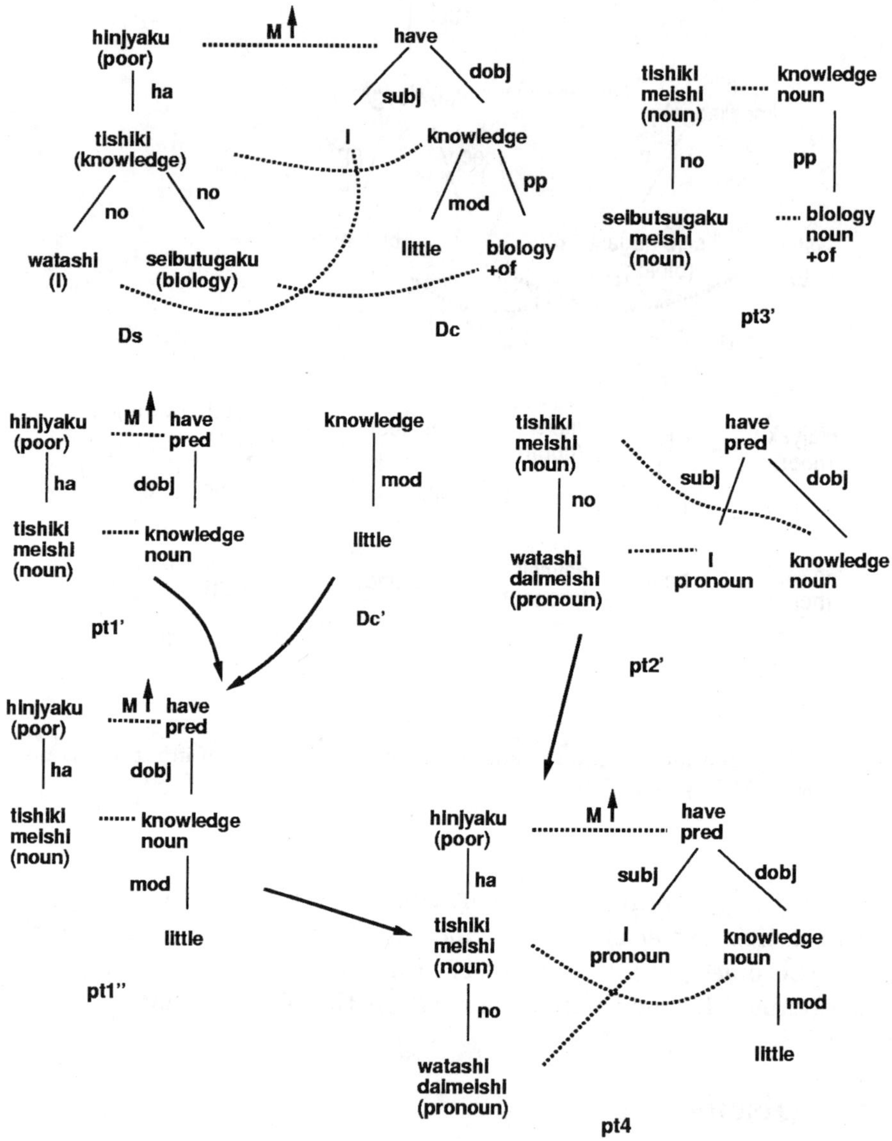

Figure 14.11. Translation patterns and dependency structures of input and correct translation

1993, Grishman, 1994, Meyers *et al.*, 1996 and Yamamoto & Matsumoto, 2000 (cf. Chapter 13, this volume).

The acquisition of translation patterns can be categorized into two types: finding translation patterns by viewing many similar translations, and finding translation patterns by comparing a correct translation and a wrong translation. An example of the former is that, given many translation instances of the Japanese word *toru* (*take*), one can obtain some translation patterns (or case frames) that are relevant for translating sentences containing *toru*. An example of the latter type, as shown in this paper, is to realize a new translation pattern by comparing a translation with its correction. The former type of method is necessary for creating a database of new translation pattern from scratch; on the other hand, the latter type is effective for enhancing a database of existing translation patterns. We have described procedures for these different types of processes in this paper.

As for the method for the former type described in Section 14.2, it is similar to these previous studies at the conceptual level, but different in other respects. Kaji *et al.*, 1992 reported a method for extracting translation templates by CKY parsing of bilingual sentences. This work is to obtain phrase-structure level phrasal correspondences, but our work is to obtain dependency-structure level phrasal correspondences. Matsumoto *et al.*, 1993 proposed a method for extracting structural matching (pairs of dependency trees) by calculating matching similarities of two dependency structures. Their work focuses on resolution of parsing ambiguity by calculating structural matching. Further, Grishman, 1994 and Meyers *et al.*, 1996 proposed structural alignment of dependency structures. Their work assumed that the least common ancestors of each fragment of a structural correspondence are preserved, but our work does not have such a structural restriction.

In addition to these differences, the main difference is to find classes (or categories) of phrasal correspondences which are highly accurate. In general, since bilingual structural alignment is a very complicated and difficult task, it is very hard to obtain more than 90% accuracy in total. If we only obtain such an accuracy rate, the result is not useful, since we need manual checks for all the correspondences retrieved. However, if we can derive some classes of phrasal correspondence with an accuracy rate of more than 90%, for instance, then we can reduce the amount of manual checking for phrasal correspondences in such classes, and this reduces the development cost of translation patterns used later in the corpus-based translation process. As shown in Section 14.2, we found that all classes of word correspondence and two subclasses of phrasal correspondence were more than 90% accurate.

When we come to use this automatically retrieved structural correspondence data in practice, we must consider (i) how to manually correct the incomplete parts, and (ii) how to reuse the manually corrected data if the results from the parser are changed.

As for the former issue, we need an easy-to-use tool to modify correspondences to reduce the cost of manual operation. We have developed a GUI tool as shown in Figure 14.12. In this figure, the bottom half presents a pair of source and target dependency structures with word correspondences (solid lines) and phrasal correspondences (sequences of shaded circles). Correspondences can easily be corrected with the aid of this graphical presentation tool.

As for the latter issue, we must develop methods for reusing the manual correction data as much as possible even if the outputs from the parser are changed. We have developed a tool for attaching phrasal correspondences into a pair of translation sentences by using existing phrasal correspondence data. This is implemented as follows: each phrasal correspondence is assigned a signature, which is a pair of source and target sentences, each of which has bracketed segments which are included in the phrasal correspondence. For instance, Figure 14.13 shows an example of a signature for a phrasal correspondence (c) in Figure 14.8: In this example, segments between square brackets represent elements which construct a phrasal correspondence.

If new parsed dependency structures for a sentence pair are given, for each phrasal correspondence signature of the sentence pair, nodes in the structures which are inside brackets of the signature are marked, and if there is a minimal subtree consisting of only marked nodes, then a phrasal correspondence is reconstructed from the phrasal correspondence signature. By using this tool, we can efficiently reuse the manually corrected data as much as possible even if parsers are updated.

As for the latter type of process, our method described in Section 14.3 is quite unique, in that it extracts new relevant translation patterns (which are not contained in the current translation pattern database) by comparing the result output by a translation system with a correct translation.

We have actually been using this system for several months to create translation patterns for the *SimTran* example-based translation system (Watanabe & Maruyama, 1994). Our experience indicates that if the mapping is correct, the result of the system can mostly be used as a translation pattern after a little editing. Most errors in the mapping

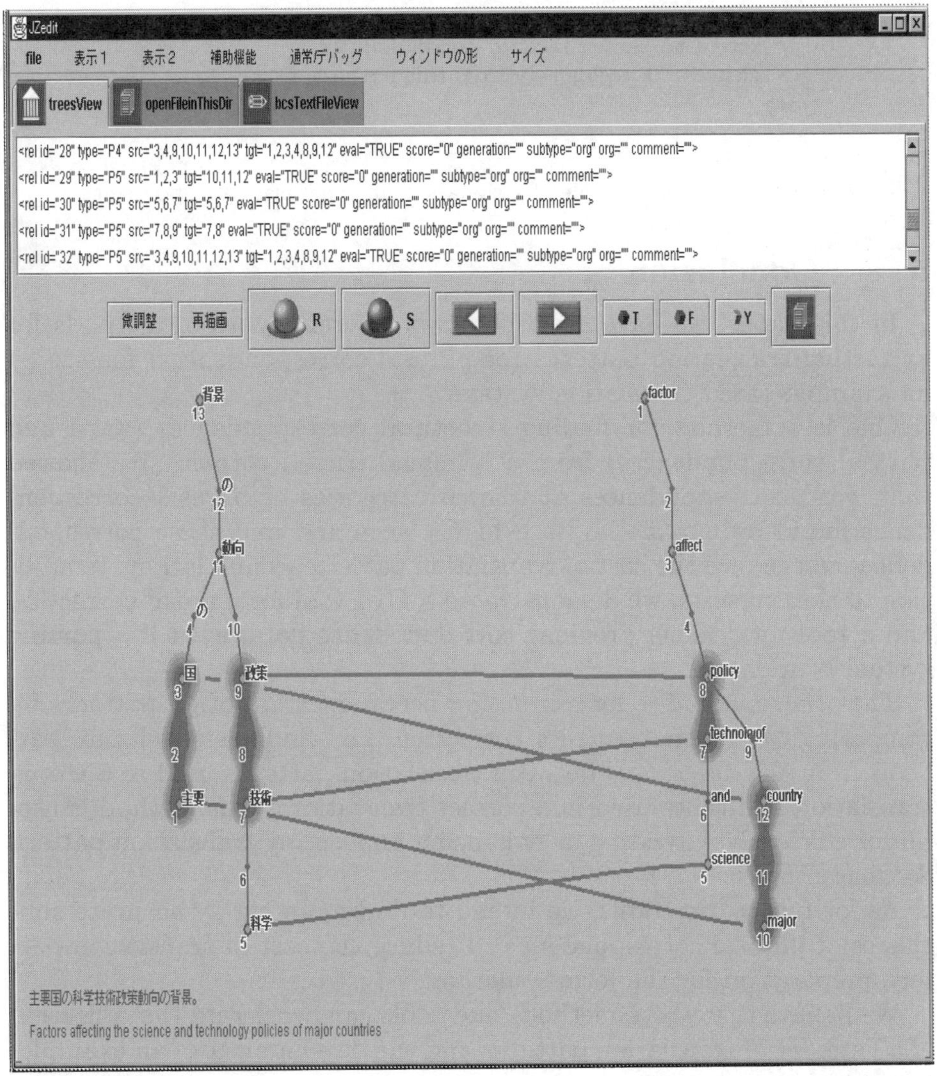

Figure 14.12. A GUI tool for presenting/manipulating structural correspondences

phase are caused (i) by a word used in a correct translation sentence not being registered in the dictionary as a translation for its source word, and (ii) by a single source word, such as a compound noun phrase, being translated as several target words. Further, creating a translation pattern by using this system takes half as much time as creating one from scratch.

⟨*sig*⟩
... [korera no kanten karano] kagaku [gijutu] ...
... science and [technology from this purpose] ...
⟨/*sig*⟩

Figure 14.13. An example of a signature for a phrasal correspondence

5. Conclusion

In this paper, we have described two different types of methods for extracting translation patterns (or phrasal correspondences) for use by an example-based translation system.

One is a method for finding structural correspondences (word and phrasal correspondences) from a bilingual parsed corpus. We showed that word correspondences and some categories of phrasal correspondence found by our method are highly accurate, and these correspondences can reduce the cost of translation pattern accumulation. In addition to these results, we demonstrated a GUI tool for manual correction and a tool for reusing previous correspondence data, even if a parsing system is updated.

The other method is for extracting necessary translation patterns by comparing MT output and its correction, i.e. finding translation patterns from the differences between translation patterns used in a wrong translation and those used in a correct translation. This method is useful for efficiently extending or enhancing an existing translation pattern database.

As for future directions, we intend to find more highly accurate subclasses of phrasal correspondence to reduce the cost of translation pattern preparation for the former method.

We believe that these methods and tools can accelerate the collection of a large set of translation patterns and the development of an example-based translation system.

References

Aramaki, E., S. Kurohashi, S. Sato and H. Watanabe. 2001. Finding translation correspondences from parallel parsed corpus for example-based translation. In *MT Summit VIII: Machine Translation in the Information Age*, Santiago de Compostela, Spain, pp.27–32.

Grishman, R. 1994. Iterative alignment of syntactic structures for a bilingual corpus. In *Proceedings of 2nd Annual Workshop on Very Large Corpora*, Kyoto, Japan, pp.57–68.

Isahara, H. and M. Haruno. 2000. Japanese-English aligned bilingual corpora. In J. Veronis (ed.) *Parallel Text Processing: Alignment and use of translation corpora* (Text, Speech and Language Technology, Vol. 13). Kluwer Academic Publishers, Dordrecht, The Netherlands, pp.313–334.

Ishimoto, H., T. Utsuro, Y. Matsumoto and M. Nagao. 1993. Structural matching between parallel sentences of English and Japanese. In *Proceedings of the Information Processing Society of Japan* **95**(11):81–88.

Kaji, H., Y. Kida and Y. Morimoto. 1992. Learning translation templates from bilingual text. In *Proceedings of the fifteenth [sic] International Conference on Computational Linguistics, COLING-92*, Nantes, France, **2**:672–678.

Kurohashi, S. and M. Nagao. 1994. A syntactic analysis method of long Japanese sentences based on the detection of conjunctive structures. *Computational Linguistics* **20**(4):507–534.

Matsumoto, Y., H. Ishimoto and T. Utsuro. 1993. Structural matching of parallel texts. In *31st Annual Meeting of the Association for Computational Linguistics*, Columbus, OH., pp.23–30.

McCord, M. 1980. Slot grammars. *Computational Linguistics* **6**:31–43.

Meyers, A., R. Yanharber and R. Grishman. 1996. Alignment of Shared Forests for Bilingual Corpora. In *COLING-96: Proceedings of the 16th International Conference on Computational Linguistics*, Copenhagen, Denmark, pp.460–465.

Nagao, M. 1984. A Framework of a Mechanical Translation between Japanese and English by Analogy Principle. In A. Elithorn and R Banerji (eds.) *Artificial and Human Intelligence*, Amsterdam: North-Holland, pp.173–180.

Sumita, E., H. Iida and H. Kohyama. 1990. Translating with examples: A new approach to machine translation. In *Third International Conference on Theoretical and Methodological Issues in Machine Translation*, Austin, TX., pp.203–212.

Takeda, K. 1996a. Pattern-based context-free grammars for machine translation. In *34th Annual Meeting of the Association for Computational Linguistics*, Santa Cruz, CA., pp.144–151.

Takeda, K. 1996b. Pattern-based machine translation. In *COLING-96: Proceedings of the 16th International Conference on Computational Linguistics*, Copenhagen, Denmark, **2**:1155–1158.

Utsuro, T., Y. Matsumoto, and M. Nagao. 1992. Lexical knowledge acquisition from bilingual corpora. In *Proceedings of the the fifteenth [sic] International Conference on Computational Linguistics, COLING-92*, Nantes, France, **2**:581–587.

Utsuro, T., Y. Matsumoto and M. Nagao. 1993. Verbal case frame acquisition from bilingual corpora. In *Proceedings of the Thirteenth International Joint Conference on Artificial Intelligence*, Chambéry, France, pp.1150–1156.

Watanabe, H. 1992. A similarity-driven transfer system. In *Proceedings of the fifteenth [sic] International Conference on Computational Linguistics, COLING-92*, Nantes, France, **2**:770–776.

Watanabe, H. 1993. A method for extracting translation patterns from translation examples. In *Fifth International Conference on Theoretical and Methodological Issues in Machine Translation TMI '93: MT in the Next Generation*, Kyoto, Japan, pp.292–301.

Watanabe, H., S. Kurohasi and E. Aramaki. 2000. Finding structural correspondences from bilingual parsed corpus for corpus-based translation. In *Proceedings of the 18th International Conference on Computational Linguistics: COLING-2000 in Europe*, Saarbrücken, Germany, **2**:906–912.

Watanabe, H. and H. Maruyama. 1994. A transfer system using example-based approach. *IEICE Transactions on Information and Systems* **E77-D**(2):247–257.

Watanabe, H. and K. Takeda. 1998. A pattern-based machine translation system extended by example-based processing. In *36th Annual Meeting of the Association for Computational Linguistics and 17th International Conference on Computational Linguistics*, Montreal, Quebec, Canada, **2**:1369–1373.

Yamamoto, K. and Y. Matsumoto. 2000. Acquisition of phrase-level bilingual correspondence using dependency relations. In *Proceedings of the 18th International Conference on Computational Linguistics: COLING-2000 in Europe*, Saarbrücken, Germany, **2**:933–939.

Chapter 15

A BEST-FIRST ALIGNMENT ALGORITHM FOR AUTOMATIC EXTRACTION OF TRANSFER MAPPINGS FROM BILINGUAL CORPORA

Arul Menezes
arulm@microsoft.com

Stephen D. Richardson
steveri@microsoft.com

Abstract Translation systems that automatically extract transfer mappings (rules or examples) from bilingual corpora have been hampered by the difficulty of achieving accurate alignment and acquiring high quality mappings. We describe an algorithm that uses a best-first strategy and a small alignment grammar to significantly improve the quality of the mappings extracted. For each mapping, frequencies are computed and sufficient context is retained to distinguish competing mappings during translation. Variants of the algorithm are run against a corpus containing 200K sentence pairs and evaluated based on the quality of resulting translations.

Keywords: logical form alignment, transfer mapping extraction, dependency structure alignment

1. Introduction

A machine translation system requires a substantial amount of translation knowledge, typically embodied in bilingual dictionaries, transfer rules, example bases, or a statistical model. In a manner similar to the many approaches to example-based MT (EBMT) discussed in this volume, our approach seeks to obtain as much of this knowledge as possible

M. Carl and A. Way (eds.), Recent Advances in Example-Based Machine Translation, 421–442.

by automatically culling examples from aligned bilingual corpora. We fall clearly into the *explicit* EBMT paradigm, which processes the bilingual corpora ahead of time, extracting translation mappings, and then storing those mappings in a database for use during translation of new sentences.

Like some of the approaches in the chapters comprising Part IV of this volume, as well as those of many others (e.g. Kaji *et al.*, 1992; Meyers *et al.*, 2000; Lavoie *et al.*, 2001), a distinctive characteristic of our system is the use of dependency structures to represent the translation knowledge stored in the system. In this regard, we abstract away from surface strings, applying sophisticated rule-based parsing techniques to obtain a *logical form* (LF), similar to that described by Jensen, 1993, for each sentence processed. One advantage of this approach, obviously, is that through the additional generality obtained by normalizing both the lexical and syntactic form of examples, they may then be matched and applied more broadly when new sentences are translated.

Early in the process of extracting mappings (or *transfer mappings*) from corpora, we also apply statistical methods to identify terminological correspondences, including both words and phrases. Our combination of rule-based, example-based, and statistical techniques firmly lands our system in the same category as other hybrid systems described in this volume (e.g., Bond & Shirai, Chapter 7).

Before the extraction of transfer mappings can be fully automated, a number of issues must be addressed. Mappings are typically acquired in systems such as ours by algorithmically aligning the nodes and arcs in LFs obtained for corresponding source and target sentences. The LF alignment and transfer mapping acquisition procedure must acquire mappings with very high precision and be robust against errors in parsing, in sentence level alignment, and in the alignment procedure itself. The procedure must also produce transfer mappings that provide sufficient context to enable the translation system utilizing these mappings to choose the appropriate translation for a given context. To address some of these same challenges, Watanabe *et al.* (Chapter 14, this volume) employ tools used by human reviewers that are designed specifically for this purpose. Recourse to manual methods, however, defeats our goal of a fully *automated* solution.

In this chapter, after providing a brief overview of the *Microsoft* Research MT (*MSR-MT*) system, we describe the LF alignment and transfer mapping acquisition algorithm used in this system, which attempts to address the issues raised above. The algorithm uses a best-first strategy and a small alignment grammar to significantly improve the quality of the mappings extracted. For each mapping, frequencies are computed and sufficient context is retained to distinguish competing mappings during translation. Variants of the algorithm are run against a corpus containing 200K sentence pairs and evaluated based on the quality of resulting translations.

2. Overview of MSR-MT

MSR-MT is a data-driven hybrid MT system, combining rule-based analysis and generation components with example-based transfer. The automatic LF alignment procedure, which is the focus of this chapter, is used to create the system's transfer example base and relies on the same parser employed during analysis. Moderately sized bilingual dictionaries, containing only word pairs and their parts of speech, provide translation candidates for the alignment procedure and are also used as a backup source of translations during transfer. Statistical techniques supply additional translation pair candidates for alignment and identify certain multi-word terms for parsing and transfer.

The robust, broad-coverage parsers used by *MSR-MT* were created originally for monolingual applications and have been used in *Microsoft* Word's grammar checker. These parsers produce an LF representation that is compatible across multiple languages (see section 3 below). Parsers now exist for seven languages (English, French, German, Spanish, Chinese, Japanese, and Korean), and active development continues to improve their accuracy and coverage.

Generation components are currently being developed for English, Spanish, Chinese, and Japanese. Given the automated learning techniques used to create *MSR-MT* transfer components, it should theoretically be possible, provided with appropriate aligned bilingual corpora, to create MT systems for any language pair for which we have the necessary parsing and generation components. In practice, we have thus far created systems that translate into English from all other languages and that translate from English to Spanish, Chinese, and Japanese. We have also experimented preliminarily with French to Spanish and with Korean and Chinese to Japanese.

Results from experiments using our Spanish to English system are reported in sections 6 and 7 of this chapter. The bilingual corpus used in these experiments comes from *Microsoft* manuals and help text. The sentence alignment of this corpus is the result of using a commercial translation memory (TM) tool during the original human translation of these texts.

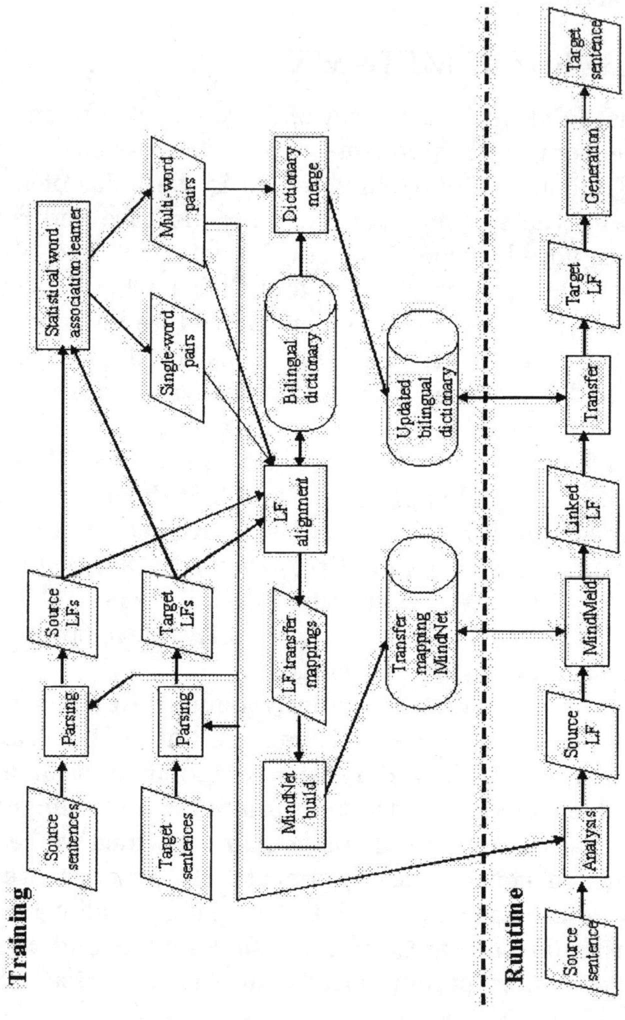

Figure 15.1. MSR-MT architecture

The architecture of *MSR-MT* is presented in Figure 15.1. For details regarding the components of the system that are mentioned below, the reader is referred to Richardson *et al.*, 2001. During the training phase, source and target sentences from the aligned bilingual corpus are parsed to produce corresponding LFs. The normalized word forms resulting from parsing are also fed to a statistical word association learner, which outputs learned single word translation pairs as well as a special class of multi-word pairs. The LFs are then aligned with the aid of translations from a bilingual dictionary and the learned single word pairs. Transfer mappings that result from LF alignment, in the form of linked source and target LF segments, are stored in a special repository known as *MindNet*. Additionally, the learned multi-word pairs are added to the bilingual dictionary for possible backup use during translation and to the main parsing lexicon to improve parse quality in certain cases.

At runtime, *MSR-MT*'s analysis component parses source sentences with the same parser used for source text during the training phase. The resulting LFs then undergo a process known as *MindMeld*, which matches them against the LF transfer mappings stored in *MindNet*. This process also links segments of source LFs with corresponding target LF segments stored in *MindNet*. These target LF segments are stitched together into a single target LF during transfer, and any translations for words or phrases not matched are searched for in the updated bilingual dictionary and inserted in the target LF. Generation receives the target LF as input, from which it produces a target sentence.

3. Logical Form

A Logical Form (LF) is an unordered graph representing the relations among the most meaningful elements of a sentence. Nodes are identified by the lemma of a content word and directed, labelled arcs indicate the underlying semantic relations. It is intended to be as independent as possible of specific languages and their grammars. In particular, LFs from different languages use the same relation types and provide similar analyses for similar constructions. The logical form abstracts away from such language-particular aspects of a sentence as constituent order, inflectional morphology, and certain function words.

Figure 15.2 depicts the LFs for the following Spanish–English pair used in example (1):

(1) *En Información del hipervínculo, haga clic en la dirección del hipervínculo* $\Longrightarrow$ *Under Hyperlink Information, click the hyperlink address.*

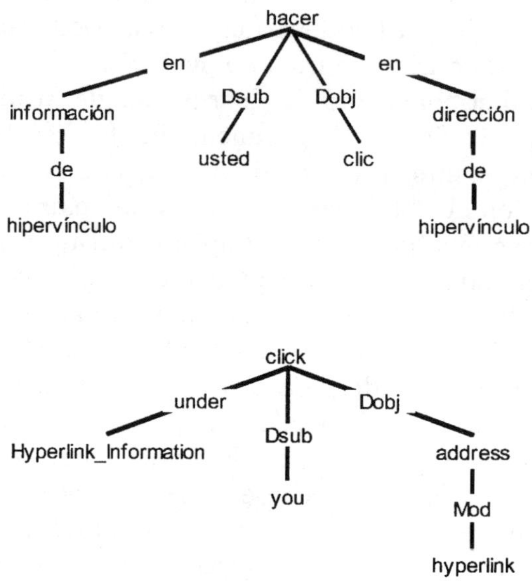

Figure 15.2. Spanish and English LFs for example sentences

4. Alignment

We consider an alignment of two LFs to be a set of mappings, such that each mapping is between a node or set of nodes (and the relations between them) in the source LF and a node or set of nodes (and the relations between them) in the target LF, where no node participates in more than one such mapping.

Our alignment algorithm proceeds in two phases. In the first phase, it establishes tentative lexical correspondences between nodes in the source and target LFs. In the second phase, it aligns nodes based on these lexical correspondences as well as structural considerations. It starts from the nodes with the tightest lexical correspondence ("best-first") and works outward from these anchor points.

We first present the algorithm, and then illustrate how it applies to the example sentence pair represented by the LFs in Figure 15.2.

4.1 Finding Tentative Lexical Correspondences

We use a bilingual lexicon that merges data from several sources (McCarthy, 1995; SoftArt, 1995; Langenscheidt, 1997), and invert target-to-source dictionaries to improve coverage. Our Spanish–English lexicon contains 88,500 translation pairs. We augment this with 9,563 translation correspondences acquired using statistical techniques described by Moore, 2001.

Like Watanabe *et al.* (Chapter 14, this volume) and Meyers *et al.*, 2000, we use this lexicon to establish initial tentative word correspondences. However, we have found that even a relatively large bilingual dictionary has only moderate coverage for our purposes. Hence, we pursue an aggressive matching strategy, using the bilingual dictionary together with the derivational morphology component of our system (Pentheroudakis & Vanderwende, 1993). We find direct translations, translations of morphological bases and derivations, and base and derived forms of translations. We find that aggressive overgeneration of correspondences at this phase is balanced by the more conservative second phase and results in improved overall alignment quality.

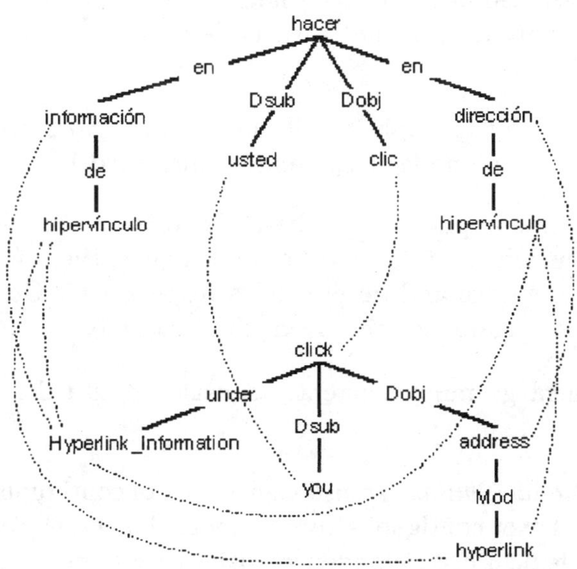

Figure 15.3. Lexical correspondences between Spanish and English LFs

We also look for matches between components of multi-word expressions and individual words. This allows us to align such expressions that may have been analysed as a single lexicalized entity in one language but as separate words in the other.

4.2 Aligning Nodes

Our alignment procedure uses the tentative lexical correspondences established above and structural cues to create affirmative node alignments. A set of alignment grammar rules licenses only linguistically meaningful alignments. The rules are ordered to create the most unambiguous alignments ("best") first and use these to disambiguate subsequent alignments. The rules, intended to be language-neutral, were developed while working primarily with Spanish–English, but have also been applied to other language pairs such as French, German, and Japanese to/from English.

The algorithm is as follows:

- Initialize the set of unaligned source and target nodes to the set of all source and target nodes respectively.

- Attempt to apply the alignment rules in the specified order, to each unaligned node or set of nodes in source and target. If a rule fails to apply to any unaligned node or set of nodes, move to the next rule.

- If all rules fail to apply to all nodes, exit. No more alignment is possible. (Some nodes may remain unaligned.)

- When a rule applies, mark the nodes or sets of nodes to which it applied as aligned to each other and remove them from the lists of unaligned source and target nodes respectively. Go to step 2 and apply rules again, starting from the first rule.

The alignment grammar currently consists of 18 rules, including the following:

1 *Bidirectionally unique translation*: A set of contiguous source nodes S and a set of contiguous target nodes T such that every node in S has a lexical correspondence with every node in T and with no other target node, and every node in T has a lexical correspondence with every node in S and with no other source node. Align S and T to each other.

2 *Translation + Children*: A source node S and a target node T that have a lexical correspondence, such that each child of S and T is already aligned to a child of the other. Align S and T to each other.

3 *Translation + Parent*: A source node S and a target node T that have a lexical correspondence, such that a parent P_s of S has already been aligned to a parent P_t of T. Align S and T to each other.

4 *Verb+Object to Verb:* A verb V_1 (from either source or target), that has child O that is not a verb, but is already aligned to a verb V_2, and either V_2 has no unaligned parents, or V_1 and V_2 have children aligned to each other. Align V_1 and O to V_2.

5 *Parent + relationship*: A source node S and a target node T, with the same part of speech, and no unaligned siblings, where a parent P_s of S is already aligned to a parent P_t of T, and the relationship between P_s and S is the same as that between P_t and T. Align S and T to each other.

6 *Child + relationship*: Same as the previous rule, but based on previously aligned children instead of parents.

7 *Verb+Verb to Verb:* A verb V_1 (from source or target) that has no lexical correspondences and has a single child verb V_2 that is already aligned to a verb V_3, where V_3 has no unaligned parents. Align V_1 and V_2 to V_3.

Note that rule 1 uses lexical correspondences only, rules 2 and 3 use both lexical and structural information, and rules 4 through 7 rely entirely on structural cues, specifically the relationships between the nodes being examined and previously aligned nodes.

4.3 Alignment Example

We now illustrate the application of the alignment procedure to the example sentences for the LFs in Figure 15.2. In the first phase, using the bilingual lexicon, we identify the lexical correspondences depicted in Figure 15.3 as dotted lines. Note that each of the two instances of *hipervínculo* has two ambiguous correspondences, and that while the correspondence from *Información* to *Hyperlink_Information* is unique, the reverse is not. Note also that neither the monolingual nor the bilingual lexicons have been customized for this domain. For example, there is no entry in either lexicon for *Hyperlink_Information.* This unit has been assembled by general rules that link sequences of capitalized words. Lexical correspondences established for this unit are based on translations found for its individual components.

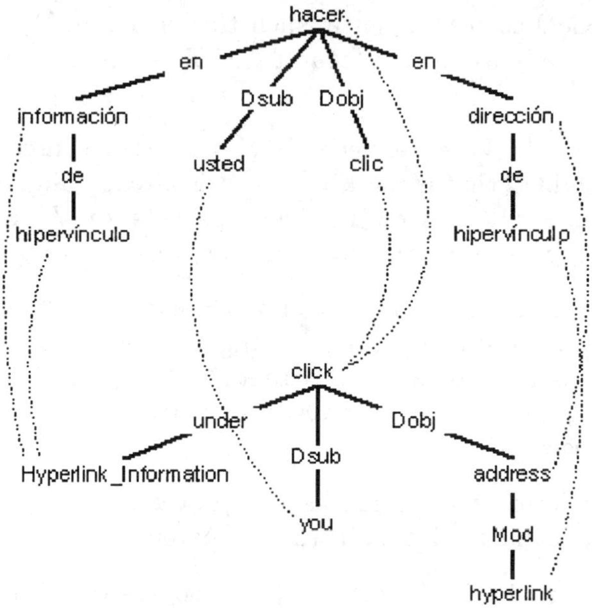

Figure 15.4. Alignment mappings between Spanish and English LFs

Next, the alignment rules apply as described below. The alignment mappings they create are depicted in Figure 15.4 as dotted lines.

- Rule-1: *Bidirectionally unique translation*, applies in three places, creating alignment mappings between *dirección* and *address, usted* and *you,* and *clic* and *click.* These are the initial 'best' alignments that provide the anchors from which we will work outwards to align the rest of the structure.

- Rule-3: *Translation + Parent*, applies next to align the instance of *hipervínculo* that is the child of *dirección* to *hyperlink*, which is the child of *address.* We leverage a previously created alignment (*dirección* to *address*) and the structure of the logical form to resolve the ambiguity present at the lexical level.

- Rule-1 now applies (where previously it did not) to create a many-to-one mapping between *información* and *hipervínculo* to *Hyperlink_Information*. The uniqueness condition in this rule is now met because the ambiguous alternative was cleared away by the prior application of Rule 3.

- Rule-4: *Verb+Object to Verb* applies to rollup *hacer* with its object *clic*, since the latter is already aligned to a verb. This produces the many-to-one alignment of *hacer* and *clic* to *click*.

5. Acquiring Alignment Mappings

Figure 15.5 shows the transfer mappings derived from the example sentences represented by the LFs in Figure 15.2.

5.1 Transfer Mappings with Context

Each mapping created during alignment forms the core of a family of mappings emitted by the transfer mapping acquisition procedure. The alignment mapping by itself represents a minimal transfer mapping with no context. In addition, we emit multiple variants, each one expanding the core mapping with varying types and amounts of local context.

We generally use linguistic constructs such as noun and verb phrases to provide the boundaries for the context we include. For example, the transfer mapping for an adjective is expanded to include the noun it modifies; the mapping for a verb may include the object as context, and mappings for noun collocations are emitted individually and as a whole. Some mappings may include 'wild card' or underspecified nodes, with a part of speech but no lemma, as shown in Figure 15.5.

5.2 Alignment Post-Processing

After we have acquired transfer mappings from our entire training corpus, we compute frequencies for all mappings. We use these to resolve conflicting mappings, i.e., mappings where the source sides of the mapping are identical, but the target sides differ. Currently we resolve the conflict by simply picking the most frequent mapping. Note that this does not imply that we are committed to a single translation for every word across the corpus, since we emitted each mapping with different types and amounts of context. Ideally at least one of these contexts

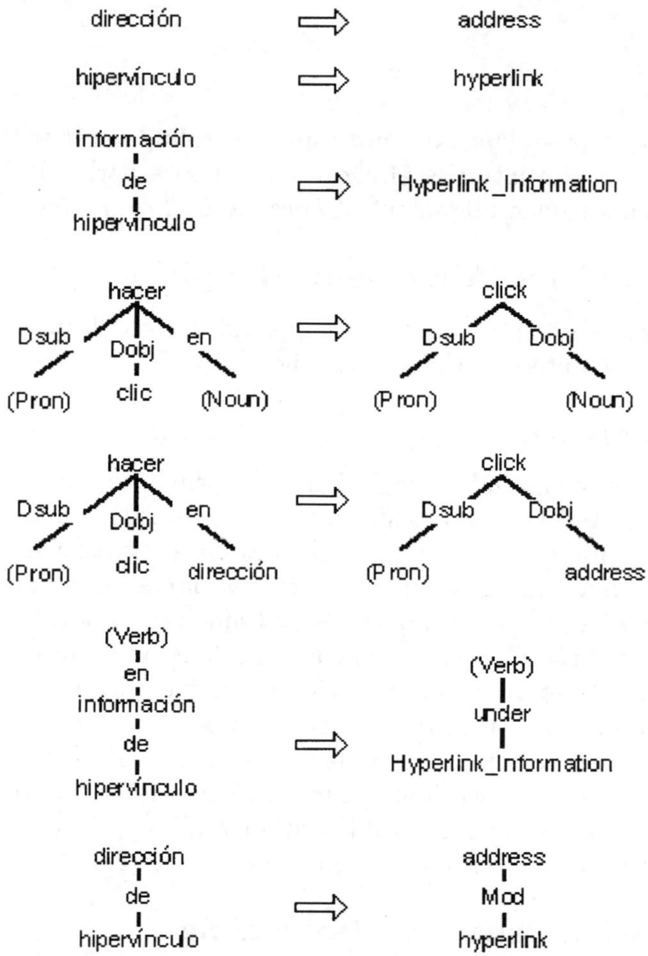

Figure 15.5. Transfer mappings acquired from Spanish and English LFs

serves to disambiguate the translation. The conflicts being resolved here are those mappings where the necessary context is not present.

A drawback of this approach is that we are relying on *a priori* linguistic heuristics to ensure that we have at least one mapping with the right context. In future work we plan to address this by using machine-learning techniques to find the precise context that serves to optimally disambiguate between conflicting mappings.

5.2.1 Frequency Threshold. During post-processing we also apply a frequency threshold, keeping only mappings seen at least N times (where N is currently 2). This frequency threshold greatly improves the speed of the runtime system, with minor impact on translation quality (see section 6.6).

6. Experiments and Results

6.1 Evaluation Methodology

In the evaluation process, we found that various evaluation metrics of alignment in isolation bore very little relationship to the quality of the translations produced by a system that used the results of such alignment. Since it is the overall translation quality that we care about, we use the output quality (as judged by humans) of the MT system incorporating the transfer mappings produced by an alignment algorithm (keeping all other aspects of the system constant) as the metric by which we evaluate the algorithm.

6.2 Translation Process

The *MSR-MT* system, described in some detail in section 2, begins by parsing an input sentence and obtaining the LF corresponding to that sentence. We then search the transfer mappings acquired during alignment for mappings that match portions of the input LF. We prefer larger (more specific) mappings to smaller (more general) mappings. Among mappings of equal size, we prefer higher-frequency mappings. We allow overlapping mappings that do not conflict. The lemmas in any portion of the LF not covered by a transfer mapping are translated using the same bilingual dictionary employed during alignment, or by a handful of hard-coded transfer rules (see Section 6.7 for a discussion of the contribution made by each of these components). Target LF fragments from matched transfer mappings and default dictionary translations are stitched together to form an output LF. From this, a rule-based generation component produces an output sentence.

The system provides output for every input sentence. Sentences for which spanning parses are not found are translated anyway, albeit with lower quality.

6.3 Training Corpus

We use a sentence-aligned Spanish–English training corpus consisting of 208,730 sentence pairs mostly from *Microsoft* technical manuals. The data was previously aligned at the sentence level by means of a translation memory tool used by human translators. The data was then parsed and aligned at the sub-sentence level by our system, using the techniques described in this paper. Our parser produces a parse in every case, but in each language roughly 15% of the parses produced are 'fitted' or non-spanning. Since we have a relatively large training corpus, we apply a conservative heuristic and only use in alignment those sentence-pairs that produced spanning parses in *both* languages. In this corpus 161,606 pairs (or 77.4% of the corpus) were used. This is a substantially larger training corpus than those used in previous work on learning transfer mappings from parsed data. Table 15.1 presents some data on the mappings extracted from this corpus using the Best-First algorithm.

Table 15.1. Best-first alignment of training corpus

Total sentence pairs	208,730
Sentence pairs used	161,606
Number of transfer mappings extracted	1,208,828
Transfer mappings per sentence pair	7.48
Number of unique transfer mappings	437,479
Number of unique mappings after eliminating conflicts	369,067
Number of unique mappings with frequency > 1	58,314
Time taken to align entire corpus not including parsing (on a 550MHz PC)	98 minutes
Alignment speed	26.9 pairs/sec

6.4 Experiments

In each experiment we used 5 human evaluators in a blind evaluation, to compare the translations produced by the test system with those produced by a comparison system. Evaluators were presented, for each sentence, with a reference human translation and with the two machine translations in random order, but not the original source language sentence. They were asked to pick the better overall translation, taking into account both content and fluency. They were allowed to choose neither if they considered both translations equally good or equally bad.

The test sentences were randomly chosen from unseen data from the same domain. Experiment 1 used 200 sentences and every sentence was evaluated by every rater. Sentences were rated better for one system or the other if a majority of the raters agreed. Experiments 2-4 used 500 sentences each, but every sentence was rated by a single rater.

For all experiments, the test system was the Spanish–English version of the *MSR-MT* system described in section 2, loaded with transfer mappings acquired using the techniques described in this paper (hereafter 'Best-First').

In the first experiment, the comparison system was a highly rated commercial system, *BabelFish.*[1] Initially, we attempted this experiment with the packaged version of the same underlying system from *Systran*, but found that on our test set it produced inferior translations to those produced by *BabelFish*, even when using its computer-domain dictionary. We speculated that the *BabelFish* website may utilize a newer version of the system or a bilingual dictionary containing additional computer terminology.

Each of the next three experiments varies some key aspect of Best-First in order to explore the properties of the algorithm. The algorithm variations are described in the next section.

6.5 Comparison Alignment Algorithms

6.5.1 Bottom Up. Experiment 2 compares Best-First to the previous algorithm we employed, which used a bottom-up approach, similar in spirit to that used by Meyers *et al.*, 1998.

This algorithm follows the procedure described in section 4.1 to establish tentative lexical correspondences. However, it does not use an alignment grammar, and relies on a bottom-up rather than a best-first strategy. It starts by aligning the leaf nodes and proceeds upwards, aligning nodes whose child nodes have already aligned. Nodes that do not align are skipped over, and later rolled-up with ancestor nodes that have successfully aligned.

[1] `http://world.altavista.com`

6.5.2 No Context. Experiment 3 uses a comparison algorithm that differs from Best First in that it retains no context (see section 5.1) when emitting transfer mappings.

6.5.3 No Threshold. The comparison algorithm used in Experiment 4 differed from Best First in that the frequency threshold (see section 5.2.1) is not applied, i.e., all transfer mappings are retained.

6.6 Discussion

The results of the four experiments are presented in Table 15.2.

Table 15.2. Translation Quality

System A	System B	Sentences where A rated better	Sentences where B rated better	Sentences where neither rated better	Net % improved sentences
Best-First	BabelFish	93 (46.5%)	73 (36.5%)	34 (17%)	10%
Best-First	Bottom-Up	224 (44.8%)	111 (22.2%)	165 (33%)	22.6%
Best-First	No-Context	187 (37.4%)	69 (13.8%)	244 (48.8%)	23.6%
Best-First	No-Threshold	112 (22.4%)	122 (24.4%)	226 (53.2%)	-2%

Experiment 1 establishes that the algorithm presented in this paper automatically acquires translation knowledge of sufficient quantity and quality as to enable translations that exceed the quality of a highly rated traditional MT system. Note however that *BabelFish/Systran* was not customized to this domain.

Experiment 2 shows that Best-First produces transfer mappings resulting in significantly better translations than Bottom-Up. Using Best-First produced better translations for a net of 22.6% of the sentences.

Experiment 3 shows that retaining sufficient context in transfer mappings is crucial to translation quality, producing better translations for a net of 23.6% of the sentences.

Experiment 4 shows that the frequency threshold does not have a statistically significant impact on the translation quality, but as shown in Table 15.3, results in a much smaller (approximally 6 times) and faster (approximally 45 times) runtime system.

Table 15.3. Comparison of size and speed (500 sentences)

	Number of Mappings (500 sentences)	Translation speed
Best-First	58,314	173 sec (0.34 sec/sent)
No-Threshold	359,528	8059 sec (17 sec/sent)

6.7 Transfer Mapping Coverage

Using end-to-end translation quality as a metric for alignment leaves open the question of how much of the translation quality obtains from alignment versus other sources of translation knowledge in our system, such as the bilingual dictionary. To address this issue we measured the contribution of each using a 3264-sentence test set. Table 15.4 presents the results. The first column indicates the total number of words or relations in each category. The next four columns indicate the percentage translated using each knowledge source, and the percentage not translated or transferred directly from source to target, respectively.

Table 15.4. Coverage of transfer mappings, dictionary, and rules

	Number of instances	Transfer mappings	Dictionary	Rules	Not translated or direct transfer
Content words	21102	96.3%	2.5%	0%	1.2%
Prepositional relations	6567	53.6%	39.5%	6.8%	0%
Other relations	17507	54.2%	0%	0%	45.8%

As the table shows, the vast majority of content words are translated using transfer mappings obtained via the LF alignment and transfer mapping acquisition procedure. The table also shows the percentage of relations covered by transfer mappings. Relations, which are represented LFs as labels on arcs (see Figure 15.2) may be labelled with a relation type (subject, direct object, etc.) and/or with a preposition.

As the table shows, though over half the relations in the input are covered by transfer mappings, the system is currently less successful at learning transfer mappings for relations than it is for content words. As a temporary measure, we have two hand-coded transfer rules that apply to some prepositional relations, which account for 6.8% of such transfers.

7. Absolute Quality

The experiments presented leave two open questions: What is the absolute quality of the translations produced by the system? And what is the relationship between translation quality and the transfer mappings learned by LF alignment?

To attempt to address these questions we conducted an absolute quality evaluation and investigated the relationship between the transfer mappings used in a translation and the absolute quality of that translation. This evaluation was conducted using a slightly newer version of the *MSR-MT* system than that used in the previous experiments.

7.1 Methodology

We used 5 human evaluators looking at translations produced from previously unseen data. Evaluators were presented, for each sentence, with a reference human translation and with the machine translation, but not the original source language sentence. They were asked to rate the machine translation on a scale of 1 to 4, taking into account both the fluency of the translation and the accuracy with which it conveyed the meaning (as compared with the reference human translation).

The scores were defined as follows:

4 *Ideal*: Fluent, all information included.

3 *Acceptable*: Comprehensible; all important information accurately transferred.

2 *Possibly Acceptable*: May be interpretable given context and time, some information transferred accurately.

1 *Unacceptable*: Not comprehensible and/or little or no information transferred accurately.

The absolute quality evaluation was run for two systems — our own system (using "Best-First") and *BabelFish*. In each case, the inter-rater agreement was good, though there was some clustering of scores around 2 and 3. The results, presented in Figure 15.6, confirm the results of Experiment 1 indicating that our system produces a significantly greater number of translations rated 3.5 to 4.0 than *BabelFish*.

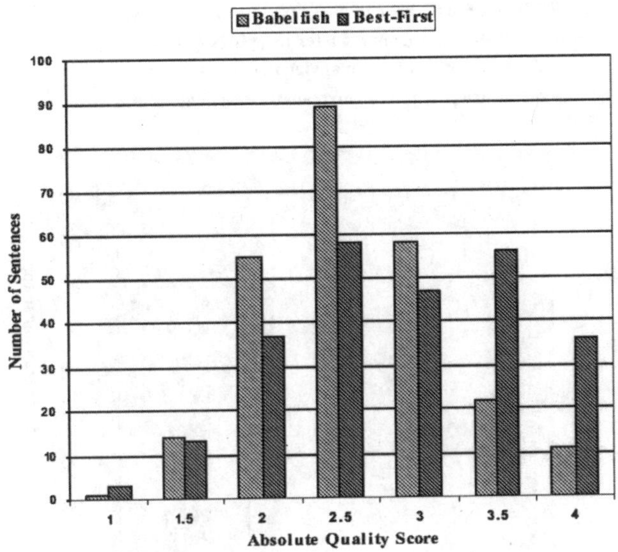

Figure 15.6. Absolute quality scores for *BabelFish* vs. Best First

7.2 Relationship between absolute quality and transfer mappings

The most interesting question for us was what relationship existed between the absolute quality of a given translation and the transfer mappings used to produce that translation.

Towards this end, we computed the following metrics for each group of sentences rated to have similar quality:

- Average number of LF nodes in the transfer mappings used in the translation. The minimum size is 1, representing word-for-word transfers with no larger context.
- Percentage of lemmas translated using transfer mappings. (The remainder are either translated using the bilingual dictionary or left untranslated.)
- Percentage of prepositional relations covered by transfer mappings (the remainder are translated using the bilingual dictionary)
- Percentage of other relations covered by transfer mappings (the remainder are, correctly or incorrectly, transferred from source to target unchanged)

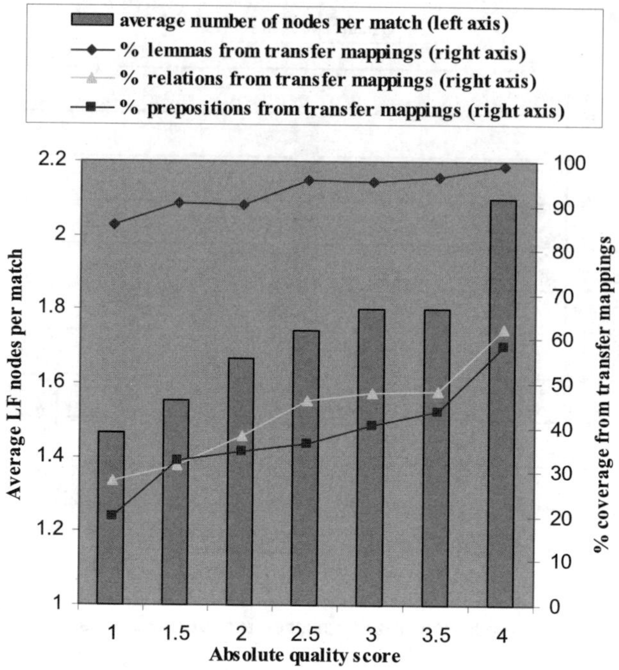

Figure 15.7. Transfer mapping metrics vs. absolute quality scores

Figure 15.7 shows these metrics plotted against the absolute quality score of the corresponding sentences. The bars represent the average number of LF nodes per match, which is plotted against the left-hand scale. The lines, plotted against the right-hand scale, represent the percentage of lemmas, prepositions and other relations, respectively, that were translated using transfer mappings.

The chart shows a strong relationship, in particular, between size of the transfer mappings used and the quality of the translation. The relationship is especially pronounced with the perfect translations. It also indicates that for sentences where most of the prepositions and relations were not covered by transfer mappings, the absolute quality was rated as low.

On the other hand, the relationship between quality and the percentage of content words translated via transfer mappings is weak, indicating that even within a specific domain, learning word-for-word translations is not enough to ensure quality. Instead larger, more contextual transfers must be learned.

8. Conclusions and Future Work

We have described an algorithm for automatically acquiring high-quality transfer mappings from sentence-aligned bilingual corpora using an alignment grammar and a best-first strategy. Results were reported from applying the algorithm to a substantially larger training corpus than that used in previously reported work on learning transfer mappings from parsed data. The results demonstrated that this approach produces transfer mappings resulting in translation quality comparable to a commercial MT system.

We also showed that a best-first, alignment grammar-based approach produced better results than a bottom-up approach, and that retaining context in the acquired transfer mappings is essential to translation quality.

Finally, we investigated the relationship between absolute translation quality and transfer mappings, and showed that larger, more contextual mappings are essential for higher quality.

We currently rely on *a priori* linguistic heuristics to determine the right context for each transfer mapping. In future work, we plan to use machine-learning techniques to discover the extent of the context that optimally disambiguates between conflicting mappings.

Acknowledgments

We gratefully acknowledge the efforts of all members of the *MSR* NLP group that participated in this project.

References

Jensen, K. 1993. PEGASUS: Deriving argument structures after syntax. In K. Jensen, G. Heidorn, & S. Richardson (eds.) *Natural Language Processing: The PLNLP Approach.* Kluwer Academic Publishers, Boston, MA.

Kaji, H., Y. Kida and Y. Morimoto. 1992. Learning translation templates from bilingual text. In *Proceedings of the fifteenth [sic] International Conference on Computational Linguistics, COLING-92*, Nantes, France, **2**:672–678..

The Langenscheidt Pocket Spanish Dictionary. 1997. Langenscheidt, Munich/Berlin, Germany.

Lavoie, B., M. White and T. Korelsky. 2001. Inducing lexico-structural transfer rules from parsed bi-texts. In *Proceedings of the Workshop on Data-Driven Machine Translation, 39th Annual Meeting and 10th*

Conference of the European Chapter of the Association for Computational Linguistics, Toulouse, France, pp.17–24.

McCarthy, M. (ed.). 1995. *Cambridge Word Selector.* Cambridge University Press, Cambridge, UK.

Meyers, A., R. Yangarber, R. Grishman, C. Macleod and A. Moreno-Sandoval. 1998. Deriving transfer rules from dominance-preserving alignments. In *36th Annual Meeting of the Association for Computational Linguistics and 17th International Conference on Computational Linguistics*, Montreal, Quebec, Canada, pp.843-847.

Meyers, A., M. Kosaka and R. Grishman. 2000. Chart-based transfer rule application in machine translation. In *Proceedings of the 18th International Conference on Computational Linguistics: COLING 2000 in Europe*, Saarbrücken, Germany, pp.537-543.

Moore, R. 2001. Towards a simple and accurate statistical approach to learning translation relationships among words. In *Proceedings of the Workshop on Data-Driven Machine Translation, 39th Annual Meeting and 10th Conference of the European Chapter of the Association for Computational Linguistics*, Toulouse, France, pp.79–86.

Pentheroudakis, J.and L. Vanderwende. 1993. Automatically identifying morphological relations in machine-readable dictionaries. In *Proceedings of the Ninth Annual conference of the University of Waterloo Center for the new OED and Text Research*, Waterloo, Ontario, Canada, pp.114-131

Richardson, S., W. Dolan, M. Corston-Oliver and A. Menezes. 2001. Overcoming the customization bottleneck using example-based MT. In *Proceedings of the Workshop on Data-Driven Machine Translation, 39th Annual Meeting and 10th Conference of the European Chapter of the Association for Computational Linguistics*, Toulouse, France, pp.9–16.

SoftArt translation dictionary, version 7. 1995. SoftArt Inc., FL.

Chapter 16

TRANSLATING WITH EXAMPLES: THE LFG-DOT MODELS OF TRANSLATION

Andy Way
away@computing.dcu.ie

Abstract Machine Translation (MT) systems based on Data-Oriented Parsing (DOP: Bod, 1998) and LFG-DOP (Bod & Kaplan, 1998) may be viewed as instances of Example-Based MT (EBMT). In both approaches, new translations are processed with respect to previously seen translations residing in the system's database. We describe the DOT models of translation (Poutsma, 1998, Poutsma, 2000) based on DOP. We demonstrate that DOT1 is not guaranteed to produce the correct translation, despite provably deriving the most probable translation. The DOT2 translation model solves most of the problems of DOT1, but suffers from limited compositionality when confronted with certain data. Notwithstanding the success of DOT2, any system based purely on trees will ultimately be found wanting as a general solution to the wide diversity of translation problems, as certain linguistic phenomena require a description at levels deeper than surface syntax. We then show how LFG-DOP can be extended to serve as a novel hybrid model for MT, LFG-DOT (Way, 2001), which promises to improve upon DOT and other EBMT systems.

Keywords: hybridity, constraint-based grammars, probabilistic language models

1. Problems for EBMT

One of the major advantages which is often claimed of EBMT is that the overall quality of translation increases incrementally as the set of stored translations increases. For example, Mima *et al.*, 1998 report that in their EBMT system, translation quality rose in an almost linear fashion, from 30% with 100 examples to 65% with all 774 examples (cf. Chapter 1, this volume). They also note that there seems to be a

M. Carl and A. Way (eds.), Recent Advances in Example-Based Machine Translation, 443–472.

limit beyond which adding further examples does not improve the overall translation quality.

While the chances of finding an exact match become greater as the corpus size increases, there are two knock-on effects whose impact on the EBMT system should be minimized. Many models of example-based MT store examples as annotated linguistic structures. These include:

- Dependency Trees (e.g. Sato & Nagao, 1990; Yamamoto & Matsumoto, Chapter 13, this volume; Watanabe, 1992, Watanabe, 1994, cf. Chapter 14, this volume; Menezes & Richardson, Chapter 15, this volume);
- CFG-trees (e.g. Poutsma, 1998, Poutsma, 2000, cf. section 2 below; Watanabe & Takeda, 1998);
- Lexicalised Tree-Adjoining Grammar Trees (e.g. Abeillé *et al.*, 1990);
- HPSG structures (e.g. Schäler, 2001);
- LFG c-structure trees and f-structures (e.g. Way, 2001, Way, 2003).

Firstly, adding more examples has a computational cost in all EBMT systems, but this is especially the case if the examples need to be parsed into linguistic representations such as those outlined above. Adding more examples also causes storage problems, and adds to the complexity of the search and retrieval stages of the EBMT process. It is, therefore, unclear that one of the purported advantages of EBMT, namely a lessening in computational cost when the size of the translation database is increased, is indeed a real benefit. Secondly, adding more examples may not be useful in practice. For example, a newly added translation pair may be identical to, or overlap other examples. Where a system involves the computation of a 'similarity metric' (e.g. Somers *et al.*, 1994), this may be influenced by the frequency of examples, so that the score attached to certain matches increases if a large number of similar examples are found. Alternatively, in other systems, identical or similar examples may just be redundant. Somers (Somers, 1999:121; cf. Chapter 1, this volume) observes that "in such systems, the examples can be seen as surrogate 'rules', so that, just as in a traditional rule-based MT system, having multiple examples (rules) covering the same phenomenon leads to overgeneration".

The two main problems for EBMT are *boundary definition* and *boundary friction.* The first of these describes the scenario where retrieved

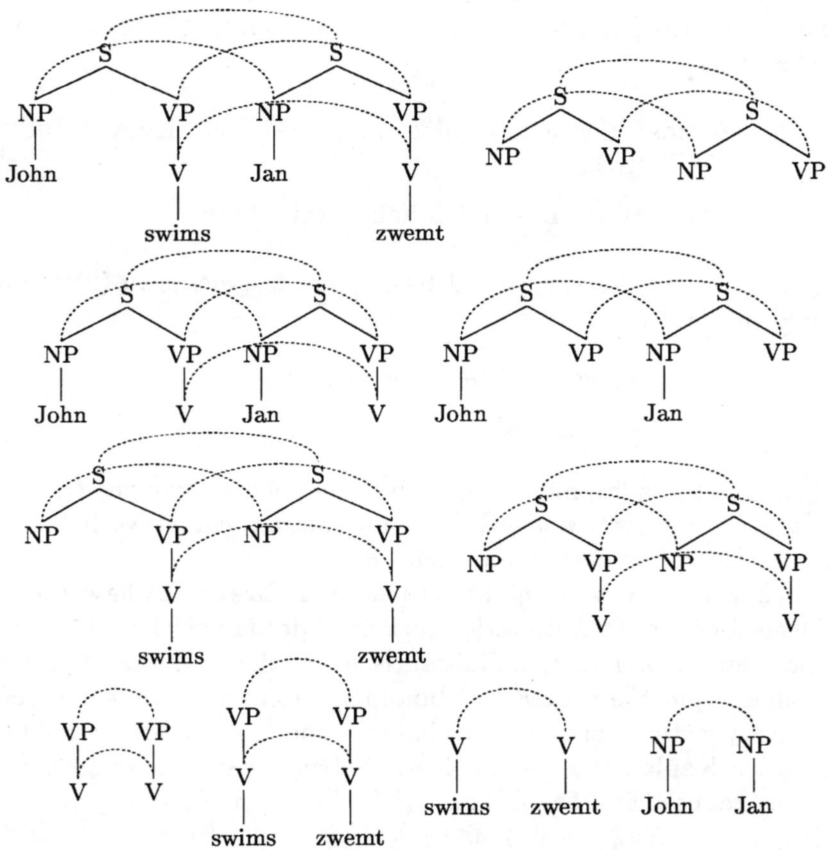

Figure 16.1. The complete DOT treebank for the linked sentence pair ⟨*John swims, Jan zwemt*⟩

fragments may not be well-formed constituents. This is a particular problem for 'pure' EBMT systems, where syntactic well-formedness needs to be ensured without grammatical information actually being employed. The second, boundary friction (cf. also Chapters 1 and 14, this volume), is a problem in the retrieval process, in that context may not be taken into account. This may be illustrated by attempting to translate *I have a small dog* into German. An EBMT system might retrieve the close matches in (1):

(1) a. A small dog eats a lot of meat ⟶ Ein kleiner Hund frisst viel Fleisch.

b. I have two ears ⟶ Ich habe zwei Ohren.

From these examples, the useful translation fragments in (2) might be isolated by the EBMT system:

(2) a. A small dog ⟶ Ein kleiner Hund

b. I have ⟶ Ich habe

In this case, these fragments would be combined to give the translation *Ich habe ein kleiner Hund*, which is ungrammatical as we have an NP bearing nominative case in object position.

We shall show how DOT and LFG-DOT fare with these two main problems for EBMT. With strict notions of decomposition of fragments, the problem of boundary definition is unproblematic. DOT, however, may suffer from the problem of boundary friction, while given the additional syntactic information available in the Lexical-Functional Grammar (LFG: Kaplan & Bresnan, 1982) f-structures, this problem is considerably reduced in LFG-DOT.

2. Data-Oriented Translation

Poutsma, 1998 and Poutsma, 2000 present a model of translation based on Tree-DOP—Data-Oriented Translation (DOT). There are two different versions of DOT. We shall describe these briefly.

2.1 DOT1

Poutsma's DOT1 model (Poutsma, 1998, Poutsma, 2000) is based on the methodology of Tree-DOP (e.g. Bod, 1998), and relates POS-fragments between two languages (English and Dutch here), with an accompanying probability. DOT1 is parameterized on similar lines to

Tree-DOP. Its **representations** are *linked* phrase-structure trees. Figure 16.1 shows the complete treebank for the linked sentence pair ⟨*John swims*, *Jan zwemt*⟩.[1]

These trees are augmented to incorporate semantic information, as a DOT1 treebank links semantically equivalent trees. It can be seen that the top left tree pair in Figure 16.1 represents the full parse trees for this translation pair. This tree pair is subjected to the DOT1 **decomposition** process (based on the DOP *Root* and *Frontier* fragmentation operations—essentially *Root* allows new tree fragments to be built by selecting a node to be the root node of a new tree, and deleting all other nodes except this new root and all nodes dominated by it, while *Frontier* selects a (possibly empty) set of nodes in the newly created subtree, excluding the root, and deletes all subtrees dominated by these selected nodes), so that the other tree pairs in Figure 16.1 are derived. Note also here that all S-rooted linked structures are derived via *Frontier*, while all others are produced via *Root*. It is these operations which delimit the boundary definitions in the DOT translation models.

Tree pair fragments are subjected to the **recombination** process in DOT using the same composition operation, namely leftmost substitution (in order to ensure the uniqueness of each derivation), as Tree-DOP (cf. the $\circ$ operator in (4), among other examples below). The target derivations are then assembled by replacing all subtrees of the source derivation by their linked target subtrees. Any pair of fragments which can legitimately combine with others results in a well formed derivation given the corpus. This causes a particular problem of boundary friction in DOT (cf. Figure 16.5) which is avoided in LFG-DOT (cf. Figure 16.7). Finally, the **probability** of target trees that are candidate translations is then calculated using the Tree-DOP probability model based on their relative frequencies in a treebank such as Figure 16.1. Importantly, therefore, DOT treebanks are *bags* of fragments, rather than sets. Accordingly, where duplication of 'similar' examples may be an impediment in other example-based systems, in DOT (and LFG-DOT) they are essential, as an increase in frequency of particular fragments directly contributes to the weight (in terms of probability) of the derivations in which they are involved. The probability of the parse tree of a particular translation is calculated by summing the probability of all possible derivations resulting in that parse tree. If different parse trees result for a particular translation, the respective probabil-

[1]Here, and in future examples, we 'translate' proper names purely in order to differentiate completely source and target representations and strings.

ities of each with respect to the others can be calculated with respect to the corpus. Similarly, if different translations are presented as candidate target strings, their respective probabilities are given. As will see with respect to (11)–(16) below, this is useful as certain MT systems (e.g. LFG-MT: Kaplan *et al.*, 1989; cf. section 4 below) cannot prevent the output of multiple translation candidates, even where some of these may be ungrammatical target strings. In such cases, an expert user is required to sift through these output strings to select the 'best' translation. This situation is avoidable where translations are output with probabilities, as in DOT and LFG-DOT, as translations may be ranked automatically (or pruned, if only the highest ranked translation is required).

Given the trivial treebank in Figure 16.1, only the one translation pair can be processed. If we assume that the treebank fragments for the translation pair *Peter laughs* ⟷ *Piet lacht* are added to those in Figure 16.1 (these new fragments would be identical except for the different lexical material on the leaves of the tree fragments), then the two new translations in (3) can be handled on the basis of fragments already in the database:

(3) a. *John laughs* ⟷ *Jan lacht*
  b. *Peter swims* ⟷ *Piet zwemt*

For example, one possible derivation of (3a) is that in (4):

(4)

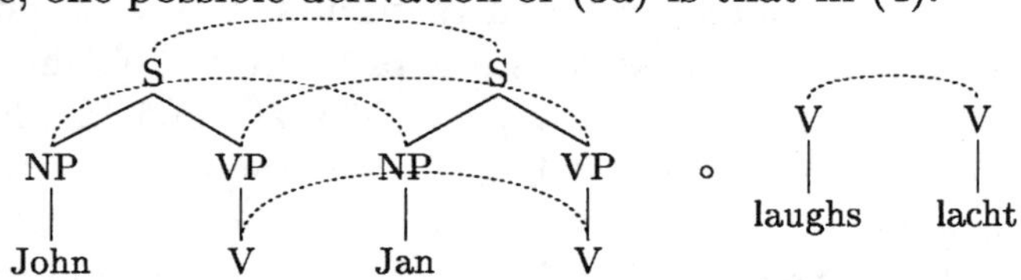

That is, the V nodes in the rightmost tree pair can be substituted at the appropriate ⟨*source, target*⟩ V nodes in the leftmost tree pair. The full parse trees for the two sentences ensue, resulting in a *bona fide* translation given this treebank. The two translations in (3) will have a slightly smaller probability than the two original translation pairs given the presence of their full linked parse trees in the treebank, each of which has a probability of $\frac{1}{12}$. That is, there is one occurrence of the actual parse trees themselves, and there are 12 trees with root `cat=s`. However, given the trivial nature of the examples, there will be no other translation candidates output so each translation will have a probability of 1. This will, of course, not always be the case with more complex examples. For instance, in section 4 we examine in two experiments the situation where multiple translations are output in LFG-DOT with accompanying probabilities given the existence of both 'default' and 'specific' fragments in the database.

2.1.1 A Problem for DOT1. The DOT1 composition operation, based on leftmost substitution in the source trees, does not deal properly with translation cases where the word order differs significantly between two languages. Such an example is the *like* $\longleftrightarrow$ *plaire* relation-changing case. As soon as the derivation in Figure 16.2 of the source sentence is arrived at, the desired linking of the English SUBJ with the French prepositional OBJ, and that of the English OBJ with the French SUBJ, are overridden by the composition operation of DOT1.

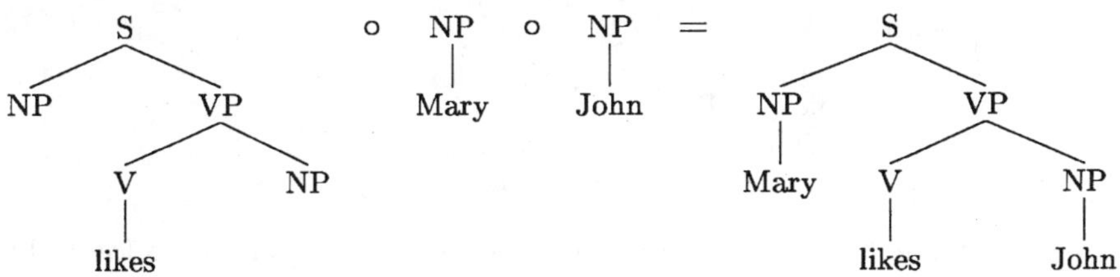

Figure 16.2. DOT derivation of the sentence *Mary likes John*

In this case the wrong translation of Figure 16.2 is derived, cf. Figure 16.3. It would appear that the adherence to leftmost substitution in the target given *a priori* leftmost substitution in the source is too strictly linked to the linear order of words, so that as soon as this deviates to any significant extent even between similar languages, DOT1 has a huge bias in favour of the incorrect translation. Even if the correct, non-compositional translation is achievable in such circumstances, it is likely to be so outranked by other wrong alternatives that it will be dismissed, unless all possible translations are maintained for later scrutiny by the user.

2.2 DOT2: An Improved Model of Translation

Poutsma overcomes this problem in DOT2 by redefining the composition operation of DOT1 to operate on *pairs* of trees, rather than on single (source) trees. This new definition of composition ensures, among other things, that relation-changing cases such as *like* $\longleftrightarrow$ *plaire* are handled correctly: instead of the wrong derivation in Figure 16.3 of the source sentence in Figure 16.2, we now obtain the correct translation *Jean plaît*

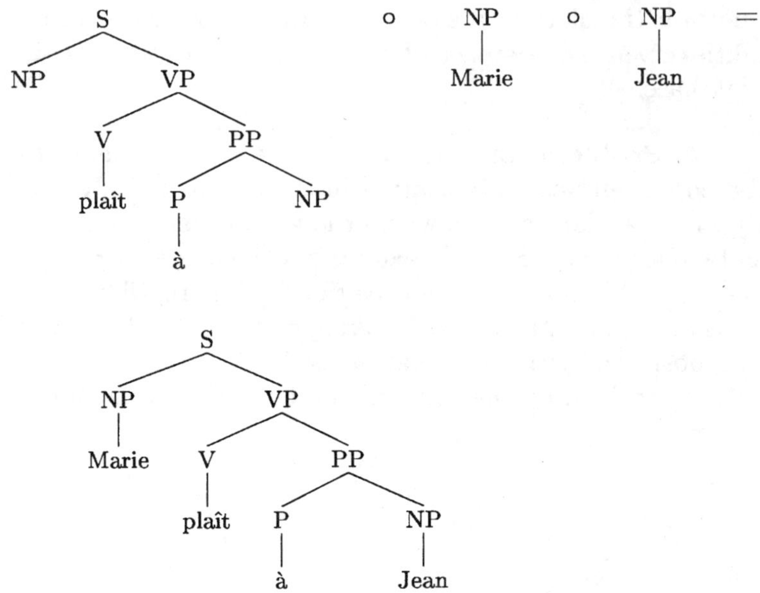

Figure 16.3. Wrong Translation of the sentence *Mary likes John* due to the DOT1 Composition Operation

à Marie. In DOT1, leftmost substitution in the source overrides the desired DOT-links between the French subject NP and the English object, as well as those between the French prepositional object and the English subject, given that composition is defined on the source tree *only.* Once pairs of trees are taken into account in DOT2, these links ensure the correct translation.

Way, 2001 shows that while DOT2 is able to handle certain 'hard' cases correctly, other examples, such as headswitching, are dealt with in a 'semi-compositional' manner. Consider the data in (5):

(5) a. DE: Johannes schwimmt gerne ⟷ EN: John likes to swim.

b. DE: Josef läuft zufällig ⟷ EN: Joseph happens to run.

Presupposing the derivation of a monolingual treebank constructed from the German examples in (5), with two different NPs, verbs and adverbs, eight sentences are possible and can receive analyses with associated probabilities with respect to that DOP corpus. However, only four of these possible sentences can receive translations in a DOT corpus, namely the examples in (5) as well as those in (6), by simple substitution of the alternate NPs into the respective subject slots:

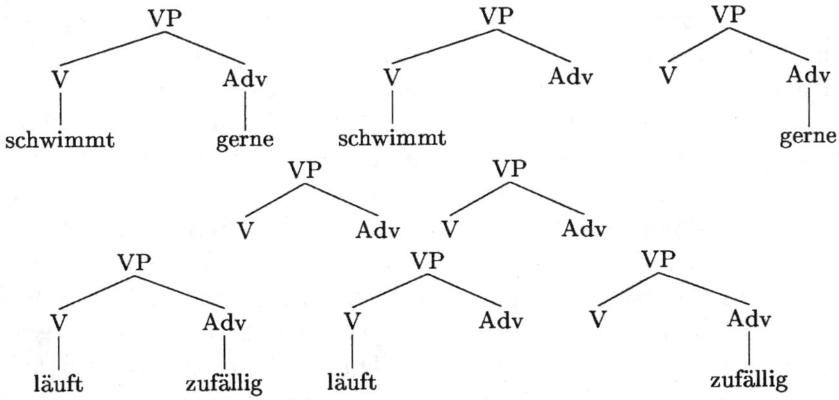

Figure 16.4. The monolingual DOP VP-fragments for a treebank built from the German examples in (5)

(6) a. DE: Josef schwimmt gerne ⟷ EN: Joseph likes to swim.

b. DE: Johannes läuft zufällig ⟷ EN: John happens to run.

The other four possible sentence pairs cannot be handled at all in a DOT treebank built from analyses of the strings in (5). This is due to the fact that the linked VP pairs are not broken down any further than at the root level. The contrast can be seen by examining the *schwimmt gerne* VP and its constituent DOP-fragments in Figure 16.4 and (7), which contains the single DOT linked VP pair:

(7)

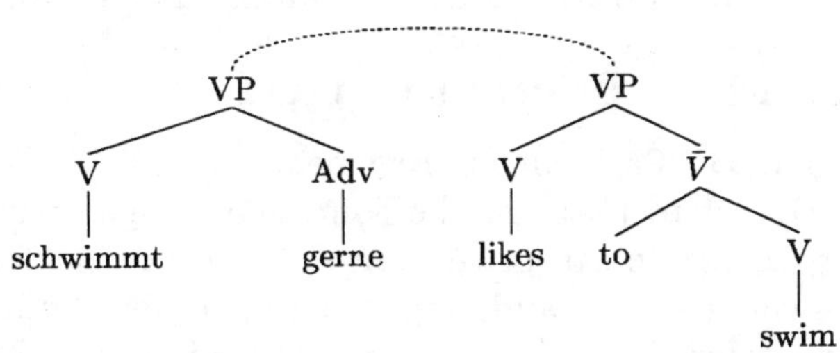

We cannot draw a link between *schwimmt* and *swim* in (7) as they are not translationally equivalent: one is a finite verb and the other an infinitive. We cannot, therefore, express the basic translation relations as ⟨*gerne, likes to*⟩ and ⟨*zufällig, happens to*⟩. Given this restriction, the only way that the other sentence pairs can be handled is if there is some prior linked pair *läuft gerne* ⟷ *likes to run* as well as a prior instance of the linked pair *schwimmt zufällig* ⟷ *happens to swim*. This is because these linked VP pairs are handled non-compositionally in DOT2 between German and English, but the monolingual VPs are treated compositionally in DOP. Contrast this situation with a DOT treebank designed to translate these 8 German strings into Dutch. Our starting point could be the German strings in (5) with their Dutch translations, as in (8):

(8) a. DE: Johannes schwimmt gerne ⟷ NL: Johan zwemt graag.

b. DE: Josef läuft zufällig ⟷ NL: Josef loopt toevallig.

Given these simple transfer (i.e. 'word for word') examples, a DOT treebank would resemble much more closely the monolingual DOP treebanks from which it is derived for the respective sentences in (8), as *every* constituent part of the German strings corresponds exactly to a constituent part of the Dutch strings. In the DOT treebank these links are made explicit. When we have a headswitching case, however, it is apparent that both DOT models would translate the sentences correctly *iff* prior examples of linked headswitching VPs exist in the treebank. Such translations would receive extremely low probabilities with respect to the corpus in the normal case as they are built with a minimal degree of compositionality (substitution of subject NP, no other derivations being possible). As these examples only ever occur rarely, the chances of DOT2 managing to translate these in practice becomes significantly lower than might otherwise be expected, as we require not only the presence of the adverb, but also its occurrence to be correlated exactly with the verb in question for translation to succeed. We shall show that the LFG-DOT4 model of translation is able to provide generalized translation fragments which enable fully compositional translation in these cases, as required.

2.3 Boundary Friction in DOT

It is clear that DOT2 is an improvement on DOT1. DOT1 cannot always explicitly relate parts of the source language structure to the corresponding, correct parts in the target structure, so fails to translate correctly where source and target strings differ significantly with respect to word order. In DOT2, correct translations are obtained along

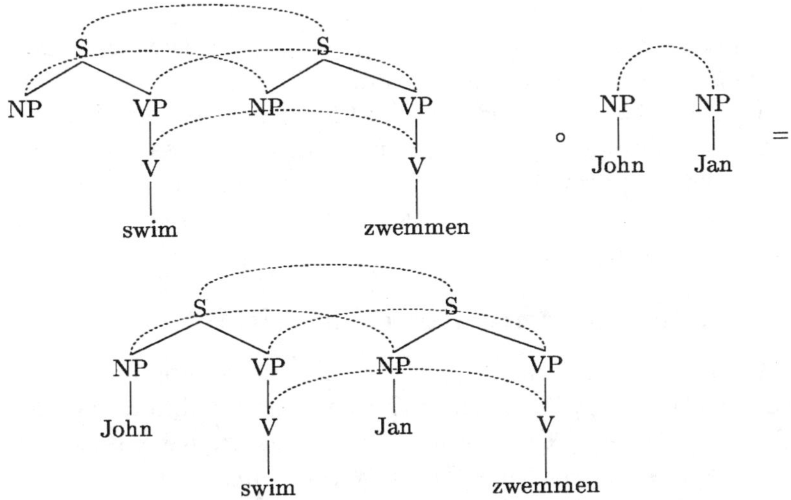

Figure 16.5. The Boundary Friction Problem in DOT

with some possible wrong alternatives. Notwithstanding the improved composition operation and probability model of DOT2, its ability to achieve the correct translation is compromised by a lesser amount of compositionality in the translation process. Given the small number of fragments playing a role in the derivation of some translations involving complex phenomena, almost the exact linked sentence pair may need to be present in order for a translation to be possible.

A further problem is that Poutsma's DOT models cannot distinguish ill-formed from well-formed input. For example, both DOT models of translation would permit the derivations in Figure 16.5. That is, with no stipulation on subject-verb agreement, it is perfectly legitimate in DOP-based models (and EBMT systems based purely on trees, e.g. Watanabe & Takeda, 1998, cf. Chapter 14, this volume), as well, of course, as systems where examples are stored as pairs of strings (e.g. Somers *et al.*, 1990) to combine a singular subject with a plural verb and end up with a well-formed object. In DOT, we end up with a translation which is well-formed given the corpus. This example illustrates that while the presence of category information alleviates the problem of boundary friction to a certain extent (compared to 'pure' example-based methods, for instance, where the examples are stored as strings with no linguistic information present at all), this continues to be problematic for DOT in certain circumstances. We show in Figure 16.7 that the analogous derivation in LFG-DOT would be deemed ungrammatical. That is, as soon as grammatical information is available via the accompanying f-structures, such a combination is impossible given the clash in NUM values for the subject and verb. Such ill-formed input can still be handled by relaxing grammaticality constraints such as these via *Discard*, but such translation pairs will be regarded as ungrammatical with respect to the corpus given their derivation via *Discard*; in DOT models, we have no such distinction.

2.4 Toward More Powerful Models

Finally, of course, translation systems which are based purely on phrase-structure (PS)-trees will ultimately not be able to handle certain linguistic phenomena. DOP-based approaches are necessarily limited to those contextual dependencies actually occurring in the corpus, which is a reflection of surface phenomena only. Purely context-free (CF) models are insufficiently powerful to deal with all aspects of human language.

Lexical Functional Grammar (Kaplan & Bresnan, 1982) is a theory of syntax which allows description of sentences at different levels—c-structure and f-structure.[2] The c-structure (*constituent* structure) is a PS-tree signifying the surface structure of the string, while the f-structure (*functional* structure) is an attribute-value matrix capturing the grammatical relations (in terms of arguments and adjuncts) inherent in the string. The mapping ϕ relates c-structure nodes onto elements of the f-structure. An example of the relevant structures for the sentence *John swims* is shown in Figure 16.6.

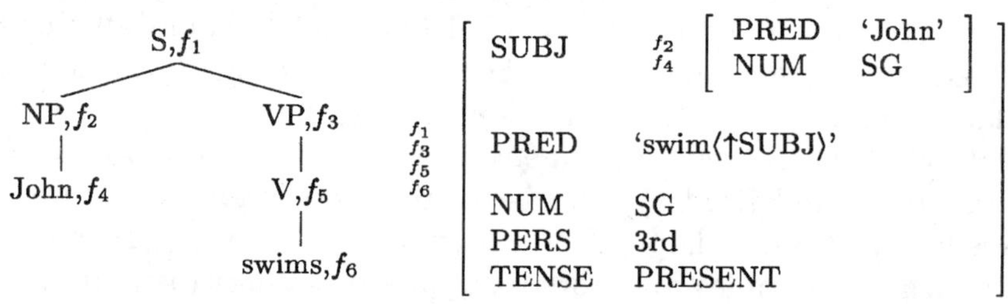

Figure 16.6. LFG Representations for the sentence *John swims*

The c-structure is built using the rules and lexical entries in (9):

[2]There is a third level, namely s-structure (semantic structure), and a second mapping σ, which relates f- and s-structures, but we omit s-structures from our translation models and will not discuss them further here.

(9)

$$\begin{array}{lll} S \longrightarrow & \underset{\uparrow\text{SUBJ}=\downarrow}{\text{NP}} & \underset{\uparrow=\downarrow}{\text{VP}} \\ \\ \text{VP} \longrightarrow & \underset{\uparrow=\downarrow}{\text{V}} & \end{array}$$

John: NP, ↑ PRED = 'John'
↑ NUM = SG

swims: V, ↑ PRED = 'swim⟨↑SUBJ⟩'
↑ NUM = SG
↑ PERS = 3rd
↑ TENSE = PRESENT

We note that the functional attributes in the lexical entry for the NP *John* appear in the SUBJ f-structure slot of the sentence's (outermost) f-structure in Figure 16.6. This is due to the equation ↑SUBJ=↓ on the NP in the S-rule in (9), which essentially states that 'the SUBJ of what is above me (the S node) is filled in by the functional attributes of what is below me (*John*)'. Note also the ϕ-links (informally, parts of the f-structure linked from a c-structure node, cf. the f_n links in Figure 16.6, for instance) showing that the NP (f_2) and *John* (f_4) nodes are linked via ϕ to the SUBJ f-structure.

The annotation ↑=↓ on the VP node in the S-rule shows that this is the functional head of the sentence. The same relation can be seen with respect to the VP rule, where the verb bears the ↑=↓ annotation. Accordingly, we see the functional information of the verb appearing at the outermost level of the f-structure, with the semantic form ↑PRED='swim⟨↑SUBJ⟩' representing the subcategorization frame for *swims*. Again, note that the S, VP, V and *swims* nodes are ϕ-linked to the outermost, sentential f-structure.

We noted above that DOT cannot handle non-CF phenomena. LFG, however, is known to be beyond context-free. It can capture and provide representations of linguistic phenomena other than those occurring at surface structure, as seen in Figure 16.6, for example. With this in mind, the functional structures of LFG have been allied to the techniques of DOP to create a new model, LFG-DOP (Bod & Kaplan, 1998), which adds a measure of robustness (both with respect to unseen as well as ill-formed input) not available to models based solely on LFG.

3. LFG-DOT Models of Translation

Way, 2001 presents four possible LFG-DOT translation models, all of which use LFG-DOP as their language models. LFG-DOP models are defined using the same four parameters as in Tree-DOP. Its **representations** are lifted *en bloc* from LFG theory, so that each string is annotated with a c-structure, an f-structure, and a mapping ϕ between them. Since we are now dealing with $\langle c, f \rangle$ pairs of structure, the *Root* and *Frontier* **decomposition** operations of DOP need to be adapted to stipulate exactly which c-structure nodes are linked to which f-structure fragments, thereby maintaining the fundamentals of c- and f-structure correspondence. Given that LFG c-structures are little more than annotated PS-trees allows us to proceed very much on the same lines as in Tree-DOP.

Root erases all nodes outside of the selected node, and in addition deletes all ϕ-links leaving the erased nodes, as well as all f-structure units that are not ϕ-accessible from the remaining nodes (for instance, features such as TENSE are deleted when the main verb is removed, as this feature—in English, at least—is inextricably linked to the verbal PRED). *Frontier* operates as in Tree-DOP, deleting all subtrees of the selected frontier nodes. Furthermore, it deletes all ϕ-links of these removed nodes together with any semantic form corresponding to the same nodes. Finally, a third, new operation, *Discard*, provides generalized fragments from those derived via *Root* and *Frontier* by freely deleting any combination of attribute-value pairs from an f-structure except those that are ϕ-linked to some remaining c-structure node, or that are governed by the local predicate. Its introduction also necessitates a new definition of the grammaticality of a sentence *with respect to a corpus*, namely any sentence having at least one derivation whose fragments are produced only by *Root* and *Frontier* and not by *Discard*. **Composition** is also a two-step operation. C-structures are combined by leftmost substitution, as in Tree-DOP, subject to the matching of their nodes. F-structures corresponding to these nodes are then recursively unified, and the resulting f-structures are subjected to the grammaticality checks of LFG. Finally, the **probability model** of LFG-DOP is again based on the relative frequency of a fragment, which in this case is a $\langle c, f \rangle$ pair. Bod & Kaplan give definitions of three possible competition sets from which fragments are sampled, depending on which point during the sampling stage the well-formedness conditions are invoked. These include the *Root* matching condition of DOP, and the following LFG conditions on grammaticality:

- *Uniqueness*: each attribute can have only one value;
- *Completeness*: all arguments of a local PRED must appear in the f-structure;

- *Coherence*: no arguments may appear in an f-structure which are not arguments of a local PRED.

Note that given the non-monotonic property of the Completeness check, this can only be enforced after all other validity sampling has taken place. The interested reader should consult Way, 2003 for details of the probability models for LFG-DOT.

3.1 LFG-DOT Model 1: Translation via τ

The first two LFG-DOT models propose the use of LFG's τ-equations to relate translation fragments between languages, the second in combination with γ, the function that links DOT source and target subtree fragments. Using τ-equations overcomes some of the problems of the DOT1 translation model. For instance, the LFG-MT solution (10) to the *like* $\longleftrightarrow$ *plaire* relation-changing case can be availed of quite straightforwardly:

(10) *like*: $(\tau \uparrow \text{PRED}) = \text{plaire}$
$\tau(\uparrow \text{SUBJ}) = (\tau \uparrow \text{OBL})$
$\tau(\uparrow \text{OBJ}) = (\tau \uparrow \text{SUBJ})$

That is, the subject of *like* is translated (via τ) as the oblique argument of *plaire*, while the object of *like* is translated as the subject of *plaire*.

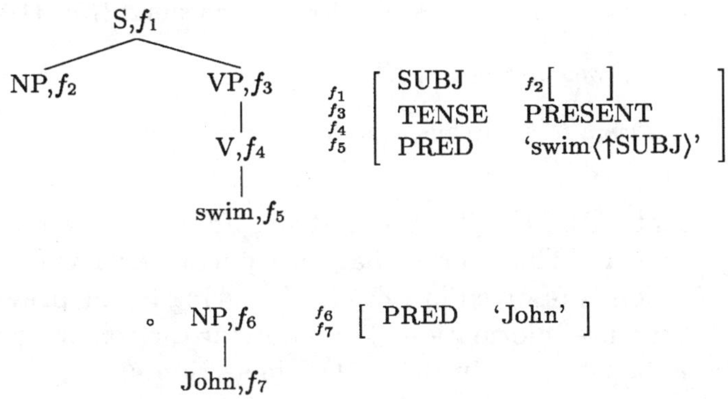

Figure 16.7. Robustness in LFG-DOP via *Discard*

In addition, DOP adds robustness to LFG-MT. LFG-DOT models of translation contain two monolingual LFG-DOP language models, so *Discard* can be run on both source and target sides. This means that LFG-DOT can cope with ill-formed or previously unseen input which LFG-MT would not be able to handle. Suppose that *John swim* is encountered as the source string, as in Figure 16.5. In LFG-DOP, this can only be interpreted if *Discard* relaxes certain constraints in the f-structures. One such derivation is shown in Figure 16.7. That is, the `SUBJ:NUM:PL` path will have been relaxed in the sentential f-structure, with the `NUM:SG` feature removed from the lower NP f-structure. The NP c-structure can be substituted at the NP node in the upper c-structure, and the f-structures unified. Given that such a derivation is possible only via *Discard*, it is regarded as ungrammatical with respect to the corpus, thereby maintaining a clear distinction between grammatical derivations permitted via *Root* and *Frontier*, and ungrammatical derivations.

Notwithstanding this, it is clear that LFG-DOT remains a robust system capable of handling unseen input, as required. The resultant f-structure would be input into the translation phase, which in LFG-DOT1 is quite simply the LFG-MT τ function. Taking the f-structure resulting from the derivation in Figure 16.7 as input, the appropriate τ-equations would build the corresponding target Dutch f-structure, which would be linked by the target language LFG-DOT model to the appropriate c-structure tree, as in Figure 16.8.

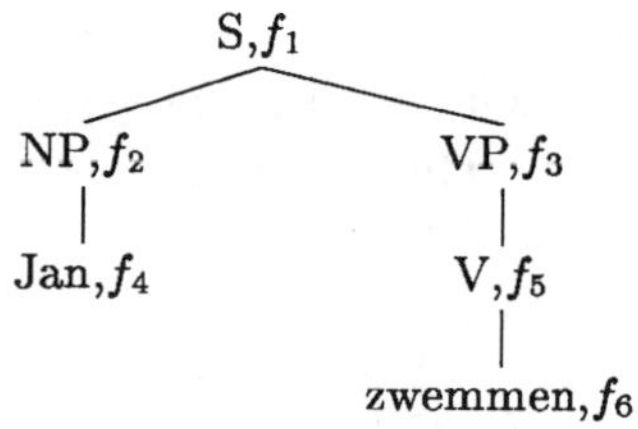

$$\begin{array}{l} f_1\\ f_3\\ f_5\\ f_6\end{array}\left[\begin{array}{ll} \text{SUBJ} & {}^{f_2}_{f_4}\left[\text{PRED} \quad \text{`Jan'}\right] \\ \text{TENSE} & \text{PRESENT}\\ \text{PRED} & \text{`zwemmen}\langle\uparrow\text{SUBJ}\rangle\text{'}\end{array}\right]$$

Figure 16.8. Robustness via *Discard* in LFG-DOT

The 'translation' of the ill-formed string *John swim* would therefore be *Jan zwemmen*. This shows that this particular DOT problem of boundary friction is resolved in LFG-DOT, owing to the presence of the syntactic f-structure information. We report further on the outstanding effect of boundary friction in LFG-DOT in section 4.

3.2 LFG-DOT Model 2: Translation via τ and γ

LFG-DOT2 requires the integration of the τ and γ mappings. Maintaining an f to f' translation engine in addition to γ adds more evidence in favour of any correct translations produced: even if these are not proposed as the most probable translations via τ, this function will only ever produce very few translation candidates (given the limited number of constraints that can play a part in the construction of translation candidates for any given source string), so we can guarantee in almost all cases that they are suggested as one of a small set of candidate translations. These can be compared to the best translation generated by γ and the highest ranking overall translation selected as output.

However, the τ mapping cannot always produce the desired translation (cf. Sadler *et al.*, 1989, Sadler *et al.*, 1990), so that most of the LFG-MT problems (notably, failure to deal successfully with certain headswitching examples, cf. Figure 16.9–Figure 16.11) are imported into both LFG-DOT1 and LFG-DOT2 models of translation.

In contrast, Way, 2001 shows that γ is always (depending, of course, on the coverage in the treebank) able to produce the correct translation, along with some possible wrong alternatives. The next two LFG-DOT models, therefore, abandon τ-equations and rely solely on γ to express the translation relation.

3.3 LFG-DOT Model 3: Translation via γ with Monolingual Filtering

The LFG-DOT3 model contains the DOT2 links between source and target c-structures, but with additional syntactic functional constraints which prevent ungrammatical structures such as Figure 16.5 from being formed (except via *Discard*, in much the same way as in Figure 16.7 above), thereby enabling truly grammatical translations to be output, as opposed to translations which are grammatical only 'with respect to the corpus'. The f-structure information can be seen, therefore, as useful for monolingual disambiguation in both source and target sides. Ill-formed or unknown input is still processable by running *Discard* over the set of linked source and target $\langle c$, LFG-DOP-$\phi, f\rangle$ fragments.

As an example, consider the *just* $\longleftrightarrow$ *venir de* headswitching case. In terms of LFG-DOT3, the translation relation is shown in Figure 16.9.[3] The semantically equivalent source and target c-structures are linked via γ only at the VP level (cf. the dotted lines linking the $\langle$*source, target*$\rangle$ VP nodes). We do not consider *fell* to be semantically equivalent to *tomber* owing to their different FIN(ite) values, added to the fact that *fell* has a TENSE value whilst *tomber* does not. Hence this translation fragment can only be reused by substituting this pair together with associated singular NP subjects at the appropriate nodes in an S-linked fragment.

[3]The solid line linking the French SUBJ with the XCOMP SUBJ indicates that the SUBJ at the outermost f-structure re-enters into the XCOMP SUBJ slot, i.e. it is the 'understood' subject of the infinitival construction.

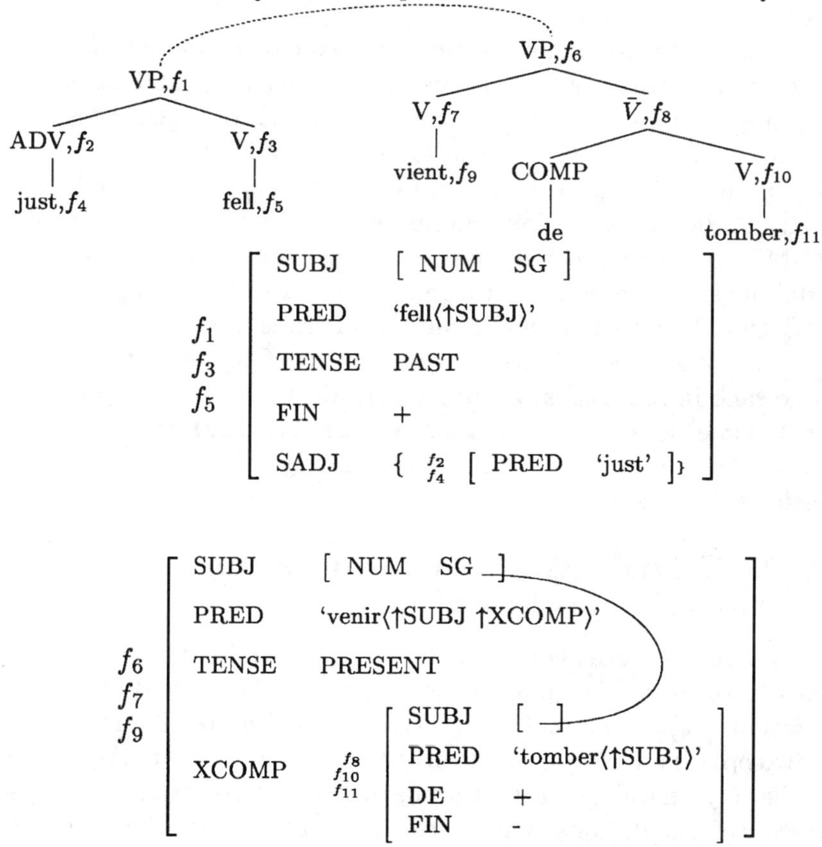

Figure 16.9. The *just* ⟷ *venir de* headswitching case in LFG-DOT3

As an example, we could combine the fragments for *the man* and *just fell*, and produce the translation *l'homme vient de tomber*, but we cannot generalize the fragments in Figure 16.9 to enable other verbs to appear in the context of *just* and *venir de.* The only way in which *just left* ⟶ *vient de partir* can be handled, for example, is if such a linked fragment already existed in the treebank—the fragments in Figure 16.9 would be of no use whatsoever in dealing with this new translation case. In this respect, as with DOT2, this LFG-DOT3 model continues to suffer from limited compositionality. We address this concern further in the next section which describes the LFG-DOT4 model.

3.4 LFG-DOT Model 4: Translation via γ and 'Extended Transfer'

In the previous section, we observed that the outstanding problem with LFG-DOT3 is its retention of the DOT2 problem of limited compositionality. Returning to the *just* $\longleftrightarrow$ *venir de* headswitching case in Figure 16.9, we would like to be able to 'relax' some of the constraints in order to map ⟨*fell,tomber*⟩ to make these linked fragments more general, and hence more useful. In so doing, we would remove this problem of limited compositionality.

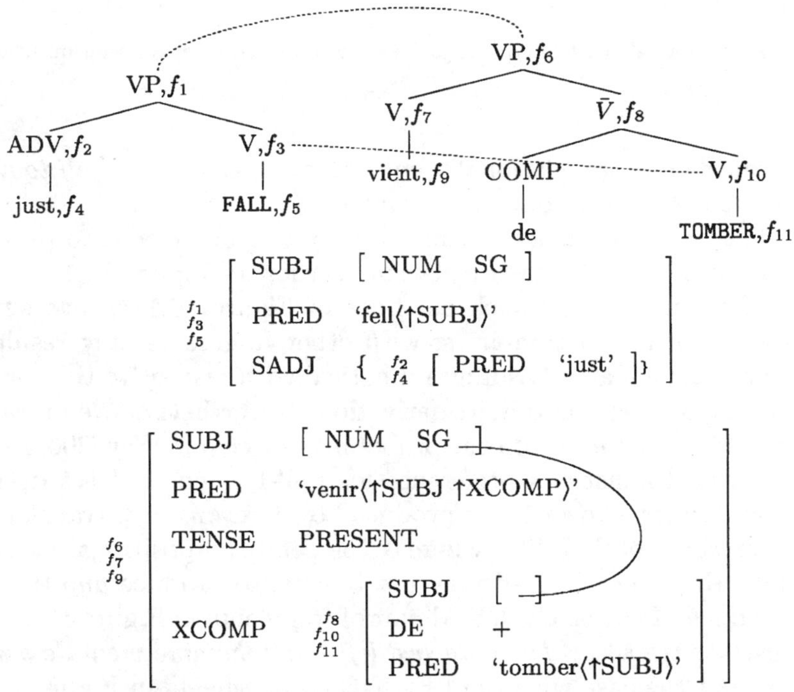

Figure 16.10. Lemmatization in LFG-DOT4

In LFG-DOT4, the basic translation relation is expressed by γ, as in LFG-DOT3. In LFG-DOT4, however, there is a second application of *Discard*, by which 'lemmatized' forms are arrived at on which 'extended transfer' can be performed. *Discard* relaxes constraints in order to produce a set of generalized fragments with the potential to deal with ill-formed or unknown input. Once the `TENSE` and `FIN` features have been relaxed on the lowest verbs in both fragments in Figure 16.9, they

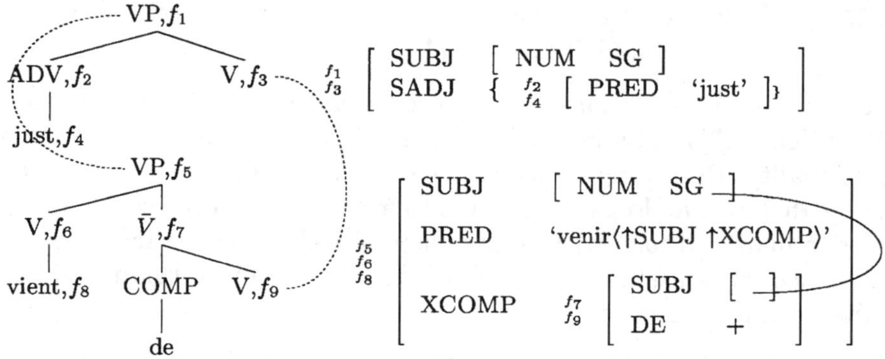

Figure 16.11. Generalized form of the *just* ⟷ *venir de* translation relation in LFG-DOT4

can be regarded as translationally equivalent. Given this, ⟨*fell,tomber*⟩ are linked and lemmatized, as in Figure 16.10.[4]

Now that ⟨`FALL,TOMBER`⟩ are linked, they can be deleted to produce the generalized form of the translation relation in Figure 16.11, as required. If fragment pairs such as those in Figure 16.11 prove subsequently to be of use in combining with other fragments, any resultant translation will be marked as ungrammatical with respect to the corpus, given that *Discard* was used in its derivation. Nevertheless, even if we restrict the impact of *Discard* on the probability space (cf. Way, 2001, Way, 2003), in order to ensure a preference for well-formed analyses derived via *Root* and *Frontier* over those produced by *Discard*, such translations will receive *some* probability, whereas the semi-compositional variants from which they were derived may not be able to produce *any* translation in practice. That is, the linked pair of fragments in Figure 16.11 can now be used to translate *The man just left* ⟶ *L'homme vient de partir*, which was not the case with the LFG-DOT3 fragments in Figure 16.9.

4. Boundary Friction in LFG-DOT: Two Experiments

Both DOT and LFG-DOT have strict definitions of fragment boundaries. We showed that whereas DOT cannot distinguish well-formed from ill-formed structures, LFG-DOT has an intuitively correct notion

[4]We ignore here the issue of the lemmatization of *vient*, cf. Way, 2001:224f. for further discussion.

of grammaticality. Nevertheless, the thorny issue of boundary friction does raise its head in LFG-DOT to a degree.

All MT systems have to decide what are legitimate translation candidates. In most rule-based systems, default rules are differentiated from specific rules, with the former applying only in those cases where a specific rule cannot. Watanabe, 1994 (cf. Chapter 14, this volume) discusses the problem of boundary friction (he calls it 'example interference'), and provides a method of distinguishing exceptional from general examples in EBMT on the basis of *similarity* of examples (cf. Sato & Nagao, 1990, who use a similar technique based on thesaurus relations). Once patterns are identified as general, exceptional or neutral, some of the side-effects of boundary friction may be overcome.

Not all rule-based systems can prevent the output of a wrong, compositional translation once a specific translation has been obtained. For instance, in LFG-MT, satisfying the requirement that only possible translations are produced is problematic where the translation of a lexical head is conditioned in some way by one of its dependants, as in (11):

(11) commit suicide $\longleftrightarrow$ se suicider

The problem is that in these cases, suppressing the wrong, compositional translation in LFG-MT is impossible. For instance, we require the default rules in (12):

(12) a. commit $\longleftrightarrow$ commettre

b. suicide $\longleftrightarrow$ suicide

Such rules are expressed in LFG-MT by the lexical entries in (13):

(13)

commit: $(\tau \uparrow \text{PRED}) = \text{commettre}$
$\tau(\uparrow \text{SUBJ}) = (\tau \uparrow \text{SUBJ})$
$\tau(\uparrow \text{OBJ}) = (\tau \uparrow \text{OBJ})$

suicide: $(\tau \uparrow \text{PRED}) = \text{suicide}$

That is, the default translation (via τ) of *commit* is *commettre*, in which case its SUBJ and OBJ NPs are translated straightforwardly as the SUBJ and OBJ respectively of *commettre*. Similarly, the default translation of the English word *suicide* in French is *suicide*. These entries show how *commit* and *suicide* are to be translated under normal ('word for word') circumstances, such as in (14):

(14) a. John commits a crime $\longleftrightarrow$ Jean commet un crime.

b. Suicide is tragic $\longleftrightarrow$ Le suicide est tragique.

Nevertheless, given the default, compositional entries in (13), LFG-MT produces the wrong translation in (15):[5]

(15) John commits suicide $\longleftrightarrow$ *Jean commet le suicide.

LFG-MT can, however, derive the correct translation *John se suicide* in such cases via the solution in (16):

(16) *commit:* $(\tau \uparrow \text{PRED}) = \text{se suicider}$
$\tau(\uparrow \text{SUBJ}) = (\tau \uparrow \text{SUBJ})$
$(\uparrow \text{OBJ PRED}) =_c \text{suicide}$

Here the collocational units '*commit + suicide*' are linked as a whole to *se suicider*. The $=_c$ equation is a constraining equation: rather than expressing mere equality, it constrains the PRED value of the OBJ of *commit* to *suicide* when it is to be translated as a whole into *se suicider*. The selective use of constraining equations enables correct translations to be derived which would only be possible in other systems by tuning. Nevertheless, the point remains that in LFG-MT we would get both translations here, i.e. a correct one and a wrong one, since it is not possible to enforce the requirement that specific rules ought to override the default translational rules where applicable. Furthermore, these translations would be output with no ranking, so linguistic expertise in both source and target languages may be required in order to select the better translation.

4.1 Experiment 1

We tested the issue of default versus specific translations in LFG-DOT3. We produced an LFG-DOT3 treebank containing all the linked fragments from the sentences in (17):

[5]Note that the rules in (12) are ***bona fide*** translation rules that any rule-based English-French MT system will require. It is, therefore, the task of the French generation component to explicitly rule out the incorrect translation in (15), ***not*** the transfer component.

(17) a. Le suicide est tragique ⟷ Suicide is tragic.

b. Jean commet le crime ⟷ John commits the crime.

c. Jean commet le meurtre ⟷ John commits the murder.

d. Jean dort ⟷ John sleeps.

e. Marie se suicide ⟷ Mary commits suicide.

f. Marie commet un attentat ⟷ Mary commits an attack.

g. Marie commet la faute ⟷ Mary commits the mistake.

h. Pierre commet un arbitre ⟷ Peter nominates an arbitrator.

i. Pierre commet une erreur ⟷ Peter commits an error.

j. Pierre commet une injustice ⟷ Peter commits an injustice.

Here there are seven instances of *commettre* (six of which translate as *commit*) as opposed to only one instance of *se suicider*.

Before examining results obtained with LFG-DOT, it is insightful to point out that in the monolingual French LFG-DOP (no *Discard*) treebank built from the French strings in (17), *Marie se suicide* is preferred about 2.6 times over the compositional alternative *Marie commet le suicide*. If these were the output translations, then ranking them against one another would favour *Marie se suicide* with a probability of 0.72 while *Mary commet le suicide* has a probability of 0.28. In the LFG-DOT3 treebank produced from the English and French sentences in (17), the specific translation is preferred even more than in the French monolingual LFG-DOP treebank. We set out to test the weight of the specific over the compositional translation for the sentences in (18):

(18) a. John commits suicide ⟷ Jean se suicide

b. Mary commits suicide ⟷ Marie se suicide

c. John commits suicide ⟷ *Jean commet le suicide

d. Mary commits suicide ⟷ *Marie commet le suicide

Translation (18a) can be built using the three derivations in Figure 16.12.[6] (18b) has the additional derivation of the full trees (and accompanying f-structures) for this sentence pair. The probabilities of (18a-b) are shown in (19):

[6]We have omitted the accompanying f-structure fragments for reasons of space.

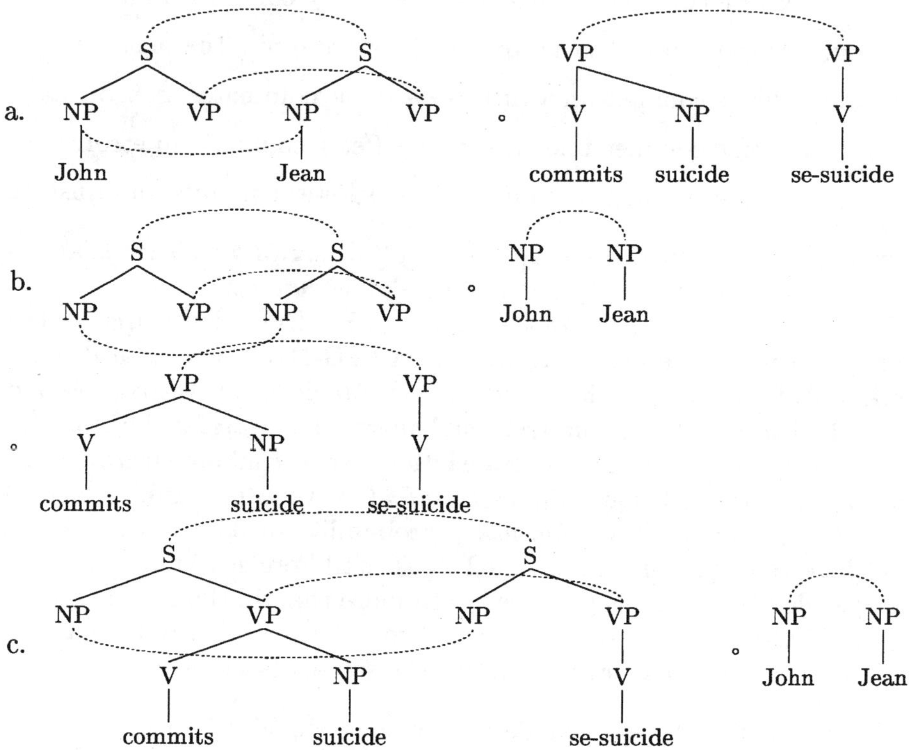

Figure 16.12. C-structure derivations for *John commits suicide* ⟺ *Jean se suicide*

(19) a. P(John commits suicide $\longleftrightarrow$ Jean se suicide) = 0.000705 ($\simeq \frac{1}{1419}$)

b. P(Mary commits suicide $\longleftrightarrow$ Marie se suicide = 0.006229 ($\simeq \frac{1}{161}$)

For each of the translations in (18c-d) there are 7 derivations with total probability 0.000501 ($\simeq \frac{1}{1998}$). Now we can rank each translation with respect to the other in (20):

(20) a. P(John commits suicide $\stackrel{T}{=}$ Jean se suicide) = 705/1206 = 0.5846

b. P(John commits suicide $\stackrel{T}{=}$ Jean commet le suicide) = 501/1206 = 0.4154

c. P(Mary commits suicide $\stackrel{T}{=}$ Marie se suicide = 6229/6750 = 0.923

d. P(Mary commits suicide $\stackrel{T}{=}$ Marie commet le suicide) = 521/6750 = 0.077

Here $\mathcal{W}\stackrel{T}{=}\mathcal{T}$ means that $\mathcal{T}$ is a translation of a word string $\mathcal{W}$. Therefore we can see that for *John commits suicide*, the correct, specific translation is about 1.4 times more likely than the wrong, default, compositional translation, whereas for *Mary commits suicide* the specific translation is preferred about 12 times more than the default translation. We see in (20) the dominance of the exact linked translation pair over the alternative translation. The presence of the exact translation (17e) is insufficient to explain the preference for the specific translation of *John commits suicide*: despite the presence of six *commit* $\longleftrightarrow$ *commettre* examples in (17) compared to only the single instance of *commits suicide* $\longleftrightarrow$ *se suicide*, the specific translation is nonetheless preferred.

4.2 Experiment 2

How many more times empirically we can expect to see *commit* $\longleftrightarrow$ *commettre* compared to *commits suicide* $\longleftrightarrow$ *se suicide*? In the LOB Corpus, there are 66 instances of *commit* (including its morphological variants), only 4 of which have *suicide* as its object, out of the 15 occurrences of *suicide* as an NP. Consequently, even for this small sample, we can see that 94% of these examples need to be translated compositionally (by *commettre* + NP), while only the *commit suicide* examples require a specific rule to apply (i.e. *se suicider*).

In the on-line *Canadian Hansards* covering 1986-1993, there are just 106 instances of *se suicider* (including its morphological variants). There will, of course, be many more instances of *commettre*. Given occurrences of *suicide* as an NP in French corpora, it is not an unreasonable hypothesis to expect that wrong translations such as (15) will be much more probable than those derived via the specific rule. However, this hypothesis is shown to be inaccurate in the above experiment.

Furthermore, it is clear from the results in (20) that a ratio of 6:1 is insufficient to achieve a bias in favour of the wrong, compositional translation in LFG-DOT. Running a new experiment with a treebank built from 5 instances of each translation pair (17a-d) and (17f-j) and just the one instance of (17e), making a total of 46 translation pairs in all, produces the results in (21):

(21) a. P(John commits suicide $\stackrel{T}{=}$ Jean se suicide) = 132/635 = 0.208

b. P(John commits suicide $\stackrel{T}{=}$ Jean commet le suicide) = 503/635 = 0.792

c. P(Mary commits suicide $\stackrel{T}{=}$ Marie se suicide = 1206/1758 = 0.686

d. P(Mary commits suicide $\stackrel{T}{=}$ Marie commet le suicide) = 552/1758 = 0.314

Now, with 30 instances of *commit* $\longleftrightarrow$ *commettre* and only the one *commits suicide* $\longleftrightarrow$ *se suicide* example, we see that the wrong, default, compositional translation for *John commits suicide* is now preferred by about 3.8 times, but the presence of the exact translation (17e) maintains the preference for the specific translation for *Mary commits suicide* by about 2.2 times. Consequently we can see that it will take many more instances of *commit* $\longleftrightarrow$ *commettre* before the specific translation for *Mary commits suicide* is outranked by the wrong, compositional alternative.

5. Conclusions and Future Work

Models of translation based on DOP and LFG-DOP translate new strings on the basis of linked ⟨*source, target*⟩ fragments already located in their databases. Accordingly, such systems may be viewed as example-based systems.

We described the DOT models of translation based on DOP. DOT1 is not guaranteed to produce the correct translation when this is non-compositional and considerably less probable than the default, compositional alternative. DOT2 addresses the failings of DOT1 by redefining the composition operation. In contrast to DOT1, DOT2 cannot fail to produce correct candidate translations, along with some possible wrong alternatives, depending of course on the corpus from which fragments are derived. Despite the presence of syntactic information in the tree-structure fragments, we showed that both DOT models continue to suffer from the problem of boundary friction in cases where singular and plural fragments are combined.

We also described a number of new hybrid models of translation which use LFG-DOP as their language models. The first, LFG-DOT1, imports the τ-equations from LFG-MT as the translation relation. LFG-DOT1 improves the robustness of LFG-MT through the use of the LFG-DOP *Discard* operator, which produces generalized fragments by discarding certain f-structure features. It can, therefore, deal with ill-formed or previously unseen input where LFG-MT cannot. Unsurprisingly, however, all of the other problems of LFG-MT are maintained in LFG-DOT1.

Given this, we augmented LFG-DOT1 with the γ function from DOT2 to give an improved model of translation. LFG-DOT2 maintains the τ translation relation to increase the chances of the correct translation being produced. Nevertheless, given that the τ-equations fail to derive the correct translation in all cases, we omitted the τ translation relation from our subsequent models.

LFG-DOT3 relies wholly on γ to express the translation relation, and uses f-structure information purely for monolingual filtering. The presence of this functional information prevents the formation of certain ill-formed structures which can be produced in DOT. LFG-DOT models, therefore, have a notion of grammaticality which is missing from DOT models. While both DOT and LFG-DOT contain strict notions of boundary definition, DOT allows the output of structures which are well-formed according to the corpus, but which are syntactically ungrammatical. The definition of well-formedness in LFG-DOT, in contrast, corresponds exactly to our understanding of grammaticality in the usual linguistic sense. However, both DOT2 and LFG-DOT3 models suffer from limited compositionality, so that in some cases the minimal statement of the translation relation is impossible.

LFG-DOT4 adds an 'Extended Transfer' phase to LFG-DOT3 by producing lemmatized forms using a second application of *Discard*. This extension overcomes the problem of limited compositionality, enabling the statement of the translation relation in an intuitive, concise fashion.

Finally, we demonstrated that LFG-DOT models of translation suffer less from the problem of boundary friction than DOT models given the presence of the additional syntactic f-structure information. In addition, we showed in two small experiments that despite attempting to 'load the dice' in favour of the wrong, compositional translation over the correct, specific alternative, LFG-DOT continues to translate in a robust fashion while maintaining a preference for the correct translation.

The work described here and in Way, 2001 uses as its evaluation metric the ability to cope with 'hard' translation cases, such as relation-changing, cf. Figure 16.2 and Figure 16.3, and headswitching, cf. (5)–(8). Special LFG-DOT corpora such as those derived to test the effect of boundary friction in section 4 needed to be created. The translation effects examined here need to be tested further on larger corpora, and the work of Frank *et al.*, 2001 and Cahill *et al.*, 2002 on semi-automatic derivation of LFG corpora from treebank resources would appear promising in this regard.

Furthermore, the hypotheses developed in Way, 2001 need to be further explored with respect to simpler translation data, such as *John swims* sentences. Different probability models will also be evaluated (cf. Bonnema *et al.*, 2000), as will the possibility of pruning the search space, by cutting down the number of fragments produced (cf. Sima'an, 1999) in order to improve the efficiency of the models proposed.

Acknowledgments

The author wishes to thank the anonymous referees whose comments led to improvements in this paper. All remaining errors are the responsibility of the author.

References

Abeillé, A., Y. Schabes and A.K. Joshi. 1990. Using Lexicalised Tags for Machine Translation. In *COLING-90, Papers Presented to the 13th International Conference on Computational Linguistics*, Helsinki, Finland, **3**:1–6.

Bod, R. 1998. *Beyond Grammar: An Experience-Based Theory of Language*, CSLI, Stanford, CA.

Bod, R. and R. Kaplan. 1998. A Probabilistic Corpus-Driven Model for Lexical-Functional Analysis. In *36th Annual Meeting of the Association for Computational Linguistics and 17th International Conference on Computational Linguistics*, Montreal, Quebec, Canada, **1**:145–151.

Bonnema, R., P. Buying and R. Scha. 2000. Parse Tree Probability in Data-Oriented Parsing. In *CICLING: Proceedings of the International Conference on Intelligent Text Processing and Computational Linguistics*, Mexico City, pp.219–232.

Cahill, A., M. McCarthy, J. van Genabith and A. Way. 2002. Automatic Annotation of the Penn-Treebank with LFG F-Structure Information. In *Proceedings of the LREC Workshop on Linguistic Knowledge Acquisition and Representation: Bootstrapping Annotated Language Data*, Las Palmas de Gran Canaria, Spain, pp.8–15.

Frank, A., J. van Genabith and A. Way. 2001. Treebank vs. X-BAR based Automatic F-Structure Annotation. In M. Butt and T. Holloway-King (eds.) *LFG-2001: Proceedings of 6th International Conference on Lexical Functional Grammar*, CSLI Publications, Stanford, CA., pp.127–146.

Kaplan, R. and J. Bresnan. 1982. Lexical Functional Grammar: A Formal System for Grammatical for Grammatical Representation. In J. Bresnan (ed.) *The Mental Representation of Grammatical Relations*, MIT Press, Cambridge, MA., pp.173–281.

Kaplan, R., K.. Netter, J. Wedekind and A. Zaenen. 1989. Translation by Structural Correspondences. In *Proceedings of the Fourth Conference of the European Association for Computational Linguistics*, Manchester, England, pp.272–281.

Mima, H, H. Iida and O. Furuse. 1998. Simultaneous Interpretation Utilizing Example-Based Incremental Transfer. In *36th Annual Meeting of the Association for Computational Linguistics and 17th International Conference on Computational Linguistics*, Montreal, Quebec, Canada, pp.855–861.

Poutsma, A. 1998. Data-Oriented Translation. In *Computational Linguistics in the Netherlands: Ninth CLIN Meeting*, Leuven, Belgium, [no page numbers].

Poutsma, A. 2000. *Data-Oriented Translation: Using the Data-Oriented Parsing framework for Machine Translation*, MSc Thesis, University of Amsterdam, Amsterdam, The Netherlands.

Sadler, L., I. Crookston, D. Arnold and A. Way. 1990. LFG and Translation. In *Third Conference on Theoretical and Methodological Issues in Machine Translation*, Austin, TX., pp.121–130.

Sadler, L., I. Crookston and A. Way. 1989. Co-description, projection, and 'difficult' translation. *Working Papers in Language Processing 8*, Department of Language and Linguistics, University of Essex, Colchester, UK.

Sato, S. and M. Nagao. 1990. Towards Memory-based Translation. In *COLING-90, Papers Presented to the 13th International Conference on Computational Linguistics*, Helsinki, Finland, **3**:247–252.

Schäler, R. 2001. Beyong Translation Memories. In M. Carl and A. Way (eds.) *Proceedings of the Workshop on Example-Based Machine Translation, MT Summit VIII*, Santiago de Compostela, Spain, pp.49–55.

Sima'an, K. 1999. *Learning Efficient Disambiguation*, PhD Thesis, University of Utrecht, Utrecht, The Netherlands.

Somers, H. 1999. Example-based Machine Translation. *Machine Translation* **14**(2):113–157 (cf. Chapter 1, this volume).

Somers, H., I. McLean and D. Jones 1994. Experiments in Multilingual Example-Based Generation. In *CSNLP-94: 3rd Conference on the Cognitive Science of Natural Language Processing*, Dublin, Ireland, [no page numbers].

Somers, H., J. Tsujii and D. Jones. 1990. Machine Translation without a source text. In *COLING-90, Papers Presented to the 13th International Conference on Computational Linguistics*, Helsinki, Finland, **3**:271–276.

Watanabe, H. 1992. A Similarity-Driven Transfer System. In *Proceedings of the fifteenth [sic] International Conference on Computational Linguistics, COLING-92*, Nantes, France, **2**:770–776

Watanabe, H. 1994. A Method for Distinguishing Exceptional and General Examples in Example-based Transfer Systems. In *COLING-94: The 15th International Conference on Computational Linguistics*, Kyoto, Japan, pp.39–44.

Watanabe, H. and K. Takeda. 1998. A Pattern-based Machine Translation System Extended by Example-based Processing. In *36th Annual Meeting of the Association for Computational Linguistics and 17th International Conference on Computational Linguistics*, Montreal, Quebec, Canada, **2**:1369–1373.

Way, A. 2001. *LFG-DOT: A Hybrid Architecture for Robust MT*, PhD Thesis, University of Essex, Colchester, UK.

Way, A. 2003. Machine Translation using LFG-DOP. In R. Bod, R. Scha and K. Sima'an (eds.) *Data-Oriented Parsing*, CSLI, Stanford, CA.

Index

Text, Speech and Language Technology

1. H. Bunt and M. Tomita (eds.): *Recent Advances in Parsing Technology.* 1996
   ISBN 0-7923-4152-X
2. S. Young and G. Bloothooft (eds.): *Corpus-Based Methods in Language and Speech Processing.* 1997 ISBN 0-7923-4463-4
3. T. Dutoit: *An Introduction to Text-to-Speech Synthesis.* 1997 ISBN 0-7923-4498-7
4. L. Lebart, A. Salem and L. Berry: *Exploring Textual Data.* 1998
   ISBN 0-7923-4840-0
5. J. Carson-Berndsen, *Time Map Phonology.* 1998 ISBN 0-7923-4883-4
6. P. Saint-Dizier (ed.): *Predicative Forms in Natural Language and in Lexical Knowledge Bases.* 1999 ISBN 0-7923-5499-0
7. T. Strzalkowski (ed.): *Natural Language Information Retrieval.* 1999
   ISBN 0-7923-5685-3
8. J. Harrington and S. Cassiday: *Techniques in Speech Acoustics.* 1999
   ISBN 0-7923-5731-0
9. H. van Halteren (ed.): *Syntactic Wordclass Tagging.* 1999 ISBN 0-7923-5896-1
10. E. Viegas (ed.): *Breadth and Depth of Semantic Lexicons.* 1999 ISBN 0-7923-6039-7
11. S. Armstrong, K. Church, P. Isabelle, S. Nanzi, E. Tzoukermann and D. Yarowsky (eds.): *Natural Language Processing Using Very Large Corpora.* 1999
    ISBN 0-7923-6055-9
12. F. Van Eynde and D. Gibbon (eds.): *Lexicon Development for Speech and Language Processing.* 2000 ISBN 0-7923-6368-X; Pb: 07923-6369-8
13. J. Véronis (ed.): *Parallel Text Processing.* Alignment and Use of Translation Corpora. 2000 ISBN 0-7923-6546-1
14. M. Horne (ed.): *Prosody: Theory and Experiment.* Studies Presented to Gösta Bruce. 2000 ISBN 0-7923-6579-8
15. A. Botinis (ed.): *Intonation.* Analysis, Modelling and Technology. 2000
    ISBN 0-7923-6605-0
16. H. Bunt and A. Nijholt (eds.): *Advances in Probabilistic and Other Parsing Technologies.* 2000 ISBN 0-7923-6616-6
17. J.-C. Junqua and G. van Noord (eds.): *Robustness in Languages and Speech Technology.* 2001 ISBN 0-7923-6790-1
18. R.H. Baayen: *Word Frequency Distributions.* 2001 ISBN 0-7923-7017-1
19. B. Granström, D. House and. I. Karlsson (eds.): *Multimodality in Language and Speech Systems.* 2002 ISBN 1-4020-0635-7

KLUWER ACADEMIC PUBLISHERS – DORDRECHT / BOSTON / LONDON